Sociology

Little, Brown and Company   Boston and Toronto

Sociology

An Introduction

J. Ross Eshleman
Wayne State University

Barbara G. Cashion
Georgetown University

Library of Congress Cataloging in Publication Data

Eshleman, J. Ross.
   Sociology, an introduction.

   Includes bibliographies and indexes.
   1. Sociology.   I. Cashion, Barbara G.   II. Title.
HM51.E84 1983   301   82-18659
ISBN 0-316-24956-4

Library of Congress Catalog Card No. 82-18659

ISBN 0-316-24956-4

9 8 7 6 5 4 3 2 1

RRD

Published simultaneously in Canada by Little, Brown & Company (Canada) Limited

Printed in the United States of America

Text Credits

Chapter 6. p. 136–137: From William
Sansom, "Happy Holiday Abroad" from
A Contest of Ladies (London: The Ho-
garth Press, 1956). Reprinted by permission of Elaine Green Ltd. on behalf of
the author's estate.

Chapter 8. p. 187: From Irving Wallace, David Wallechinsky, and Amy

(continued on page 583)

To Janet, Jill, and Sid
and
to Janet and Libby

Preface

Sociology is an exciting discipline. We wouldn't be in this field if it weren't. However, we know you won't accept our choice as evidence that sociology is exciting — after all, both authors have taught it regularly for many years. Quite simply, the excitement of sociology comes from its subject matter: social life and social organization. Sociology encompasses all aspects of society including those that involve you in a direct and personal way: family life, community change, religion, and sexual inequality, to name just a few. It involves a unique way of looking at the world in which we live, forcing us to question the obvious and understand how society and behavior is patterned and organized. More and more people are discovering that sociology provides them with unique skills and abilities: in research methods, in applying social theory in the working world, and in using their knowledge and understanding of social processes, organization, and change.

Our purpose in writing this introductory text is to convey to the beginning student this excitement; this unique way of looking at society; and these skills and abilities. For many students, this text may be their first exposure to the discipline. For other students, who studied sociology in a high school course, this text will broaden their knowledge of the field. In any case, for an introductory textbook to succeed with today's students, it must respond to their special demands. We believe we have met those demands by writing a text that is:

1. *comprehensive and with depth and detail.* Survey data collected prior to writing this text indicated the chapter and topical areas most desired by instructors of introductory sociology. These have been included. In covering these areas we have included enough depth and detail to enable the reader to understand, compare, and question without getting bogged down in insignificant trivia.

2. *readable and interesting.* The readability level of an introductory text should not be so elementary as to be inapproppriate for a college student, nor should it be so sophisticated that the student can't understand it. We feel we've reached a happy medium: our text challenges students to broaden their understanding of society in a manner that holds their interest and encourages them to read on.

3. *eclectic in theoretical orientation.* A temptation often exists to expound on the particular theoretical orientation most familiar to the writer. To a certain extent this has happened, but we feel with positive results. Both authors have been trained in an interactionist perspective, yet one relies heavily on a functionalist perspective and the other tends to stress a conflict perspective. The result is a text that covers these three perspectives throughout and also includes perspectives such as exchange theory, phenomenology, and others, when appropriate to the topic.

4. *up-to-date and well organized.* How to organize chapters and integrate material in the best way possible are difficult tasks. How does one talk about norms, roles, change, and culture in early chapters when they are described in later chapters? Should social inequalities based on age and sex be included early in a text, in the middle, the end, or not at all? If included, how can they be related to socialization, deviance, or collective behavior? We have placed topics in the order preferred by a consensus of instructors and grouped them so that one topic and chapter flows into the next. In addition, although basic concepts and theories may change little over time, we have made sure that the examples, illustrations, research, and data in the text are both up to date and relevant to today's student.

5. *cross-cultural.* As you might expect in a text aimed primarily at American students, many research findings and data are from the United States. However, the discipline of sociology conveys the idea that we can only understand ourselves or our own society by noting variations in behavior patterns and social organization in other societies. These cross-cultural references and illustrations are an integral part of the text.

Organization

This book is divided into five parts. Part I begins by looking at what the sociological perspective is, how sociology differs from the other social sciences, and what sociologists do. From this beginning, we examine the development of sociology in Europe, focusing on a number of the leading early theorists and their ideas, and then turn to the American scene with an overview of the major theoretical perspectives in sociology today. Part I concludes with a chapter on methods of studying society, including the components and standards of scientific inquiry, types of sociological research, and the research process itself.

Given this background, in Part II we look at culture and the individual within the social context. What are the elements of culture and how do we interpret our own and that of others? We then address the question of how individuals learn to interact in their culture and society. How significant is interaction in the development of the self? This part concludes with an analysis of deviance, including theories on the nature of deviance and ways that society controls the deviant individual.

Part III contains three chapters on social inequality, covering social differentiation and stratification, racial and ethnic differentiatiation, and age and gender differentiation. Although many aspects of social inequality are covered in the chapters on socialization, family, and collective behavior, Part III devotes in-depth attention to these issues.

To many sociologists, the first chapter in Part IV is the core of the discipline: groups and organizations. Here we examine types of groups and formal organizations, including bureaucracies, and the meaning of social institutions. Then we cover the five most basic institutions: the systems of family, religion, education, politics, and economics. In each chapter we present cross-cultural material and several theoretical perspectives to enrich the understanding of those basic components of society.

Our text concludes with four chapters on human ecology and change. Part V begins with an examination of collective behavior. How does it develop and why? What are the major types of collective behavior? A chapter on population and health follows in which we discuss the major aspects of health and the world population explosion. The final two chapters cover the changing community and social change in general. Again, cross-cultural material, particularly third world data, is presented to clarify the nature of change and modernization.

Although we have organized our text in a particular manner, the chapters or parts can be used in a different order. Some instructors may wish to focus much earlier on social change, or on groups and organizations. Others may wish to reverse the chapters on the institutions and social inequalities, whereas still others may want to cover research methods later in the course. Concepts introduced in any early chapters that are covered later in the course may be looked up in the glossary by the student.

Features

The key features we have included in our text will significantly enhance its effectiveness for both instructor and student. These include:

□ *Sociologists at Work.* What career options are available to sociologists? Some teach, but others are working as sociologists in areas outside of academia. In our text, each chapter contains the profile of an individual whose training has been in sociology at the BA, MA, or PhD level. In the first two chapters we profile two recent college graduates: One has decided to go on for her PhD; the other is applying his sociological training in a home for troubled children. In each of the remaining chapters we introduce a person whose career relates to the chapter topic. Instructors and students alike will be fascinated by the range of careers these people have chosen. This feature is not found in any other introductory sociology text.

□ *Summaries.* Each chapter is followed by a summary that highlights the key ideas and concepts discussed in the chapter. These can be helpful to students who want a quick review of the chapter.

□ *Key Terms.* Following each chapter summary is a list of the terms and concepts discussed in the chapter. Like the summaries, these lists can serve as useful review tools for the student. Each of these terms is defined in the Glossary at the end of the text.

□ *Suggested Readings.* Following the key terms, each chapter provides a list of sources that students can read to supplement the material in the chapter. Each of the suggestions is annotated with a brief description of the suggested material. Instructors may want to refer to some of these for more extensive classroom material. The suggested readings can serve as a starting point for research papers or simply as an easy source for students who want to investigate a particular topic in greater depth.

□ *Boxed Inserts.* Each chapter contains supplemental materials in the form of boxed inserts. Most are short excerpts from books or newspapers and illustrate a point under discussion. We think you will find them both contemporary and interesting.

□ *Tables and Figures.* The chapters include a number of tables and figures to supplement the written content. Frequent use is made of 1980 census material. The graphic displays in the figures and the detailed data in the tables should enhance the presentation of a particular topic and increase the interest of the student.

□ *Full-Color Art Program.* Careful thought went into selecting photographs, fine art, and movie stills that will be of interest to students and reinforce concepts discussed in each chapter. We are also pleased to have commissioned a well-known Boston artist, Karen Watson, to create original art for the cover and part-opening pieces.

□ *End-of-Part Readings.* Each of the five parts concludes with one or two brief readings. We have chosen a mix of contemporary and classic articles that students should enjoy. By including readings in the text, there is no need for a separate readings text.

□ *Appendix: Exploring a Career in Sociology.* Students frequently ask for practical advice on careers for sociology majors, the level of degree needed for jobs in sociology, finding a job, locating professional organizations, and sources available to assist in educational training and career advancement. Our Appendix answers these questions and in greater detail than do other texts. This Appendix, in conjunction with our "Sociologists at Work" feature, provides students with a real sense of the timeliness and relevance of sociology.

□ *Glossary.* Probably no introductory textbook has a more extensive glossary than this one. Over 400 definitions of important concepts are found at the end of the book for quick and easy reference. The glossary is useful for ready reference, for checking on the meanings of terms listed at the end of each chapter, and for reviewing purposes.

Supplements

1. *Study Guide.* A thorough and practical student study guide includes learning objectives, chapter outlines, and a special feature called "Workshops" that applies sociological concepts to everyday life by using newspaper articles and raising questions based on them.

2. *Instructor's Manual.* A comprehensive manual provides a wealth of teaching suggestions, objectives and resources, outside activities stressing the importance of sociology to personal lives, suggested readings from short stories and novels, a guide to films, and much more.

3. *Test Bank.* An extensive test bank of approximately 2000 items is available to instructors, in both booklet and computerized format. The questions are primarily multiple choice with many true-false and a number of short essays as well. The test bank is in two parts so that differently worded but similar questions can be given to different classes. Each question is referenced to the appropriate text page to make verification quick and easy.

Acknowledgments

Few ideas in an introductory textbook stem from the authors alone. How does one express an intellectual debt to the scholars, researchers, teachers, and students who provided the ideas, data, and findings expressed here? Obviously that is impossible. One can, however, acknowledge those people who have specifically helped in the preparation of some aspect of this book.

Of course, we thank our own personal groups, our families and friends who have supported our efforts as we have studied and worked in our chosen field. We especially thank our children who have taught us as much as we have taught them. We also thank our teachers, those people who have sparked our interest in sociology and helped us develop our ability to think through the issues of the discipline. Certain professors have been especially influential: Professors Muriel Cantor, Edward Dager, John Pease, Barbara Hetrick, Larry Hunt, Jennie McIntyre, A. R. Mangus, Leonard Kercher, and numerous colleagues at Wilson College, Western Michigan University, Georgetown University, and Wayne State University.

Special thanks are due to two persons who were instrumental in organizing and writing a first draft of one chapter. Dr. Melinda Bacol-Montilla, a part-time instructor at Wayne State University, wrote an original draft for the chapter on racial and ethnic differentiation. Dr. James E. Gruber, a professor at the University of Michigan-Dearborn, wrote the original draft for the chapter on the changing community. A third person, Dr. Elizabeth Nall, provided assistance for the chapter on religious groups and systems. A special note of appreciation due to Doris Seifert and Terri Krutell, who typed several chapters, and to Maureen Preuss, who typed the glossary. With their help we were able to meet the deadlines involved in a major project such as this.

This book owes much to the constructive criticisms and suggestions offered by text reviewers. In particular, we wish to thank: David Alcorn (Angelo State University); Henry Barlow (Cleveland State University); David Brinkerhoff (University of Nebraska, Lincoln); Stephen Green (North Adams State College); Arthur Greil (Alfred University); David Karp (Boston College); Mark Kassop (Bergen Community College); Abraham Lavender (University of Miami); Anthony Orum (University of Texas-Austin); Brian Pendleton (University of Akron); Beth Rubin (Indiana University-Bloomington); Richard Shaffer (California Polytechnic State University-San Luis Obispo); Robert Smith (Framingham State College); Charles Tolbert (Baylor University); Thomas Van Valey (Western Michigan University); Charles Vedder (Stetson University); and Joan Weston (Brookhaven Community College).

A special word of thanks go to people behind the scenes who made significant contributions to the text and played a major part in the final product. None of them perceived themselves as sociologists several years ago but several of them must feel they now qualify. Katherine Carlone, a former editor at Little, Brown, convinced one of us to sign a book contract. Madelyn Leopold very ably replaced Katie and provided the editorial assistance and direction necessary to produce a text. And Garret White, the editor-in-chief, gave us invaluable support. Many other individuals made specific contributions and need to be recognized. Daniel Otis took our submitted drafts and did the reorganizing, rewriting, and polishing essential for publication. Timothy Kenslea edited the "Sociologists at Work." Victor Curran designed the book. Donna McCormick researched and wrote the appendix on sociology careers. And two very special people, with whom we exchanged more phone calls and letters than most teenagers or separated lovers, are Lesley Ripley and Dana Norton. We have indeed been fortunate to have Lee as Developmental Editor and Dana as Book Editor. Their remarkable skills and support as well as their enthusiasm made the project proceed smoothly and resulted in a final product that we believe is superior to any of the competing texts.

J.R.E.
B.G.C.

Contents

Chapter 3
Methods of Studying Society   46

Part I Reading

Part II
Individuals
Within Society   78

Chapter 4
Culture and Society   80

Part II Readings

Part III
Social Inequality   184

Chapter 8
Social Differentiation
and Stratification   186

SOCIOLOGISTS AT WORK
Planning and Social Change   544

Part V Reading

Appendix: Exploring a Career in Sociology   553

Glossary   561

References   575

Name Index   585

Subject Index   589

Sociology

John Boyle, *first son, seated at Hereford.*

Part I

Sociology: Perspectives and Methods

Sociology is about people, but we learn about people in history, psychology, business, anthropology, political science, biology, and many other disciplines. So why study sociology? Because the perspective is different. Sociologists study people as they interact with other people, at work, at play, at home or in school, in small groups, in large groups, or in large organizations. Using this unique perspective, we learn not only about people but also about social groups and social systems, a major goal in sociology.

The first chapter in this textbook describes what sociology is, what sociologists do, and how sociology differs from other disciplines. Chapter 2 introduces you to the history of sociology and the development of a variety of theories sociologists use to describe social groups and social systems and how people interact in them. The third chapter explains how sociologists gather and use evidence to test their theories.

Welcome to the perspective of sociology. We hope that as you begin to learn how sociologists view people and their activities, you too will use this perspective in your own observations of people. We believe that with a sociological perspective you will better understand yourself and others and realize how social groups and social systems shape your life and the lives of those around you.

Chapter 1
The Nature and Uses of Sociology

People who like to avoid shocking discoveries, who prefer to believe that society is just what they were taught in Sunday School, who like the safety of the rules . . . should stay away from sociology.

— Peter Berger

Have you ever wondered how your life would be different if you had been born in a different country? What would it be like to speak French instead of English, to enjoy blood pudding instead of ice cream, or to have your spouse chosen for you by your parents without your having any say in the matter? Have you ever asked yourself why people do things they know will harm their health — smoke cigarettes, overeat, or fail to exercise? What type of person joins the Hare Krishnas or the Sun Myung Moon church? Have you ever considered how your life is affected by forces beyond your own control — the air you breathe, the price of gasoline, the wars you fight, or the color of your skin?

Questions such as these — about the society in which you live and the social forces that shape your life — are the subject of sociology. If you are curious about your community, about the causes of crime and violence, about the people who hold power in society, or about the behavior of people of different cultures, ages, sexes, races, or socio-economic levels, then you should enjoy a course in sociology.

What Is Sociology?

What is *sociology*? There are several ways to try to answer this question. The dictionary will tell you that it is the study of social relationships, social institutions, and society. The term itself, often credited to Auguste Comte (1798–1857), the founder of sociology, is derived from two root words: *socius*, which means "companion" or "associate," and *logos*, which means "word." At its most basic, then, it means "words about human associations or society." Robert Bierstedt (1970, p. 4) has noted that the combination of these two roots is unfortunate, because *socius* is Latin and *logos* is Greek. As a result, the name of the discipline is the illegitimate offspring of two languages.

Another way to find out what sociology is would be to check the table of contents of an introductory sociology text. There you would find that it is concerned with such topics as social interaction, culture, stratification, bureaucracy, population, age and sex roles, collective behavior, ecology, power and politics, norms and values, urban development, and crime and deviance.

A third method would be simply to ask people. You might get such responses as "Sociology is much like social work" and "Sociology is similar to socialism, I think."

Another procedure would be to find some sociologists and observe them at work. Some might spend most of their time poring over volumes from the census bureau or travel to northern Alaska every year to talk to Eskimos about their hunting practices. Some might investigate sexual behavior in a clinic or study kinship systems among natives of the South Pacific. Others might look into how college students perceive their professors or how television has influenced family life in the United States.

If you pursued all these approaches, you would probably find yourself with a bewildering variety of responses. What do they have in common? They all suggest that sociology is concerned with every aspect of the self in relationships with others and every aspect of the social world that affects a person's thoughts or actions. As stated by the American Sociological Association in a booklet called *Careers in Sociology* (1977), sociology is the study of social life and the social causes and consequences of human behavior. The term *social life* encompasses all interpersonal relationships, all groups or collections of persons, and all types of social organizations. The "causes and consequences of human behavior" encompass how these relationships, groups, and organizations are interrelated; how they influence personal and interpersonal behavior; how they affect and are affected by the larger society; how they change or why they remain static; and what the consequences of these factors are. This definition reflects the belief that people can be understood only in the context of their contacts, associations, and communications with other people.

Thus, sociologists may consider questions such as the following (general topics are followed by specific studies that a sociologist might undertake):

□ How do groups influence individual human behavior? (How do patterns of social interaction and behavior change when a person moves from his or her home to a college dormitory?)

□ What are the causes and consequences of a particular system of social order? (Why are women the principal landowners in some societies while men are in others?)

□ What social factors contributed to a particular social change? (Why is it that a larger percentage of women have been working outside the home during the last thirty years?)

□ What purpose is served by a particular social organization? (Why do people join the Rotary Club?)

□ What are the causes and consequences of a particular social system? (How do the patterns of social interaction in a small village differ from those in a large city?)

Other areas investigated by sociologists include racial and ethnic relationships, prejudice and discrimination, power and politics, jobs and income, families and family life, school systems and the educational process, social control, organizations, bureaucracies, groups and group dynamics, leisure, health, military systems, women's movements, and labor movements. The stratification of people by wealth, education, and power

Sociologists attempt to understand social life and social organization in a variety of settings. Consider, for example, how human interaction, employment patterns, or child-rearing practices in a Columbian village (right) may differ from those in a city such as San Francisco (below). Or consider how the contrasting types of housing, modes of transportation, or number of people in each area affect social life. These are some of the types of questions that sociologists try to answer.

and differences due to sex or age may also be examined. As you can see, sociology is an extremely broad field. In its most comprehensive sense, it can be regarded as including every aspect of social life — its causes, its forms and structures, its effects, and its changes and transformations.

The Sociological Perspective

Up to this point, we have been discussing the content of sociology. Sociology is also a perspective, a way of looking at society and social behav-

ior. Like the blind men who described the elephant differently depending on whether they felt its trunk, tail, body, or leg, everyone regards the world from his or her own point of view. A school building may be seen as a place of work by a teacher, as a place of study by a student, as a tax liability by a homeowner, as a fire hazard by a firefighter, and as a particular structural design by a builder. In the same way, sociologists consider the social world from their own unique perspective.

What is *the sociological perspective?* It is a conscious effort to question the obvious, to remove ourselves from familiar experiences and examine them critically and objectively. This sort of empirical (based on observation or experiment) investigation enables us to determine whether our generalizations about society are accurate. These investigations could involve asking questions about poverty in a wealthy nation, about the social forces leading to unionization, or about the effects of divorce on family life and children.

This perspective also entails efforts to see beyond individual experiences. The sociologist tries to interpret patterns, the regular, recurrent aspects of social life. An awareness of interaction patterns and group processes can help us understand the relationship between our personal experiences and the society we live in.

Human behavior is to a large extent shaped by the groups people belong to, by the social interactions that occur, and by the social and cultural context in which the behavior takes place. Apart from the social and cultural context, for example, it may be extremely difficult to understand the spontaneous, simultaneous, and collective shout that occurs when a person with a wooden stick hits a round object over the head of a person wearing a glove on one hand but not the other. It may be difficult to understand the anger of people in a neighborhood when children are bused to a school in a different neighborhood. Behaviors such as these reflect the group, the institution, and the society in which they occur. Since individual behavior can be understood only in its social and cultural context, the sociological perspective considers the individual as part of the larger society. It notes how the society is reflected in individuals and attempts to discover patterned behaviors and regularity in events.

The sociological perspective operates at two levels, which sociologists term *macro* and *micro*. The difference is related to the size of the unit of analysis. *Macrosociology* deals with large-scale structures and processes: broad social categories, institutions, and social systems such as war, unemployment, and divorce; solutions to these problems are sought at the structural or organizational level.

Microsociology, on the other hand, is concerned with how individuals behave in social situations. The social problems of a veteran, unemployed worker, or divorcé would be subjects for microsociological research; solutions would be sought at the personal or interpersonal level. The sociological perspective involves investigations of problems on both scales.

Perhaps the macrosociological/microsociological distinction can be clarified by elaborating on the issue of divorce. At a microlevel we can observe husbands and wives in interaction and note that divorce is more likely to occur if the persons involved can't agree on important issues, if one person takes a rigid or inflexible stance, of if the personalities of the persons involved are incompatible. At a macrolevel we can observe how divorce rates vary crossculturally by degree of societal modernization or how divorce rates are related to various systems of mate selection, lineage, or place of residence. At microlevels the unit of analysis is the person or persons in interaction; thus "solutions" to divorce may be related to personal counseling, marital education programs, or small group workshops. At macrolevels the unit of analysis is the organization, institution, or system, and solutions to divorce may be related to decreasing "free choice" of mates in favor of "parental choice," or moving to a single (patrilineal or matrilineal) lineage system rather than a multilineal one, or living with the kin group rather than in a separate residence or locale. At a microlevel we may try to change the person, the behavior, or the interaction pattern. At the macrolevel we may attempt to change the structure, the organization, or the social system. Sociologists study and analyze society and social life at both levels.

Macrosociology deals with large-scale structures and processes. At this level the sociological perspective might involve examining how systems such as the military influence or are influenced by types of governments or cooperation between nations, or how events such as war affect marriage and divorce rates or the gross national product. Macrosociology focuses on patterns of behavior and forms of organization that characterize entire societies.

Microsociology deals with people's everyday interactions. It focuses on individuals in the workplace, in marriage, or in any group interaction. It is concerned with how acts, motives, and meanings of individuals shape their social interactions, which in turn maintain or change social structures.

Sociology and Popular Wisdom

It is widely assumed, sometimes accurately so, that research findings tend to support what we already know. We all have some idea why people act the way they do and understand how society works. As social beings, most of us were raised in families and communities. Everyone has learned to obey traffic signals and danger signs. We have all heard the debate and rhetoric of presidential and local political campaigns. We have all read newspapers and heard television reports that remind us continually of crime, racial conflicts, poverty, inflation, pollution, and teenage pregnancies. We all understand social life — our own experiences make us experts in human behavior and in the nature of society. Let us examine a few examples to prove our point. Is it not obvious that

1. with divorce at an all-time high, the institution of marriage is breaking down and the number of families is decreasing drastically?

2. since the Catholic church opposes the use of artificial means of contraception, far fewer Catholics than Protestants in the United States use contraceptive devices?

3. since capital punishment leads people to give serious thought to the consequences before comitting crimes, crime rates are much lower in states that have capital punishment than in those that do not?

4. since women in most societies are confined to the home, receive relatively low pay, and are highly dependent and oppressed compared with men, more women than men commit suicide?

Many other examples could be given, but these common sense ideas should illustrate our point. Although you may agree with all of them, research findings indicate that all these statements are false. It is true that divorce rates are at an all-time high, but it is not true that marriage is breaking down, nor that the number of families is greatly decreasing. Most people who divorce remarry. People are tending to marry at a later age, and an increasing number of young people are choosing to remain single longer, but most people eventually marry. Combined with the increasing number of persons in society, neither the number of marriages nor the rate of marriages per thousand people is decreasing (see Table 1-1).

The second statement suggests that because the Catholic church opposes contraception, the proportion of Catholic users would be far lower than that of Protestants. This "obviously true" statement was accurate until fairly recently. Today, however, national survey data of married women under age forty-five show that except for sterilization, Catholic and non-Catholic contraceptive practices are quite similar (Westoff and Jones, 1977). In 1975, between 75 and 80 percent of each group were using contraception. Only slight differences exist in the use of the pill (34 percent for both non-Catholic and Catholic), IUD (9 percent versus 7.6 percent), diaphragm (4.1 percent versus 3.5 percent), condom (9.6 percent versus 14.9 percent), or foam (3.9 percent versus 2.6 percent). Thus, in this regard, the position of the church is not followed by most persons who define themselves as Catholics, at least in the United States.

The third statement suggests that crime rates are lower in states that have capital punishment than in states that do not. The evidence, however, suggests that there is very little relationship between the rate of murder and other crimes and the use of capital punishment. The murder rates in states that have the death penalty are not consistently lower than in states that do not have it. In general, the death penalty is not a deterrent to murder or other crimes. Even imprisonment does not seem to be a major deterrent, as is evident from the recidivism (repeat) rate of people who have been in prison. Rather than changing people's attitudes, punishment may make them more cautious and promote extra efforts to avoid apprehension.

The fourth statement, that women are more likely than men to commit suicide, is also without support. For a variety of reasons, the suicide rate is much higher among men than among women (see Table 1-2). This is true regardless of race for both the number and rate of suicides. In 1978, for example, of 27,294 suicides, 20,188 were by males (74 percent). The rate of suicide per 100,000 population is approximately three times as high for men as for women.

These examples illustrate that although some popular observations may be true, many others are not supported by empirical data. Without social research (see Chapter 3), it is extremely difficult to distinguish what is actually true from what our common sense tells us should be true. Even if this is the only sociology course you ever take, I hope that, after completing it, you will have a far greater understanding of yourself, of your society,

Table 1-1
Marriages, divorces, and rates: United States, 1958–1979

YEAR	MARRIAGE		DIVORCE	
	NUMBER	RATE	NUMBER	RATE[a]
1979	2,359,000	10.7	1,170,000	5.3
1978	2,282,272	10.5	1,130,000	5.2
1977	2,178,367	10.1	1,091,000	5.0
1976	2,154,807	10.0	1,083,000	5.0
1975	2,152,662	10.1	1,036,000	4.9
1974	2,229,667	10.5	977,000	4.6
1973	2,284,108	10.9	915,000	4.4
1972	2,282,154	11.0	845,000	4.1
1971	2,190,481	10.6	773,000	3.7
1970	2,158,802	10.6	708,000	3.5
1969	2,145,000	10.6	639,000	3.2
1968	2,069,000	10.4	584,000	2.9
1967	1,927,000	9.7	523,000	2.6
1966	1,857,000	9.5	499,000	2.5
1965	1,800,000	9.3	479,000	2.5
1964	1,725,000	9.0	450,000	2.4
1963	1,654,000	8.8	428,000	2.3
1962	1,577,000	8.5	413,000	2.2
1961	1,548,000	8.5	414,000	2.3
1960	1,523,000	8.5	393,000	2.2
1959	1,494,000	8.5	395,000	2.2
1958	1,451,000	8.4	368,000	2.1

[a] Rates are based on an annual basis per 1,000 population.
SOURCE: Monthly Vital Statistics Report, *Annual Summary for the United States, 1979, Births, Deaths, Marriages and Divorces,* DHHS Publication No. (PHS) 81–1120, vol. 28, no. 13, November 13, 1980, Table M, p. 9.

and of human behavior, as well as an increased ability to question many of the popular observations widely accepted as truth by the press and by our citizens.

Sociology and the Other Social Sciences

All branches of science attempt to discover general truths, propositions, or laws through methods based on observation and experimentation (see Chapter 3). Science is often divided into two categories: the social sciences and what are often referred to as the natural sciences. The natural sciences include (1) the biological sciences — biology, eugenics, botany, bacteriology, etc., which deal with living organisms, both human and nonhuman; and (2) the physical sciences — physics, chemistry, astronomy, geology, and so on, which deal with the nonliving physical world. The word "natural" must be applied to these sciences with caution, however. The *social sciences* are just as natural as those that comprise the natu-

Table 1-2
Number of suicides by race and sex, 1950–1978

YEAR	TOTAL	WHITE MALE	WHITE FEMALE	BLACK AND OTHER MALE	BLACK AND OTHER FEMALE
1950	17,145	12,755	3,713	542	135
1960	19,041	13,825	4,296	714	206
1970	23,480	15,591	6,468	1,038	383
1975	27,963	18,206	6,967	1,416	474
1978	27,294	18,619	6,631	1,569	475

	RATE PER 100,000 POPULATION				
1950	11.3	19.0	5.5	6.8	1.6
1960	10.6	17.6	5.3	7.1	1.9
1970	11.5	17.9	7.1	8.6	2.9
1975	12.7	20.1	7.4	10.6	3.3
1978	12.5	20.2	6.9	11.1	3.1

SOURCE: U.S. Bureau of the Census, *Statistical Abstract of the United States: 1980*, 101st ed., Washington, D.C., U.S. Government Printing Office, 1980, no. 310, p. 186.

ral sciences. The organization of cities, the collective action of a football team, and the patterns of interaction in a family system are just as natural as electricity, magnetism, and the behavior of insects.

Sociology is a social science, but it is important to realize that a complete understanding of a society or of social relationships would be impossible without an understanding of the physical world in which societies exist and an understanding of the biological factors that affect humans. Like the other social sciences — psychology, anthropology, economics, and political science — sociology deals with human relationships, social systems, and societies. Although the boundaries among the various social sciences are sometimes hazy, each tends to focus on a particular aspect of the world and tries to understand it. Scientists who devote their lives to the study of rocks, birds, plants, childrearing, or poverty do not deny

the importance of other aspects of the world. They find, rather, that the area they have chosen to study requires their full concentration.

Each social science focuses on selected aspects of social relationships or social systems. Scientists in each field generally devote their attention to "what is" rather than "what should be." The social sciences are also likely to have as a goal the acquisition of knowledge rather than the direct utilization of that knowledge. Each is likely to seek general laws or principles instead of isolated descriptions of particular cases or events. Thus they differ little in their focus on social phenomena, in their methods, and in their goals, but they do vary in their particular focus of attention. Also, it's not unusual for the social sciences to overlap somewhat. People living in poverty, for example, may be of equal interest to the sociologist, the demographer, and the historian. Each of them, however, would concentrate on a different aspect of the situation. As a result, an introductory course in sociology is very different from an introductory course in economics, political science, anthropology or psychology, and a brief description of the other social sciences may help us understand the nature of social science in general as well as the nature of sociology in particular.

Economics is the study of how goods, services, and wealth are produced, consumed, and distributed within societies. Figures about the gross national product, balance of payment deficits, or per capita income may seem to belong more to the realm of statistics or mathematics than to a social science, but these statistics reflect individual behavior, the relationships among groups, and the functioning of society. The effect of supply and demand on prices and the distribution and consumption of material goods serve as indicators of social exchange. Although sociologists also study factors such as these, they devote their attention to different aspects of them. Few economists, unlike sociologists, pay much attention to actual behavior or attitudes, to business enterprises as social organizations, or to the impact of religion or education on levels of productivity or consumption. Economists may provide us with import and export figures, ratios of savings to investment, and information about the rate at which money changes hands, but they would be unlikely to interpret these factors as the results of people buying new cars to gain prestige or starting new businesses because they are frustrated with their jobs or their bosses.

Political science studies power, governments, and political processes. Political scientists study different kinds of governments as well as interpersonal processes and means through which power is exercised, focusing on both abstract theory and the actual operation of government. During elections, it is political scientists who provide us with information about voting patterns, changes from previous elections, and the characteristics of voters. Traditionally, political scientists have been interested primarily in political theory and government administration. Recently, however, they have begun to devote more attention to matters of interest to the sociologist, such as the acquisition of political beliefs, the social backgrounds of the political activists, and the role of women and minorities in political outcomes.

Anthropology, like sociology, is a broad and varied discipline. It includes physical anthropology, archaeology, cultural history, social linguistics, and social and cultural anthropology. Physical anthropologists attempt to understand both primitive and modern cultures by studying physical traits such as the shape and size of skulls, artifacts such as pottery and weapons, and genetic mutations of both human and nonhuman forms of life. The work of cultural or social anthropologists, on the other hand, is very similar to that of sociologists. Like sociologists, they are concerned with social institutions, patterns of organization, and other aspects of society. There are differences in the two fields, however. Anthropologists generally study a society as a whole, whereas sociologists are likely to concentrate on one aspect of a society. Also anthropologists often live in the culture or community they are studying so that they can observe behavior directly. Sociologists are more likely to rely on statistics, questionnaires, or secondary data, and are frequently interested in comparing information about the social processes and structures of different cultures, whereas anthropologists often study cultures or communities individually.

Psychology is concerned primarily with human mental processes and individual human behavior. Frequent areas of study include learning, human development, behavior disorders, perception, emotion, motivation, creativity, personality, and a wide range of other psychic and behavioral processes. In addition to being studied by psychologists, some of these areas are also studied by sociologists and by members of a field known as *social psychology*. These three branches of social science have different emphases, however. Psychology is concerned with individuals. Social psychology is the study of how an individual influences his or her social interactions with other individuals or with groups, and of how social behavior influences the individual. Sociology deals primarily with groups and social systems. Much of the material covered in sociology textbooks is technically social psychology.

History is considered either a social science or one of the humanities and provides a chronological record of important past events. Sociology is an analytical discipline that tries to derive general truths about society. History, on the other hand, is basically descriptive; historians traditionally consider every event to be unique, assuming that attempts at classification or generalization may impair their ability to understand exactly what happened. A sociologist studying the Bolshevik revolution, therefore, might try to determine whether revolutions evolve through a standard series of stages or whether certain social situations are common to most prerevolutionary societies. A historian studying the same revolution would be more interested in discovering the exact sequence of the events that actually occurred.

Increasingly, however, many historians are becoming more sociological in their orientation. Instead of concentrating exclusively on events — names, dates, successions of kings, details of battles — they are analyzing broad social movements and general social patterns. Many are turning to sociological methods of analysis to determine what social forces influenced specific historical events.

Geography is concerned with the physical environment and the distribution of plants and animals, including humans. Geographers may study such things as why a particular trade route evolved or how the formation of nations is influenced by the physical landscape. The physical geographer investigates climate, agriculture, the distribution of plant species, and oceanography. Social and cultural geographers, like sociologists, may be interested in how the distribution of people in a particular area influences social relationships. Sometimes urban geographers and urban sociologists work together on such problems as how various types of housing affect family life and how a given transportation system affects employment and productivity. Although often not considered a social science, social geography clearly shares many areas of interest with the other social sciences.

Is *social work* a social science? Technically, it is not. Social work is the field in which the principles of the social sciences, especially sociology, are applied to actual social problems in the same way the principles of physiology are applied in medicine and principles of economics are applied in business. The *applied sciences* — those that directly use these principles — are often considered distinct from the *pure sciences* — those that seek knowledge for its own sake — but they can actually be considered to occupy different points on the same continuum. At one end of the continuum would be the disciplines that use knowledge to solve actual problems. A social worker might, for example, use information obtained from family research to try to place children in foster homes or to establish centers of spouse abuse. At the other end of the continuum would be the disciplines involved in research, not to solve a specific problem, but simply to increase our understanding of the world. A researcher of this sort might study child rearing or spouse abuse as a function of income or education levels. But few social scientists do only pure research and few social workers do *only* applied science. For example, social workers devise their own research and techniques to help people solve personal and group problems, and the resulting applications contribute to our existing body of knowledge. For their part, sociologists have recently begun to become more involved in applied research. Sociologists

The Sociologist's Image

It is, of course, true that some Boy Scout types have become sociologists. It is also true that a benevolent interest in people could be the biographical starting point for sociological studies. But it is important to point out that a malevolent and misanthropic outlook could serve just as well. Sociological insights are valuable to anyone concerned with action in society. But this action need not be particularly humanitarian. Some American sociologists today are employed by governmental agencies seeking to plan more livable communities for the nation. Other American sociologists are employed by governmental agencies concerned with wiping communi-

ties of hostile nations off the map, if and when the necessity should arise. Whatever the moral implications of these respective activities may be, there is no reason why interesting sociological studies could not be carried on in both. Similarly, criminology, as a special field within sociology, has uncovered valuable information about processes of crime in modern society. This information is equally valuable for those seeking to fight crime as it would be for those interested in promoting it. The fact that more criminologists have been employed by the police than by gangsters can be ascribed to the ethical bias of the criminologists themselves, the public rela-

tions of the police and perhaps the lack of scientific sophistication of the gangsters. It has nothing to do with the character of the information itself. In sum, "working with people" can mean getting them out of slums or getting them into jail, selling them propaganda or robbing them of their money (be it legally or illegally), making them produce better automobiles or making them better bomber pilots. As an image of the sociologist, then, the phrase leaves something to be desired, even though it may serve to describe at least the initial impulse as a result of which some people turn to the study of sociology.

SOURCE: Peter Berger, *Invitation to Sociology: A Humanistic Perspective*. Garden City, New York: Doubleday, Copyright © 1963 by Peter L. Berger. pp. 2–3. Reprinted by permission of Doubleday & Company, Inc.

and social workers do share some common tasks, then, but it is a mistake (albeit a common one) to regard sociology as equivalent to social work or social welfare.

Sociological Careers and the Uses of Sociology

Beginning students of sociology often ask a number of related questions. Some of the more common ones are (1) "Why should I take sociology? If I'm not interested in a sociological career, what use will it be to me?" (2) "What is the value of sociology to society? Why should this field be supported?" (3) "What do sociologists do? If I de-

cided to become one, what career options would be open to me?" Let us explore some answers to these questions.

What Sociologists Do

First, we should separate the discipline from the person. Sociology is the discipline. Sociologists are the people who have been trained in the discipline and practice it. They perform a wide variety of tasks. Most are employed as teachers, researchers, administrators, or policy consultants, but as we will demonstrate in our "Sociologists at Work" sections (at the end of each chapter), sociologists hold jobs in a whole range of different areas.

Sociologists as Teachers. More sociologists are employed as teachers than in any other capacity. There are more than fifteen thousand in the United States today, and at least two-thirds of them consider teaching their primary responsibility. Most teaching sociologists also serve other functions — researcher, administrator, or social critic, perhaps. Most teaching positions are found in liberal arts colleges or colleges of arts and sciences, in departments devoted to sociology exclusively or to some combination of sociology, anthropology, and social work. Increasingly, sociologists are being hired in professional schools of such fields as medicine, nursing, law, social work, business administration, theology, and education.

Sociologists as Researchers. In addition to teaching, most sociologists do or have done research. The research function is often regarded as contributing to the society at large by providing new knowledge about society. Most researchers engage in *basic or pure research,* the acquisition of knowledge for its own sake with little thought about how the results will be used. Increasingly, funding and social agencies are asking for *applied research* that will provide directives, suggestions, or answers related to a particular problem. Both types of researchers, for example, may be interested in crime. The basic researcher may seek information about the causes of crime, its prevalence, and its distribution by age, sex, or ge-

Most sociologists teach and/or do research. Here David Reisman, a sociologist at Harvard, does dictation in connection with his research. A significant segment of teachers' or researchers' time is spent not only in the classroom or at a computer terminal but alone in an office surrounded by the key tools of the profession: books and journals.

ography. The applied researcher may study existing social policies, police or court practices, or ways to decrease or eliminate a particular type of criminal activity. Both types of research make important contributions to our society.

Sociologists as Administrators. Sociologists serving as administrators work as coordinators, decision makers, or managers of a social organization. Increasingly, they are applying their knowledge of interpersonal relationships, bureaucracies, and organizations to improve employment practices in hospitals, schools, businesses, and government agencies. The trained sociologist should have a solid understanding of organizational structure, role conflicts, status differentiations, primary group relationships, both material and symbolic rewards, and the relationship of a particular institution or organization to the larger community and society. Although not all sociologists make good administrators, sociological training should provide many of the intellectual resources and conceptual tools necessary to serve effectively in this capacity.

Sociologists as Policy Consultants. As an outgrowth of their role as academicians and researchers, sociologists are often sought out by governments, businesses, and communities to offer suggestions or advice. Their services have been requested in court decisions on busing, in neighborhood programs for crime prevention, in the development of personnel policies for insurance companies, in discrimination cases involving automotive companies, and in the creation of community mental health centers. Sociologists seldom work as full-time consultants, however. They are used in specific situations such as to offer methodological advice to groups doing evaluation studies, assist in data analysis, or explain the probable consequences of a set of alternative courses of action. Many people consider this capability of social scientists to be an underutilized na-

Sociologists are often called upon to provide advice in their areas of expertise. A criminologist with a PhD in sociology worked with the Detroit Police Department to set up this neighborhood crime watch program.

tional resource. Sociologists, economists, political scientists, anthropologists, and psychologists, all of whom are experts in a particular aspect of society, could often make a much greater contribution to society than they are given an opportunity to make.

Uses of Sociology

As can be seen from the previous discussion, sociologists serve in a variety of capacities. Although teaching, research, administration, and consulting are not reserved exclusively for the sociologist, they have a unique contribution to make in these roles. Most of you are not studying sociology to make it a career. What does it have to offer you?

An Editor Speaks Out on Sociology and the Promotion of Public Policy

Sociology at its best is the study of the development and structure of society and social relationships. While not a precise science that can predict behavior, it is nonetheless a valuable discipline assisting the search for more rational social arrangements.

Sociologists invite trouble, however, when they break out of such a useful supporting role into the stardom of advocacy based on their fallible predictions. The fact that they can walk away from a failed policy and go back to the drawing board — a luxury politicians can't afford — underscores the risk of too close a relationship between research and policymaking.

This is why so much interest and controversy have been raised by the various studies of schools and society by Professor James Coleman, now of the University of Chicago. When he reported in 1966 that black children appeared to learn better in integrated classrooms, politicians and judges paid heed. They listened again, in 1978, when Professor Coleman said further research had raised questions about the earlier findings, and that desegregation was not having the desired educational result. And policymakers paid attention again this month when a new Coleman report held that private high schools seemed to provide a better education than public ones.

Responding more quickly this time than before to critics who questioned his methods and findings, Mr. Coleman has already rephrased some of his conclusions. He said the new study did not prove any inherent superiority of private schools, only that they were more likely to stress things like discipline, homework and high standards, which are the hallmarks of effective schools, whether private or public.

Put that way, the Coleman study only confirms many other studies, such as John Goodlad's "Study of Schooling," conducted for the past seven years at the University of California, Los Angeles, and a 1979 British report entitled "Fifteen Thousand Hours." It also confirms the common-sense experience of many like Abe Lass, retired principal of Brooklyn's Abraham Lincoln High School, who has long insisted that the first requirement of a good school is that children be able to go to the toilet unafraid.

But in reconsidering his report, Mr. Coleman also conceded that he "wanted to address the policy issue of whether public funds should be used to encourage private education." That statement of political purpose at a time of controversy over his findings of fact was hardly a service to sociology. If those who wield political power are to make use of sociological studies — and they should — the research should be neutral both in fact and appearance. The situation is not unlike that in 1972, when Christopher Jencks confused the discussion of a school study called "Inequality." He said he had found that public schools were a poor instrument for eliminating economic and social inequalities, but instead of resting on his findings, he made them the basis of sweeping policy recommendations for redistribution of income and socialism.

Sociology gains in prestige and value when it keeps its distance from the political battles of the day. Mr. Coleman himself proved the value of such restraint in his study of "The Adolescent Society" in 1961. That landmark study of adolescent behavior, peer pressures and their effect on school and society offered the first coherent analysis of the youth culture that became such a prominent feature of American life in the Sixties. Without presuming to recommend, it still helped educators and others to shape youth and school policies for years to come.

SOURCE: Fred M. Hechinger, The Editorial Notebook, *The New York Times,* May 18, 1981, p. 18. © 1981 by The New York Times Company. Reprinted by permission.

First, because it is concerned with every aspect of social life, sociology should interest every social being. Just as we should have an understanding of sickness without being doctors and an understanding of money without being economists, an understanding of sociological principles can be useful to us in our daily lives because they are concerned with an enormous range of events. Sociologists may study topics as diverse as the intimacy of husband and wife and the dynamics of mob violence. Violent crime may be the subject of one study, the communion of persons in a religious institution the subject of another. One investigator may be concerned with the inequities of race, age, and sex, while another may investigate the shared beliefs of common culture. Sociology is interested in both the typical or normal and the unusual or bizarre.

Second, even if you are not interested in a career in sociology, it offers valuable preparation for other types of careers. If your interest lies in business, law, education, medicine, architecture, ministry, social work, public administration, politics, or any profession dealing with people, social life, or the social order, sociology can be a useful major since it provides a wealth of knowledge that can be applied to any of these fields.

Third, sociology can teach us to consider perspectives other than our own and to look beyond the individual in our efforts to understand individual behavior. It encourages us to look not merely at how people and events are unique and different, but at how people share perceptions and how events occur in patterns. It familiarizes us with a range of theoretical explanations of how people think and act, how societies' structures change, and how society operates.

Fourth, since research is basic to sociology, even a brief introduction to the field will acquaint you with a range of research techniques and methods that can be applied to any social area: family, education, poverty, delinquency, war, ecology, and so on. Whether we use simple observation, formal structured interviews, content analysis, experimental designs, or elaborate statistical computations, a knowledge of the variety of research techniques available should be useful in many settings.

Fifth, and perhaps most important, sociology can help us understand ourselves. Humans are social animals, and people can understand themselves only in the context of the society in which they live. A knowledge of the social constraints that bind us can be frustrating — we may feel trapped, angry about our inability to control our lives, and disappointed at the social inequities that surround us. It is only through understanding our society, however, that we can appreciate what is good about it and try to improve conditions we believe to be bad.

Joel Charon (1980) provided a good summary of the uses of sociology when he listed some of the insights he has gained from his studies in this field:

1. To be different is not to be wrong. Others may think us funny, immoral, or dumb, but these judgments are merely aspects of their social definition, not absolute truths.

2. We are prisoners of social organization. Much of what we do is determined by the structures of the cultures we live in. This knowledge can be liberating, however — through understanding society we can achieve the freedom to live as we choose.

3. Things are not what they seem to be. We adopt the views transmitted to us by our culture, but these views are often limited and superficial and do not constitute understanding.

The study of sociology also made Charon more realistic about what is possible in society. Certain ideals are worth working for and can be achieved. By devoting our efforts to conditions that can be changed, we can influence the direction of the social evolution that is always occurring, both in our own lives and in the larger society.

SOCIOLOGISTS AT WORK
Pursuing a Graduate Degree

Mary Lisa Carrico is a student of sociology. In 1982 she earned an undergraduate degree in sociology from Angelo State University in San Angelo, Texas, and made plans to enroll in the graduate program at Texas Christian University. She will be a departmental teaching assistant and a candidate for a master's degree. She expects to continue her studies and earn a doctorate.

What drew Carrico to the study of sociology? "I'd never even thought about sociology as a major," she admits, "until I took an introductory class. The professor made it so interesting that I wanted to learn more about the field. After I had taken about four sociology classes, I decided to major in sociology. My parents weren't too thrilled. They were sure I'd never get a job — they thought of sociology as a very limited field, in which my options would be confined mainly to teaching. But I stuck with it, and the more I learn, the more possibilities I see for work in sociology."

And not just for work, Carrico finds. "Sociology can be applied to every interaction between two or more people, so of course my study of sociology has helped me in other areas. It has helped me learn to deal with people better and to be more open to new situations. Specifically, sociology has helped me very much in journalism, which was my minor. The things I learned in studying sociology have helped me in conducting interviews and looking at stories from new angles."

Carrico has not decided exactly what areas of sociology she will concentrate on in graduate school, but she has narrowed the field down. "The interactions of small groups fascinate me, and social psychology teaches us a lot about that. I grew up in an area with a high minority population and I've seen the problem of prejudice working from both sides, so I'm interested in the sociology of minority groups. And I guess I've been interested in deviant subcultures — strictly from a sociological viewpoint, of course!"

What comes next for Mary Lisa Carrico? "I'd like to be involved in research, and to teach at the university level," she says. "I also plan to continue my work in journalism. Being able to communicate the results of research is as important in its own way as the research itself. Before I settle down in a somewhat permanent position, though, I plan to get as much experience as possible. Internships, assistantships, and other jobs will give me a chance to explore the various job possibilities in sociology. I see my years in graduate school as the perfect time to get involved in a variety of projects so I can decide exactly how I will apply my study of sociology in my life."

Summary

Sociology is the study of society, social life, and the causes and consequences of human social behavior. The terms society and social life are assumed to include interpersonal relations within and among groups and social systems. Sociology is concerned with all aspects of the social world. Concerns range from such subjects as the family, sibling rivalry, and small-group dynamics to international conflict, organizational processes, and bureaucracies like the federal government.

In their efforts to understand social life, sociologists question the obvious, seek patterns and regularities, and look beyond individuals to social interactions and group processes. They try to assess individual behavior in the context of the larger society. This perspective is applied both to microsociology, which considers problems at the level of interpersonal and small-group processes, and to macrosociology, which considers large-scale problems, structures, social organizations, and social systems.

Although many people believe that the structure and workings of society are a matter of common knowledge, countless sociological findings disprove popular conceptions and provide surprising insights.

Sociology is one of the social sciences, disciplines that try to systematically and objectively understand social life and predict how various influences will affect it. Each social science attempts to accumulate a body of knowledge about a particular aspect of society and the social world. Economics deals with the production, consumption, and distribution of goods and services. Political science deals with power, governments, and political processes. Anthropology deals with social and physical aspects of both primitive and contemporary cultures. Psychology is concerned with the bases of individual human behavior and with mental and psychic processes. History explores past events, and geography investigates the relationship between people and their physical environment. Strictly speaking, social work is not a social science — it is not concerned chiefly with accumulating a body of basic knowledge. Rather, it is considered an applied discipline that uses the knowledge of the social scientist to improve social life.

At the end of the chapter, we raised and answered three questions about sociology: (1) What do sociologists do and what career options are available to them? (2) Why should students who are not interested in sociology as a career take it as a course? (3) What is the value of sociology to society? In answering these questions, we noted that most sociologists are employed as teachers, researchers, administrators, consultants, or some

combination of these roles. Sociology is of value to people uninterested in making it their career because it (1) provides a basic understanding of social life, (2) is a useful preparation for other careers, (3) broadens the range of perspectives from which we try to understand the social world, (4) provides an orientation to the use of research techniques applicable in a wide variety of contexts, and (5) helps us understand ourselves and our positions in society.

In the next chapter, we consider sociology from a historical perspective, noting its development in Europe and America and examining the theoretical orientations predominant in the field today.

Key Terms

anthropology
economics
geography
history
macrosociology
microsociology
political science
psychology and social psychology
pure and applied science
social science
social work
sociology
the sociological perspective

Suggested Readings

Berger, Peter. **Invitation to Sociology: A Humanistic Perspective.** *Garden City, N.Y.: Doubleday Anchor, 1963.* A brief introduction to sociology, written in a nontechnical, easily understood style.

Careers in Sociology. *A publication of the American Sociological Association, Washington, D.C., 1977.* A booklet providing a series of vignettes that illustrate careers in sociology at various levels of education.

Charon, Joel M. **The Meaning of Sociology.** *Sherman Oaks, Calif.: Alfred Publishing 1980.* A concise, easy-to-read overview of the field of sociology.

Harris, C. C. **The Sociological Enterprise.** *New York: St. Martin's Press, 1980.* This book critically examines sociological inquiry and some of its fundamental concepts. It may be difficult reading for undergraduates.

Inkeles, Alex. **What Is Sociology?** *Englewood Cliffs, N.J.: Prentice-Hall, 1964.* A brief overview of the history, approaches, and schools of sociological thought.

Lazarsfeld, Paul F. and Jeffrey G. Reitz. **An Introduction to Applied Sociology.** *New York: Else-vier, 1975.* A book about applying the principles of sociology to real problems.

Mills, C. Wright. **The Sociological Imagination.** *New York: Grove Press, 1959.* This brief book, a classic in sociology, provides a readable overview of the sociological perspective.

Scott, Robert A. and Arnold R. Shore. **Why Sociology Does Not Apply: A Study of the Use of Sociology in Public Policy.** *New York: Elsevier, 1979.* A serious critique of the purpose of sociology in society. The authors are particularly concerned with the relationship between pure and applied research and their actual relevance to social policy (as distinct from their relevance to intradisciplinary concerns).

Chapter 2
The Development of Sociology

The facts will eventually test all our theories; and they form, after all, the only impartial jury to which we can appeal.

— Jean Louis Rodolphe Agassiz

The Development of Sociology in Europe

The study of sociology is a recent development in social history. Philosophers such as Aristotle and Plato had much to say about society and human relationships, but until the late nineteenth century, no writer we know of could appropriately be considered a sociologist. In fact, the label "sociologist" was not applied to the early practitioners of the field in their own time — they have been identified as such only in retrospect. Most early writers were interdisciplinary in orientation, drawing their ideas from philosophy and the physical and biological sciences. As a result of developments in the natural sciences, much early writing in sociology was based on the assumption that laws of human behavior could be discovered in the same way that laws of nature had been discovered by astronomers, physicists, and other natural scientists. These early writers also had great faith in the power of reason, assuming that it could be used to formulate laws that could be applied to improve social life and eliminate or diminish social problems.

These assumptions were rapidly put to a test as the industrial revolution presented new challenges and social problems. People began to migrate to towns and cities for factory jobs. With many of these jobs came low wages, long working hours, child labor practices, housing and sanitation problems, social alienation, social conflict, crime, and a range of other social problems that provided an abundance of conditions for concern, study, and solution. The industrial revolution that began in England, social revolutions in France under Napoleon, and political upheavals throughout Europe provide the backdrop for the emergence of the discipline known today as sociology.

We can begin to understand this discipline, now less than two hundred years old, by briefly examining a few of the early writers who were influential in its development. An understanding of the origins of sociology may improve our grasp of what the discipline is today. We will discuss the ideas of five theorists: Comte, Marx, Spencer, Durkheim, and Weber. These men all lived in the nineteenth century, and their ideas stemmed from their personal circumstances and social settings.

Auguste Comte

Auguste Comte (1798–1857) was born in southern France, the son of a minor government official. Educated in Paris, his studies were concentrated in mathematics and the natural sciences. Before completing his schooling, he was expelled for participating in a student insurrection against the school's administration. He then became secretary to Henri Comte de Saint-Simon, an influential political leader and advocate of a pre-Marxist version of socialism — a system in which the means of production (e.g., industry) is owned by the people. Comte was greatly influenced by Saint-Simon, but their relationship ended when Comte was accused of plagiarism, a charge he denied. He held another job in Paris for approximately twelve years, but was again dismissed. He had made too many enemies and too few friends.

Comte is usually credited with being the "father of sociology" since he coined the term sociology. He first called this new social science "social physics" because he believed that society must be studied in the same scientific manner as the world of the natural sciences. Like the natural sciences, Comte said, sociology would use empirical methods to discover basic laws of society, which would benefit mankind by playing a major part in the improvement of the human condition.

Comte is best known for his law of human progress, which states that each of our leading conceptions, each branch of our knowledge, all human intellectual development, passes successively through three different theoretical conditions: the *theological,* or fictitious; the *metaphysical,* or abstract; and the *scientific,* or positive. In addition, each mental age of mankind is accompanied by a specific type of social organization and political dominance. In the first stage, the theological, everything is explained and understood through the supernatural. The family is the prototypical social unit (the model or standard to which others conform) and the political dominance is held by priests and military men. In the second stage, the metaphysical, abstract forces are assumed to be the source of explanation and understanding. The state replaces the family as the prototypical social unit and, as in the Middle Ages and the Renaissance, the political dominance is held by churchmen and lawyers. In the third and highest stage, the scientific, the laws of the universe are studied through observation, experimentation, and comparison. The whole human race replaces the state as the operative social unit, and the political dominance is held by industrial administrators and scientific moral guides. It was Comte's assertion that the scientific stage of human knowledge and intellectual development was just beginning in his day. According to Comte, sociology, like the natural sciences, could henceforth draw on the methods of science to explain and understand the laws of progress and the social order.

A related concept originated by Comte was the view that society was a type of "organism." Like plants and animals, society had a structure consisting of many interrelated parts, and it evolved from simpler to more complex forms. Using this organic model as a base, he reasoned that sociology should focus on *social statics,* the structure of the organism, and on *social dynamics,* the organism's processes and forms of change.

Comte believed that sociology was the means by which a more just and rational social order could be achieved.

Karl Marx

Karl Marx (1818–1883) was born in Germany. His father, a lawyer, and his mother were both descended from long lines of rabbis. Marx attended college, planning to practice law, but after becoming involved with a radical antireligious group he decided to devote his life to philosophy. Unable to get a university position, he became a writer for a radical publication and wrote a series of articles on certain inhumane social conditions. His articles attracted the attention of government officials who opposed his views, and he lost his job. Shortly thereafter he moved to Paris and met the leading intellectuals of the radical movements of Europe, completing his conversion to socialism. He began his lifelong friendship with Engels, with whom he wrote the now famous *Communist Manifesto* (1847). Having joined the Communist League in Brussels, he returned to Germany. He was again exiled for his activities. He moved to London where, with his friend Engels, he continued to promote his views until his death in 1883.

The theme common to all the writings of Marx and Engels was a profound sense of moral outrage at the misery produced in the lower classes by the new industrial order. Marx concluded that political revolution was a vital necessity in the evolutionary process of society and that it was the only means by which the improvement of social conditions could be achieved.

Marx was a major social theorist and contributor to economic and philosophical thought. He believed that *social conflict* — struggles and strife — were at the core of society, the source of all social change. He asserted that all history was marked by economic determinism, the idea that all change, social conditions, and even society it-

Karl Marx (1818–1883) addressed his writings to the inequalities between the producers of wealth (labor) and the owners of its production (management). He believed that as a social scientist he should not only observe, but work to change the inequalities that existed between the different classes.

self are based on economic factors and that economic inequality results in class struggles between the *bourgeoisie,* or owners and rulers, and the *proletariat,* the industrial workers. These conflicts between the rich and the poor, the managers and the workers, lead to feelings of alienation among the workers. The recognition among workers that they share the same plight leads to a sense of "class consciousness" and ultimately, according to Marx, to revolution.

These ideas were in sharp contrast to those of Comte and many other key figures of the nineteenth century. Comte proposed that the social order be modified by science and research findings, but Marx believed that conflict, revolution, and the overthrow of capitalism were inevitable.

Today, regardless of whether they agree or disagree with Marx's ideas, few sociologists deny the importance of the contributions he made. Sociologists are still trying to understand the influence of economic determinism, social conflict, social structure, social class, and social change on society.

Herbert Spencer

Herbert Spencer (1820-1903) was born in England, the son of a school teacher. Like Comte, he received considerable training in mathematics and the natural sciences but little in history and none in English. Feeling unfit for a university career, he worked as a railway engineer, a draftsman, and finally as a journalist and writer.

One of Spencer's major concerns was with the evolutionary nature of changes in social structure and social institutions. He believed that human societies pass through an evolutionary process similar to the process Darwin explained in his theory of natural selection. It was Spencer who coined the phrase "survival of the fittest," and he was the first to believe that human societies evolved according to the principles of natural laws. Just as natural selection favors certain organisms and permits them to survive and multiply, societies that have adapted to their surroundings and can compete will survive. Those that have not adapted and cannot compete will encounter difficulties and eventually die.

Spencer's *evolutionary scheme* paralleled Darwin's theory of biological evolution in other ways. He believed that societies evolved from relative homogeneity and simplicity to heterogeneity and complexity. As simple societies progress, they become increasingly complex and differentiated. Spencer viewed societies not simply as collections of individuals, but as organisms with a life and vitality of their own.

In sharp contrast to Comte, the idea of survival of the fittest led Spencer to argue for a policy of noninterference in human affairs and society. He opposed legislation designed to solve social problems, believing it would interfere with the natural selection process. He also opposed free public education, assuming that those who really wanted to learn would find the means. Just as societies that could not adapt would die out, Spencer contended, individuals who could not fit in did not deserve to flourish.

As you can imagine, Spencer's ideas had the support of people of wealth and power. His theories strengthened the position of those who wanted to keep the majority of the population impoverished and minimally educated. His ideas also tended to support a discriminatory policy — was it not a natural evolutionary law that kept people unequal? Like Marx, Spencer thought conflict and change were necessary parts of the evolutionary process. Unlike Marx, however, he believed that planned change would disrupt the orderly evolution of society, which he thought would eventually improve the social order. His goals are a radical departure from those of Marx in other respects, too, of course.

Spencer was one of the earlier writers to be concerned with the special problem of objectivity in the social sciences. Comte never seemed concerned with potential conflicts among his personal views, his religious mission, and his analysis of society. Marx denied that objective social science was possible, believing that theory was inseparable from socialist practice. Spencer, however, devoted attention specifically to the problem of bias and other difficulties that sociologists face in their work.

Those familiar with contemporary politics in the United States will recognize a recent resurgence of ideas similar to those espoused by Spencer, but today few sociologists accept his ultraconservative theory of noninterference in social change. There is, however, widespread acceptance of the idea that societies grow progressively more complex as they evolve.

Emile Durkheim

Emile Durkheim (1858–1917) can be considered the first French academic sociologist. Before Durkheim, sociology was not a part of the French education system, although such related fields as education, social philosophy, and psychology were studied. In 1892, the University of Paris granted him its first doctor's degree in sociology. Six years later he became the first French scholar to hold a chair in sociology. In addition to teaching, Durkheim wrote critical reviews and published important papers and books. His best known books include *The Division of Labor in Society, The Rules of Sociological Method, Suicide,* and *Elementary Forms of Religious Life.*

Durkheim is responsible for several important ideas. He refused to explain social events by assuming that they operated according to the same rules as biology or psychology. To Durkheim, social phenomena are *social facts* that have distinctive social characteristics and determinants. He defined social facts as "every way of acting, fixed or not, capable of exercising on the individual an external constraint" (1950, p. 2). Being external to the individual, they outlive individuals and endure over time. They include such things as customs, laws, and the general rules of behavior that people accept without question. Stopping at traffic lights, wearing shirts, and combing one's hair are behaviors most people perform without dissent. In short, individuals are more the products of society than the creators of it.

Although an individual can come to know and be a part of society, society itself is external to the individual. For this reason, Durkheim concentrated on examining characteristics of groups and structures rather than individual attributes. Instead of looking at the personal traits of religious believers, for example, he focused on the cohesion or lack of cohesion of specific religious groups.

Emile Durkheim (1858–1917) advanced social theory as well as social methodology in central ways. He was especially concerned with the problem of social order: how individuals can live together in a harmonious society. He advanced sociological research with a classic statistical study that showed how the incidence of suicide will vary from one population group to another, influenced by social forces.

Durkheim's work *Suicide* deserves special attention for several reasons. It established a unique model for social research, and it clearly demonstrated that human behavior, although it may seem very individual, can be understood only by investigating the social context in which the behavior takes place. After looking at numerous statistics on different countries and different groups of people, Durkheim concluded that suicide was a *social* phenomenon, related somehow to the individual's involvement in group life and the extent to which he or she was part of some cohesive social unit. Durkheim's central thesis was that the more a person is integrated into intimate social groups, the less likely he or she is to commit suicide. Thus, people who have a low level of social integration and group involvement, such as the unmarried and those without strong religious convictions, would be expected to have higher suicide rates. Durkheim found that this was true.

He believed that social integration was achieved through people's mutual dependence and acceptance of a system of common beliefs. An important element in the system of beliefs was religion, whose ceremonies become common experiences, symbols shared by the association of a group of people.

Durkheim played a key role in the founding of sociology. Although Comte, Marx, and Spencer introduced new ideas about society and helped convince the public that sociology and the other social sciences deserved a hearing, it was Durkheim who made sociology a legitimate academic enterprise.

Max Weber

Max Weber (1864–1920) was born in Germany, the son of a wealthy German politician. He was trained in law and economics, receiving his doctorate from the University of Heidelberg at the age of twenty-five. For the next several years he taught economics, but he soon succumbed to the severe mental illness that kept him an invalid

Max Weber (1864–1920) developed a sociological perspective that balanced two views. On the one hand he believed that social scientists should study the subjective values and meanings that individuals attach to their own behavior and that of others. At the same time he believed that social scientists should study these values and meanings objectively, remaining morally neutral or value-free. His own investigations covered very diverse fields, including law, politics, economics, religion, and authority.

and recluse for much of his life. Despite this condition, Weber was a prolific writer. His best known works in sociology include *The Protestant Ethic and the Spirit of Capitalism, The Sociology of Hinduism and Buddhism, Theory of Social and Economic Organization,* and *Methodology of the Social Sciences.*

Weber's mixed feelings toward authority, familial or political, are reflected in his writings on the topic of power and authority. Weber discussed why men claim authority and expect their wishes to be obeyed. (Typically for his period, women were not considered.) His approach to sociology, however, has probably been as influential as his ideas. His predecessors considered societies in terms of their large social structures, social divisions, and social movements. Spencer based his studies on the belief that societies evolved like organisms, Marx considered society in terms of class conflicts, and Durkheim was concerned with the institutional arrangements that maintain the cohesion of social structures. These theorists assumed that society, although composed of individuals, existed apart from them. In Weber's work, the *subjective* meanings that humans attach to their interactions with other humans played a much greater role. Weber believed that sociologists must study not just social facts and social structures, but *social actions*, the external objective behaviors as well as the internalized values, motives, and subjective meanings that individuals attach to their own behavior and to the behavior of others. He also contended that social actions should be studied through qualitative, subjective methods as well as objective and quantitative techniques. The goal, Weber believed, was to achieve a "sympathetic understanding" of the minds of others. He called this approach *verstehen:* understanding human action by examining the subjective meanings that people attach to their own behavior and to the behavior of others. Once values, motives, and intentions were identified, Weber contended, sociologists could treat them objectively and scientifically.

This approach is evident in Weber's interpretation of social class. Whereas Marx saw class as rooted in economic determinism, particularly as related to property ownership, Weber argued that social class involves subjective perceptions of power, wealth, ownership, and social prestige, as well as the objective aspects of these factors.

Besides the scholars we have discussed, many other European thinkers have made important contributions to sociology, including Georg Simmel, Henri de Saint-Simon, Vilfredo Pareto, Ferdinand Tönnies, and Karl Mannheim. With rare exceptions, they viewed society as a social unit that transcended the individual or was greater than the sum of individuals. It was for this reason, in part, that they did not investigate the means by which individual humans come to accept and reflect the fundamental conditions and structures of their societies — a question that was an important concern of some early American sociologists.

The Development of Sociology in America

The earliest sociologists were Europeans, but much of the development of sociology took place in the United States. The first department of sociology was established in 1893 at the University of Chicago, and many important early figures of the discipline were associated with that institution. Sociology is such a young discipline that your instructors may have met or studied with many of the leading early sociologists.

Most of the earlier American sociologists shared with their European forerunners an interest in social problems and social reform, in part because of the rapid social change that had been taking place in this country. These scholars focused on urbanization and urban problems — ghettos, prostitution, drug addiction, juvenile delinquency, immigration, and race relations.

The Chicago School

Until the 1940s, the University of Chicago was the leading sociological training and research center in America. Seven of the first twenty-seven presidents of the American Sociological Association taught or were educated at that institution. The city of Chicago served as a living laboratory for the study of many early social problems.

One leading figure in this group was Robert E. Park (1864–1944), who studied in Germany with a sociologist named Georg Simmel. Park worked as a secretary to Booker T. Washington, and also as a journalist, before beginning his work at the University in 1914, and he was the author of several important books. With another writer he wrote an early textbook in sociology (1921) and a book called *The City* (1925), which showed how urban communities are areas of both cooperation and competition much like ecological habitats that occur in nature. The multidisciplinary approach he established became known as *social ecology* (described in Chapter 19).

After World War I, a group of scholars at the University of Chicago developed an approach

Robert E. Park (1864–1944) was one of the most influential members of the "Chicago School" of sociology. He brought his interest in the city and in urban processes into the university and into the lives of his students more than any other scholar.

to social psychology known today simply as the "Chicago School." Previously, human behavior had been explained primarily in terms of instincts, drives, unconscious processes, and other innate characteristics. The Chicago School, whose members included Charles Horton Cooley, George Herbert Mead, and W. I. Thomas, emphasized instead the importance of social interactions in the development of human thought and action. Mead was the chief advocate of the view that humans respond to symbolic and abstract meanings as well as concrete experiences, and that self and society are one and the same in that individuals internalize social role expectations, social values, and norms. Humans are both actors and reactors, they are self-stimulating and can produce their own actions, responses, and definitions. To most members of society, for example, the act of burning a flag is more than a need for heat. People have learned to attach a special significance and meaning to a flag and respond with agreement or anger over a particular symbolic act, in this case, burning the flag. They might turn to others to ask why this is happening or to tell others what to do. This ability to internalize norms, share meanings, and anticipate responses is what makes social order and social systems possible. These ideas are basic to what was later called the *symbolic interactionist perspective,* which is explained in more detail in this chapter and those that follow.

The decade of the 1930s was a period of rapid change in American sociology. It was during this time that the field developed its "service" relationship to national public policy, its theoretical focus on macro systems, and its methods of large-scale quantification. In the words of Lengermann (1979, p. 196), "The societal crisis of the thirties raised new empirical and theoretical questions for sociologists, brought new demands from public and state to bear on the professional community, opened up new sources of employment and research support, created career anxiety for many sociologists and helped produce the regional associations." Lengermann claims, however, that the depression of the 1930s was not the cause of changes in sociology during this decade, since the methodological, theoretical, and professional transformation was in process prior to 1929. Rather the changes were brought about by factors such as the growth and differentiation of the profession, by emerging elitist coalitions, and by the loss of momentum of the Chicago scholars.

The Shift of Influence to the East

In the 1940s the center of sociological research shifted from Chicago to schools like Harvard and Columbia. Talcott Parsons (1902–1979), who founded the sociology department at Harvard, rapidly became the leading social theorist in America, if not the world. Drawing heavily on the work of European thinkers such as Weber and Durkheim, he developed a very broad "general theory of action" (Parsons and Shils, 1951), in which he attempted to analyze the influence of a great variety of social factors. He applied his conclusions in many areas, including the family, health, education, the economy, religion, and race relations. Although generations of graduate students have joked about the difficulty of understanding his complex abstract writing style, he had an undeniable influence on American sociology.

Robert K. Merton (1910–   ), a student of Parsons, began his teaching career at Harvard. From 1941 until his official retirement in the 1970s, however, Merton was affiliated with Columbia University. Although his general orientation was similar to Parson's, Merton was much less abstract and more concerned with linking general theory to empirical testing. This approach came to be known as the *middle range theory*. His contributions to our understanding of such concepts as social structures, self-fulfilling prophecies, deviance, and bureaucracies place him among the leading American social theroists.

C. Wright Mills, Lewis Coser, George Homans, Erving Goffman, and Herbert Blumer will also be mentioned throughout the book as

Talcott Parsons (1902–1979) (top) is recognized as the most important abstract theorist in America. He developed a general theory of action that analyzed social phenomena ranging from individual behaviors to large structures of society. Robert K. Merton (1910–   ) (below) is an American sociologist who developed sociological theories of the "middle range." These theories are less abstract that those of Parsons. Merton is one of the major contributors to structural-functional theory.

A Sociological Parable: Merton's Self-fulfilling Prophecy

It is the year 1932. The Last National Bank is a flourishing institution. A large part of its resources is liquid without being watered. Cartwright Millingville has ample reason to be proud of the banking institution over which he presides. Until Black Wednesday. As he enters his bank, he notices that business is unusually brisk. A little odd, that, since the men at the A.M.O.K. steel plant and the K.O.M.A. mattress factory are not usually paid until Saturday. Yet here are two dozen men, obviously from the factories, queued up in front of the tellers' cages. As he turns into his private office, the president muses rather compassionately: "Hope they haven't been laid off in midweek. They should be in the shop at this hour."

But speculations of this sort have never made for a thriving bank, and Millingville turns to the pile of documents upon his desk. His precise signature is affixed to fewer than a score of papers when he is disturbed by the absence of something familiar and the intrusion of something alien. The low discreet hum of bank business has given way to a strange and annoying stridency of many voices. A situation has been defined as real. And that is the beginning of what ends as Black Wednesday — the last Wednesday, it might be noted, of the Last National Bank.

Cartwright Millingville had never heard of the Thomas Theorem ["If men define situations as real, they are real in their consequences"]. But he had no difficulty in recognizing its workings. He knew that, despite the comparative liquidity of the bank's assets, a rumor of insolvency, once believed by enough depositors, would result in the insolvency of the bank. And by the close of Black Wednesday — and Blacker Thursday — when the long lines of anxious depositors, each frantically seeking to salvage his own, grew to longer lines of even more anxious depositors, it turned out that he was right.

The stable financial structure of the bank had depended upon one set of definitions of the situation: belief in the validity of the interlocking system of economic promises men live by. Once depositors had defined the situation otherwise, once they questioned the possibility of having these promises fulfilled, the conse-

major contributors to the development of sociology. These are just a few of the many influential scholars we do not have room to discuss. It is perhaps sufficient to say that sociology is stronger in the United States than in any other country although the field is also well established in many other parts of the world. The American Sociological Association currently has about fourteen thousand members, a number far greater than in any other country.

Contemporary sociology, like most academic disciplines, is concerned with many subject areas. It uses a wide variety of methodological tools and procedures and offers a range of theories to explain the phenomena it deals with. These social theories and major theoretical orientations are discussed in the next section.

The Major Theoretical Perspectives in Sociology

Theories are explanations offered to account for a set of phenomena. Social theories are explanations of social phenomena — why people choose to marry as they do or why people behave differently in different social situations.

We all develop theories (to use the term in its broadest sense) to help us explain a wide variety

quences of this unreal definition were real enough.

A familiar type-case this, and one doesn't need the Thomas theorem to understand how it happened — not, at least, if one is old enough to have voted for Franklin Roosevelt in 1932. But with the aid of the theorem the tragic history of Millingville's bank can perhaps be converted into a sociological parable which may help us understand not only what happened to hundreds of banks in the '30's but also what happens to the relations between Negro and white, between Protestant and Catholic and Jew in these days.

The parable tells us that public definitions of a situation (prophecies or predictions) become an integral part of the situation and thus affect subsequent developments. This is peculiar to human affairs. It is not found in the world of nature, untouched by human hands. Predictions of the

return of Halley's comet do not influence its orbit. But the rumored insolvency of Millingville's bank did affect the actual outcome. The prophecy of collapse led to its own fulfillment.

So common is the pattern of the self-fulfilling prophecy that each of us has his favored specimen. Consider the case of the examination neurosis. Convinced that he is destined to fail, the anxious student devotes more time to worry than to study and then turns in a poor examination. The initially fallacious anxiety is transformed into an entirely justified fear. Or it is believed that war between two nations is inevitable. Actuated by this conviction, representatives of the two nations become progressively alienated, apprehensively countering each "offensive" move of the other with a "defensive" move of their own. Stockpiles of armaments, raw materials, and armed men grow larger and eventually the anticipa-

tion of war helps create the actuality.

The self-fulfilling prophecy is, in the beginning, a *false* definition of the situation evoking a new behavior which makes the originally false conception come *true*. The specious validity of the self-fulfilling prophecy perpetuates a reign of error. For the prophet will cite the actual course of events as proof that he was right from the very beginning. (Yet we know that Millingville's bank was solvent, that it would have survived for many years had not the misleading rumor *created* the very conditions of its own fulfillment.) Such are the perversities of social logic.

SOURCE: Robert K. Merton, "The Self-fulfilling Prophecy," *Social Theory and Social Structure*, Revised and Enlarged Ed. Glencoe, Ill.: The Free Press, a Corporation, 1957, pp. 422–423. Reprinted with permission of Macmillan Publishing Co., Inc.

---

of events. Even when the explanations are wrong, they may help us develop guidelines for behavior and hypotheses that can be tested.

Suppose, for example, that several sociologists are trying to determine why the rate of armed robbery has risen in Metropolis in the last ten years. One sociologist might suggest the proposition that it was due to the increase in unemployment, which forced people to rob to get money for food. Another might hypothesize that the crime rate is largely the result of the increased availability of heroin — addicts are robbing to get money for a fix. A third might suggest that armed robbery is related to the incidence of divorce —

children from broken homes are spending too much time on the street and getting into trouble.

After they develop their theories, the sociologists would begin to test them. They could examine statistics, interview parents, check police records, and use other means to acquire information. In this greatly oversimplified example, let us assume that the sociologist with the "broken home" idea discovers that most of the robbers who have been caught are in their twenties and thirties. This conclusion argues against his theory — the robbers would probably have been living away from their families. Is it possible, though, that the robbers are alienated and incapable of holding jobs because of experiences they had as children? (This is an example of a theory leading to new avenues of exploration even though it appears to be wrong.) The sociologist, upon further investigation, determines that the divorce rate in Metropolis underwent a sharp decline in the 1940s and 1950s, contrary to the national trend. This assumption means that his secondary theory — that the robbers are the victims of homes disrupted by divorce when they were children — is also wrong.

Let us assume, however, that the other propositions are supported by the information discovered. The robbery rate began to climb shortly after the local air conditioner factory closed, and it jumped dramatically at about the time the police say heroin began to be sold on the street.

Does the fact that both of these theories received support from research mean that one of them is wrong? Not necessarily. Sociology offers multiple explanations of most phenomena. Explanations can be different without being incompatible, and even those that seem unlikely or illogical should be evaluated in the context of the events they were designed to explain.

In the example given above, the term theory is used rather broadly. To be more precise: a theory is a set of interrelated statements or propositions intended to explain a given phenomenon. It is based on a set of assumptions and self-evident truths, includes definitions, and describes the conditions in which the phenomenon exists.

Although sociological theories exist to explain everything from childrearing to automobile sales, a small number of basic theories predominate in the field. These are explained below and will be described in more detail and applied to specific topics later in the book.

Evolutionary Theory

The evolutionary approach is associated with biological concepts and concerned with long-term change. *Evolutionary theory* suggests that societies, like biological organisms, progress through stages of increasing complexity. As with ecologists, evolutionists suggest that societies, again like organisms, are interdependent with their environments.

Most of the early sociologists and some recent ones adhere to an evolutionary view. Early sociologists often equated evolution with progress and improvement, believing that natural selection would eliminate weak societies and those that could not adapt. The strong societies, they believed, deserved to survive because they were better. It was for this reason that early theorists such as Spencer opposed any sort of interference that would protect the weak and interfere with natural evolutionary processes.

Contemporary evolutionists, on the other hand, rarely oppose all types of intervention. They tend to view evolution as a process that results in change, but they do not assume that the changes are necessarily for the better. Almost all would agree that society is becoming more complex, for example, but they might argue that the complexity brings about bad things as well as good. The telephone is a good illustration of a technological improvement that makes our lives more complex. Surely it is an improvement — it permits us to be in contact with the whole world without stirring from our homes — but a contemporary evolutionist might point out that a phone can also be an annoyance, as students trying to study and harried office workers can attest. Early evolutionists, on the other hand, would have been more likely to regard the telephone as a sign of progress and hence an unmixed blessing.

Evolutionary theory provides us with a structural perspective from which to judge a wide range of social influences. If its basic premises of directional change and increasing complexity are valid, it should provide better comprehension of current trends, and even help us predict the future.

Structural Functional Theory

Structural functionalism also has its roots in the work of the early sociologists, especially Durkheim and Weber. Among contemporary scholars, it is most closely associated with the work of Parsons and Merton. Many would argue that structural functionalism is the dominant theoretical view in sociology today. It is sometimes referred to as *social systems theory, equilibrium theory,* or simply *functionalism.*

The terms *structure* and *function* refer to two separate but closely related concepts. Structures can be compared with the organs or parts of the body of an animal, and functions can be compared with the purposes of these structures. The stomach is the structure; digestion is its function. In the same way, health care organizations and the military are social structures (or social systems), and caring for the sick and defending the country are their functions. Like a biological structure, a social system is composed of many interrelated and interdependent parts or structures.

Social structures include any component or part of society: clubs, families, nations, groups, and so forth. Central to an understanding of social structures are the concepts of *status* and *role.* Simply defined, a status is a socially defined position: female, student, lawyer, or Catholic. Some of these are *ascribed statuses,* that is, given to us at birth (age, sex, race) whereas others are *achieved statuses* (college graduate, father, teacher). Sets of interrelated statuses or positions are *social systems.* For example, the interrelated statuses of mother, father, and children constitute a family system. The interrelated statuses of teachers, students, and school administrators constitute an educational system.

You can easily list many personal statuses, such as age, sex, marital status, education, occupation, or religion. Each of these statuses has a dynamic aspect, a set of expectations and behaviors associated with it in a given group or society. These are termed *roles.* As a result, different roles (expectations for behavior) are associated with different statuses (positions) such as infant or adult, male or female, student or teacher, married or single. To occupy certain statuses is to have a general idea of appropriate behavior. The roles or expectations of a baseball team manager, for instance, differ from that of the batter, pitcher, or fielder.

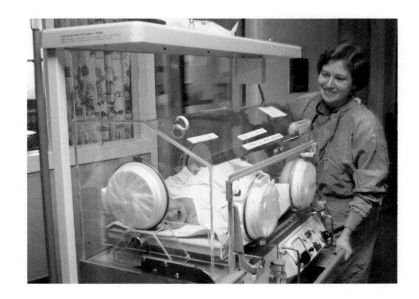

All social systems are made up of interrelated statuses, with certain behaviors attached to them. The structural functionalist, in analyzing our health care system, notes that people who occupy different statuses — physicians, nurses, technicians — have different role expectations and perform different functions. Here, a health care specialist fulfills one of her functions in caring for newborn infants.

What is expected of a pitcher or batter, however, and what that pitcher or batter actually does may differ. In other words, role performance does not always match role expectations. The learning of these role expectations and behaviors is accomplished through the socialization process, described in Chapter 5.

As we mentioned earlier, interrelated statuses constitute social systems. Each social system performs certain functions that make it possible for society and the people who comprise that society to exist. Each serves a function that leads to the maintenance or stability of the larger society. The educational system is intended to provide literary and technical skills, the religious system is intended to provide emotional support and answer questions about the unknown, families are intended to socialize infants, and so on. The functionalist perspective assumes that these social systems have an underlying tendency to be in equilibrium or balance; any system that fails to fulfill its functions will result in an imbalance or disequilibrium. In extreme cases, the entire system can break down when a change or failure in any one part of the system affects its interrelated parts.

A social system can be regarded as having two types of functions: (1) what the system does and (2) the consequences that result from a particular type of structure or organization. In a biological system, the function of the eyes is to obtain information about the environment. This function provides one with the ability to seek food and shelter and the ability to avoid danger. In a social system, one function of government might be to maintain order. An advantage of this function is that people can carry on their affairs — running businesses, raising families — without having their lives disrupted.

According to Merton, a social system can have both *manifest functions* and *latent functions*. Manifest functions are intended and recognized; latent functions are neither intended nor recognized. One manifest function of education systems is to teach literary and technical skills. They also perform the latent functions of "sitting" for children while parents work and providing contacts for dating and marriage. Correctional institutions have the manifest functions of punishment and removing criminals from social interaction with the larger society. They may also perform the latent functions of providing advanced training in breaking and entering.

Merton recognized that not all consequences of systems are functional — that is, they do not all lead to the maintenance of the system. Some lead to instability or the breakdown of a system. These consequences he termed *dysfunctions*. Families have a manifest function of rearing children. The intensity of family interactions, however, can lead to the dysfunction, or negative consequence, of violence and child abuse. This dysfunction may lead to the disruption of relationships within the family system or even to the total breakdown of the system.

Sociologists who adhere to the functionalist perspective examine the parts of a given system and try to determine how they are related to one another and to the whole. They observe the results of a given cluster or arrangement of parts, attempting to discover both the intended (manifest) and the unintended (latent) functions of these parts. In addition, they analyze which of these consequences contribute to the maintenance of a given system and which lead to the breakdown of the system. It should be noted that what may be functional in one system may be dysfunctional in another. A function that is good for corporate profits may not be good for family solidarity, while one that is good for religious unity may not be good for ethnic integration.

According to the functionalist perspective, social systems exist because they fulfill some function for the society. Functionalists focus on order and stability, which has led some critics to argue that it supports the status quo. With the emphasis on equilibrium and the maintenance of the system, the process of change, critics say, receives little attention. In this respect, functionalism differs greatly from conflict theory, which is described below.

Conflict Theory

Conflict theory also had its origins in early sociology, especially in the work of Marx. Among its more recent proponents are such people as Mills, Coser, and Dahrendorf. They share the view that society is best understood and analyzed in terms of conflict and power.

Karl Marx began with a very simple assumption: the structure of society is determined by economic organization, particularly the ownership of property. Religious dogmas, cultural values, personal beliefs, institutional arrangements, class structures — all are basically reflections of the economic organization of a society. Inherent in any economic system that supports inequality are forces that generate revolutionary class conflict, according to Marx. The exploited classes eventually recognize their submissive and inferior status and revolt against the dominant class of property owners and employers. The story of history, then, is the story of class struggle between the owners and workers, the dominators and the dominated, the powerful and the powerless.

Contemporary conflict theorists assume that conflict is a permanent feature of social life and that as a result societies are in a state of constant change. Unlike Marx, however, these theorists rarely assume that conflict is always based on class or that it always reflects economic organization and ownership. Conflicts are assumed to involve a broad range of groups or interests: young against old, male against female, or one racial group against another, as well as workers against employers. These conflicts result because things like power, wealth, and prestige are not available to everyone — they are limited commodities, and the demand exceeds the supply. Conflict theory also assumes that those who have or control desirable

Competition for limited resources and inequalities between persons or groups may lead to disharmony, even violence, but they may also be a source of constructive change. Shown here is one situation of status and power inequality.

goods and services will defend and protect their own interests at the expense of others.

In this view, conflict does not mean the sort of event that makes headlines, such as war, violence, or open hostility. It is instead regarded as the struggle that occurs day after day as people try to maintain and improve their positions in life. Neither should conflict be regarded as a destructive process that leads to disorder and the breakdown of society. Theorists like Dahrendorf and

Coser have focused on the integrative nature of conflict, its value as a force that contributes to order and stability. How can conflict be a constructive force? The answer is basically that people with common interests join together to seek gains that will benefit them all. By the same token, conflict among groups focuses attention on inequalities and social problems that might never be resolved without conflict. Racial conflicts, for example, may serve to bind people with common interests together and also lead to constructive social change.

There is an obvious contrast between the views of the functionalists, who regard society as balanced and in a state of equilibrium, and the views of conflict theorists, who assume that society is an arena of constant competition and change. Functionalists believe the social process is a continual effort to maintain harmony; conflict theorists believe it is a continual struggle to "get ahead." Functionalists view society as basically consensual, integrated, and static; conflict theorists believe it is characterized by constraint, conflict, and change. Whereas functionalists have been criticized for focusing on stability and the status quo, conflict theorists have been criticized for overlooking the less controversial and more orderly aspects of society.

Symbolic Interaction Theory

Symbolic interaction theory, although influenced somewhat by early European sociologists, was developed largely through the efforts of Mead, Thomas, and Cooley, who all belonged to The Chicago School. The key difference between this perspective and those discussed earlier revolves around the size of the units used in investigation and analysis. Macrosociological orientations — the evolutionary, structural-functional, and conflict theories — interpret society in terms of its large structures: organizations, institutions, social classes, communities, and nations. Microsociological orientations such as symbolic interaction theory, on the other hand, study individuals in

society and their definitions of situations, meanings, roles, interaction patterns, and the like. Although these levels of analysis overlap considerably, they operate from different assumptions and premises.

The question of how individuals influence society and how society influences individuals is central to sociology. As you recall, early sociologists (Spencer, Durkheim, and Marx, for example) regarded society as an entity existing apart from the individual. Symbolic interactionists, however, assume that society exists within every socialized individual and that its external forms and structures arise through the social interactions taking place among individuals at the symbolic level.

What is meant by "the symbolic level"? It can be explained this way: suppose you are driving down the road in your car and you come upon a brick wall running across the road. You stop, of course, because you have learned you cannot pass through a physical object. If, however, you perceive the brick wall to be a mental picture, a mirage, you won't "of course" stop. Let us suppose next that you are riding down the same road and you come to a stoplight. Once again you stop — but why? There is nothing physical to keep you from progressing. Your reason for stopping is that you have learned that the red light is a *symbol* that means stop. The world around us can be said to consist of these two elements: physical objects and abstract symbols. Thus language is a system of symbols. It represents physical objects or concepts that can be used to communicate.

According to George Herbert Mead, who played an important role in the development of symbolic interactionism, it is the ability of humans to use symbols that sets us apart from animals and allows us to create social institutions, societies, and cultures. People in a society share an understanding of certain symbols (the stoplight, for example). Social learning takes place at both symbolic and nonsymbolic levels. In interaction with others, we learn (internalize) social expectations, a specific language, and social values. In interaction with others, we learn to share meanings and to communicate symbolically through words and gestures. As humans, we can interact at both a physical (a slap) as well as a symbolic level (showing a fist or making a verbal threat). Because we can relate symbolically, we can carry on conversations with ourselves. We can also imagine the effects of different courses of action. We can imagine what will happen if we throw a rotten tomato in the face of a police officer. By thinking through alternate courses of actions, we can choose those believed to be most appropriate for a given situation. The fact that others share similar expectations makes life patterned and relatively predictable. Those who fail to recognize that red traffic lights mean stop will have trouble getting any place safely in their cars.

The interactionist perspective examines patterns and processes of everyday life that are generally ignored by many other perspectives. It raises questions about the self, the self in relationships with others, and the self and others in the wider social context. Why do some of us have negative feelings about ourselves? Why can we relate more easily with some persons than others? Why do we feel more comfortable around friends than strangers? How is it possible to interact with complete strangers or to know what to do in new situations? How are decisions made in families? Symbolic interactionists try to answer such questions by examining the individual in a social context. The starting point of this examination is the social setting in which an individual is born and the interactions he or she has with parents, siblings, teachers, neighbors or others. From these interactions, we learn what is proper or improper, whether we are "good" or "bad," who is important, and so forth. A more complete explanation of this perspective is given in Chapters 5 and 6 and in other sections throughout the book.

Although symbolic interaction theory is the most widely used and recognized interaction perspective, exchange theory also falls within this general orientation.

Exchange Theory

Exchange theory has a diverse intellectual heritage, drawing from sources in economics, anthropology, and psychology as well as sociology. This perspective is based on the belief that life is a series of exchanges involving rewards and costs. In economic exchanges, people exchange money, goods, and services, hoping to profit or at least break even in the exchange. In anthropological, psychological, and sociological exchanges, the items of exchange include social and psychic factors as well. In return for your companionship, I'll invite you to my house. In return for your positive teacher evaluation, I'll work extra hard to be a good instructor. Work, gifts, money, affection, ideas — all are offered in the hope of getting something in return.

Social exchange theory seeks to explain why behavioral outcomes like marriage, employment, and religious involvement occur, given a set of structural conditions (age, race, gender, class) and interactional possibilities. This theory assumes:

- Most human gratification is derived from the actions of other humans.
- New associations are begun because they are expected to be rewarding, and old associations continue because they are rewarding.
- When we receive rewards or benefits from others, we're obliged to reciprocate by supplying benefits to them in return.
- In general, giving is more blessed than receiving, because having social credit is preferable to being socially indebted (Eshleman, 1981).

Although people may work selflessly for others with no thought of reward, it is quite unusual. The social exchange perspective assumes that voluntary social interactions are contingent on rewarding reactions from others. When rewarding reactions cease, either the actions end or dissatisfaction results.

There are two different schools of thought in the exchange theory perspective. George Homans,

SOCIOLOGISTS AT WORK

Helping Children Live Within the System

Henry Lewis is a group leader and counselor at New Horizons Ranch and Center, outside Goldthwaite, Texas. New Horizons is a residential treatment center for children who have problems living within "the system" — be it their family, their school, or the community at large. The center's goal is simple. As Lewis puts it, "We help them get their act together." The people who run the center think Henry Lewis has a solid credential that can help them achieve that goal: a B.A. in sociology, which he earned at Angelo State University in nearby San Angelo.

If New Horizon's goal is simple, the ways of reaching it are not. "Every child comes here with a different problem, and every child is dealt with differently," says Lewis. "They're referred to us by their school systems, by the Texas Department of Human Resources, and by the Texas Youth Council. We're a private, nonprofit organization. We're not an institution per se. We're located out in the country, and there are no locks, no fences,

nothing like that. We run a school, and we get the kids involved in work around the ranch or for businesses in town. We go fishing, we go skating, we go to movies — we try to set up a family environment. And we do a lot of individual counseling."

There are about fifty children at New Horizons at any given time. "They come to us because they've had school problems or home problems," Lewis says. "Or they might have been taken out of their homes because they've been neglected or physically or sexually abused. Or they might have been abandoned. None of our kids have criminal records. They've come to the Texas Youth Council because there's no other place for them to go at the time. Students who are referred to us have to come up here for pre-placement — we accept about one in ten. They have to assure us that they *want* to work on their problems, that they *want* to be in our program. Then we draw up an individual treatment plan." The average stay

the theorist responsible for originating exchange theory, represents a perspective consistent with that of behavioral psychologists, who believe that behavior can be explained in terms of rewards and punishments. Behaviorists focus their attention on actual behavior, not on processes that can be inferred from behavior but cannot be observed. In exchange theory, the rewards and punishments are the behavior of other people, and

those involved in exchanges assume that their rewards will be proportional to their costs.

Peter Blau is the advocate of a different school of exchange theory, one that is consistent with symbolic interactionism. Blau does not attempt to explain all exchanges in terms of observable behavior. He argues that the exchange is more subjective and interpretative and that the exchanges occur on the symbolic level. As a re-

at the center is about eleven months, although some children stay only a month or two and some have stayed as long as three years. Then they move back to their homes, or on to foster homes or to other treatment centers. One girl left recently to enroll in Henry Lewis's alma mater, Angelo State University. At present there are about forty-five boys and nine girls at the center. They are divided into groups according to age, background, educational level, and size — four groups of boys and one of girls. Lewis is the group leader for the youngest group, eight boys aged ten to fourteen.

The staff of thirty includes people with degrees in psychology and sociology and other counseling backgrounds, and others with no degrees who have been with the center from the beginning (in 1971) and understand and are committed to its ideal of treatment in a family atmosphere. When they were looking for someone with training in sociology, a friend in the Texas Department of Corrections referred them to Lewis. "My study of sociology really helped me prepare for this work," he says. "I was interested in juvenile deliquency, family violence, and that whole spectrum of social problems. The most important thing is to understand the reality — that the sort of stuff we deal with really does happen. To a lot of people it's hidden. Studying sociology, studying families and children *in* families and in

groups, gave me an awareness of the problem and the need."

The problems Lewis encounters are a varied lot. He cites the case of a young black boy who grew up in a completely segregated setting and had little experience of white people. "He grew up in an environment where whites were foreign, the bad guys. We had to work with him just to get him to the point where he could feel comfortable around a white person." Another boy was adopted at a young age. After three or four years it became clear that his adoptive family didn't want him. He was neglected and abused. He reacted to this several ways: soiling his underwear, fighting in school, attacking his teachers. "We had here a child who could not really fit in with any social group. Wherever he went — to school, to the store — you could be sure he would cause some disturbance." The center set a goal for him: to increase his patience and his attention span. After about a year the results were noticeable. "Now you can send him into a store and know he's not going to pull anything. We had to offer him an alternative to his behavior. We had to show him that he *could* go out with a group, that he *could* live in a world of families and groups." That is something New Horizons Ranch and Center excels at. "For some of these children, this is the only real home, the only family, they've ever had."

---

sult, money may be a just reward only if it is defined by the receiver as such, and psychic rewards of satisfaction with doing a good job or of pleasing someone may be as important as money, gifts, or outward responses of praise.

Both Homans and Blau agree that what is important is that each party receives in the exchange something perceived as equivalent to that which is given (to Homans, *distributive justice;* to Blau,

fair exchange). All exchange involves a mutually held expectation that reciprocation will occur. If resources or exchange criteria are unequal, one person is at a distinct disadvantage and the other has power over and controls the relationship. As a result, in marriage, unequal exchanges between husband and wife are likely to result in dominance of one over the other or may even end the relationship. In employment, if employee and employer do not recognize a fair exchange of rewards and costs, dissatisfaction may result, the employee may quit, or the employer may dismiss the employee.

In exchange theory, then, social life is viewed as a process of bargaining or negotiation, and social relationships are based on trust and mutual interests.

Summary

Compared with the other sciences, sociology is of recent origin. Not until the 1800s was a scientific methodology applied to social phenomena. The industrial revolution and political upheavals in Europe encouraged various scholars to try to explain social change and the social order. Five theorists had an especially important influence on the development of sociology: Comte, Marx, Spencer, Durkheim, and Weber.

Auguste Comte is credited with being the father of sociology. He first called it social physics because he believed society must be studied in the same scientific manner as the natural sciences. He believed that human progress evolved through three stages: the theological, the metaphysical, and the scientific. Karl Marx, one of the most radical thinkers of his time, made major contributions to our understanding of social conflict. He believed that all history was based on economic determinism, which resulted in class struggles between the rich and powerful bourgeoisie and the working class proletariat. Herbert Spencer, like Comte, focused his attention on evolutionary schemes, emphasizing in particular the social survival of the fittest. Unlike Comte, however, he argued for a policy of government noninterference in the course of human history and change.

Emile Durkheim made major contributions to our understanding of social facts. He rejected explanations of social events that assumed that society operated in a fashion parallel to biology. In a classic study, he demonstrated that suicide was re-lated to the degree of involvement in a cohesive group or social unit. Max Weber focused his writing on a new methodology for studying social life. He emphasized the need to focus on subjective meanings (*verstehen*) in studying human interaction and social systems.

The development of sociology in America drew heavily from European writers, especially at the macrosociological level, but America was also very influential in the development of microsociology. Important contributions were made by men like Cooley, Mead, and Thomas who stressed the importance of social interaction and the influence of society on human thought and action. Not until the 1930s did sociology shift from the University of Chicago to other major educational institutions. In the East, Parsons, Merton, Mills, Coser, Homans, and Blau were influential in the development of social theory.

A social theory is a systematically interrelated proposition that seeks to explain a process or phenomena. Five major theories, three at the macro level and two at the micro level, have had an important influence on contemporary sociology. These are the evolutionary-ecological theory, structural functional theory, conflict theory, symbolic interactional theory, and exchange theory.

An evolutionary theory suggests that societies, like biological organisms, go through transitions or stages and are interdependent with the environment or world about them. A structural functional theory focuses on the parts of a system, the relationships among these parts, and the functions or consequences of social structures. These functions can be either intended and recognized (manifest) or unintended and unrecognized (latent). Some consequences are dysfunctional in that they lead to the instability and breakdown of the system. Structural functional theories assume that systems have a tendency toward equilibrium and balance.

Conflict theory assumes that conflict is a permanent feature of social life and a key source of change. The Marxist orientation toward conflict assumes that it is rooted in a class struggle between the employers and the workers or between the powerful and the powerless. Many conflict theorists assume that conflict serves an integrative function and acts as a source of constructive change. Symbolic interactionism, a micro theory, emphasizes relationships between individuals and between individuals and society. According to this theory, society has as its basis shared meanings, language, social interaction, and symbolic processes. It is the mind that differentiates humans from nonhumans and permits people to develop a social self, to assume the role of others, and to imaginatively consider alternative courses of action.

The basic assumption of an exchange theory is that social life involves a series of reciprocal exchanges involving rewards and costs. Exchange theories endeavor to explain why certain behavioral outcomes result from a given set of structural conditions and interactional possibilities.

The next chapter looks at methods of studying society. Upon completion of this first part of the book, you will have a clearer understanding of sociology and the close relationship between theory and research.

Key Terms

ascribed and achieved status
bourgeoisie and proletariat
Comte's law of human progress
conflict theory
social facts
dysfunctions
Economic Determinism
evolutionary theory
exchange theory
manifest and latent functions
Marx and social conflict
middle range theory
role
social statics and social dynamics
social system
Spencer's evolutionary scheme
structural functional theory
symbolic interaction theory
The Chicago School
theories
verstehen

Suggested Readings

Coser, Lewis A. **Masters of Sociological Thought: Ideas in Historical and Social Context.** *New York: Harcourt Brace Jovanovich, 2nd ed., 1977.* A look at the lives and ideas of major figures in the development of sociological theory.

Hinkle, Roscoe C. **Founding Theory of American Sociology 1881–1915.** *Boston: Routledge and Kegan Paul, 1980.* An advanced work that compares, contrasts, and classifies the theories of early American sociologists.

Merton, Robert K. **Social Theory and Social Structure.** *Glencoe, Ill.: The Free Press, revised and enlarged ed., 1957.* The original statement of structural functionalism. Merton also discusses the development of his theory of the middle range, the consequences of anomie, and the self-fulfilling prophecy.

Poloma, Margaret M. **Contemporary Sociological Theory.** *New York: Macmillan, 1979.* A text designed and written for undergraduate students of sociology covering the major sociological theories.

Rossides, Daniel W. **The History and Nature of Sociological Theory.** *Boston: Houghton Mifflin, 1978.* An introduction to social theory with an emphasis on a critical investigation of problems of social science.

Turner, Jonathan H. **The Structure of Sociological Theory.** *Homewood, Ill.: The Dorsey Press, revised ed., 1978.* An analysis of the historical roots and contemporary forms of four dominant paradigms of social theory: functionalism, conflict, interactionism, and exchange.

Warshay, Leon H. **The Current State of Sociological Theory: A Critical Interpretation.** *New York: David McKay, 1975.* A comprehensive and integrated overview of the present state of contemporary sociological theory, with a discussion of current trends.

Chapter 3
Methods of Studying Society

It is a capital mistake to theorize before one has data.
— Sir Arthur Conan Doyle

People arrive at their opinions and beliefs through a number of different routes, and notions about reality vary greatly. Some people believe that politicians are crooked, others that they are dedicated public servants. Some believe that hard work will lead to success, others that it is a waste of time and that for them, failure is inevitable.

We get ideas such as these from a number of different sources. We derive some from everyday experiences and common sense: our past experiences and personal observations convince us that certain things are true. We see blondes having a good time and are convinced that blondes have more fun. We talk to women who want children and assume that a desire for children is instinctive in women. Experience and common sense may lead these women to different conclusions, however.

We get other ideas from "authorities," people assumed to be knowledgeable because of their experience or position. We may consider the Pope, the President of the United States, our personal physician, our professor, or our parents to be authority figures. We seldom bother to investigate the source of their expertise or the information they used to reach their conclusions because we feel that their information is not subject to question. Like ideas derived from common sense, however, the opinions of authorities may differ. The conclusions of one doctor are not always identical to those of another doctor. Parents sometimes do not agree with each other, much less with other parents.

A third source of ideas or knowledge is revelation. Revelation may be thought to result from divine experiences, prayer, or magic. Knowledge acquired through revelation is often thought to be sacred and absolute, so it is not subject to question. Some people, for example, believe that wives should submit to their husbands' authority because the Bible says they should do so.

A fourth source of ideas is tradition. The wisdom of previous generations is passed on and accepted as accurate. We may plant corn by the phase of the moon and take a sip of brandy to cure a chest cold. Why? Because that's the way it's always been done.

A fifth source of knowledge is research that uses empirical methods. Some sociologists do not reject personal experience, common sense, authority, revelation, and tradition as sources of knowledge, but most rely heavily on methods considered empirical or scientific. Empirical methods focus on observable phenomena, which means that others should be able to observe the same phenomena and check our observations for accuracy. Unlike the common sense observations made as part of our daily experience, however, researchers using empirical methods strive to be objective. In this chapter, we will consider the use of scientific methods in sociology. We will also examine standards of scientific inquiry, types of sociological research, research methods, and the process of research.

Is Sociology a Science?

Sociology differs from disciplines such as religion, philosophy, and the humanities in its commitment to the scientific method. Whenever possible, researchers use methods highly similar to those used in the physical and biological sciences. Rather than basing our social knowledge on tradition, hearsay, or intuition, sociologists base their understanding of social life on observation and empirical evidence, which is accomplished through systematically collecting and analyzing data.

Most sociology textbooks include the term *science* in their definition of sociology, claiming that it is the scientific study of human behavior.

As we saw in the previous chapter, sociology has modeled itself after the natural sciences since its inception in the nineteenth century, largely because the natural sciences had been successful in formulating laws, principles, and theories about the physical world by systematically formulating problems, collecting data through observation and experiment, and devising and testing hypotheses. The success of these procedures, known as the *scientific method,* encouraged early social scholars to use the same procedures in developing laws, principles, and theories about human behavior and the social world.

The scientific method was used in sociology for other reasons as well. The goals of sociological investigation are often said to be explanation and prediction. Since men like Darwin and Newton successfully developed principles of evolution and gravity that were both highly explanatory and predictive, science appeared to be the logical model of inquiry to adopt in attempts to explain and predict social phenomena. There were also practical reasons for adopting science as the model of inquiry. In much of the Western world, particularly in American society, science has been regarded as almost sacred. Sociologists, seeking legitimacy for their young discipline, tried to convey to a skeptical world that they too could be objective, systematic, precise, and predictive in their field of study. It was also shown that science worked. Just as physical technology had been developed by scientific means, it was thought that a social technology could be developed that could change the social order, either by resolving social problems or by modifying existing processes or structures. Sociologists, therefore, generally consider themselves to be engaged in a scientific pursuit.

Not everyone regards sociology as a science, however. Van Den Berghe (1978) argues that if by the word "science" we mean a logically inherent body of generalizations concerning causal relationships among observable, measurable, and

The invention and widespread dissemination of computers for reading and processing data have greatly expanded the research capabilities of social scientists. Today, sociologists can work with thousands of cases and engage in sophisticated statistical analysis in a relatively brief time due to the hardware and programming technology readily available to them.

life is too complex and unpredictable to be studied scientifically. It has also been argued that sociology, unlike astronomy and other physical sciences that have existed for hundreds of years, is too young a discipline to have developed the kinds of laws and principles found in the natural sciences. Any subject may seem complex to an untrained observer, however, and people have been "doing" sociology for thousands of years. The real difficulties in studying sociology scientifically involve different issues, for example, the "free will" of human beings. Although individual behavior is constrained by innumerable biological and social factors, humans retain a sufficient measure of autonomy and free will so that behavior is often difficult to predict. A second issue is the closeness of the subject matter of sociology to the observer: sociologists are part of the societies they are observing, which makes it extremely difficult for them to prevent bias from affecting their perceptions.

Defenders of sociology as a science argue that although individuals have free will, collectives, aggregates, social structures, and social organizations do not. Although it may be impossible to predict exactly how an individual will behave in a particular situation, certain groups tend to behave in predictable ways in similar situations. We can't say how a divorce is going to affect a particular child in a unique family situation, but we may be able to predict the probable effects of divorce on children from similar families. In response to the second criticism, that sociologists must be biased because of their closeness to their subject matter, it can be argued that they can be objective by separating themselves from the subject, by repeating studies using multiple observers, and by making crosscultural and historical comparisons. Thus, although one can argue correctly that many sociologists are biased, naive, simplistic, limited in cultural perspective, and bound by the present, this type of argument tells us little about whether sociology can be considered a science.

predictable phenomena, then sociology is not a science. For sociology to qualify, he contends, the meaning of science would have to include observations, descriptions, hunches, opinions, tautologies, statistical tendencies, concepts, and taxonomies. Science as generally defined does not include all these dimensions.

Other arguments are often heard about why sociology is not a science. It is sometimes said that the subject matter of human behavior and social

How then does one proceed? To determine whether sociology is or is not a science, we have to rephrase the question, asking what distinguishes the scientific mode of inquiry from non-scientific modes of inquiry. Can sociology and the other social sciences follow the scientific mode? To answer this question, we will consider the nature of scientific theories and standards of scientific inquiry.

The Components of Scientific Theory

Scientists try to organize and test their accumulated knowledge by developing and refining concepts, generalizations, and laws. Like other scientists, social scientists organize concepts, develop hypotheses and propositions, and look at relationships among these propositions to study and explain a particular phenomenon. Concepts, conceptual frameworks, frames of reference, and theory all contribute toward providing explanations of events and letting scholars know where to focus their attention.

Theories are not inherently correct or incorrect — they are simply ways of looking at and rationally explaining different phenomena. They can enable the researcher to conduct empirical studies in an organized and logical fashion. A theory is an attempt to find patterns and consistencies in seemingly idiosyncratic and inconsistent events. Good theory is much more than speculation. It is a key source of ideas for testing by researchers who, in turn, modify and refine the theory. As described in Merton's middle range theories, there is an important link between general theory and empirical testing.

Concepts and Variables

Concepts are the bases of all theories. A *concept* is a miniature "system of meaning" symbolized by a word, phrase, or label that enables us to perceive a phenomenon in a certain way. Concepts are tools by which one can share meanings. They are abstractions used as building blocks for the development of hypotheses, propositions, and theories, but concepts themselves do not explain, predict, or state relationships. Most of the terms in the glossary of this text are sociological concepts: norms, statuses, stratification, groups, mobs, or folkways, for example. When these concepts can have two or more degrees or values, they are referred to as *variables*. "Husband" is a concept; "years married" is a variable. "Dollar" is a concept; "level of income" is a variable. "Years of marriage" and "level of income" can both vary, but the meanings of the words "husband" and "dollar" remain constant.

Concepts and variables are continually revised and refined, and new concepts must often be invented to express new ideas. Thus, although the concept "family" may serve as an adequate term for lay people, professional sociologists must differentiate nuclear, extended, conjugal, and other types of families. Because the concept used will affect how things are observed, it must be constructed in a way that will not distort "reality." One of the sociologist's major tasks as theorist or as researcher is to label phenomena in ways that avoid undesired connotations. (For example, think about the different connotations of labels such as nigger, colored, Negro, black, and Afro-American, or the varying meanings attached to the words honky, whitey, WASP, palefaced, uncolored, white, or German-American.)

Conceptual Frameworks

When a set of concepts is interrelated to describe and classify phenomena, the concepts are generally referred to as a *conceptual framework*, which might be defined as a cluster of interrelated concepts for viewing a phenomenon and for describing and classifying its parts. In the strictest sense of the term, a conceptual framework is not a theory. It is more often descriptive than explanatory, and it is generally employed as a classification scheme or taxonomy. Conceptual frameworks facilitate both theory and research by providing definitions of concepts and describing the range of variables that might be employed within a given theory or area. It has been debated, for example, whether structural functionalism is a theory or a conceptual framework. Theories explain, conceptual frameworks do not. For purposes of research, using a particular concept or variable within a framework of related concepts or variables proves to be useful in understanding the meaning of or the manner in which the concept is used. The concept "role," for example, when used within a structural-functional framework, is generally defined as an expectation for behavior associated with a given status such as male, married, or student. Role to an interactionist, however, may mean expectations for behavior developed in interaction between persons and mutually shared by them.

Propositions and Hypotheses

It is from conceptual frameworks that propositions, hypotheses, and theories can most readily be established. A *proposition* is a statement about the nature of some phenomenon. It generally consists of a statement about the relationship between two or more concepts. The statement "Social activity is related to student grades" would be a proposition. If this proposition is formulated so that it can be tested, it is considered a *hypothesis*. A testable hypothesis would be "Students who attend more than one social activity a week have higher grade point averages than those who do not." Hypotheses and propositions are identical, except that hypotheses indicate how the stated relations can be tested. Hypotheses serve as the important link between theory and empirical inquiry. Both hypotheses and propositions are formed by combining concepts into statements that describe a meaningful relationship.

Frequently, as in the example above, a hypothesis states that if one variable changes in some regular fashion, a predictable change will occur. Thus, as social activity goes up, grade point averages go up. This is known as a *direct relationship*. *Inverse relationships* are also possible — as social activity goes up, grade point averages go down. Hypotheses that involve direct or inverse relationships are called *directional hypotheses*. *Null hypotheses,* which state that there is no relationship between the variables of interest, can also be formulated: there is no relationship between social activity and grade point averages.

Theory

A *theory* results when a series of propositions that explain some particular process can be logically and systematically interrelated. A good theory should be testable, cumulative, and widely applicable. It should also be stated in abstract terms, and allow predictions to be made. Thus, a theory is far more than mere speculation or a random collection of concepts and variables. It is a set of logically interrelated propositions that explains some process or set of phenomena in a testable fashion. Like propositions, theories not only provide explanations of observed reality but serve as important sources of new hypotheses.

The formulation of theories is just one aspect of the scientific method. Measured against this standard alone, sociology would certainly be considered a science. Most sociologists are keenly aware of the importance of organizing concepts, testing hypotheses, and developing theories. In addition to using this framework for their investigations, however, scientists adhere to a number of widely accepted standards of inquiry.

The Standards of Scientific Inquiry

Objectivity

The scientific standard of objectivity asserts that in the study of any phenomenon, social or nonsocial, the personal biases and values of the people doing the research must never influence the data reported or the interpretation of results.

The political, religious, racial, or other beliefs of the investigators should in no way determine the findings of a study. Two independent researchers who study the same phenomena should produce identical results, therefore, regardless of their differences in status, belief, or personal behavior.

Whether totally objective social research is possible has been seriously questioned. The literature from social psychology itself shows that people's interests and perceptions are influenced by their social background, social class, level of education, and numerous other factors. It also indicates that we are selective in what we perceive, remember, and report. Male and female researchers studying marriage often report different perceptions of the same married couple. Sociologists studying race relations have found that a journalistic account of an event by a black writer differs from an account of the same event by a white writer. It is argued that human beings cannot be totally objective.

If absolute objectivity is to be regarded as a requirement, then sociology can be dismissed from the realm of scientific inquiry. All scientists are social beings, however, regardless of their discipline. In addition, there are many procedures for minimizing the level of subjectivity. One procedure is to recognize the influence of existing biases and assumptions and strive to eliminate the influence of those we can control. Another procedure is to base research on a particular theory and test it by seeking evidence that could either support or reject it. Other methods of minimizing the level of bias and subjectivity will be discussed in the following sections on the other standards of science and the scientific method.

Replication

The scientific standard of *replication* asserts that research should be conducted and reported in such a way that someone else can duplicate it. The use of similar subjects and measuring procedures under similar conditions should produce results virtually identical to those of the original study. Thus, another way to reduce investigator bias is to have identical or similar studies undertaken by people who have differing biases and personal values.

In the physical sciences, replication of studies under identical conditions is often easier than it is in the social sciences, but even in the physical sciences it is sometimes impossible to re-create identical conditions. A California earthquake or a space shuttle explosion cannot be duplicated. In the social sciences, the problems of replication are compounded by human factors. Some studies may be impossible to duplicate because of the nature of the problems studied. It may not be possible, for example, to duplicate studies done of the wives of husbands held hostage in Iran. It is possible, however, to duplicate studies of wives whose husbands are temporarily absent due to hospitalization, imprisonment, or other factors and to note patterns of psychological adjustment, points of greatest stress, changes in kin and child relationships, or other conditions. The principle of replication of studies is based on the conviction that similar conditions and circumstances should produce highly similar results.

Precision of Measurement

The scientific standard of *precision of measurement* asserts that the phenomenon being studied should be measured in precise, reliable, and valid ways. The more accurate our measurements, the better we are able to test our ideas about the social world. An ability to test or study anything, whether it be height, a religious practice, or a theory, is in large part dependent on the ability to measure it accurately. Theories could be debated endlessly without progress if no one determined how to observe and measure the ideas or concepts central to them. No one has developed a precise, reliable, or valid measurement of the influence of angels, for example, so there is no way to prove or disprove their existence.

All aspects of social life are areas for sociological research. Some events, however, may be difficult to replicate since they may happen only once. This may be the case in studies of wives whose husbands were held hostage in Iran or studies of these marriages following the hostages' reunion with their families.

Some concepts or variables are much easier to measure than others. We all agree on how to measure the number of males and females in a room, because we know how to measure quantities of people and how to determine gender, but how would we proceed with a study of the relationship between gender and happiness? *Happiness* is an abstract term that means different things to different people, and opinions would vary on how to measure it. In general, the more abstract a variable is, and the further it is removed from direct observation, the more difficult it is to reach a consensus on how it should be measured. This is not to say that the variable happiness cannot be measured — it can.

The process of arriving at a means of measuring a concept or variable is referred to as *operationalization*. In this procedure, the sociologist selects quantitative indicators of an abstract concept determining what will be observed and how it will be measured. In the example given above, this would involve determining some criteria for assessing happiness. We might decide that happiness is whatever the individuals themselves think it is and simply ask them whether they are happy or not, or ask them to rate their own happiness on a five-point scale. On the other hand, we might decide that factors such as absence of depression, high levels of self-esteem, or the ability to function successfully are indicators of happiness and attempt to measure those. Although opinions may differ on whether the criteria selected actually reflect happiness, the operationalization of the definition ensures that we understand what we are considering happiness and what we are measuring. The development of an *operational definition* makes an abstract variable measurable and observable and permits another researcher to objectively replicate our study. This process also improves the precision of our measurements.

Attitude of Researcher

In their introductory textbook on social science methods, Williamson et al. (1977) state that scientific inquiry involves a particular attitude on the part of the researcher. Researchers adopt a critical attitude, continually questioning the accuracy of the data being collected. They ask such questions as: Is my data correct? What errors might be influencing my findings? What kinds of data will cause me to reevaluate my theoretical ideas? A researcher operating within a scientific framework will demand empirical evidence that is observable and verifiable. Without acquiring data, theoretical, theological, philosophical and other types of speculation are nonscientific.

Williamson et al. also indicate that scientific researchers should adopt an analytical attitude toward the subject of inquiry. Scientists are rarely concerned with simply describing the phenomena being studied. Instead, they seek to understand the structures and dimensions underlying the empirical observations. Sociologists would not be interested in simply describing what happened during the Miami riots of 1980, for example; they would try to determine what factors caused or influenced the riots. Scientists do not merely describe, but attempt to explain and predict as well.

Now that we have discussed some of the methods and attributes of scientific inquiry, we can return to our original question. Should sociology be considered a science? Like most questions, this one cannot be answered with a simple yes or no. The issue is not so much whether sociology is a science, but to what extent it is pursued with scientific modes of inquiry. According to the criteria we have discussed, some sociological studies would certainly be regarded as scientific. A sociologist studying the correlation between age at marriage and divorce rates would develop operational definitions and precise measurements to objectively examine a phenomenon in a replicable study. Studying a problem such as the relationship between gender and happiness might have to use methods that, strictly speaking, would not be considered scientific. In short, the techniques used by sociologists range from those that meet the strictest standards of scientific inquiry to those that, although still useful, fall short of that standard.

Now that we have discussed the basic procedures of science and sociology, we will turn our attention more specifically to research methods and the logic of proof.

Types of Sociological Research

The distinction between scientific and unscientific sociology can be clarified by examining the methods used to prove a hypothesis. One criterion that social scientists use to evaluate theories and propositions is the extent to which they can be empirically investigated or researched. This research is of two basic types, descriptive and explanatory.

Descriptive Research

Descriptive research describes social reality or provides facts about the social world. A descriptive study would be undertaken to determine whether people who have served time in prison have more trouble finding jobs than people who have not been in prison, or to determine what percentage of college students smoke marijuana more than once a week. All descriptive studies share the goal of providing data on social facts.

Just what are *social facts?* Facts are reliable and valid items of information. A fact could be a behavior (John scored three touchdowns), an attitude (women want equal pay for equal work), a law (the speed limit is 55), or even a statistic (the median family income in 1980 was $21,023). The information must be reliable and valid. *Reliability* is the extent to which repeated observations of the same phenomena yield similar results. *Validity* is the extent to which observations actually yield measures of what they are supposed to measure. If a bathroom scale registers different weights each time you step on it, it is not reliable. If it gives the same weight each time but it isn't an accurate measure, the bathroom scale may be reliable (same results each time) but not valid (inaccurate weight). For a measure of your weight to be considered a fact, the scales must be reliable (consistent) and valid (accurate). A key goal of descriptive research is to provide an accurate view of social reality by providing social facts that are both valid and reliable.

Explanatory Research

Explanatory research attempts to explain *why* things happen or don't happen. Why do people with prison records have trouble finding jobs? What factors are related to students smoking marijuana? Questions like these are concerned with

Oh my! I hope and pray that if this scale is reliable it's not valid. (Note: The scale is reliable if it gives the same results each time she steps on it and valid if those results are the accurate weight.)

the problem of causation. What factors make a designated phenomenon happen or change? What is the cause of a given effect?

In all scientific studies, the variable that *causes* an effect is known as the *independent variable.* The variable that is affected by the independent variable is the *dependent variable.* In a study of child abuse, the abuse itself would be the dependent variable, the effect, and the causes of child abuse — perhaps such factors as stress and the abuse of parents when they were children themselves — would be the independent variables. In another study, lung cancer (effect) would be the dependent variable and smoking (cause) the independent variable.

The same variable may be independent in one context and dependent in another. In a study of the causes of divorce, for example, divorce would be considered the dependent variable (effect), and the causes of divorce, the independent variable. In a study of factors that influence job performance, however, divorce might be found to be an independent variable (a cause), and job performance (the effect) the dependent variable.

Sometimes independent variables are known and the investigator focuses on dependent variables. A study of this sort was undertaken to determine whether soldiers exposed to atomic fallout during nuclear tests suffered any ill effects. The cause, or independent variable (nuclear radiation) was known and the effect, or dependent variable, was being investigated: did these soldiers develop health problems?

In other cases, dependent variables are known, and investigators focus on independent variables. A study of this sort was undertaken at the Love Canal community, near Buffalo, New York. The investigators knew that people in this area were suffering from an unusual number of health problems, including cancer and miscarriages; that is, they knew the effect, the dependent variable. They had to search for the independent variable, the cause of the health problems. They

Citizens of the Love Canal community in New York determined that their disproportionate number of health problems (dependent variable) were caused by (independent variable) chemicals dumped close to their homes. The homeowners joined together to get legal assistance, increase public awareness of the seriousness of the problem, and find a solution to their dilemma.

found that homes in the community had been built on the site of a chemical dump and that the chemical residue was causing serious health problems.

When a clear relationship in time exists between an independent and a dependent variable, they are easy to distinguish. The independent variable (cause) must precede the dependent variable (effect). Lung cancer does not cause smoking. In the social sciences, however, cause and effect are sometimes hard to distinguish clearly. For example, do sexual problems cause marital problems, or do marital problems cause sexual problems?

To establish a cause-effect relationship, researchers must establish an *association* between two variables. Variables that are not associated cannot be causally related. The age of one's grandparents is not related to one's driving ability — obviously, neither causes the other. Even when two variables can be associated, however, it is not safe to assume that one causes the other. Hours of daylight begin to increase at the same time the rate of drowning begins to increase, but it would be absurd to argue that one causes the other, however, and thus we can see that there must also be a *logical rationale* for relating two variables before they can be considered to comprise a cause-effect relationship.

How do sociologists go about their research, whether it is descriptive or explanatory? How do they determine facts, associations, or cause-effect relationships? What procedures do they use to observe and generalize in a scientific manner? Some of the methods used in sociological research are reviewed in the following section.

Sociological Research Methods

Sociological research involves methods of two types, qualitative and quantitative. *Qualitative methods* are used to study conditions or processes that are hard to measure with numbers, such as self-image, manners, how police make a decision to arrest someone, or the pain parents feel as they spank a child. This type of research often involves case studies and participant observation, in which the observer takes part in the activity being observed. *Quantitative methods* are designed to study variables that can be measured in numbers: age, income, years married, or crime rates, for example. This type of research usually involves surveys or experiments.

Sociologists probably use surveys to obtain information about the social world more than any other procedure, but observation studies, case studies, and experimental designs are also used. Throughout the research process, careful consideration must be given to the range of alternative methods or procedures that might meet one's objectives, and there are a variety of procedures and methods that may suit one's need. Expense, facilities, access to people with computer and statistical skills, time, and other factors will influence the choices made. By carefully choosing a research design and methods, a great deal of time and money can be saved, and the research can be done more efficiently. Observation studies, survey research, and experimental designs are the three research options considered most often.

Observation Studies

One qualitative method of obtaining information about social processes is through observation. The researcher or research team watches what is happening with no attempt to control, modify, or influence the ongoing activity. The researcher systematically observes what is happening, and the focus is specifically on the variables or dimensions defined by the hypotheses, propositions, or theory.

Systematic observations may take several forms. One type is the *laboratory observation,* where the sociologist controls the environment in which a particular activity takes place. Sometimes one-way windows are used to reduce the chances

that the activity will be influenced by the researcher. This technique might be employed to study how aggression in children's play is influenced by their watching violence on television, or to explore interactions between men and women in a small group.

A second type of observation takes place in a natural setting rather than in a laboratory. Often termed *field observation,* this type is done by the researcher "on location." One might observe student behavior in a classroom or the interactions between salespersons and customers at a store, for example.

A third observation technique is *participant observation,* in which the researcher is an active participant in the event being studied. Anthropologists frequently use this method to study a particular community or subculture. Sociologists have been participant observers in studies of nudist camps, bars, prisons, the drug trade, and entire communities. Unlike laboratory or field observers, the researchers become directly involved in the group or community activities. As participants, they may learn about some of the subtleties involved in personal interactions. The researcher may therefore acquire a deeper understanding of the emotions and beliefs that bind the group together than would be possible if observations were made by a person not participating in the group.

Most participant observation research takes the form of a *case study,* in which an individual, a single group, community, or activity is observed. Although case studies and participant observation generate new insights and hypotheses, they also present serious difficulties. It may be impossible to generalize on the basis of observations of a single group because an examination of a single case or example may not prove or illustrate anything. Furthermore, a researcher who is also a participant can have difficulty remaining objective and making unbiased observations. It may be impossible to separate personal emotions and feelings from actual events: we tend to see what we want to see. Another problem is that in some instances the researcher is more an intruder than a long-time member of a group. Does the presence of a newcomer affect what takes place? In spite of difficulties such as these, however, participant observation can familiarize us with certain social realities that would be impossible to understand with other data-gathering procedures.

Survey Research

The procedure used most frequently to obtain information about the social world is *survey research*. This quantitative technique involves systematically asking people about their attitudes, feelings, ideas, opinions, behaviors, or anything else. Usually, the researcher uses a questionnaire to guide the questioning. You may have participated in a survey at some point, either an informal survey in a magazine — "How masculine or feminine are you?" — or a formal survey of your attitudes toward birth control or some other issue.

Surveys have a number of advantages over many other data-gathering procedures. They are usually easy to administer and often permit researchers to gather data on identical variables from many people simultaneously. Unlike most participant observation studies, which may take months or years, surveys provide a lot of information in periods ranging from a few minutes to several hours. When highly structured, survey responses are uniformly categorized, which makes tabulation easier. Finally, the precise categorical data provided by surveys is highly amenable to statistical quantitative analysis.

There are problems with surveys too, of course. If questions concern personal information about age, income, sex life, or criminal activities, for example, the respondents may not answer honestly. Second, if the questions or responses are highly structured, the results of the survey may reflect not the actual beliefs of the people being questioned but the researcher's conceptions of how the questions should be asked and what people's answers are likely to be. To give an exaggerated example, a survey question about attitudes toward abortion that listed as the only possible answers "I think abortion should not be allowed under any circumstances" and "I think abortion is permissible in situations involving rape or danger to mothers' health" would not yield valid information. Third, do surveys assess only the most superficial aspects of social life or cover only a limited part of the respondents' thoughts on a subject? Surveys may fail to assess areas that are difficult to examine, and people's beliefs may be far more complex than a survey indicates.

Despite problems such as these, survey research has gained increasing methodological sophistication and is widely used by social scientists. Public opinion pollsters use surveys to gather information about the popularity of politicians. Market researchers employ them to discover why people use a particular soap product, and census takers use them to find out the characteristics and size of the population. They are helpful to sociologists in getting information on a great variety of factors and in testing hypotheses as well.

One major problem in research is identifying a group of people to be studied. The group might be doctors, students, taxpayers, voters in a given election, or any selected group that can provide the information needed to prove or disprove the hypotheses. This group is called the *population,* or, more rarely, the *universe* to be studied. Since we can rarely study all doctors, students, or taxpayers due to such factors as cost and time, we must pick an appropriate sample. A *sample* is a group of people chosen from the population who are thought to represent the population. The sample is then questioned, and their answers should reflect the beliefs of the population as a whole.

Samples are chosen by a variety of methods. A *random sample* is chosen by chance, so that every member of a group has an equal chance of being selected. Since it is usually impossible to place all names in a hat, as is often done at prize drawings, sociologists often assign a number to each name and use a table of random numbers to select which persons should be included. They may also use a method know as *systematic sampling*, in which a specific pattern of selection is followed, such as selecting every twentieth name. A third method is *stratified sampling*, in which the population is divided into groups and then chosen at random from within those groups. If our population were students, we might stratify them by class rank, sex, or race and then randomly select from each of these groups. Regardless of how the sample is chosen, if every person has an equal chance of being chosen, it should be a *representative sample* — it should reflect the attitudes of the total population. A small representative sample is likely to provide far more accurate data about a population than a large nonrepresentative one. There are obvious benefits in being able to study a few hundred people and make accurate generalizations about an entire population on the basis of one's findings. These procedures are used daily in the ratings of television programs, by market researchers of consumer purchasing patterns, and by sociologists testing hypotheses.

The survey is not completed with the selection of a sample, of course. It is necessary to administer our tests or ask our questions of the sample. The questions themselves must be formulated according to the principles of scientific inquiry, which were discussed earlier. Our questions must be carefully worded, precise, operationally defined, free from investigator bias, valid, reliable, and so forth. Imagine how the responses might be influenced if we were to ask a question such as this: "Do you agree with my view and that of all patriotic Americans that an increase in the military budget is vital to our national defense?" As you can see, it is important to ask questions that aren't slanted toward a particular type of response,

or are unclear. Care should be taken to ensure a complete set of possible response choices. The use of improper questions, regardless of the representativeness of the sample, will yield data that cannot be used to prove or disprove a hypothesis and adequately complete the research process.

Experimental Designs

A third procedure for obtaining information about the social world is through the *experimental design*, a classic scientific procedure used to determine cause-effect relationships in carefully controlled situations. In an ideal experiment, it is possible to control all relevant factors and manipulate, statistically or in the society itself, one variable to determine its effect. To carry out an experiment, two matched groups of subjects are selected. In the *experimental group*, an independent variable is introduced, and it is the effect of this variable that is tested. The *control group* is identical to the experimental group in every respect, except that the variable is not introduced into this group. If we were studying the effects of dim lighting on social interaction, for example, we might randomly choose two groups of students. The experimental group would be placed in a dimly lit room, whereas the control group would be in a normally lit room. The researcher would note differences in the behavior of the two groups: frequency of interaction, level of noise, number of subgroups formed, and other behaviors considered germane. Differences in the social behavior of the two groups would presumably be due to the influence of the independent variable, dim lighting.

Experiments are most frequently done in a laboratory setting where it is easier to control conditions than it is in a natural or field (nonlaboratory) setting. It has been argued, however, that laboratory settings are artificial and yield distorted results. Among the social sciences, the experimental type of design is used most often in psychology, and extensive experimental work has been

Experiments are often done by social psychologists in laboratory settings with the observer using a one-way mirror. In this way the observer will not influence the interactions of the people being observed.

done in the study of learning, perceptions, attachments, frustration, and similar behaviors. Students often ask how it is possible to conduct experiments with humans in either a laboratory or non-laboratory setting. Can we lock people in rooms, withhold food, punish them, or remove them from friends and family? We can't, of course, because such research would be highly unethical. Scientists, however, can study circumstances that already exist in the social world: populations of starving people, families who abuse their children, jobs that provide little variation in activity, neighborhoods destroyed by floods or fire, hospitals that isolate people from their loved ones, and prisons that put people in solitary confinement. The social world also contains populations of well-fed people, families that do not abuse their children, and so forth. It is often possible to find existing experimental and control groups that have all characteristics in common except the independent variable chosen for observation.

Suppose we wish to find out whether playing music to workers in a factory influences their pro-ductivity. We could design an experiment in which music was played to one group (the experimental group) and withheld from another group. An alternative method would be to find existing settings in which music was provided or not provided and compare their productivity. A third method would be to statistically compare two groups in which the selected variables could be controlled. Sociologists have used each of these procedures, and, as you can see, a variety of alternatives are available with an experimental type of design.

One of the best-known experiments in sociology resulted in what is widely referred to as the "Hawthorne Effect." Before World War II at the Hawthorne plant of Western Electric, Elton Mayo separated a group of women (the experimental group) from the other workers and systematically varied their lighting, coffee breaks, lunch hours, and other environmental factors (Roethlisberger and Dickson, 1939). In the control group, work conditions went on as usual. Much to the amazement of the researchers, the productivity of the experimental group (the dependent variable) increased regardless of the variables that were introduced, including returning the workers to their original conditions. Obviously, the desired result, increased productivity, was not being caused by a specific independent variable. On the one hand, the experiment seemed like a success — the experimental group differed from the control group when independent variables such as lighting and coffee breaks were introduced. The experiment seemed like a failure, however, in that one independent variable seemed to have as much influence as another. The researchers concluded that the women were trying to please the researchers and enjoyed the attention they were getting. The very presence of the researchers "contaminated" the experiment to the point where they became a significant independent variable and caused a change in the dependent variable — work productivity. The "Hawthorne Effect," then, can be a potential problem whenever an experiment is conducted.

The Research Process

Most research proceeds in accordance with a sequence of rules and procedures basic to the scientific method. Following these procedures does not ensure that a research project will flow smoothly from beginning to end, of course. Researchers must often make changes and adjust to unforeseen difficulties once the study is underway. The general sequence of most research projects is as follows:

1. Formulate the problem.
2. Review the literature.
3. Develop hypotheses for testing.
4. Choose a research design.
5. Collect the data.
6. Analyze the results.
7. Interpret the findings, draw conclusions, and disseminate results.

Formulate the Problem

All research begins with a desire to discover or explain something. To a sociologist using scientific methods, only problems that are amenable to observation and testing would be considered fit subjects for research.

Problems may originate from a number of different sources. They may be selected because they deal with problems that need to be solved: How can child abuse be prevented? How can racial tensions in high schools be diminished? They may also be formulated to test aspects of a theory. Role theory suggests that marital problems are related to a lack of consensus between husband and wife about expectations and the acceptability of certain behaviors. Is this proposition true?

Problems may also be formulated on the basis of previous research findings. Divorce rates dropped during the depression of the 1930s, but will they also drop during the recessions in the 1980s? More adolescent boys than girls smoke cigarettes, but has this changed with the rise of the women's movement? A fourth source of problems is personal experience or general curiosity. A problem need not concern a social ill, a theory, or previously investigated phenomena. We may simply be curious about what type of person burns crosses on other people's lawns or whether married professional athletes are more likely than nonathletes to have extramarital affairs. Whatever the source of the problem researchers seek to investigate, the problem must be articulated in such a way that they know exactly what they are trying to determine.

Review the Literature

This aspect of the research process is closely associated with formulating the problem and also with the next step, developing a hypothesis for testing. By reviewing relevant literature, we learn what studies have already been completed, where, when, and with whom they were done, and what

Not all experiements or research data gathered by observation require laboratories or one-way mirrors. In fact, many of the observation studies conducted by sociologists use nonlaboratory settings. An observation study of smokers and nonsmokers, for example, might be done at a dinner party.

theoretical orientation explained the researchers' findings. We discover what scientists and non-scientific writers have reported in the area. This review alerts us to what is already known, gives us clues about existing gaps in our knowledge, and helps us more clearly define the boundaries of our own investigation.

Develop Hypotheses for Testing

Hypotheses, as you will remember, are statements of relationships between two or more variables. They are formulated such that they can be empirically proved or disproved. Propositions tend to be abstract, but hypotheses are specific, testable assertions of theory. They state what we want to test as well as what we expect to find. Unless they are in the null form (factor A is not related to factor B), they predict a relationship between two or more variables. Deriving hypotheses from a theory involves knowing what variables are important, how they are interrelated, and what regularities to look for. Suppose, for example, we wanted to know why people smoke cigarettes. A psychoanalytic theory would suggest that we examine early childhood experiences, particularly as related to gratification during the oral stage of development. A symbolic interaction theory would suggest that we examine the reference groups (particularly peers) of the smokers or that we examine the definition or meaning that smoking has to the persons who smoke. Frustration theory may direct us to examine sources of stress or conflict.

When hypotheses are not developed, studies by social researchers may still provide descriptive and useful data, but this result increases the likelihood of gathering useless and unnecessary information. Investigators who do not operate according to a preconceived rationale are less likely to achieve results that can be used to make predictions, and their findings are also less likely to contribute to our accumulated knowledge about a particular social phenomenon.

If hypotheses include variables that can be tested, these variables must be provided with operational definitions that specify what procedures will be used to identify the variable. Operationally defined variables are oriented toward the empirical (i.e., observable) world. An exceptional student, therefore, might be operationally defined as one who has a grade point average of 3.5 or better on a scale of 4.0, an old car might be operationally defined as one that is more than eight years old, and an adjusted person may be operationally defined as one who scores above a specified level on a given personality test. The development of hypotheses is the link between the abstract world of theory and propositions and the more specific and concrete world of empirical testing.

Choose a Research Design

After the problem has been formulated, the literature has been reviewed, and precise hypotheses have been developed for testing, we must establish the procedures by which evidence can be gathered to support or reject the hypotheses. This is our research design, our plan for the collection and analysis of data. Choosing a research design can be compared with the process of planning a trip — once we have decided where we want to go and how to get there. Like people planning their travels, researchers have to take many factors into account: time, expense, flexibility, number of people involved, interests, and so on. They must consider the various methods of research and choose the one that is best for their

studies. Is observation a good method, or would a survey or experiment be better? If the experiment involves a certain population, how will these people be located? Is a sampling procedure necessary, or can the entire population be questioned? Can the researcher pursue the study alone, or will help be needed? The answers to questions like these will serve as the blueprint for action. It is important to keep in mind that aspects of the design may have to be changed once the process is begun, just as travelers may have to change their itinerary after leaving for a trip.

Collect the Data

After a tentative design is established, the next step is to carry it out. Data about social phenomena can be drawn from a wide variety of sources. Labovitz and Hagedorn (1981) divided data into three types: (1) responses elicited directly from subjects by questioning, through questionnaires or interview guides (a listing of specific questions to direct the interviewer); (2) facts acquired by human observers (participant observers or judges) or mechanical observers (cameras or tape recorders); and (3) physical trace evidence (litter and fossils, for example). Data can be further classified according to their sources. *Primary source data* are gathered by the researchers themselves. *Secondary source data* are used by the researcher but gathered from elsewhere — census reports, vital statistics records, company files, and sales receipts, for example. Gathering data from multiple sources is one way to check validity because more confidence can be placed in our data if information is corroborated by several different sources.

Analyze the Results

After the data are collected, they must be assembled, organized, and classified in such a way that the hypotheses can be tested. If the study is

A Research Note on Street-Level Justice, *or,* Do Police Invoke the Law Consistently?

Introduction

Police are legally mandated to enforce the law uniformly, but do they? Unlike other decision makers in the criminal justice system, such as prosecutors and judges, police officers make legal decisions in a context of low visibility, and they have wide discretionary power over who will be subject to legal intervention and control. Most scholars agree that selective enforcement is routine.

Problem

A research study was conducted by Smith and Visher to examine variations in police arrest practices. They wanted to see if arrest practices are influenced by such variables as: (1) the dispositional preferences of victims; (2) the race of the suspect; and (3) the presence of bystanders.

Literature Review

From a review of more than forty publications dealing with the particular topic of police-citizen encounters, the authors discovered that most encounters involve minor offenses, are reactive rather than proactive (that is, involving response to, rather than prevention of, crime), and are influenced by the location of the encounter, by the presence of an audience, and by the seriousness of the offense. Some debate has been generated by the literature that deals with characteristics such as race, age, and gender; the demeanor of the suspect; the presence and actions of complainants; and the relationship between the victim and the suspect.

Conflicting Models for Arrest Decisions

Given the norm of selective enforcement, what criteria play a role in arrest decisions? A conflict model suggests that enforcement reflects the underlying dimensions of social stratification; that is, members of socially disadvantaged groups, such as blacks, are more likely to be arrested. An opposing view — a consensus model — assumes that the police are equally responsive to the interests of all groups and that their arrest decisions are based on the seriousness of the violations rather than on the situation or characteristics of the violator. Given the absence of an integrated theoretical model, the contribution of various predictors of the arrest decision remains problematic.

Sample and Data

The data for the Smith and Visher study were gathered in relatively small and involves few cases or observations, the researchers may be able to process and analyze the data themselves without the aid of computer or statistical techniques. Large-scale studies may involve thousands of cases and dozens of variables, however, and personal data manipulation is impossible in such cases.

Suppose we are concerned with population control, and our review of the literature indicates that people who marry later have fewer children. We might state our hypothesis as follows: "Age at marriage is negatively related to family size." In other words, the older people are when they marry, the smaller the ultimate size of their family. We chose a design that included checking marriage and public birth records and then gathered data on one thousand cases. This information included data on each person's birth date, marital status, date of marriage, and number of children. Case number 1, for example, was born

1977 by trained civilians riding on nine-hundred patrol shifts representing twenty-four police departments in the metropolitan areas of St. Louis, Missouri; Rochester, New York; and Tampa-St. Petersburg, Florida. Excluding traffic stops where arrest occurs rarely and any case where the characteristics of the suspect were in question, the final sample contained 742 encounters. The majority of the encounters were responses to citizen requests for police service. Detailed data was gathered on such variables as police entry; location; bystanders; informal and formal disposition; suspect sex, age, and antagonism; the victim-suspect relationship; the seriousness of the offense (felony or misdemeanor); and whether or not arrest was made.

Findings

The findings were presented at various levels. At a descriptive level it was found that encounters occur in public places and involve misdemeanors. Half of the encounters involved bystanders who observed but were not directly involved in the police-suspect interaction. Half of these bystanders were white, four-fifths were male, and the predominant age was nineteen to thirty-five years. The presence of bystanders increased the probability of arrest. The probability of arrest was greatly increased for suspects who were antagonistic and who failed to display deference toward an officer. Race was also a factor, with black suspects more likely to be arrested. In contradiction to other findings, the police did not discriminate in favor of women. In the matter of citizen inputs, police were more likely to make arrests if the victim requested it and less likely to do so if the victim requested the suspect's release. If the victim and suspect were acquainted, arrest was less likely. Finally, the data support the view that the amount of discretion available to the officer is inversely related to the seriousness of the offense: that is, the more serious the offense, the less discretion available to the officer and the more likely the arrest.

Discussion

The research lends some support to both the consensus and the conflict models of police behavior. Police *do* respond to the legal seriousness of the offense and the preferences of victims when making arrest decisions. But police also systematically apply more formal sanctions against persons who are socially disadvantaged. Other factors affecting arrest decisions were: antagonistic suspects (requiring police to react to this challenge of their authority), the presence of bystanders (amplifying the need of police to appear in control of the encounter), and victim-suspect acquaintance (reflecting police perceptions that the victim may not cooperate in subsequent adjudication). The evidence repeatedly demonstrated that arrests are not applied randomly to individuals. Selection bias *does* exist at the arrest stage.

SOURCE: Douglas A. Smith and Christy A. Visher, "Street Level Justice: Situational Determinants of Police Arrest Decisions," *Social Problems*, 29 (December 1981): pp. 167–177.

December 25, 1918, married May 22, 1948, and had five children. Case number 2 was born April 11, 1936, married May 31, 1958, and had two children. Similar data were obtained for the rest of the cases. Now that all these data are available, how do we go about proving or disproving our hypothesis?

In most cases, it is necessary to arrange the data in a manageable form. For our purposes, the exact dates of birth and marriage are superfluous since we are interested in the age at which a person married. Case number 1 was married at age twenty-nine, case number 2 at age twenty-two, and so on. It might also be desirable to organize age information into different categories — those married before age twenty and those married after age twenty, perhaps (see Table 3-1). Age at marriage might also be categorized at five-year intervals, or in any other way that might help us test hypotheses. It would then be a simple matter to

Table 3·1
Examples of categories for age at first marriage

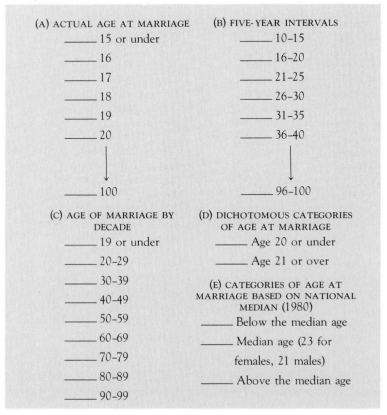

(A) ACTUAL AGE AT MARRIAGE	(B) FIVE-YEAR INTERVALS
_____ 15 or under	_____ 10–15
_____ 16	_____ 16–20
_____ 17	_____ 21–25
_____ 18	_____ 26–30
_____ 19	_____ 31–35
_____ 20	_____ 36–40
↓	↓
_____ 100	_____ 96–100

(C) AGE OF MARRIAGE BY DECADE	(D) DICHOTOMOUS CATEGORIES OF AGE AT MARRIAGE
_____ 19 or under	_____ Age 20 or under
_____ 20–29	_____ Age 21 or over
_____ 30–39	**(E) CATEGORIES OF AGE AT MARRIAGE BASED ON NATIONAL MEDIAN (1980)**
_____ 40–49	_____ Below the median age
_____ 50–59	_____ Median age (23 for
_____ 60–69	females, 21 males)
_____ 70–79	_____ Above the median age
_____ 80–89	
_____ 90–99	

make a graph or table of results that could easily be interpreted.

In addition, we might want to include some descriptive data about each of the variables. The *mode* is the most frequent response. We might discover that the mode of male age at marriage was twenty; that is, more males married at twenty than at any other age. The *median* is the point where one-half of the respondents are above and one-half are below. We might discover that half the women were married before age eighteen and half after age eighteen. The *mean* is the average, the sum of the age at marriage divided by the number of people involved. Suppose, for example, that the first seven people in our study were married at ages 30, 22, 20, 18, 16, 16, and 16. The most frequent age at marriage (mode) is 16. The age at which half are below and half are above (median) is 18. The average age (mean) is 19.7 — the sum of the ages divided by seven. These figures are measures of central tendency.

The mean, mode, or the median age at marriage as a measure of central tendency is important to social scientists as well as to the public at large for a variety of reasons. At a personal level, students may be interested in knowing if they are younger, older, or the same age as others who marry. Business people and marketing specialists are interested in knowing the number who marry and the specific age of marriage for both men and women in terms of the increased potential that results for housing, honeymoon travel, baby clothes, food, and the like. Insurance agents recognize the impact of marriage on auto accident rates or life expectancy and frequently take into account marital status in addition to age in determining risk. Legislators and lawyers are influenced in their decision making on the legal ages of marriage, drinking, or adult status based on the actual ages of marriage. Social scientists have discovered a wide range of variables (family size, divorce rates, level of education, etc.) to be related to age at marriage. Any of these persons or groups may be most interested in that which is most frequent (mode), the average (mean), or the point at which half are above and half are below (median) depending on their intended use.

Finally, we may wish to discover the *range* of a variable, the distance between the largest and smallest amount. We might discover that everyone in our study was married between the ages of twelve and eighty, or eighteen and thirty. The most commonly used measure of range is the *standard deviation,* a statistical measure that indicates the proportion of cases that fall within a standard unit of measurement from the mean. It indicates the *variance* in the distribution of cases. Variance refers to the extent to which scores, ages, or results differ. If everyone gets the same exam score, is the same age, or runs a race in the same time, there is no variance nor is there any degree of deviation from the mean. Perhaps variance can be illustrated by looking at the bar graphs in Figure 3-1.

Similar results exist with any variable. Returning to the example of age at marriage, the variance would be very small if two-thirds of our cases were married between seventeen and twenty-one, even if the range was between twelve and eighty. The standard deviation would indicate how much the age at marriage deviated from the mean.

Figure 3-1
Variability on exam scores: Three examples

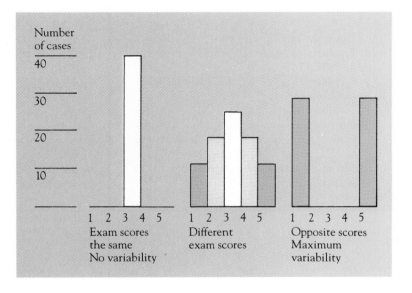

SOCIOLOGISTS AT WORK
Using Research Methods in Health Care

Lana S. Leggett is a research consultant for Northeast Central Ohio Emergency Medical Services, Inc. (NECOEMS) in Wooster, Ohio. NECOEMS is designing and implementing an emergency medical system that covers an eight-county area in the northeastern part of that state. Lana Leggett is also a sociologist, holding a doctorate in applied sociology from Kent State University.

How does Leggett use her sociological training in her work at NECOEMS? "My primary responsibility," she says, "is to develop and implement research projects to establish and maintain this emergency medical system." This involves setting up special studies, in which she applies the research design and methodology she learned as a student of sociology. She lists the following as the essential steps:

□ Define the problem.
□ Become familiar with existing literature in the field.
□ Formulate testable hypotheses and define the variables of study.
□ Develop a research design. (A research design must use a methodology that is *appropriate* to the material being studied and *workable* in the field.)
□ Aid in the collection and processing of research data.
□ Analyze the results, interpreting and summarizing the findings.
□ Draw conclusions, discussing the significance of the findings.

In addition, she must monitor and evaluate the functioning of the overall NECOEMS system. "As part of my job, I develop research instruments to measure the functioning of the system." She also develops instructions and training materials to aid in the use of report forms, oversees the training of those who will use them, and aids in the development of a program for processing the data collected. Then she provides written summaries of the findings reported on the forms. She compiles appropriate statistics for decision-making purposes, and presents her findings to interested groups. "For example, I developed an ambulance run report form that is used to document any medical care given before a patient arrives at the hospital. This form can be used to evaluate the quality of care given. It is one link in tracing the patient from the scene of a sudden illness or injury through admission and treatment to discharge from a medical facility." In developing this form she used the interviewing, scaling, and data selection and refinement techniques and procedures she learned while studying sociology. "My sociological background," Leggett says, "has given me the foundation for carrying out the responsibilities of my present position."

Interpret Findings, Draw Conclusions, and Disseminate Results

After the analysis of the data, the final activities of the research process are begun. We interpret our findings, draw our conclusions, and confirm, reject, or reformulate our original hypothesis, proposition, and theory. Then the results are also made available to others. These final activities can be very difficult, however. Suppose, for example, we found that people who married at a young age did have larger families but that they were only slightly larger than the families of those who married when they were older. If people who married before age twenty had an average of 1.9 children, and those who married after age twenty had an average of 1.8 children, should we accept our hypothesis? Would this finding be significant, or could the difference be the result of chance or a bias in the sample we investigated? If the community we examined consisted largely of an ethnic group that encourages early marriage, we may not be able to generalize our findings to the entire state or country. Interpretations must take into account any factor in the research process that could have influenced our results. Some projects inevitably fail, but even a research project that does not prove what it set out to prove may teach us something important — witness the research that resulted in what we now call the Hawthorne Effect (see page 60). By doing careful, detailed research and reporting it completely and accurately, however, we allow our studies to be replicated and can discover if other studies yield similar results.

By reporting our findings and conclusions, we make them subject to public review, criticism, and application. Sociologists frequently publish their results in professional journals, where they are reviewed by other sociologists. Sometimes the results are published in books, monographs, or popular magazines. When the results have been disseminated, the research process is complete.

The steps of the research process that we have described are general guidelines. In practice, researchers develop their own styles and use methodologies that best meet the objectives of the research. It is dangerous to become so interested in a particular technique, theory, measuring device, or other element of research that the basic substantive issues of the project are overlooked. As Peter Berger (1963) wrote: In the social sciences, as in love, an overemphasis on technique can lead to impotence.

Summary

Although we learn about society from everyday experiences, common sense, authority, revelation, and tradition, sociology is heavily dependent on empirical research that uses the scientific method.

Is sociology a science? Some argue that it is, some argue that it isn't. It may be more constructive to note what distinguishes scientific modes of inquiry from nonscientific modes of inquiry and then consider whether sociology can follow a scientific mode.

There are certain standards of inquiry basic to science. Objectivity involves excluding personal values, beliefs, and biases from the research process, findings, and interpretations. The standard of replication requires that research be undertaken and reported such that someone else can duplicate it. The precision in measurement standard requires that whatever is studied be measurable and that measurements be precise, reliable, and valid. The adoption of a critical attitude leads researchers to question their data and methods throughout the entire process. Scientists also adopt an analytical orientation toward their research.

Sociological research is of two basic types: descriptive and explanatory. Descriptive research provides reliable, valid data on social facts — the way things are. Explanatory research goes beyond description in order to determine why a certain social situation occurs and to discover cause-effect relationships. Dependent variables in explanatory research are those the investigator wants to explain; they are dependent on or determined by other variables. Independent variables are those that cause the variations in the dependent variable.

Sociological methods are often categorized into two types: qualitative and quantitative. Qualitative methods are used to study variables that cannot be measured in numbers without great difficulty. These methods include case studies, laboratory observations, field observations, and participatory observations. Quantitative methods are used to study variables that can be measured in numbers. Experimental research and surveys are quantitative methods. Surveys, the most frequently used method of sociological research, involve systematically asking people about their attitudes or behaviors, which is usually accomplished with the use of questionnaires. Choosing an appropriate sample and wording questions carefully are crucial parts of the survey method. The experimental method involves the use of two or more similar groups. An independent variable is introduced into the experimental group but withheld from the control group.

Research generally involves a sequence of tasks, including the following: formulating the problem, reviewing the literature, developing hypotheses for testing, choosing a research design, collecting data, analyzing the findings, drawing conclusions, and disseminating the results. There are often many different ways to categorize the data, formulate tables, and use statistical measures such as the mode, median, mean, range, and standard deviation. When the data analysis is finished, conclusions are drawn and the results are made available to the public.

Key Terms

case study
concept
conceptual framework
control group
dependent variable
descriptive research
direct relationship
directional hypotheses
experimental design
experimental group
explanatory research
field observation
hypothesis
independent variable
inverse relationship
laboratory observation
mean
median
mode
null hypotheses
objectivity
operational definition
operationalization
participant observation
population or universe
precision of measurement
proposition
qualitative methods
quantitative methods
random sample
range
reliability
replication
sample
scientific method
social facts
standard deviation
stratified sampling
survey research
systematic sampling

validity
variables
variance

Suggested Readings

Bailey, Kenneth D. **Methods of Social Research.** *New York: Macmillan, 1978.* A survey of sociological methodology, with an emphasis on quantitative methods.

Cole, Stephen. **The Sociological Method. 3rd ed.** *Chicago: Rand McNally, 1980.* A short book designed to give the beginning student a conceptual understanding of empirical social research. Paperback.

Denzin, Norman K. **The Research Art.** *New York: McGraw-Hill, 1978.* A look at sociological research methods from an interactionist point of view, with an emphasis on qualitative methods.

Hoover, Kenneth R. **The Elements of Social Scientific Thinking. 2nd ed.** *New York: St. Martin's Press, 1980.* A short explanation of social science for those who use the results of social science research and those who are beginning their own research. Paperback.

Labovitz, Sanford and Robert Hagedorn. **Introduction to Social Research. 3rd ed.** *New York: McGraw-Hill, 1981.* A brief, understandable introduction to social research. Paperback.

Walizer, Michael H. and Paul L. Wienir. **Research Methods and Analysis: Searching for Relationships.** *New York: Harper & Row, 1978.* A textbook that integrates methodological considerations with statistical processes.

Weiss, Carol H. **Evaluation Research: Methods of Assessing Program Effectiveness.** *Englewood Cliffs, N.J.: Prentice-Hall, 1972.* A brief paperback that discusses the application of research methods to the evaluation of social programs.

Williamson, John B., David A. Karp, and John R. Dalphin. **The Research Craft: An Introduction to Social Science Methods.** *Boston: Little, Brown, 1977.* A comprehensive textbook designed for use in a first course on social research methods.

The Sociologist as Detective

by William B. Sanders

In this reading, sociologist William B. Sanders compares the work of sociologists to that of detectives. An unlikely comparison? Read and find out.

In the course of their work, both detectives and sociologists must gather and analyze information. For detectives, the object is to identify and locate criminals and to collect evidence to ensure that the identification is correct. Sociologists, on the other hand, develop theories and methods to help them understand social behavior. Although their specific goals differ, both sociologists and detectives formulate theories and develop methods in an attempt to answer two general questions: "Why did it happen?" and "In what circumstances is it likely to happen again?" — that is, to explain and predict. Detectives' theories consider such questions as: "What motives would explain a specific type of crime?" "What do certain crimes have in common?" "Where is a given type of crime likely to occur?" Sociological theories are developed around such questions as: "How is social order possible?" "How is social conflict regulated?" "What forms are displayed in social interaction?"

To test their theories, detectives and sociologists rely on empirical evidence and logical modes of analysis as well as on their imagination. Both employ observation techniques, interviews, experiments, and other empirical methods to test the validity of their theories. Nevertheless, there are differences in their methods of gathering and

analyzing information, and each can profit from techniques developed by the other. Sociologists, for example, rarely if ever employ such devices as the polygraph machine (lie detector), and detectives do not use multivariate analysis (charting several causal variables). Detectives have made much more use of physical evidence than have sociologists, who have seldom bothered to analyze the physical features of social phenomena. (The work of Webb and his associates [1966] stands as a notable exception.)*

In investigating a crime, detectives interview victims, witnesses, informants, and suspects. They compare these interviews with physical evidence that they gather in order to piece together a consistent account of what took place and to determine whether the people they interviewed were telling the truth. They may conduct an experiment to see whether a crime could have occurred in the way suggested by the accounts and the physical evidence. Finally, the detectives may discern a pattern from several cases involving crimes of the same sort. (A pattern would include the typical method used to commit the crime, the type of place in which the crime occurred, and the time the crime occurred.) Knowing this pattern, the detectives would then observe ("stake out") certain areas during the times the crime is likely to occur.

---

* Modern detectives use more sophisticated modes of analysis than did Sherlock Holmes, who was able to detect that Dr. Watson had been in Afghanistan after merely shaking hands with him, or Charlie Chan, who could tell whether a person was left- or right-handed by noting how matches had been torn from a matchbook, but they devote the same attention to details and basic reasoning.

Sociologists, on the other hand, generally use only a single method and only a single source of data. Survey researchers will use only the data gathered in interviews, experimental researchers will only conduct an experiment, and participant observers will conduct no surveys or experiments and will report their findings solely in terms of their field notes. Moreover, it is unlikely that any of them will use available physical evidence. However, the sociologist could greatly profit from using multiple methods and measurements in a single study. Each method or source of data has its strengths and weaknesses. Experiments have questionable external validity, attitudes elicited by interviews often have no relation to people's actual behavior, and observational studies lack control. By using more than one method and source of data in a single study, as detectives do, sociologists can discover and compensate for the weaknesses of the various methods and will multiply their strengths.

Theory

The stereotype of the detective who asks for "just the facts" is inaccurate, for detectives are always working with and testing theory. In any investigation a detective would be at a loss for questions to ask and interviewees without at least a rudimentary theory. For instance, in homicide cases, the first people generally contacted by detectives are friends, relatives, or acquaintances of the victim. Behind such investigative procedures is the theory that most homicides are committed by people who are socially close to the victim. Theory even determines what facts are noted. For example, in "Silver Blaze," a case of a stolen racehorse, Sherlock Holmes's observation of the fact that a dog was *not* barking was directed by the theory that dogs do not bark at people they know. The "fact" that the thief must have been known to the dog was overlooked by Dr. Watson and readers who were not guided by that theory.

Similarly, sociologists develop theories that

lead them to ask certain questions and not others, and these questions in turn lead them to notice certain "facts" and not others. For example, Max Weber's theory of the relationship between religious belief systems and economic systems led him to formulate certain questions concerning the economic structures of societies with and without predominantly Protestant beliefs. Likewise, Durkheim's theory of anomic suicide led him to examine suicide rates in various countries in terms of each country's dominant religion. In both of these theories, religion was a fact to be noticed. In Goffman's examination of mental hospitals, on the other hand, the focus of his theory on the social world of patients in a mental hospital as they developed and sustained it led him to ignore the issue of what bearing their religious background had on their being committed. Problems relevant to certain theories are not relevant to others, and certain questions are relevant to certain problems and not to others. The facts that are located in research stem from the researcher's theory.

Central to theories and research are concepts, which Blumer calls "fashioners of perception," in that they direct the researcher to "see" the world in certain terms and configurations. For instance, the concept of "social class" directs the researcher to look at elements that give some people power and deny it to others. The concept of "the situation" directs the observer's attention to the context to encounters between people rather than just to the individuals in interaction. Concepts provide the crucial link between theory and research, in that they tell the researcher what is of theoretical interest and what to look for. If a theory states, for example, that there is a relationship between associations and criminal behavior, the researcher will not look at head shapes, economic position, or family size, but will concentrate on whom criminals associate with.

Detectives' investigations are also guided by certain concepts. The concept of "motive," for example, plays a central role in many investigations. Assuming that people are generally rational, detectives attempt to identify those who would benefit from a crime. This conceptual view leads them to certain people as possible suspects and away from others. For example, in an arson case, detectives try to determine whether the owner of the house or business or anyone else would benefit more from the building's absence than its presence. Without such a guiding concept, there would be no starting point for an investigation and no grounds on which to build a theory or finish an investigation.

Evidence

Just as theories direct researchers to facts and give meaning and relevance to facts, so facts in turn give validity and shape to theories. And since sociology, like detecting, is an empirical enterprise, sociological theories require evidence for them to be considered valid, just as detectives' theories do.

Beginning with a hypothesis, the researcher gathers concrete evidence to either substantiate or disprove it. For example, detectives may hypothesize that the butler was responsible for the murder of the lord of the manor. Before they can arrest him, however, they must locate evidence to show that there is "probable cause" for considering him a suspect. For conviction, they must show that the butler was guilty beyond a reasonable doubt. If the butler's fingerprints are found on the murder weapon, for example, this would stand as cause for arresting him; however, if the murder weapon is found to be something the butler normally handled, such as a poker for tending the fire, other corroborating evidence would have to be located to prove the hypothesis that he was guilty.

Similarly, sociologists must prove their hypotheses. For example, in attempting to discover whether there is a relationship between amount of education and income, the sociologist might hypothesize that the more education an individual has, the greater his income will be. But he gathers evidence to prove or disprove this hypothesis, not by showing that one person with a college degree has a greater income than another person with less education, but by taking the average amount of education of several people and comparing it with their average income. Thus, instead of working with single cases, sociologists typically work with several cases.

An important feature of detective investigations is the practices involved in recognizing evidence as evidence. At a crime scene and in the course of an investigation, there are numerous elements that may or may not be regarded as evidence. Physical artifacts, statements by witnesses, and written documents can all turn out to be evidence, but whether they are so treated depends on the formulated circumstances of the case. For example, in an investigation of a burglary with attempted homicide, detectives searched an area around the crime scene for evidence. Overlooked but quite visible was a plastic bleach bottle that had been partially ripped apart. Later, when a suspect was arrested, a similar piece of plastic was found in his possession.* The old bleach bottle was now seen retrospectively in an entirely new light. If the piece of plastic found on the suspect could be matched to the piece missing from the bottle found on the crime scene, the suspect could be linked to the crime. Thus, from being merely a piece of trash, the bleach bottle was elevated to a piece of evidence.

Because what comes to be seen as evidence depends on the context of the situation and what will be evidence is often unclear until a context has been provided or a hypothesis is more fully developed, detectives keep everything that ap-

---

* Credit cards, plastic playing cards, and other flat, thin pieces of plastic are commonly used by burglars to slip open door locks.

pears to be potentially useful. Intelligence units, for instance, keep all sorts of information in their files. Much of it is never used or even seen as useful at the time it is collected, but if a situation comes up where they need the information, they will have it. In a crude way, much of what is collected by detectives is like using seat belts. They do nothing for the driver until he has an accident, but, for the value they have on the occasions when they are needed, they are worth the little inconvenience they cause.

Similarly, sociologists know that concepts may be indicated in different ways, depending on the research situation. Using the concept of social status, the sociologist cannot assume that the status symbols of one group will be the same for another group. For example, having a big, expensive automobile may indicate status among most Americans, but status among environmentalists may be indicated by the lack of such a car. Thus, before specifying big cars as an indicator of social status, the sociologist sensitizes the concept to the research situation. In this way he ensures that what is taken to indicate an instance of a conceptual phenomenon actually does so.

Related to this is the issue of contextual embeddedness of meaning and evidence. That is to say, what something means and whether or not it is seen as evidence depend on the context of the situation. For instance, consider the question "Do you have a match?" If the sociologist is studying pickup strategies in bars, this would be taken as an indicator of an attempt to initiate a conversation. In the context of male-female bar interaction, the question has a certain meaning. However, in another context — say, in a conversation between two old friends or in a gymnasium where boxers train — it has an entirely different sense. In a study of pinball players, the author found that the term "match" generally refers to a free game. Hence, what is defined as evidence for the sociologist as well as for the detective depends on the context of the situation.

Purposes and Problems of Research

In the very broadest sense, the purpose of sociological research is to test and develop sociological theory. Theory, in turn, explains and predicts social behavior. However, there is a good deal of sociological research that only indirectly tests or develops theory. A researcher may collect data to determine the *frequency* and *distribution* of various features of social life. For example, a researcher may conduct a survey to find how many students smoke marijuana. On the other hand, a sociologist may want to conduct a study simply in order to *describe* the forms of behavior in a given setting, such as bars, airports, laundromats, or department stores. Both of these types of studies, though, are related to theory. In looking at the frequency and distribution of marijuana smokers, the researcher may find that students who live in urban areas are more likely to smoke marijuana than are rural students. Such findings would serve as tests for a theory linking crime with population density. Similarly, by describing typical forms of behavior in various social settings, the researcher may test the theory that social settings determine the type of behavior to be found in a given setting.

Let us turn now to some of the problems in sociological research. Some of these issues are specific to certain kinds of research, and they will be explained in other parts of the book. Here only the general problems common to all research will be considered.

Validity. Simply stated, validity refers to the correspondence between the researcher's collected data and the real world. The extent to which the collected data reflect naturally occurring social behavior and processes determines its validity. For example, if for some reason respondents to a questionnaire elected not to tell the truth, the data collected by the researcher would not reflect the real world and would be considered invalid. *Internal validity* is generally considered in the context of measurement, but here it will be used to entail description as well. If data have internal validity, any significant differences observed in a comparison can be attributed to a predicted cause, and not to measurement or description error. For example, in a study of assembly workers, the researchers predicted that the workers would increase production if the lighting were heightened. As the lighting improved, so did production; however, work production also went up when the lights were dimmed. The researchers concluded that the assembly workers increased their efforts as a result of the presence of the researchers. The increased production had nothing to do with the lights. Thus, the prediction that work production increased with lighting proved to be erroneous. Similarly, in descriptive studies, notably participant-observation research, often what the researcher describes is due to the researcher's presence rather than being a picture of normal behavior that occurs in the researcher's absence. Field experiments and unobtrusive measures have features that avoid some of the problems of internal validity.

External validity, on the other hand, refers to the generalizability of the findings. If the data cannot be generalized to other, theoretically similar settings, situations, organizations, or populations, then the study lacks external validity. For example, if a researcher were interested in finding out the attitudes of a given community but interviewed only members of the upper class, he would have no way of knowing whether the attitudes he found were truly representative of the entire community. Thus, he could not generalize his findings to the entire community, and the study would lack external validity.

In order to increase external validity, researchers employ *randomization* procedures. Used mainly in surveys but occasionally in other methods as well, randomization is a procedure that gives every unit in the universe of interest an equal chance at being included in the sample to be interviewed, tested, or observed. The *universe* is the population in which the researcher is interested, and the *sample* is that part of the universe that will be researched. If the sample is random, it is assumed that all of the various relevant aspects of the universe will be proportionately represented; therefore, the findings can be generalized to the entire universe and be considered externally valid.

Reliability. Another problem encountered in research is that of reliability. Reliability is the ability of a method to replicate results when it is used by different researchers. For example, a researcher in California conducts an experiment and finds that individuals under a specific set of conditions will conform to group norms even though they do not personally agree with them. The researcher sends his experimental design to a researcher in New York who conducts the same experiment under the same conditions and finds the same results. The experiment is then considered reliable, since different researchers using the same instrument found the same thing. Fixed-choice questionnaires are considered highly reliable, whereas participant-observation studies are considered to have lower reliability.

Ethics. A final problem that should be discussed here involves research on human beings. This problem is in part an interactional one pertaining to such issues as soliciting subjects to participate in experiments, gaining access to an observation setting, and getting people to respond to interviews.... Here we will deal with ethical problems.

Unlike the detective, the sociologist does not face legal constraints in gathering evidence. The sociologist's data will not be invalidated if he does not warn his subjects that what they say may be used against them, nor do defense lawyers instruct subjects not to speak to sociologists. However, sociologists do have an unwritten code by which they attempt to abide.

Sociological researchers should not invade the privacy of others without their permission. For instance, even if they were legally able to do so, sociologists should not plant bugs in people's homes or locate themselves so that they can secretly observe others in private places. Similarly, sociologists should avoid lying, cheating, and stealing as resources for gathering data. Often it may seem that the only way to get information is by using techniques that are unethical and rationalizing their use in the name of sociology. Not only is such behavior unethical, but if sociologists began to engage regularly in these practices, they would soon lose their position of trust and would find it difficult to persuade informants to reveal information.

While sociologists are not ethically required to announce their research intentions in public places, in some situations it may be difficult to differentiate between private and public settings; some very private business takes place in public. An excellent example is the research by Laud Humphreys in which Humphreys, in the role of a "watch queen," or voyeur, observed impersonal sex between men in public toilets. On the one hand, Humphreys was not invading a private space, and that criterion alone justified his presence without announcing that he was a sociologist engaging in research. On the other hand, the sexual activity was private, and it was not the type of behavior with which most of the participants would want their names associated; therefore, in this sense the research can be taken as an invasion of privacy. The resolution of where the invasion of privacy begins and where the public domain ends must be in terms of the general standards of the members' understanding of public and private places. Thus, since no one needs special permis-

sion to enter a public toilet as one would need for entering a private home, it can be argued that observation of such domains should not be forbidden to the unannounced researcher.

This does not, however, exclude the sociologist from using data from private places that have been discarded and from which inferences can be made as to what takes place in those places. By analyzing what people put in their trash, for example, sociologists have found certain private activities that, although unseen, are easily inferred. Sawyer, for example, estimated drinking habits from the frequency and distribution of liquor bottles found in trash cans. Thus, like detectives, who are barred from invading privacy without permission, either in the form of a search warrant or by the controller of the private space, sociologists need to develop methods for *seeing more than that to which they have access.*

A final ethical consideration lies in the confidentiality of the sociologist's subjects. Much of the information gathered by sociologists may be harmful to those who were observed or questioned. In order to protect their subjects, sociologists do not reveal the names of their subjects, the names of the organizations, or (sometimes) even the location of the study. Confidentiality, besides having ethical implications, has practical ones as well. Much of the information gathered by detectives is based on what their informants tell them. If detectives revealed the names of their informants, soon there would be no informants. Similarly, if sociologists made public the names and places of their studies that uncovered adverse information, soon no one would speak to them.

SOURCE: Sanders, William B., ed., *The Sociologist as Detective: An Introduction to Research Methods.* Copyright © 1967 by Praeger Publishers, Inc., New York, a division of Holt, Rinehart and Winston. Reprinted by permission of Holt, Rinehart and Winston, CBS College Publishing.

Part II

Individuals Within Society

There would be no society if there were no people talking to one another, acting and interacting, cooperating with one another, and competing with one another. But how do people know how to behave in their own society? How does society teach them what is right and what is wrong, what is appropriate behavior and what is not? Each society has its own special set of rules, its own customs and traditions, its own set of values and beliefs, and each must teach its members how to fit into the society. Chapter 4 looks at the variety of cultures in societies. Chapter 5 reviews the many ways society uses to teach its members appropriate behavior.

If we understand the customs of the society and understand how people learn these customs, we can better understand how people interact with one another. Chapter 6 in this section describes how sociologists study interaction, what they look for in the interaction, and whether interaction is consistent with the rules, customs, traditions, and beliefs of the society. But what about those people who do not conform? Most of us at some time or other do not behave as expected, and some of us never seem to behave according to any of society's rules. When and why people deviate from what is considered normal behavior is taken up in the final chapter of this section.

Chapter 4
Culture and Society

We think according to nature; we speak according to rules; we act according to custom.

— Francis Bacon

The term *culture* means different things to different people. In the minds of many people, it is associated with such activities as attending the opera, listening to classical music, and going to art museums. According to this definition, relatively few of us have culture. If one wanted to acquire it, one might begin by studying Mozart, Rembrandt, and Chaucer.

As used by sociologists and cultural anthropologists, however, culture has a different meaning. To a sociologist, a culture is a system of ideas, values, beliefs, knowledge, norms, customs, and technology shared by almost everyone in a particular *society*. A society is a social group; a culture is a society's system of common heritage. Each of us has a culture, because we were all raised in society. We express our culture continuously in our dress, food, work, language, and other activities. We learn our culture from our forebears and contemporaries and then we pass it on to future generations.

In general terms, a culture can be said to include all the human phenomena in a society that are not the products of biological inheritance. Culture includes all learned behavior, not just the behavior of the wealthy or the highly educated. It consists of both the nonmaterial aspects of a society such as language, ideas, and values, and the material aspects, such as houses, clothes, and tools. Both the skills needed to make a product and the product itself are parts of culture. Sociologists do not judge culture on the basis of the taste or refinement of the society it is a part of. Bowling and fox hunting, rock groups and symphony orchestras, wood carvings and museum paintings — all are human products and all reflect culture.

Elements of Culture

In most discussions of culture it is assumed that the various groups of people within a society share certain expectations about how it works and how its members should behave. In America, people live in houses or apartments. We buy food in a supermarket or grow it ourselves, we have jobs, and we generally expect our spouses to be sexually faithful to us. In traditional Eskimo culture, by contrast, people lived for part of the year in houses made of snow. They hunted for food because no one had jobs in our sense of the word. In some circumstances, sexual infidelity was not merely tolerated, it was encouraged. Since behaviors of these types vary from one group or society to another, they are viewed as products of culture rather than as basic aspects of human nature. In other words, these behaviors are not programmed genetically, as in most animal life — they are determined by the culture. Humans are not born knowing which beliefs and behaviors are appropriate. They must be learned.

Symbols

The existence of culture is dependent on people's ability to create and understand symbols. A *symbol* is something that is used to represent something else. Words, numbers, flags, crosses, and kisses are symbols. During World War II, raising the middle and index fingers of one hand was the symbol "V" for victory. During the 1960s, the same gesture came to symbolize a message of "peace." Raising the middle finger, putting thumbs up or thumbs down, and spreading one's thumb and little finger ("hang loose" in Hawaii), all convey a particular meaning. In the same way, a stop sign is a symbol meaning "halt" and a cross is a symbol of Christianity. The ability to use symbols is uniquely human. Unlike animals, human beings can use symbols to understand reality, to transmit messages, to store complex information, and to deal with an abstract symbolic world.

Symbols are arbitrary designations. There is no necessary connection between a symbol and what it represents. There is nothing inherent in the act of holding one's thumb up that indicates we approve of something. Similarly, the word "tree" is just a label we give to an object. If a group of children designate a tree a "goal," it becomes a goal. Symbols are often completely unrelated to the objects they represent.

As stated in Chapter 2 in our discussion of the symbolic interaction perspective, only humans can assign symbols to represent the objects around them, which is what makes humans different from animals and enables us to create cultures. The difference is not one of degree. It is not that humans have better reasoning ability than animals. Rather, it is a fundamental difference in kind. Most sociologists would argue that animals do not reason, communicate symbolically, or deal with abstractions. If they did, they too could develop art, music, sports, social institutions, laws, and other aspects of culture.

Language

The most important set of symbols is *language*. Language, among humans, refers to the systematized usage of speech and hearing to convey, communicate, or express feelings and ideas. It is through language that our ideas, values, beliefs, and knowledge are transmitted, expressed, and shared. Other media such as music, art, and dance are also important means of communication, but language is uniquely flexible and precise. It permits us to share our experiences in the past and present, to convey our hopes for the future, and to describe dreams and fantasies that may bear little resemblance to reality. (Some scientists have questioned whether thought is even possible without language.) Although language can be used imprecisely and seem hard to understand, it is the chief factor in our ability to transmit culture.

All human societies have languages. Although there are thousands of different languages in the world, linguistic behavior as such is universal. Some societies cannot read or write their language, but they all have a spoken language. Like symbols, the use of language is uniquely human, which is one of the most basic distinctions between human beings and other forms of life.

The importance of language to humans and to our cultural heritage is illustrated by the reports of two experiments in which young chimpanzees were reared for a time in the homes of psychologists (Kellogg and Kellogg, 1933; Hayes, 1951). The first study, conducted in the 1930s, involved a husband and wife, both psychologists, who raised their own child with an infant chimpanzee. The infants were the same age, and careful attention was given to treating them similarly. In many

Two of the key elements of culture are symbols and language. Both are abstractions used to represent or communicate some aspect of the culture. Fingers, for example, are used symbolically to point, indicate numbers, convey approval or disapproval, or represent a variety of meanings. Perhaps you know people who "talk with their hands." Most of our talking, however, occurs with verbal symbols we refer to as language.

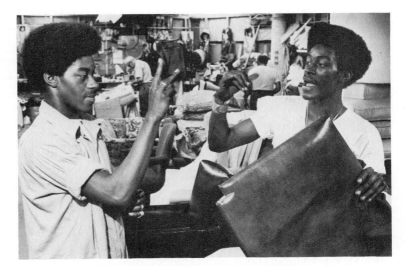

respects, their development was almost identical. In motor skills, the chimpanzee even outpaced the child, but as soon as the child began to speak, the child's cognitive development greatly outpaced that of the chimpanzee. Efforts were made to teach the chimp to speak, but the psychologists reported that they were completely unable to train their animal to utter any words or to imitate human speech.

A similar experiment was conducted in the 1940s, again with a human infant and a chimpanzee and a husband-and-wife team of psychologists. The results were about the same, but this research team reported that their chimpanzee acquired a vocabulary of three words: mama, papa, and cup. Observers reported, however, that the imitation of words was so crude that the sounds could hardly be identified and could be called words only by a stretch of the imagination. It was also clear that these words were used mechanically and without understanding.

These studies demonstrated a major gap between the human infant and the chimpanzee, a difference in kind, not merely in degree. The chimpanzee, one of the most intelligent animals, lacked the neural equipment to either generate or comprehend language. Although chimps emit sounds and respond to commands, their sounds do not constitute a system of symbols and their responses do not involve a system of shared definitions and meanings. Chimpanzees also lack the type of pharynx found in humans, whose size, shape, and mobility are crucial to the production of speech.

More recently, studies have been done on teaching chimpanzees to use sign language. The most famous of these chimpanzees was Washoe. Washoe was taught to use American Sign Language, a system of hand signs used by the deaf. During the four years that Beatrice and Allen Gardner worked with her, Washoe amassed a vocabulary of 160 signs (Gardner and Gardner, 1969). She not only used the appropriate sign for an object but also put signs together in meaningful ways and occasionally invented her own names for objects. Since Washoe, other chimps have been taught to use different types of symbols to communicate. Some of the most exciting research has involved teaching two chimpanzees to use sign language with each other. However, the verdict is still out on whether the use of sign language by chimpanzees really constitutes "language." As yet, chimpanzees have not used their sign language to share ideas or transmit knowledge, nor have they passed on this language to their offspring. But we may eventually find ourselves changing our description of language as uniquely human.

Language is so basic to culture and essential for human interaction and social organization that it is often taken for granted, but we have only speculative explanations of its origins. Did it begin with the imitation of sounds of nature such as running water or wind in the trees? Did it start with the utterance of grunts, sighs, coughs, and groans? Did it originate in calls and sounds that came to be shared by group members and later expanded to include new experiences and objects? We don't know, but there do seem to be attributes shared by many of the world's languages.

By studying the structures and other characteristics of the world's languages, linguists have been able to classify them into about nine families on the basis of their similarity. Languages in these families are spoken by almost 90 percent of the world's population. English belongs to the Indo-European family, which also includes Hindi, Sanskrit, Greek, Russian, French, German, and a number of other languages. The inclusion of certain languages in a common language family was determined by noting regular phonemic changes that took place from one language to another over time and place. For example, the Sanskrit word brata (brother) became phrater in Greek, frater in Latin, broder in Old English, and bratu in Slavonic. Regularities such as these suggest that these languages are related and descended from a single original Indo-European tongue. In addition, related words for milk, yoke, and wheel, which are widespread, suggest the availability of cattle and wagons in most cultural communities. These regularities of words over time and place, and the widespread use of selected ones, indicate that language is an integral and universal part of culture. Linguistic traits are learned and shared just like other cultural traits.

Language influences people's thought and experience to a greater degree than is generally recognized. In 1929, Edward Sapir argued that people see and interpret the world through the grammatical forms, labels, and categories provided by their language. He contended that societies with different languages actually perceive the world differently; that is, they don't just use a different set of labels to describe the same things. This idea is known as the *Sapir-Whorf Hypothesis*. Benjamin Whorf, a student of Sapir, noted while working for an insurance company that workmen handling barrels of gasoline were very careful about matches and cigarettes when the barrels were full but that they became careless and caused many accidents once the label "empty" had been applied to a barrel. In other words, the application of the word "empty" to a barrel influenced the workers' perception and consequent behavior (Whorf, 1941). Intrigued by this finding, he began to study different cultures to see whether people's behavior was influenced by the language they used. He found that language does influence the way we perceive things and how we behave. The Eskimos, for example, have no general word for snow, but they have more than twenty words for different kinds of snow, depending on whether it is falling, drifting, fresh, crumbling, and so on. To most Americans, a banana is just a banana, but Filipinos have different words for bananas of different sizes, colors, and uses. Interpreters of languages such as Hebrew, Russian, or German often find that no parallel word exists in English for the word they are trying to translate. Thus they can only try to convey in English the "reality" of the word they are translating. The Sapir-Whorf Hypothesis appears to be valid: our perceptions of reality are greatly influenced by our language. Languages are learned, shared, and transmitted from one generation to another and they are a central element of culture.

Values

Values are ideas shared by the people in a society on what is important and worthwhile. Our values are the basis of our judgments about what is desirable, beautiful, correct, and good as well as what is undesirable, ugly, incorrect, and bad. Most values have both positive and negative counterparts, which are reciprocally related. If you place a high positive value on fighting for one's country, for example, you probably place a high negative value on those who refuse to fight. If you value marital sexual exclusiveness, you probably disapprove of those who engage in extramarital sexual relationships. Values are often emotionally charged because they stand for things we believe to be worth defending.

Most of our basic values are learned early in life from family, friends, the mass media, and other sources within society. These values become part of our personalities, and because we learn them from society, few people possess unique sets of values. They are generally shared and reinforced by those with whom we interact. Placing a high value on God, money, honesty, cleanliness, freedom, children, education, or work serves as a general guide for our behavior and the formation of specific attitudes. Since values indicate what is proper or improper, they tend to justify certain types of behavior and forbid others.

When basic values are in conflict, we usually place them in a hierarchy of importance and behave in ways consistent with those defined as most important. During a war, for example, the value of patriotism may overcome the value that human life is precious. When it is impossible to place our values in a hierarchy to resolve a conflict, we may feel guilty or suffer mental stress.

To give another example of value conflict, consider the case of a husband who enjoys spending time with his family. If job demands take him away from his family for extended periods, he is likely to feel stress. To avoid stress, he could quit his job, take the family along on job trips, justify the job demands as in the best interests of the family, compromise on both family and job demands, or leave the family. Some of these choices may be impossible, however. Quitting the job or taking the family along may not be realistic alternatives, and divorce may conflict with social and religious values. Mental stress is likely to result when choices are impossible. The alternative courses of action, as well as the choice selected, will generally be consistent with the values of the society and those most important to us.

Sometimes our stated values and our behavior are inconsistent. We may place a high value on freedom of the press but want to censor communist writings. We may place a high value on individualism but want to punish people whose behavior is inconsistent with our definition of appropriate behavior. Our true values are often reflected more by what we do than by what we say. If we say we value education but have no interest in attending classes, or if we say we value simplicity but spend money conspicuously to display our wealth, it is our actions that expose our real values.

Since values are learned cultural products, they differ from one society to another. One society may value political independence, another may place a higher value on political conformity and obedience. One society may value individual achievement, another may emphasize family unity and kin support. In the United States, despite the tremendous diversity of our population, certain

Values are ideas shared by people in a society about what is important or worthwhile. Sometimes certain books and other literature are believed to violate values of sexual morality, patriotism, racial purity, or religious doctrines. In such instances it is not uncommon to ban, even destroy, such literature. A scene from the movie Fahrenheit 451 *vividly portrays this situation.*

value patterns tend to be shared by almost everyone. Robin M. Williams, Jr., in a sociological interpretation of American society (1970), described fifteen major value orientations in our culture. These included a belief in *achievement and success*, stressing personal achievement, especially secular occupational achievement; *external conformity*, emphasizing the adherence to similarity and uniformity in speech, manners, housing, dress, recreation, politically expressed ideas, and group patterns; and *democracy*, advocating majority rule, representative institutions, and the rejection of monarchical and aristocratic principles. Other American values are described in Table 4-1. It must be kept in mind that these are general themes in American values, which change constantly. They are often in conflict, and they are not all exhibited in a single person's behavior. As you

Table 4-1.
General themes in American values

Achievement and Success — An emphasis on personal achievement, especially secular occupational achievement.

External Conformity — An emphasis on the adherence to similarity and uniformity in speech, manners, housing, dress, recreation, politically expressed ideas, and group patterns.

Democracy — Advocacy of majority rule, representative institutions, and the rejection of monarchical and aristocratic principles.

Activity and Work — An emphasis on haste and bustle, strenuous competition, ceaseless activity, busyness.

Moral Orientation — Thinking in terms of ethics: right or wrong, good or bad.

Humanitarian Mores — An emphasis on any type of disinterested concern and helpfulness such as personal kindliness and comfort, spontaneous aid in mass disasters, philanthropy, etc.

Efficiency and Practicality — An emphasis on getting things done, standardization, mass production, technological innovation, adaptability, expediency.

Progress — An emphasis on the future rather than the past or present; a belief that forward is better than backward, that new is better than old, and that changes proceed in a definite direction and make life better.

Material Comfort — A focus on adequate nutrition, medical care, shelter, transportation, and an increasing emphasis on obtaining maximum pleasure with minimum effort.

Equality — An emphasis on equality of opportunity rather than equality of condition, and a rejection of rigid class distinctions — particularly on the level of overt interpersonal relationships.

Freedom — A belief that people should run their own lives and be independent, that government should not deny freedom of the press, freedom of worship, or freedom of private enterprise.

Science and Secular Rationality — An interest in controlling nature, and a belief in an ordered universe in which human beings can improve their situation and themselves by approaching problems rationally and scientifically.

Nationalism-Patriotism — Preferential treatment for one's own culture, demanding loyalty and allegiance to national symbols and slogans and pride in one's country.

Individual Personality — Placing a high value on the individual development of responsibility, independence, and self-respect.

Racism and Related Group-Superiority Themes — The ascription of value and privilege to individuals on the basis of race or membership in a particular group.

SOURCE: Robin M. Williams, Jr. "Values in American Society" in *American Society: A Sociological Interpretation*, 3rd ed. Copyright © 1951, 1960, 1970 by Alfred Knopf, Inc. Reprinted by permission.

may have noted, some of them appear to be inconsistent. How can we value both independence and conformity, or equality and racism? Some of the explanations for these inconsistencies lie in whether the value is applied generally or specifically. For example, a person might say, "Our society believes strongly in freedom of the press, but I don't want my town library to carry novels with explicit sex in them." Other explanations may reflect the beliefs of different regions of the country. Williams states that most conflicts between value systems in the United States occur between those centering around individual personalities and those organized around categorical themes or conceptions. Group discrimination and racism, as a categorical theme, is contrary to other central values of the society. Each of these values has a historical base and a complexity far greater than is evident in this brief discussion. Evidence does suggest, however, a decline in racist beliefs over several decades: legislation has forced movements away from enforced segregation and public discrimination, and Congress has passed a civil rights act and a series of laws that forbid discrimination because of race, sex, religion, nationality, place of birth, or place of residence. Thus, while a central value may continue to exist that grants privilege based on group or racial affiliation, some evidence suggests that this particular theme may be fading.

Norms

Social *norms* are another element of culture. Norms are rules of conduct or social expectations for behavior. These rules and social expectations specify how people should and should not behave in various social situations. They are both prescriptive — they tell people what they should do — and proscriptive — they tell people what they should not do. Examples of important changes in the norms guiding American life can be seen in Figure 4-1.

Whereas values are abstract conceptions of what is important and worthwhile, social norms are standards, rules, guides, and expectations for actual behavior. Norms and values are likely to be conceptually consistent, but values are less situation-bound and more general and abstract. Norms link values with actual events. "Honesty" is a general value; the expectation that students will not cheat on tests is a norm. Most norms permit a range of behaviors; that is, certain kinds and degrees of overconformity and underconformity are expected and tolerated. We would not criticize a starving man for lying to get food, for example.

An early American sociologist, William G. Sumner (1840–1910) identified two types of norms, which he labeled "folkways" and "mores." They are distinguished not by their content but by the degree to which group members are compelled to conform to them, by their degree of importance, by the severity of punishment if they are violated, or by the intensity of feeling associated with adherence to them. *Folkways* are customs or conventions. They are norms in that they provide rules for conduct, but violations of folkways bring only mild censure. In the United States, most adults are expected to eat vegetables with a fork rather than a spoon or knife, and most students attend classes in pants or skirts rather than gowns or bathing suits. If you eat vegetables with a spoon or attend class in a gown or bathing suit, the chances are you will not be arrested or beaten, but you may receive some smiles, glances, or occasional comments from others. Why? It may be easier to use a spoon for eating vegetables, and on hot days a bathing suit may be more comfortable attire. The reason people would express mild disapproval is that these behaviors violate middle-class folkways.

Like other norms, folkways are learned in interaction with others and are passed down from generation to generation. Folkways change as culture changes or when we enter different situa-

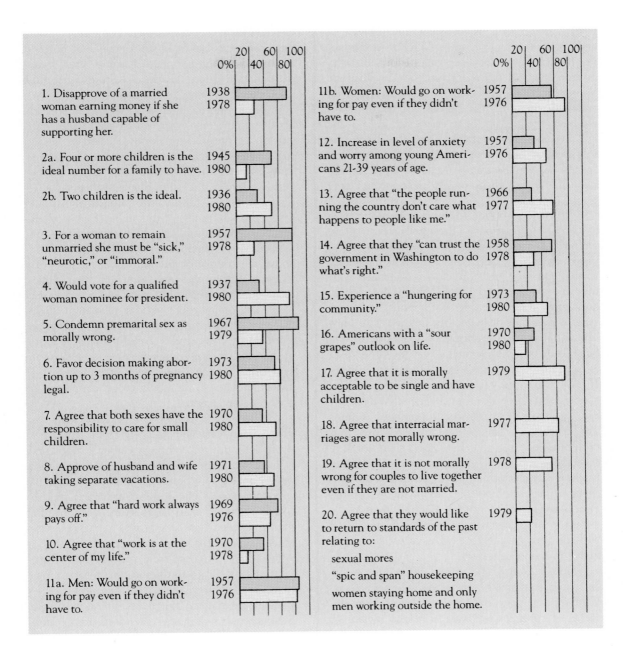

Figure 4·1
Twenty major changes in the norms guiding American life

tions. Our tendency is to accept the folkways as appropriate without question. Why do suburbanites fertilize lawns and keep them trimmed? Why do people avoid facing one another in elevators? Why are people expected to chew food quietly and with their mouths closed? No written rules are being violated in these situations, and no one is being physically harmed. These are simply the folkways of our culture, the set of norms that specify the way things are usually done, and people who violate these norms are punished only mildly if at all.

Mores are considered more important than folkways, and reactions to their violation are more serious. They are more likely than folkways to involve clear-cut distinctions between right and wrong, and they are more closely associated with the values a society considers important. Violations of mores inspire intense reactions, and some type of punishment inevitably follows. The punishment may involve expulsion from the group, harsh ridicule, imprisonment, or in some cases even death. Why don't people masturbate in public? Why don't physicians end the life of elderly people who have a terminal illness? Why don't people betray their country for money? Actions such as these violate cultural mores. Mores that prohibit something, that state "thou shalt not," are called *taboos*. To love and care for one's children is a mos (singular of mores); to commit incest with them or neglect them is a taboo. In the United States, people who murder, commit treason, or engage in incest are widely regarded as sinful and wicked. They violated the mores of society by engaging in taboo behaviors.

Since folkways and mores differ only in degree, it is sometimes difficult to tell them apart. Furthermore, since folkways and mores are elements of culture, they vary from one society or subculture to another. The physical punishment of children may be a folkway in some cultures and a taboo in others. Killing may be rewarded in war

but condemned in one's local community. Marriage between blacks and whites may be a norm in Hawaii and a strong taboo in some other states. To function effectively in a culture, one must learn the appropriate folkways and mores.

Certain norms that a society feels strongly about may become *laws,* which are formal, standardized expressions of norms enacted by legislative bodies to regulate certain types of behaviors. Laws do not merely state what behaviors are not permitted; they also state the punishment for violating the law. Ideally, the punishment should reflect the seriousness of the crime or civil offense and be carried out by a judicial system. This system, however, legitimizes physical coercion and is above the control of any individual member of a society. Within the boundaries of their duties, members of a judicial system can use physical force, kill, or imprison without retaliation. Laws, therefore, are formalized legislated norms that are enforced by a group designated for that purpose. In contrast, folkways and mores (unless they are made into laws) are enforced by the members of society themselves, not by a group designated to do the enforcement.

When a law does not reflect folkways and mores, its enforcement is likely to be ignored or given low priority. Although certain actions may be formally defined as illegal in certain communities (shopping on Sundays, smoking marijuana, premarital sexual relationships), enforcement is ignored because of changing folkways or mores that grant a degree of social approval to the behavior, which suggests that conformity to the norms of society does not come from formal law enforcement officials but from the informal interaction of members of society. Most norms are followed by members of society, but adherence is not rigid. Adaptations to changing conditions are possible, and a certain degree of deviation from existing norms is both possible and beneficial for the effective functioning of society. The process of violating norms beyond the range of group acceptability is termed *deviance,* and the process of applying sanctions to obtain social conformity is known as *social control.* These topics are explored in Chapter 7.

Technology and Material Culture

In addition to the nonmaterial aspects of culture — symbols, language, values, norms, and laws — there are certain material techniques and products used by societies to maintain their standards of living and lifestyles. The practical production and application of these techniques and products is a culture's *technology.* Technology applies the knowledge gained by science in ways that influence all aspects of culture. It includes social customs and practical techniques for converting raw materials to finished products. The production and use of food, shelter, clothing and the commodities, physical structures, and fabrics are also aspects of a society's technology. These physical productions are called *artifacts.* A society's artifacts can be very diverse: beer cans, religious objects, pottery, art, pictures, buildings and building materials, clothes, books, and even contraceptive devices. Material artifacts reflect the nonmaterial culture — symbols, beliefs, values, norms, and behaviors — shared by the members of a society.

Artifacts provide clues to a society's level of technological development. Americans, especially those of European descent, take great pride in their level of technology. The ability to perform heart transplants, split atoms, and produce sophisticated nuclear weapons, supersonic jets, computers, and environmentally controlled living and working conditions leads us to perceive our type of culture as superior, advanced, and progressive. This perception is often accompanied by a belief that cultures with a low level of technological development are inferior and nonprogressive. These are subjective perceptions, however, not scientific

criteria for evaluating cultures. A more objective evaluation of "less developed" cultures indicates that they possess an amazing degree of skill and ingenuity in dealing with the environment. Many apparently crude techniques are based on fundamental principles of engineering. Today, people marvel at the rice terraces built several thousand years ago on mountainsides in Asia, which included water distribution systems that seem difficult to improve upon today. These rice fields produced food for generations of families and communities without the aid of diesel tractors, complex machinery, or hybrid rice plants, and many are still in use. Anthropologists know of countless instances of the survival of people under conditions that few members of "highly developed" cultures could endure. The adobe huts of American Indians, the igloos of the Eskimos, or the bamboo houses of rural southeast Asia, none of which have indoor plumbing, heating, or air conditioning, would be inadequate homes for most members of more technologically advanced cultures. Yet these people's technology is suited to and perfectly adequate for their particular lifestyles. It could be argued that in more developed nations the technology is developed by a handful of specialists, so the general population is less technologically proficient than members of "primitive" groups.

The goals and consequences of technology and the production of material goods are being seriously questioned today. Does a high level of technology increase happiness and improve family life? Do complex technologies bring us clean air and pure water and help us conserve natural resources? All cultures possess a technology so that they can apply knowledge to master the environment and control nature. It is a mistake to dismiss a culture's technological system because it is less developed or complex than our own.

Technology and material culture are cumulative; that is, when a more efficient method or tool

This African village has no large buildings, vehicles, or streets. It may be perceived by some as a culture with an inferior and nonprogressive level of technological development. Yet ethnographic investigations disclose a highly sophisticated culture with architecture that expresses communal organization and human figures sculpted from tree trunks that rank among the best of African art.

is found, the old one is replaced. The new method or tool must be consistent with the values and beliefs of the culture it is used in, however. Many effective means of controlling population have been developed, for example, but these means have not been adopted in some cultures because they are inconsistent with societal beliefs and values. In the United States, for instance, contraceptive devices such as condoms, IUDs, diaphragms, foams, jellies, and birth control pills are widely used and available to the general population. Yet the value system of a large segment of the adult population views their use among adolescents as inappropriate and immoral as well as being the cause of high rates of illegitimacy among teenagers. These same contraceptive devices are not suitable to many cultures in Latin America because of their inconsistency with religious values, even though these devices are available and proven to be highly effective when properly used. This phenomenon is known as *cultural lag* (Ogburn, 1950). Cultural lag occurs when changes in technology and material culture come more rapidly than changes in nonmaterial culture: customs, beliefs, values, and laws. In rapidly changing societies, cultural lag is inevitable. The development of nuclear weapons, for example, may surpass our techniques of world diplomacy and statesmanship. Medical advances that prolong life may surpass our ability to provide meaningful tasks for the elderly. The production of handguns may surpass our willingness or ability to control their sale, distribution, and use. Cultural lag indicates that various elements of culture change at different rates and shows how the technological and material aspects of culture affect and are affected by the nonmaterial aspects of culture.

Our attention is often focused on material aspects of culture because of their concrete nature. When archeologists dig up the remains of an ancient civilization, they may find pots, shells, stones, jewelry, building foundations, and bones. When people visit other countries, they notice the goods in the markets, the means of transportation, and the types of housing, whereas the values, beliefs, and meanings associated with symbols and the language system are less visible. The material and nonmaterial are both significant elements of culture, however, and they have a strong influence on each other.

Interpreting Culture: Our Own and Others

There is an enormous variety of cultural symbols, languages, values, norms, and technologies available to us. How do members of a society decide which to accept or use? When a society chooses one cultural system, how do its members perceive the systems of other cultures? Answers to such questions can be found by examining such concepts as ethnocentrism, xenocentrism, temporocentrism, and cultural relativism.

Ethnocentrism

Do you know of any culture that is better than your own? Do you think other types of families, religions, races, school systems, athletes, or artists are superior to those found in your society? Most people assume that their own culture, group, and behaviors are superior to those of others. The attitude that one's own culture is superior to others, that one's own beliefs, values, and behaviors are more correct than others, and

Rapidly changing societies retain old aspects of culture amid new technological and material developments, On the road between Agra and Delhi, India, one may see three modes of transportation illustrating different levels of technological development.

that other people and cultures can be evaluated in terms of one's own culture is known as *ethnocentrism*. Ethnocentrism was defined by Sumner (1906) as "that view of things in which one's own group is the center of everything and all others are scaled and rated with reference to it" (p. 13).

Most groups in any society tend to be ethnocentric. Religious groups believe they have the "truth" and are more moral than others. Some even send our missionaries to convert the "heathen" and change the pagan lifestyles of the "backward" and "lost" people of the world. Scientists are equally likely to believe that their methods are the best way to approach problems. Countries spend vast sums to defend their eco-

Flag-waving Americans believe that the values and behavior of their culture are the best and should be honored and respected. This ethnocentrism is also illustrated by bumper stickers reading: "Buy American," and "God Loves America."

nomic and political system, believing that their way of life is worth dying for. Most Americans believe that monogamy is more "proper" than polygamy and that capitalism is far superior to communism. Most of us consider the practice of eating worms disgusting and consider people who scar their bodies to be masochists. We are likely to believe that people who refuse to drink milk are ignorant and that people who walk around half-naked are shameless. Each of these views illustrates ethnocentrism: we judge other cultures according to the perspectives and standards of our own. We think it quite natural that American women paint their lips and hang jewelry from their ears, that men tie a strip of cloth around their necks, and that people eat corn, which is considered chicken food in many cultures.

Most people spend their entire lives in the culture in which they were born, and ethnicentrism is particularly strong among people who have had little contact with other cultures. Yet ethnocentric attitudes are maintained even among people who have considerable formal education, access to the mass media, and extensive experience traveling in other countries. Functionalists might argue that this is so because ethnocentrism is functional for a society's and a group's existence since it promotes group loyalty, cohesiveness, and unity. It also improves morale, encourages conformity, and reinforces nationalism and patriotism. Ethnocentric cultures have confidence in their own traditions; they discourage outsiders and thus protect themselves against change. Cultures that consider themselves superior tend to maintain the status quo — if our culture is already best, why change it?

On the other hand, some aspects of ethnocentrism are dysfunctional and have negative consequences. Ethnocentrism can increase resistance to change and encourage the exclusion of outsiders who may have something good to contribute. It can encourage racism, discourage integration

Body Ritual Among the Nacirema

In the hierarchy of magical practitioners, and below the medicine men in prestige, are specialists whose designation is best translated as "holy-mouth-men." The Nacirema have an almost pathological horror of and fascination with the mouth, the condition of which is believed to have a supernatural influence on all social relationships. Were it not for the rituals of the mouth, they believe that their teeth would fall out, their gums bleed, their jaws shrink, their friends desert them, and their lovers reject them. They also believe that a strong relationship exists between oral and moral characteristics. For example, there is a ritual ablution of the mouth for children which is supposed to improve their moral fiber.

The daily body ritual performed by everyone includes a mouth-rite. Despite the fact that these people are so punctilious about care of the mouth, this rite involves a practice which strikes the uninitiated stranger as revolting. It was reported to me that the ritual consists of inserting a small bundle of hog hairs into the mouth, along with certain magical powders, and then moving the bundle in a highly formalized series of gestures.

In addition to the private mouth-rite, the people seek out a holy-mouth-man once or twice a year. These practitioners have an impressive set of paraphernalia, consisting of a variety of augers, awls, probes, and prods. The use of these objects in the exorcism of the evils of the mouth involves almost unbelievable ritual torture of the client. The holy-mouth-man opens the client's mouth and, using the above mentioned tools, enlarges any holes which decay may have created in the teeth. Magical materials are put into these holes. If there are no naturally occurring holes in the teeth, large sections of one or more teeth are gouged out so that the supernatural substance can be applied. In the client's view, the purpose of these ministrations is to arrest decay and to draw friends. The extremely sacred and traditional character of the rite is evident in the fact that the natives return to the holy-mouth-men year after year, despite the fact that their teeth continue to decay.

It is to be hoped that, when a thorough study of the Nacirema is made, there will be careful inquiry into the personality structure of these people. One has but to watch the gleam in the eye of a holy-mouth-man, as he jabs an awl into an exposed nerve, to suspect that a certain amount of sadism is involved. If this can be established, a very interesting pattern emerges, for most of the population shows definite masochistic tendencies.

Note: If you didn't recognize who the Nacirema are, try spelling their name backwards.

SOURCE: Horace Miner, "Body Ritual Among the Nacirema," *American Anthropologist* 58 (3) (June 1956): pp. 503–507. Reprinted by permission.

---

efforts, increase hostility and conflicts among groups, and prevent changes that could be beneficial at all. Carried to an extreme ethnocentrism is destructive, as evidenced by the Nazis in Germany who believed in the absolute superiority of the "white Aryan" race and culture. The result was the death of millions of people who didn't fit this category.

Xenocentrism

The opposite of ethnocentrism is *xenocentrism*. Xenocentrism is the belief that what is foreign is best, that one's own lifestyle, products, or ideas are inferior to those of others. The strange, distant, and exotic are regarded as having special value: cars made in Japan, watches made in

Switzerland, beer brewed in Germany, fashions created in France, silks imported from India and Thailand, and gymnasts from eastern European countries are believed to be superior to our own. In some instances, feelings of xenocentrism are so strong that people reject their own group. Thus we find anti-American Americans, anti-Semitic Jews, priests who revolt against the church, blacks who reject a black identity, and family members who scorn the kin network. Xenocentrism may focus on a product, an idea, or a lifestyle. Regardless of the focus, it is assumed that native techniques and concepts are inferior.

Temporocentrism

Temporocentrism is the temporal equivalent of ethnocentrism. It is the belief that one's own time is more important than the past or future. Accordingly, historical events are judged not in their own context but on the basis of contemporary standards. As Bierstedt (1970) stated, "We are all inclined to assume that the present is more important than the past and that the whole of historical time is significant only for what it means to us" (p. 177). Our tendency toward temporocentrism leads us to assume that current crises are more crucial than those of other periods, that problems need to be solved now before it is too late. An associated belief is that actions taken now will have an enormous impact on life in the future. This belief could conceivably be warranted, but in most cases what we do in our time will later be viewed as only a minor ripple on the stream of history.

Since ethnocentrism is strongest among people with little education or exposure to other nations, temporocentrism is most prevalent among people who lack historical perspective. Even people with extensive educational training and a strong grasp of history tend to focus on the present, however. Politicians, and social scientists view today as the critical period. Sermons, newspapers, and teachers stress that we are living in perilous times, that this is the age of transition.

Cultural Relativism

Social scientists who study other cultures tend to be highly temporocentric, but most make special efforts to avoid ethnocentrism and xenocentrism. They attempt to view all behaviors, lifestyles, and ideas in their own context. The belief that cultures must be judged on their own terms rather than by the standards of another culture is called *cultural relativism.*

According to the cultural relativistic perspective, an act, idea, form of dress, or other cultural manifestation is not inherently right or wrong, correct or incorrect. They should be judged only in the context in which they occur; what is appropriate in one culture or context may be inappropriate in another. Nudity in the shower is appropriate, but nudity in the classroom is inappropriate. In some hunting societies, being fat may have survival value and serve as a source of admiration. In America, however, fatness is regarded as unhealthful and rarely serves as a source of admiration. The practice of abandoning unwanted infants would be viewed as intolerable by most contemporary cultures, but many cultures used to follow this practice and some still do. The point is that any aspect of a culture must be considered within its larger cultural context. The aspect may be regarded as good if it is acceptable to the members and if it helps attain desired goals and bad if it is unacceptable or fails to achieve these goals.

Cultural relativity does *not* mean that a behavior appropriate in one place is appropriate everywhere. It is not a license to do as one wishes. Even though having three wives is acceptable for Moslem men, killing female infants is acceptable in a Brazilian tribe, and wearing loin cloths is acceptable to African bushmen, these behaviors are not acceptable to most Americans in New York or Los Angeles. They are appropriate in some societies because they are part of a larger belief and value system and are consistent with other norms appropriate to that cultural setting. Cultural relativism makes us less likely to ridicule or scorn the beliefs and habits of people from other cultures.

The Organization of Culture

A culture is not simply an accumulation of isolated symbols, languages, values, norms, behaviors, and technology. It is an organized system of many interdependent factors, and its organization is influenced by physical circumstances — climate, geography, population, and plant and animal life. Eskimos eat meat almost exclusively, live in igloos or huts made of skins, and dress in furs. Many societies in tropical rain forests have diets composed primarily of fruits and vegetables, live in shelters made of leaves and branches, and wear few clothes. Physical circumstances, however, may have less influence on a culture's organization than such social factors as contact with other cultures, the stage of technological development, or the prevailing ideologies — the assertions and theories characteristic of the group.

Although cultures vary in their symbols, language, behavior, and the way these factors are organized, all cultures share some basic concerns, which are known as *cultural universals*. People in all cultures must have food, shelter, and protection. All people face illness and death, and every society has a kinship system. Like American suburbanites, African bushmen and Mongolian nomads socialize and train their members in the ways of the culture, provide for work and leisure activities, and establish leaders and rulers. Basic institutions such as these are explored more fully in chapters that follow. At this point we will examine some of the ways that culture, the learned social heritage of a society, is organized.

Cultural Traits and Complexes

Cultural traits are the smallest unit of culture. Traits of the material culture would include such items as a handshake or a kiss. Traits such as a salute, handshake, or kiss can be of many different types and have many different meanings. A *cultural complex* is a combination of related traits. Baseballs, bats, and gloves are parts of a sports complex. Kissing, holding hands, and sharing verbal intimacies are parts of a love complex. Textbooks, papers, lectures, and classrooms form part of the complex related to students and education.

Social institutions consist of related cultural traits and complexes. One way to analyze a culture's organization is to examine the traits and complexes that comprise it. These factors are not arranged randomly; the technologies, skills, values, behaviors, and other characteristics of a culture tend to complement one another, and all are integrated into a larger unit. The extent of the complementarity of units is often referred to as the degree of *cultural integration.*

As you might expect, the extent of cultural integration varies widely. Preindustrial, traditional societies are more likely to be highly integrated than less traditional industrial societies, which are generally larger and more complex, and they contain a greater variety of groups and lifestyles. They are more heterogeneous and possess a wide range of values, work patterns, mate selection procedures, religious rituals, and other conditions. The variety of forces at work in an industrial culture make integration more difficult. Although entire cultures may share many cultural complexes, certain variations in a culture's values, languages, families, and other elements can be discovered through an examination of subcultures, countercultures, and idiocultures.

Subcultures

It is rare to find a society that has a single culture shared equally by all its members. This could happen only in small, isolated, nonindustrial societies, but most societies include groups who share some of the cultural complexes of the larger society yet also have their own distinctive set of cultural complexes. These units of culture are called *subcultures*. Although subcultures exist within the confines of a larger culture, they also have their own norms, values, and lifestyles. They often reflect racial or ethnic differences such as those found among black, Polish, or Chinese Americans. Other subcultures develop around occupations: athletics, the military, medicine, or factory work. The Mormons, Amish, Hutterites, and other groups form religious subcultures; some are based on geography, such as those found in the South and New England; others are based on wealth and age. There are also drinking, drug, disco, and homosexual subcultures. Every society that has diverse languages, religions, ethnic or racial groups, or varying economic levels has subcultures.

All subcultures participate in the larger, dominant culture but possess their own set of cultural elements: symbols, languages, values, norms, and technologies. In heterogeneous societies, a person may be a member of several subcultures at any one time or at different times in his or her life. In the United States, a black adolescent male living in poverty may speak a black dialect, have an Afro haircut, wear African dress, enjoy "soul" food, and obtain money by means considered appropriate to his culture but unacceptable to the dominant culture. An Amish adolescent male living on a Pennsylvania farm might speak a form of German, wear a black suit and hat, part his hair in the middle cut to shoulder length, enjoy sauerkraut and potatoes, be forbidden to dance or go to movies, and turn all earnings over to his father. Both the black and the Amish adolescent are required to abide by the laws of the dominant society, however.

At times, the dominant culture and the subculture may conflict to such a degree that tremendous stresses occur and a crisis results. Members of the subculture may be required by the dominant culture to register for the military even though they value pacifism. The subculture may value the use of certain drugs but be forbidden by the dominant culture to obtain them, or speak a language not used in the public schools. It is important to realize that, in addition to the differences among cultures, there are great variations within cultures as well.

Countercultures

A *counterculture* is a subculture that adheres to "a set of norms and values that sharply contradict the dominant norms and values of the society of which that group is a part" (Yinger, 1977, p. 833). Ideologically, countercultures adhere to a set of beliefs and values that radically reject the society's dominant culture and prescribe an alternative one. Because they accept such beliefs and values, members of a counterculture behave in such radically nonconformist ways that they tend to drop out of society (Westhues, 1972). Dropping out may mean either physically leaving or ideologically and behaviorally "leaving" by rejecting the dominant values and working to change them.

"But it is an emergency, Ed: The gold washed off the best china."

Delinquent gangs, the Hare Krishna religious sect, and the youth movement of the 1960s can be classified as countercultures. The norms and values of each of these groups contrast sharply with those held by conventional middle-class groups. Often, these values are not merely different from those of the dominant culture, but in opposition to them. Delinquent gangs may grant prestige and social approval for lawbreaking, violence, theft, or the use of drugs to achieve their goals of dominance and material success. The stated goal of the Hare Krishna religious sect is the salvation of the world through its conversion to Krishna Consciousness. The Krishna counterculture entails considerable ritualism, ceremony, shaved heads, chant-ins, proselytizing in airports, and other activities often viewed as countercultural. The youth movement of the 1960s, which included political activists, dropouts, and hippies, actively challenged the dominant cultural norms of hard work, financial success, dress conformity, sexual restrictiveness, military superiority, and white supremacy. Flacks (1971) indicated that the youth movement of the 1960s stressed cooperation over competition, expression over success, communalism over individualism, being over doing, making art over making money, and autonomy over obedience. Now, however, the hippies have all but vanished and their flourishing communities such as Haight-Ashbury in San Francisco and the East Village in New York have disappeared. Studies of the values expressed in counterculture and dominant culture magazines indicate that the counterculture did not appreciably influence the values of the dominant culture (Spates, 1976). It appears that today the pendulum has swung away from countercultural trends among youth.

Idiocultures

Gary Fine (1979) argues that every group forms its own culture to a certain extent. He called these created cultures *idiocultures*. An idio-culture is a system of knowledge, beliefs, behaviors, and customs created through group interactions. Members of a group share certain experiences and recognize that references to a shared experience will be understood by other members. Members of one group, for example, might roar with laughter whenever the word "cashew" is mentioned. All small groups have a culture unique to themselves but which is nevertheless part of a larger cultural pattern. A group's idioculture is formed by the group itself, so idiocultures do not exist when a group is first formed. They are created from the opening moments of group interaction when people begin to learn names and other information about one another. With time, rules are established, opinions expressed, information exchanged, and members experience events together.

Suppose, for example, that a newspaper has just been established and that the editors, reporters, typesetters, and other employees have come together for the first time. Initially, they will have shared no experiences, but as they work together they will develop certain unique ways of interacting. At first, the reporters may go out for coffee individually, but eventually they might decide to delegate one person to get coffee for everyone. "Gathering background information" might become a euphemism for wasting time. When the Johnson Warehouse is destroyed in the biggest fire that ever happened in the town, they might come to refer to any big story as a "Johnson." Similarly, stories dealing with improper behavior by politicians might come to be called "Watergates," and the task of writing the relatively uninteresting daily reports about weddings, funerals, and meetings might come to be called the "trivia." After a few unpleasant arguments, the reporters might agree never to comment on one another's stories. After working together for an extended period, the group would develop its own jargon and set of customs that would not be intelligible to an outsider.

SOCIOLOGISTS AT WORK
Evaluating Sex Education Programs

Sandra Baxter is a senior researcher at Advanced Technology, Inc., in McLean, Virginia, where she conducts program evaluations for federal government agencies. Previously, she worked at MATHTECH, Inc., in Bethesda, Maryland, as a sociologist researching the effectiveness of sex education programs for adolescents and their parents. Before that, she taught sociology at the university level for five years. She has an undergraduate degree from the University of Chicago and graduate degrees from American University and the University of Michigan — all in sociology.

How did this sociologist get into the business of consulting for the federal government? "I left teaching because my heart was always in research," Sandra Baxter says, "and teaching leaves little time for thoughtful research. I learned about the position at MATHTECH from a friend there. I asked him what the position entailed, and when he told me I remarked that I couldn't have written a better job description for myself. So, like the majority of job changes, this one came

through informal knowledge of a vacancy and the encouragement of a friend already located in the new job setting. I was interested in the subject matter because of my training in social psychology and political sociology, but my background in research methodology and statistics is what actually qualified me for the job.

"Initially, my job was to design the evaluation of parent sex education courses my colleagues were constructing and to implement the evaluation at ten sites around the country. One major problem was to identify good teachers who already were offering or were interested in offering a course for parents. Once we indentified them we tried to help them gain access to a group of parents, or create a group. How do you create demand for a new course? The answer depends on the characteristics of the communities you've chosen to work in. We offered a course to Hispanic parents in New York City. With knowledge of the importance of the church in Hispanic communities, we knew that the best strategy was to obtain the sponsorship of a local church, or at

Ideal and Real Culture

In most cultures, differences exist between what people are supposed to do and what they actually do; that is, there is a discrepancy between the *ideal culture* and the *real culture*. If you were asked to tell a foreign visitor about the norms and values of Americans, for example, you would probably describe the ideal culture, mentioning such topics as freedom, democracy, equal rights, monogamy, marital fidelity, and educational op-

portunity for all. The actual culture differs considerably from the ideal, however. The very poor are less likely to get a good education, marital infidelity is common, and many people have several spouses during their lives.

This distinction between real and ideal culture is expressed by some anthropologists in terms of *explicit* culture and *implicit* culture. These terms may be more accurate than "real" and "ideal" — both types of culture are real in the sense that they actually exist. The point is that stated cul-

least get permission to hold the course in their building. Who was likely to attend, and how should the course materials be focused? Again, sociological insight suggests that mothers have the primary responsibility for rearing children in Hispanic cultures, so we could expect only mothers at the New York course. The norm in white middle-class communities is for both parents to play some role in overseeing children's development, so we planned to have both mothers and fathers in attendance at those sites. We were correct in both assumptions, and so were able to tailor the courses correctly for their different audiences.

"I also provided methodological and statistical background for an evaluation of exemplary sex education courses taught to adolescents nationwide. I eventually headed my own project, working with local school districts in Maryland to assess their sex education curricula, conduct training for their teachers, and evaluate how their programs improved with our assistance. All of these jobs required some travel, a quick course in the teaching of sex education, sensitivity to the political volatility of our research, and a firm basis in research techniques.

"Research on any educational program is tricky," Baxter warns. "You have to disentangle learning effects from developmental effects. In sex education, the desired end result of the course — 'responsible sexual behavior' — may not appear for years in adolescents who are not sexually active. How do you measure whether the course has accomplished its goal? There are intermediate indicators, of course, but the challenge lies in identifying them and measuring them. My knowledge of social psychology, particularly peer group dynamics and family sociology, was invaluable. My background in political sociology gave me a broad perspective on sex education as a social movement, the resistance to it that could be expected, and the strategies sex education professionals could follow to ensure their acceptance in communities. My training in sociology gave me an awareness of the social context in which adolescents, their parents, educators, and researchers functioned. It also gave me the tools to identify, measure, and evaluate the complex dynamics of attitudes and behaviors of all these sets of actors.

"But insights alone wouldn't have answered the questions we were contracted to answer: What effects do sex education courses have on adolescents and on parents? These questions could only be satisfactorily answered through solid, scientifically defensible research designs and procedures. The training I received as a quantitative researcher was crucial to doing the job well."

tural traits and complexes are not always practiced. Students should be sensitive to distinctions of this sort. The speed limit may be 55, but many people drive at 65. Honesty in the classroom may be the norm, but cribbing may be widespread. Clashes between ideal and actual practices may be avoided through rationalizations or flexibility in social control. A student might defend cheating on a test by arguing that "everyone does it." Police rarely arrest everyone who exceeds the speed limit, concentrating instead on extreme violations.

Summary

A culture is a society's social heritage, the system of ideas, values, beliefs, knowledge, norms, customs, and technology that everyone in a society shares. A society is a group of people who share a common culture. Some of the most significant elements of a culture are symbols, language, values, norms, and technology.

Symbols are arbitrary designations that represent something. The use of symbols is a uniquely human capability that allows us to make sense of reality, transmit messages, store complex information, and deal with an abstract world. Our most important set of symbols is language, which enables us to transmit and store our social heritage. The importance of language to humans is illustrated in studies comparing the development of children and chimpanzees. The humans outpaced the chimps as soon as they began to speak. It has been demonstrated that language influences how we perceive and experience the world. The Sapir-Whorf Hypothesis suggests that the use of different languages by different societies causes them to perceive the world very differently. Rather than simply seeing the same world with different labels, they actually perceive different realities.

Values are conceptions about what is important and of worth. They are learned and shared cultural products that justify certain types of behavior. People in the United States tend to value achievement, success, work, a moral orientation, humanitarian concerns, practicality, progress, material comfort, equality, freedom, external conformity, science, nationalism, democracy, and individualism. Americans also tend to believe that some groups are superior to others. Values indicate what is important, whereas norms are rules of conduct, the standards and expectations of behavior. Norms are of two types: folkways, which are customs or conventions that are only mildly censured if violated, and mores, which are far more important and severely punished if violated. Laws are the formalized and standardized expressions of norms.

In addition to the nonmaterial aspects of culture such as these, there are material and technological aspects as well. Cultural lag occurs when changes in technology come more rapidly than changes in the nonmaterial aspects.

Members of a society tend to view their own culture in certain ways. Ethnocentrism is the belief that one's own culture is superior to others and applies its own cultural standards in judging other cultures. Xenocentrism is the belief that what is foreign is best, that one's own lifestyle, products, or ideas are inferior to those of others. Temporocentrism is the belief that the past should be judged in terms of the present, that one's own time is exceptionally important. The idea of cultural relativism suggests that cultures must be judged on their own terms, not by the standards of another culture. Acts, ideas, and products are not inherently good or bad; they must be judged in the cultural context in which they happen.

A culture is not simply a collection of isolated ideas and values. It is an organized system in which all components are interrelated and interdependent. Some aspects of culture are common to all societies, but in other respects cultures are extremely varied. The smallest units of a culture are called traits; a combination of related traits is known as a cultural complex. The extent to which these complexes are complementary is an index of a society's degree of cultural integration.

Subcultures are groups within a society that share the common culture but have their own distinctive set of cultural complexes. A counterculture is a type of subculture adhering to a set of norms and values that sharply contradict the dominant norms and values of the society of which the group is a part. To a certain extent, all groups possess localized cultures of their own, which are known as idiocultures.

There are differences between a culture's ideals and its members' actual behavior. In the following chapters, we will discuss the individual in a societal and cultural context as well as examining how culture is learned, how people are socialized, and how we come to identify ourselves and behave as males or females.

Key Terms

artifacts
counterculture
cultural complex

cultural lag
cultural relativism
cultural traits
cultural universals
culture
ethnocentrism
folkways
ideal and real culture
idiocultures
language
laws
mores
norms
Sapir-Whorf Hypothesis
society
subcultures
symbol
taboos
technology
temporocentrism
values
xenocentrism

Suggested Readings

Gordon, Milton M. (ed). Special Issue, "America As a Multicultural Society," **The Annals of the American Academy of Political and Social Science** 454 (March 1981): 1–205. A special issue devoted to subcultures in America: blacks, Jews, Catholics, Hispanics, Mexicans, Asians, native Americans, Muslims, and others.

Hammond, Peter B. **An Introduction to Cultural and Social Anthropology. 2nd ed.** New York: Macmillan, 1978. An anthropology textbook emphasizing both cultural evolutionary and cultural ecological interpretations of how cultures develop, how societies "act," and how people behave.

McCready, William C. and Andrew M. Greeley. **The Ultimate Values of the American Population.** Beverly Hills, Calif.: Sage Publications, 1976. A national survey research study of the values held by people in the United States.

Mead, Margaret. **Sex and Temperament in Three Primitive Societies.** New York: Morrow, 1935. A pioneering work by the most famous anthropologist of this century.

Miller, Elmer S. and Charles A. Weitz. **Introduction to Anthropology.** Englewood Cliffs, N.J.: Prentice-Hall, 1979. An anthropology textbook covering human biological evolution and cultural variation in today's world.

Spradley, James P. and Michael A. Rynkiewich. **The Nacirema: Readings on American Culture.** Boston: Little, Brown, 1975. A look at the complexity of American culture from an anthropological perspective.

Westhues, Kenneth. **Society's Shadow: Studies in the Sociology of Countercultures.** Toronto: McGraw-Hill Ryerson, 1972. A book about countercultural movements that discusses definitions, conditions that give rise to them, what happens once they get started, followed by an examination of the hippie movement.

Williams, Robin M., Jr. **American Society: A Sociological Interpretation. 3rd ed.** New York: Alfred Knopf, 1970. An excellent sociological analysis of the people and society of the United States, including a discussion of geography, social institutions, value systems, and cultural change.

Chapter 5
Socialization as a Lifelong Process

Training is everything. The peach was once a bitter almond; cauliflower is nothing but a cabbage with a college education.

— Mark Twain

What Is Socialization?

Socialization is the process of learning how to interact in society. In the United States, most people learn to speak the English language and to eat with a fork. They learn that cereal, bacon, and eggs are breakfast foods and that sandwiches are appropriate for lunch. They find out that worthwhile people do worthwhile work and that those who don't do anything are of less value. They discover that certain countries and people are friendly and others are dangerous. Women learn to smile when they are tense and to cry at good news that relieves the tension. Men learn that they should not cry at all, although some do so at times.

Sociologists are interested in socialization because by studying how people interact and learn the complicated behaviors regarded as suitable in their society, they hope to understand people better. By examining what we have learned about our society, ourselves, and our place in society, we can better understand why we think and act the way we do. The study of socialization is also of value in our everyday lives. If we understand why we act as we do, we can change our values, our beliefs, our expectations, and our behavior in ways that might otherwise never occur to us. The study of socialization is a very liberating part of a liberal education.

Is Human Interaction Necessary?

Normal human infants are born with the muscles, bones, vital organs, and all the other biological parts needed to live. They are utterly helpless, however, and cannot survive without human interaction. Babies not only need food and warmth to survive physically, they also need physical stimulation to grow. When they are handled physically by an adult, they are stimulated by tones of voice and facial expressions, which make them aware of their environment, and stimulate them to respond to it. Observations of infants who were comparatively isolated from human contact have shown that a lack of social interaction can have very serious consequences.

Children in Institutions

Rene Spitz (1946) observed children who had apparently been healthy when they were born and who had been living in a foundling home for two years. Clothing, bedding, and room temperatures in the home were suitable, and every child was seen by a physician at least once a day. A small nursing staff took care of the physical needs of the children, but other interaction with the babies was very limited. Nutritious food was carefully prepared and provided, and all infants were breast-fed until they were three months old. Newborn infants were isolated from older infants in a special ward until they were six weeks old. They were then transferred to the baby ward, where they were kept in glass-enclosed cubicles until they were fifteen to eighteen months old.

In spite of this excellent physical care, 38 percent of the ninety-one children in the home died within two years of the study. Of the surviving infants, thirty-six had returned home or been moved elsewhere and twenty-one were still at the institution. These twenty-one children showed slow physical and social development. They were small, and some could not walk or even sit up. Those who could talk could say only a few words, and some could not talk at all. They had not developed either physically or socially.

Spitz compared these children with infants brought up in another institution, where their mothers were being held for delinquency. Physical care was basically the same as in the foundling home, but these babies were not as isolated from other people. They were transferred into rooms with other infants at the relatively early age of six months, and they spent a great deal of time with their mothers. The mothers, who had little else to occupy them, enjoyed playing with their children for hours. The infants received a great deal of social stimulation, and their development was normal. Spitz concluded that the difference between the foundling home and the nursing home was the amount of attention the children received, which illustrates the crucial importance of social interactions in child development.

Feral Children

The importance of social interaction has also been demonstrated in studies of feral children, those who have grown up in the wild. Several feral children were reportedly found in Europe during the past few centuries. Probably the most famous was the wild boy of Aveyron, found in the wilderness in France in 1800 (Shattuck, 1980). It is not known when the boy was separated from other humans or how he survived in the wilderness until he reached puberty, but he did not know any language, so he might have been separated from humans while very young.

The boy's behavior seemed very strange to those who found him. When given a choice of food to eat, he rejected most of it. His choice was potatoes, which he threw into a fire and then picked out with his bare hands, eating them while they were very hot. In addition to tolerating heat, he could tolerate cold, and he was happy to be outdoors in the winter without clothes. He could swing from tree to tree easily, and he was excited by the wind and the moon.

A young doctor took an interest in the boy and taught him to eat a wider variety of foods, to sleep at regular hours, and to wear clothes. It was determined that he could hear noises and make

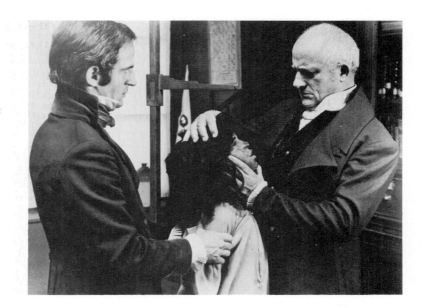

A doctor is shown examining the wild boy of Aveyron in the movie The Wild Child. *The child was apparently healthy yet did not behave at all like a normal boy. Because human behavior develops as a result of social interaction, this boy and others brought up without it do not learn behavior patterns considered to be natural and normal. Our behavior results from our socialization, not from instincts that are present at birth.*

sounds, so an effort was made to teach him to talk. He learned to say a word for milk, but only after he had been given milk — he never learned to use the word to ask for it. After five years of training he had not learned to talk. He did, however, learn to cry occasionally and to hug his teacher. He survived for twenty-two years after the training stopped, living a quiet life in a cottage with a housekeeper, but he never advanced his learning. Those who studied him were interested to note that he never showed any interest in sexual behavior.

Since human development was poorly understood in 1800, when this child was found, the descriptions we have of him are not very useful to us. We don't know whether the boy was healthy when he was born or when he was found, and we can't say to what extent his problems were the result of early isolation. Social scientists have been able to examine more recent cases of early isolation more closely, however.

Isolated Children

Two children who had been hidden in the attics of their family homes because they were illegitimate and unwanted were discovered in the 1930s. The subsequent development of these children was described by Kingsley Davis (1940, 1947).

The first child, Anna, had been deprived of normal contact and had received little human care for most of her six years. When Anna was found she was in poor physical condition. She made no gestures such as pointing or waving, and she had no understanding of speech. She could not walk or feed herself even when food was put in front of her. She was so apathetic that it was hard to tell whether she could hear. She was believed to be feeble-minded and was sent to a school for the retarded where she died at age ten and a half of hemorrhagic jaundice. Before she died, however, she learned to follow directions, string beads, identify a few colors, build with blocks, and enjoy pictures. She had a good sense of rhythm and had become attached to a doll. She talked mainly in phrases, but she did try to carry on conversations. She learned to wash her hands and brush her teeth. She walked well, could run fairly well, and learned a good many things in spite of her isolation and her illness.

The second case involved Isabelle, who had been kept in seclusion until age six and a half. Her mother was deaf and mute, and because Isabelle had been confined in a dark room with her mother, she had no chance to develop speech. She communicated with her mother by gestures and could make only a strange croaking sound.

Although it was established that Isabelle could hear, specialists working with her believed she was retarded because she had not developed any social skills. They thought she could not be educated and that any attempt to teach her to speak would fail after so long a period of silence. Nevertheless, the people in charge of Isabelle launched a systematic and skillful program of training that involved pantomime and dramatization. After one week of intensive effort, she made her first attempt to speak, and in two months she was putting sentences together.

Eighteen months after her discovery, she spoke well, walked, ran, and sang with gusto. Once she learned speech, she developed rapidly, and at age fourteen she completed the sixth grade in public school.

Why did these children develop so little when they were isolated? Many people assume that the feral boy and the isolated girls had something physically wrong with them, that they did not develop normally because they were retarded. Sociologists believe that the lack of social interaction was quite sufficient to produce their stunted growth. Any physically healthy child as isolated as these children could not develop what we consider to be normal behavior. This is not a new or revolutionary debate. For centuries, philosophers and social scientists have been arguing whether human development is determined by biological factors or environmental influences. This is known as the *nature-nurture debate*.

Sociobiology and the Nature-Nurture Debate

Interest in the nature-nurture debate has been renewed recently by the science of *sociobiology* (Wilson, 1975). Sociobiologists are biologists by training, although some sociologists and other social scientists support their views. Sociobiologists believe that social behavior is determined by inborn genetic traits, which influence human behavior in much the same way that animals are influenced by their genetic inheritance. An example in sociology would be that sexual preference is determined genetically and that humans have a genetic tendency to have only one or a very few mates (Van den Berg, 1979). Sociobiologists also think that homosexuality is genetically determined, although temporary homosexual behavior, occurring, for example, when opposite-sex partners are not available, may be environmental. They also believe that altruistic behavior (behavior performed to benefit others without regard for oneself) and warlike behavior are biologically based.

Most sociologists criticize the sociobiological viewpoint on the grounds that behavior varies greatly from culture to culture, and sexual behavior, whether with the same sex or the opposite sex, varies enormously. Altruistic behavior also varies widely and is entirely lacking in humans and monkeys who have been raised in isolation. As for warlike behavior, it is completely absent in many societies.

In addition, many physiologists believe that there is no genetic basis for human behavior. Biological drives or instincts that dictate behavior are supposedly very powerful, but so far no powerful, fixed drives or instincts have been discovered in human beings. Insects and birds perform many complex behaviors even when they have been reared in isolation. Honeybees do complicated dances to show other bees where food is located, and birds build intricate nests in the same manner as others of their species. Humans who have been raised in isolation, however, do almost nothing, as the studies we discussed indicated.

Money (1980), a physiologist and a psychologist, believes that the nature-nurture controversy is based on an illusion, because environmental factors become part of our biology when we perceive them. When a piece of information enters our minds, it is translated into a biochemical form. Although we don't fully understand the workings of the brain, we do know that the brain stores information permanently and that information in the brain can cause physiological changes in other parts of our bodies. Money contends that the information in our brain shapes our behavior and that distinctions between nature and nurture are irrelevant.

Although a few sociologists emphasize the sociobiological perspective, most believe that human behavior develops through what people have learned from social interactions.

The Development of the Self

The development of our personal identity — or self — is a complicated process. Two theorists who were among the first to explore how this process developed in interaction were Charles Horton Cooley and George Herbert Mead.

Charles Horton Cooley: The Looking-Glass Self

Charles Horton Cooley (1864–1929) pointed out that when we refer to the self, when we use the word "I," we are usually not referring to our physical body. We use the word "I" to refer to opinions, desires, ideas, or feelings — I think, I

feel, I want — or we associate the idea of the self with roles, with what the self is doing. We feel satisfaction as we work well on a project, or frustration when things are not going well. We also have our sense of self in relation to other people. We compare and contrast ourselves with others, and our uniqueness is based on that comparison. Cooley argues that it is difficult to think about the self at all except to view the self as doing things, acting in society, thinking about ideas learned in society, and otherwise being a part of it. Even the word "I" that we use to refer to ourselves must be learned from other people.

From these conclusions, Cooley theorized that the idea of the self develops in a process that requires reference to other people, a process he called the *looking-glass self*. According to Cooley, the looking-glass self has three components: (1) how we think our behavior appears to others, (2) how we think others judge our behavior, and (3) how we feel about their judgments. We know that we exist, that we are beautiful or ugly, serious or funny, lively or dull, intelligent or stupid, through the way other people treat us. We never know exactly what other people think of us, of course, but we can imagine how we appear to them and how they evaluate our appearance. We often respond to these imagined evaluations with pride, mortification, embarrassment, or some other feeling. The looking-glass self means that we see ourselves and we respond to ourselves, not as we are, and not as others think we are, but as we *imagine* others think we are.

George Herbert Mead: Role Taking

George Herbert Mead (1863–1931), like Cooley, recognized how important it is for people to interact with others in the development of the self. When infants are first born, they cannot differentiate between all the objects they see from their crib. The world appears as a kaleidoscope of color and movement. Very soon, however, they learn to distinguish important objects, such as the bottle and the mother who brings it. Infants can observe the mother and from her actions begin to understand when she is bringing a bottle. In other words, they begin to have expectations about the mother's behavior.

Since a set of expectations about how a person in a certain situation will behave is known as a *role,* Mead used the term *role taking* to describe the process of figuring out how others will act. As infants role-take, they recognize, through the actions of others, that they themselves are objects in this world. They learn to differentiate self from the kaleidoscope of movement and color. Infants thus learn about the self through the way others treat them.

At first an infant sees self only as the object of the mother's attention, but soon it learns that it can control that self, can use the hand to pick things up, can pull self up to a standing position, can walk, and can say "no." The self has power over the self, can act independently, and can control its own behavior in ways that will shape the behavior of others. It can cry for attention, smile for praise, show off, or do things that please others. The self has become a consciously acting self.

The ability to role-take is extremely important to children. As children grow, they practice role taking in *play.* They often play "house" or "school," taking the role of mother, father, or any other person important to them — *significant others.* By taking the roles of these significant others, they can better understand their own roles as children, students, sons, or daughters. By practicing the roles of others in play, they learn to understand what others expect of them, and they learn how to behave to meet those expectations.

A child who responded differently to each person in his or her life would never develop an integrated sense of identity and would never know how to behave with strangers. Thus the child learns to see others not as individuals with separate expectations but as a group, all of whom have the same expectations. This hypothetical group is known as *the generalized other.* The influence of the generalized other is evident in the actions of a child playing a game. A child playing baseball does not respond to each team member

Children may not learn to read or write when they play school, but they do learn about the roles of teacher and student. These children have even recruited their dolls and stuffed animals to play the role of student, lining them up in an orderly fashion to face the teacher. By learning to take different roles, the children will know what to expect from other people in these roles.

differently, even though they are different people playing different roles. Instead, he or she treats them all as a team with the same set of expectations. Because they have just one set of expectations, the child has just one consistent role. As seen through the eyes of this generalized other, the self becomes consistent and unified.

Psychological Theories of Socialization

In addition to the views of Cooley and Mead, two schools of psychological thought have influenced the study of socialization. Unlike sociologists, psychologists focus primarily on individual behavior rather than on interaction among individuals. The psychological perspectives we will consider are *behaviorism* and *developmental theory*.

Behaviorism

The focus of behaviorism is on observable actions. Behaviorists make no assumptions about the thoughts or interpretations presumed to underlie observable behavior. They distrust efforts to find out what is in someone's mind. Sociologists who are not behaviorists have also benefited from the behavioral stance that caution is necessary in efforts to understand what people are thinking.

Behaviorists believe that children acquire all behaviors through learning. They study how behaviors are learned and what stimulates learning. *Classical conditioning*, first described by the Russian psychologist Ivan Pavlov, involves pairing one stimulus with another. Pavlov realized that dogs salivate in response to food, and when he gave them food, he also rang a bell. The dogs learned to associate the bell with the food; eventually they salivated at the sound of the bell even when no food was present. Similarly, an infant may wiggle and coo when she sees her mother's face, because she has learned to associate her face

with being fed just as Pavlov's dogs associated the bell with food.

Classical conditioning is concerned with the response that follows a stimulus. *Operant conditioning,* on the other hand, is concerned with the reinforcement or reward that follows a response. B. F. Skinner, a famous researcher in this field, found that behavior that is reinforced usually occurs again. If you study carefully and receive an A in all your courses, you will probably continue to study because you have been rewarded. If you receive a D in all your courses, you might soon stop studying. Children's behavior is most likely to be reinforced when they behave in ways that gain their parents' attention, and they repeat behaviors if they are praised. Sometimes an undesirable behavior is reinforced when a parent attends to it, because the child seeks parental attention in any form — even punishment.

Behavior modification is a technique based on the premise that a behavior can be changed by changing the response to it. Psychologists can teach parents how to reinforce children's good behaviors without reinforcing their undesirable ones.

Sociologists agree that classical and operant conditioning come into play in the socialization process, but we must have some knowledge of a person's thoughts if we are to understand that person's responses to a stimulus. Conditioning may work with very young children because they don't have language and cannot analyze situations. Older children, however, have learned a great deal and attach their own meanings to events. These interpretations of events also influence behavior and should be taken into account.

Developmental Theory

Developmental theory deals with the stages of development people pass through as they mature. Developmental theorists generally agree that, although social learning is influential, the stages of development are determined largely by biological factors. They assume that development proceeds from stage to stage and that the developmental tasks of each stage must be successfully resolved before a person can advance to the next stage. There are a number of important developmental theorists, but we will concentrate on only two: Sigmund Freud and Jean Piaget.

Sigmund Freud (1856–1939) was a physician whose contribution to our understanding of personality development has been very influential. *Freudian theory* contends that people possess a number of drives or urges connected with satisfying basic needs, such as the need for food or sexual release. These urges, known collectively as the *id,* seek immediate satisfaction. In society, however, instant gratification is rarely possible, and the id must be controlled. This control is accomplished by what Freud called the *superego,* the part of the mind that incorporates society's rules. The id and the superego are in continual conflict. When you are hungry, for example, your id urges you to satisfy your hunger in the quickest way possible, perhaps by grabbing food from someone else's plate. Your superego, however, tells you that this is an unacceptable way to satisfy your hunger. Freud stated that normally developing children develop an *ego,* which reconciles the demands of the id and superego as much as possible.

According to Freud, children develop through a series of five stages, which are the oral, anal, phallic, latency, and genital. He said that a child developing normally progresses through the five stages, but that under- or overgratification of the child at any stage can cause him or her to remain, or become fixated, at that stage. These fixations can result from improper weaning or toilet training, from demanding too much or too little dependency, from having poor adult models, or from other factors. It is these factors that influence the development of children and shape their personalities.

Jean Piaget (1896–1980), a Swiss psychologist, also contended that development comes in stages

A child who is frustrated will often throw a temper tantrum. Freud believed this happened because the child has not yet learned to control the natural desires of the id. Eventually the child will develop a superego by learning that society does not find temper tantrums to be acceptable behavior. Then the child will develop an ego, or the ability to deal with frustration in a more socially acceptable manner.

as the child develops biologically. Piaget was concerned chiefly with the development of the mind, or *cognitive* development.

According to *Piagetian theory,* there are qualitative differences in the ways children think at different ages. As they mature, they build upon the learning that took place during previous stages. The first stage, known as the *sensorimotor period,* lasts from birth until about age two. During this period, infants are incapable of the process adults call "thinking." They learn about their physical environment, their movements, and the effects of their movements on the environment and often engage in the same behavior repeatedly if they find that it produces an interesting effect. A baby girl may shake her crib again and again to see the attached mobile rotate. Piaget's studies show that infants and older children seem to enjoy challenges for their own sake, not just because they yield a reward. They also prefer situations that are moderately novel — those that are too familiar may seem boring, and those that are too unfamiliar may be frightening.

The second stage, the *preoperational period,* lasts from about age two to age six or seven. Although children become capable of thought during this period, their thinking is illogical and dependent on observable phenomena. They may play with rattles when they see them, but if a rattle is out of sight they don't know how or where to look for it. Their developing ability to use language reflects their growing understanding of symbols, but they do not have a complete understanding of cause-effect relationships or of many other basic concepts, and they tend to be highly egocentric — they cannot distinguish between their own thoughts and perceptions and those of others.

It is during the third stage of cognitive development, the *concrete operational period,* that children learn to process information logically and systematically. They can do this, however, only when the information is presented in concrete form because problems presented in abstract form

are beyond their capabilities. This period lasts from about age seven to age twelve.

The fourth and final stage, according to Piaget, is the *formal operational period,* which begins at about age twelve and which is the level of thinking characteristic of adults. People who have reached this stage can solve complex problems stated in abstract terms. They are capable of thinking logically, so they can test hypotheses, draw inferences, and construct generalizations.

Sociologists are less inclined to believe that stages of development are biologically determined. The studies of isolated children indicate that they don't develop at all if they do not interact. Sociologists have found the study of child development extremely useful, however, and the stages of development described by some psychologists are quite compatible with the stages of development described by Cooley and Mead.

Agencies of Socialization

Socialization is found in all interaction, but the most influential interaction occurs in particular groups, which are referred to as *agencies of socialization.* Among the most important are the family, the schools, peer groups, and the mass media.

The Family

The family is the primary agency of socialization. It is the first socializing influence encountered by most children and affects them for the rest of their lives. A family that teaches children that their goals should be subjugated to those of the family teaches them a set of norms that will remain even after they learn elsewhere that their primary responsibility is to take care of themselves.

Families also give children their geographical location, as easterners or westerners, for example, and their urban or rural background. In addition, the family determines the child's social class, race, religious background, and ethnic group. Each of these factors can have a profound influence on children. They may learn to speak a particular dialect, to prefer certain foods, and to pursue certain types of leisure activities. The child's knowledge of appropriate work habits may be determined by the type of job the parents have. Some studies show that working-class parents emphasize obedience, which is necessary in working-class occupations, whereas middle-class parents emphasize exploration and experimentation, which develop the problem-solving skills necessary in middle-class jobs (Kohn, 1959).

Families also teach children values they will hold throughout life. They frequently adopt their parents' attitudes not only about work but also about the importance of education, patriotism, and religion. Even a child's sense of worth is determined, at least in part, by the child's parents.

One of the values instilled in the children of most American families concerns the worth of the unique individual. We are taught that we possess a set of talents, personality characteristics, strengths, and weaknesses peculiar to ourselves and that we are responsible for developing these traits. This view of the value of the individual is not found in all cultures, however. Many people who emigrated from southern Europe, for example, believe that one's primary responsibility is to the family, not to oneself. The son of a European farm family is expected to be loyal and obedient to the family, to work for its benefit, and someday to take over the farm, but in our culture, staying with the family is often regarded as a sign of weakness or lack of ambition. Both beliefs are just two of the many values that people learn primarily through the family.

While taking a walk through the woods, the members of this family are socializing with each other. They are teaching each other how they value nature, recreation, and time spent together. Parents who do not share outdoor activities with their children will teach them something quite different about their values, attitudes, and beliefs regarding the outdoors and use of leisure time.

The Schools

In some societies, socialization takes place almost entirely within the family, but in highly technical societies children are also socialized by the educational system. Schools in the United States teach more than reading, writing, arithmetic, and other basic skills. They also teach students to develop themselves, to test their achievements through competition, to discipline themselves, to cooperate with others, and to obey rules, all of which are necessary if a youngster is to achieve success in a society dominated by large organizations.

Schools teach sets of expectations about the work children will do when they mature. They begin by learning about the work roles of community helpers such as firefighters and doctors, and later they learn about occupations more formally. They take aptitude tests to discover their unique talents, and, with the help of guidance counselors, they set occupational goals.

Schools also teach citizenship in countless ways: they encourage children to take pride in their communities; to feel patriotic about their nation; to learn about the country's geography, history, and national holidays; to study government, explain the role of good citizens, urge their parents to vote and to pledge allegiance to the flag; to become informed about community and school leaders; and to respect school property.

It has been suggested that learning at home is on a personal, emotional level, whereas learning at school is basically intellectual. Evidence suggests, however, that learning at school also involves personal factors, such as a student's self-image and the teacher's perceptions of the student. In other words, students form a looking-glass self and perform in response to teacher expectations. In one experimental study in the classroom (Rosenthal and Jacobson, 1968), students were randomly divided into two groups. The teacher was told that those in the first group were bright and that those in the second group were not. The students believed to be highly intelligent by the teacher performed significantly better than those believed to be less intelligent. The teacher's expectations of the students influenced their performance.

Most school administrators and teachers reinforce our cultural emphasis on the uniqueness of individuals. Thus they try to identify the unique talents of students through comparison and competition with other students and then attempt to develop these talents so that they will become useful to the larger society.

Peer Groups

Young people spend considerable time in school, and their *peer group*, people their own age, is an important influence on their socialization.

Peer group socialization has been increasing in this century because young people have been attending school for a longer period. They no longer drop out at fourteen — most finish high school and about half go on to college.

Young people today also spend more time with one another outside of school. Unlike young people of earlier decades, few are isolated on farms. Most live in cities or suburbs, and, increasingly, they have access to automobiles so they can spend time together away from their families. Teenagers' most intimate relationships are often those they have with their peers, and they influence one another greatly. In fact, some young people create their own unique subcultures. Coleman (1974), who refers to these simply as cultures, lists as examples the cultures of athletic groups in high schools, the college campus culture, the drug culture, motorcycle cults, the culture of surfers, and religious cultures. In part because teenagers are often unsure of themselves, the sense of belonging that they get from their subculture may be extremely important to them, although the pressures to conform to group expectations can be quite severe.

The Mass Media

The American *mass media* — television, popular magazines, and other forms of communication intended for a large audience — are paid for by advertising. When dress, music, and other aspects of the youth subculture became big business, advertisers began directing their programs to young people. Radio stations brought new kinds of music not only to youth but also to a wider audience, thus socializing other age groups to the music of the youth subculture. The media also advertised youthful styles of dress. Young people who rejected fashion in favor of blue jeans, however, were later socialized to buy high fashion blue jeans and other garments with designer names. This type of interaction occurs constantly in the socialization process. As young people de-

Students who spend a great deal of time together socialize each other. These students have all learned appropriate dress and hairstyle from other members of their peer group. The styles they have agreed on are not necessarily those encouraged by parents or school officials.

velop their unique talents, they influence society. Society in turn socializes them to use their unique talents in ways consistent with the values and norms of the society.

Young people are socialized to pursue activities apart from the family. As a result, the movie industry can rely on them to attend movies in theaters and also at school. Because youngsters have learned to be active and competitive, they prefer movies that show action and competition, and movies in turn reinforce this aspect of socialization. Violent horror films have been particularly popular over the last few years. Movies with themes of violent revenge also draw a lot of young people to the theaters, and actors like Clint Eastwood and Charles Bronson have made their reputations by acting in this type of movie.

Television also uses violent programming to appeal to teenagers, but teenagers do not stay home as much as younger children, so they watch less television. Younger children, who watch an average of almost four hours of television a day, urge their parents to buy the cereals, snack foods, and toys they see advertised. The shows children watch reinforce the norms of the larger society.

Programs about the family teach children

what an American family should be like. Children may develop their conception of the family from what they see on television rather than from the home they live in. They learn, for example, that families include both a mother and a father, even though one-fifth of children have only one parent, and that families live in houses, even though many children live in apartments. Some mothers on television often stay home and wear aprons, while many others work and wear jeans rather than aprons. We do not know precisely how much children learn about the ideal family from television, but these family shows are undoubtedly influential.

The effects of television violence cannot be measured accurately because children also learn competition and violence from other sources, and television both socializes and reinforces the socialization they receive elsewhere. Studies do indicate, however, that children can learn new techniques for being violent from watching a movie in an experimental situation, as shown in the classic experiment done by Bandura (1965). A group of children who watched a movie in which a doll was treated aggressively in unusual ways later imitated these unusual aggressive behaviors. Although the mass media are not the only teachers of violence in America, viewers can certainly learn about violence from the media just as they learn it from other experiences.

Socialization of Gender Roles

Socialization plays an especially important part in determining what children believe to be acceptable behaviors for members of their sex. Even though the situation has begun to change, our environment bombards both men and women with subtle and not so subtle suggestions that certain types of behavior are acceptable for women and certain types of behavior are acceptable for men.

People who diverge significantly from traditional roles often meet with resistance from individuals and the social system as a whole throughout their lives. The same sources of socialization that influence people in other areas of their lives — work, the mass media, education, interactions with others — also affect the socialization of gender roles.

Infant and Childhood Experiences

Gender-role socialization in our society begins at birth. When a baby is born, he or she is wrapped in a blue or pink blanket, and from that moment on parents respond to the infant on the basis of its sex (Bem and Bem, 1976). Parents can better predict what infant girls will be doing in twenty-five years — being a wife and mother — than they can tell what boys will be doing, since boys have many more options and opportunities. Boys will be expected to be more aggressive, better in mathematics, better problem solvers, and more athletic than girls. When they grow up they will be expected to concentrate primarily on their career, to be task-oriented, and to be interested in performing tasks that lead to the goals they have set for themselves. This conception of males has been labeled an *instrumental role* by sociologists. Girls will be expected to be more verbal, more expressive, more emotional, and when they grow up more interested in interpersonal relationships, a conception labeled an *expressive role* by sociologists (Zelditch, 1955). Infant boys are often described as big, athletic, strong, or alert, but girls are usually described as tiny, dainty, sweet, pretty, delicate, inattentive, or weak. Parents tend to notice the dainty fingernails of the baby girl, even though those of the baby boy look identical. Boy and girl infants are also treated differently. Boys are handled roughly and tossed around playfully, but girls are held more, cuddled, talked to, and treated as if they were very fragile. Even the tone of voice used is different. Boys are talked to in loud voices, while girls are spoken to gently.

Out in Right Field

Throughout my entire school career, the time of day I dreaded most was Gym class. Whereas other kids seemed to look forward to Gym as some sort of relief from sitting at a desk and listening to a teacher, I dreaded the thought of sports.

The curse followed me throughout my entire life. In elementary school, part of the year we played baseball outdoors. The two best players (never me) were captains and they chose — one by one — players for their teams. The choosing went on and on, the better players getting picked first and me and my type last.

During the game I always played the outfield. Right field. Far right field. And there I would stand in the hot sun wishing I was anyplace else in the world. Every so often a ball looked like it was coming in my direction and I prayed to god that it wouldn't happen. If it did come, I promised god to be good for the next thirty-seven years if he let me catch it — especially if it was a fly-ball. The same thing occurred when it was my turn to bat. It was bad enough, but if there were any runners on base — or any outs — and it all depended on me — I knew we were lost.

The rest of the year in elementary school consisted of indoor Gym class, some of which were coed. The coed Gym classes consisted of things like dance lessons. The teachers would teach us essential dances like the fox trot, the mambo and the merengue. These were always a chore because it was you and your girl partner — usually matched by height — and I of course was the shortest — and matched up with the shortest girl — who towered over me anyway. Dances like the Virginia Reel and square dancing, which were a group thing, I usually enjoyed a lot. A lot, that is, until it became clear from the actions of the rest of the guys in dance class that I was the only one having a good time. After that even that type of dancing was awful.

Junior high school was equally awful. For it was in junior high that real Gym classes started — Gym class with lockers and smelly locker rooms and gym uniforms and showers with eight million other guys.

I hated the sight of my gym uniform. The locker room stench

Infants respond differently to these very early variations in treatment (Rubin, Provenzano, and Luria, 1974). Children who are touched and talked to cling to their mothers and talk to them more, regardless of their sex, and since girls are held and talked to more than boys, they tend to reciprocate with this kind of behavior (Goldberg and Lewis, 1969; Moss, 1967).

Parents continue to teach children proper gender-role behavior, either consciously or unconsciously, throughout childhood. Girls are often told not to get dirty and not to be rough. Boys are usually told not to cry. Studies have shown that fathers are more concerned than mothers about gender-role behavior (Aberle and Naegele, 1952).

Fathers often want their little girls to be gentle and dependent, but they are sometimes very concerned if their sons show a lack of responsibility and initiative or if they are too passive or cry a lot. Mothers too, however, are concerned about proper gender-role behavior. They treat their daughters with more warmth and indulgence and allow their sons to be much more aggressive. Sons are encouraged to fight back if another child starts a fight, but daughters are not (Sears, Maccoby, and Levin, 1957).

Children also learn gender-role behavior in nursery schools (Serbin and O'Leary, 1975). Classroom observations of fifteen nursery schools showed that the teachers (all women) treated boys

almost knocked me out. And during Gym class I tried my best not to exert myself, so I wouldn't sweat too much, so I wouldn't have to take a shower with eight million other guys.

In junior high we still did things like play baseball. But things started to get rougher and rougher. We did things like wrestling. And gymnastics. To this day I can't climb a pole or a rope. Calisthenics were and are a bore.

High school was the same old stuff. However, in high school, sports started taking on new dimensions because the most highly prized girls looked to the best athletes. The football and basketball players. I was out of the competition from the beginning, but that didn't make it any the less awful.

There was absolutely no relief from sports in the early part of my life, for it happened not only in school, but also at home. My older brother was a good athlete.

He went to ballgames and even tried out for and made some teams. He plastered our room with hateful pictures of the Dodgers at bat. Sports consumed his entire life, and he would get home from school, change his clothes and run out to play.

My father related to my brother completely in this way. They had a fine sports relationship, and would go off to ballgames together — or talk at the dinner table of the day's ballgames or the latest standings, which they both knew by heart. I was completely left out of this. After a while I grew resentful and wanted no part of it. Yet, every so often my father would try. He would take me out back for a while with a ball, bat and glove and try to make a man out of me. Patiently he would throw a ball in my direction and I swung and missed it. After he quickly grew tired of that he would once again explain to

me how to use the fielding glove he stuck on my hand and I would try my hand at catching. I soon grew tired of this — mainly because I missed so often and had to go chasing down the block after the ball. These sessions never lasted very long. Even Sundays were no relief — the television was usually on and blasting a ballgame. I grew to hate the sound of Mel Allen's voice.

My father and brother seemed to have a great relationship. I didn't. Neither with my father, nor with my brother. I guess I was left to my mother. We seemed to get along fine.

SOURCE: *Unbecoming Men: A Men's Consciousness-Raising Group Writes on Oppression and Themselves.* Albion, Ca.: Times Change Press. Copyright © 1971. Reprinted by permission. 36–38. Reprinted in Joseph H. Pleck and Jack Sawyer, eds., *Men and Masculinity*, Englewood Cliffs, N.J.: Prentice-Hall, 1974, 17–18.

and girls differently. Teachers responded three times more often to disruptive behavior by boys than by girls. The boys usually got a loud public reprimand, whereas the girls were given a quiet rebuke that others could not hear. Disruptive behavior is often an attempt to gain attention, and because the boys received the attention they were seeking, they continued to behave disruptively. When the teacher paid less attention to the boys, this behavior diminished.

Teachers were also more willing to help the boys find something to do. The girls who were not doing anything were ignored and received attention only when they were literally clinging to the teacher's skirts.

The teachers spent more time teaching boys. In one instance, the teacher showed boys how to use a stapler, but when a girl did not know how to use it, the teacher took the materials, stapled them herself, and handed them back to the girl. Problem solving and analytical ability are related to active participation, but girls were not given the opportunity to try things as often as boys.

The story books read to preschool children also teach gender-role behavior. Weitzman (1972), in a review of picture books, found that little girls were admired for their attractiveness, while little boys were admired for their achievements. Men were admired for their accomplishments, while women were admired for being the

Even in the most loving parent-child relationships, a variety of gender roles can be taught unwittingly. Did this father help the daughter onto the tire, and is he being careful that she does not fall? Would he be more likely to expect a son to climb onto the tire, stand on it and swing himself? Or would this father treat a son and a daughter in exactly the same way? We need more research to learn how the social behavior of fathers teaches gender roles to their children.

wives or daughters of kings, judges, adventurers, or explorers. Women were typically shown as wives and mothers, never as pursuing goals outside of the home. Studies of award-winning children's books have shown that the girls in the stories are usually indoors doing domestic chores or passively watching someone else's activities, while boys do interesting and exciting things like rescuing animals or building space ships.

Textbooks likewise subtly teach gender-role behavior. In a review of mathematics texts published between 1970 and 1975, females were generally portrayed as emotional and domestic. In most textbooks, little boys were shown as significantly taller than little girls of the same age, even though in reality children before puberty are about the same height.

Schools teach gender roles in other ways as well. Most teachers are women, but principals and superintendents are men. Women teachers are more likely to teach young children, but as subject matter becomes more difficult and specialized, more men are found teaching. Children receive subtle messages about the capability of men and women as they observe the jobs they hold. School counselors also encourage children to follow expected gender roles. Girls who want to enter masculine occupations or boys who want to enter traditionally feminine occupations will be defined by career counselors as in need of more extensive guidance. Efforts are sometimes made to steer them into more "appropriate" occupations.

Mass Media and Socialization for Gender Roles

From childhood on, Americans spend thousands of hours watching television, which has a strong tendency to portray gender-role stereotypes. In children's television programming, studies showed that male characters are usually portrayed as aggressive, constructive, and helpful, whereas the female characters are passive and deferring to males (Sternglanz and Serbin, 1974). On "Sesame Street," considered to be one of the best children's shows, the male characters are likely to have valued personality characteristics — honesty, loyalty, and so on — whereas the female characters are usually passive, silly, or inept.

Adult programs, especially the situation comedies, are watched by many children and adults. "I Love Lucy," which was originally produced in the fifties and is still seen in reruns, featured Lucille Ball as a consistently inept housewife who has to be rescued by the harassed but tolerant Ricky, her husband. Every episode revolved around Lucy's getting into some sort of trouble. Current situation comedies are a little more subtle. In "MASH", for example, the main female character, Major Margaret Houlihan, holds a position with a lot of responsibility and is of a higher military rank than most of the other characters, but she is head nurse and must defer to the judgments of the doctors as well as endure sexist comments.

In general, nighttime television has more male than female characters. The emphasis is on male achievement, which often involves violence. The male characters' physical attractiveness is relatively unimportant. Such heroes as Quincy and Lou Grant are not handsome by conventional standards. Women characters, on the other hand, are almost always physically attractive. Even when they are portrayed as competent individuals, they either get themselves into situations where they must be rescued by men or else they work for men. The part of Joyce Davenport, the assistant district attorney on "Hill Street Blues," is one of the few roles on television where a woman is competent and independent.

Advertising on television and in the press also tends to stereotype both men and women. Women are usually beautiful, bewildered homemakers, even when they work outside the home. The ads show them arriving home from work to cook the family meal or do the family wash, but they don't know what to serve or which soap to

Public defender Joyce Davenport, played by Veronica Hamel, interviews a prisoner on the television program "Hill Street Blues." Joyce Davenport is one of the few competent, professional women portrayed on television during prime time. Both men and women are socialized to expect less competent behavior from women, and television usually confirms these expectations. It could, however, teach us that women can be competent by portraying more women like Joyce Davenport.

use to get shirt collars really clean. A male voice heard in the background tells the woman how to solve her problem. Men in ads are stereotyped as forceful, athletic, involved in business of some kind, or at least actively watching a ball game, but always knowing exactly what they want or which beer has more gusto.

Many popular songs also reflect male and female gender-role stereotypes. Men sing songs of achievement about how they will be number one and won't be pushed around, while women sing more fatalistic songs about accepting life because there's not much they can do about it. Women sing about giving everything up for love, while men sing about not letting any woman get the better of them. Here are just a few song titles from the past few decades: "I Did It My Way," "I Want to Be Bobby's Girl," "Under My Thumb," "I Will Follow Him." Although more recently songs such as "I Am Woman" and "I Will Survive" have been popular, songs that point up women's strength and self-sufficiency are rare.

Socialization in Adulthood

The knowledge we acquire as children shapes the meanings we give to ourselves and the world, and it can continue to influence us for the rest of our lives. We never stop learning new things, however — every day we have new experiences, learn new information, and add the meanings of these new facts to what we already know. Although new knowledge may be different from knowledge acquired as children, the same agencies of socialization are at work.

Types of Adult Socialization

Like children, adults are socialized by their families. Single people must be socialized when they marry in order to live intimately with their spouses and to share living arrangements. If they have children, they learn the role of parents and will probably rely on the knowledge of child care they acquired from their own parents. Since the two parents were themselves brought up by different sets of parents, they will have learned different child-rearing techniques and therefore will have to socialize each other to reach agreement about child-care practices. As the children grow up, the parents must be socialized to allow their children to become independent after years of dependency. All of this learning is a part of *adult socialization.*

Children themselves are often very active socializers of their parents. As infants, they let their parents know when they need attention. Beginning at about age two, they become aware of themselves, learn to say no, and begin to let their parents know when they need some independence. This process of demanding both attention and independence continues as long as the children are at home. It can result in serious conflicts in some youths, particularly those who rebel, fight, take drugs, or run away from home. The socialization of parents can be quite dramatic.

Adult socialization also occurs in schools. Colleges teach adults of all ages, and the move from home to college can be a period of intense socialization. College freshmen must adapt to their new independence from the family and make their own decisions about health, food, sleep, class attendance, study habits, exercise, and social relationships. They must learn to live in crowded situations and compete with peers. Some avoid these decisions by going along with the crowd. Others drop the values they learned in the family and adopt a new set of values, whereas some continue to maintain family values in the new setting. Each choice entails a certain amount of socialization.

Another type of adult socialization is *occupational training,* which teaches the attitudes and values associated with an occupation, as well as skills. Medical schools, for example, teach students the technical knowledge required to practice medicine, but they also convey the values of the profession. As students proceed through medical school, the number who want to be general practitioners decreases and the number who want to enter a specialty increases, partly because specialists need to keep up with only a small part of the overwhelming volume of new medical information. In addition, medicine is taught by specialists, who tend to encourage students to enter a specialty.

Rules and values must also be learned in fields that require less training than medicine. A new employee in an office has to learn how to conform to the expectations of the other workers and to the written and unwritten rules. Are men and women expected to wear suits or is less formal clothing acceptable? Do employees address one another by their first names? Is rigid adherence to established procedures expected? Are some department heads more accommodating than others? During socialization, the employee will discover the answers to questions such as these.

Adults, like children, get a great deal of factual information from the mass media — radio, television, books, and newspapers. The news media not only report what is happening, they tell people what to consider important. News items based on press releases may convey only what the agency issuing the release wants to make public, and news broadcasts may not present competing unofficial views. Thus, whether we realize it or not, we may learn to define as important whatever officials are telling us is important.

Soap operas are directed toward working-class women, high school students, and college students who are home during the day. These programs display an upper-middle-class lifestyle to working-class people. The styles of dress and decor and people's conduct in social situations are characteristic of the well-to-do. In subtle ways, soap operas show viewers the evils of drugs and alcohol, proper child-rearing techniques, and how to behave during a divorce or other tragedy, to name just a few of the topics they cover. People tend to be either good or evil; generally the good are loved by family and friends whereas the evil suffer as a result of their bad behavior.

Resocialization

Another adaptation to new situations that adults must sometimes make is known as *resocialization*. The changes people undergo during this period are much more pervasive than the gradual adaptations characteristic of regular socialization. Resocialization usually follows a major break in a person's customary life, one which requires that the person adopt an entirely new set of meanings to understand his or her new life. *Mortification of self* (Goffman, 1961), the most dramatic type of resocialization, occurs in such institutions as the armed forces, prisons, and mental hospitals. People entering these institutions are totally stripped of their old selves. Physically, they are required to strip, shower, and don institutional clothing. All personal possessions are taken away, and they must leave behind family, friends, and work roles. They must live in a new environment under a new set of rules and adopt a new role as a military person, prisoner, or mental patient. Their previous learning must be completely reorganized.

The "midlife crisis" is another example of a dramatic resocialization. Men may have been socialized by families, schools, peers, the media, and other life experiences to believe that they are unique individuals with special talents that must be developed if they are to be superior to others and attain important positions in society. Men who have learned this — those who have been well socialized — develop their talents and hold important positions, adding more each day to their wealth of knowledge. At some point in middle age, however, a few men learn a revolutionary new set of meanings. They may decide they are unique and valuable people even without their special abilities, important jobs, and high salaries.

SOCIOLOGISTS AT WORK
Youth Guidance

Barbara Monsor is coordinator of research and statistics at Youth Guidance, a school-based social service program for adolescents in Chicago. A private nonprofit organization founded in 1924, Youth Guidance has offices in middle schools and high schools in five Chicago school districts. Monsor joined them in 1978, after earning a master's degree in sociology at the University of Illinois at Chicago Circle.

Does Monsor find uses for her sociological background in her work at Youth Guidance? "Constantly," she says, "It's an integral part of what I do. My interest — both theoretical and pragmatic — in the field of human development, and particularly child development, is engaged daily." Youth Guidance provides a vast array of services to the children who are referred to it by teachers and school administrators, hospitals, and other professionals. Monsor enumerates some of these services: "We do counseling, we run creative arts programs, we do group counseling and family therapy, we provide referrals to outside therapists and hospitals for problems that are bigger than we can handle, we provide counseling and other services to teachers and counselors who are already in the schools and help them with their counseling overload, and we run a training program for social workers and graduate students in social work."

Being located in the schools is a great help to Youth Guidance in delivering these services. "It's almost axiomatic," Monsor says, "that adolescents don't get these services unless you grab them where they are. We used to have all our offices downtown. Our first move into a school — long before I came here — was something we negotiated with the school district. After that we were asked to move into several other schools. Our office space is an in-kind contribution from the schools, in return for the services we provide."

Children in the schools are referred to Youth Guidance for a wide range of reasons. "They may just have unexplained bad grades," Monsor says. "They may be acting aggressively in the classroom. They may not be showing up for class and be on the verge of dropping out. They may be EMH children — educably mentally handicapped, with many adjustment problems. They may have threatened suicide or have threatened their peers with violence. They may have just been released from the hospital and have problems related to that. They may be pregnant — we have one whole group of pregnant girls. They may have language and cultural problems, especially if they're recent immigrants."

Monsor's role in all this is a busy one. "I am responsible for statistics, in-house evaluation and research, and data to be used in contracts with government and private funders and in meeting their monitoring requirements. I do mainly qualitative research — an annual evaluation of our counseling program based on interviews with clients and school staff people, for example."

Monsor is happy in her job, which she first learned of from the director of Youth Guidance, who is married to one of her professors at Chicago Circle. "I accepted the job," she says, "because I felt I would be able to make use of my academic background, training, and interests, and to work in a setting where I could subscribe to organizational goals. When we deal with children in trouble, we have a systemic approach to *trouble*. We find that problems occur for family, cultural, and economic reasons. We're not one of those mental health agencies that defines our children as 'sick' and wants to lock them up somewhere."

Once they change the basic set of meanings they have been acting on, everything else changes. Some quit their jobs and take off for the north woods to farm or work with their hands. Most change in less dramatic ways, but they have still changed the basic set of meanings they learned as children and have begun to act on a new set of meanings.

Retirement from work is sometimes an easy process of socialization to a new situation, but it often requires a great deal of resocialization. Retired people often lose at least part of their income, so they may have to adapt to a new standard of living. With the loss of work, new sources of self-esteem may have to be developed, but society may help in this process by providing education on financial management, health, and housing. Counseling services and support groups for retired persons may also be provided, often by employers, especially when they want employees to retire.

Besides loss of income and self-esteem, retirement creates another resocialization problem. Most roles involve social expectations and provide rewards for meeting those expectations. Retirement, however, is a *"roleless"* role (Riley et al., 1969). There are no social expectations associated with retirement other than the loss of a previous role; as a result, the satisfactory performance of the retirement role goes unrecognized. To compound the problem, the retired person's spouse often dies during this period, so he or she must relinquish the family role as well as the work role. But if the retired person has enough money to buy nice clothes, enjoy hobbies, and afford travel for social events or volunteer work, then he or she can create a new role that is rewarding.

Summary

Socialization is the process of learning how to interact in society. Infants must interact in order to survive, and as they interact they learn about society. Children who have been isolated or who received little attention when very young do not learn to walk, talk, or otherwise respond to people because social interactions are crucial to development.

Sociobiologists believe that inborn genetic traits direct human behavior just as they direct the behavior of animals. They contend that sexual, altruistic, and warlike behaviors occur in humans because they exist in our genetic makeup. Most biologists and social scientists, however, think that there is no nature-nurture debate but that people's behavior is determined by their biological capacity to learn socially.

Charles Horton Cooley used the phrase looking-glass self to describe how people learn about themselves; that is, our identities are heavily influenced by our perceptions of how others view us. We see ourselves, not as we are, and not as others see us, but as we think others see us.

Mead used the term role taking to describe the process of figuring out how others think and perceive us. According to Mead, children take the role of only one other person at a time at first. Eventually, however, they develop a conception of a generalized other, a hypothetical group assumed to share the same expectations of the child. Children practice role taking in play and learn to generalize in team games.

Although psychologists are interested in the behavior of individuals rather than social interactions, several psychological orientations are of interest to sociologists. Behaviorists focus on people's observable actions, making no assumptions about underlying processes. They study how behaviors are learned and what stimulates learning. Developmental psychologists deal with the stages of development from infancy on through the life cycle. They study both physical development and cognitive development, the development of thought processes. Many developmental theorists believe that development is predominantly biological rather than social. Freud said that development passes through a series of stages characterized by different sources of drive gratification. Piaget found that the nature of cognitive processes changes as children mature.

As youngsters grow, assume the roles of others, and learn about themselves, they are being socialized — learning cultural values and norms. Some of the important agencies of socialization are the family, schools, peer groups, and the mass media.

People's perceptions of behavior appropriate for members of their sex are the result of socialization. From birth, males and females are treated differently. Men are expected to be active and task-oriented, whereas women are expected to be nurturing and people-oriented. Socialization for these roles occurs in every aspect of American society, from children's storybooks to the mass media. From this socialization, children learn what is expected of themselves and others.

Socialization continues throughout life. Resocialization may be necessary when a person's life changes dramatically and abruptly, such as going to prison or entering retirement.

Key Terms

behavior modification
behaviorism
classical conditioning
developmental theory
expressive role
Freudian theory
id, ego, superego
instrumental role
mass media
mortification of self
nature-nurture debate
operant conditioning
peer group
Piagetian theory
play
resocialization

role taking
"roleless" role
significant others
socialization
sociobiology
the generalized other
the looking-glass self

Suggested Readings

Campbell, Ernest Q. **Socialization: Culture and Personality.** *Dubuque, Iowa: Wm. C. Brown, 1975.* This is a very brief book, but it summarizes well the topic discussed in this chapter.

Coleman, James S. **Adolescent Society.** *New York: The Free Press, 1960.* This is a classic study of the youth subculture, and although it is now almost twenty-five years old, it is interesting to read and to learn how little has changed.

Goslin, David (ed.). **Handbook of Socialization Theory and Research.** *Chicago: Rand McNally, 1969.* This is an encyclopedia rather than a reading book, but it is so respected in this area of study, you may enjoy browsing through it to see the depth of study undertaken in socialization.

Money, John. **Love and Love Sickness. The Science of Sex, Gender Difference and Pair-Bonding.** *Baltimore: Johns Hopkins University Press, 1980.* A discussion of the development of sex differences from a leading researcher in the field.

Pleck, Joseph H. and Jack Sawyer (eds.) **Men and Masculinity.** *Englewood Cliffs, N.J.: Prentice-Hall, 1974.* A collection of readings on male socialization.

Shattuck, Roger. **The Forbidden Experiment: The Story of the Wild Boy of Aveyron.** *New York: Farrar, Straus, Giroux, 1980.* This is a recent description of a wild boy found in 1800 in France. It provides insights into the behavior of a child who knew no language.

Weitzman, Lenore J. **Sex Role Socialization.** *Palo Alto, Calif.: Mayfield Publishing, 1979.* A brief overview of socialization with emphasis on feminine behavior.

Chapter 6
The Individual and Social Interaction

It is thus with most of us; we are what other people say we are. We know ourselves chiefly by hearsay.

— Eric Hoffer

As discussed in the last chapter, the people around us play a vital part in the socialization process and, more specifically, in our sense of who we are and how we should act. Suppose, for example, that you arrive at a party where you don't know anybody. You would probably find that you are attracted to a certain group of people. How do you decide whether or not to approach them? What do you say if you do approach them? How do you want these people to perceive you? As bright and amusing? As mysterious and brooding? At parties, as in every other situation, we interact continually — with ourselves, the environment, and with other people. The list of questions we can raise about individual feelings and behavior, about social expectations (norms), and about social groups is endless. The interactionist perspective answers some of these questions by examining, at a microsociological level, the individual in a social context. This perspective directs our attention to the individual, who is born into a certain society, who interacts with others, who learns what behaviors are expected, and who acts on the basis of what he or she has learned.

Social interactionists study the relationship between society and the individual. They study how society shapes or controls individuals and how, in turn, individuals create and change society. As you may recall from Chapter 2, early sociologists such as Spencer, Durkheim, and Marx examined society as existing apart from the individual. Social interactionists such as Mead, Cooley, and Blumer examined the relationship *between* societies and individuals. They perceived the individual and society as different sides of the same coin. Society cannot exist without individuals, but neither can individuals exist outside of society. We must be born into a society of at least one other person if we are to survive.

Symbolic Interaction

All animals interact, but no animals except humans have built societies, cultures, and social institutions. We are also unique in our capacity to use language. It was George Herbert Mead who first described why language makes humans different from all other animals. In *Mind, Self and Society* (1934), a compilation of Mead's lectures published by his students after his death, Mead demonstrated that the unique feature of the human mind is its capacity to use *symbols,* both verbal and nonverbal. As discussed in Chapter 4, language is a symbol system. The words in a language have meaning, and when we know the meanings of words we can communicate with others who share the same language. Language, however, is not the only type of symbol we use. The Christian cross is a symbol to Christians. It has a special meaning for people who understand the Christian religion, just as the American flag has meaning for most people. Any meaningful thing that can be used to represent something else is a symbol.

Because we can communicate with symbols we can work cooperatively. We can indicate with words what we want to do and how we can share a task. We can say, "George, you lift up the chair while I move the rug." Animals are incapable of this sort of cooperation. If food is tied to the end of a rope, two chimps in a cage can work together to pull on the rope, but should the food at the end of the rope get caught on the side of the cage, the chimps cannot work cooperatively so that one would push and the other would pull (Lindesmith and Strauss, 1968). They cannot build anything if the task requires that one hold something while the other put something on top of it, which calls for planning and cooperation, and language is necessary to carry out such a task.

Lindesmith and Strauss (1968) point out that one reason why animals have not developed symbol systems and language is that most animals are mute. They do not have the physiological capacity to make the sounds that human beings can make. They cannot articulate a variety of sounds and join them in various ways.

It is more than the physical ability to speak that enables people to interact symbolically, however. As indicated by Mead, the ability to talk to ourselves and reason things out is a distinctly human feature. When we see another person in the street, we do not simply react to the person instinctively. We think, "Is this someone I know, or is it a stranger? Do I want to know this person, ignore her, say hello to her?" We give a meaning to the situation and act according to that meaning. If we say "hello" to the other person, we are using a symbol that means, "I wish to greet you in a friendly manner." The other person knows the meaning of the symbol and can understand and share with us in this *symbolic interaction.* It is the mind that permits people to develop a social self, to take the roles of others, and to imaginatively consider alternative courses of action by talking to ourselves. It is the mind that allows us to share ideas about ways to use objects, to decide what is good and what is bad, what is beautiful and what is ugly. We can talk ourselves into doing one thing and not another.

By using our minds in interaction with others, we develop our definitions of self and our expectations of appropriate behavior for ourselves and others. The fact that others share similar expectations makes life patterned and relatively predictable. Within this general pattern of predictability, however, a number of factors change constantly. One of these factors is the social self and how we perceive it.

The Social Self and Interaction

The Social Self

All human beings who can function in society have a social self. This *social self* consists of our internalized self-concepts and develops as a result of our socialization and through the process known as the looking-glass self (Cooley, 1902). We have a *self-image,* an image of ourselves as male or female, athletic, intelligent, beautiful, ugly, literate, or whatever. We base this self-image on things we have learned in the past — how well we performed in school, how well we got along with family and friends, what interests and hobbies we have developed, and on all our other past experiences.

In addition to our general self-image, we have a self-image based on how we believe we are functioning in our present situation. Are we performing well or incompetently, are we interested in this but bored with that, can we do one thing but not another, do we look good or are we poorly dressed? Our evaluations of ourselves on the basis of our past history and our behavior in the present situation yield our feelings of *self-esteem.* As you can see, our ideas about ourselves tend to vary from situation to situation.

One of the ways in which the self changes in different situations is through role taking. We assume other people's roles to understand what they will do and how they will respond to us (see Chapter 5). We also take roles when we intend to interact with someone else. We have certain expectations about other people's roles, and we act in accordance with them. If the person is a friend, for example, we expect him or her to act in accordance with the "friend" status-role and show concern for our well-being. The same person may also act in a variety of other status-roles — son, student, employee, and so on — each of which requires a different set of interactions. Friends may act very differently with their parents than with peers. Sometimes behavior varies so much from situation to situation that it is hard to believe the same person is involved.

Because we are continually redefining ourselves on the basis of our interactions with others, sociologists consider the self as a *process.* In different situations, we may consider ourselves to be a warm and friendly person, a competitive person, or a dependent person. Sometimes we will feel

Frederic March in the dual movie roles of Dr. Jekyll and Mr. Hyde. Most people do not change so radically, but we all change our behavior somewhat. Kindness and gentleness toward friends and family may change to aggressiveness on the playing field.

awkward and shy; if we think a situation is dangerous, we may be very cold and unfriendly. Even if we generally define ourselves as competitive, we may relax with friends and may not bother to compete in situations we don't care about. An adult who is generally competitive may have no desire to compete with children playing hopscotch. Even the most dependent person in a group will occasionally be assertive, persuading friends to see a particular movie or attend a particular sporting event. The structure of the group we are interacting with — its size and the age, sex, power, and prestige of its members — as well as the role we play in the group influence our behavior and the behavior of the other group members.

The key process of self is *interpretation,* how we interpret ourselves and others. We do not notice everything around us; we focus our attention on the things we consider meaningful or on only one idea. When we are thinking about what we will write on an exam or what we will say in a job interview, we may notice little else. We are constantly interpreting our environment, and these interpretations shape how we act.

Defining the Situation

To determine how to act, we must be able to define the situation we are involved in. Is the situation important? We act differently when we collide with a student in the hallway than when we collide with our professor. These people are likely to have different expectations of how we should act. In a given situation, should we define ourselves as a serious, hard-working student or a wise-cracking friend? Our answers to questions such as these determine how we act and how we expect others to act.

Research has shown that we do form opinions about others on the basis of what we expect of them, which may be most obvious when we consider gender-role expectations. Studies in this area show how extensively we rely on our expectations of others in making evaluations of them.

In one series of investigations about college student expectations of appropriate gender-role behavior (Rosenkrantz et al., 1968; Broverman et al., 1972), students were asked to rate men and women on certain characteristics. Men were typically rated high on such characteristics as aggressiveness, objectivity, independence, competitiveness, ambition, activeness, dominance, and self-confidence. Women were described as gentle, sensitive, emotional, expressive, neat, tactful, passive, dependent, and submissive.

College students often use these stereotypes when they evaluate professors and tend to praise or criticize them in accordance with their gender-role expectations. Male professors are praised more often for being stimulating, dynamic, demanding, respected, and effective, whereas female professors are praised for being kind, sensitive, and bright. Male professors are criticized for being sarcastic, arrogant, abrasive, pompous, obnoxious, egotistical, or overbearing. Female professors are criticized as unorganized, ineffective, confused, unfocused, or as having problems relating to the students (*Georgetown Law Weekly*, 1981).

The fact that students may define interactions with professors on the basis of gender may lead them to value their opinions differently. Suppose a student has similar disagreements with two professors, one male and one female. They may leave her feeling very differently. In the interaction with the woman professor, she may feel that the professor was overreacting or approaching the issue too emotionally. The same interaction with a male professor is likely to leave the student feeling that she is the one who was wrong. Situations such as this result from a student's defining male professors as more intellectual than female professors.

Our definitions of situations are influenced in ways other than evaluating others, of course. We also define situations in terms of what we think social norms expect of us. If we believe that we must be individuals who are worth attention, we will often try to draw attention to ourselves in a conversation. The following conversation, taken from a study by Derber (1979), demonstrates how two friends talk to each other on the basis of this definition of the situation. In this conversation, each is trying to get the other's attention. When they respond to each other, they use their response to shift attention to themselves.

JOHN: I've got such a huge appetite.

BILL: I couldn't eat a thing.

JOHN: My father would take me every two weeks to a game and I spent every minute looking forward to it.

BILL: I remember the first game my father took me to. I made so much noise that he didn't want to take me anymore. (p. 27)

Notice how often the word "I" is used in American conversations. Try carrying on a conversation without using the word "I" or any other word that refers to the self: "me," "my," "mine," "myself," "we," "us," "our," or "ourselves." In a very competitive society such as ours, we often feel the need to draw attention to ourselves.

Conforming to Expectations

To how great an extent do we conform to the expectations of others? This question is not easy to answer because it depends on how we define the situation and the other people involved in it. Researchers have examined the extent to which individuals are influenced by others whom they respect. In one study, Asch (1955) showed groups of college students two cards, one with one line on it, the other with three lines (see Figure 6-1). One of the lines on the three-line card matched the length of the single line on the other card. The others were obviously of a different length. In each group, all the students except one were instructed to name a wrong line as the matching line. The "naive" subject, upon hearing the other students name two lines that were obviously not the same length, could either agree with them or act independently and disagree with them.

In 36.8 percent of the trials, the subjects went along with the majority. Some of these subjects believed that the majority must be right, that they were seeing something wrong. Others assumed they hadn't understood the instructions, or went along with the majority rather than cause disagreement in the group.

Almost all of those who did not go along with the group felt very uncomfortable. Rather than expecting the group to justify its behavior, they tried to justify their own behavior. They thought they were seeing something wrong or had misunderstood instructions. Convinced that they could not agree with the group, they felt dis-

Figure 6-1
Subjects were shown two cards. One bore a standard line. The other bore three lines, one of which was the same length as the standard. The subjects were asked to choose this line.

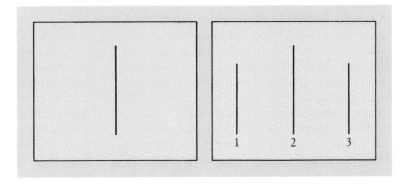

turbed, puzzled, separated, like outcasts. The fact that they could not understand the group's behavior affected their own behavior.

In another experiment, Milgram (1963) asked subjects to administer increasingly severe electric shocks to a victim in another room. The victim was a confederate of the experimenter and did not actually receive shocks, but he would pound and kick on the wall as the severity of the "shocks" increased. The procedure caused extreme nervous tension in some subjects — sweating, trembling, stuttering, nervous laughter, and even uncontrollable laughing seizures. Other subjects remained calm throughout. Of the forty subjects, twenty-six obeyed the orders of the experimenter and administered the most potent shock on the generator, which was labeled 450 volts, two steps beyond the designation: "Danger: Severe Shock."

Milgram concluded that the subjects willingly gave shocks to a victim more because of their definition of the situation they found themselves in than because they were cruel. The subjects defined the situation as a respectable experiment, in which the experimenter was a legitimate researcher who knew what should be done, and they defined their own role as a volunteer who had agreed to cooperate in the experiment. These definitions of the situation, the experimenter, and the self had to change before the subjects could refuse to cooperate.

Before these experiments were conducted, psychiatrists did not believe that people would follow the instructions of the experimenter. As it turned out, many subjects did follow the instructions but then felt terrible about what they had done and required help to overcome their feelings. We now realize that any type of experiment that encourages people to do what they would not do in other situations is unethical.

David Riesman (1953) has gathered evidence that we have become a society that puts more emphasis on the expectations of others. In the nineteenth century, people were taught to be "inner directed," to find their own direction in the world. Those who worked on their own small farm, ran a family store, or started their own small businesses were dependent on their own initiative to succeed. In the twentieth century, as more people live in urban areas and work in large corporations, they are becoming "other directed." They have to get along with others, to cooperate, to take instructions, and to be aware of others' expectations. Just as nineteenth-century people learned to act independently, we are learning to consider the expectations of others.

The Dramaturgical Approach

To explain the complexity of social interaction, Goffman (1959) compared interaction to a drama on stage — a comparison known as the *dramaturgical approach*. Every act involves interaction, whether the audience involves other people or just the self. We present ourselves so that our audience will define us as we wish to be defined. We prepare our presentation backstage in the privacy of our rooms when we shower, wash our hair, and use deodorant — in our society, cleanliness and a lack of odor are important factors. Complexions must be smooth, so men shave, women put on makeup, and adolescents use cosmetics to cover up acne. Suitable clothing is selected so that we can present ourselves formally in formal situations and casually in casual situations. We want to present ourselves so that others will interpret our role accurately.

The Presentation of Self

After we have prepared ourselves backstage, we present ourselves onstage, and the setting is very important. A formal setting such as a church, a more informal setting such as a classroom, and a casual setting such as the arena where a basketball game is being held require very different presentations. In some settings, one can race for a front row seat, talk loudly, wave to friends, and eat or drink. In other settings, these behaviors would be quite inappropriate.

The church setting requires a different self-presentation than the setting of a sporting event. In church people are more formally dressed, quieter, reverent, and attentive. The same people at a sporting event will dress casually, laugh, talk, look around, and make more noise. Much of our behavior is shaped by the particular setting we are in.

A woman in a bar presents herself as casual and friendly, giving cues with her appearance. The athletic attire and the beer cup give the impression that she has time to relax; the half smile and the turn of the eyes give the impression that she is ready to turn her full attention to her companion. Her interpretation of the situation may not, however, coincide with her presentation of self. We don't know what she is thinking.

Some students present themselves in the classroom very carefully in an effort to show the acceptable amount of interest. They do not arrive too early lest they appear too eager to other students, but they do not wish to be late because they may irritate the professor. Most students prefer not to sit in the front row since that might also indicate overeagerness. They prefer to sit toward the back of the room, but not so far back that they appear disinterested. They also avoid participating too eagerly in classroom discussions, but on the other hand they try to avoid sleeping soundly. Most present themselves as showing a moderate amount of interest in the classroom.

The way we present ourselves — the *presentation of self* — gives other people cues about the type of interaction we expect. In formal situations, we usually greet friends with a handshake or a remark, whereas in informal situations we may greet friends with a hug or a kiss. If we are with friends, we talk and laugh, but on a bus or in an elevator we do not speak to strangers and keep a social distance even when space is crowded and we cannot keep physically distant. Psychologists refer to our manner of presentation as *body language*. We give cues about ourselves in the way we present and use our bodies in interaction. This topic will be discussed further in the section on nonverbal communication later in this chapter.

In illustrating the dramaturgical approach, Goffman described a character called Preedy as he presented himself on a beach on the Riviera. Preedy very consciously tried to make an impression on the people around him. It was his first day on vacation and he knew no one. He wanted to meet some people, but he didn't want to appear too lonely or too eager, so he presented himself as perfectly content in his solitary state.

The following excerpt from Goffman (1959) describes Preedy's behavior:

> If by chance a ball was thrown his way, he looked surprised; then let a smile of amusement lighten his face (Kindly Preedy), looked round dazed to see that there *were* people on the beach, tossed it back with a smile to himself and not a smile *at* the people, and then resumed carelessly his nonchalant survey of space.
>
> But it was time to institute a little parade, the parade of the Ideal Preedy. By devious handlings he gave any who wanted to look a chance to see the title of his book — a Spanish translation of Homer, classic thus, but not daring, cosmopolitan too — and then gathered together his beach-wrap and bag into a neat sand-resistant pile (Methodical and Sensible Preedy), rose slowly to stretch at ease his huge frame (Big-Cat Preedy), and tossed aside his sandals (Carefree Preedy, after all).
>
> The marriage of Preedy and the sea! There were alternative rituals. The first involved the stroll that turns into a run and a dive straight into the water, thereafter smoothing into a strong splashless crawl towards the horizon. But of

Appearance and Attraction

The aphorism that "beauty is only skin deep" no doubt provides psychological comfort to some persons. However, research evidence suggests, to the contrary, that physical attractiveness has a definitive effect on our self-images and on the quality of our social relationships. Among the findings of several studies on body image and physical appearance, the following are particularly worth noting:

1. Physical appearance is strongly related to the likelihood of attracting a mate and this is most especially true for women in American society. (Walster et al., 1966; Berscheid et al., 1971; Elder, 1969)

2. Persons who view themselves as unattractive have more difficulty establishing relationships with others, and particularly persons of the opposite sex. (Walster et al., 1966; Brislin, 1968)

3. Men and women of equal levels of physical attractiveness (and so equal levels of "social desirability") tend to pair off in courtship and marriage. (Silverman, 1971; Murstein, 1971; Berscheid et al., 1973)

4. All other things being equal, one's chances for economic and occupational success is strongly related to one's physical attractiveness. (Feldman, 1975)

5. Persons who are dissatisfied with the level of their own physical attractiveness report themselves as generally less happy than persons satisfied with their body image. (Berscheid et al., 1973)

6. Overall, women show greater dissatisfaction with their bodies than men. (Calden et al., 1959; Berscheid et al., 1973)

7. The more physically attractive persons are judged to be, the more they are perceived as intelligent, personable and likeable. (Miller, 1970)

SOURCE: Karp, David A. and William C. Yoels, *Symbols, Selves, and Society. Understanding Interaction*, p. 63. Copyright © 1979 by David A. Karp and William C. Yoels. Reprinted by permission of Harper & Row, Publishers, Inc., New York.

---

course not really to the horizon. Quite suddenly he would turn on to his back and thrash great white splashes with his legs, somehow thus showing that he could have swum further had he wanted to, and then would stand up a quarter out of water for all to see who it was.

The alternative course was simpler, it avoided the cold-water shock and it avoided the risk of appearing too high-spirited. The point was to appear to be so used to the sea, the Mediterranean, and this particular beach, that one might as well be in the sea as out of it. It involved a slow stroll down and into the edge of the water — not even noticing his toes were wet, land and water all the same to *him!* — with his eyes up at the sky gravely surveying portents, invisible to others, of the weather (Local Fisherman Preedy). (p. 5)

Notice how much Preedy could tell about himself without saying a word. Whether anyone

enters the water in as calculated a manner as Preedy is questionable, but whoever watches someone like Preedy will form an opinion of him from his presentation. Likewise we would form an opinion of some other man after watching him walk on the beach. His age, weight, posture, muscle size, suntan, and facial expression will lead us to suppose that he is a newcomer, a beachcomber, athletic, friendly, lonely, happy, or sad. If we interact with him, we would enter the interaction with a preconceived set of expectations about his behavior. Manner and appearance shape interaction in very important ways.

Maintaining the Self

Once we have presented ourselves in a particular role and have begun to interact, we must maintain our presentation. In class, students cannot begin to shake hands with fellow students, wander around the room, or write on the blackboard. It would not only disrupt the class, it would spoil the presentation of the student, who would be considered disruptive, strange, or worse. If students or others want to maintain the definitions others have of them, they must maintain a performance in accord with the definition.

Sometimes we inadvertently give the impression that we are not maintaining our performance. Since we don't want others to develop expectations about us that we are not prepared to meet (Scott and Lyman, 1968), we try to account for any behavior that does not match our presentation. If we are late and want to avoid giving the impression that we are always late, we make excuses: "I am usually very prompt, but my car ran out of gas," or "I thought the meeting was at eight o'clock, not seven o'clock." We may be more fatalistic and say, "I tried to arrive on time, but everyone in my family is late. It's our nature." Or we may blame someone else and say, "The bus was late." On the other hand, we may try to justify our lateness by saying, "These meetings never start on time" or "It doesn't matter. No harm done." We expect others to see us not as irresponsible and inconsiderate but as prompt and considerate, in spite of our lateness, and others often support our claims about ourselves and ignore the contradictory presentation.

We also try to maintain our presentations by *disclaimers,* that is, disclaiming a role even while we are acting in that role. "I usually don't drink, but this punch is so good" disclaims the role of drinker. "I'm not prejudiced, but . . ." followed by a racist remark or "I'm no expert, but . . ." followed by a remark only an expert could make are phrases that tell the audience that the self is not what it appears to be.

Often the audience accepts a person's accounts or disclaimers and the interaction proceeds smoothly, but sometimes the drama does not work out so well. We may present ourselves in the role of someone who knows how to act in social situations but not live up to those claims. We may fall down a flight of stairs as we make our grand entrance. We may stand up at a meeting to give a class report, claiming to be an expert, but our trembling hands and factual errors will not support these claims. A speaker and those in the audience may attempt to ignore the errors, but at some point the speaker may get too flustered to continue the pretense of living up to the role or become embarrassed and laugh, cry, faint, or blush. When a group can no longer support an individual's claims, the whole group may become embarrassed or angry (Goffman, 1967).

Implicit in interactions is the assumption that presentations will be maintained. Each person agrees to maintain the self and to support the presentations of others. If people's presentations are not supported by the people themselves or by others, it may be followed by an emotional response. In some situations, we may become embarrassed, and if our presentation is ridiculed we may get angry. If someone seems to fill a person's image of the ideal romantic love, we may fall in love with that individual. If the person is cruel or unfaithful or behaves in some other way that tarnishes our image of him or her, we may grow angry and eventually fall out of love.

Our feelings about ourselves and others are learned (Hochschild, 1975). Just as we learn self-esteem by understanding how others evaluate us, we learn when to be embarrassed, when to be angry, when to fall in love and with what type of person. If we are angry at someone who deserves our respect, we feel guilty about our own behavior. If we love someone whom others define as entirely inappropriate, we become confused. Again, we have expectations about maintaining performances, both our own and others, and we respond emotionally when these expectations are not met.

Humans have very complex minds, of course. People learn a varied set of meanings during their lives, and they interpret each situation on the basis of their own biography and their own definition of the situation. They may be very involved in their presentations, or they may separate their selves from the particular roles they are playing and keep a certain amount of *role-distance*, as Goffman (1961) terms it. While children thoroughly enjoy the merry-go-round in an amusement park, for example, adults sit on the horse looking bored or perhaps feeling somewhat foolish. They cannot get totally involved in the act of riding a horse. How a person presents self and maintains interaction depends on his or her unique interpretation of self, others, and the situation. It is this ability to interpret that makes interaction such a varied, interesting, and challenging area of study.

Nonverbal Behavior

In Goffman's dramaturgical approach it is evident that nonverbal behavior is an important aspect of how we present ourselves to others. Nonverbal behavior includes facial expressions, gestures, and how close we stand to one another when we interact. Nonverbal cues can make a difference in how we feel about an interaction. If, for example, your professor sat back in his chair with his arms folded across his chest and his legs crossed, you might feel that he was not at all open to the idea you were presenting.

Some types of body language, specifically facial expressions, are universally understood — a smile has the same meaning throughout the world — but most types of body language are culture specific. LaBarre (1974), an anthropologist, noted that in many cultures a rocking of the head up and down does not mean "yes" as it does in our culture. The Abyssinians nod "yes" by throwing the head back and raising their eyebrows, and they say "no" by jerking the head toward the right shoulder. The Maori say "yes" by raising the head and chin, but Sicilians mean "no" when they do the very same thing. The Ainu of Northern Japan use their hands to gesture "yes" and "no." They gracefully raise both hands up, palms up, when they wish to agree, but the right hand passed back and forth in front of themselves means they disagree.

Two men in Florence, Italy, carry on a conversation. We might assume from the closeness of the people, and one man's arm blocking the movement of the other, that these men are having an argument. However, Italians typically require much less personal space than Americans.

The way people greet strangers also varies in different societies. In the United States we shake hands. The Eskimos welcome strangers by lightly hitting them on the head or shoulders with a fist. A Polynesian man greets another man by rubbing him on the back. Amazon men slap one another on the back, and in Borneo men clasp hands, raise them, and then kiss each other on the back of their raised hands.

Edward T. Hall, in his book *The Silent Language* (1959), noted that the use of personal space — how close we stand to each other — differs from culture to culture. In the United States, distances between individuals vary according to their relationship. Generally, the more intimate the relationship, the closer people stand to each other.

This type of personal space can also be manipulated to display power. In order to clearly delineate their position of authority, employers might stand a little closer to a new employee than is usually accepted in a formal situation. By moving into a less formal distance, they throw the new employee off balance and assert their power. They must be careful not to stand too close, however, since it might be misinterpreted as flirtation. In other countries this manipulation of personal space might be meaningless.

In Latin America people normally stand much closer to each other to carry on a normal conversation. An American may feel uncomfortable at this distance, as if the Latin American were breathing down his or her neck. If the

Americans appear to require a great deal of personal space. Even while having a casual drink at a bar, and even while chatting with each other, these people keep their distance. It is no wonder that in other societies the distance shown here might be considered very unfriendly.

American steps back to a more comfortable distance, the Latin American may interpret this as an unfriendly gesture.

We often want to assume that nonverbal language is universal, that an individual who has a strong handshake is either self-assured or perhaps dominating and controlling, or someone with a weak handshake is a weak person, or perhaps a gentle person. We may assume that people who look us straight in the eye are self-confident or bold and that those who look away are either demure or sneaky. Whatever our interpretation of these nonverbal gestures, we must remember that they are culturally learned and that the meaning we give to the gesture of another person may not, in fact, be the meaning that person intends to give us.

Ethnomethodology

One of the interaction perspectives covered in this chapter, ethnomethodology is the most recently developed as well as the most misunderstood. In sociology, this perspective is most closely identified with Harold Garfinkel (1967), who questioned existing theories by asking how sociologists and people in everyday life create and sustain the presumption that the social world is orderly and patterned, the presumption that people share meanings. This approach, rather than focusing on patterns themselves, draws attention to how humans construct, maintain, and change the *appearance* of an orderly and patterned social world. Ethnomethodology, then, is concerned with the methods people commonly use in everyday life to create a sense of order.

According to ethnomethodologists, all common social interactions are governed by certain "folk" rules, which involve a wide variety of background assumptions and implicit expectations that people have about one another. These assumptions and understandings are taken so much for

People line up for a bus in London, following unwritten rules that maintain order. The rules in London are different from those in cities of the United States, where bus riders cluster around the door. We learn the rules of our society for even such small matters and must learn new rules if we are to fit smoothly into another society. Americans would be considered pushy in London if they clustered at the door.

granted they are rarely noticed — until they are disrupted. In an experiment reported by Garfinkel (1967) students were asked to challenge every statement made in conversation with selected subjects. The following is a typical exchange:

SUBJECT: I had a flat tire.
EXPERIMENTER: What do you mean, you had a flat tire?
SUBJECT: (Appears momentarily stunned and then replies in a hostile manner) What do you mean, "What do you mean?" A flat tire is a flat tire. That is what I meant. Nothing special. What a crazy question. (p. 42)

In this example, the experimenter was apparently violating an implicit rule for this type of social interaction, a rule that certain types of common expressions should not be challenged. The results were a hostile subject and a negative response: "What a crazy question." The point is that all interaction is based on hidden assumptions and understandings that should be accepted without question. If someone says to you, "How do you do?" try responding with "What do you mean, 'how do you do?'" The result is likely to be frustration, puzzlement, anger, and an end to the conversation. Why? Because we get upset when others refuse to accept the underlying assumptions we supposedly share.

SOCIOLOGISTS AT WORK
Clinical Sociology and Personal Change

Roger A. Straus is a clinical sociologist. He made that career choice while a graduate student at the University of California at Davis. "I became increasingly committed to the principle that all our theories, concepts, and knowledge, if they are truly worth anything, can be applied to resolving problems in the real world. I came to feel that the test of valid theory and knowledge was in its ability to be brought back into the real world usefully. At the time, however, I had no interest in working for the state or federal government or for a consulting firm. My commitment was to the development and practice of sociologically grounded interventions to serve people and their groups. There was no such institutionalized role. Even now there is none."

What Straus did, therefore, was to create his own role. He set up a private practice as a clinical sociologist. "My goals in turning to clinical practice," he explains, "involved an extension of my conventionally sociological interests. I wanted to discover realistic theory through clinical data and feedback from theoretically guided interventions, and I wanted to do something useful with sociological perspective and methods." As an undergraduate and later as a graduate student he had done research on the nature of religious conversion and the function of new religious movements. He concluded that such groups were successful not because they brainwash or process recruits "like pigs being converted into so much bacon," but because they hold out to potential recruits what he calls "proprietary technologies for personal transformation" — that is, methods, prac-

Ethnomethodologists try to discover these processes and rules that people take for granted without challenging since they are significant not just in face-to-face encounters but in social organizations as well.

Ethnomethodologists have attempted to show how hospitals, police departments, courts, suicide prevention centers, and other agencies develop special procedures for handling their clients. These and similar organizations have a tendency to fit clients and events into patterns and categories that complement the ongoing action of the agency. Cicourel (1968), for example, noted that agencies created to process juvenile delinquents routinely based their judgments on conversations with the delinquent, the parents, the arresting officer, the counselor, and the judge. This procedure was taken for granted; the information gathered was used in official reports, and the delinquents were then classified into the categories devised by the agency. Thus the classification of delinquency depended less on the acts of the delinquent than on the definitions that arose from the procedures and interactions used in the agency. Yet the rules, the procedures, and agreed-upon assumptions of the agency had not been questioned or analyzed.

The rules we follow in personal interactions and organizations may be so obvious that they are viewed as insignificant, but they do affect what

tices, or answers that only they claim to offer. Outsiders who are seeking to change or improve their lives may then choose (or be persuaded) to become involved with one of these groups in order to realize those promises for themselves.

"Following up this line led me to the phenomenon of hypnosis," Straus says. "I found myself getting involved in working with hypnosis at the same time that I was conducting research into the nature of hypnosis and personal change processes generally. I operated within the context of a hypnosis practitioner — although this was quickly transformed into a much wider role." One application was weight loss counseling. Straus would focus on the social origins of weight problems in America. "I'd typically begin by discussing how we are trained as children to use food to reward ourselves, to compensate for difficulties or illness, and to manage stress and make ourselves feel better, generally." The client would then be guided to replace such definitions with new ones facilitating the desired self-control.

After three years of private practice, Straus closed his office and shifted gears. "I had found out what I wanted to learn," he says. "Since 1980 I have directed my efforts at writing for the general public and working with community groups. In both cases, my aim has been to do clinical sociology on a wider scale than would be possible in a conventional practice." He has had one book published (*Strategic Self-Hypnosis,* 1981) and is at work on a second, a self-help book on weight control. He has organized the Center for Clinical Sociology, which serves as a resource center for the clinical sociology movement. And he has expanded his clinical activities to the areas of community mental health and politics. "My role is a logical extension of traditional sociology to interventions designed to empower individuals and their groups to deal with the social systems, problems, and dynamics affecting their lives," he says. "Conventional sociology has almost invariably stopped at seeking to define the ways social context influences, shapes, and constrains human beings. That's only half the story. Clinical sociology is an extension of the educational function, but we must extend our concept of education to embrace pragmatic training — showing people how to translate theory and concept and perspective into action."

happens. Ethnomethodologists contend that the essence of interaction and society itself can be captured by focusing on the methods people use to construct, maintain, or change the appearance of an orderly and connected social world.

The Construction of Reality

When sociologists study the details of verbal and nonverbal social interaction — the presentation of self, role taking, maintaining presentations, the meanings people give to objects, and the rules with which they order their lives — they sometimes seem to have moved a long way from the study of society. Their work is clearly sociological, however, because they are investigating how people construct an orderly society. It is by giving meanings to people and things that we are able to develop a *construction of reality* (Berger and Luckman, 1966).

When we assign a meaning to something and act in accordance with that meaning, we behave in a predictable way. Most of us, for example, have learned certain meanings about the United States, and in accord with these meanings we criticize our country at election time and boast about it on the Fourth of July. Similarly, we have learned the meaning of work, and we arrive at work on time and expect to be paid for our efforts. We also interact with our families on the basis of the meanings we attach to them. We maintain an orderly society by learning the social meanings of country, work, family, and other social systems and acting according to these meanings.

People commonly treat the meanings they give to people and things as objective facts. Sociologists call this process *reification*. Is it a fact that our country is the best in the world, or is this the meaning we give to it? Is it a fact that work is honorable, or is this the meaning we give to it?

People in other societies give different meanings to country, work, and other social entities, which suggests that meanings are not based on fact. When we attribute a meaning to something and act in accordance with this meaning, however, we treat it as if it actually were a fact.

To give an everyday example, Saturday night has a different meaning than other evenings. It is a night to be with friends, to go to parties, relax, and have fun. It might be pleasant to work in the library or read in one's own room on other evenings, but on Saturday night the same activities might indicate rejection or lack of friends. Many people struggle with a loneliness on Saturday nights that did not affect them on other nights of the week even though Saturday is actually no different from any other night. The sun sets in the same way, and the moon, stars, animals, and plants do as they always do at night, but people in our culture, because they have given a particular meaning to Saturday night, change their behavior, their mood, and their feelings about themselves on Saturday night.

Some people do not share the generally accepted meanings of the rest of society. If they carry this to an extreme, if they don't share our meanings of country, work, and family, they may refuse to work, live in a family, or even have a home. In other words, they may not maintain the social order. The power of our shared meanings is such, however, that rather than questioning our meanings, we label these people deviant, although a little deviance might be a good thing if it allows us to realize that social meanings are not objective facts. Intelligent people can suspend belief in the social meanings, ask if these meanings are facts, and redefine them when they are destructive rather than constructive. An understanding of how we learn meanings and how they shape our behavior can be very liberating, because it permits us to change meanings, redefine situations, and act in ways that will better meet our own goals.

Summary

Sociologists study social interaction in order to better understand the relationship between individuals and society. Our ability to act socially and build culture is based on our ability to use symbols, and language is our most important symbol system. Our symbols allow us to share meanings with one another, to think about the past and the future, and to work cooperatively. Animals cannot do these things because they lack the physical capacity to create a variety of sounds and the cognitive ability to think abstractly. Being able to interact symbolically makes humans unique among all forms of animal life.

Through socialization and the use of symbols, a person develops a social self, a self-image based on previous experiences and interaction. People also develop images of themselves in various situations, a situational self, and their evaluation of their self-image is their self-esteem. Because a person's self-image, self-esteem, and behavior vary from situation to situation, the self is understood better as a process of interpretation rather than as a fixed collection of traits.

When the self interacts, it interprets through role taking, how others will act in a given situation. Many studies have shown that we have certain expectations of how males and females will act, and we tend to evaluate their performance on the basis of our expectations. We also adjust our behavior to meet our own expectations and those of others. We may dominate a conversation when we think we deserve attention, or we may ignore others if we decide they do not merit attention. Interaction would be impossible if we did not assume roles and adjust our behavior to meet expectations.

Research has shown that people sometimes change their behavior to cooperate with a group, even when it involves denying one's perceptions. In the Milgram studies, some people were willing to give electric shocks to a victim because they defined the situation as a respectable experiment and agreed to cooperate. Over the past century, Americans have become more willing to conform to the expectations of others.

Erving Goffman compared our everyday interactions to dramas enacted on stage. The setting, our appearance, and our manner, including our body language, convey to the audience the role we wish to play. We must maintain our presentation throughout the interaction or else account for behavior not in accord with our presentation by using excuses or justifications. We also disclaim roles that we might appear to be playing but do not want to play. If we cannot maintain our presentation, we may become embarrassed or angry or otherwise respond emotionally, depending on our definition of the situation.

Ethnomethodologists, rather than assuming that we share meanings when we interact, try to understand the social rules we use to maintain the assumptions that the world is orderly and that others share our meanings. Their insights and research have shown that the assumptions we take for granted may distort our judgment about what is really happening in a situation. We construct a social reality by the meanings we give to objects, and then we reify these meanings — we assume that our meanings are fact. Anyone who does not share these meanings is suspected of not being in touch with reality, and we are more apt to label these people as deviant than we are to question our own meanings.

Key Terms

construction of reality
disclaimers
dramaturgical approach
ethnomethodology
interpretation

presentation of self
reification
self-esteem
self-image
symbolic interaction

Suggested Readings

Derber, Charles. **The Pursuit of Attention. Power and Individualism in Everyday Life.** *Cambridge, Mass. Schenkman, 1979.* An important book, delightful to read, and full of insights into how society shapes individual conversations.

Goffman, Erving. **The Presentation of Self in Everyday Life.** *Garden City, N.Y.: Doubleday, 1959.* This book describes the dramaturgical approach to the study of social interaction and analyzes interaction in great detail.

Goffman, Erving. **Stigma.** *Englewood Cliffs, N.J.: Prentice-Hall, 1963.* This book describes how those who are different — the physically deformed, drug addicts, prostitutes, ugly people, and others — constantly socialize others and are socialized themselves as they interact.

Hewitt, John P. **Self and Society: A Symbolic Interactionist Social Psychology,** *2nd ed. Boston: Allyn & Bacon, 1979.* This very readable text discusses symbolic interaction and expands on some of the topics discussed in this chapter.

Komarovsky, Mirra. **Dilemmas of Masculinity: A Study of College Youth.** *New York: Norton, 1976.* Excellent research by a sociologist on the effects of changing sex roles on college men.

Schur, Edwin. **The Awareness Trap.** *New York: McGraw-Hill, 1976.* Schur convincingly argues that we cannot change our emotional lives, the way we feel about ourselves, by analyzing the self alone but that we must understand our place in society and how society has shaped our behavior.

Chapter 7
Deviance and Social Control

There is nothing either good or bad, but thinking makes it so.

— William Shakespeare

Deviance is universal. It exists in all societies, wherever people interact and live in groups. It is found in complex, industrialized, urban areas as well as in tribal, folk, and agrarian regions. Although it is sometimes claimed that people in certain societies cooperate in complete harmony and peace, anthropologists claim that no society or culture, large or small, rural or urban, has complete behavioral conformity and a total absence of deviance.

What Is Deviance?

The term *deviance* means different things to different people. The definition we use influences our explanations of its causes and our attempts to control it. Does deviance reside in the individual? Is it a particular type of act or behavior? Is it defined socially? Are certain groups immune from being labeled deviants? Our answers to questions such as these will influence how we analyze deviance and whether we ultimately understand it.

Our definition of deviance will be concerned with the extent of variation, or deviance, from a set of norms or shared social expectations. It involves a social audience that defines certain people and behaviors as going beyond the tolerance limits of social norms. Socials norms, rules, and expectations about appropriate and inappropriate behavior exist in all societies. People everywhere have social controls to enforce the rules and punish those who do not conform.

Norms rarely state exactly which behaviors are acceptable and which are unacceptable, and universal adherence to them is unknown. All societies permit variations in the behavior demanded by the norms. Where variations are possible, people will test their range, and some

In the U.S., prostitution is viewed as deviant behavior, but in Amsterdam (above), Hamburg, and other cities in Europe, prostitutes can operate openly in certain areas. This view of prostitution as nondeviant may be due to its positive functions: income for women, sexual gratification for men, a safety valve for marriages, and an impersonal, commitment-free relationship.

will inevitably exceed the boundaries of permissible and approved behavior. Deviance consists of these norm violations; the norm violators are the deviants. People's perceptions of deviance rarely correspond to its reality, however, as we will see in the following disscusion of certain traditional views of deviance and deviants.

Traditional Views of Deviance and Deviants

There are many approaches to the study of deviance. Different explanations focus variously on people, behavior, or the social context of people and behavior. Other theories describe the socialization of deviancy and its causes, support, and transmission. In addition, theorists have described how such social conditions as conflict, anomie, and labeling contribute to deviance and how it is formally and informally controlled. As you might guess, there are also biological, psychological, and sociological theories, to say nothing of the explanations brought forth by lawyers, the clergy, and others who counsel, treat, punish, or work with those defined as deviant. Four of the more common traditional views of deviance are discussed below.

The Absolutist View

Until the middle of this century, most social scientists assumed that social rules were clear and obvious to most members of society. Certain behaviors were considered deviant regardless of the social context in which they occurred. This perspective, known as the *absolutist view*, was based on the assumption that everyone agreed on certain norms and that certain behaviors are clearly deviant and others are clearly not. Thus prostitution, homosexuality, and the use of drugs might be assumed to be deviant at all times and in all cultures, and chastity, heterosexuality, and abstinence from drugs might be regarded as nonde-

Widespread Misconceptions About Certain Deviant Behaviors

Most persons defined as "mentally ill" have hereditary defects.

Abortion is always a dangerous operation (this was widely believed prior to the recent "legalization" rulings and the attendant spread of more accurate information; it probably still is the predominant belief in certain restricted social circles).

Most "child molesters" are homosexuals.

People who smoke marijuana run a high risk of becoming heroin addicts.

Nudists are sex-obsessed voyeurs ("peepers").

All persons diagnosed as "legally blind" are totally unable to see.

Lesbians (female homosexuals) regard themselves as men and display behavior patterns similar to those of men.

Corporate "price-fixers" do not really understand that price-fixing is against the law.

Beginning drinking while young is the main cause of alcoholism.

Prisons and mental hospitals are so comfortable today that they are no longer effective.

SOURCE: Edwin M. Schur, *Interpreting Deviance: A Sociological Introduction*, p. 31. Copyright © 1979 by Edwin M. Schur. Reprinted by permission of Harper & Row, Publishers, Inc.

---

viant. This view, however, fails to take into account variations in social norms and people's perceptions of them. In some cultures, homosexuality, certain types of prostitution, and the use of drugs are considered perfectly acceptable. The absolutist perspective has been rejected by most sociologists, but many laymen continue to assess deviance in these terms.

The Moral View

A second view, *the moral view*, is that deviance is *immoral and antisocial*. As in the absolutist perspective, certain behaviors are regarded as being deviant in all situations, but it is also as-

sumed that deviance is bad or evil and that people who commit deviant acts lack morals and are depraved and antisocial. Like the absolutist, the moralist assumes that there are just two kinds of people and two kinds of behavior: the moral nondeviant and the immoral deviant. Deviant people are regarded as inherently different from others, that is, deviant by nature. They are considered innately antisocial and evil, and their behavior is believed harmful to others and to society. Today, many groups or categories of people in the United States are viewed as inherently deviant. Many people define Iranian students, homosexuals, and political liberals as innately evil and their behavior as antisocial and harmful to U.S. interests. Likewise, unwed mothers and marijuana smokers are sometimes viewed as different from others and lacking in moral judgment and moral behavior.

This view has also been rejected by social scientists. As we shall discuss later in this chapter, deviance is not inherent in persons or in acts. Even if it were, it is not necessarily antisocial, evil, or immoral. In fact, deviance has positive functions and desirable consequences for society, which will also be discussed later.

The Medical and Social Pathological Views

A third approach to deviance applies a *medical view* to behavior and society. Deviance is assumed to be essentially pathological, evidence that a society is unhealthy. Just as healthy humans function efficiently without pain or discomfort, healthy societies are thought to function smoothly without problems. The prevalence of child abuse, rape, robbery, mental disorders, and alcoholism are thought to indicate that a society has a sickness. This perspective closely parallels the *social pathological view* of the early 1900s.

Like the moral view, the medical view is absolutist. It assumes that people are either deviant or not deviant − there is no grey area − but this polarity is expressed in terms of health or illness. Today, it is not uncommon to hear references to a "sick" society, but few people agree on how to cure the sickness or on what constitutes a healthy society. Even among individuals, psychiatrists and doctors often have trouble distinguishing who is healthy and who is not.

The Statistical View

A fourth view of deviance relies on statistics. Any behavior that is atypical, that varies from the average or mode, is considered deviant. This view is not absolutist: deviance is assumed to be a variable characteristic that increases the further a behavior is removed from the average. Deviants are viewed not as sick people, as in the medical view, but simply as being different. According to the *statistical view*, any variation from a statistical norm is deviant. Thus a person who is left-handed, who has red hair, or who belongs to a minority group is defined as a deviant. (See Table 7-1 for additional examples.) Everyone fails to conform to the average in some respect, however, so according to this definition, we are all deviants.

Is this little girl deviant? The answer is yes, if "deviant" means atypical, in the minority, or different from the average. Children under age five comprise only about 7 percent of the total U.S. population and female children under five comprise only 3.5 percent of the total U.S. population.

Table 7-1

Statistical deviants in the United States, based on variation from the median or the most common characteristic, 1980

CHARACTERISTIC	MEDIAN OR MOST COMMON	STATISTICAL DEVIANTS, PERCENT	
1. Age	Median = 30.0	Under age 5	7.2
		Age 65 and over	11.3
2. Years school completed	Median = 12.5	Less than 5 years	3.4
		4 years or more of college	17.0
3. Marital Status	Married 65.7%	Single	20.1
		Widowed and divorced	14.2
4. Persons in household	1–3 = 71.3%	6 or more	5.4
5. Household income (1979)	Median = $16,553	Less than $5,000	13.2
		More than $35,000	12.4

SOURCE: U.S. Bureau of the Census, *Statistical Abstract of the United States: 1981* (102nd ed.), Washington, D.C., 1981. (1) No. 29, p. 26; (2) No. 232, p. 142; (3) No. 46, p. 37; (4) No. 65, p. 46; (5) No. 720, p. 432.

Although this view avoids absolutism, judgments about morality, and analogies with medicine, it fails on several counts. It does not take into account the meanings people attach to behaviors, and it ignores situations in which deviance is defined by a powerful group that is a numerical minority. Variations in the enforcement of rules are not considered, nor are interpersonal interactions, societal standards, or public awareness of or response to the deviance. Although much socially defined deviance falls outside of the average, the degree of variation may be less significant than the social definitions and social judgments attached to the variation.

The Relative Nature of Deviance

More recently, sociologists have begun to advocate a relativistic model. As we stated in Chapter 4, cultural relativism is the assumption that behaviors, ideas, and products can be understood or evaluated only within the context of the culture and society of which they are a part. A *relativistic view* suggests that deviance likewise can be interpreted only in the sociocultural context in which it happens. Is a person seven feet tall a deviant in the context of professional basketball? Is a person without a bathing suit a deviant at a nudist beach?

Is killing deviant in the context of war? Context is influential in all of these determinations.

By assessing deviance in a particular social context, the relativistic model avoids the problems of the absolute, moral, medical, and statistical models. If deviance is relative rather than absolute, an act that is deviant in one context may not be deviant in another. A behavior considered "sick" in one society could be thought healthy in a different society. A certain act might be statistically deviant in one culture but not in another. As is generally true of cultural relativism, however, the fact that an act is defined as nondeviant in one situation does not mean that it is nondeviant everywhere. By the same token, acts that are defined as deviant in some places are not defined as such everywhere. Thus deviance does not consist merely of acts or behaviors, but of group responses, definitions, and the meanings attached to behaviors and therefore we can expect definitions of deviance to vary with circumstances. Some of the most important variations that affect these definitions concern time, place, situation, and social status.

Variation by Time

An act considered deviant in one time period may be considered nondeviant in another. Cigarette smoking, for example, has a long history of changing normative definitions. Nuehring and Markle (1974) note that in the United States between 1895 and 1921, fourteen states completely banned cigarette smoking and all other states except Texas passed laws regulating the sale of cigarettes to minors. In the early years of this century, stop-smoking clinics were opened in several cities and antismoking campaigns were widespread. Following World War I, however, cigarette sales increased and public attitudes toward smoking changed. Through the mass media, the tobacco industry appealed to women, weightwatchers, and even to health seekers. States began to realize that tobacco could be a rich source of revenue, and by 1927 the fourteen states that banned cigarettes had repealed their laws. By the end of World War II, smoking had become acceptable, and in many contexts it was thought socially desirable.

In the 1950s, scientists found that smoking could cause a variety of diseases, including lung cancer and heart disease. In 1964 the Surgeon General published a landmark report on smoking and health, and soon thereafter some states began passing anticigarette legislation again. Laws were passed requiring a health warning on cigarette packages, and in 1973 the National Association of Broadcasters agreed to phase out cigarette advertising. Since then, airlines, restaurants, and other public places have begun to designate segregated sections for smokers and nonsmokers, and in many states smoking is completely prohibited in such places as elevators, concert halls, museums, and physicians' offices (Markle and Troyer, 1979), which suggests that smoking is beginning once again to be considered a deviant behavior. Many other examples could be given of how behaviors defined as deviant at one time may be ignored or even encouraged at another time.

Variation by Place

Behaviors viewed as deviant in one location, society, or culture may be considered nondeviant in others. In many cultures, having more than one wife is a sign of wealth, prestige, and high status. In the United States, however, having more than one wife at once is a punishable offense. Certain sexual acts that are deemed immoral, criminal, or delinquent in American society are accepted in Scandinavian countries. Bullfighting in Spain and Mexico and cockfighting in the Philippines are festive, legal gambling activities that produce income, but they are forbidden in the United States. On the other hand, American dating practices, divorce rates, and bathing attire are thought shocking by much of the non-Western world. Table 7-2 provides the result of research in six countries where the people were asked how they

Table 7-2
Legal prohibition of various acts: Views in six countries

"DO YOU THINK THIS ACT SHOULD BE PROHIBITED BY THE LAW?"
(PERCENT DISTRIBUTION: "DON'T KNOW" CATEGORY EXCLUDED)

	INDIA (N = 509)		INDONESIA (N = 500)		IRAN (N = 475)		ITALY (SARDINIA) (N = 200)		U.S.A. (N = 169)		YUGOSLAVIA (N = 500)	
	YES	NO	YES	NO	YES	NO	YES	NO	YES	NO	YES	NO
Incest	94.3	5.7	98.0	0.6	98.1	1.9	97.5	2.0	71.0	20.7	95.0	0.8
Robbery	97.3	2.7	99.2	0.0	97.9	2.1	100.0	0.0	100.0	0.0	98.4	0.4
Appropriation[a]	96.6	1.2	99.8	0.2	97.1	2.9	100.0	0.0	92.3	7.1	98.0	0.0
Homosexuality	74.1	25.0	85.9	7.2	90.3	9.7	86.5	12.5	18.3	66.9	71.6	13.6
Abortion	40.9	58.7	95.3	3.0	83.9	16.1	76.5	21.5	21.9	74.5	24.8	63.2
Taking drugs	74.9	24.6	93.3	2.4	89.8	10.2	92.0	3.0	89.6	11.8	89.2	4.2
Factory pollution	98.8	1.2	94.9	1.0	97.7	2.3	96.0	3.5	96.4	3.0	92.8	1.6
Public protest	33.3	65.8	72.3	20.9	77.0	23.0	34.5	64.5	5.9	91.1	46.2	38.4
Not helping	44.5	53.9	67.7	24.4	56.4	43.6	79.5	20.0	27.8	52.7	76.6	12.2

[a] Taking over someone else's property for your own use.

SOURCE: Graeme Newman, *Comparative Deviance: Perception and Law in Six Cultures*, New York: Elsevier, 1976, p. 116. Copyright 1976 by Elsevier Science Publishing Co., Inc. Reprinted by permission.

Deviance does not reside in acts or behaviors per se, but in the meanings attached to them. In U.S. society, most people define nudity in public places as deviant. In a culture that stresses cleanliness, to cover oneself with mud is considered deviant as well. But what is viewed as deviant may depend on the situation: identical behavior among two-year-olds would be seen in a different light.

felt about the legal prohibition of specific acts. Note the extent to which the people in the United States differed from other countries in their response to the issues.

There are also variations in definitions of deviance within cultures as well as among them. Vast differences exist among regions of the United States in the approval granted to interracial dating, among states in the approval of teenage smoking, and among rural and urban areas in the acceptance of theaters showing pornographic films. Different subcultures often have norms that are viewed as deviant by other subcultures in the same society.

Variation by Situation

Behavior defined as deviant in one situation may not be in another, even in the same time period and geographical area. A man who dresses in women's clothes to act in a play would be considered normal, but a man who dressed in women's clothes in the audience would not. Sex between husband and wife in the home is granted social approval, but sex at a public beach or on the church altar might land you in jail or a mental hospital.

Variations in the acceptance of marijuana and alcohol use by college students were studied by

Orcutt (1975). Their degree of acceptance varied widely, depending on such factors as (1) the social goals of the drug use, (2) the regularity of use in certain situations, and (3) the user's motivation for using drugs. Most students, for example, accepted marijuana or alcohol use at small parties with friends who were also using them. They tended not to accept a person's use of drugs or alcohol every day before going to a job to help cope with work, however (see Table 7-3 for student response in more detail). The social relativity of deviance reminds us that we must carefully select the time, place, and situation in which we behave in certain ways.

Variation by Social Status

Deviance also varies with *social status,* the position in society that one occupies. As described in Chapter 2, ascribed statuses are given at birth: age, sex, race, and so on. Achieved statuses are "gained" or "achieved": marital, educational, occupational, and so on. Prince Charles of England's social status, for example, is ascribed — he was born into royalty. Sandra Day O'Connor's status has been achieved by her appointment to the Supreme Court. Until recently, a woman or a black person who aspired to be a bank president might have been considered deviant, but such an aspira-

Table 7-3

Percentages accepting or indifferent to marijuana and alcohol use by situational item variations

SITUATIONAL ITEMS	% ACCEPTING OR INDIFFERENT	
	MARIJUANA	ALCOHOL
1. — A college student smokes marijuana (drinks alcohol) at a small party with his friends who are also using marijuana (alcohol).	82.8	97.0
2 — A college student working as a salesman smokes marijuana (drinks alcohol) with one of his clients who has offered it to him.	39.0	81.0
3 — A college student smokes marijuana (drinks alcohol) two or three times a week when he gets together with friends in the evening.	70.9	79.0
4 — During a boring party, a college student withdraws to a quiet corner to get high on marijuana (alcohol) to help him feel better.	41.7	34.9
5 — A college student uses marijuana (alcohol) to ease his anxieties about meeting others before going to any kind of a party.	39.6	48.5
6 — A college student working in an office regularly smokes marijuana (drinks alcohol) with his co-workers during their lunch break.	29.6	31.5
7 — On a particularly trying day at his part-time job, a college student smokes marijuana (drinks alcohol) during his lunch break to help him face the rest of his work.	26.5	20.9
8 — Every day before going to his job, a college student smokes marijuana (drinks alcohol) to help him cope with his work situation.	9.3	4.9

SOURCE: James D. Orcutt, "Deviance as a Situated Phenomenon: Variations in the Social Interpretation of Marijuana and Alcohol Use," *Social Problems* 22 (February 1975):351. An adaptation of Table 1. Reprinted by permission.

tion might have been encouraged in a white male. Similarly, members of a country club might try to encourage a rich Mafia member to join but treat the drug dealers and prostitutes who made the Mafia's money with contempt. The status associated with a person's sex, race, age, and income will influence which of his or her behaviors are considered deviant.

An examination of how deviance varies by social status can be seen by noting differences in appropriate behaviors for males and females. While recognizing variations by time, place, and situation, certain behaviors are given greater approval for women than men, whereas others are given greater approval for men than women. It is acceptable for women — but not men — to wear high heels, panty hose, and earrings, for example, but whereas men can go topless to any beach, women who do so would be considered deviant. Although in the past men and women differed greatly in types and degree of deviant behavior, there is evidence that this is changing. A review of forty-four studies (Smith and Visher, 1980) dealing with the relationship between sex (male-female) and deviance/criminality indicates that women are closing the gap in the involvement of personal offenses (e.g., drug and alcohol violations), youth offenses (e.g., truancy, school problems), and property offenses (e.g., theft, embezzlement, fraud) but differ considerably in involvement with violent offenses. This general narrowing of female-male differences seems consistent with the view that women may be experiencing greater structural opportunities to engage in deviant behaviors because the social roles of men and women are changing. If and when total sexual equality is obtained, variation in deviance by sexual status may disappear.

The relativistic perspective acknowledges the diversity of behaviors, convictions, and sanctions that can be found in society, and also the variety of meanings and definitions attributed to behav-iors and sanctions. This view also recognizes the potential for conflict in a society or a single person in attempting to conform to the norms of different groups. A teenager may be encouraged to smoke marijuana by peers but not by parents. A Catholic couple may wish to use only "natural" contraceptive methods to conform to church norms, yet want to use "artificial" methods to conform to their own norms and those of their friends and society.

From the relativistic perspective, deviance is not assumed to reside exclusively in either people or actions. It is, rather, an interactive process involving people's behavior, an audience, norms and definitions, and society as a whole. To understand deviance, we must focus not only on people or acts but also on the conditions in which deviance occurs and how others react to it. Many factors must be taken into account: the social setting; the society's structure, definitions, and labels; the way people learn norms and the variation from norms that society permits; and the means by which behaviors within the range of variability are controlled and behaviors outside of this range are punished.

Theories of Deviance

As we have illustrated, deviance varies by time, place, situation, and social status. Given the wide variations in deviance, how can it be explained? What causes deviance? Why do people violate social norms? Equally important, why do people conform and obey social norms? Most people do conform, and conformity is granted greater social approval in most circumstances, so theories have tended to focus more on the deviant than the nondeviant. The two are not easily separated, however, and explanations of one are equally applicable to the other.

Scientists have developed a variety of theories to explain deviance, but the fact that many theories exist does not mean that one is correct and the others incorrect. Theories often reflect the discipline from which they developed. Biological theories tend to focus on genetic, anatomical, or physiological factors. Psychological theories tend to emphasize personality, motives, aggression, frustration, or ego strength. Sociologists usually emphasize sociocultural, organizational, environmental, or group factors. Although some theories have more empirical support than others, all can increase our understanding of the complexities of human behavior, whether deviant or nondeviant, and the social order.

Biological Theories of Deviance

Several of the traditional views discussed earlier in this chapter involved biological factors. The view that deviance is a sickness adhered to a medical model, which assumed not just a social pathology or a mental illness but an unhealthy biological organism as well. Similarly, the moral model implied that certain people possess a biologically-based resistance to conformity. These views share the assumption that certain defects or weaknesses in an individual's physical constitution produce deviant behaviors.

Biological theories of deviance are often traced back to the Italian physician-psychiatrist Cesare Lombroso (1835–1909). Lombroso, sometimes referred to as the father of modern criminology, was interested in the scientific study of crime. He believed that attention should be shifted from the criminal act to the criminal — specifically to the physical characteristics of the criminal. He was convinced that the major determinants of crime (or deviance) were biological — that there was a "born criminal type." These conclusions were based on a comparison of four hundred prison inmates with a group of Italian soldiers. Lombroso found that the prisoners displayed physical abnormalities such as deviations in head size and shape, eye defects, receding chins,

and excessively long arms, which led him to the belief that criminal tendencies are hereditary and that potential criminals could be recognized by certain physical characteristics or *body types*. Several years after Lombroso published his work, an English research team headed by Charles Goring published the results of a study comparing prisoners with a group of nonprisoners that included undergraduate students at Oxford and Cambridge. This study revealed practically no physical differences between the two groups. Goring's group concluded that "there is no such thing as a physical type." Nevertheless, Lombroso's findings were influential for many years.

Other research on biological factors followed. In the 1930s, the American anthropologist Ernest Hooton claimed that criminals were organically inferior to "normal" people (Vold, 1958). In the 1940s, an American psychologist-physician, William Sheldon, attempted to link body type to behavior. He classified people in terms of three types of physique: the *endomorph* who is soft, round, and usually fat; the *mesomorph* who is muscular, stocky, and athletic; and the *ectomorph* who is skinny and fragile (see Figure 7-1). He associated these body types with certain temperamental and behavioral tendencies. A disproportionately high percentage of criminals were found to be mesomorphs with stocky, muscular bodies. This statistical correlation is not a cause-effect explanation, however; other factors may also be at work. Physically fit boys may be recruited to delinquency more often, or judges may see muscular boys as more of a threat than unhealthy, skinny, or obese boys.

More recently, considerable excitement has been generated by claims that a specific genetic condition may be associated with crimes of physical violence (Suchar, 1978). Some violent criminals have been found to have an extra Y chromosome: they have XYY *chromosomes* rather than the usual XY. Other findings, however, indi-

Figure 7-1
Sheldon's body types

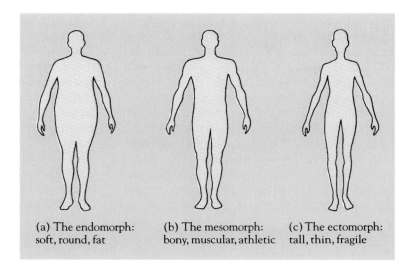

(a) The endomorph:
soft, round, fat

(b) The mesomorph:
bony, muscular, athletic

(c) The ectomorph:
tall, thin, fragile

cate that the great majority of XYY males have never been convicted of any crime, which suggests that the XYY factor is not a cause of deviance.

As you may have guessed, there are many problems with biological theories of crime, delinquency, and deviance, but the recent interest in the new science of sociobiology testifies to the continuing appeal of biological approaches. There are theories suggesting that sexual behaviors, both deviant and nondeviant, are biologically rooted, and that alcohol and drug abuse are caused by some chromosome component or genetic deficiency. Most of these explanations fail to explain, however, why others with a similar biological makeup do not exhibit the same forms of behaviors. In other words, biological explanations do not clearly differentiate the deviant from the nondeviant, and they fail to explain the tremendous variation in deviance as well as its relative nature. Today, most sociologists reject the notion that biology, heredity, or constitutional factors cause deviance.

Psychological Theories of Deviance

Like biological explanations, psychological theories tend to focus on the person who engages in deviant behavior. Some psychological theories share with biological approaches the notion that the causes of behavior are rooted in a person's physiological or genetic makeup: instincts, needs, drives, and impulses. In psychological theories, however, the emphasis is on the mind rather than the body. These theories focus on such factors as personality structure, learning, goals, interests, motivations, willpower, frustration, anxiety, guilt, and other psychic conditions and responses. Social psychologists often consider the social context of behavior, in addition to these factors.

Psychological theories often associate deviance with a sickness, arguing that deviance results from a psychological abnormality, a psychopathic personality, or a mental illness. This explanation, following the medical model described earlier, assumes that deviant behaviors such as alcoholism, child abuse, and crime are the consequences of mental illness. It is certainly true that mentally ill people may commit deviant acts, but this theory does not account for deviancy among people who are not mentally ill, nor does it explain why some mentally ill people are not deviant.

Some psychological explanations suggest that deviance results from *frustration*. When needs are not fulfilled, frustration results, which in turn leads to *aggression* and often antisocial, deviant behaviors. The greater the frustration, the more extreme the aggression. Frustration over the lack of money, the loss of a job, or a failure in love can lead to aggressive acts: speeding, child abuse, robbery, or even murder. One difficulty with this explanation is that frustration is defined so broadly that it includes almost any behavior. Another problem is that it does not account for people who are frustrated but do not act deviantly.

Other psychological explanations exist as well. Freudian theorists linked deviance with defects of the superego or conscience. People with weak egos were said to be unable to control their impulses, defer gratification, or adhere to planned rational courses of action. Other theorists have associated deviance with such factors as motivation, intelligence, stress, unconscious needs, and personality traits. In general, these psychological explanations are not very useful, because theories involving instinct and unconscious needs are extremely difficult if not impossible to test empirically. Explanations based on frustration and aggression or illness fail to differentiate the deviant from the nondeviant. Another major difficulty with most biological and psychological theories is that they ignore the relative nature of deviance: the influence of social context, variations in rates of deviance, and social responses to deviance. Several sociological theories, some of which incorporate psychological components, consider factors other than acts and actors.

Sociological Theories of Deviance

Sociological theories attempt to explain deviance by looking at sociocultural processes and organizational structures, although acts and actors are considered as well. Anomie theory, a structural-functional theory, focuses on value conflicts between culturally prescribed goals and socially approved ways of achieving them. Conflict theory contends that groups in power define the acts of the weaker groups as deviant in order to exploit them. Sociocultural learning theories are concerned with how people interact and learn deviance. Labeling theory regards deviance as a process of symbolic interaction and focuses on the meanings, definitions, and interpretations applied to people and acts. Control theories concentrate more on conformity than on deviance and deal with internal and external social controls that inhibit people's involvement in deviance.

Anomie Theory

In Chapter 2 we discussed Durkheim's conclusion that suicide is a social phenomenon related to a person's involvement in group life and membership in a cohesive social unit. Anomic suicide, he said, happens because of social and personal disorganization. People feel lost when the values of a society or group are confused or norms break down. Under most conditions, norms are clear and most people adhere to them, but during times of social turmoil people find themselves in unfamiliar situations. Making distinctions between the possible and the impossible, between desires and fulfilling those desires, becomes impossible. This condition of social normlessness is termed *anomie*.

Merton (1957), extending Durkheim's explanation of anomie, argues that anomie arises from an incongruence between a society's emphasis on attaining certain goals and the availability of legitimate, institutionalized means of reaching these goals. Such groups as the poor, teenagers, racial minorities, and blue-collar workers are constantly informed through education, the media, and friends that material success is an important goal, but legitimate means for achieving it are often unavailable. Thus deviance is the result of a strain between a society's culture and its social structure, between culturally prescribed goals and the socially approved ways of achieving them.

Merton listed five ways that people adapt to the goals of a culture and the institutionalized means of achieving them (see Table 7-4). Only *conformity* to both the goals and the means is nondeviant. The other methods of adaptations are all varieties of deviant behavior.

A second mode of adaptation is *innovation*. Innovators accept social goals but reject the normatively prescribed means of achieving them. Students who want to get good grades are adhering to widely held values, but if they cheat, they are violating a norm.

A third mode of adaptation is *ritualism*. Ritualists follow rules rigidly without regard for the

Table 7-4

Merton's typology of modes of individual adaptation

MODES OF ADAPTATION	CULTURE GOALS	INSTITUTIONALIZED MEANS
I. *Conformity*	+	+
II. *Innovation*	+	−
III. *Ritualism*	−	+
IV. *Retreatism*	−	−
V. *Rebellion*	±	±

Note: In this typology Merton used the symbol + to signify "acceptance," − to signify "rejection," and ± to signify "rejection of prevailing values and substitution of new values."

SOURCE: Robert K. Merton, *Social Theory and Structure.* Revised and Enlarged Edition, Copyright 1957, by The Free Press, a Corporation. Reprinted with permission of Macmillan Publishing Co., Inc.

ends for which they were designed. The office manager who spends all his or her time making sure employees come to work on time, don't drink coffee at their desks, and don't make personal phone calls is a ritualist. By focusing on petty rules, he or she loses sight of the real goal of the office. Ritualists conform to traditions and never take chances. Merton suggests that lower-middle-class Americans are likely to be ritualists, because parents in this group pressure their children to compulsively abide by the moral mandates and mores of society. This form of adaptation is not generally considered a serious form of deviant behavior. People cling to safe routines and institutional norms, thereby avoiding dangers and frustrations that they feel are inherent in the competition for major cultural goals.

Retreatism is a more drastic mode of adaptation. Retreatists such as tramps, psychotics, alcoholics, and drug addicts reject both the cultural goals and the institutional means. These people are truly aliens: they are *in* the society but not *of* it. They are members of their society only in that they live in the same place. Retreatism is probably the least common form of adaptation, and it is heartily condemned by conventional representatives of society. Retreatist deviants are widely regarded as a social liability. According to Merton (1957), this fourth mode of adaptation "is that of the socially disinherited who if they have none of the rewards held out by society also have few of the frustrations attendant upon continuing to seek these rewards" (p. 155).

The fifth and final mode of adaptation is *rebellion*. Rebels such as members of revolutionary movements withdraw their allegiance to a society they feel is unjust and seek to bring into being a new, greatly modified social structure. Most social movements such as the gay rights or women's liberation movements fall short of what Merton considered rebellion since these activists do not reject most societal goals. These movements do advocate substituting new values in certain parts

Robert Merton explained deviance as the result of the strain that arises from an incongruence between the goals of a culture and the legitimate means of attaining them. Bag ladies, tramps, alcoholics, and psychotics are examples of deviants who neither conform to socially approved cultural goals nor have or use legitimate means for achieving them. These people are aliens in society and are viewed as social liabilities.

of society, however. Merton suggests it is typically members of a rising class rather than the most depressed strata who organize the resentful and the rebellious into a revolutionary group.

Merton's theory has been criticized on a number of different grounds (Schur, 1979; Thio, 1978). Critics argue that it erroneously assumes that a single system of "cultural goals" is shared by the entire society. It has also been faulted for failing to explain why some people choose one response while others choose a different one. Another weakness is that certain types of deviance — rape, the behavior of hippies in the 1960s — do not neatly fall into any of his five modes of adaptation. Other critics argue that Merton's theory ignores the influence of societal reactions in the shaping of deviance and the fact that much perceived deviance involves collective rather than individual action. Finally, much criticism has been leveled at Merton's underlying assumption that deviance is disproportionately concentrated in the lower socioeconomic levels.

Anomic theory does have some strengths. It provides a framework for examining a wide range of social behavior, it has stimulated many research studies, and it has raised the social consciousness of deviance analysts. This last-mentioned point is particularly true of some members of the new generation of sociologists. These theorists have devised conflict theories of deviance that emphasize the widespread social oppression and basic contradictions found at the heart of our socioeconomic system.

Conflict Theory

Conflict theorists are the major critics of the assumption of the functionalist and anomie theories that a society shares a single set of values. *Conflict theory* contends that most societies contain many groups which have different, often conflicting, values and that the strongest groups in a society have the power to define the values of weaker groups as deviant. Conflict theorists emphasize the repression of the weak by the powerful, the exploitation of the masses by strong interest groups, and the influential and often wealthy groups who use laws, courts, and other agencies to oppose the interests and activities of lower socioeconomic groups and minorities. Most businesses exist to make a profit, and if in making a profit they (intentionally or nonintentionally) provide jobs, raise the level of personal gratification, and improve the community as well, little conflict may result. If, however, high taxes, high wages, fringe benefits, safety requirements, or pollution controls disrupt profits, then lobbying groups, political contributions, and media campaigns are used to influence legislation, taxation, and controls. Part-time workers may be used extensively to eliminate fringe benefits. Women and blacks may be hired at lower wages than is necessary for men and whites. Community tax incentives may be granted to keep the businesses or industries at the expense of the individual. The powerful exploit those with less power, and this exploitation by the elite produces racism, sexism, inequality, and institutionalized violence. The conflict between the powerful and the weak, therefore, influences both the creation of deviance and our response to it.

Chambliss (1969) contends that many legal scholars and social scientists are not even aware of this class domination. Most assume that the law is based on the consensus of its citizens, that it represents the public interest, and that it treats citizens as equal and serves the best interests of society. Conflict theorists, however, argue that the law means just that legal authorities *ought* to be fair and just. Chambliss and Seidman (1971) found that they are actually unfair and unjust, favoring the rich and powerful over the poor and weak. This condition exists, they say, not because law enforcement officials are cruel or evil but because they would antagonize members of the middle and upper classes if they arrested them for their white-collar offenses. These classes might then withdraw their support from law enforcement agencies, thus leading to loss of jobs.

Quinney (1979) and Spitzer (1975), who agree that deviance and deviants are defined and controlled by the powerful, go a step further and blame the lack of justice directly on the capitalist system. Drawing heavily from Marx, Spitzer contends that populations are considered deviant by capitalists when they disturb, hinder, or question any of the following: (1) capitalist modes of appropriating the products of human labor, (2) the social conditions under which capitalist production takes place, (3) patterns of distribution and consumption in capitalist society, (4) the socialization of productive and nonproductive roles, or (5) the ideology that supports capitalist society.

According to the conflict perspective, deviance *definitions* are determined largely by the dominant class, deviance *rates* are determined primarily by the extent to which certain behaviors threaten dominant class interests, and deviance *control* is in large part determined by the extent to which the powerful can socialize and reward those who follow their demands. Many conflict theorists perceive their theory as a call for political action to raise a revolutionary consciousness and end the oppression of the powerless by the powerful.

Like other theories, conflict theory has its critics, who fault it for not searching for the causes of deviant behavior. They also say it does not explain the crimes and deviances that are basically nonpolitical (vices, trivial deviations). In addition, conflict theorists have been criticized for assuming that in the utopian Communist society murder, robbery, rape, and other crimes will disappear after the power to criminalize them is abolished.

Sociocultural Learning Theories

Sociocultural learning theories deal with the processes through which deviant acts are learned and the conditions under which learning takes place. Deviant behaviors are learned through essentially the same processes as other behaviors (see Chapter 5). Unlike anomie and conflict theories, sociocultural learning theories emphasize the groups people belong to and how they learn the norms prescribed by those groups. Three of these theories focus specifically on deviance: cultural transmission theory, differential association theory, and social learning theory.

Cultural transmission theory, sometimes called subculture theory, stems from the Chicago School of sociology described in Chapter 2. Shaw and McKay (1929) noted that high crime rates persisted in certain Chicago neighborhoods over several decades even though the areas changed in ethnic composition and other ways. To explain this phenomenon, they suggested that when deviance is part of a community's cultural pattern, it is culturally transmitted to newcomers as they move into the area. When there is a tradition of deviance in a subculture, the norms of that subculture are passed on by the gang, peer group, or play group during interaction with newcomers. As a result, they too become deviant, not by violating norms but by conforming to the norms of the subculture.

Other sociologists quickly picked up on the idea that deviance is transmitted culturally through learning and socialization. These scientists extended the theory, suggesting that people learn not only from gangs or peer groups but also from other agents of socialization: parents, teachers, church leaders, business colleagues, and others. A person could learn deviant attitudes by observing that people throw away parking tickets, keep incorrect change in a supermarket, or find ways to avoid paying taxes. One primary source of learning about deviance may be institutions designed to correct deviance, such as juvenile homes, detention centers, reformatories, prisons, and mental hospitals. Even people within these subcultures, however, are exposed to and learn conforming behaviors, so why are some people attracted to deviant behaviors while others are not?

The *differential association theory* was devised by Sutherland (1939; Sutherland and Cressey, 1970) to answer this question and explain how deviance and crime are culturally transmitted. More specifically, Sutherland attempted to determine why crime rates vary among different groups of people. Why is the crime rate higher in the city than the country, in impoverished areas than other areas? Why do more males than females, more blacks than whites, commit crimes? Sutherland also wanted to explain individual criminality: why some individuals become criminals and others do not.

He contended that criminal behavior is learned rather than inherited or invented. The learning takes place through verbal and nonverbal communications, primarily in intimate groups. Learning a criminal behavior involves acquiring a set of motives, drives, rationalizations, and attitudes, as well as specific techniques for committing the act itself. Lawbreaking is defined as either acceptable or unacceptable. People are considered deviant when they acquire more definitions that favor violating norms and laws than oppose such violations. The deviant behavior of individuals in this group may vary in frequency, duration, priority, and intensity, depending on the amount of time they spend with groups possessing different norms. These variations in group involvement are known as *differential association*.

Sutherland did not believe that contact with criminals was necessary for a person to become deviant; exposure to definitions favoring deviance was sufficient, and the influence and frequency of these exposures varies from person to person. According to this theory, deviance is a learned behavior, a set of behaviors transmitted to people through their interactions with others.

The *social learning theory* is a revision of Sutherland's differential association theory in accordance with the principles of behavioral theory (Akers, 1977; Akers et al., 1979). Social learning theory focuses on the influence of operant (instrumental) conditioning, in which behavior is shaped by the stimuli that follow it. Behavior is acquired through direct conditioning, through imitation, or through modeling the behavior of others. A behavior is strengthened by rewards (positive reinforcement) or the avoidance of punishment (negative reinforcement) and weakened by aversive stimuli (positive punishment) or loss of rewards (negative punishment). Akers et al. (1979) state that the acquisition and persistence of either deviant or conforming behavior are a function of what particular behaviors have been rewarded or punished, which is known as *differential reinforcement*. The norms and attitudes people learn from others, especially peers and family, are also influential.

Suppose, for example, that a fifteen-year-old, John, has just moved to a new neighborhood. Initially, he has no friends. One day, unhappy and lonely, he defies a teacher and gets into a violent argument with him. After class, several of his peers comment admiringly on the way he told the teacher off. The attention serves as positive reinforcement: John needs friends. He tells his mother what happened, but she says only that she wishes she could tell her boss to go to hell once in a while, which encourages John to think that his behavior is acceptable. He begins to deliberately provoke arguments with teachers, and gradually he gets a reputation as a rebel. Girls begin to pay attention to him (positive reinforcement). Eventually, however, he is suspended from school for two weeks, which then deprives him of the attention of his friends (negative punishment). When he returns, he finds that his teachers have collectively decided to ask him to leave the room whenever he acts up, so he learns to be more cautious (negative reinforcement). He is also required to clean the bathrooms after school every time he gets into trouble (positive punishment). The positive reinforcement encouraged him to act in a mildly deviant fashion, but the negative punishment, negative reinforcement, and positive reinforcement encouraged him to conform to school standards. Eventually, he finds a level of disruption that maintains his reputation without forcing his teachers to try to change his behavior. Akers et al. (1979) assessed social learning theory of deviant behavior with data on factors that influenced the drinking and drug use of three thousand adolescents. They found that alcohol and drug use were both positively correlated with exposure to users and association with users.

Sutherland, in his differential association theory of deviance, suggested that criminal and deviant behaviors are learned in group interaction. Members of gangs, for example, socialize one another as to what type of behaviors are appropriate or inappropriate and what norms and laws can be violated.

They also found that drug and alcohol use increased when it was reinforced more than punished and when use was defined positively or neutrally. Although differential association accounted for most of the adolescents' variations in drug and alcohol use, differential reinforcement, definitions, and imitation were also influential.

Sociocultural learning theories focus on how deviance is learned. Critics argue that these theories do not explain how deviance originated or how certain behaviors came to be defined as deviant. It has also been argued that they do not deal adequately with those who commit deviant acts in isolation rather than as part of a group. Furthermore, these theories are often difficult to test empirically without engaging in circular reasoning: deviance is caused by a tradition of deviance caused by earlier deviance. Another weakness is that it is very difficult to determine precisely what stimuli or learning experiences cause a person to initially commit a deviant instead of a conforming act. Nevertheless, sociocultural learning theories have contributed to our understanding of the nature of deviance.

Labeling Theory

The theories of deviance discussed so far have focused on deviant people, deviant acts, the process of learning deviance, and the causes of deviance. *Labeling theory* is concerned primarily with the effects of labeling a person "deviant." How does society formulate definitions of deviance? How and by whom are these labels applied to certain people? How does being labeled deviant influence a person's behavior?

Most labeling theorists interpret deviance in terms of symbolic interaction processes (see Chapter 2). Like other behaviors, deviant behavior is not regarded as a certain type of act undertaken by a person in isolation. It is, rather, a result of human interactions, people's interpretations and definitions of their own actions and those of others. As Kitsuse (1962) stated it, "Forms of behavior *per se* do not differentiate deviants from non-deviants; it is the responses of the conventional and conforming members of the society who identify and interpret behavior as deviant which sociologically transform persons into deviants" (p. 253).

Note that, according to this perspective, deviance is a relative condition. It is not a certain type of act, it is the consequence of applying a certain label. As Becker (1963) noted, "Social groups create deviance by making the rules whose infraction constitutes deviance and by applying those rules to particular people and labeling them as outsiders" (p. 9). Thus if two people commit the same act, one might be labeled a deviant and the other might not, depending on the meaning given to the act by their social groups.

Edwin Lemert (1951), one of the first labeling theorists, identified two categories of deviance. *Primary deviance* involves behavior that violates social norms but is temporary and sporadic. Most important, individuals who are involved in primary deviance do not regard themselves as deviant, nor are they regarded as such by those around them. *Secondary deviance* involves habitual violation of norms by individuals who not only consider themselves deviant but also are labeled deviant by others. Secondary deviance becomes a routine resulting in a label that leads to further deviance. Thus we have the development of a *deviant career* and a label that becomes a master status: cheat, prostitute, liar, and so on. Getting so labeled leads others to view you in terms of that deviant status, overlooking other qualities or statuses, and then other "career" options may become closed and you may have little choice but to live up to the label and behave accordingly. The behavior, for example, of a student who buys one term paper to turn in to his history professor might be primary deviance. If this student consistently cheated on tests and turned in papers that he had not written himself, his behavior would be considered deviant by his peers, his professors, and himself and would therefore constitute secondary deviance.

Who labels whom? Speaking from the conflict perspective, Becker (1974) says: "A major element in every aspect of the drama of deviance is the imposition of definitions — of situations, acts, and people — by those powerful enough or legitimated to be able to do so (p. 62). The labelers, therefore, would include such social control agents as police, judges, prison guards, and psychiatrists, whereas the labeled would include criminals, delinquents, drug addicts, prostitutes, mental patients, and others. Generally, rich, white, or powerful people are more likely to apply labels and the poor, blacks, and the powerless are more likely to be labeled. A poor or black person is more apt to be arrested, prosecuted, and convicted than a rich or a white person for committing the same act. Data from the U.S. Bureau of the Census, for example, showed that approximately 9.7 million arrests took place in 1980. While blacks constituted 11.7 percent of the population, they were involved in approximately 26 percent of the arrests (*Statistical Abstract*, 1981, No. 309, p. 180). Of the total number of inmates, 41 percent were black (No. 334, p. 190). Of the prisoners under sentence of death, 39 percent were black (No. 338, p. 192). Similar statistics lend support to a higher arrest, prosecution, and conviction rate among men, the young, the less

Sociologists indicate that certain groups or categories of persons are more likely to be defined as deviant than others. Males, teenagers, the poor, and blacks and other minority persons are disproportionately represented in arrests, convictions, and imprisonment.

educated, and the poor. Jail inmates, for example, consisted of 94 percent male, 70 percent under 30 years of age, 61 percent with less than 12 years of schooling, 49 percent with no prearrest income or a prearrest income of under $3,000, and 87 percent with a prearrest income of under $10,000 (No. 334, p. 190).

What are the consequences of labeling? According to theorists, being labeled deviant has negative consequences because these people tend to see themselves as deviant, which leads them to continue their so-called deviant behavior (Thio, 1978, p. 58). The application of a label may therefore play a part in originating and continuing deviant behavior. Ridicule, humiliation, harassment, or imprisonment may also result from labeling. Labeled people may no longer be treated as respectable parents, teachers, or community members; they may lose their jobs, be rejected by friends, or be sent to a prison or mental hospital. Responses of this sort often push labeled people further into the deviant activity. Ex-convicts who cannot get jobs may return to robbery or drug dealing. Those labeled as mentally ill lose many of the social supports necessary for mental health. Drug addicts, alcoholics, and prostitutes may turn to others who share the same label for support and companionship, which leads them to organize their lives around their deviance.

Although it is accepted by many sociologists, labeling theory has its critics. It does not explain the *causes* of deviance, nor can it be used to predict who will be labeled and in what context. Like other symbolic interaction theories, labeling theory is difficult to test empirically. Another criticism is one that also applies to conflict theory: if the powerful create and impose the deviant label, how is it possible that powerful people are also labeled deviant? Critics have also questioned the extent to which deviance encourages rather than deters deviant behavior. Finally, are all persons in prisons or mental hospitals there simply because someone chose to label them, or are some behaviors so disruptive that severe sanctions such as institutionalization must be imposed to maintain social order? Other social consequences of deviance are discussed in the next section.

The Social Consequences of Deviance

As we stated in our discussion of structural-functional theory in Chapter 2, social systems are composed of many parts, which exist because they perform some function in the maintenance of the system. Any part of a social system may be dysfunctional in some respects, but the part continues to exist because it performs a function that leads to the maintenance and stability of the system. Also, as we stated earlier in this chapter, deviance is universal — it exists in all societies and therefore it seems logical to assume that deviance continues to exist because it serves certain functions in the maintenance of societies.

Social Functions of Deviance

The notion that deviance may have positive effects runs counter to the traditional views described earlier. According to these views, deviance is harmful, immoral, antisocial, and a sickness in society. Deviance is not merely a sickness, however; it is part of the nature of all social systems. It has also been traditionally regarded as evidence of social disorganization, but many deviant subcultures such as gangs, organized crime, prostitution, or police corruption may be found in highly organized societies and be highly organized themselves. Durkheim pointed out as early as 1894 that deviations should be regarded as a normal part of a society (Kelly, 1979). It appears that deviance performs various social functions, some of which are described below.

It helps define the limits of social tolerance. By indicating the extent to which norms can be violated without provoking a reaction, it helps clarify the boundaries of social norms and the limits of behaviorial diversity. Methods of social control such as arrests, psychiatric counseling, criminal trials, and social ostracism help define these limits. Arrests and trials indicate to the public the seriousness of certain deviations and the extent to which violations of norms are tolerated. Driving 57 miles per hour when the speed limit is 55, for example, is tolerated by police, and driving 60 usually is tolerated, but driving 80 or 100 is likely to lead to punishment. Spanking a child may be acceptable, but a parent who injures a child can be arrested. By observing societal reactions to deviance, members learn the limits of acceptable variation from norms.

Deviance can increase the solidarity and integration of a group. Such a label can unite the people who share it. Certain deviants find emotional support and a sense of community among others who share their values and behavior patterns. Student protesters, homosexuals, and members of religious cults and other subcultures tend to defend and protect one another and derive their identities from their deviant group. By the same token, highly integrated groups may form in an attempt to defeat or eliminate deviants because having a common enemy tends to unite group members.

Deviance can serve as a "safety valve" for social discontent. When people desire things that the social norms do not permit them to have, they may become frustrated and angry and attack norms or even attempt to destroy the social system. Certain types of deviance permit people to escape from conventional norms and rid themselves of frustration without disrupting the social system as a whole. Cheating on one's income tax may be an outlet for frustration with government spending on wasteful projects or with being underpaid. The use of illegal drugs may be a safety valve against job frustrations or a poor marriage. Income tax cheating and drug use involve risk to individuals, but they may prevent expressions of frustration more injurious to society. Thus they tend to indirectly support such basic institutions as marriage, the economy, and the government. By funneling off anger and discontent, deviance may remove some of the strain produced by social mores.

Deviance can indicate defects or inadequacies in the existing social organization and bring about changes. High rates of certain kinds of deviance may expose problems in the social order. Large numbers of parking violations may indicate that there is not enough parking space. Outbreaks of violence in prison serve as a warning that the system is inadequate. Activities such as freedom marches by blacks in the South, the burning of draft cards by young men in the 1960s, and the hunger strikes of IRA members in Ireland were organized acts of defiance (and deviance) intended to force leaders and the public to address perceived problems in the social system. Another functional aspect of deviance, therefore, is that it can set in motion steps that lead to social change, and these changes can occur in many different forms. They can involve modifications in the existing structure, modifications in behavior, or changes in the definitions of deviance. Until the early 1960s, a black person who tried to sit in the front of a bus in Alabama was regarded as deviant. Following court cases and rulings against segregation, this behavior is no longer considered deviant. As social norms change, so do their definitions and folkways and mores may be modified as a consequence of deviant acts.

Social Dysfunctions of Deviance

Some consequences of deviance are dysfunctional: they can disrupt, destabilize, or lead to the complete breakdown of a social system. Given the range of tolerance of norm violations, isolated in-

Jackson: The Rioting Is an Ugly Reminder That Changes Must Be Made

The rioting Friday at Southern Michigan State Prison underscored a critical problem: The prison is too big, too crowded, too difficult to patrol. Whatever were the factors underlying this particular violence, the truth is that the Jackson prison ought to be replaced.

Conditions at the prison were dramatically presented to the public last year by Free Press photographer Taro Yamasaki, who won a Pulitzer Prize for his depictions of weapons in the possession of prisoners, grim cell blocks, depressing jams of humanity. Life within the world's largest walled prison is not merely tough; it is frightening and debasing.

None of that fully explains — and certainly it does not justify — the violence that broke out Friday. A day earlier, two guards were assaulted and injured. Prisoners are not the only ones who suffer from the violence and from conditions that make the prison unmanageable.

As efforts are made to determine what went wrong this time and why, the probability is that there can be no single explanation. In an outmoded prison with almost 6,000 inmates, about half of them inside the walls of the central facility, it is not realistic to expect anything much better than ongoing tensions that inevitably boil over.

Size alone makes it almost impossible for those who run the prison to detect and confiscate weapons manufactured inside or slipped in from outside, or to prevent harassment of some prisoners by others.

Michigan voters last year turned down a ballot proposal that would have provided $500 million to build four 550-bed prisons. The Legislature then approved, even so, a prison construction plan to be financed by other means. But the state budget becomes tighter and tighter.

Somehow, in some way, means must be found to replace the prison at Jackson and to end the overcrowding throughout the system. Whatever the immediate causes of this week's rioting, the harsh truth is that danger is always impending at Southern Michigan State Prison.

SOURCE: Editorial, *Detroit Free Press*, May 23, 1981, p. 6A. Reprinted by permission.

---

stances of deviance generally have little effect on the stability of systems. Widespread, long-term, and more extreme norm violations can impair the functioning of groups or entire systems.

Deviance can disrupt the social order. Violations of norms can disturb the status quo, make social life unpredictable, and create tension and conflict. Teachers who refuse to teach, parents who ignore their children, or workers who fail to do their appointed tasks can keep the system from functioning smoothly. The effect of an alcoholic father on a family system is a good example. The family's income may decrease, the wife may have to assume full responsibility for raising the children, and the children may be ashamed to bring friends home. All routines are subject to being disturbed by him. Deviance is often dysfunctional because it disrupts the order and predictability of life.

Deviance can disrupt the will of others to conform. If norm violations are unpunished or if members of society refuse to obey established rules, the desire to conform is decreased. Studying for an exam may seem pointless if you know other students are going to cheat. Obeying the speed limit can be frustrating if other drivers blow their horns to get you out of the way so they can speed by. To work hard when others are lazy, to be honest when others are dishonest, or to obey the rules when others ignore them can make one's efforts seem pointless. When deviance and conformity are not differentiated, deviance disappears. If they receive the same response or reward, what is the motivation to conform? Conformity to a given norm, rule, or law makes sense only if (1) others conform as well, (2) those who conform are differentiated from those who do not in some way, or (3) norm violators receive some type of punishment. Deviance that erodes the desire to follow rules and conform to social norms is dysfunctional.

Deviance can destroy trust. Social life is based in part on the assumption that other people are honest and trustworthy. When interpersonal trust decreases, people become more dependent on the legal system to define, interpret, support, and enforce the law. If all car dealers (or car buyers) were honest, written contracts would not be necessary and a few judges and lawyers would be out of work. In this sense, deviance is functional for the legal system, but it is dysfunctional to the society as a whole. Widespread deviance, just as it disrupts the will to conform, destroys our confidence and trust in others.

Deviance diverts resources that could be used elsewhere into social rehabilitation and control efforts. It may be functional in that it provides thousands of jobs for those who rehabilitate and control criminals, drug addicts, the mentally ill, and others, but it is dysfunctional in that the money used to deal with deviance cannot be used for other constructive and productive purposes. Criminal activities alone cost billions of dollars every year. Most would agree that these funds could be used more profitably elsewhere.

Clearly, deviance is neither all good nor all bad. Some of its consequences lead to the stability and maintenance of the system, others tend to disrupt it. Whatever the case, it is here to stay, an inevitable part of every society. Because it exists in every society, certain methods of keeping it under control have evolved.

Deviance and Social Control

The fact that deviance is universal and sometimes has positive social functions does not eliminate the need to control it. If societies are to survive, they must have ways of making people conform to social norms. Control is maintained by encouraging conformity, not by directly discouraging deviance, and the absence of motivation to conform results in deviance.

Conformity to social norms is generally explained in terms of two social control processes. *Internal controls* cause members of society themselves to want to conform to the norms of society. *External controls* are pressures or sanctions that are applied to members by others. The two types of control tend to operate simultaneously.

Internal Controls of Deviance

Internal controls are those that exist inside individuals. They include a wide range of factors: positive self-image, self-control, ego strength, high frustration tolerance, and a sense of social responsibility, among others. The workings of internal controls can be explained in part by the socialization theories discussed in Chapter 5. These theories explained how we internalize norms, learn the expectations of others, and develop a desire to conform to them. Some types of deviance, such as criminality and mental illness, are widely believed to be caused by inadequate socialization, especially in early childhood.

Most social control is directly related to a person's social self — our definitions of who we are in relation to the society we live in. Internal motivations to conformity result not from a fear of being caught or fear of punishment but because people have been socialized to see themselves in a certain way and to believe that stealing, cheating, murder, and certain other behaviors are wrong. In a study of deterrents to shoplifting, for example, Kraut (1976) concluded as follows: "People's definitions of themselves and of deviant behavior seem to act as internal constraints on shoplifting. When respondents explained why they hadn't stolen the last time they bought an item in a store, the two most important reasons they gave were their own honesty and their belief that shoplifting was unacceptable behavior" (p. 365).

Our feelings about right and wrong are sometimes referred to as our conscience. The saying "Let your conscience be your guide" assumes that you have internalized certain notions about deviant and nondeviant behavior. For most people, the conscience develops as a direct result of socialization experiences in early childhood and later in one's life. Social institutions such as the family and religion are significant in internalizing social norms. Once social norms are internalized, deviations produce feelings of guilt, remorse, or conflict. The relatively high prevalence of conformity in comparison to deviance is due largely to internal controls.

External Controls of Deviance

External controls are those that come from outside an individual. They can be either informal or formal. *Informal external controls* involve peers, friends, parents, or the other people one associates with regularly. These persons or groups apply pressure to encourage individuals to obey the rules and conform to social expectations. The same techniques can be used to encourage conformity to deviant norms. In the shoplifting study just mentioned, Kraut (1976) found that external constraints are also very important and that informal sanctions are a stronger deterrent than formal sanctions. Shoplifting was strongly correlated with the subjects' perception of their friends' involvement in and approval of shoplifting. In other words, subjects whose friends shoplifted or approved of it were more apt to shoplift than subjects whose friends disapproved of it, which suggests that friends have a powerful influence on the acceptance or rejection of deviant behavior.

Informal social controls have been found to be the major cause of the low rates of alcoholism found among Jews. Glassner and Berg (1980) found that American Jews avoid alcohol problems through four protective social processes: (1) they associate alcohol abuse with non-Jews; (2) they learn moderate drinking norms, practices, and symbolism during childhood through religious and secular rituals; (3) they form adult relationships primarily with other moderate drinkers; and (4) they use a repertoire of techniques to avoid excessive drinking under social pressure. These techniques included reprimands by the spouse, developing reputations as nondrinkers by making jokes, avoiding many drinking situations, and finding rationalizations for not drinking. Alcoholism is a common form of deviance, but the low rate of alcoholism among Jews indicates that informal social controls can exert a powerful influence in controlling it.

Formal external controls, the systems created by society specifically to control deviance, are probably the least influential. Courts, police officers, and prisons are formal external controls. Unlike internal controls and informal external controls, formal controls are supposed to be impersonal and just. In actuality, however, the legal system tends to favor certain groups of people, as conflict theory suggests. Even in prisons, guards tend to overlook rule violations by certain prisoners and enforce rules with others. The discretionary power of police officers, prosecutors, judges, and other officials in arresting, prosecuting, and convicting people is often used arbitrarily. It may be highly dependent on factors other than deviance per se. Age, race, sex, social status, prior deviations, and other factors have all been shown to affect the nature and outcome of formal control mechanisms.

SOCIOLOGISTS AT WORK
Redirecting Juvenile Offenders

Linda Myers is a juvenile probation officer with the Geauga County Juvenile Court in Chardon, Ohio. "According to my job description," says Myers, "I see to it that juvenile offenders placed on probation follow the orders of the court. In fact, my job involves much more than that." Myers works with not only her probationers but also their families and teachers to gain insights into how the probationers interact with those around them — from authority figures to peers — and to formulate the most effective programs for helping the offenders overcome their deviant behavior.

After completing her bachelor's degree at Lake Erie College with a concentration in sociology and psychology, Myers was hired as an intake officer with the Geauga County Juvenile Court. As intake officer she screened incoming complaints against juveniles, conducted home and school investigations, and provided the judge with a social history of the juvenile as well as a recommendation on the handling of the case. Myers' sociological background in family systems and relationships helped her objectively assess home environments and their effect on the adolescents brought to court.

Although Myers' bachelor's degree also qualified her for her next job — the county typically hires bachelor's-level sociologists as probation officers — she decided to pursue a master's degree in applied sociology at Kent State University. She credits the program with giving her a greater understanding of social systems and social agencies, how they work and interact. At Kent she explored the "diversity of programs offered by the human services along with the organizational framework of such institutions and the numerous roles available to sociologists within the social services." This training is particularly useful to her in directing her probationers to the community services and agencies that she feels best fit their needs.

As part of her master's program, Myers also undertook an internship in which she investigated one of her main concerns — the relationship between substance abuse and the variety of offenses

Summary

Deviance is universal, and every society has people who commit acts defined as exceeding the tolerance limits of social norms. There are several traditional views of deviance. The absolutist view assumes that certain acts or people are deviant in all contexts and at all times. Deviance has also been seen as immoral; that is, nonconforming personal behavior is evil and antisocial. According to the medical model, deviance is evidence that a society is unhealthy. A statistical model defines deviance as any behavior that varies from the average or mode.

The relativisitic view, a more sociological perspective, assumes that deviance can be defined only in the context of the society or group in which it takes place. Deviance is not thought to be a certain type of act or person. It is, rather, a relative condition that varies according to time,

for which juveniles are brought to court. Geauga County's high recidivism rate — 48 percent of juvenile offenders end up in court two or more times — convinced her that treatment was often misdirected toward an obvious offense like truancy while ignoring a more serious cause — drug abuse. Her study revealed that indeed 69 percent of juvenile offenses were drug-related. One thirteen-year-old girl, for example, was found guilty of unruliness, as charged by her parents who could not control her, and placed on probation. According to her social history, she had been involved in increasingly serious offenses since the age of ten — running away, truancy, shoplifting, and assault and battery. No one before Myers recognized the possibility of drug abuse as the problem. The girl had denied it vehemently and her parents agreed, pointing out that she didn't even smoke cigarettes. At one point, however, the girl asked Myers, "Do you think I'm insane?" "No," was Myers' response, "but I'm convinced you're on drugs." Shocked by Myers' detection of the problem, the girl admitted she'd been taking drugs for three years. Subsequent testing revealed that she was chemically addicted and only then did she begin receiving treatment.

Myers currently has a caseload of fifty-three female offenders, who are expected to obey a set of standardized rules, such as observing a curfew, making restitution in cases of vandalism, and not associating with others on probation. In addition, Myers and her probationers formulate an individualized set of goals and agree to the terms of a behavior contract that might include regular school attendance, involvement in at least one extracurricular activity, or doing chores at home. Myers also strongly believes in clearly defining the consequences of violating the agreement — from a warning to a return to court and possible incarceration.

Myers maintains close contact with her probationers through weekly meetings. At least half of each day she visits homes and schools, talking to parents, teachers, and friends to gain ongoing insights into her probationers' environment, progress, and needs. As she points out, however, "Crises have a way of not occurring between 8:30 and 4:30, and I spend many evening and weekend hours on the phone trying to defuse explosive situations." The long hours, however, are a price Myers is willing to pay to develop the close, supportive relationship through which she can best help her probationers and that often lasts long after the official relationship has ended.

Myers feels she will continue to work within the court system for some time. Her future may involve a private practice or involvement in preventive approaches to delinquency. Whatever she chooses, she is convinced her sociological training will continue to serve her well.

place, situation, and social status. This view takes into account the great diversity of meanings that can be associated with people or acts in different situations.

Many theories have been developed to explain who is deviant, the causes of deviance, and how it can be controlled or modified. Biological theories have attempted to associate it with body type, physical abnormalities, and chromosome aberrations. Psychological theories emphasize such factors as personality, motivation, willpower, frustration, aggression, and ego strength. Sociological theorists do not ignore biological and psychological factors, but they tend to view theories based on these factors as insufficient. Sociological theories focus on the interactional, organizational, and social normative factors through which people learn definitions of deviance. These factors also determine people's behavior, which a social audience labels as either deviant or nondeviant.

Anomie theory links deviance to conflicts between culturally valued goals and institutionalized means of achieving them. Innovation, ritualism, retreatism, and rebellion are deviant modes of adaptation.

Conflict theorists say that definitions of deviance are devised by the powerful to repress and exploit the weak. An influential, wealthy elite is assumed to oppose and control the powerless, the poor, and minorities.

Sociocultural learning theories, which are basically both social and psychological in nature, emphasize the processes through which deviant acts are learned and the types of conditions under which they are learned. Cultural transmission theory, sometimes called subculture theory, explains the continuity of crime and deviance in certain geographical areas as the result of the transmission of deviant norms from one generation to the next. Differential association theory contends that deviance is learned through verbal and nonverbal communication. According to this theory, we learn either deviant or nondeviant attitudes and behaviors by associating differentially with deviant or nondeviant individuals and groups. The social learning theory of deviance, which draws heavily on differential association theory, suggests that operant (instrumental) conditioning and imitation play important roles in the learning of behaviors. Differential rewards and punishments and exposure to conforming or deviant models greatly influence whether we develop deviant or conforming attitudes and behaviors.

Labeling theory, rather than emphasizing acts or individuals in isolation, focuses on why certain people and acts are singled out as deviant and also on the effects of being labeled deviant. This approach, which is based on the principles of symbolic interaction, assumes that defining deviance and other behaviors is a collective process. People in social contexts define and interpret their own behavior and that of others and apply labels on the basis of their definitions. These labels have a significant effect on the continuation of deviant behavior for both those defined as deviant and the audience who labels them.

Deviance can influence social systems in several different ways. Some of the consequences are functional: they can help define the limits of social tolerance, increase the solidarity and integration of groups, indicate inadequacies in the system, and bring about constructive change. Other consequences are dysfunctional: deviance can disrupt the social order, decrease the will of others to conform, destroy trust, and divert resources that could be used elsewhere into social rehabilitation and control efforts.

The control of deviance is generally explained in terms of two factors, internal controls and external controls. Internal controls, which are exerted by individuals on themselves, involve such factors as self-concept, ego strength, high frustration tolerance, and conscience. These controls are believed to be acquired through socialization. External controls include both informal interactions with people, such as family and friends, and formal controls, which are carried out by the agencies designated by society to maintain law and order.

Key Terms

absolutist view
anomie theory
cultural transmission theory
deviance
differential association
differential reinforcement
formal external controls
frustration, aggression
informal external controls
internal controls
labeling theory
Lombroso's body types

social learning theory
sociocultural learning theories
XYY chromosomes

Suggested Readings

Becker, Howard S. **Outsiders: Studies in the Sociology of Deviance.** *New York: The Free Press, 1963.* This is one of the pioneering works of labeling theory applied specifically to marijuana use and the careers of dance musicians.

Douglas, Jack D. and Frances Chopert Waksler. **The Sociology of Deviance: An Introduction.** *Boston: Little, Brown, 1982.* An examination of a broad range of sociological theories that have been developed to explain deviance and the application of these theories to selected varieties of deviance.

Ferrell, Ronald A. and Victoria L. Swigert. **Deviance and Social Control.** *Glenview, Ill.: Scott, Foresman, 1982.* An interpretation of the major classic and contemporary theories of deviance and social control, emphasizing structural, interactional, and social-psychological influences.

Goode, Erich. **Deviant Behavior: An Interactional Approach.** *Englewood Cliffs, N.J.: Prentice-Hall, 1978.* A textbook covering deviance from an interactionist-labeling perspective.

Hills, Stuart L. **Demystifying Social Deviance.** *New York: McGraw-Hill, 1980.* A look at the special creation of deviance from the interactionist, conflict, and humanist perspectives. The book covers the meanings people impute to behavior, the distribution of power, and the economic, legal, and political structure of society, and an emphasis on creating a more humane and just society.

Kelly, Delos H. **Deviant Behavior: Readings in the Sociology of Deviance.** *New York: St. Martin's Press, 1979.* An anthology concerned with social responses to deviant behavior and why certain individuals violate social norms.

Rosenberg, M. Michael, Robert A. Stebbins and Alan Turowetz (eds.) **The Sociology of Deviance.** *New York: St. Martin's Press, 1982.* Eleven essays covering deviant careers, subcultures, power, conflict, social control, social change, and trends in deviance research.

Rubington, Earl and Martin S. Weinberg. **Deviance: The Interactionist Perspective.** *4th ed. New York: Macmillan, 1981.* A collection of forty readings on the interactionist approach to deviance.

Schur, Edwin M. **Interpreting Deviance: A Sociological Introduction.** *New York: Harper & Row, 1979.* A systematic, comprehensive textbook on the interpretation of deviance.

Thio, Alex. **Deviant Behavior.** *Boston: Houghton Mifflin, 1978.* A relatively comprehensive textbook on deviance, covering the major theories of deviance, the relevant literature, and specific forms of deviant behavior including murder, rape, robbery, prostitution, homosexuality, suicide, mental disorder, swinging, illegal drug use, and alcoholism.

Traub, Stuart H. and Craig B. Little (eds.). **Theories of Deviance.** *2nd ed. Itasca, Ill.: F. E. Peacock, 1980.* A look at major theoretical perspectives on deviance: functionalism, social disorganization, cultural conflict, anomie, differential association, and labeling.

Part II Readings

On Being Friends
by Constantina Safilios-Rothschild

Can men and women ever really be friends in American society? Sociologist Constantina Safilios-Rothschild looks at how socialization affects the way the sexes interact.

Within the context of the American society, men and women have been provided with hardly any socialization experiences that prepare them for being good friends with each other. From very early adolescence, when girls and boys for the first time become interested in associating with each other, they are pressured to date and to think in terms of romance. There is no institutionalized alternative that allows them to consider friendship without romantic overtones. This is a serious socialization handicap, and it has long-range consequences for the possible man-woman relationships.

There is evidence that in some societies, boys and girls learn how to value friendship sometimes even more than sexual and love relationships. In urban Greece, for example, as well as in other Mediterranean societies, middle- and upper-middle-class boys and girls enjoy the institution of *parea* from the time they are 15 or 16 years old. *Parea* usually replaces or supplements dating (which is exclusive rather than multiple) and is composed of a number of boys and girls whose pairing is taboo. *Parea* members go out together socially, spend hours talking and playing together and learn to associate with peers of both sexes and to enjoy them as friends and persons rather than as dates. The crucial socialization function of *parea* is evident in the adult men's and women's ability to have and enjoy friendships with both sexes and a *parea* throughout life, in addition to sexual, love, and marital relationships.

It must be noted, however, that despite the fact that *parea* members are not supposed to develop romantic interest in each other, occasionally this happens. The pair then either drops from the *parea* or maintains the friendship appearance within the context of the *parea*, while at the same time dating each other outside of it.

There are some sporadic reports that at least some teenagers and young people have started going out in groups without any special pairing arrangement. Although no systematic research data are available, to the extent that this is the trend, it is encouraging, since it can be expected to facilitate and enhance the intrinsic value of friendships between men and women. But the fact remains that American men and women have not known how to enjoy and appreciate nonromantic friendships. Some women, especially those who are well-educated, have tried to establish this kind of friendship, but usually the response has been either sexual and love proposals or a total lack of interest. Because they valued the interaction with the men involved, some reluctantly accepted a sexual and affective relationship. However, in some cases in which women have formed a friendship with a man (especially with an attractive man), they have felt insulted and rejected if there was no clear indication that the man was sexually or affectively interested in them (even if he did not behaviorally express those interests owing to a variety of social constraints). Thus, while women have been relatively more interested in and appreciative of other-sex friendships than men, they have also tended to be ambivalent and dissatisfied when these friendships were totally devoid of underlying or potential sexual and love elements.

Here it must be noted that the reasons for which men have not typically sought or especially valued friendships with women are not limited to their masculine sex-role stereotypes and socialization experiences. Women have not particularly valued other women's friendship either because of the prevailing notion that women are of less value than men. Thus, men were the "desirable" friends for both men and women and women felt quite proud of a male friend.

In traditional societies in which women have been and are almost entirely excluded from the world of men (except as sexual objects or servants), they have learned to value and depend upon close relationships with other women. But whenever it is possible to have men as friends, women have clearly preferred them over women. Their motivations have been complex. Men have always been desirable as friends because such friendships were often viewed as a prelude to or potential for future love relationships. In fact, many women report that long and close friendships between men and women that eventually develop into romantic love relationships tend to be strong and good. In a way, friendships with men were some sort of insurance for the future, in case actual love or marital relationships did not work out satisfactorily or were disrupted. Also, women enjoy friendships with men because such relationships sometimes represent their acceptance by men as an equal and a worthwhile partner and companion without the contaminating influence of expressed sexuality. Any underlying sexual overtones reassure women, on the other hand, of their attractiveness for men other than their husband and/or lover.

The existence of sexual and affective overtones need not interfere with the establishment and enjoyment of friendships between men and women. As a matter of fact, they may be necessary for some friendships; or they may add considerably to the dimensions and enjoyment of the relationship. However, what *can* interfere are the expectations the friends, as well as the people around them, hold concerning the realization of sexual and love interests. When men and women can handle the existence of these overtones and when those around them can accept such friendships at face value, it is possible to relax and appreciate the relationship, even with the occasional sexual and/or romantic overtones.

When people believe, as a result of their upbringing and the prevailing sex-role stereotypes, that "something is wrong" unless a sexual or a love relationship develops between a man and woman who are in a nonromantic friendship, the situation will be strained and difficult. In fact, the two involved may grow to see the friendship as a "stalemate" or a failure, and cease eventually to appreciate what it offers. To avoid this, as we have mentioned above, friends must resist the pressures of those around them to gravitate toward a sexual relationship, if they are both unmarried. If friends are already married to other people, then the pressures on them to dissolve their friendship are enormous. Marital partners, relatives, and acquaintances find it hard to accept the existence of such friendships. Spouses particularly resent them because of the existing close ties and the sharing of experiences, even when they are convinced that there are no sexual or love elements. They typically feel that another person is taking over an important part of the intimate relationship with "their" mate. Furthermore, men and women friends (especially if they are not married to other people) usually spend a lot of time together and share many experiences that are usually shared by lovers. This becomes an additional factor that conditions them and pushes them toward a romantic relationship or the breakup of the friendship.

Other types of complications that threaten the survival of a friendship between a man and a woman emerge when only one of them wants and attempts to transform the friendship into a sexual or love relationship but the other is reluctant to do so. In these cases, only rarely does the friendship survive because the one who proposes the changes may feel rejected. This is particularly true for men, whose idea of masculinity does not allow them to accept that a woman's lifelong friendship may be as (or more) valuable than a short-lived sexual or love relationship. Too many friendships have been wasted in this way — rich and meaningful relationships that would have provided wonderful experiences for the people involved.

A fundamental difficulty in the establishment and survival of friendships between men and women is the monolithic love model by which we have been taught to abide. The Western version of the love model requires not only sexual and affective exclusivity but also companionship exclusivity, so that there is little room even for close, intimate friends. As we have already mentioned, this tendency has sometimes been carried so far in the United States that very close friendships even with members of the same sex have been considered undesirable and suspect. American couples are expected to *be* best friends; they usually have other friends whom they see socially, but even when any of these become close, the couple shares them so that one spouse does not feel left out. Exclusive friends aren't allowed.

In view of all the structural and psychological obstacles that interfere with the establishment and survival of nonromantic friendships between men and women, it seems almost a miracle when they succeed. Up to now, there have been some special situations that tended to facilitate such friendships. Men and women sometimes found it easier to become good friends after they had stopped being lovers or spouses. The earlier sexual or love relationship can help reduce or minimize the sexual tension between them and leave them free and relaxed to enjoy a relationship without hangups and inhibitions. As a matter of fact, in some cases, previously mismatched lovers and spouses have been known to form healthy friendships once the sexual and love elements were removed. Another special situation has been the ease some men found in having nonsexual relationships with older women. Such friendships were not only socially approved but even encouraged, and enriched the lives of both people. Today, however, in our present transitional stage, the sexuality of older women is increasingly recognized, so with the introduction of sexual possibilities such friendships may experience considerable strain. There are indications that older women, especially if they are vital and interesting, are increasingly viewed as attractive and desirable.

Probably, as many more men and women come to enjoy an equal social status, we can expect that many more will want to develop friendships with the other sex. Only when such friendships have become a perfectly acceptable and highly valued form of interaction between men and women will sexual and love relationships truly become options. As long as male-female friendships are strenuous, difficult, and at best ambiguous, men and women who are attracted to each other for a variety of reasons will be pressured and obliged to opt for sex and/or love when many might have preferred a fulfilling friendship.

SOURCE: Safilios-Rothschild, Constantina, ed., *Love, Sex, and Sex Roles,* © Prentice-Hall, Englewood Cliffs, N.J., 1977. Reprinted by permission.

Boot Camp

*Peter Rose, Myron Glazer,
and Penina Migdal Glazer*

*Resocialization is one of the most disrupting pro-
cesses that a person can go through. In this article,
the authors describe a marine recruit's experience.*

Becoming a Soldier

The armed forces prepare men (and some
women) to endure hardship, obey orders, achieve
group solidarity, and acquire the skills and attitudes necessary for military service. To do this,
authorities demand that recruits leave behind
their families, possessions, ideas — indeed, their
whole civilian selves — and forge new identities as
military personnel.

Life in a Marine Boot Camp

How resocialization in the military occurs is
well described by Steven Warner, a conscientious
objector drafted in 1972 by the marine corps. (At
this stage of the Vietnam War, the draft was still
operating, though bitterly opposed by many
Americans.) Warner, like the other recruits, found
that many of his previous beliefs were challenged
as the corps attempted to turn him from a citizen
who hated war into a soldier who would obey
on command. The experience made a strong
impression.

> Our Greyhound drove onto Parris Island at
> ten that night. A few seconds after we stopped, a
> staff sergeant wearing the Smokey Bear hat all
> drill instructors wear came on the bus and said:
> "You're on Parris Island. There are two ways to
> leave here: on a bus like this in eight or nine
> weeks or in a box. . . . If you have any cigarettes,
> put them out. If you have any gum, swallow
> it. . . . You have ten seconds to get into that
> building. . . . Move! . . .

> A staff sergeant began . . . telling us how we
> were to behave from that moment on. . . .
> Recruits must stand at attention at all times.
> Recruits will not eyeball. Recruits will double-
> time everywhere. Recruits will do nothing with-
> out permission: they will not speak or swat bugs
> or wipe off sweat or faint without permission.
> Recruits will call everyone, except other recruits,
> "Sir." Recruits will never use the word "you" be-
> cause "you" is a female sheep and there are no
> ewes on Parris Island. Recruits will never use the
> word "I" because "I" is what a recruit sees with,
> not what he calls himself.

An initial part of the resocialization process
began with **depersonalization** — depriving people of their individuality. The young men were no
longer called by their names. Their personal possessions were taken away, and a hundred rules
(that is, new norms) were thrown at them. Merg-
ing with the group was stressed. A recruit had to
speak, look, and act like every other recruit — or
else. Uniforms and haircuts were important components of that transformation. Former roles and
identities did not count. It no longer mattered
whether a recruit had been a high school football
captain, the owner of a custom sports car, or a
promising writer. The sooner the past was forgotten, the better the recruit would get along.

The resocialization process included another
crucial component made clear right at the beginning. The drill instructor (DI) immediately became
the recruits' most important significant other. His
welcoming speech not only set out a whole series
of new norms but also established that he controlled rewards and punishments. If the recruit did
not live up to his role obligations, he would be
observed and quickly reprimanded. The DI's
opinion and reactions were what counted now.
He and his fellow DIs were in control.

The subjugation of the recruits was immediately reinforced when the men were ordered to
pick up their gear and follow their DI after the
initial speech. Those recruits who couldn't keep

the double-time pace were cajoled, cursed, and punished. The message was clear. Tough days were ahead. The DIs had the difficult task of turning soft individual civilians into a disciplined fighting unit. It may not have been a task they relished, but it was necessary, and they did it in a relentless manner.

The DIs' definition of their own roles reflected their sensitivity to the process of resocialization. The recruits brought with them a vast baggage of previous roles and cultural definitions. The armed forces assumed that all of these had to be broken down and discarded if the recruits were to become military men capable of responding to orders, working as a group, and living together. New norms had to be repeated continually and appropriate behavior demanded. There could be no exceptions. The DIs had to be constantly alert for infractions of the rules and ready to "chew out" (or "ream") offenders. The DIs' vigilance and consistency in playing their roles were important defenses against letting the recruits slide into former patterns of civilian behavior.

The controlled environment began to have its effect on Warner. The recruits were constantly warned about the cunning and toughness of North Vietnamese soldiers. Although Warner had come to boot camp unafraid of the "enemy" in Southeast Asia, the training sessions instilled fear in him. Other things were also happening. A sense of group solidarity was beginning to take shape. The men reached out to help one another in time of trouble. As in actual combat, recruits acted out the belief that they could depend on their buddies. Primary group relations were developing under the supervision of the authorities.

Since the first days of boot camp, we had been warned about the PRT [Physical Readiness Test] we would take during the last week. This would be our initiation into the Marine Corps. . . .

We climbed some ropes in full gear, carried one another over our shoulders for a while, crawled a lot. . . . Then came the last hurdle: a three-mile run in full gear — steel helmet, boots, pack rifle.

Everyone was grim. Our commanding officer, also in full gear, ran in front of the company. Gordon [the DI] was in front of our platoon. . . . We ran silently for a while. The only sounds were heavy breathing and boots hitting the ground. Then Gordon started us on our chants: "Here we go-o! HERE WE GO-O! Long Road! LONG ROAD! Hard Road! HARD ROAD! Won't Stop! WON'T STOP! Gimme More! GIMME MORE! Marine Corps! MARINE CORPS!"

Two or three recruits were having a hard time. They had run the distance many times before, but now they gasped for air and stumbled trying to keep up. Other recruits took turns, carrying their rifles, their packs, and even their helmets. If the stragglers continued to fade, they were held up by the arms, even carried. . . . The point was, the platoon kept on running, and no one was left behind. We had learned our lesson.

When it was over, everybody was grins and backslapping. Gordon, sweating more than I had ever seen before, came into the barracks and gave us a small smile and said: "MARINES . . . take a shower." It was the first time he had ever called us that.

This episode includes some telling points about the process of resocialization. The men's new status required more than putting aside previous statuses. It required them to forge a new identity as marines. This included the belief that the recruit could overcome difficult physical challenges, that he must and could make sure that his buddies handled them too, and that success would be achieved under the leadership of competent authorities. The reward was a shared satisfaction that the unit had succeeded and that each member could be proud of his part in the achievement. Thus, while former statuses had been suppressed, the new one — marine — made all the sacrifices easier to bear.

In this effort, the peer group played a central part. Feelings of interdependence — that "We're in it together" — reinforced the authorities' value that the unit was more important than the individual. In a controlled environment, resocialization of participants is more effective if the peer group supports the values of the authorities.

How do the characteristics of a controlled environment described earlier apply to military basic training? All aspects of the recruit's life are conducted at one particular place — the military base — and under the control of one authority — the DI. Every aspect of the recruit's life takes place in the company of other recruits who are in the same circumstances and playing the same role. All daily activities are scheduled by the authorities without the consent of the recruits. Finally, all these activities fulfill the main purpose of the military — to prepare men to fight in wars. This means socializing them to respond to authority even when their lives are at stake. Behavior that had been acceptable in civilian life was now defined as deviant and subject to punishment. Even a conscientious objector like Steven Warner found his previous beliefs undermined. In a particularly revealing final statement, he wrote that if his own son ever had to be in the armed forces, he hoped the boy would serve in the marines.

Warner's experiences reveal other characteristics of controlled environments. For one thing, depersonalization is central to resocialization. It forces the recruit to leave behind former statuses and the roles and identities associated with them. Warner's experience also shows that unlearning former role behavior is a painful procedure that people are likely to resist. Significant others are crucial in the unlearning process. They in turn succeed best when they set out their expectations clearly and consistently and when they have the resources to reward conformity and punish deviance. And an individual is more willing to play a new role if it is shown to have some positive relation to past definitions of the self. In other words, recruits may vehemently dislike obeying orders, but they are more likely to do so if they can be convinced that this shows they "can take it" and are now fit to be called "marine." Resocialization occurs more easily if conformity to the rules of the new position is perceived as competence rather than subservience. Finally, resocialization proceeds more smoothly if the individual finds new groups with which to identify within the controlled environment.

SOURCE: From Rose, P. I., Glazer, M., and Glazer P. M., *Sociology: Inquiring into Society,* 2nd ed. Copyright © 1982 by St. Martin's Press and reprinted by permission of the publisher. Excerpted material from Warner, Steven, "A Conscientious Objector at Parris Island." *The Atlantic Monthly,* June 1972. Reprinted by permission of Paul R. Reynolds, Inc.

Part III

Social Inequality

We are not all equal. Some people are rich and some are poor. Some are respected and others are despised. Some are powerful and others are powerless. Being born into a rich family, a poor family, a respected family, or a powerful family makes a difference in the way we live our lives. This is true even in the United States where equality is valued.

Inequality is found in most societies and persists from generation to generation. Is it good for society? Does it serve any useful purpose? Or does it continue in spite of the conflicts and suffering it causes? This section on social inequality explores the answers to these questions. Chapter 8 provides a general overview of inequality, how it develops, and how it persists. We look at how the structure of society maintains social differences, sometimes by force but usually because we are socialized to believe that things are as they should be. In Chapters 9 and 10 we describe specific groups who are differentiated on the basis of wealth, status, and power — women, the elderly, and members of certain racial and ethnic groups. Through a variety of events in history, all these groups are held in positions in the lower strata of our society.

Chapter 8
Social Differentiation and Stratification

All animals are equal, but some animals are more equal than others.

— George Orwell

Social Stratification

Leonid Brezhnev may be the leader of the most powerful communist country in the world, but his lifestyle is so extravagant that Marx and Engels, the founders of communism, would surely have condemned him as an enemy of the people.

Although Brezhnev continues to mouth the myth that the USSR is a classless society, he personally owns two yachts and maintains a fleet of fancy foreign cars, including a Rolls-Royce Silver Cloud, a Citroen-Maserati, a Mercedes 450 SCL and two gifts from Richard Nixon: a Cadillac and a Lincoln Continental.

While most citizens of the Soviet Union wait in line for rationed products, Brezhnev and other Communist Party leaders shop at special stores, paying their bills with funds from "open accounts" at the State Bank. Brezhnev's Moscow apartment and his country house are tended by servants and furnished with the latest Western style gadgets as well as his famous collection of antique clocks.

His favorite gadget helps him to fight his tobacco habit. It's a locked cigarette case with a timer that forces Brezhnev to wait for his next smoke. However, unlike the rest of the people in the USSR, who have no choice but to wait for goods, Leonid Brezhnev sets his own timer. (*Parade* magazine, May 31, 1981, p. 16)

Leonid Brezhnev is certainly different from other communists. The powerful leader of a powerful nation, he lives far more comfortably than his fellow citizens. Why is he so powerful that he can rule a nation and attain great prosperity while other citizens must wait in line for their basic necessities? In the United States, the Rockefellers and the Kennedys control great wealth and live lives of luxury in summer and winter mansions. Nelson Rockefeller became a vice-president and

John Kennedy became a president of the United States. Why are they so rich and powerful, while other Americans are in prison or live in shacks?

Inequality — the unequal distribution of scarce goods or resources — is found in many different types of cultures. Certain goods and resources are hard to come by in certain societies. In some countries meat is scarce; in others it is plentiful. Land is a scarce resource in some areas of the world, but in others it is so plentiful that no one even bothers to claim ownership. There are not enough workers in some societies, which makes children a valuable resource. They work on the family farm and provide for their parents in old age, so a man who has many children may be a rich man. Some commodities are scarce in many cultures. In both the United States and in communist countries, for example, mansions and luxury cars are scarce commodities.

A person who controls scarce resources has power. *Power* is the ability to achieve one's desires, even when others resist. People who can grow food, raise armies, or cure illness have power over those who cannot.

We rank people according to the scarce resources they control. Money and property are scarce resources in our society, and those who own a great deal of money and property, wealthy people, can use this resource to gain power. It has been said that very respected people also control another scarce resource — public respect — and that they can use this resource to gain power. Political leaders are likewise powerful because they are in a position to control the members of a political party. This ranking of people according to their wealth, prestige, or party position is known as *social stratification*. Stratification separates the rich from the poor, the powerful from the powerless. Those who possess scarce resources have a high rank, and those who do not possess them have a low rank.

Our place in the stratification system influences every part of our lives: where we live, go to school, and work; what we eat, how we vote; and whom we marry. Our sexual behavior, sports, hobbies, and health are all affected by the rank society gives us. It is therefore not surprising that social stratification is an area of great interest to sociologists.

Sources of Power

According to Weber (1946), the scarce resources that are the sources of power in society are of three types: social class, status, and party.

Social Class

Social class is based on several closely related factors: wealth, the power derived from wealth, and "life chances" to acquire wealth. *Life chances* are the opportunities people have to improve their income. A woman from the upper-middle class, for example, has a better opportunity to get a good education and thus a good job than a woman from the lower classes.

Marx and Engels, in *The Communist Manifesto* (1848), argued that social class was based entirely on wealth. The bourgeoisie, the rich, formed a class because they were the exclusive owners of the means of production — the farms and factories that produced needed food and supplies. The poor, the proletariat, formed a class because they had no land to produce food and no means to manufacture the supplies they needed. They could only sell their labor to the owners of the factories.

Because the rich had control of the means of production, they had power. They could hire the poor when it was profitable and fire them when they were no longer needed. The rich could make a profit on the labor of the poor. The poor, by contrast, had no power to claim the profits of their labor.

Max Weber (1946) agreed that social class is based on wealth, but he argued that a chance to acquire wealth is just as important as wealth itself.

Regardless of social class, boys pass free time in conversation with one another like the prep school youths and the ghetto youths in these photos. The wealth of the prep school students, however, increases their life chances — they are more likely to get an advanced education and to meet influential people. They will therefore have a better opportunity to develop their talents and sell themselves in the job market.

He said that a "life-chance" to acquire wealth is dependent on the possibility of making a profit in the marketplace. People who have a scarce resource other than wealth, such as an advanced education, a special skill, or a talent or service to sell, have power in the marketplace. They can sell when the price is right or sell to the highest bidder, and they can refuse to sell when the price is too low. Social class, then, is determined by life chances to acquire wealth as well as wealth itself.

Social Status

According to Weber, *social status* is another important source of power. Whereas class is based on economics, status is social. It is a function of the honor and prestige a person receives from others in the community. Prestige is acquired by being born into a highly respected family, living in a high-status neighborhood, attending the right schools, or joining high-status groups or clubs. People also gain prestige by being able to buy consumer goods that others admire, such as expensive houses, yachts, or airplanes. In short, status is acquired by doing things and buying things that others admire. People who have status have power because they can influence those who respect them. They can use this influence to get a better job or increase their chances of marrying into wealthy or high-status families and thus use their power to increase their wealth.

Parties

Parties are Weber's third source of power. A person can gain power in the community by being politically active in national, state, or local parties, in special interest groups, in influential clubs, or in any other type of organization in which decisions are made to reach certain goals. By developing power in parties, people can increase their status by winning respect and increase their social class by reaching goals that are profitable to them.

Class, status, and party are often closely interrelated. Status and party can be used to increase wealth. Wealth can be used to buy consumer goods and increase status or to join prestigious clubs and increase political power. These three sources of power do not always go together, however. Wealthy people who are criminals, who live reclusive lives, or who are otherwise atypical have low status if no one respects them. Priests, ministers, college professors, and community leaders may be poor but still have a high status. Party leaders who use their position to increase their wealth sometimes do so in such a way that they lose status and the respect of others.

You may better understand characteristics of stratification — class, social status, party — if you think back to high school days and the ways that students could gain recognition. Some students gained recognition in dimensions of class, others gained recognition in dimensions of status, and still others, in dimensions of political activities. Table 8-1 provides examples of these dimensions of stratification.

Socioeconomic Status

It is difficult to place individuals in a particular social stratum because class, status, and party affiliations can all influence where they might be placed. Is the widower of a distinguished scholar

Table 8-1

Dimensions of stratification in a high school elite

CLASS (WEALTH OR SKILLS FOR THE MARKETPLACE)	
Wealthy students	Most likely to succeed
Valedictorian	Best athletes
Honor Society members	Best actors and actresses

STATUS (HONOR AND RESPECT)	
Most popular	Best dressed
Best looking	Members of sororities and
Most poised	fraternities
	Prom queens

PARTIES (POLITICAL ACTIVITY)	
Student body officers and	Club officers
delegates	Newspaper editors
Class officers	
Sorority and fraternity	
officers	

who lives on a small retirement income in the same class as a mail carrier or a shoplifter who has the same income? Does a rural doctor who serves the poor and receives a small income have the same class position as a suburban doctor who serves the rich and has a large income? Does a prostitute have the same class position as the owner of a small employment agency? As you can see, class boundaries can be difficult to determine. A person who has a high position in one category may have a low position in a different category. Where, then, should that person be placed?

To resolve this problem, sociologists have developed the concept of *socioeconomic status* (SES). This measure considers income, education, and occupation when assessing a person's status. Someone who earns $50,000 will be ranked higher than a person earning $10,000, a college graduate will be ranked higher than a high school graduate, and anybody in a professional or management occupation will be ranked higher than a laborer. Usually there is a consistent pattern among these three rankings of status. People with many years of education hold occupations that afford high status and high incomes. One of the more interesting problems sociologists study, however, is how to categorize people who have *status inconsistency*, for example, many years of advanced education but a very low income.

Theories of Social Stratification

Why are societies stratified? This question was widely debated by early sociologists, and their differing viewpoints have shaped current debates on the subject. As you will remember from Chapter 2, Spencer believed that superior people would educate themselves and become leaders, whereas inferior people would remain in the bottom ranks of society. Society, he said, developed through an evolutionary process, and those who profited

from natural selection — "survival of the fittest" — came out on top. This process of natural selection was good for social progress, he argued, and society should not interfere with it.

The opposing view was formulated by Marx, who argued that stratification would eventually create revolution. The upper class in industrial society hired the proletariat to work in their factories, exploited them for profit, and drove them into poverty. As the proletariat became poorer, Marx contended, they would become aware of their plight and would revolt. The theories of these early writers have had a strong influence on the two prevailing modern theories of stratification, structural functionalism and conflict theory.

Structural-Functional Theory

Structural functionalists have refined Spencer's notion that society, like any other organism, is self-regulating and self-maintaining and that it consists of interrelated parts that serve a function in maintaining the system as a whole.

According to this view, stratification is necessary for society to function. Complex industrial systems need to be centralized, and power is placed in the hands of people who are capable of being leaders. Leadership requires advanced learning, hard work, and the ability to assume responsibility. Society rewards those who serve as leaders by giving them *wealth*. Wealth and status, both scarce resources, provide power, so those who serve society by providing scarce skills become the powerful people. Thus, inequality is created by the needs of the society, not by the desires and needs of individuals (Davis and Moore, 1945). If society had an equal need for all types of work, then all its members would be equal.

Conflict Theory

Conflict theorists reject the functional viewpoint (Duberman, 1976), arguing that inequality develops as a result of people's desire for scarce resources, and close-knit groups compete with one another to gain possession of these resources. According to this view, resources are not rewards for talent or for assuming difficult tasks but are acquired through inheritance, coercion, or exploitation. Inequality results when one group acquires more resources than other groups.

Once the dominant group gets power, it tries to make its power appear legitimate by using propaganda to appeal to the masses through education, the mass media, religion, and politics. It tries to convince the masses to support the leadership of the dominant group for the good of the country, promising to protect the country from enemies such as capitalists or communists. The dominant group may also base its appeals for support on religious or moral grounds, claiming the divine right of kings or the moral right of the electoral system.

If the masses are influenced by the propaganda of the upper class, they are said to have what Marx called *false consciousness*, a belief that the upper class is superior and has the right to rule. If, on the other hand, the masses reject the propaganda of the upper classes and are aware that they are being exploited, they are said to have *class consciousness*. Regardless of their consciousness, there is little conflict if the masses have jobs and can live lives they find satisfactory. Serious conflicts develop only when the masses are severely exploited and possess class consciousness.

Attempts at Synthesis

Some sociologists are trying to reconcile the functional and conflict theories of stratification (Lenski, 1966; Dahrendorf, 1951; Tumin, 1963). Accumulating research suggests that stratification has a wide variety of causes, some based on conflict, some on cooperation. A stratification system based on religion, for example, may stress feelings of community and selflessness. Others, based on land ownership or accumulation of money, may tend to emphasize competition and the efforts of individuals. As our understanding of the nature

and development of stratification improves, it is becoming increasingly apparent that stratification is influenced by a great many different factors: how food is grown, how supplies are manufactured and distributed, how much wealth accumulates, and how people use their leisure time, to name a few. Neither functional nor conflict theory offers us a full understanding of how stratification systems develop.

There is, however, widespread agreement that all stratification systems are based on the accumulation of wealth. Wealth creates leisure time, time to do something besides work. It also encourages division of labor — people spend their leisure time in diverse ways and develop special skills that enable them to do certain jobs better than others. Lenski (1966), who has classified societies into five types on the basis of their complexity, has shown that wealth, division of labor, and stratification increase as societies grow more complex. These five types of society are discussed next.

Types of Societies and Social Differentiation

Very simple societies have simple divisions of labor, and all people have about the same tasks and possessions; as a result there is little social differentiation. Societies grow more complex as their wealth increases, however, since there are many different jobs to be done. In a complex society such as our own there is a wide division of labor, which creates a wide array of social positions, and thus stratification develops as we rank these positions in order of importance. Lenski (1966) has shown that stratification increases as societies grow more complex and wealthy. He discerned five basic types of society.

Hunting and gathering societies consist of fifty people or less who live on what they can find to eat. They are often nomadic, moving from place to place in search of food. They are usually very

A Gathering Society: The Tasaday

Sometime during the 1960s, a Filipino hunter named Dafal discovered three naked men digging roots deep in a rain forest. Dafal made friends with the men, exchanged some food, and parted. Dafal mentioned this meeting to Philippine officials, who asked to meet the forest people, and the Tasaday Cave-Dwellers became known to modern society.

The Tasaday numbered about two dozen people, living in three caves in the side of a mountain overlooking a large stream. They survived by foraging in the forest. Their basic food was a root they called *biking*, which was dug and eaten either raw or cooked. They also gathered fruits and wild yams, and from the stream they gathered frogs, tadpoles, crabs, fish, and grubs. All food was shared among the members of the group.

Their tools were sticks and stones, their clothing was grass. They had no healing ceremonies, no elaborate marriage ceremonies, no burial ceremonies, apparently no ceremonies of any kind. They had no known magical or religious traditions.

The only division of labor observed among the Tasaday was that women swept the caves and men gathered firewood. Men, women, and children searched for food. Men and women were equally responsible for the children. Decision making was a group process based on discussion, and all men and women expressed their opinions. They did not argue.

One woman appeared to exert more influence over the group than any other person. Her opinions were highly regarded, and her recommendations were followed more often than anyone else's. She usually divided up the supply of food. While she had influence, she did not have any power. She could not make anyone do anything they did not wish to do. The Tasaday were highly egalitarian.

SOURCE: Vivilo, Frank Robert, *Cultural Anthropology Handbook: A Basic Introduction,* New York, McGraw-Hill, 1978.

A Tasaday family rest in their cave. From left are Lubo, Ivet (the mother), a baby who has not yet been named, Lolo sitting in the rear, Natek lying down, and Bilangen (the father). The Tasaday hunt and gather food using the simplest stone age tools. They have no wealth and therefore no class distinctions, although some members of the society may be considered more able and talented at the work of gathering food.

poor and must share what they find to eat in order to survive. No one can be excused from work. Surpluses of food or supplies are not accumulated, so no one can become wealthy. Some people may gain special respect because of their age, wisdom, skill in hunting, or magical abilities, but they do not derive any power from their status because there is no area to exercise their authority and little to do except work. With so little differentiation in these societies, there is little stratification.

In *simple horticultural societies,* the people farm using a digging stick as their basic tool. They have a fairly reliable source of food and may even have a surplus from time to time. Thus, they can remain in one location, build shelters, and make tools. A surplus of food and supplies allows them some leisure time, which they use in sports and ceremonial activities. They also occasionally fight wars to protect their land. Certain specialized occupations develop: warriors and ceremonial and political leaders. Ceremonial leaders are sometimes paid for performing ceremonies, especially those involving healing, and they may become wealthy. Political leaders, with the assistance of warriors, can capture slaves and enforce their edicts. As labor is divided among different groups and wealth and status accumulate, a stratification system develops.

Advanced horticultural societies farm with irrigation, terracing, and fertilization. These techniques increase the food supply, so the size of the population can grow. Societies at this level have learned how to work metals, which increases the variety of material goods and also the variety of occupations. As the size and wealth of the population increase and a greater variety of occupations develops, stratification increases. The king becomes a very powerful person. He has a larger army and can capture more slaves and force them to do whatever he chooses. Social differentiation and stratification are much greater in these societies than in simple horticultural societies.

Agrarian societies, such as those found in Europe in the Middle Ages, have far more sophisticated technology than horticultural societies. This advanced technology increases the development of centralized power in two ways. As defenses and weapons are improved, arming a warrior with the materials needed to win battles becomes an expensive proposition. By supplying the weapons, the rich are able to develop armies, which they use to conquer land and slaves and to control farmers, who become the serfs of the society. Second, as the variety of goods grows, a merchant class develops to trade them. The more powerful rulers tax the wealth accumulated by the merchant class and become extremely rich.

As wealth and power become concentrated in the hands of very few people, society becomes severely stratified. The ruler and governing classes probably received from a quarter to a half of the national income in the agrarian societies of the Middle Ages (Lenski, 1966).

Industrial societies such as the United States have the greatest division of labor and the most wealth and hence the most stratification. Industrialization, structured as it is on the factory system of production and the assembly line, requires workers to perform very specialized tasks. They specialize in operating a particular piece of equipment, or packing a manufactured product, or driving a truck to market, or keeping records, or advertising the product, or selling the product, and so on. Workers do not produce goods for personal consumption. Instead, they do a specific job in exchange for money and then buy personal goods with that money.

Durkheim (1947) believed that the division of labor created a more integrated society, one having what he called *organic solidarity.* Because no worker produced all the food, clothing, housing, and other goods needed to survive, each worker was dependent on other workers to produce the needed products. The interdependence among workers would create, Durkheim believed, a more integrated society. This interdependence does not, however, create a system of equality. The variety of specialized jobs in an industrial society, when ranked in a complex hierarchy of high to low status having great differences in salaries, creates a very complex stratification system.

Industrial societies also have a wide gap between those at the top and those at the bottom because of the great production of wealth in these systems. The surplus of goods produced, when accumulated in the hands of a few people, will make those people very wealthy compared with others. There is a huge gap between the American families who have enormous fortunes and the poor who have accumulated no wealth.

Types of Stratification

There are three basic types of stratification: estate, caste, and class. These are ideal types that do not exist in pure form in any society, but, rather, are found in combination.

The *estate system*, practiced in Europe during the Middle Ages, was based on a family's relation to the land. People were born to a certain rank — noble, serf, or slave — but there was some opportunity for rank to change. A commoner could be knighted; a serf could be freed or sold into slavery.

In a *caste system*, class is ascribed at birth. An individual's worth is judged on the basis of religious or traditional beliefs about the person or the person's family. The caste system is very rigid: no one can move into another caste.

This system is found in India and South Africa. In India, there are some three thousand castes. People must marry within their own caste, and their caste determines their status, identity, education, occupation, and trade union. It affects what kind of food they eat, where they live, what kind of medical care they receive, how they are supported in old age, and how they are buried. While economic or social success does not change an individual's caste, the caste as a whole can raise

In a caste system of stratification, a person cannot move from one caste to another. In this photograph we see evidence of the stratification system in India, as one man takes his leisure while being pedaled by a man of lower caste.

its status by changing its customs to imitate a higher caste, but this process takes several generations.

The *class stystem* is found only in industrial societies, and social level is defined in terms of wealth or status. This system allows movement among classes. Although wealth and the life chances to acquire wealth are often inherited, it is also possible to acquire wealth or status through one's own achievements.

While the United States is predominantly a class system, women and blacks have had some of the characteristics of a caste system. These minority groups have rarely been able to achieve wealth by entering the prestigious professions, and they have rarely been accepted for top positions in business or government because of the ascribed status of the group into which they were born. Even in those instances when an individual woman or black did gain a position that would ordinarily bring wealth or status, women and blacks have not received the income and status associated with such achievement. Like castes, the advancement of individual women and blacks will depend to a great extent on raising the status of the entire group.

The fact that some groups in the United States have castelike characteristics demonstrates that the typologies of caste and class are ideal types. Some systems are *open systems,* allowing a great deal of mobility, some are *closed systems,* allowing little or no mobility. Sociologists use the ideal types in order to compare and contrast different social systems, recognizing that every system has variations within it.

Inequality in the United States

Social inequality in the United States is based on family background, wealth, education, occupation, and a variety of other characteristics. People can move from one class to another. For these reasons, there is no widely accepted system for describing class in this country. The best way to understand the class system is to look at its various dimensions separately.

Social Status in American Society

The earliest studies of stratification in America were based on the concept of status, people's opinions of other people. It was found that status was conferred on others on the basis of their wealth. In a study of a New England town called Yankee City (Warner and Lunt, 1942), the local citizens described six classes:

1. *The upper-upper.* People who had inherited family wealth and high status.
2. *The lower-upper.* People who had income comparable to that of the upper class but who had acquired wealth recently and lacked a distinguished family background.
3. *Upper-middle.* Moderately successful business and professional people.
4. *Lower-middle.* People who were respectable, who lived in nice homes, and worked as low-ranking white-collar workers, foremen, or craftsmen.
5. *Upper-lower.* People who were factory and service workers; some low-ranking white-collar workers.
6. *Lower-lower.* Intermittent workers, families on welfare, and transients.

The Warner studies and others have found that people at different status levels have different lifestyles. They belong to different churches, read different magazines, have different leisure-time activities, and hold different political attitudes. They also tend to respect their own group above other groups. The upper classes consider themselves good, honest, hard-working people, and

Occupational Prestige

Beginning in 1947, groups of researchers have asked samples of Americans to rank the prestige of an assortment of occupations. These surveys have found that Americans have maintained consistent opinions over the years about the relative prestige of various occupations. The results of a 1963 survey, from most to least prestigious, are listed below.

U.S. Supreme Court Justice
Physician
Nuclear physicist
Scientist
Government scientist
State governor
Cabinet member in the federal government
College professor
U.S. Representative in Congress
Chemist
U.S. Foreign Service Diplomat
Lawyer
Architect
County judge
Dentist
Mayor of a large city
Member of the board of directors of a large corporation
Minister
Psychologist
Airline pilot
Civil engineer
Head of a department in a state government
Priest
Banker
Biologist

Sociologist
Captain in the regular army
Accountant for a large business
Public schoolteacher
Building contractor
Owner of a factory that employs about 100 people
Artist who paints pictures that are exhibited in galleries
Author of novels
Economist
Musician in a symphony orchestra
Official of an international labor union
County agricultural agent
Electrician
Railroad engineer
Owner-operator of a printing shop
Trained machinist
Farm owner and operator
Undertaker
Welfare worker for a city government
Newspaper columnist
Policeman
Reporter on a daily newspaper
Bookkeeper
Radio announcer
Insurance agent
Tenant farmer (one who owns livestock and machinery and manages a farm owned by someone else)
Carpenter
Local official of a labor union
Manager of a small store in a city
Mail carrier
Railroad conductor
Traveling salesman for a wholesale concern

Plumber
Automobile repairman
Barber
Machine operator in a factory
Owner-operator of a lunch stand
Playground director
Corporal in the regular army
Garage mechanic
Truck driver
Fisherman who owns his own boat
Clerk in a store
Milk route man
Streetcar motorman
Lumberjack
Restaurant cook
Singer in a nightclub
Filling station attendant
Coal miner
Dock worker
Night watchman
Railroad section hand
Restaurant waiter
Taxi driver
Bartender
Farmhand
Janitor
Clothes presser in a laundry
Soda fountain clerk
Sharecropper (one who owns no livestock or equipment and works on a farm owned by someone else)
Garbage collector
Street sweeper
Shoe shiner

SOURCE: Hodge, R. W.; Siegel, P. M.; Rossi, P. H. "Occupational Prestige in the United States, 1925–1963," *American Journal of Sociology* 70 (November 1964). Reprinted by permission of the publisher, The University of Chicago.

they may regard the lower classes as inferior. The lower classes also believe they are good, honest, average, hard-working people and tend to regard the upper classes as hypocrites who think they are superior.

The Distribution of Income

In 1980, the median income in the United States for people with full-time jobs was $19,173 for men and $11,591 for women (U.S. Dept. of Commerce, 1981). As you will remember, the median is the amount at which half of a given population falls above and half falls below. The distribution of this income was very unequal (see Table 8-2). Over half of the individuals who did not live with relatives made less than $10,000. Only 0.9 percent of such individuals made $50,000 or more. Table 8-2 also shows that families have an advantage over unrelated individuals in earning power, but, even so, 18.9 percent of families earn less than $10,000.

In 1980, the median income of families in which the wife did not work at a paying job was $18,972. In families where the wife did work, the median income was $26,879. In one-parent families headed by a man, median income was $17,519. In one-parent families headed by a woman, however, the median income was only $10,408 (U.S. Dept. of Commerce, 1981).

Another way to look at income distribution is to consider the share of income received by each 20 percent of the population. Table 8-3 shows that the poorest 30 percent of the population received only 5.1 percent of the total avail-

America's Richest People

Estimated Worth

$3 Billion to $5 Billion
du Ponts, Wilmington, Del. *Chemicals.*
Mellons, Pittsburgh, Pa. *Mellon National Bank.*

$2 Billion to $3 Billion
Gettys, Los Angeles, Cal. *Getty Oil.*
Daniel K. Ludwig, N.Y., N.Y. *Shipping, real estate.*

$1 Billion to $2 Billion
Rockefellers, N.Y., N.Y. *Standard Oil.*

$600 Million to $1 Billion
Fords, Detroit, Mich. *Ford Motor Company.*
Hunts, Dallas, Tx. *Oil.*
Pews, Philadelphia, Pa. *Sun Oil.*

Pritzkers, Chicago, Ill. *Hyatt Hotels, real estate.*

$400 Million to $600 Million
Bechtels, San Francisco, Cal. *Engineering and construction management.*
Henry Crown, Chicago, Ill. *General Dynamics.*
Marvin Davis, Col. *Colorado Oil.*
Michel Fribourg, N.Y., N.Y. *Continental Grain.*
William R. Hewlett, Palo Alto, Cal. *Hewlett-Packard.*
Keibergs, Kingsville, Tx. *King Ranch, real estate.*

SOURCE: From Dan Rottenberg in *Town and Country*, May 1978. © 1978. Reprinted by permission.

Table 8-2
Distribution of families and unrelated individuals by income, 1980

INCOME	FAMILIES IN EACH CATEGORY, PERCENT	UNRELATED INDIVIDUALS IN EACH CATEGORY, PERCENT
$50,000 and over	6.7	0.9
$35,000–$49,999	12.8	1.3
$25,000–$34,999	19.8	4.7
$20,000–$24,999	13.7	6.5
$15,000–$19,999	14.0	11.0
$10,000–$14,999	14.1	17.9
Under $10,000	18.9	57.6

SOURCE: U.S. Department of Commerce, Bureau of the Census. Washington, D.C.: U.S. Government Printing Office, 1981.

Table 8-3
Percent of income and percent of wealth for each fifth of population, 1980

TOTAL POPULATION	TOTAL AVAILABLE INCOME	TOTAL AVAILABLE WEALTH[a]
Highest fifth	41.6%	76%
Second highest fifth	24.3%	
Middle fifth	17.5%	24%
Second lowest fifth	11.6%	
Lowest fifth	5.1%	

[a] Assets such as property, including stocks, bonds, and real estate.
SOURCE: U.S. Bureau of the Census, Current Population Reports, Series P-60, 1981; Rossides, Daniel W., *The American Class System: An Introduction to Social Stratification.* Boston: Houghton Mifflin, 1976.

able income in 1980, whereas the richest 20 percent of the population received 41.6 percent of the available income. This distribution of income has remained very stable over the past forty years.

The Distribution of Wealth

Wealth consists of personal property as well as income. Personal property includes liquid assets (cash in bank accounts), real estate, stocks, bonds, and other owned assets. Families in the top 20

percent income bracket possess 76 percent of the wealth in this country (Rossides, 1976). Even in this group of high earners, however, the wealth is not distributed evenly. Families whose income is in the top 1 percent earn 19 percent of the total income. They own 60 percent of all corporate bonds and 57 percent of all corporate stocks.

According to Rossides (1976), the very wealthy actually control even more money than they possess. By owning many shares of the major

Mrs. Richard C. duPont leads Politely, one of her money-making thoroughbreds, to the barn after winning the Aqueduct in 1967. Wealthy people are able not only to enjoy very expensive sports, but also to turn these activities into profitable ventures. The leisure activities of the rich contrast sharply with the leisure activities of the poor.

corporations, they influence not just their own fortunes but those of many others. The Rockefeller family, one of the wealthiest families in the United States, has estimated assets of at least one billion dollars. Because the family dominates key banks and corporations, they control assets of more than fifteen times their personal wealth (Szymanski, 1978).

Class Consciousness

Class consciousness is the awareness that different classes exist in society. In the United States, people can identify a variety of classes, at least in the smaller communities studied by Warner and Lunt (1942). Most people, however, assign themselves to the middle class.

Form and Huber (1969) studied the attitudes of people from all income groups to learn who they thought should rule in the United States and who they thought actually did rule. They found that more than half of all poor and middle-class people believed that big business and the rich ruled the country, but very few felt that they should. Most Americans tend to believe that the middle class should rule the country. More than half of the rich believed that unions run the country, but most of them thought that unions should not.

Conflict theorists maintain that when the members of a society think that the powerful have a right to their power, those members will act in ways that maintain the system of stratification. When people believe that the power structure is not legitimate, they are more likely to resist that rule.

In the United States, people are aware of the rich, but they do not appear to support the power of the rich, according to the study done by Form and Huber. At the same time, Americans are less aware of the impoverished class and assume that most people are middle class. Thus Americans are not very class conscious, do not differentiate between classes to a great extent, and appear to be willing to maintain the system of stratification.

The Upper-Middle Class

The upper-middle class consists of professional and technical workers, managers, and a few highly skilled workers and supervisors. Professional and technical workers include doctors, lawyers, engineers, and other highly educated people. Managers are the higher ranking workers in larger organizations. The vast majority of workers in the upper-middle class are white males.

Early in the 1970s, a study of very highly paid managers in a large corporation (Margolis, 1979) indicated that most earned $30,000 to $45,000 per year, placing them in the top 20 percent of earners. These managers could afford the high-budget lifestyle as reported in Table 8-4. Many people think of this class as the typical American manager: educated white-collar workers who earn a comfortable living, own their own home, and send their children to college. In 1980, however, male managers and administrators had a median income of $23,558, higher than the median income for all males. Most people in these occupations, however, would need a second worker in the family to enter the higher budget group, and if there were no second worker, these managers would have a median income only slightly higher than the intermediate budget. Female managers and administrators have a median income of $12,936.

Table 8-4
Urban budgets for a four-person family, 1980[a]

	LOWER BUDGET	INTERMEDIATE BUDGET	HIGHER BUDGET
Food	4,321	5,571	7,024
Housing	2,608	5,106	7,747
Transportation	1,160	2,116	2,751
Clothing and personal care	1,259	1,763	2,556
Medical care	1,298	1,303	1,359
Other consumption	597	1,109	1,829
Other costs (gifts, occupational expenses, etc.)	583	957	1,610
Social Security and disability insurance	881	1,427	1,608
Income tax	1,337	3,781	7,924
Total cost (as of autumn 1980)	14,044	23,134	34,409

[a] Note: These figures, prepared by the federal government, are useful in delineating various classes and status groups. The rich, of course, spend more than the higher budget and the very poor spend less than the lower budget.

SOURCE: U.S. Bureau of the Census, *Statistical Abstract of the United States: 1981* (102nd ed.). Washington, D.C.: 1981, No. 785, p. 471.

The Working-Class Majority

The working-class includes workers in industry, craftsmen, foremen, and laborers, both skilled and unskilled. It also includes service workers, who provide cleaning, maintenance, and other services. These groups make up about 58 percent of the male work force (Levison, 1974). Some sociologists argue that clerical workers, most of whom are women with routine jobs and low pay, should also be considered a part of the working class. Although strictly speaking they are not blue-collar workers, they have more in common with the working class than they have with white-collar professional and managerial workers.

The working class is generally poorly paid, susceptible to layoffs, and subject to poor working conditions. The average income for production workers in the United States in 1980 was $9.92 an hour, a figure higher than those in all other industrial countries except Belgium, Germany, the Netherlands, and Sweden. Assuming that there are no layoffs during the year, the income of production workers would be about $20,000. This figure puts them in the intermediate budget range.

Other working-class occupations pay considerably less. These workers make less than the median income and fall in the lower budget range, even if there are no layoffs, and many blue-collar workers are laid off during a typical year. In 1970, when the unemployment rate was 4.9 percent, more than 30 percent of the working class were laid off for fifteen weeks or more, which is an especially severe problem for construction workers, and it severely reduces the total income earned during the year (Levinson, 1974). Many low-paid working-class people fall below the poverty line and enter the class that has come to be called the "working poor."

Jane Fonda, portraying a clerical worker in the movie Nine to Five, works in a setting that more nearly resembles an assembly line than it does a managerial position. Most clerical workers receive low pay, have low status, and receive little opportunity to manage their own work, let alone that of others. Many argue that clerical staff should be considered working-class rather than middle-class workers.

Poverty

The U.S. government has developed a measure of poverty that takes into account the size of the family, the number of children, and whether the family lives on a farm. The income level considered impoverished varies with these factors. For a family of four not living on a farm, the poverty line in 1980 was $8,414, about half of the lower budget figure. The government reports that in 1980, 29.3 million people, or 13 percent of the population, were living in poverty.

Most poor people either work at low-paying jobs or cannot find jobs. Some are too ill to work, and others are single mothers who cannot earn enough to support their children. The poor cannot get loans, thus cannot buy cars, and lacking transportation, they cannot seek employment where work is available.

The poor also pay more for most of what they buy (Caplovitz, 1963). A larger percentage of their income is spent on food, and the food they purchase is often bought in more expensive inner-city locations. Without cars, they do not have transportation to more economical stores.

The hand-to-mouth existence of the poor requires only one emergency to create a downward spiral of trouble. If a mother cannot find adequate care for her child, even for a brief period, she may have to stay home. If she loses her job, her utilities may be turned off, there may be no money for food, and she may be evicted from her apartment. The poor have no assets to protect them from the collapse of their precarious financial situation.

Inequality and Life Chances

Housing and Lifestyle

The rich often own several homes: a family estate, an estate in an exclusive resort area, and a large apartment in an exclusive apartment building in the center of a major city. They spend their leisure time with their wealthy friends and neighbors, and they work together on the boards of banks and corporations. They manage their business affairs with much mutual respect and close cooperation. Their children usually marry the children of other wealthy families, so rich families are usually related to one another, and their wealth remains in the same group.

Upper-middle-class managers and professionals, who are near the top 20 percent of earners, are most likely to own homes in the suburbs. In addition to providing a nice place to live, owning a home has proved to be a good investment because homes increase in value with inflation, and they provide income tax deductions. Managers, who are often transferred, prefer to buy very conventional suburban homes since they are easier to sell (Margolis, 1979).

Working-class people are also likely to live in the suburbs, but they are less apt to own their own homes. Those who rent houses or apartments do not benefit from inflation or tax deductions. Instead, as prices go up, their rents go up, and they may find it very difficult to improve their standard of living. Some working-class people who cannot afford homes buy trailers and move to trailer parks in order to escape rising rents.

Poor people have a very difficult time finding adequate housing. They may live in substandard housing in rural areas or in urban slums and often pay high rents for it. Sometimes two families share the same apartment, which may be very overcrowded. The poor spend more money for roach killers than any other class of people.

The poorest people in the United States do not even have homes or apartments. They live on the street. The number of street people is not known, but it is estimated that there are four thousand homeless women and a considerably larger number of homeless men in New York City. In Washington, D.C., approximately ten thousand women came to a shelter for homeless women during one year. These people have either lost contact with their families or they have no families. They also have no income — a person must have an address to receive welfare. They sleep in subways, doorways, or on park benches. They are often raped or assaulted, and in winter they sometimes freeze to death.

Education

The children of the rich are the group most likely to go to private preparatory schools and elite colleges, regardless of their grades. Middle-class children ordinarily graduate from public or parochial high schools, and they have an excellent chance of going to college if their grades are satisfactory. Working-class children usually complete high school, but only those who achieve very high grades are likely to attend college. Poor children tend to drop out of high school and often live in neighboorhoods with poor schools, at which they may not even learn to read or write. Seeing that high school graduates often have trouble getting jobs, they become discouraged and quit as soon as they are old enough. It appears that education is a life chance very closely associated with family wealth.

Medical Care

The rich and the middle classes who are regularly employed are usually covered by medical insurance through their employers. Insurance covers most medical expenses, and members of these classes generally receive good medical care. They can afford to go to private doctors and private hospitals. They can comfortably discuss their health problems with doctors, and they understand the medical advice they receive. Most doctors are from the middle or upper classes themselves and they understand best the problems of people from the same background.

The poor have major health problems. They usually suffer from nutritional problems because they cannot afford meat and vegetables, substituting such starchy foods as beans, bread, and macaroni. They suffer from assaults, rat and dog bites, inadequate heating, and other hazards of living in poverty, and they are more likely to commit suicide.

In the middle 1960s, the U.S. government developed Medicaid, a health insurance program for the poor, and Medicare, a health insurance program for the elderly. Since these programs began, the poor have visited doctors more frequently and are receiving better medical care. In poor neighborhoods, however, public clinics and hospitals are likely to be overcrowded, under-staffed, and poorly equipped, and those who go to

A woman rests on a city street next to her bundle of possessions. She is one of the thousands of people in the United States too poor to have a home. Many homeless people were once members of the middle class but have become widowed or divorced, have no family to support them, and are unable to find work to support themselves.

these facilities may have to wait four to six hours for treatment. They see whatever doctor is on duty, not necessarily the one they have dealt with before. In addition, they often have trouble communicating with doctors about their symptoms and problems, and they may have difficulty understanding the medical advice they receive. Doctors who work in public hospitals and clinics are often foreign born, and some speak English poorly. Those who were born in this country rarely come from working-class or impoverished backgrounds.

The working classes suffer most from job-related diseases and injuries. They visit doctors less frequently than either the rich or the poor and tend to treat themselves unless they are seriously ill. Those who do not work in the best unionized manufacturing jobs or who work irregularly because of layoffs and job changes may not have health insurance. They cannot afford private doctors, and public hospitals and clinics are usually not located in their neighborhoods. They may also feel uncomfortable discussing their complaints with upper-class doctors. Like the poor, they may have trouble understanding medical advice about their illness and its treatment.

The very poor and homeless see doctors only when they are picked up by the police and brought to public clinics. Among the most unfortunate cases seen in emergency rooms are homeless people who are frostbite victims. They may have to have a toe or a foot amputated, only to return to the streets to suffer frostbite again.

Social Mobility in the United States

Social mobility — changing one's social position — can occur in a variety of ways. *Geographic mobility* involves moving from one location to another. A move from one job to another job of equal rank is *horizontal mobility*. A change to a job of higher rank is *upward mobility*, and a movement to a job of lower rank is *downward mobility*. Each of these illustrates *vertical mobility*. Mobility between generations is traditionally measured by comparing the social positions of fathers and sons. (Daughters usually are not studied.) If a son has a higher position than his father had, the son is upwardly mobile; if the son's position is lower, he is downwardly mobile. Both the social structure and individual characteristics influence upward and downward mobility.

In the United States in the twentieth century, many structural changes have increased the wealth of the nation and the standard of living has improved. Many sons have achieved a higher standard of living than their fathers had as a result of these structural changes. Most children, however, have remained in the same social class as their fathers. It is only occasionally that a son has been able to achieve a position in a higher social status than his father.

Structural Characteristics of Mobility in the United States

Mobility in this country is influenced by (1) increased technology, (2) the growth of large corporations, (3) an increased standard of living, (4) the growth of urban areas, and (5) the maintenance of a split labor market.

Increased technology has eliminated some jobs involving manual labor and increased the number of white-collar clerical and service jobs. Should a move from a boring, low-paying assembly-line job to a boring, low-paying desk job be considered upward mobility, or is it, rather, horizontal mobility, movement that does not bring with it any real advantages? Some sociologists urge that white-collar work has a higher status, but others contend that this shift merely changes the nature of work, not the class or status of the worker.

The growth of large corporations has influenced the wages people are paid. Those who work in large organizations often earn more than those who work in small firms. People in supervisory positions earn a percentage more than the people they supervise, and their earnings generally increase as the number of people they supervise increases. Thus, as corporations grow larger, supervisors earn more. Many qualified people in large organizations never have the opportunity to be supervisors, however, and despite their high qualifications, they will never be able to earn the income of the supervisor. In a smaller organization they would more likely be promoted.

The increasing standard of living over the past century has improved the lives of most workers in the United States, even though their relative class or status remains unchanged. This improvement is especially true of factory workers, whose wages and living conditions today have improved dramatically since the turn of the century.

The growth of urban areas, in which the cost of living is higher, has led to higher wages for city dwellers. Equally qualified people doing the same work are likely to earn more money in the city than in the country. Doctors, for example, earn

SOCIOLOGISTS AT WORK
Co-hosting on National Public Radio

Susan Stamberg is the co-host of *All Things Considered,* a nightly news and public affairs program broadcast on the National Public Radio network. She has been with the program since it was born in 1971, except for an eight-month break in 1981 to write her first book, *Every Night at Five: Susan Stamberg's "All Things Considered" Book* (Pantheon). She was the first woman to host a nationally broadcast nightly news program. The road that led Stamberg to *All Things Considered* includes along the way a bachelor's degree from Barnard College, with a double major — in English and sociology.

Why sociology? "I found it extremely absorbing, a way to make some sense out of my experience," says Stamberg. "I was intrigued with the idea of trying to sort out a lot of apparently disparate and incoherent information, of trying to create a framework for that information. That's sociology's greatest strength, but also its greatest weakness. Bernard Barber, who headed Barnard's excellent sociology department when I was there,

would create these lovely charts and try to pull *everything* into one of three columns. It was a brilliant attempt to impose order on life, even though sometimes large chunks of experience were left dangling."

Has Stamberg's study of sociology helped her in her work on *All Things Considered?* "It's funny," she says. "I split my major, but I would bury the sociology half of it, in college conversations. I'd say I majored in English and then I'd mumble the other part, largely because I couldn't stand the twitting I'd get — especially from the Columbia boys who had little respect for social sciences. They'd say, 'Sociology? Nothing but a command of the obvious. An aggressive obscuring of perfectly obvious facts.' But it was as important as the English in teaching me to deal with ideas. I felt it at the time, and I feel it even more strongly today. Just knowing that there are such things as social institutions, that actions are rarely random or entirely isolated, helps in my radio work. It was always clear, for instance, that every-

considerably more in large metropolitan areas than in rural areas.

A *split labor market* is one in which some jobs afford upward mobility and others do not. A management trainee job, may lead to management jobs of higher and higher rank, and ultimately to the presidency of a company. A secretarial position, however, is much less likely to lead to an administrative job than it was formerly. The development of labor markets is a great obstacle to higher earnings for women and minorities, who fill most of the jobs that have no career lines.

Individual Characteristics and Upward Mobility

A basic assumption of structural-functional theory is that society rewards people who develop leadership skills through education and hard work. Researchers have conducted many studies in order to learn about the characteristics of individuals who succeed. These studies, most of which were concerned with men, have examined the influence of such factors as family background, grades in school, years of education, and

---

one has a family, but I was never aware of *the family* as an institution until I looked at it the way a sociologist looks at it. I can't really be specific about how that knowledge helps me in the course of asking questions" — Stamberg is renowned among her listeners as an insightful and thought-provoking interviewer — "but it does." It also helps her bring a fresh viewpoint to specific stories. "Reading Emile Durkheim was important. In my senior thesis at Barnard I took his concept of *anomie*, that feeling of public rolelessness and alienation from social institutions, and applied it to the works of some modern authors — André Gide, Albert Camus, and others. That concept was helpful in approaching contemporary stories about suicide, especially teenage suicide. It also helped with Watergate and the subsequent public apathy toward politics."

Stamberg's first job after graduation was as an editorial assistant at *Daedalus*, the journal of the American Academy of Arts and Sciences. Then she got married and moved to Washington, where she took a similar job at the *New Republic*. After a short while she moved over to radio — "I fell into radio" is the way she puts it — as the producer of a weekly news and public affairs program at a local public radio station. It was

there she got her first air time, as a last-minute substitute when the weather girl got sick. She reflects on the experience of going on the air: "I couldn't just go out and say, 'All right, I'm about to talk to millions of people.' I would have got lockjaw. Instead, I concentrated on talking to one person — my husband. He was a perfect audience: he's intelligent, he's interested in a lot of things, he likes to laugh." This practice helped her when she moved to the national network and *All Things Considered*. "Most of our listeners are as curious and information-hungry as I am. They also follow the demographic profile of the country. People have a stereotype of public radio listeners as PhD, pipe-smoking professors. The average American is a high-school graduate. Our average listener is a high-school graduate. We reach everyone — blue-collar workers, white-collar workers, pink-collar workers, black-collar workers, you name it."

The impulse that drew Susan Stamberg to her work in radio is the same one that drew her to sociology. "It was interesting to me because it dealt with real people and what they were doing. It dealt with *today*." That interest makes millions of listeners tune in to *All Things Considered* every night at five.

personality (Jencks, 1979). The studies show that family background is the factor that most accurately predicts the future earnings of men. Anywhere from 15 to 50 percent of the variation in men's earnings appears to be related to family background. Men from families with high incomes generally make more money than those from families with low incomes. The studies do not, however, explain why family income is related to a son's future earnings. Structural functionalists argue that sons from families with high income usually have all of the advantages believed to contribute to future money-making ability. Their parents can teach their sons important skills, and they live in neighborhoods where their friends have the same advantages. Because of family advantages, they are likely to do well in high school and attend college.

Structural functionalists believe that the best way to increase upward mobility in this country is to increase the opportunities available to children from poor families. Such a move would involve providing better preschool education, better public school education (including the opportunity to attend schools with young people from wealthier backgrounds), and the opportunity to go on to college or technical schools.

Conflict theorists criticize the notion that sons from high-income families succeed because they are more qualified. They argue that social class in the United States is an ascribed status and maintain that the poor cannot enter the upper class through increased education, as has been demonstrated by women and blacks. Members of minority groups may find it difficult to spend the time and money required to receive a higher education if they believe they will not be rewarded for their efforts. Conflict theorists contend that opportunity and equality for the poor will be brought about only through changes in the stratification system and in the redistribution of wealth.

Summary

People's differing ranks in society are based on class and status. Class rankings are based on wealth, income, and life chances to acquire wealth and income. Status comes from the honor and respect people receive from others. Class and status are sources of power, and they are the criteria used to rank people in a system of stratification.

Structural functionalists believe that systems of stratification develop because societies need scarce leadership skills and reward those who are willing to assume the responsibility of leadership. Conflict theorists contend that stratification develops because certain groups gain a monopoly of the scarce resources through inheritance or conflict and use those resources to maintain their high positions.

Research indicates that stratification becomes more pronounced as wealth and the division of labor increase. Very simple societies have little division of labor and little stratification. Agrarian and industrial societies have more wealth, greater division of labor, and more stratification.

There are several types of stratification systems. In a caste system, positions are assigned at birth according to the position of the caste, and a person's caste is fixed for life. The class system is found only in industrial societies and allows movement into higher or lower strata through the accumulation or loss of wealth and status.

Inequality in the United States stems from wealth, income, education, and status — especially occupational status. Although most people identify themselves as middle class, the lifestyles of Americans vary widely. The differences are especially profound between the rich and the poor, and the most important ones are found in housing, health care, and educational opportunity. It is these variations that affect life chances.

The American class system has been quite stable for at least fifty years. Those born into wealthy families remain wealthy, and those born in poverty are likely to remain poor. The most important determinant of one's class position in this country is family background.

Key Terms

caste system
class consciousness
class system
closed system
downward mobility
estate system
false consciousness
horizontal mobility
inequality
life chances
open system
organic solidarity
parties
power
split labor market
social class
social status
socioeconomic status (SES)
social stratification
upward mobility

Suggested Readings

Duberman, Lucile. **Social Inequality: Class and Caste in America.** *Philadelphia: Lippincott, 1976.* A good basic text on stratification, including excellent sections on minority groups and women.

George, Susan. **How the Other Half Dies: The Real Reasons for World Hunger.** *Montclair, N.J.: Allanheld, Osmun, 1977.* This book discusses the exploitation of the world's poor by large international banks and businesses.

Howell, Joseph T. **Hard Living on Clay Street: Portraits of Blue Collar Families.** *Garden City, N.Y.: Doubleday/Anchor, 1973.* Howell, who lived in a neighborhood of southern working-class people tells the moving, sometimes funny, sometimes sad story of their lives.

Margolis, Diane Rothbard. **The Manager: Corporate Life in America.** *New York: Morrow, 1979.* This study of eighty managers reveals how the corporation has shaped their professional and personal lives.

Piven, Frances Fox and Richard A. Cloward. **Regulating the Poor: The Functions of Public Welfare.** *New York, Vintage, 1971.* Piven and Cloward argue that throughout history welfare payments have been used to ease the discontent of the poor in hard times and then reduced to make the poor take low-paying jobs when they are available.

Rossides, Daniel W. **The American Class System: An Introduction to Social Stratification.** *Boston: Houghton Mifflin, 1976.* A thorough text with good references for the student desiring further study in stratification.

Sexton, Patricia Cayo and Brendan Sexton. **Blue Collars and Hard Hats: The Working Class and the Future of American Politics.** *New York: Vintage, 1971.* A sympathetic discussion of the problems of the working class, this book argues for policies promoting downward mobility rather than upward mobility in order to reduce inequality.

Chapter 9
Racial and Ethnic Differentiation

After all there is but one race — humanity.

— George Moore

The United States is aptly called "a nation of nations." The diversity of the country's social and cultural life is a result of the many different groups who have migrated here. Can you imagine how monotonous life would be if people were all the same? Almost everyone enjoys the exotic sights, sounds, and smells of Chinatown. Greek, Italian, or Japanese cuisine is a welcomed change from the usual American diet of hamburger or steak. We also benefit from our diverse cultural heritage in many more important ways as well.

Race and ethnic relations in the United States, however, are far from smooth. Our history has been marked by conflict, competition, prejudice, and discrimination. In this chapter we will identify the major minority groups in North America and discuss some of the causes and consequences of stereotyping, racism, prejudice, discrimination, and racial inequality. We will also consider two approaches: the pluralistic and integrationist perspectives, which may help reduce racial and ethnic inequality.

Racial, Ethnic, and Minority Groups

The terms *race* and *ethnic* are often used rather loosely. Although they may be treated as equivalent or overlapping concepts, it is important to differentiate these terms before we discuss the more substantive issues of race and ethnic relations.

Racial Groups

The concept of race is extremely unclear. Anthropologists and biologists remain deadlocked over the issue of whether race is a meaningful

211

biological concept. The essential question is whether there are significant variations in the traits of different populations of humans. The focus of investigation has ranged from obvious characteristics such as skin and hair coloring to less obvious traits such as blood type and genetically transmitted diseases (Newman, 1973). In pursuing their research, scientists have measured heads, examined eye color, and even examined ear wax. A wet type of ear wax was found to be common among East Asian groups, especially among the Chinese and Japanese, whereas a drier type was found among European and black populations.

Classification of peoples by skin color has been complicated by the effects of climate. It has been found that variations in skin shading are caused by varying degrees of exposure to sunlight. Asians and Africans have darker coloring because they live in tropical climates. Classification by skin color is further complicated by intermarriage. Many populations are the results of biological mixing — for example, the Creoles of Alabama and Mississippi, the Red Bones of Louisiana, the Croatians of North Carolina, and the Mestizos of South America. Whether members of these groups have Indian or black ancestors is a matter of dispute.

In reality, a social definition of *racial groups* takes precedence over biological criteria. From the biological standpoint, only those who had more than 50 percent black ancestry would be considered black. There was a time when Georgia and a number of other southern states classified as "colored" any individuals who had a known black ancestor, regardless of whether they were 60 percent black or 6 percent black.

Even the U.S. Bureau of Census used the concept of race loosely in its 1980 census in which race was equated with national origin. Hence, "Filipino," "Korean," and "Vietnamese" were treated as racial classifications. Moreover, classification by race was a matter of self-identifi-

cation. There was no scientific definition to use in determining which category to check on the census form.

In sum, social definitions far outweigh biological definitions of race but these social definitions are based on some combination of certain inherited physical traits. Some physical traits such as red hair, height, and size of feet, for example, may be inherited but these are rarely used to differentiate people into one racial category or another, while other physical traits such as skin color may be used. Taking these considerations into account, biological differences per se do not constitute racial differences. Rather, race is a socially defined group or category of people distinguished by selected inherited physical characteristics.

Ethnic Groups

The word "ethnic" is derived from the Greek word *ethnikos,* which translates to "nations" in English. The word was initially equated with national origin and applied to European immigrants such as the Italians, Germans, Poles, and other national groups who came to the United States in large numbers, especially between 1900 and 1925. Today, ethnicity is given a wider definition and may also refer to group membership based on religion, language, or region. Using the word in this sense, Jews, Mormons, Latinos, and white Southerners can be considered as *ethnic groups.*

Whereas race is based on selected physical characteristics such as skin color, hair texture, or eye shape, ethnicity is based on cultural traits that reflect national origin, religion, and language. Cultural traits may be apparent in the manner of dress, speech patterns, and modes of emotional expression. Other cultural traits are less obvious but still vital to the group's heritage — such characteristics as ethical values, folklore, and literature.

Some authors prefer to focus on "sense of peoplehood" or "consciousness of kind" as the defining characteristic of ethnicity. Defined in this way, ethnicity may encompass both biological and cultural characteristics. Thus, Patterson (1975) defined ethnicity as a condition in a society in which certain members choose and emphasize a cultural, racial, or national tie as their primary identity outside the family. We take as our definition of ethnicity that of Milton M. Gordon, who likewise focused on the "sense of peoplehood" criterion. According to Gordon (1964), an ethnic group is

> any group which is defined or set off by race, religion, or national origin, or some combination of these categories. . . . All of these categories have a common social-psychological referent, in that all of them serve to create, through historical circumstances, a sense of peoplehood. (p. 27)

Minority Groups

Describing racial and ethnic relations in terms of minorities and majorities can be misleading. In common usage, the terms *majority* and *minority* pertain to number, which may be irrelevant to majority or minority status in a society. Numerical superiority, although it is influential, does not necessarily ensure majority status. Women, for example, are a numerical majority in American society, yet they have a minority status. In the Republic of South Africa, whites comprise less than one-fifth of the total population but they are in a position of dominance.

Subordination appears to be the key characteristic of *minority groups*. The minority is subordinate to the majority in power and privilege; the norms, values, cultural patterns, and laws that are observed and enforced are those of the majority. In the United States, Newman (1973) observed, the most highly valued norms or archetypes (standard patterns of behavior) are those of the white, Anglo-Saxon Protestant (WASP) middle classes (see Chapter 4). Minority groups are distinguished on the basis of the extent of their departure from these norms. They are also set apart on the basis of power and size. Using all three criteria — social

norms, power, and size — Newman (1973) defined *minority groups* as those

> that vary from the social norms or archetypes in some manner, are subordinate with regard to the distribution of social power, and rarely constitute more than one-half of the population of the society in which they are found. (p. 20)

According to this definition, the aged poor, poor people in Appalachia, southern whites, the handicapped, and homosexuals are minority groups. The minorities discussed in this chapter, however, were selected on the basis of racial and ethnic criteria.

Major Minority Groups in the United States

The black population is the largest minority group in the United States (see Table 9-1), constituting nearly 12 percent of the total population. The Spanish-speaking population is second to the black community in size, constituting approximately 6.4 percent of the population. The Spanish classification, however, overlaps with other racial categories.

The third largest group, the Asian community, increased phenomenally during the past ten years. Twice as many Asian ethnics were counted in 1980 as in 1970. Following this group in size are the Native Americans, categorized in the U.S. Census as American Indians and grouped with the Eskimos and Aleuts (native Eskimoan tribes from the Aleutian Islands, which is a chain of volcanic islands extending some 1,100 miles from the tip of the Alaska Peninsula). These Native American groups included about one and a half million people in 1980, slightly more than one-half of 1 percent of the U.S. population. Unfortunately, comparable figures for white ethnics are not available. As a racial group, they are considered white and lumped together with the white native born.

Table 9-1

Distribution of the various minority groups in the United States for 1970 and 1980

RACE	1970		1980	
	NUMBER	PERCENTAGE	NUMBER	PERCENTAGE
Total	203,211,926	100.0	226,504,825	100.0
White	177,748,975	87.4	188,340,790	83.2
Black	22,580,289	11.1	26,488,218	11.7
Asian and Pacific Islander	1,538,721	0.8	3,500,636	1.5
American Indian, Eskimo, and Aleut	827,268	0.4	1,418,195	0.6
Other	516,673	0.3	6,756,986	3.0
Spanish origin (may be of any race)	9,072,602	4.5	14,605,883	6.4

SOURCE: U.S. Bureau of the Census, Current Population Reports, Series P-20, No. 363, *Population Profile of the United States: 1980*, Washington, D.C.: U.S. Government Printing Office, 1981, Table 3, p. 9.

Black Americans

Black Americans comprise the largest racial minority in the United States. Because of such unique historical experiences as slavery, legal and social segregation, and economic discrimination, many blacks have lifestyles and value patterns that differ from those of the white majority. The relations between whites and blacks have been the source of a number of major social issues in the past several decades: busing, segregation, job discrimination and interracial marriage, to mention a few.

In an examination of black families, Eshleman (1981), expanding on the work of Billingsley (1968), identified six major social transitions that have affected or will affect black Americans. The first transition was the movement from Africa to America, which is significant because of three factors: color, cultural discontinuity, and slavery. *Color* is the most obvious characteristic that sets whites and blacks apart. *Cultural discontinuity* was the abrupt shift from the culture learned and

accepted in Africa to the cultural system of America. Rarely has any ethnic or racial group faced such a severe disruption of cultural patterns. *Slavery* was the unique circumstance that brought many blacks to America. Unlike almost all other groups, Africans did not come to this country by choice. Most were brought as slaves to work on southern plantations. Unlike many free blacks in the North, slaves in the southern states had few legal rights. Southern blacks were considered the property of their white owners, who had complete control over every aspect of their lives.

A second major transition was from slavery to emancipation. In 1863, a proclamation issued by President Lincoln freed the slaves in all territories still at war with the Union. Although the slaves were legally free, emancipation presented a major crisis for many blacks because most were faced with the difficult choice of either remaining on the plantations as tenants with little or no wages for their labor or searching beyond the plantation for jobs, food, and housing. Many men left to search for jobs, so women became the

Black Americans comprise the largest racial minority in the United States. They share the aspirations and values of the dominant culture: home ownership, regular employment, and pride in one's achievements. The extent to which these can be achieved, however, goes beyond individual initiative and a personal work ethic to the types of support structures available in the larger society: educational and job training opportunities, employment availability, home loans, nondiscriminatory neighborhoods, housing availability, and the like.

major source of family stability. The shift to emancipation from slavery contributed to the third and fourth transitions.

The third transition was from rural to urban areas. For many blacks this shift had both good and bad effects. Cities were much more impersonal than the rural areas most blacks moved from, but they also provided more jobs, better schools, improved health facilities, a greater tolerance of racial minorities, and a chance for vertical social mobility. Today, 73 percent of America's black population live in urban areas.

A closely related shift was the fourth transition, from southern to northern communities. The job opportunities created by World War I and World War II were the major impetus for the exodus of southern blacks to the North, a trend that continued through the 1960s. In 1900, nine out of ten blacks lived in the South. By 1970, the ratio had dropped to five out of ten (Shaefer, 1979). Today, there are more blacks in New York City and Chicago than in any other cities in the world, including African cities, and

these cities have retained their top rankings for thirty years. In 1980, Detroit displaced Philadelphia as the city with the third largest black population.

The fifth transition was from negative to positive social status. The black middle class has been growing in recent years and resembles the white middle class in terms of education, job level, and other factors. A high proportion of blacks remain in the lower income brackets, however, because of the prejudice, segregation, and discriminatory practices endured by blacks throughout most of their time in this country. Only in the past twenty-five years have they achieved a measure of equality. Previously, they were routinely denied equal protection under the law, equal access to schools and housing, and equal wages. Discrimination has by no means been eradicated, but few would deny today that substantial progress has been made. Many social reform movements have been led by black leaders, perhaps because blacks have had the strongest grievances of any American ethnic group.

The final transition was from negative to positive self-image. A basic tenet of the symbolic interaction approach is that we develop ourselves, our identities, and our feelings of self-worth through our interactions with others. Throughout most of our history, blacks have been the last to be hired and the first to be fired. As black children interact in a society in which racism is still widespread, they may internalize feelings of inferiority and low self-worth. One major consequence of cuts in social programs under the Reagan Administration is that they may have conveyed a message to all minority groups in the United States that they are of little importance compared with the interests of the dominant white middle and upper classes.

Spanish Americans

There are over fourteen and a half million people in the United States today who claim Spanish origins. This category includes those who classify themselves as Mexican, Puerto Rican, or Cuban and those from Spain or the Spanish-speaking countries of Central and South America. It also includes those who simply identify themselves as Spanish American, Hispanic, or Latino. Our discussion will focus on Mexican Americans, who constitute approximately 60 percent of this group.

Mexican Americans are also identified as Chicanos, an abbreviated form of Mexicano. Over one million Mexican Americans are descendants of the Mexicans who lived in the Southwest before it became part of the United States. They became Americans in 1848, when Texas, California, New Mexico, and most of Arizona became U.S. territory. These four states plus Colorado contain the largest concentrations of this group today. Most urban Mexican Americans live in California, especially in Los Angeles.

Other Mexican Americans came from Mexico. They can be classified into three types: (1) legal immigrants; (2) braceros, or temporary workers; and (3) illegal aliens. Large-scale migration in

Most Spanish-Americans in the United States today come from Mexico as legal immigrants, temporary workers, or illegal aliens. One of their cultural characteristics is an emphasis on strong family ties, and the extended family is pervasive throughout the subculture. Ties between extended families often take the form of coparenthood, where godparents (compadres) are chosen from outside the kin network as a source of assistance and support.

the early 1900s was caused by the revolution and unsettled economic conditions in Mexico and by the demand for labor on cotton farms and railroads in California. Before the minimum wage law was passed, agricultural employers preferred braceros to local workers because they could be paid less, and the braceros were not a burden to the federal government inasmuch as they returned to Mexico when their services were no longer needed. Referring to the braceros, one grower remarked, "We used to own slaves but now we rent them from the government" (Dinnerstein and Reimers, 1975, p. 101).

The number of illegal aliens from Mexico is not known, and estimates range from one to ten million. Immigration policy concerning legal and illegal Mexican immigrants generally varies with the need for labor, which in turn depends on economic conditions. When the demand for Mexican labor was high, immigration was encouraged. When times were bad, illegal aliens were tracked down, rounded up, and deported. They were scapegoats in the depression of the 1930s, and they are again in today's recession.

Traditional Mexican-American culture is characterized by strong family ties, large families, *machismo,* and a practice known as *compadrazgo.* The extended family is the most important institution in the Chicano community. The theme of family honor and unity diffuses throughout Mexican-American society irrespective of social class variation or geographical location. Madsen (1964) says that the upper-class rancher and the lower-class crop picker both think of themselves first as family members and second as individuals. This familism extends beyond the nuclear family unit of husband, wife, and children to relatives on both sides and persists even when the dominance of the male becomes weakened. It serves as a primary source of emotional and economic support as well as serving as the primary focus of obligations.

Large families are a second major characteristic of traditional Mexican-American culture. While large is a relative term, five- and seven-child families are large when compared with the two- and three-child families common to the majority of U.S. families. Families of this size, when linked with minimal skills and low levels of income, make it difficult for the Mexican American to enjoy life at a level equal to the dominant groups in American society.

Machismo is an exaggerated sense of masculinity. Some Mexican males and husbands are believed to assert their *machismo* by being the aloof authoritarian head of the family, directing its activities, arbitrating disputes, and representing the family to community and society. Queen and Habenstein (1974) state:

> . . . the husband, having long been socialized in the tradition of the sexual conquest of "bad" girls and the ascetic veneration of the "good," finds it difficult to assimilate sexual intercourse with the wife as an act of mutuality involving gratification and fulfillment equally shared; the wife, aware from earliest socialization that as a weaker female she cannot trust herself in sexual matters, denies herself or makes no sexual advances toward the spouse. The husband, free to continue the social activities enjoyed before marriage, finds conquests of other females ego building, and, as he makes no effort to deny such activities to his friends, they become just another means of demonstrating *machismo.* (p. 435)

One consequence of *machismo* is to take the husband out of the home and force upon the wife an early and permanent role of motherhood. Even as a grandparent, in contrast to the father and his relationship to the children, the mother continues to be the nurturing, warm parent even when her children are adults with children of their own.

Compadrazgo (godparenthood) is a social system that promotes ties between extended families.

Its most common form is co-parenthood, linking two families through the baptismal ritual. The godparents, *compadres,* are chosen with care from outside the immediate kinship network. The male, the most important *compadre,* will hopefully be a man of influence, status, and respect in the community. *Compadres* are expected to develop close relationships and in times of trouble have the right to call on one another for assistance. *Compadrazgo* is most likely to exist among rural families.

Urban Chicanos conform more closely to the Anglo-Saxon nuclear family and egalitarian norms. The extended family and the *compadrazgo* system are considered less important, and the *machismo* syndrome has given way to more egalitarian husband-wife relationships.

A vigorous Mexican-American political movement emerged around 1966. The Chicanos have achieved a number of goals such as having bilingual instruction introduced at the elementary level. Cesar Chavez, one of the best-known Chi-

cano leaders, organized Mexican farm workers in 1962 and started a lettuce boycott in 1972 that received nationwide publicity. The primary goal of Chicano political movements is to restore pride in Mexican-American heritage.

Asian Americans

The Asian community in the United States is a highly diverse group. The most numerous groups within it are the Chinese and Japanese. Also included in the Asian category are Filipinos, Asian Indians, Koreans, Hawaiians, and Guamanians. In the past decade, more immigrants have come from the Philippines, Korea, and Vietnam than from any country outside of North and South America (see Table 9-2). The Chinese, particularly those from Taiwan, also have represented a major share of Asian immigration.

The Chinese were the first Asians to enter this country in large numbers. Unlike the Japanese, the Chinese resist assimilation and tend to uphold traditional values such as filial duty, ven-

Table 9-2

Top ten countries outside of North and South America sending immigrants to the United States: 1970, 1975, and 1979

1970		1975		1979	
Philippines	31,200	Philippines	31,800	Philippines	41,300
Italy	25,000	Korea	28,400	Korea	29,200
Greece	16,500	China	18,500	China	24,300
United Kingdom	14,200	India	15,800	Vietnam	22,500
China	14,100	Portugal	11,800	India	19,700
Portugal	13,200	Italy	11,600	United Kingdom	13,900
India	10,100	United Kingdom	10,800	Iran	8,500
Germany	9,700	Greece	10,000	Portugal	7,100
Korea	9,300	Germany	5,200	Germany	6,300
Yugoslavia	8,600	U.S.S.R.	5,100	Italy	6,200

Notes: All immigrants are listed by country of birth. China includes both mainland China and Taiwan.

SOURCE: U.S. Bureau of the Census, *Statistical Abstract of the United States, 1981,* (102nd ed.) Washington, D.C.: U.S. Government Printing Office, 1981, No. 131, p. 88.

In the second World War, the federal government placed more than 110,000 people of Japanese ancestry in relocation camps. Here, members of the Moshida family are shown awaiting the evacuation bus.

eration of the aged and deceased ancestors, and arranged marriages. Chinese-American families tend to be male dominated, and extended family patterns are the rule. The traditional family structure is difficult to maintain in the United States, however, in part because of political legislation. In early migrations, married Chinese males usually came alone with the intention of having their wives and children follow. The Immigration Act of 1904 made it impossible for them to send for their families, however, which resulted in what Betty Sung (1967) called the "mutilated family."

Today, most Chinese live in large urban enclaves in Hawaii, San Francisco, Los Angeles, and New York. A tourist visiting a Chinatown is likely to notice only the exotic sights, smells, and sounds; the problems prevalent in Chinatowns are less evident. There is often overcrowding, poverty, poor health, rundown housing, and inadequate care for the elderly. Not all Chinese live in Chinatowns, however. Those who have "made it" live in the suburbs.

At present, the Chinese have no national organizations. Their local organizations, which are based on previous village ties or common family name, wield little power outside their communities.

Like the Chinese, most early Japanese immigrants were males imported for their labor, but important differences between these two groups resulted in different experiences (Kitano, 1980):

1. The Japanese came from a developing, industrial nation, the Chinese came from a primarily agricultural one.
2. The Japanese used their embassy and consular officials as resources. The Chinese relied on informal organizations.
3. The Japanese started families almost immediately after they arrived. For the sake of their children, the Japanese had to accept American norms. The "split family syndrome" experienced by the Chinese precluded their beginning families, however. (p. 255)

As a result of these factors, Japanese Americans are today more fully integrated into American culture and have higher incomes than the Chinese or other Asian groups.

The traditional family system of the Japanese resembles that of the Chinese. It is characterized by male dominance, reverence for the aged, preference for male offspring, and strong family ties.

During World War II, fearing that there might be Japanese Americans working against the American war effort, the federal government moved most of them to "relocation camps." Regardless of their political views or how long they had been in this country, families were forced to pack up and move to camps in Utah, Arizona, California, Idaho, Wyoming, Colorado, and Arkansas, which severely disrupted their lives, of course. Many were incensed at the suggestion that they were not loyal Americans capable of making valuable contributions to the American war effort. Some of the relocated families had sons serving in the armed forces. Altogether, more than 110,000 people of Japanese ancestry, 70,000 of them U.S. citizens by birth, were moved. After the war, the Japanese were allowed to return to their homes, but they were never compensated for the time, businesses, or property that they lost.

Native Americans

Today, half of the Native American (Indian) population live in the states of California, Arizona, New Mexico, and North Carolina. The Native-American population is actually a varied group of tribes having different languages, cultures, and levels of civilization and at the time of the European invasion could be divided into six major geographical areas (Feagin, 1978):

1. the Eastern tribes who hunted, farmed, and fished
2. the Great Plains hunters and agriculturists
3. the fishing societies of the Pacific Northwest
4. the seed gatherers of the California area
5. The shepherd and pueblo farmers in the Arizona and New Mexico area
6. the desert societies of Southern Arizona and New Mexico (p. 191)
7. the Alaskan groups, including the Eskimos (p. 191)

By the 1960s, Native Americans were no longer regarded as nations to be dealt with through treaties — they were considered "wards" of the U.S. government. They were rounded up and forced to move to reservations where most remain today. The isolated life of the reservation made it difficult to cope with the rapid growth of industry and caused many other problems.

The Indian equivalent to the family is the band, which includes a number of related families who live in close proximity. The band is composed of kinspeople who share property, jointly organize rituals and festivals, and provide mutual support and assistance. Bands are egalitarian and arrive at decisions collectively.

In the 1960s and 1970s, many Native Americans banded into organized collectives to demand a better life for their people. Several tribes have banded together to bargain more effectively with the federal government, and they have sometimes used militant tactics to get results.

Estimates of the number of Native Americans in the United States at the time of the European settlement range from one to ten million. By 1800, the population had declined to 600,000, and by 1850 it had dwindled to 250,000. In 1970, the Native-American population exceeded the one million mark for the first time since the period of European expansion.

White Ethnics

Most white ethnics in the United States today emigrated as a result of the European expansionist policy of the last 350 years. Earlier immigrants came mainly from northern and western European countries such as Britain, Ireland, Germany, France, and Switzerland. More recent im-grants came largely from southern and eastern European countries: Italy, Greece, the U.S.S.R., Yugoslavia, and Portugal (refer back to Table 9-2).

The majority of these immigrants discarded their roots and adopted American norms and values. Many dropped their European names in favor of names that sounded more "American," and most white ethnics have successfully assimilated. Michael Novak (1975), who is of Slovak ancestry, wrote the following about his experiences.

> Under challenge in grammar school concerning my nationality, I had been instructed by my father to announce proudly: "American." When my family moved from the Slovak ghetto of Johnston to the WASP suburb on the hill, my mother impressed upon us how well we must be dressed, and show good manners, and behave — people think of us as "different" and we mustn't give them any cause. (p. 593)

The emerging assertiveness of blacks and other nonwhites in the 1960s induced many white ethnics to reexamine their positions. John Goering (1971) found in interviews with Irish and Italian Catholics that ethnicity was more important to members of the third generation than it was to the migrants themselves. Novak (1975), a third-generation ethnic American, expressed the feeling of being deprived of his roots, his history:

> Odd that I should have such shallow knowledge of my roots. Amazing to me that I do not know what my family suffered, endured, learned, hoped these past six or seven generations. . . . As if history, in some way, began with my father and with me. (p. 592)

Today, many American ethnic communities emphasize more than their folk culture, native food, dance, costume, and religious traditions in establishing their ethnic identities. They have sought a more structured means of expressing, preserving, and expanding their cultures, and

many have formed fraternal organizations, museums, and native-language newspapers in an effort to preserve their heritage (Lopata, 1976).

One of the predominant white ethnic groups is the Jewish American. America has the largest Jewish population in the world, its estimated six million exceeding the approximately three and a half million Jews in Israel. They are heavily concentrated in New York City and its surrounding areas.

Jewish Americans are basically ethnic in nature in that they share cultural traits to a greater extent than physical features or religious beliefs. As a minority group they have a strong sense of group solidarity, tend to marry one another, and experience unequal treatment from non-Jews in the form of prejudice, discrimination, and segregation. While Jews are generally perceived to be affiliated with one of the three religious groups, the Orthodox, the Reform, or the Conservative, many, if not the majority of Jews, do not participate as adults in religious services or belong to a temple or synagogue. Yet they do not cease to think of themselves as Jews. The trend in the United States seems to be the substitution of cultural traditions for religion as the binding and solidifying force among Jewish Americans.

Injustices to Jewish people have existed for centuries all over the world. The most tragic example of anti-Semitism was during World War II, when Adolf Hitler ordered the extermination of six million Jewish civilians — what Jews call the Holocaust. While anti-Semitism in the United States never reached the extreme of Germany, it did exist. As early as the 1870s certain colleges excluded Jewish Americans. In the 1920s and 1930s a myth of international Jewry emerged that suggested Jews were going to conquer all governments throughout the world, using the vehicle of communism, believed by anti-Semites to be a Jewish movement. At this same time, Henry Ford, the Catholic priest Charles E. Coughlin, and groups like the Ku Klux Klan published,

Jewish Americans are a predominant white ethnic group in the United States. Cultural and religious celebrations serve as binding and solidifying events for the Jewish people and other ethnic minorities. One such event is Sukkoth, a Jewish harvest festival that commemorates the wandering of the Jews in the desert after their expulsion from Egypt (circa 1200 B.C.). During this holiday the Jewish people build and eat in sukkas — booths with roofs of branches and leaves that recall the temporary shelters used by their forbears in the wilderness.

preached, and spoke about the Jewish conspiracy as if it were fact. Unlike Europe, however, the United States government never publicly promoted anti-Semitism and Jewish Americans were more likely to face the question of whether to assimilate than how to survive.

Concern about anti-Semitism seemed to decrease drastically following World War II through the 1960s, but in the 1970s and continuing today, anti-Semitic sentiments and behaviors appear to be on the increase. The extent to which this is due to Jewish individuals occupying positions of power, the Middle East conflict, black power activists, the rise of religious fundamentalist preachings, or some other reason is a subject for debate. Whatever the cause, racial or ethnic hostility tends to unify the victims against the at-

tacker and Jewish Americans are no exception. Attitudes and their influence and some theories of prejudice and discrimination are discussed in the section that follows.

Attitudes and Their Influence

One of the most serious problems faced by most ethnic groups in America concerns how they are perceived by others. For a number of reasons, people tend to treat those they perceive to be different in ways they would not treat members of their own group. Not infrequently, this has led to inequalities and increased the strains that society must deal with. To pursue the American ideal of equality, we must understand how the attitudes underlying unfair practices are formed. Sociologists are among those who have addressed this problem, and we begin by discussing their findings on the nature of prejudice.

Prejudice

A *prejudice* is a preconceived judgment, either good or bad, about another group. More specifically, it is "an attitude that predisposes a person to think, perceive, feel, and act in favorable or unfavorable ways towards a group or its individual members" (Secord and Backman, 1964, p. 165). We are concerned here chiefly with the negative connotation of the word — ethnic relations in this country are characterized more by antipathy than by empathy — as witnessed by the fact that a number of ethnic slurs such as "wetback" and "nigger" exist, but there are few ethnic nicknames that express positive feelings.

A variety of theories have been offered to explain prejudice. Early theories were often based on the premise that prejudiced attitudes are innate or biological, but more recent explanations tend to attribute the development of prejudices to the social environment.

Economic theories of prejudice are based on the supposition that competition and conflict among groups are inevitable when different groups desire commodities that are in short supply. These theories explain why racial prejudice is most salient during periods of depression and economic turmoil. In California, for example, from the 1840s through the depression of the 1930s, economic relations between whites and Chinese Americans were tolerant and amiable as long as the Chinese confined themselves to occupations such as laundry and curio shops. When they began to compete with whites in gold mining and other business enterprises, however, violent racial conflicts erupted. Japanese Americans had a similar experience.

The "exploitation" variant of economic theory argues that prejudice is used to stigmatize a group as inferior to put its members in a subordinate position and justify their exploitation. The exploitation theme explains how capitalists have traditionally justified exploiting recent immigrants who had little money, few skills, and serious language problems.

Psychological theories of prejudice suggest that prejudice satisfies psychic needs or compensates for some defect in the personality. *Scapegoating* involves blaming another person or group for one's own problems. Another psychological theory of prejudice is *projection*, attributing one's own unacceptable traits or behaviors to another person. This theory suggests that people transfer responsibility for their own failures to a vulnerable group, often a racial or ethnic group, and it closely resembles the *frustration-aggression* theory (Dollard et al., 1939). In this view, groups who strive repeatedly to achieve certain goals become frustrated after failing a number of times. When the frustration reaches a high intensity, the group seeks an outlet for their frustration by displacing their aggressive behavior to a socially approved target, a racial or ethnic group. Thus the Germans, frustrated by runaway inflation and the failure of their nationalist ambitions, vented their aggressive feelings by persecuting the Jews. Poor whites, frustrated by their unproductive lands and financial problems, drained off their hostilities through antiblack prejudices.

The *authoritarian personality theory* argues that some people are more inclined to prejudice than others due to differences in personality. According to the authors of the theory (Adorno et al., 1950) prejudiced individuals are characterized by rigidity of outlook, intolerance, suggestibility, dislike for ambiguity, and irrational attitudes. They tend to be authoritarian, preferring stability and orderliness to the indefiniteness that accompanies social change. Simpson and Yinger (1972) questioned whether these traits cause prejudice and suggested that they may in fact be an effect of prejudice or completely unrelated to it.

Regardless of what theory one accepts, prejudice is sustained through *stereotypes*, which are widely held beliefs about the character and behavior of all members of a group. They are usually based on readily discernible characteristics such as physical appearance and are oversimplifications that seldom correspond to the facts. A prejudiced person might say of one group, "They breed like rabbits," of another, "They are a bunch of hoodlums," overlooking the great range of individual differences found in every group. They tend "to think of people in bunches as though they were bananas" (Berry and Tischler, 1978, p. 236).

Stereotypes of the majority are usually more favorable than those of minorities. Whites may be portrayed as industrious, intelligent, ambitious, and progressive, while blacks may be described as lazy, happy-go-lucky, and ignorant. There are several stereotypes associated with Native Americans. One image often projected to the public by the movies and television advertising is of the Native American who is strong and stoical, who has a special relationship to nature. A stereotype more common in the past was of the ruthless, blood-thirsty savage cruelly murdering innocent (white) settlers. A third suggests that all Native Americans are alcoholics who live in self-induced poverty. Needless to say, none of these stereotypes even begins to reflect the great diversity of behavior that exists now and has always existed among Native Americans as among other groups.

Stereotyping is not entirely dysfunctional. Albrecht et al. (1980) have argued that "stereotypes afford us the comfort of recognition and save us

Stereotypes are widely held beliefs about the character and behavior of members of a group. In movies and on television, conformity to stereotypes perpetuates viewers' beliefs. The black mammy portrayed in the Jerome Kern musical Show Boat *is the stereotypical overweight happy servant.*

the time and effort of interpreting masses of new stimuli hourly" (p. 254). They help us mentally sort people into predictable categories, making social interaction easier and minimizing social errors. Most of our encounters are dominated by stereotyped conceptions of how we should act and how others should respond, whether we are dealing with bank tellers, employers, or family members.

Most would agree, however, that the dysfunctional aspects of stereotyping far outweigh the functional aspects. In addition to pointing out how stereotyping is functional, Albrecht et al. (1980) cited several harmful consequences. First, stereotypes are often based on inaccurate information, and distorting reality could very well interfere with a person's adjustment to his or her social environment. Second, they are used to justify discrimination against members of various ethnic and racial groups. The stereotype that blacks are lazy and unintelligent, for example, could be used as a basis for categorically barring blacks from highly paid executive and managerial positions.

A third damaging effect of stereotyping is that it may contribute to the development of an inferior self-concept. The symbolic interaction viewpoint tells us that self-perceptions are created through internalizing the attitudes, responses, and definitions one believes are held by others. An inferior self-concept may be developed through the process described by Robert Merton in Chapter 2 as a *self-fulfilling prophecy*. The stereotyped false definitions influence behavior and make the prediction come true. The behavior outcome is then used to confirm the original prophecy.

Radke and Trager's (1950) early studies of black children support the idea that members of a stereotyped minority tend to internalize the definitions attached to them. In these studies, the children were asked to evaluate black and white dolls and to tell stories about black and white persons in photographs. The children overwhelmingly preferred the white dolls to the black. The white dolls were described as good, the black dolls as bad. The black individuals in the photographs were given inferior roles as servants, maids, or gardeners.

More recent studies of self-esteem found little or no difference between blacks and whites. Zirkel (1971) reviewed over a dozen studies of black and white students attending grammar and secondary schools and concluded that black and white children now have similar levels of self-esteem. Simmons et al. (1978) found that minority students have even stronger self-concepts than majority students. This change in attitudes can be linked to the civil rights movements of the late 1960s and early 1970s, when emerging ethnic pride began to be expressed in such slogans as "Red Power" and "Black is beautiful."

Discrimination

Prejudice is a judgment, an attitude. *Discrimination*, on the other hand, is overt behavior or actions. It is the categorical exclusion of "all members of a group from certain rights, opportunities, or privileges" (Schaefer, 1979, p. 53). According to the conflict perspective, the dominant group in a society practices discrimination to protect its advantages, privileges, and vested interests.

A number of authors (e.g., Allport, 1954; Kintoch, 1974) have argued that discrimination is a possible but not inevitable outcome of prejudice; that is, prejudiced people are likely to be discriminatory, but exceptions do occur. Recognizing the possible independence of these two concepts, Robert Merton (1976) classified people into four categories.

1. The unprejudiced nondiscriminator: all-weather liberal
2. The unprejudiced discriminator: reluctant liberal
3. The prejudiced nondiscriminator: timid bigot
4. The prejudiced discriminator: all-weather bigot (pp. 189–216)

People in categories 1 and 2 believe in the American creed of equality, human rights, human dignity, freedom, and justice. The all-weather liberals practice what they believe in and are likely to urge others to abide by the same American ideals. Reluctant liberals, although holding the same beliefs as the all-weather liberals, are prone to social pressure. Reluctant liberals are silent in the presence of articulate bigots and exercise discrimination in order "not to hurt the business." The overture "I don't have anything against you personally, but . . ." is familiar to many of us.

Like reluctant liberals, the timid bigots are susceptible to situational factors and will not discriminate when in the company of nonbigots. Also, bigoted employers are now deterred from discriminatory hiring practices by affirmative action laws. All-weather bigots are blatant bigots through and through. They do not believe that members of certain racial and ethnic groups are their equals, and they do not bother to conceal the antagonism they feel for these groups. They express their intolerance freely in their speech and their actions

Racism

Whereas prejudice is an attitude, *racism* is a system of beliefs and actions based on those beliefs, although the distinction is sometimes difficult to grasp. Essentially, racism can be regarded as having three major components. First, it involves the belief that one's own race is superior to other racial groups. This component may involve racial prejudice, but it is not synonymous with it. Racial prejudice is an attitude, usually negative, toward the members of other racial groups. The belief in the superiority of one's own group may also involve ethnocentrism, which was defined in Chapter 4 as a belief in the superiority of one's own

group on the basis of cultural criteria. A person's own group may be an ethnic group, but it need not be. Thus racial prejudice and ethnocentrism can be regarded as properties of racism, not synonyms for it.

The second property of racism is that it has an *ideology,* or set of beliefs, that justifies the subjugation and exploitation of another group. According to Rothman (1978), a racist ideology serves five functions.

1. It provides a moral rationale for systematic deprivation.
2. It allows the dominant group to reconcile values and behavior.
3. It discourages the subordinate group from challenging the system.
4. It rallies adherence in support of a "just" cause.
5. It defends the existing division of labor. (p. 51)

Perpetuators of racist ideologies claim that they are based on scientific evidence. One pseudo-scientific theory, for example, held that the various races evolved at different times. Blacks, who presumably evolved first, were regarded as the most primitive race. As such, they were believed to be incapable of creating a superior culture or carrying on the culture of the higher, white races, but the theory also argued that some benefits could accrue to the blacks by serving members of the white race. This theory is obviously self-serving and completely without scientific foundation.

The third element in racism is that the beliefs are acted upon. Many examples of racist actions in this country could be given. The lynching of blacks in the South and the destruction of entire tribes of Native Americans who were regarded as little more than animals are two of the more extreme instances.

Racism can be of two types. *Individual racism* originates in the racist beliefs of a single person.

Racist store owners, for example, might refuse to hire black employees because they regard them as inferior beings. *Institutional racism* occurs when racist ideas and practices are embodied in the folkways, mores, or legal structures of various institutions. The policy of apartheid in the Republic of South Africa (described by Berry and Tischler, 1978, pp. 7–8) is one of the most notorious examples of institutional racism. The policy of apartheid, reminiscent of Jim Crow legislation in this country, calls for biological, territorial, social, educational, economic, and political separation of the various racial groups that compose the Republic of South Africa.

Does Skin Color Make a Difference?

Gergen (1967) indicates that there are numerous physical dimensions such as height and weight along which people within any society vary. For these there is a single norm within a society and fewer and fewer cases exist as one moves away from this norm. Unlike the physical dimensions of height and weight, skin color is not normally distributed within most contemporary societies. Rather, the distribution tends to be multimodal; that is, classified as white, black, yellow and so on, with the tendency to treat as equivalent all those who fall within a given color.

Gergen analyzes the research done on the extent to which variations in skin color convey or elicit positive or negative feelings. Are negative evaluations associated with members of groups other than one's own based on pigmentation groupings? Studies of color symbolism in the Western tradition associate the following with black: woe, doom, darkness, dread, death, terror, horror, wickedness, curse, mourning, and mortification with "despair" as the major association elicited by black. These stand in marked contrast to those associated with white: triumph, light, innocence, joy, divine power, purity, regeneration, happiness, gaiety, peace, chastity, truth, modesty, femininity, and delicacy. From the Bible to major writers of poetry and literature, the tendency has been to use white in expressing forms of goodness and black in connoting evil.

Studies also demonstrate that not only is white rated more positively than black but that both blacks as well as whites feel similarly in this regard (though whites are more extreme in their differential evaluation of the colors). These color preferences seem to be established at a very early age. Studies of elementary and preschool children showed a preference for white dolls to brown ones and black children preferred to see themselves as white and to have white friends. The often noted tendency for the dark-skinned to feel inferior may have an initial basis in color symbolism, which implies that while race prejudice may be learned, people may also have to be taught *not* to be prejudiced. It further implies that the tendency of the dark-skinned to feel inferior may require an extended process of relearning. As Gergen indicates (p. 401), "The difficulties in breaking through such categorizations are considerable. In Buber's terms, the person who is classified on the basis of skin color becomes an *It* rather than a *Thou*."

SOURCE: Kenneth J. Gergen, "The Significance of Skin Color in Human Relations," *Daedalus* 96 (Spring 1967): 390–406.

South African Non-Persons: Suppression by Banning

For most of the past 20 years, Winnie Mandela has lived in a uniquely South African limbo. She is "banned," an exile within her own country. The wife of Nelson Mandela, imprisoned leader of the African National Congress, the black 47-year-old former social worker is considered to be a threat to public order and white supremacy. Since 1962 she has enjoyed real freedom for a total of only eleven months, and she is now beginning another five-year term as a banned person. Thus she, along with 114 other black and white opponents of apartheid,

remains an outcast, a legal leper with few rights and many restrictions.

Banning is one of the most chilling methods for suppressing dissent in South Africa. There is no requirement for formal charges, no trial, no appeal. Individual cases vary, but banned people may be confined to specific districts away from their homes and are often restricted to their quarters at night or on weekends. They must report regularly to the police and are never permitted to meet socially with more than one person at a time. (The authorities recently

made a brief exception: Mrs. Mandela was allowed to attend her brother's funeral. On her way home, she was in an automobile accident and suffered a broken arm.)

Those who are banned are forbidden to write anything, even a diary, and the press is prohibited from quoting them — even after death. Their freedom to work is restricted; they are under constant police surveillance; their homes, telephones and cars are often bugged and their mail is intercepted. "Old friends would see me and cross the street to walk on the other side," recalls one former victim. Adds another, "You become a non-person."

While the privations of banning are harsh, they are not as unpleasant in most cases as the more common punishment of indefinite detention without trial. In 1960

Racism can take many different forms — separatism, segregation, subjugation, exploitation, expulsion, and others. We will focus on two forms considered the most extreme: genocide and mass expulsion.

Genocide is the practice of deliberately destroying a whole race or ethnic group. The term was coined by Raphael Lemkin to describe the heinous crimes committed by the Nazis during World War II against the Jewish people, which is the supreme example of racism. Of the 9,600,000 Jews who lived in Nazi-dominated Europe between 1933 and 1945, 60 percent died in concentration camps (Berry and Tischler, 1978). The British also solved race problems through annihilation during their colonization campaigns over-

seas. During the period 1803 to 1876, for example, they practically wiped out the native population of Tasmania. The aborigines were believed to be a degenerate race, wild beasts to be hunted and killed. One colonist regularly hunted natives to feed his dogs, but we don't have to go to Australia for illustrations. As early as 1717, the United States government was giving incentives to private citizens for exterminating the "troublesome" native Indians, and Americans were paid generous bounties for Indian scalps.

The Convention on Genocide of the United Nations formulated international legislation in the 1970s declaring genocide a punishable crime. More than seventy nations ratified the convention, but the United States, surprisingly, was not

the government began to practice detention in addition to banning, which was ten years old. The two repressive measures have become part of the grim pattern of national life. Over the years, banning and detention have been used to silence more than 1,500 critics of the regime, including 350 people seized during the Soweto riots in 1976 and scores of journalists, clergymen and antiapartheid leaders following the death in custody of Stephen Biko in 1977.

Following a wave of riots and demonstrations that disrupted official celebrations of the 20th anniversary of South Africa as an independent republic last May, the security police have stepped up their campaign of repression. Since then, Winnie Mandela has been joined in her unusual exile by a dozen or so people, including Student Leader Andrew Boraine, son of an opposition member of parliament. At the same time, nearly 600 people have been detained without trial, some of them for as long as seven months. Among those arrested: 18 union and student leaders and, embarrassingly enough for the government, the niece of Pieter Koornhof, Pretoria's Minister for Race Relations. Last week the government moved again, slapping a five-year banning order on David Johnson, president of the black students' society at Johannesburg's University of the Witwatersrand. Protested one angry student: "No words can adequately express the revulsion we feel at such state action."

The rebanning of Winnie Mandela prompted sharp criticism from church leaders and liberal politicians. David Dalling, spokesman for the opposition Progressive Federal Party, called the decision "vicious and personally malicious." The Right Reverend Philip Russell, the Anglican archbishop of Cape Town, publicly deplored "the whole diabolical detention-banning machinery." The protests, however, made little difference. The government clearly intends to continue stifling all opposition to apartheid.

But in her own quiet way, Winnie Mandela rose to the challenge. She reported to the police station for the first time under the new banning order by deliberately walking through the door marked "white," a practice she intends to continue for at least the next five years.

Institutionalized racism is embodied in the norms of a culture. The policy of apartheid in the Republic of South Africa has government support for racial segregation and discrimination against nonwhites. Overt indications of these practices can be seen in the signs of rest rooms for non-Europeans, that is, blacks, coloreds, and Asians.

Mass expulsion was forced on the Cherokee Indians as seen in this illustration of the "Trail of Tears." President Jackson saw the Indians as a nuisance and an impediment to growth and progress. In 1817, he began to force them to give up large tribal tracts and move west to areas that were seen as remote and of little interest to white settlers.

one of them. This country did not sign the genocide convention primarily because of the legal objections raised by American lawyers and the American Bar Association. The objections were based on technical questions about the definitions of such concepts as "group," "mental harm," and "physical harm."

Mass expulsion is the practice of expelling racial or ethnic groups from their homeland. The United States routinely used expulsion to solve conflicts with the Indians. In an incident known as "the trail of tears," the Cherokees were forced out of their homeland in the region where Georgia meets Tennessee and North Carolina. The removal was triggered by the discovery of gold in the Georgia mountains and the determination of whites to take possession of it. The exodus went to the Ohio River and then to the Mississippi, ending in what is now Oklahoma. Of the ten thousand Cherokees rounded up, about four thousand perished during the exodus.

Racist thinking and racist doctrine were rampant between 1850 and 1950, which is aptly called "the century of racism." Since 1950, it has declined in many parts of the world, but there is no question that it still exists.

Patterns of Group Interaction

When different racial and ethnic groups live in the same area, widespread and continuous contact among groups is inevitable and it rarely results in equilibrium. Generally, one group seizes power and dominates the other groups. Race relations are usually affected by government, however. In the United States, legislation has played an important role in shaping the destiny of American minorities. During most of our history, the goal has generally been to merge the various minorities into the American mainstream. Today, the country is experimenting with a different aim, the "separate-but-equal" approach.

Stratification

As we saw in Chapter 8, stratification in a society takes a variety of forms. Sometimes it is based on rank such as an estate system, sometimes it is based on ascribed status at birth such as in a caste system, and sometimes it is based on acquired status such as income or occupation, as in many industralized societies. Some societies, including our own, stratify people on the basis of ascribed statuses like race and ethnic heritage in addition to the achieved statuses of education and income. We call this rating system *racial and ethnic stratification*.

In American society, the predominant norms, values, beliefs, ideas, and character traits are those of the majority — the white, Anglo-Saxon, Protestant middle class. The more a group diverges from the norms of the majority, the lower its rank in the social hierarchy. Thus it may be less desirable to be Chinese or Mexican than to be German or Irish, and less desirable to be German or Irish than a white Anglo-Saxon Protestant.

The consequences of allocating status on the basis of ethnic or racial membership are most evident in the different lifestyles, life chances, and opportunities of different groups. When social inequality is based on racial lines, the majority gets the more desirable positions and minorities get the less desirable ones.

Donald L. Noel (1975) contends that three conditions are necessary for ethnic stratification to occur in a society: ethnocentrism, competition for resources, and inequalities in power. The inevitable outcome of ethnocentrism is that other groups are disparaged to a greater or lesser degree, depending on the extent of their difference from the majority.

Competition among groups is found when they must vie for the same scarce resources or goals, but it need not lead to ethnic stratification if values concerning freedom and equality are held and enforced.

According to Noel, it is the third condition, inequality in power, that enables one group to impose its will upon the others. Power permits the dominant group to render the subordinate groups ineffectual as competitors and to institutionalize the distribution of rewards and opportunities to consolidate their position.

What positions, then, do ethnic and racial groups occupy in the stratification system of the United States? This question can be addressed through considering the statistics in Table 9-3 on the education, occupation, and income of various ethnic groups.

In our society, education is an important vehicle of social advancement. It is the key to high-paying, prestigious, and self-fulfilling jobs. Native Americans, blacks, and Mexican Americans were significantly below white males in college comple-

Table 9-3

Education, occupation, and income indexes for the major minority groups in the United States when compared with white males

	COLLEGE COMPLETION RATE (1976)	OCCUPATIONAL SEGREGATION (1976)	EARNINGS DIFFERENTIALS FOR COLLEGE EDUCATED (1975)
Males			
American Indian/Alaskan natives	.24[a]	35.7[b]	.77[c]
Blacks	.32	37.9	.81
Mexican Americans	.32	38.2	.71
Japanese Americans	1.56	41.5	.94
Chinese Americans	1.76	61.4	.84
Filipino Americans	1.00	59.7	.86
Majority (white)	1.00	0.0	1.00
Females			
American Indian/Alaskan natives	.12	69.4	.68
Blacks	.32	69.3	.65
Mexican Americans	.15	73.1	.46
Japanese Americans	1.03	72.1	.55
Chinese Americans	1.29	79.7	.42
Filipino Americans	1.50	99.2	.60
Majority (white)	.65	66.1	.53

[a] This can be interpreted as follows: In 1976 the college completion rate for American Indian and Alaskan native males was 24 percent of (or 76 percent below) the rate for majority (white) males.

[b] This can be interpreted as follows: In 1976, at least 35.7 percent of American Indian and Alaskan native males would have had to change occupations in order to have an occupational distribution identical to the majority (white) males.

[c] This can be interpreted as follows: In 1975, American Indian and Alaskan native males with four or more years of college earned 77 percent of the average for majority males with the same educational attainment.

SOURCE: U.S. Commission on Civil Rights, August 1978.

tion rates. Asian Americans, both males and females, had a college completion rate higher than that of white males. These high rates reflect the emphasis placed on education by Asian Americans and probably also reflect the changes in immigration policy in the mid-1960s that gave priority to highly skilled and professional immigrants.

The occupational segregation indexes indicate that minorities are overrepresented in certain occupational categories compared with white males, which reflects the highly skewed occupational distribution of the minorities. Minorities, especially Native Americans, blacks, and Mexican Americans, are usually found in low-paying, less prestigious occupations.

As for income, in all groups both males and females who had four or more years of college earned less than white male college graduates. These figures imply that members of the minorities are less able to convert schooling into earnings, and although nonwhites still have a long way to go before catching up with white men, nonwhite men and women have made considerable strides in absolute income during the last thirty years. Burstein (1979) attributed these gains to improvements in education, changes in interracial attitudes and the law, and to the enforcement of Equal Employment Opportunity (EEO) legislation in the 1960s and 1970s.

Integration

Integration comes about when ethnicity becomes insignificant and everyone can freely and fully participate in the social, economic, and political mainstream. To accomplish this goal, the removal of legal barriers has to be complemented by the elimination of the prejudiced attitudes and social pressures that maintain ethnic barriers, and many Americans do feel that assimilation should be the basis for an integrated society. There are two variants of assimilation in the United States: the *melting pot* and *Anglo-conformity*. The formulations below differentiate these two terms.

Melting pot: $A + B + C = D$
Anglo-conformity: $A + B + C = A$

In melting pot assimilation, each group contributes a bit of its own culture and absorbs aspects of other cultures such that the whole is a combination of all the groups. Anglo-conformity is equated with "Americanization," whereby the minority loses its identity completely to the dominant WASP culture, and it has been the more prevalent integrationist policy in this country during recent decades.

Integration is a two-way process: the immigrants must want to assimilate and the host society must be willing to have them assimilate. The immigrant must undergo cultural *assimilation,* learning the day-to-day norms of the WASP culture

pertaining to dress, language, food, and sports. This process also involves internalizing the more critical aspects of the culture such as values, ideas, beliefs, and attitudes. *Structural assimilation* involves developing patterns of intimate contact between the "guest" and "host" groups in clubs, organizations, and institutions of the host society. Cultural assimilation generally precedes structural assimilation, although the two sometimes happen simultaneously.

Gordon (1964) has observed that cultural assimilation has occurred on a large scale in American society. The various minorities, however, differ in the pace at which they are assimilating. With white ethnics of European origin, cultural assimilation went hand in hand with amalgamation (biological mixing through large-scale intermarriage). Among Asian ethnics, Japanese Americans seem to have assimilated most completely and are being rewarded with high socioeconomic statuses. In contrast, Chinese Americans, particularly first-generation migrants, have resisted assimilation and retained strong ties to their cultural tradition. The existence of Chinatowns in many cities reflects this desire for cultural continuity.

Assimilation involves more than just culture borrowing, however. Immigrants want access to the host's institutional privileges, and the issue of integration is particularly relevant in three areas: schooling, housing, and employment.

Members of most ethnic groups live in segregated housing. *Segregation* is the act of separating a group from the main body and results in ethnic enclaves such as little Italies, black ghettos, and Hispanic barrios. The most significant division, however, is between the whites in the suburbs and the blacks and other minorities in the inner cities. At the institutional level, segregation can be attributed to discriminatory practices and policies of the federal housing agencies and mortgage-lending institutions. Suburban zoning patterns that tend to keep out poorer families are also influential. At the individual level, segregation is the result of some whites' refusal to sell their houses to nonwhites or the desire of minorities themselves to live in ethnic communities.

The city-suburb polarization of blacks and whites declined, however, during the mid-1970s, partly because of the antisegregation efforts of the U.S. government. Since 1965, federal law has prohibited discrimination in the rental, sale, or financing of suburban housing. In Chicago, all banks and savings and loan associations bidding for deposits of federal funds were requested to sign anti-red lining pledges. *Red lining* is the practice among mortgage-lending institutions of imposing artificial restrictions on housing loans for areas where minorities have started to buy (Vitarello, 1975), but despite these and other advances American society has a long way to go in desegregating housing patterns.

Busing legislation is designed to eliminate racial segregation in schools. Defenders of the legislation argue that minority students who are exposed to highly achieving white, middle-class students will do better academically (Coleman et al., 1966). They also contend that desegregation by busing is a way for whites and minority groups to learn about each other, which may diminish stereotypes and racist attitudes.

Opinion surveys indicate that opposition to integration is not the major concern of many people who oppose busing. A 1975 Harris survey found that 56 percent of adults were in favor of desegregating public schools and 35 percent were opposed. On the issue of busing, however, the overwhelming majority were opposed, 74 percent to 20 percent. Even among blacks themselves, while 40 percent were in favor of busing, a substantial proportion (47 percent) were opposed to it.

Concerning jobs, Hogan and Featherman (1977) and Featherman and Hauser (1976) believe that blacks will eventually be integrated into the stratification system of the majority, but prior to the early 1970s, ethnic group membership was a much more influential factor in determining what sort of job blacks could get. As Hogan and Featherman (1977) observed, "Black men have experienced a perverse sort of egalitarianism — neither the disadvantages of lower socioeconomic origins nor the advantages of high social origins and edu-

Integration occurs when ethnicity becomes insignificant and everyone can freely and fully participate in the social, economic, and political mainstream. Indications of the extent of racial integration can be witnessed in neighborhoods, jobs, churches, and the general community. In the field of education, busing, which was a heated political issue, brought a greater number of black and white students together.

cation weigh as heavily in the status attainments of Blacks as they do in those of Whites" (p. 101).

In the 1970s, particularly among young workers, patterns of socioeconomic stratification varied less by race than they did in previous years. The economic integration of blacks began first and has proceeded furthest among blacks born in the north. Internal differentiation of the black population and its development of more distinct socioeconomic strata also indicate that blacks have made gains in socioeconomic integration.

Pluralism

Cultural pluralism may be expressed with the formula $A + B + C = A + B + C$ where the various groups maintain their distinctive cultural patterns, subsystems, and institutions. Whereas an integrationist seeks to eliminate ethnic boundaries, a pluralist wants to retain them. Pluralists argue that groups can coexist by accepting their differences, however. Basic to cultural pluralism are beliefs that individuals never forget or escape their social origin, that all groups bring positive contributions that enrich the larger society, and that groups have the right to be different but equal.

Two types of cultural pluralism may be distinguished on the basis of the nature of the contact among groups (Gordon, 1978). Cultural pluralism at the *tolerance* level is primarily characterized by secondary contact across ethnic lines involving formal, nonintimate associations. This form of pluralism was found among blacks and whites in the old South. At the *good group relations* level, there is considerably more contact among groups. At this level, Gordon (1978) argues that pluralism and some forms of integration can coexist. This type of pluralism would involve "employment integration, common use of public accommodations, inter-ethnic composition of civic organizations and frequent symbolic demonstrations of inter-group harmony which emphasize common goals and values" (p. 161).

Several authorities believe that assimilation and pluralism are happening simultaneously in American society. Glazer and Moynihan (1970) perceive the process of becoming "hyphenated" Americans as involving cultural assimilation. Thus a Russian American is different from a Russian in Russia and a black American is not the same as a black in Africa. On the other hand, they perceive the emergence of minority groups as political interest groups as a pluralistic trend. Similarly, Gordon (1978) contends that assimilation of minorities is the prevailing trend in economic, political, and educational institutions, whereas cultural pluralism prevails in religion, the family, and recreation.

Cultural pluralism results in separate ethnic communities, many of which are characterized by a high degree of *institutional completeness;* that is, they include institutions and services that meet the needs of the group such as ethnic churches, newspapers, mutual aid societies, and recreational groups. These ethnic enclaves are particularly attractive to recent immigrants who have language problems and few skills. Schaefer (1979) compared ethnic communities to decompression chambers. "Just as divers use the chambers to adjust to the rapid change in water pressure, immigrants use the communities to adjust to cultural change they are forced to make upon arriving in a new country" (p. 45).

Today, we are witnessing a resurgence of interest by various ethnic groups in almost forgotten languages, customs, and traditions. Greeley (1971) calls this resurgence of ethnicity "a new tribalism," characterized by increased interest in the "high culture" of one's ethnic group, visits to ancestral homes, the increased use of ethnic names, and renewed interest in the native language of one's group (pp. 148–151).

The general rule has been for American minorities to assimilate, however. Most ethnic groups are oriented toward the future, not toward the past. American ethnics are far more interested in shaping their future within the American structure than in maintaining cultural ties with the past.

What of the future of ethnic groups and integration in the United States? Most observers agree that serious problems remain to be overcome. Racism continues to have a powerful influence on individual lives and the interactions of different ethnic groups, and each step in the process presents new problems. One recent twist, for example, involves allegations of *reverse discrimination,* in which members of the majority claim to be vic-

tims of racial discrimination. In the most celebrated of these cases, Alan Bakke brought suit against the state of California for denying him admission to medical school while accepting members of minorities with lower scores on admissions tests. The busing controversy of the past decade is another well-known example of a shift in the nature of race relations.

Despite the new problems that crop up, there is reason for optimism. Just as few would argue that race relations are not everything they should be in this country, few would refute the fact that progress has been made during the past three dec-

SOCIOLOGISTS AT WORK
Assessing Services for the Hispanic Population

JoAnne Willette is a senior research specialist for Development Associates, Inc., an international management and government consulting firm in the Washington, D.C. area. She does survey research, program evaluation, and policy analysis, mostly for the federal government. In her work she applies the theoretical, methodological, and statistical training in sociology she received as an undergraduate at George Washington University and a graduate student at the University of Maryland.

What tasks does Willette bring this training to bear on? In the area of policy analysis, she has worked on a study for the U.S. Department of Health and Human Services (HHS) to improve services to the Hispanic population in this country. One of the first tasks in the study was to

review all the major programs in HHS, including Social Security, Medicare, Medicaid, Aid to Families with Dependent Children, Adolescent Pregnancy Prevention, Family Planning, Programs for the Aging, Head Start, Migrant Health, Child Welfare Services, and seven HHS block grants to the states.

For each of these programs she reviewed the legislation, guidelines, and funding. She also interviewed federal, state, and local program administrators, and people in the target populations. She did further interviewing on the block grants, funds that are given to the states with relatively few strings attached. In these interviews she tried to find the different ways states were planning to spend the funds, the criteria they were using to distribute the funds, and the amount of input the

ades. A number of barriers to equality have been eliminated. Civil rights activism during the 1960s and 1970s brought about reforms in laws and government policies. In 1963 Affirmative Action was established, and President Kennedy issued an executive order calling for the disregard of race, creed, color, or national origin in hiring procedures as well as in the treatment of employees. Affirmative Action has since become a principal government instrument in eradicating institutional racism (Feagin, 1978), and its laws were later amended to include women so that today the laws prohibit discrimination on the basis of sex.

The reduction of institutional racism has had indirect as well as direct effects. According to the *contact hypothesis,* interracial contact leads to reductions in prejudice under the following conditions: (1) that the parties involved be of equal status and (2) that the situation in which the contact occurs be pleasant (Schaefer, 1979). Rokeach, Smith, and Evans (1960) take a similar position, arguing that prejudiced people do not reject others because of their ethnic membership per se but because they perceive others as having different values and beliefs. These authors hypothesize that if people of different races encounter one

target population for these programs had in the decision.

Another part of this project was an in-depth study of the demographic and socioeconomic characteristics of the Hispanic population in the United States from 1950 to 1980. Trends in the Hispanic population were compared to those in the black, white, and total populations. Trends among the various Hispanic ethnic groups (Mexican-Americans, Puerto Ricans, Cubans, and those of other Spanish origins) were also compared to each other.

The analysis was based on census reports and other national statistics collected by the federal government. Tracing trends in the population was a challenge: methods of collecting data and defining variables change over time, and this affects the comparability of the data. For example, even the definition of Hispanic was changed between 1950 to 1980. In a statistical sense, the concept *Hispanic* is relatively new; the 1970 census was the first to ask people to classify themselves as Hispanic or non-Hispanic. Before this, Mexican-Americans in five southwestern states were identified using a manual coding system and

a list of Spanish surnames. Puerto Ricans in New York City were identified by birth and parentage questions during coding procedures. Other Hispanics were not counted at all. The result was an undercount of unknown proportions.

A third part of this study was annual projections of Hispanic population from 1980 to 1990, derived from 1980 census data by some of Willette's demographer colleagues at Development Associates.

How did her training prepare her for this work? "I entered sociology with the intention of using it as an applied rather than an academic discipline," she says. "My sociological background has been useful in studying government programs whose effects can be seen in social changes. We ask such questions as: What needs to be done in a particular area or for a particular population? What is being done or what programs are in place? How effective are these programs? Sociology showed me how to move from the conceptual to the operational level, so you can measure things reliably and validly. My knowledge of sociological theory, research methods, statistics, and computer programming are very useful."

another under conditions favoring the perception of similar beliefs, racial prejudice will be substantially reduced. Both these theories stress that the contacts must be amiable to reduce prejudice.

Changes in the way minorities are portrayed in the mass media have also influenced levels of prejudice. During the 1950s and 1960s, when blacks and other minorities were portrayed at all, it was usually in stereotyped roles as servants or other low-status workers. Today, although it could be argued that portrayals of minorities in the media still tend to reflect stereotypes, the situation has improved considerably.

Another cause for optimism is the frequent finding of research studies that more educated people are more likely to express liking for groups other than their own. It may be that the educated have a more cosmopolitan outlook and are more likely to question the accuracy of racial stereotypes. It is to be hoped that the trend in this country toward a more educated population, along with the other advances that have been made, will contribute to a reduction in prejudice and the more complete realization of the American ideals of freedom and equal opportunity for all.

Summary

Race refers to a socially defined group or category of people distinguished by selected inherited physical characteristics. An ethnic group is a number of individuals who feel they are one people because they have a common race, religion, national origin, or language. Racial and ethnic groups are considered minorities when they are subordinate to another group in terms of power, social status, and privilege and when their norms, values, and other characteristics differ from those that prevail in a society.

The major ethnic groups in the United States are the blacks, Hispanics, Asians, American Indians, and European ethnics. The black and Spanish-speaking populations are the largest. Due to changes in the immigration policies in the mid-1960s, most immigrants today come from Asian countries, and the population of Asian Americans has increased dramatically.

A prejudice is a preconceived judgment about another group. A variety of theories have been offered to explain prejudice, including economic and psychological ones. Prejudice often involves acceptance of ethnic stereotypes, widely held beliefs about the character and behavior of all members of a group. Whereas prejudice is an attitude, discrimination is overt behavior that is usually (but not always) based on prejudice.

Racism is a system of beliefs and actions based on those beliefs. It has three distinguishing characteristics: (1) the idea that one's own race is superior to any other race, (2) an ideology, and (3) actions based on the racist beliefs. Genocide and mass expulsion are consequences of extreme forms of racism.

Stratification in the United States runs to a large extent along racial and ethnic lines and is found only when three conditions are present: ethnocentrism, competition, and, most important, inequalities in power. Inequalities can be resolved through either integration or pluralism. Integration involves assimilation: acceptance of the norms, values, and customs of the majority. Pluralism is the assumption that separate-but-equal coexistence is possible. Various ethnic groups have adopted different routes in their efforts to participate in the mainstream of American society, but some have not adapted as completely as others. Several authorities believe that integration and pluralism are occurring simultaneously in American society today, and, in the past twenty years, American ethnic groups have experienced a renewed interest in their heritage.

Although relations among ethnic groups are far from perfect in this country, some progress has been made in the last few decades. Recent government regulations make it more likely that members of different groups will interact as equals, which several authorities suggest will lower levels of prejudice. Changes in the portrayal of minorities in the media and the trend toward a better-educated population may lead to further progress in this area.

Key Terms

Anglo-conformity
assimilation
cultural pluralism
discrimination
ethnic groups
genocide
integration
mass expulsion
melting pot
minority groups
prejudice
projection
racial groups
racism
scapegoating
segregation
stereotypes
structural assimilation

Suggested Readings

Burstein, Paul. **"Equal Employment Opportunity Legislation and the Income of Women and NonWhites,"** American Sociological Review 44 *(June 1979):367–391.* Based on census, labor, and survey data, this study assesses the impact of federal Equal Employment Opportunity (EEO) laws passed in the 1960s and 1970s on the income of minorities and women.

Gergen, Kenneth J. **"The Significance of Color in Human Relations,"** Daedalus 96 *(1969):387–421.* This study uses a social-psychological framework to examine prejudices associated with skin color.

Gordon, Milton M. **Human Nature, Class, and Ethnicity.** *New York: Oxford University Press, 1978.* This book covers the author's general theory of racial and ethnic relations. It includes a collection of essays on social stratification, the nature of pluralistic group life, and assimilation in American society.

Killian, Lewis M. **The Impossible Revolution: Phase II,** *New York: Random House, 1975.* A powerful book relating black protest to four areas of concern to blacks: psychological well-being, political recognition, economic security, and social status.

Kitano, Harry H. L. **Race Relations,** *Englewood Cliffs, N.J.: Prentice-Hall, 1980.* A textbook considering race relations from the viewpoint of a minority-group member. It includes excellent accounts of the history and current statuses of the various Asian-American groups in the United States.

Newman, William M. **American Pluralism: A Study of Minority Groups and Social Theory.** *New York: Harper & Row, 1973.* A look at the United States as a pluralistic society.

Torhman, Robert A. **Inequality and Stratification in the United States.** *Englewood Cliffs, N.J.: Prentice-Hall, 1978.* A book on social stratification that includes definitions of key concepts and a discussion of theories. It focuses on three types of inequality: racial and ethnic, occupational, and gender-based.

Schaefer, Richard T. **Racial and Ethnic Groups.** *Boston: Little, Brown, 1979.* A textbook on race and ethnic relations that assesses recent development in the context of a historical framework and existing theoretical orientations.

Schermerhorn, R. A. **Comparative Ethnic Relations: A Framework for Theory and Research.** *Chicago: The University of Chicago Press, 1978.* A book examining intergroup relations at a macrosociological level from the functionalist and conflict perspectives.

Wolf, Eleanor P. **Trial and Error: The Detroit School Segregation Case.** *Detroit: Wayne State University Press, 1981.* An extensive study of the Detroit busing case, this book examines courtroom testimony on residential segregation, education, and the use of social science evidence in judicial proceedings.

Chapter 10
Gender and Age Differentiation

Youth is a gift of nature, but age is a work of art.
— Garson Kanin

In simple horticultural societies, people tend to work together and play together; there is little division of labor by age or gender. In complex industrial societies, however, people are differentiated on the basis of the roles they play. Young people are segregated from the larger community in age-graded schools. Old people are expected to leave the work force and are becoming increasingly segregated from the mainstream of society. Women have traditionally stayed at home as housewives, caring for home and family, and men have traditionally provided the family income. In recent decades, women have been entering the work force in large numbers, but they are often denied equal opportunities in the job market. This chapter is about how these three groups — children, women, and old people — are affected by the way society differentiates them.

Gender Differentiation

Although women bear children and assume most of the responsibility for rearing them — buying food and clothes, making meals, and caring for the home — the role of housewife has a low status. Many women who work outside the home also find that their work is valued less than that of men. Waiters have a higher status than waitresses. Bricklayers are considered skilled workers, but typists are not. Doctors, who are mostly male, have much higher status than nurses, who are mostly female. In the Soviet Union, the majority of doctors are women, but they do not have the high status of doctors in the United States. On the other hand, many Americans would not vote for a woman for president.

Why does society tend to devalue women and the work they do? Why do so many women

241

hold low-status jobs that pay poorly? Why are they often respected and rewarded less highly than men? Are there basic differences between the sexes that justify this situation?

Biological Bases of Gender Differences

Males and females differ from the moment of conception, when sex is determined. The ovum of the mother always carries an X chromosome, which bears the genetic material to develop a female. The father's sperm may carry either an X or a Y chromosome. If the sperm carries an X chromosome, the fetus will develop into a female. If the sperm carries a Y chromosome, testes develop that secrete a hormone that causes the embryo to develop as a male. The question physiologists and psychologists have struggled with is whether the sex hormones in the fetus affect the central nervous system and therefore influence how males and females behave.

We do know that children who are biologically of one sex can be socialized to behave as normal children of the opposite sex. One such case involved identical twin boys, one of whom lost his entire penis during a circumcision operation. He was brought to Johns Hopkins Hospital for treatment, where it was recommended that he be raised as a girl. Through surgery, it was possible to build him a vagina so that he could function as a female. Biologically, however, he was still a male and would never be able to bear children. The child was raised as a girl while her twin brother was raised as a boy. Money and Ehrhardt (1972) describe the process of change as follows:

> The first items of change were clothes and hairdo. The mother reported: "I started dressing her not in dresses but, you know, in little pink slacks and frilly blouses ... and letting her hair grow." A year and six months later, the mother wrote that she had made a special effort at keeping her girl in dresses, almost exclusively, changing any item of clothing into something that was

clearly feminine. "I even made all her nightwear into granny gowns and she wears bracelets and hair ribbons." (p. 124)

The little girl later came to prefer dresses to slacks, and she took pride in her hair. She loved to have her hair set and she would sit under the dryer "all day long." She became very neat and clean and, unlike her brother, she loved to have her face washed.

According to the Money and Ehrhardt (1972) study, the mother reported that she hoped both children would go to college and "have some kind of career. That's what I would like for both of them. . . . As long as they get their high school, at least my daughter. My son, it's almost essential, since he will be earning a living for the rest of his life" (p. 127). The son chose very masculine career goals, such as a policeman or fireman. He wanted to do what his father did, work where his father worked, carry a lunch kit, and drive a car. The daughter assumed she would get married and wanted to be a doctor, which her mother thought was a nice feminine occupation.

At birth, the girl had been the dominant twin, but by age three she was less rough than her brother, and her dominance took the form of being "a mother hen" to her brother. The boy, however, protected his sister if anyone threatened her. Money and Ehrhardt also reported that the mother wanted to "teach her to be polite and quiet. I always wanted those virtues. I never did manage, but I'm going to try to teach my daughter to be more quiet and ladylike" (p. 128).

Sociological Bases of Gender Differences

The twins in the study described above were both genetically male, and they received normal male hormones during the fetal period. (Hormonal treatment did not begin until puberty.) This study and others like it indicate that sex hormones do not affect the human nervous system in such a way that either masculine or feminine behavior is inevitable. This child's feminine behavior was clearly the result of socialization, some of it intentional, some of it unconscious.

These findings are corroborated by certain crosscultural studies. The influence of hormones on the nervous system is presumably the same in all humans, but in some cultures men and women occupy roles in ways very unlike those typically found in the United States. In the Chambri (formerly *Tchambuli*) society of New Guinea, for example, the women are the workers. They do the fishing, weaving, planting, harvesting, and cooking, carrying and caring for their children all the while. They are generally confident, laughing, brisk, good-natured, and efficient. They have a jolly comradeship that involves much rough joking. The men, on the other hand, are more involved in producing arts and crafts and planning ceremonies. They tend to be more emotional than the women and also more responsive to the needs of others. The women typically have an attitude of kindly toleration toward the men, enjoying the men's games and parties but remaining rather remote emotionally (Mead, 1935).

In many African societies, it is the women who have traditionally owned much of the land. Europeans have often tried to impose their own system of ownership on these tribes, sometimes with dire consequences. When Europeans introduced modern farming methods to the Ibo tribe of Nigeria, they took the land from the women and gave it to the men. The men raised cash crops, which they sold, and the women were left without their traditional means of subsistence. In 1923, the Ibo women rioted. Ten thousand women looted shops and released prisoners from jail. In two days of intense rioting, fifty people

Chambri women do most of the work necessary for survival in their society. Some of this work is considered by other societies to be appropriate for men. Chambri women grow and harvest crops, cook the food, care for the children, and do it all with good-natured confidence. In this picture Chambri women are shown going to market.

were killed and another fifty were injured. Later, the women became more organized and continued their revolt against land reforms and taxation with more riots, strikes, cursing, and ridicule (Leavitt, 1971). In certain other societies, men and women both share what we would consider a traditional feminine role or a traditional masculine role. The point is that the *gender roles* assumed by men and women in different societies vary enormously, so much so that the existence of a powerful hereditary predisposition among men and women for certain gender roles seems unlikely.

The gender-role socialization of the members of a society seems to be related to its structure. In hunting and gathering societies in which survival depends on the constant search for food, both males and females are socialized to be assertive and independent. Women must stay near their infants in order to nurse them while men assume the tasks of hunting and fighting, probably because they are stronger. Yet as societies grow wealthier and more complex, as the division of labor increases and hunting is no longer necessary to provide food for people, gender-role differentiation increases. If both men and women are capable of meeting the demands of almost all positions or statuses without being constrained by biological factors, why does role differentiation increase? Why do women have lower status in modern society than men? Sociologists begin with their theoretical perspectives in order to explore these questions.

Theories of Gender Differentiation

Structural-Functional Theory

Structural functionalists, you will recall, believe that society consists of interrelated parts that perform a function in maintaining the whole system. They assume, accordingly, that women have traditionally made important contributions to so-

ciety. They raised children, maintained the home, and provided food, clean clothing, and other necessities of daily living. They have also played an expressive role, nurturing and providing emotional support for husbands and children returning home from work or school. The woman in the family created the atmosphere of close interpersonal relationships necessary to a worthwhile human existence, relationships lacking in the competitive workplace (Parsons and Bales, 1955). Although these skills are vital to society, they are outside of the marketplace, since they do not command a price.

According to this perspective, the traditional function of a man was to protect and provide for his wife and children. He was the head of the household, controlling where the family lived, how money was spent, and making other decisions important to the survival of the family. He also made the political and economic decisions in the community by serving in powerful decision-making positions.

Technological advances have reduced the workload of women in the household, making it possible for them to enter the work force outside of the home. Technology has also reduced the number of hours that men have to work, so they can spend more time with their children and in other activities. As a result, the family has become more egalitarian (Goode, 1970). Both men and women can spend time at home caring for children, and both share in the role of provider. Because women have only recently entered the work force, they tend to be in low-paying jobs, but structural-functional theorists believe women should make rapid gains in earning power as they gain experience and skills.

Some functional theorists and others are concerned about changes in traditional family roles, fearing that equality between men and women will cause the disintegration of the family. They foresee increases in adultery and divorce, declining birth rates, increased juvenile delinquency, neglect of aging parents, and a host of other family-linked problems. Most functionalists, however, believe the family will survive as equality increases between men and women, although it may assume a different form than it has had in the past.

Conflict Theory

Conflict theorists believe that women have low status because they have been exploited by more powerful men (Hartmann, 1977). Very early in the development of societies, military force was used to protect land and other valuable private property and also to capture women from other tribes. Women were prized possessions who could work for their captors to increase wealth and provide children who would grow into future workers. At the same time, they could increase the prestige of the men who owned them, especially if they were beautiful and desired by other men.

It was not just as future workers that children were important. Men needed children to look after the property when they grew old and to inherit it when they died. To know who his children were, a man needed to isolate his women from other men. Thus women became the protected property of men so that they could accumulate wealth and have children to inherit it. According to this perspective, women were from earliest times exploited by men for the work they did and the children they bore.

The process of industrialization removed work from the family, but, conflict theorists argue, men were not willing to lose their control over the labor of women. They tried to either keep women out of the work force entirely or allowed them to hold only the lowest-paying jobs. They passed laws regulating the kind of work women could do and the hours they could work. They also passed laws regulating women's rights to income, property ownership, and birth control, and made them exclusively responsible for domestic tasks. Men forbade women from joining unions and entering professions. Legally and by tradition, they prevented them from gaining high positions in the work force.

Less powerful men were also hurt by the practice of keeping women in the positions with low pay. The existence of a labor force of poorly paid women meant that men who asked for higher wages could easily be replaced by lower-paid women. Conflict theorists believe that powerful men will have to be forced to give up their dominant position in the labor force and at home if women are to make any gains toward equality.

Gender Differentiation and the Workplace

Sociologists study gender differentiation in order to understand which theoretical perspective of society is more accurate. If the structural-functional perspective is correct, then as industrial society develops women should move into the work force and attain equality with men. If conflict theory is right, then as industrial society creates more wealth and power for men, they will use the wealth and power to improve their own position and women will lag farther and farther behind.

At the very beginning of this book we pointed out that sociologists sometimes study the obvious. Perhaps studying whether women are improving their position in society is one of those obvious questions, because we are always hearing in the press and elsewhere that the position of women today is improving rapidly. But is it really? Compared with the Middle Ages in Europe, the twentieth century in the United States is a period of great wealth. Men, women, and children live richer, fuller lives, and there is no question that the lives of women are more pleasant than they used to be. That is not the question. What we want to know is whether women are becoming equal to men as they participate fully in industrial society or whether the gap between men and women is growing larger as the wealth in society increases. This is not an easy question to answer. We must look at the position of women throughout the history of industrialization and we must look at the position of women today, keeping in mind that we want to know if the gap between men and women is growing wider or becoming narrower.

A Brief History of Women and Work

Regardless of their legal status, whether free or slave, women have always played an important economic role in society by producing many valuable goods and services. In the agrarian society of Europe during the Middle Ages, they produced much of what was needed in the home. They carried water from the well, prepared the food, and sometimes grew it too. They prepared the wool, manufactured the clothing, cared for the children, healed the sick with their herbs and medicines, and did many other tasks essential to the survival of the family. They also produced items for sale in the marketplace. If their husbands went off to war, women completely took over managment of the farms.

Toward the end of the Middle Ages, peasants began leaving the land and moving to the developing cities, which opened new choices to women (Bernard, 1981). They became vagabonds, traders, innkeepers, and occasionally ran breweries and blacksmith shops. They often became members of a guild, a type of medieval trade union. Women who did not wish to marry could enter *Beguines*. These were communes of seven or eight women located in urban areas. The women vowed celibacy upon joining the Beguine, which provided a secure workplace. They pursued such occupations as sewing, baking, spinning, and weaving and sold their products in the marketplace. They formed guilds to bargain with the cities, the Catholic church, and the overlords for the right to practice their trades.

Women from upper-class families could enter *convents* and become nuns. At that time, convents had great scholarly reputations; the women who entered them could be educated and pursue re-

spected political or scholarly careers. The convents were also known for their achievement in poetry, drama, weaving, and needlework, and the nuns enjoyed fine clothing and jewelry. Poor girls could also enter the convent as boarders, lay sisters, or servants. They did the more arduous labor involved in the production of food and other necessities, sometimes becoming a personal servant to one of the nuns.

By the fifteenth century, the plague had swept through Europe. There was a shortage of workers for the developing industries, and the birthrate was very low. The success of the Beguines and convents provided considerable competition to the new industries. Beguines were regulated to the point where they could no longer survive. Convents were regulated by the Catholic church to become more austere establishments. Scholarship and art gave way to menial labor, service to the poor, and simple dress. Family life became the only secure option left to women.

It was during this period that the great European witch hunts took place (Nelson, 1975). Witches were women who healed. They also served as midwives, advisors on birth control, and abortionists. They used a combination of magical practices inherited from earlier times as well as various herbs and medicines. Some, such as belladonna, are still in use today. These healers became enemies of the Catholic church because they were not Christian and enemies of the state because they helped keep the birth rate low — which limited the supply of children who could grow up to be the future soldiers and cheap laborers in the newly industrializing nations. During the years 1400 and 1700 approximately half a million people, most of them women, were burned as witches. While the loss of Beguines and communes restricted them to family life, the witch hunts intimidated and further reduced the status of women.

The goods traditionally produced by women in the home were the first to be manufactured in

By the 1920s the American garment industry had grown large and employed many women to operate sewing machines. The fine needlework skills used in the home to make clothing, quilts, and other domestic articles were no longer in demand. Instead, women who needed to earn money worked in factories that were hot, crowded and unsafe, doing tedious work for poor wages, but it was one of the few ways a woman could earn money. Most women preferred to stay out of the labor force.

factories at the beginning of the industrial revolution, the most important of which were textiles. Poor, young, single women went to work in the mills and were forced to work under terrible working conditions and for very little pay. Married women could not leave the home for the twelve-hour work days required in the mills and still maintain their homes, so married women lost their ability to earn income. As industry and the population grew, good farm land became scarce, so men also became available for factory work. Protective labor laws were passed that limited the number of hours women and children could work and the types of work they could do. As men became the preferred workers in factories, women, who already found it difficult to earn money inside the home, found it increasingly difficult to obtain work outside the home. For most of the nineteenth century, the vast majority of women were without income, and the only alternative that provided economic well-being was marriage. The family thus ceased to be an economic unit producing goods for itself and for trade. It came to be separate from the economy, an escape from the world, a group that bought goods rather than sold them.

Women in the Workplace in the Twentieth Century

At the beginning of the twentieth century, many upper-class women received an education, and some worked in the professions. Poor women who worked were usually employed as servants. The vast majority of women, however, were married and worked in the home to meet the needs of their families. They produced few goods for the marketplace and had little income. By 1980, 50 percent of women in the United States were working. They comprised 40 percent of the labor force (Smirlock, 1980). The major reason women take jobs is, like men, for economic necessity. Nearly two-thirds of all women workers are either single, separated, or divorced. They must support themselves and sometimes their families. About 50 percent of all married women are now in the work force, but research indicates that they too work for economic reasons and not just to escape boredom.

Income

The median income for women working full time in 1980 was $11,591, only 60 percent of the median for men — $19,173. The gap between men and women varies from state to state, as shown in Table 10-1, but overall it has been widening: in 1958, women earned 64 percent of what men earned. There are three major reasons for this widening gap.

1. Women are entering the work force in low-paying occupations. More women than men work in low-paying clerical service, or blue-collar work. Often these jobs have no career lines, so women cannot advance to higher positions.

2. People with low salaries receive smaller raises. A 10 percent raise on $10,000 is smaller than a 10 percent raise on $20,000 and the gap widens.

3. Women are sometimes paid less than men when they hold equivalent jobs.

The percentage of women making low and high salaries can be seen in Figure 10-1.

During the 1960s, the federal government made a considerable effort to create equal opportunity for men and women. President Kennedy established Affirmative Action in the federal service, and President Johnson continued the ef-

Table 10-1
The wage gap by state

WOMEN'S EARNINGS AS PERCENT OF MEN'S					
Washington, D.C.	78.4%	Oklahoma	58.6%	Rhode Island	56.6%
New Jersey	66.1	California	58.4	Missouri	56.5
Vermont	65.4	Kentucky	58.4	North Dakota	56.0
New York	64.9	Minnesota	58.2	Iowa	55.7
Tennessee	63.8	Nevada	58.2	Idaho	55.4
Maryland	62.2	New Mexico	58.0	Montana	55.3
North Carolina	61.1	Ohio	57.9	Oregon	55.3
Michigan	61.1	Colorado	57.9	Alaska	55.2
South Carolina	60.9	Kansas	57.8	Delaware	55.1
Arkansas	60.7	Hawaii	57.7	West Virginia	55.0
Massachusetts	60.7	Arizona	57.6	Washington	54.7
Florida	60.0	Connecticut	57.5	Indiana	53.8
Mississippi	60.0	Illinois	57.5	Wyoming	53.7
Virginia	59.8	Wisconsin	57.5	Utah	53.3
Pennsylvania	59.7	Nebraska	57.2	Louisiana	49.8
New Hampshire	59.3	South Dakota	57.1		
Alabama	59.2	Texas	57.0		
Maine	59.1				

SOURCE: *What Women Earn.* Copyright © 1981 by Thelma Kandel. Reprinted by permission of the Linden Press, a Simon & Schuster division of Gulf and Western Corporation.

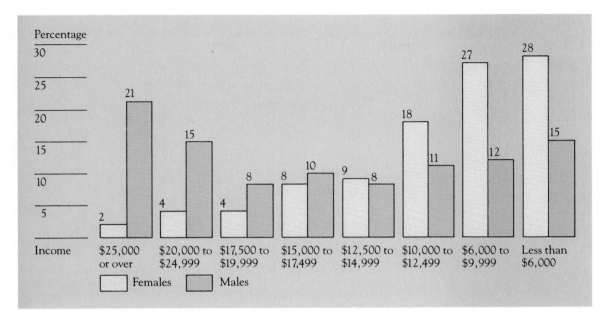

Figure 10-1
Percentage of workers with income from full-time jobs, by sex, 1980.

fort with his Great Society programs. Despite these efforts, men entering the federal service during this period received salaries $800 to $1,300 higher than women entering equivalent positions with equal qualifications and experience. In a carefully done study (Grandjean, 1981) tracing the careers of these men and women from the time they entered federal service until 1977, it was found that at each stage of their careers, the gap between men and women widened by an additional $600 to $2,000. The differences in income for males and females for each job category can be seen in Table 10-2.

Occupation

Women could improve their income if they worked in occupations that paid more money. While more and more women have been entering

the labor force, the vast majority have taken low-paying jobs involving typing or filing, or they have entered service occupations such as being a waitress, a beautician, or a cleaning woman. While the number of women in all fields has grown, the proportion of women in the more highly paid occupations is very low, as shown in Table 10-3.

In 1940, 4 percent of all executives were women. In 1980, 5.6 percent were women. Why are there so few women moving into management jobs in corporations? One reason is that relatively few women have been employed long enough to work their way up to top positions. Another reason, however, is that women at work tend to be viewed by men in their positions as wives and mothers, not as serious workers (Kanter, 1979), which, of course, affects their chances of promo-

Table 10-2

Median income of full-time workers by occupation and sex, 1980

	FEMALES	MALES
Professional, technical, kindred	$15,285	$23,026
Managers and administrators, except farm	12,936	23,558
Sales	9,748	19,910
Clerical, kindred	10,997	18,247
Craft, kindred	11,701	18,671
Operatives	9,440	15,702
Laborers, except farm	9,747	12,757
Service workers, except household	7,982	13,097
Private household workers	4,562	Not available

SOURCE: U.S. Department of Commerce, Bureau of the Census. *Current Population Reports.* Series P-60. No. 127. "Money Income and Poverty Status of Families and Persons in the United States: 1980." Washington, D.C.: U.S. Government Printing Office, 1981.

Table 10-3

Percentage of men and women in each occupational category, 1980

OCCUPATION	MEN	WOMEN
Professional and technical workers	62%	38%
Nonfarm managers and administrators	77	23
Clerical workers	22	78
Sales workers	72	28
Craft and kindred workers	95	5
Operatives, including transportation	73	27
Service workers (except private household)	52	48
Private household workers	5	95
Nonfarm laborers	89	11

SOURCE: U.S. Department of Commerce, Bureau of the Census, *Current Population Reports.* Series P-60. No. 127. "Money Income & Poverty Status of Families and Persons in the United States: 1980." Washington, D.C.: U.S. Government Printing Office, 1981.

tion. Men often do not want to promote married women because they might become pregnant and leave. Those who already have children tend not to be promoted because they may take time off from work to care for them, although studies show that women are not absent more than men. Divorced or single women are not promoted be-cause they might get married and leave. Often, men judge women not on the basis of their com-petency but on the basis of their traditional family role, and women are found lacking.

Furthermore, decisions that affect their work performance are frequently made at meetings that the women do not attend, although men would

Today women work in a variety of occupations. Profes-sional women, such as the architect working at her desk, earn more than most women, but very few archi-tects are women. On the other hand, the waitress works in a field dominated by women, but the pay is low. Blue-collar female workers like the auto mechanic usually earn more than they could in traditional female occupa-tions, but often less than men in blue-collar jobs.

normally expect to participate in decisions that affected their own work performance (Shockley and Staley, 1980). Men continue to assume that they should make the important decisions and do not include women in these meetings. If they do have the opportunity to participate in the decision-making process, their suggestions are more often challenged than men's, and if men and women disagree on an issue, men are expected to be the winners. Men continue to see themselves as managers, and they continue to see women in the traditional roles of wives, mothers, and assistants to men.

The influence of traditional gender-role attitudes is evident in other occupations also. The largest number of women in white-collar work are secretaries, stenographers, or typists. Typists and stenographers often work in a group or pool. Work to be typed is distributed to the pool, or if

someone in management wants to dictate, a stenographer will go to his or her office, take dictation, and bring it back to the pool to type it.

In the large corporation studied by Kanter (1979), which is considered a typical corporation in the way it structures its work force, secretaries are promoted out of the pool and assigned to one manager. They have no job description other than to do what the boss wants done and they may or may not type or take shorthand. They may file, fill out forms, greet visitors, bring coffee, and run errands for the boss, who assigns the work and makes judgments about raises. The way to succeed as a secretary in this corporation is to get assigned to a boss who gets promoted. As the boss is promoted, the secretary is promoted too. The rank of the secretary is based not on her work but on the rank of her boss.

In her study of secretaries, Kanter (1979)

The Cocktail Waitress

Spradley and Mann (1975) studied cocktail waitresses and found that while their work was devalued, their work was more difficult than the bartender's and designed to make his job easier. The cocktail waitress takes drink orders from the customer, then she goes to the bar and orders the drinks from the bartender, not as the customer named them, but naming them as the bartender recognizes them. She orders them, not in the order she receives them, but in the order the bartender will mix them, such as giving him brandy drinks

together and beer orders together. While he makes the drinks, she puts fruits and straws in the drinks as required, stirs them and adds up the bill in her head, even though he could do it on the cash register. Then she must put the drinks on the tray, not in the order they were mixed, but in the order placed by the customers.

If the bartender wants a drink during working hours, he has one, but the waitresses are not allowed to drink. If the bartender wants a break, he can ask a waitress to fill in behind the bar, but he would

never be expected to fill in for a waitress. When she helps him, she feels honored and thanks him for the opportunity. If he should on occasion help her, she thanks him for helping her. Spradley and Mann found that whenever there is an exchange of roles, the woman must show her appreciation to the man. Just as when a man "lets a woman drive" she thanks him, but when he helps her cook, she thanks him. The work and status of the cocktail waitress in many ways reflect the work and status of women in society.

SOURCE: James P. Spradley and Brenda J. Mann, *The Cocktail Waitress. Woman's Work in a Man's World.* New York: Wiley, 1975.

found the following: that because secretaries were considered expendable, they had to develop their own tactics for getting what they wanted from their bosses.

> This was a game some secretaries played extremely well. Whether or not they, as women, were intrinsically any more "emotional" than men, they learned to display their emotions as a very useful way to get what they wanted. As a former executive secretary said, "Women, like men, learned what the rules of the game are. A secretary goes in to see her boss and quivers and cries. Not because she's so emotional, but because she knows the rules. She gets the raise because he can't stand to see her cry.... We have to use the rules we have available to us. Women in business use what they can." (p. 96)

In her book *Men and Women of the Corporation,* Kanter (1979) argues that if women are to become upwardly mobile, not only must jobs be restructured, but interpersonal relationships in the corporation must be changed.

Women who do blue-collar work seem to play the least "feminine role" in their work because they often do hard physical labor. Studs Terkel (1974) tells of a "sparrow of a woman" in her mid-forties who has worked in a factory for twenty-one years as a punch press operator, oven unloader, sander, riveter, and stapler. She describes her job making luggage as follows:

> In forty seconds you have to take the wet felt out of the felter, put the blanket on — a rubber sheeting — to draw out the excess moisture, wait two, three seconds, take the blanket off, pick the wet felt up, balance it on your shoulder — there is no way of holding it without it tearing it all to pieces, it is wet and will collapse — reach over, get the hose, spray the inside of this copper screen to keep it from plugging, turn around, walk to the hot dry die behind you, take the hot piece off with your opposite hand, set it on the floor — this wet thing is still balanced on my shoulder — put the wet piece on the dry die, push this button

that lets the dry press down, inspect the piece we just took off the hot piece, stack it, and count it — when you get a stack of ten, you push it over and start another stack of ten — then go back and put our blanket on the wet piece coming up from the tank ... and start all over. Forty seconds. We also have to weigh every third piece in that time. It has to be within so many grams. We are constantly standing and moving. If you talk during working, you get a reprimand, because it is easy to make a reject if you're talking. (p. 290)

She suffers from constant burns, falls from slipping on the wet floor, arthritis in her hands from handling the hot pieces, fainting in the heat, and deafness from the noise of the factory. She says, "They can't keep the men on the tanks, we've never been able to keep a man over a week." Nevertheless, she has men for supervisors and a husband and children to cook for when she goes home at night.

Sexual Harassment

Women in all types of jobs suffer from *sexual harassment,* sexual advances made by coworkers or superiors at work. Women who reject sexual advances may be denied a job, intimidated, given poor work evaluations, denied raises or promotions, or fired.

Sexual harassment is much more widespread than is generally realized. The first questionnaire ever devoted solely to this topic surveyed working women in 1975 (Farley, 1978). The results were startling: 92 percent of respondents cited sexual harassment as a serious problem, and 70 percent reported that they had personally experienced some form of harrassment. In a January 1976 Redbook magazine survey, again over 92 percent reported sexual harassment as a problem, with a majority describing it as serious. Other studies indicate that sexual harassment is also a major problem in offices of the United Nations, in the United States military, in civil service jobs, and in private industry.

In deciding how to respond to sexual harassment, the victim must consider the economic necessity of keeping the job, the opportunities for getting another job, the likelihood of achieving decent work evaluations and future promotions, the possibility of being fired, and the attitudes of family and friends to her situation. The victim usually decides to quit, transfer to another job within the organization, or do nothing and suffer in silence because probably no one will believe her if she makes a complaint.

Women Below the Poverty Line

Given the many problems women face in the workplace, it's not surprising that more than a third of all women who are heads of families have incomes below the poverty line. (Women are said to be heads of families if they have children to support and if there is no man in the family.) In *female-headed families,* 64.3 percent of the children under six live in poverty, compared with 9.4 percent of the children living in families headed by a male. Also the proportion of children living in poverty in black families is much higher than in white families: 70.4 percent as against 59.2 percent of the children in white female-headed families.

Many women living in poverty receive welfare, but many more are working full time for a living. One-third of the female labor force is employed in the lowest-paying jobs in the economy — household labor (maids), agriculture (field workers), retail sales, and service jobs (women who clean offices, do shampoos in a beauty shop, etc.). Many of these jobs are not covered by minimum wage laws, pay very low salaries, and do not provide fringe benefits such as overtime pay, sick leave, unemployment insurance, paid vacations, and medical plans, which add another 20 to 30 percent to the salaries of other workers (Shortridge, 1975). Most women are now eligible for

Social Security if they work in one job steadily, but many employers do not pay Social Security, partly because they do not want to make the necessary contribution and partly because they do not want to deduct the necessary contribution from their workers' very small paychecks.

Why do women remain in these low-paying occupations? There are a number of reasons. Many women do not have the education or skills necessary to move to other occupations, and the jobs they have do not provide experience that permits them to eventually move to a paying position. The experience of a day worker or a migrant farm worker cannot be transferred to other occupations. Another reason is discrimination. Many women are simply not hired for better-paying jobs because of their sex, age, or race, and those in low-paying jobs are likely to be laid off from time to time rather than be given promotions or fringe benefits. Thus they must reenter the work force at beginning salaries.

Shortridge (1975) suggests four alternatives for women who have to work at low pay: welfare, marriage, government regulation, and organization. None of these alternatives is very satisfactory. Welfare is sometimes difficult to qualify for, and in some rural areas, welfare payments are extremely low and available only in the winter. When spring planting jobs become available, welfare payments are cut off and the women must return to the fields and work for very low wages. Even if welfare continues to be available, it may be so degrading that the worst jobs are preferable.

Marriage is not an alternative for all women and becomes progressively less likely as women grow older. There are more women than men in the older age brackets, and five million more women than men in the United States. Also, older men sometimes prefer to marry younger women.

Government regulations are of little help to these women. Some are not protected by minimum wage laws, and there is little government support for programs that would pay them supplementary wages. During the 1960s, the Johnson Administration began the Job Corps to train men for better-paying jobs, but this program specifically excluded women until women in Congress protested this discrimination.

Organizing women for better pay and improved working conditions is very difficult, especially among day workers who do not work for the same employer. Unions have sometimes resisted organizing women and allowing them to join existing unions. In some cases employers have fired them if they attempted to form unions. Nevertheless, the number of unions for women is increasing, and more women are joining them all the time.

The Status of Women

Judging the status of women presents many problems to sociologists. Women are often assumed to have the same status as their husbands, and to some extent this is a useful assumption. Certainly a company president's wife has higher status than a company vice-president's wife, and both rank higher than the wife of a businessman or blue-collar worker. But does the president's wife rank higher than the vice-president, businessman, or blue-collar worker? Assuming that a wife has the same status as her husband may indicate her relationship to other married women, but it does not indicate her relationship to men.

A second problem with this system of ranking women is that it does not indicate the women's relative power. Class and status are important because they are means of achieving power and influence, but what are the powers of the president's wife? Can she make decisions about the organization or its members? Can she decide how money will be spent or invested? Does

she have money at her disposal, or must she get money and permission to spend it from her husband? A president's wife may have far less power and influence than the ordinary worker in the organization.

Third, how does one rank the working wife? If her occupation has a different status than her husband's, does she have her own occupational status or that of her husband?

And finally, how does one rank an unmarried woman? She is often ranked according to her occupation and education, but this also creates problems. A woman executive may be of the same rank as a male executive, but because she is a woman she may not receive the honor and prestige he receives. And how does she rank compared with other women? Is she of the same rank as the nonworking wife of another executive?

Jesse Bernard (1981) contends that the status of women cannot be compared with the status of men and suggests an alternative system. At the top of this system she places society women, who determine which individuals will be accepted into the elite. Beneath this stratum she places celebrities, famous actresses, sports stars, and others who have a great deal of money and power. Intellectuals, the next level, are those who originate and disseminate ideas, such as writers, professors, lawyers, artists, judges, business people, and civil servants. Housewives are placed in fourth place because they play a vital role in society. White- and blue-collar women are placed in the same class below housewives because they generally have comparable income and educational status, although some would consider their position higher than that of housewives. Below working women, Bernard places two groups: welfare recipients and outcasts such as bag ladies and beggars. This system does not, of course, resolve the problems of the relative rank of men and women, but it may be a useful system for analyzing the status of women compared with other women, and it may also be useful, if in future years research is done to determine which, if any, of these status groups can use their status to acquire political power.

Women and Political Power

During the twentieth century a growing number of women in this country have been entering the work force, and in 1980 more than half were employed. Like the men who immigrated to America in the nineteenth century, women usually enter the work force in the lowest-paying jobs.

To improve their position in society, women have organized now and then, and from the time of the Civil War *women's movements* have worked to gain political power. Women finally gained the right to vote in the 1920s, and the women's movement began a resurgence in the 1960s.

Most of the women who have been active in these movements are from the upper-middle class. Educated women have the organizational skills and the economic security to pressure government and corporations for legal and economic gains. They have fought for the *Equal Rights Amendment (ERA),* for the right to enter jobs and the professions, for unbiased hiring practices, for equal pay, and for the right to abortions. They have worked to fight poverty, to make day care centers available for the children of working mothers, and to make marriage and divorce laws more equitable. Although working-class women generally support most of the goals of the women's movement, they have been less active in pursuing them. Their economic security is so precarious and so dependent on the family that conflicts are extremely threatening to their position.

As a result of their struggles, women have gained many rights. They won the right to vote. They can now hold many jobs that in the past were barred to them. Today there are female bartenders, construction workers, and bus drivers, to mention just a few. In all these occupations, however, they are greatly outnumbered by men.

Many states continue to limit the amount of weight women can lift and restrict their work in other ways, but laws have been passed guaranteeing them equal pay for equal work, and they have gained the right to practice birth control and obtain abortions. Except for the right to vote, however, these rights are not guaranteed under the Constitution, and the laws that grant these rights could be changed at any time by Congress.

In 1972, the Equal Rights Amendment was approved by Congress. The ERA states that "Equality of rights under the law shall not be denied or abridged by the United States or any state on account of sex." Although the majority of Americans supported the ERA, by 1982 it was not ratified by the required number of states to become a part of the U.S. constitution. Arguments for the ERA emphasize the necessity of giving women equality under the law. Arguments against it emphasize the need to protect women and their traditional family role.

To summarize this section, the research evidence indicates that the gap in income between men and women is widening, that women continue, for the most part, to work in low-paying jobs that are designed to maintain the role of women in society as helpers and caregivers, rather than as decisive and powerful people. They have been active politically, but as yet have very precarious political power, which may come as a surprise to most people — something we would assume to be otherwise if we assumed women were improving their status. Maybe changes will take place in the next few years, maybe evidence will be found to show that the differentiation between men and women is decreasing, but until we have such evidence, we must conclude that the events we have seen during the history of industrialization support a conflict perspective of society.

The Social Differentiation of the Elderly

The Elderly in Other Societies

Like women, the elderly often played an important economic role in preindustrial societies. They were part of the basic economic unit, the family, and all family members worked to the best of their ability. As parents grew older, their children assumed greater responsibility for work. If parents became physically less able, they did different work, but they continued their usefulness.

Even in the United States on the few remaining family farms, much work is done by the elderly. People in their eighties can tend livestock, garden, prepare food, cook, sew, and otherwise help support the family. People confined to a rocking chair can also do a great deal: shell peas, string beans, husk corn, knit, sew, mend, and do many other time-consuming tasks.

In some societies, the elderly have very high status, and in those that practice ancestor worship, the elderly can become very powerful. They are the matriarchs or patriarchs and form the councils of ruling elders. They are considered to have great wisdom, and people come to them for advice.

In societies where resources are scarce, the elderly become a burden when they cannot work. Although they are usually taken care of, they are not respected. In a few societies, such as the Ik of Uganda, resources are extremely scarce and the environment is very harsh. Rather than be a burden that could threaten the existence of the entire group, the elderly are expected to commit suicide or are left to die from starvation or exposure to the elements. In other societies, they may be killed by their younger relatives.

A Japanese grandmother plays a shamisen for her grandchildren. The Japanese have a great deal of respect for the wisdom and talents of the elderly, as shown by the rapt attention these children pay to their grandmother. In the United States, grandparents would more likely be the listeners and their grandchildren the performers.

In modern industrial societies, the elderly are expected to retire. If they have enough money, they may enjoy retirement, but retirement can cause a serious problem for those without financial security. It can also cause problems for a society with increasing numbers of old people. In 1900 the average life expectancy was 47, but now it is over 73 years of age. In 1900 there were very few old people, but today more than 11 percent of the population are over 65, and as people live longer, the number of old people in the population will increase. Society now must deal with the problem of large numbers of old people who do not have enough money. Why, then, do we expect old people to retire?

Theories of Age Differentiation

Structural-Functional Theory

Structural-functionalists believe that society functions best when it uses its most skilled workers in the labor force. Thus it is good for both society and the elderly that they retire. Society benefits because younger workers can be brought into the work force to replace those retiring, and retirees benefit because they don't have to work anymore.

The belief that the elderly are better off not working is founded on the assumption that they decline physically and mentally and that as they do they isolate themselves from social activity. This *disengagement* theory (Cumming and Henry, 1961) is based on evidence that people spend less time with family and friends as they get older.

Conflict Theory

Conflict theorists believe that the elderly are a minority who are powerless to protect their jobs. After a lifetime of service to a corporation, they are simply dismissed from the work force.

The corporate elite would rather hire younger workers who are stronger, healthier, and can be hired for less pay than older, experienced workers receive. Younger workers, concerned about the scarcity of jobs, encourage laws to force the elderly to vacate jobs the younger workers need. On the other hand, younger workers do not want to pay high taxes to support large numbers of elderly people. The elderly, thus, are left without work and often with little or no income.

Age Differentiation in Income, Status, and Class

Income of the Elderly

The median income in 1979 for men over sixty-five was $6,430. For women, it was $4,759. Most people over sixty-five are retired, and most of their income is received from the Social Security program. In 1978, the average retired worker received $243.83 per month, and the average married couple received $404 per month. If people work to earn additional income, their Social Security may be reduced or eliminated. If retired people are not eligible for Social Security and have no other income, they are eligible for Supplemental Security Income (SSI), which pays a single person about $144 a month.

The United States began the Social Security program during the depression of the 1930s, when millions of people were out of work and unable to support themselves. It was designed such that working citizens covered by the program paid a part of their wages into the program and at sixty-five became eligible to receive income based on the amount they had contributed. It was not designed, however, to provide an adequate income. It was assumed that savings or pensions accumulated during the working years would also be used during the retirement years and that Social Security would provide a secure base on which to

build a retirement income. Soon after Social Security was established, the government set a mandatory retirement age of sixty-five, which was raised to seventy in 1978 for all workers with the exception of government workers, who are not required to retire.

Social Security benefits have increased steadily since the program began in order to reduce the number of people living in poverty. Whether these benefits will continue to increase is of serious concern to the elderly. As the number of older people increases, it is expected that the costs involved in paying benefits will put pressure on the Social Security system, and many expect to see benefits reduced severely.

Millions of workers in the lowest-paying jobs were never covered by Social Security. Often, these workers were employed by companies that did not have pensions, or they lost their pensions when they were laid off. The meager wages earned during their working years did not permit them to save money. Today, many of these people live in poverty, even when they are assisted by the small Supplemental Security Income payments.

Married women who did not work receive half of their husband's Social Security benefits after he dies, and sometimes the pensions of husbands are often stopped when the husband dies. Working women often receive low benefits from Social Security or none at all because they earned low wages or worked in occupations not covered by Social Security. Thus, on the average, women collect much lower Social Security benefits than men.

Status

Status in the United States is usually derived from occupation and income. As we have seen, the elderly generally have very low incomes and no occupation. Society provides them with few roles in which they can earn the respect of others. In fact, as we discussed in Chapter 5, they have been described (Riley et al, 1969) as occupying a roleless role. They are generally required to retire and sometimes pressured to do so before the mandatory retirement age. Although businesses and counselors often give advice on planning for future income, planning on how future time will be spent, and planning for future health care, society has no expectations of the elderly. They are not expected to contribute to the nation's welfare, so they have no structured way to gain honor and respect from society.

A variety of myths have developed about the elderly to explain their low status, as, for example,

Aging in Children's Books

One of the youngest groups in the continual succession of antidiscrimination movements since the 1960s is made up of aging men and women. The effectiveness of old people in making the rest of society conscious of the prejudice against age showed most clearly in the recent law that raised the mandatory retirement age from 65 to 70. The new law acknowledges the fact that chronological age often bears little relation to capability and that many old people make excellent employees.

Although impressive advances against age discrimination have been made in legislatures and courts, the image of the elderly seems to be unchanged. At the University of Chicago Phyllis Barnum, a doctoral candidate in educational psychology, found evidence that an image of the elderly as passive, incompetent, and sickly was being created and reinforced in the pages of children's books.

Barnum analyzed the characterization of old people in 100 books written for children from preschool through the first grade. She selected at random five books published each year from 1950 to 1959 and from 1965 to 1974, which were listed in the *Children's Catalog,* and found that their portrayal of the aged contradicts reality in nearly all areas of life. For one thing, old people are not fairly represented: Although people older than 65 made up 9.3 percent of the population, they appeared as characters only 3.3 percent of the time and in only 5.3 percent of the illustrations. Aging men and women are shown involved in little social activity and interaction with other adults (in only 18 out of 2,500 drawings), and when they are active, they are employed at low-level jobs, working as "janitors, shopkeepers, and elephant riders." They appear more sickly, passive, and incompetent, and less self-reliant than do other adults. Barnum says, "The combination of greater passivity, more sickness, and less self-reliance ... gives an unnecessarily gloomy cast to old age in children's literature."

When she turned to books that featured the elderly as main characters, the image did not improve much. In a few cases a grandparent is shown to be wise and able, but whether wise or in-being ill a great deal of the time. Actually, only 5 percent of the elderly are in nursing homes, and most elderly people are very healthy. It is often assumed that people deteriorate as they age, but there are great variations in the ages at which people begin to decline physically. Typically, the eyes change in the decade after age forty, the ears and skin change in the decade following age sixty, but other organs do not typically deteriorate until after age seventy. Thus, chronological age is not a sure indicator of physical condition. The elderly do suffer more than younger people from chronic illnesses such as arthritis and high blood pressure, but only 21 percent of them consider health a serious problem whereas 50 percent of young people think health is a problem for the elderly (Manion, 1972).

Because of their presumed ill health, they are often viewed by others as being slow, inactive, and uninterested in sex or the larger world. They are thought to be unable to work and content to sit day after day by themselves. In fact, however, many elderly people jog, bowl, swim, travel, are active in politics, and can do anything others do.

The elderly are also assumed to suffer from mental illness or senility. Older people do make decisions more slowly and deliberately than younger people, but most of their supposed de-

competent, they are "almost un-failingly pleasant." Barnum believes that this placid portrayal lacks humaneness, because old people in children's books are not allowed to show a realistic range of emotions.

Her study follows a recent tradition of examining children's books for evidence of prevailing attitudes in society. Dick and Jane first got their comeuppance in the early civil-rights years, when activists pointed out that, except for red-caps and servants, the population of the books that taught children to read was exclusively white. Following the black-rights movements came feminists, who were concerned about the image of mothers as invariably tied to kitchens and kids, and disturbed by the absence of girls who were self-reliant, adventurous, and physically active. Now old people are taking their turn.

The greatest misrepresentation of all may be in showing all grandparents as elderly. Many people became grandparents in their 40s, which can hardly be considered old age. Barnum's evidence comes from books written for children up to eight years old. When children of that age open their books and find a meek, gray-haired, cookie-baking grandmother and a grandfather who sits in a rocking chair and whittles, they may have trouble reconciling those images with their own grandmothers, who might just have returned to work, and with their grandfathers, who may be at the height of their careers. Lillian Carter has become a symbol of the vitality of the elderly, but it is rarely pointed out that her son and daughter-in-law, who are both active and involved people, are also grandparents.

The prevalence of smiling old grandparents raises an additional point. Children are never shown to have relationships with old people who are not related to them. The absence of the unrelated elderly raises a question about age stratifaction in our society. *Do* children have relationships with old people to whom they are not related? In fact, do they see old people at all? Books generally reflect the society around them, and perhaps the increasing popularity of retirement communities and the segregation of inactive old people in homes for the aged is leading the United States toward a society that will have less and less contact between the very young and the very old.

SOURCE: *Human Nature*, Sept. 9, 1978, p. 13. Copyright © 1978 by Human Nature, Inc. Reprinted by permission of the publisher.

cline in intelligence is a myth. Older people, like everyone else, suffer mentally if they are isolated, if they are confined to their homes, or if they live in institutions. The majority of old people, however, are not isolated. They maintain contact with family and friends, and in general their interactions begin to decrease only after age seventy. Senior citizen programs are designed to give them opportunities to interact with others, since an active social life helps keep them alert and mentally healthy. The myths about the physical and mental health of older people decrease their status, self-confidence, ability to interact with others, and feelings of life satisfaction.

Sex Roles and Aging

The fact that women tend to be judged on the basis of their appearance and men by their achievements creates marked differences in status as they grow older. Men gain status during middle age. The physical changes that occur — the development of a more rugged-looking face, the graying temples — may be considered signs of maturity and handsomeness. Women, however, are encouraged to hide all signs of aging by using a variety of skin creams, mudpacks, makeups, rinses and dyes to wash away the gray, and hand creams to keep their hands young and soft-looking. Both men and women may gain weight, but men can hide their shape under business suits, which are not revealing. Many women's clothes, however, are designed to emphasize the figure, so a changing physique is not so easily hidden.

The stress on achievement as a source of status for men hurts them when they retire. Men who have defined their status on the basis of their careers suddenly have no careers. Money is an indication of career success, and upon retirement income usually decreases. Unless they have developed other activities to maintain their identities, they often feel at a loss when they retire. Women have not traditionally had to make this transition.

They continue in their homemaking role, and except for having to learn to live with a man who is home all day, their daily routine and identity are not significantly changed by retirement.

Lifestyles of the Elderly by Class

The lifestyles of the elderly resemble those of other adult age groups. The very wealthy are often exempt from mandatory retirement laws, which cover white-collar and blue-collar workers but not top executives, people running their own businesses, members of Congress, or people in other elite positions. The wealthy are better able

SOCIOLOGISTS AT WORK
Evaluating Programs for the Elderly

Francis G. Caro is the director of the Institute for Social Welfare Research at the Community Service Society of New York. He also serves as principal investigator on several of the institute's research projects. He joined the institute in 1974 after teaching sociology at Brandeis University and the University of Colorado and working as a community researcher in New Haven, Connecticut and Kansas City, Missouri.

Frank Caro has long been interested in the study of age groupings. In his student days (at Marquette as an undergraduate, at the University of Minnesota as a graduate student) he studied the way teenage boys approached educational and occupational decisions. More recently he has been involved in studying the special problems of the elderly, and in particular the disabled elderly. "I

got involved in this area while I was at Brandeis," he says. "When I came to New York City, I came to a setting where there was a substantial commitment to providing home care for functionally disabled older people. In the rest of the country this is being done on a small scale, in demonstration programs. Here, without a lot of visibility, the city's Human Resources Administration just went out and did it. They started with a program created for disabled younger adults, but then they opened the program to the elderly and it has grown rapidly. The city's program now has 30,000 clients and spends upwards of $200 million a year. We want to know how it's working."

The Community Service Society is an old private social welfare agency, founded in the middle of the nineteenth century. As more and more

than others to live with their families and continue the activities they previously enjoyed.

The middle classes usually leave their suburban homes when they retire because their income is reduced sufficiently that they cannot continue to maintain a house, or they may move from urban to rural areas, where the cost of living is lower, especially to the warmer climates of the south. Many have enough money to move to retirement villages where they can enjoy a variety of activities and the companionship of other elderly people. Others do not like the age segregation and retire to small towns or rural areas.

People who have always been poor usually continue to live in the same poor areas when they grow old. They may be in subsidized housing for the elderly, in cheap hotels or rooming houses in the city, or in rural housing. The rural poor occasionally migrate to the city because of the shortage of housing and services in rural areas, and the elderly poor in general are most likely to suffer from social isolation. They often have no network of friends for socializing and no money to spend on activities. They frequently live in crime-ridden areas and are afraid to venture out into the streets. Their nutrition may be inadequate, so they are more apt to be ill than wealthier people. The elderly poor suffer from poverty in much the same way that younger groups suffer from poverty.

direct services were taken over by government agencies, CSS shifted its aims to trying to exert a constructive influence on government programs, conducting or studying pioneer programs. "We have a great deal of credibility in the city," Caro says, "so we have access to a lot of information, and we get an attentive audience when we publish our results."

Caro is serving as principal investigator in CSS's study of the city's program for the disabled elderly. "We are dealing with a group that has serious self-care limitations. They have trouble with the problems of daily living — walking, eating, toilet functions — and with using the telephone, paying bills, taking medicine. These are especially serious problems among the disabled elderly, who are faced with the illnesses, weakness, and loss of mental capacity that often accompany aging. The city provides homemakers and home attendants to help these clients manage the tasks of daily living. They do shopping, cleaning, and cooking; they make beds, provide companionship, serve as escorts. All are nonprofessional services."

"One area we're studying is the way family members, if they are available, work with the public service agency. We're concerned with the intergenerational relationship. Throughout the life cycle, intergenerational family relations tend to be quite strong. There is a great deal of reciprocity over the years, but until very late in their lives, parents tend to give more help to their adult children than they receive in return. When parents are very old, they often can't manage on their own, and need help. To what extent do they get it? Do they get it from spouses? Adult children? Other informal supports? Organized services? What is the division of labor between the family and the service agency, and what should it be? We draw on sociological insights regarding intergenerational patterns of family bonds. A sociological perspective helps us understand what family members are committed to doing on behalf of a disabled relative and the circumstances under which they seek outside assistance."

The Very Old

In the previous section we discussed the income, status, and lifestyle of the majority of elderly people to make the point that most are healthy and active. Their status does not result from their biological age, but rather it results from the structure of society, especially the structure of work. As life expectancy increases, however, the number of people living to the age of 85 and beyond is also increasing. These are the people who are the most likely to suffer from debilitating illnesses and are usually in institutions such as nursing homes for the aged.

The practice of putting the elderly in nursing homes is a twentieth-century phenomenon, and they have developed partly because they have received government support. During the Great Depression, when Social Security was established, old people used their pensions to pay for nursing care. In 1965 Medicare and Medicaid were established, and these medical insurance policies for the aged and the poor provided additional funds to be used for nursing home care. Nursing homes also developed because in the twentieth century families in urban areas could not care for a disabled elderly person. People have to go to work, and no one could stay home to care for the patient. Also to be considered is the fact that the number of elderly is increasing.

Most people dread the idea of spending the last days, months, or years of their lives in a nursing home. They fear the loss of familiar surroundings, personal possessions, the freedom to come and go as they please, and the treatment they will receive. Nursing homes must earn profit if they are to stay in business. They must heat their buildings, buy food, and pay salaries to their staff. In order to do this they may cut their food budgets to a minimum, hire poorly trained staff and pay them very low wages, and crowd as many paying patients into the building as they possibly can. Some nursing homes can manage very well on their budgets, some must cut corners in order to stay in business. How much money the patient can afford to pay will often determine the kind of care a patient can buy.

But what are the alternatives? The patients can sometimes be cared for by the family, but some are very difficult to care for. They may need extensive nursing care or they may not have either the physical or mental capacity to cooperate with the care giver, and the family may find it impossible to provide the needed care. Furthermore, the family may suffer economic hardship if one of its members is required to leave a job in order to stay home, or if round-the-clock care requires hiring nursing staff to come to the home.

Although not an alternative to either nursing homes or home care, *hospices* are institutions designed to care for the terminally ill. They try to alleviate pain and emotional suffering for the patient and the family until the patient dies. They are innovative, using a new approach in treating the terminally ill, but they are very expensive and they do not care for chronically ill people who are expected to live for a year or more.

Euthanasia, mercifully ending the life of a suffering person, is also not an alternative for the long-term patient who is chronically ill, and it is a much debated topic. Should someone's life be ended when there is no hope of recovery? Even the strongest proponents of euthanasia support its use only for patients whose death is imminent. There are no serious proposals for using euthanasia to be rid of the chronic patient who is expected to live for many months or even years.

While only 5 percent of the elderly live in institutions, most people believe this is not a suitable way to live out one's life, and yet society has provided no satisfactory alternative social structure for these people. As the population lives longer and more and more people reach old age, one of our great challenges will be to devise social structures that will allow the elderly to lead active lives for as long as possible, and to live graciously even when they can no longer be active.

Summary

Modern society differentiates people on the basis of age and sex. Children are required to go to school, and women are usually expected to take care of children when they are not in school. Women have been entering the work force in increasing numbers throughout the twentieth century, but their status has remained low.

Most working women are employed in white-collar clerical positions, in service positions as cleaning women or waitresses, or in factories. The majority receive low wages, many live in poverty, and children who live with women heads of families are likely to live in poverty.

The status of women has traditionally been linked to the status of their husbands, but this system of ranking presents many problems, and Jessie Bernard has suggested that women should be classified according to a different system.

Women have little political power because they rarely hold high offices in government or business. Although many laws have been passed in recent years to improve their legal status, these laws are not guaranteed by the Constitution. The Equal Rights Amendment (ERA) was ratified by Congress to provide constitutional protection for women, and although it is favored by most citizens, it was not ratified by the required number of state legislatures.

For the past one hundred years, women have actively worked to improve their position in society. The contemporary women's movement has helped pass many of the laws that protect them today.

The elderly are usually required to retire, which sometimes creates economic hardships for them. Social Security provides some income for many elderly people, but the program was not designed to provide an adequate income in old age. Many elderly people are not eligible for Social Security because they worked in occupations not covered by the program. Often, these occupations were low paying or temporary jobs, so these people generally have no savings. Some receive Supplementary Security Income (SSI) payments, but they are very low, and these elderly people are usually poor.

The aged suffer low status because they do not work and because they are viewed by the rest of the population as sickly, feeble, disinterested in life, and often senile. Although they suffer from more chronic diseases than other age groups, they are typically healthy, active, interested, and interesting people who are capable of playing active roles in society.

The very old, who are most apt to be seriously ill, may spend their last days in nursing homes. Most people believe this is not a satisfactory way to care for the aged, but to date our society has not devised a satisfactory alternative for caring for the old and ill.

Key Terms

Beguines
convents
disengagement
Equal Rights Amendment (ERA)
euthanasia
gender roles
hospice
sexual harassment
women's movements

Suggested Readings

Bernard, Jessie. **The Female World.** *New York: The Free Press, 1981.* This book treats women as living in a world very different from the world of men and emphasizes the assets women can offer to make a more human world for everyone.

Boserup, Ester. **Woman's Role in Economic Development.** *London: Allen and Unwin, 1970.* This is an excellent discussion of how women suffer as a result of economic development in modernizing countries.

Kantor, Rosabeth M. **Men and Women of the Corporation.** *New York: Basic Books, 1979.* This book is an excellent discussion of the pressures and problems of work in a large corporation for both men and women.

Kreps, Juanita M. **Women and the American Economy, a Look to the 1980s.** *Englewood Cliffs, N.J.: Prentice-Hall, 1976.* Written by an economist, this book concisely discusses the class position of women today.

Rosseau, Ann Marie. **Shopping Bag Ladies: Homeless Women Speak About Their Lives.** *New York: The Pilgrim Press. 1981.* A moving collection of photographs depicting homeless women in the United States.

Spadley, James P. and Brenda J. Mann. **The Cocktail Waitress, Women's Work in a Man's World.** *New York; Wiley, 1975.* Good reading, especially for anyone who thinks this is an easy job. It will make cocktail waitresses aware of their job in a new way.

Sayre, Anne. **Rosalind Franklin and DNA.** *New York: Norton, 1975.* An excellent book on one woman's experiences in scientific research.

Schwartz, Arthur N. and James A. Peterson. **Introduction to Gerontology.** *New York: Holt, Rinehart & Winston, 1979.* A good basic text on aging.

Relating the Two Worlds

by Jessie Bernard

> *According to sociologist Jessie Bernard, there is a male style of dealing with the world which emphasizes competition and a female style which stresses cooperation. Bernard makes the case that society might well benefit from a shift to the female style.*

Annie Oakley may have been right when she sang to her male counterpart, "Anything you can do I can do better" — a form of braggadocio that proved her point — but for most women a more nearly accurate version would probably be: "Anything you can do I can do, too, but I'd do it differently." There are many ways to skin a cat. Or manage an economy. Or operate a polity. Sometimes the way women do it might even be better than the other ways.

There are bits and pieces of research, however limited in practical applicability controlled research necessarily has to be, that at least give us hints with respect to the efficacy of the female style. These cases-in-point are not intended as a justification for greater sharing by women in decision making in the polity, as proof that they deserve it, or as a demonstration of their worthiness, as in the old redemptionist argument. I do not believe women have to prove their credentials for full participation. It is their right. But it is reassuring to know there is evidence that their participation can improve the quality of decisions.

It may be a far cry from the research laboratory to the real world, but not too far to be relevant. One study, for example, found that laboratory games structured according to the tenets of the male ethos as delineated by Peter Blau's exchange model produced expectably sexist behavior in both men and women. The goal sought in this rigidly structured game was exchange of social control. The goal of a second, more open and liberally structured, game was more consonant with the style of the female ethos: that is, exchange of trust and information. In this second type of game, scores were consistently higher and interplayer differences in scores significantly smaller than in the rigidly stereotyped male kind of game. The authors conclude that "sexist behavior is a response to the structure of the game [social system] and the rules [norms] of play [interaction]." And, further, that "a change in game structure and rules results in a change in game behavior — regardless of social psychological attitudes."

Another laboratory study of game bahavior produced similar results. . . . we reported the aggressive, power-oriented style of male behavior in laboratory game situations as contrasted with the more accommodative or collaborative style of females. The results obtained are relevant at this point: the payoff from the female style was better than that from the male style:

> In terms of which style produces a better outcome, it is quite clear that the female arrives at a relatively more favorable position than does the male (most striking when she forms the minority).

267

Male strategy may be called self-defeating when it encounters female strategy. By competing against each other in the majority situation, the males place the female at an advantage, for their attempts to exploit her merely mean that she more often obtains points through coalition. One male may defeat the other, but the female thereby gains. In groups with a female majority, the same result does not occur, because, evidently, the aggressive play of the male minority, seeking to exploit his rivals, forces the two females into a comparatively solidary alliance against him, either as a simple means to avoid undue competition (i.e., to solve the problem of outcome in the female manner) or as a defense against his perceived strength. In either case, he loses.

In brief, "all of these phenomena may be understood as a function of male 'exploitative' strategy vs. female 'accommodative' strategy. The former appears to be self-defeating when it encounters the latter."

A third experimental study had to do with success in a pencil-and-paper test dealing with survival problems on a desert. Six teams of five individuals each, with different sex-ratios — five women: no man; four women: one man; three women: two men; two women: three men; one woman: four men; five men — were asked to rank fifteen items according to their importance for survival in a contrived desert situation, first individually, without group discussion, and then together as a team after group discussion. The individual scores for each team were averaged, so that there were two scores for each team, one the average of the five individual, prediscussion scores and the other the postdiscussion, consensual team score. The standard of correctness was the ranking of an experienced expert on survival in desert conditions. The lower the score, the more nearly it coincided with his rankings. The averaged prediscussion individual scores were about the same for men (69.9) and women (69.1). The all-female team score (53.8) was better than the all-male team score (62.8). Although team discussion improved the performance of both sexes, it improved female scores (15.3) more than twice as much as it improved male scores (7.1). The "male bond" did not seem to work as well among the men as the "female bond" did among the women. As I read the results it seems to me that perhaps the women were more open to the arguments made by other members of the group, more amenable to persuasion by discussion, that the men may have been more reluctant to change their minds or concede a point in discussion, that having once made a point it was harder for the men to admit that another point of view might be better. I picture the men therefore as less amenable than women to correction by group discussion.

In another study, this time observational, Raphaela Best found that while a group of third-grade boys were fighting it out to see who was going to be in charge of the line-up for watching the long-awaited hatching of chicks, and thus missing the whole show, the girls, unencumbered by the need to boss the operation, were quietly watching the whole process in an orderly fashion. Again, a branch bank run by women in a Maryland suburb, designed to serve its customers in ways reassuring to them rather than intimidating, grew faster than any other branch. And, finally, the radical women who dissociated themselves from the macho Weathermen in the 1960s had greater ultimate success in terms of survival and duration of impact than the men themselves had.

The style of the female world, in brief, can pass even the male-world test — winning. It may be in fact that the win-at-any-cost competitive pattern of the male ethos detracts from rather than adds to its efficiency and productivity. It is just possible that incorporating the style of the female world into the economy and the polity would have a benign rather than a hazardous effect. On the male as well as on the female world. For it does appear that where important issues are being delineated and great decisions being made, the contribution of the female as well as of the male style could greatly improve the result, whatever the content of the decision itself might be. It is not the substance of the issue alone that is important but the style of arriving at it as well. It may well be desirable that there be enough representatives of the female world in legislatures and on benches to have an impact on both the decisions and the styles of arriving at them. Granted then, that incorporating the style of the female world would be desirable, is it feasible?

The Possibility of Cultural Change: Cases in Point

The inertia of culture seems to trap us in the present pattern of relationship between the ethos of the male world and the ethos of the female world. Still, we do know that whole cultures sometimes do change, and fairly rapidly at that.

Some years ago Margaret Mead described the Arapesh of New Guinea, among whom both men and women were nurturing in the way we define as female. But only a few years earlier they had been head hunters, a far cry from a female kind of pursuit. She later revisited and reported equally remarkable changes in other cultures she had studied originally a generation earlier. Since then a reversal of the kind of change reported among the Arapesh — from an essentially female style to a male style — has also been reported this time among the Fore in Papua, New Guinea.

In the early 1960s E. Richard Sorenson lived among the Fore and recorded their life on film. They gathered and gardened for a living. Although he himself does not label Fore society of the early 1960s as maternal, he does say that women constituted a "benevolent sanctuary" to children. There were "no chiefs, patriarchs, priests, or medicine men." The single men's house sheltered ten to twenty men, boys, and friends; several smaller women's houses provided shelter to the women and small children. The older boys and young men explored and roamed, but also gardened. There was a "spontaneous urge to share food, affection, work, trust, toils; and pleasure was the social cement that held the Fore hamlets together." Friendship ties were more important than kinship bonds. When land was plentiful the Fore left a place rather than fight for it, though when land became scarce they would fight if they had to. But they considered warfare a curse. There was a division of labor, the men and boys doing the selecting of the garden sites, the slashing and burning, and the fencing; the women and girls cleared the weeds and grass, prepared the soil, transplanted, cultivated, and harvested. There were no monetary units. "Sharing was informal and voluntary among friends and close associates. There was no attempt to qualify value to facilitate repayment. With outsiders exchange took the form of feasts."

This almost archetypically "female" kind of world disintegrated with the coming of a road which opened the Fore up to the outside world, introducing coffee culture to them and bringing them into the world market economy. The Fore world — from child rearing to forms of social bonding — was completely transformed. Now there were "repeated incidents of anger, withdrawal, aggressiveness and stinginess." Sorenson attributes the changes to differences in child-rearing practices introduced after the coffee revolution. But far more was involved. A "male" style succeeded the old "female"-style world. Exchange superseded sharing. The sexual division of labor changed. It was primarily the men who went forth into the outside world to work on the coffee plantations, who learned how to cultivate the coffee, and who brought it back to their own communities. The transformation did not involve a dissolution or abolition of the sexual division of labor but rather a reformulation of it.

The new "male" society that came with the coffee revolution was wealthier in that it supplied the community with more material goods. But it was also more competitive, less loving, less relaxed. There were, in brief, costs as well as benefits from the change.

Changing Times

Granted that change in a highly complex society like ours is altogether different from that of change among the Fore and that we could hardly expect so much change in style so rapidly. Still, change in our society has been occurring ever since the beginning of the nineteenth century. If the pristine self-interest ethos of the Gesellschaft had been left to operate in full force, the whole system would long since have collapsed. It was too lethal; it left too many casualties. When the catastrophic concomitants of the new capitalistic system had first begun to surface in the nineteenth century, a wide variety of reform movements with a wide variety of programs had arisen to pick up the pieces left in the wake of rampant industrialization. Women had done much of the salvage work, the "friendly visiting," the philanthropy, the social work, the social reform that had kept the new economy viable. The self-interest ethos had not been permitted to operate in pristine form. It had had to be restricted. The current cries of men like Sorokin, Bezdek, Strodtbeck, Sennett, and Cobb remind us that the time may now be ripe for accelerated change.

For some time now the economy has been moving in the direction of the pole here labelled female. The ethos of the Gesellschaft is becoming more congruent with the ethos of the female world. A "people-oriented" style of management has been found essential in administering the economic system. It began to evolve in the 1920s in the form of a so-called human-nature-in-industry

movement even before women were in a position to make their views felt. By the first quarter of the century workers were already protesting the social and psychological conditions of the work site. Researchers were asking what was on the workers' mind and they were telling anyone who would listen what it was. In the present context all this can be seen retrospectively as a recognition of the values embodied in the female ethos, a concern for workers as human beings. It was still motivated, however, by self-interest since it was profit — not love and/or duty — that ultimately motivated the human-nature-in-industry good deeds.

We are now being told that the newer kinds of work call for qualities reflected in the female ethos; that such qualities are needed at all occupational levels, and not only vis-à-vis workers but vis-à-vis everyone. Qualities heretofore condemned as feminine are now in demand. Whether brought to bear on either the economy or the polity by men or by women or by both or by some intrinsic logic of the systems themselves, the female style may prove to be just what a lot of doctors — male and female — have been ordering for quite some time. This conclusion is not intended to resuscitate the redemptive role of women but to suggest that the direction present-day economic and political trends are taking may just happen to coincide with the style and ethos of the female world.

If it is, indeed, true that the "logic of events" is leading in the direction of greater recognition of the style of the female world, is there any need for women to push it themselves? If the economy and the polity increasingly are being pulled in the direction of the female ethos, if the necessity for altruism is crowned with scientific recognition, even accorded adaptive status, if some men are even converts to the female approach, should women complain if this movement is not recognized as such? If they are not given a share of the credit?

There is a story that circulates in the female world, so common that it has become a cliché, of a woman who has proposed an idea to a male group only to have it fall on deaf ears. They listen politely but then as politely ignore the suggestion. Several minutes later the same idea is proposed by a male member of the group and now it is enthusiastically embraced. Should the woman be elated that her idea has prevailed? Or should she be angry that she is not credited with it? The first response would conform to the old interpretation of the female culture's ethos. A woman should be satisfied with a "redemptive" role. Right — in the form of her idea — has prevailed. Why care who gets the credit for it? Shouldn't she just rejoice in knowing that the ethos of the female world is infiltrating the male world? Or is that much self-effacement beyond the call of — even feminist — duty? Yes, it is. We want, in Jean Baker Miller's words, "a new form of living . . . [and] the ways of achieving this new form of living will . . . have to include more mutuality, cooperation, and affiliation, on both a personal and a larger social scale." The new ways should not be manipulative or have to be bootlegged in as though illegitimate.

No Promise of Utopia

Despite the dreams of the utopists and idealists, there is no all-purpose, perfect way for the two worlds to relate to one another; no ultimately true, correct, basic, permanent, final way toward which we are groping and which we will some day achieve. The relationship between the two worlds in gathering societies was just as "true" as that between male and female peasant worlds in the middle ages or male and female Victorian worlds in the nineteenth century, or male and female worlds in the recent past. However different the relationship between them, they are all "true." But a relationship that is suitable for one age is not necessarily so for another.

To say that the relationship between the worlds will change does not mean that they will necessarily converge, that they will come to resemble one another in all ways, that they will become identical, indistinguishable, that all differences will disappear. They will no doubt continue to differ. And they will relate to one another in different ways. Sometimes a whole culture may "tilt" in the direction of the male ethos, sometimes in the direction of the female, sometimes in a direction different from both.

Carpe Diem

I am sometimes criticized by my *consoeurs* for what seems to them my irrational optimism. How can I sustain such a mood in the face of so many setbacks in the female world, so much defeat, so much backlash, such slow headway? The obstacles from the male world — in both economy and polity — sometimes seem all but insuperable. Well, for one thing because I have lived a great many years and know how long it takes to effect change, how bumpy the road is, and how much patience it takes. For another thing, I retain my faith in human intelligence. I think, for example, that the male world can change. If it is capable of putting a man on the moon, it is surely capable of modifying itself.

I allow a male — a sociobiologist to boot — to state my case here on the assumption that it will have more credibility coming from a "hawk" — representing the male world — than it would coming from a "dove" — representing the female world.

> [E]ven if we look on the dark side and assume that individual man [*sic*] is fundamentally selfish, our conscious foresight — our capacity to simulate the future in imagination — could save us from the worst selfish excesses. . . . We have at least the mental equipment to foster our long-term selfish interests rather than merely our short-term selfish interests. We can see the long-term benefits of participating in a "conspiracy of doves," and we can sit down together to discuss ways of making the "conspiracy" work. We

have the power to defy the selfish genes of our birth. ... We can even discuss ways of deliberately cultivating and nurturing pure, disinterested altruism — something that has no place in nature, something that has never existed before in the whole history of the world.

Translated into the idiom of the present context, his message is that the male world is capable of participating in the goals of the female world. It can learn that its own best interests lie in sharing the values of the female world. I believe that the "doves" — regardless of their sex — are becoming increasingly persuasive.

Some moments in history seem to be more open to change than others. As Harris sees it, "We are rapidly moving toward such an opening."

The present is a time when "a mode of production ... is reaching its limits of growth and a new mode of production must soon be adopted." It may be a propitious time for "reining in" the male ethos. The odds for success, I recognize, may not be favorable. Still, "in the meantime, people [read: women] with deep personal commitments to a particular vision of the future are perfectly justified in struggling toward their goals, even if the outcome depends on both luck and skill; the rational response to bad odds is to try harder." *Carpe diem* might well be the best motto.

The Elderly Poor: An Example of What Happens to the Unproductive in Capitalist Society

by Harold Freeman

The golden years? Sociologist Harold Freeman discusses the tragic circumstances that make the golden years a nightmare for the 50 percent of America's elderly who live in poverty.

Consider a single group of damaged participants, the elderly poor. Of the 26 million Americans below the federal poverty line, approximately 5 million are over 65; 50 percent of all elderly Americans, 33 percent of all rural elderly and 60 percent of all elderly blacks live in poverty.

The urban elderly poor find it hard to get around; in many smaller communities bus service

during the middle hours of the day is infrequent. So, for food, they shop in nearer, smaller, and more expensive stores. If hot food is served at a center few can get to it. They are particularly vulnerable to assault and theft; to the dissident young, as Dr. Marvin Wolfgang has explained, the elderly poor are attractive targets. In the view of the elderly themselves, their most serious concern is fear of crime against them — more serious than concern over money, health, or loneliness. They fear to leave their homes and they fear to stay in them. And they have reason for fear. In a recent study financed by the Law Enforcement Assistance Administration and the Department of Housing and Urban Development, elderly poor living in multiple housing occupied also by young adults are 3½ times more vulnerable to crime by the young than are other residents. In a period of one year, 1973 to 1974, Americans 65 and older experienced a 46 percent increase in assault. In 1975, 35 percent of New York City's elderly lived in its 26 poorest neighborhoods; of the sample interviewed 40 percent had been criminally victimized. These are among the scores of grim facts documented in the subcommittee inquiry, directed by Congressmen Edward Roybal and John Hammerschmidt, for the House Select Committee on Aging.

Occupational opportunities are few, though a surprising part of their small current income does come from whatever work they can get — often as part-time janitors, watchmen, house- and babysitters. The work-at-home offers to which some are drawn are often fraudulent. They cannot read the fine print, they have slender legal recourse against misrepresentation. They are many among the 15 million who come annually to the bar of justice with anxious complaints but without funds, and now even the limited capacity of the legal remainder of the Office of Economic Opportunity to provide help for them has been reduced by the elimination of its vital back-up research funds. In the United States, one lawyer is available to 9,570 poor, a ratio one-twelfth of that holding for the general population. In some States the ratio is even lower — in North Carolina one lawyer to 67,000 poor. These figures need to be considered alongside (a) 23 percent of the poor have at least one legal problem per year; (b) public funding for such problems is $2.16 per poor person.

Medical burdens are particularly heavy on the elderly poor. According to the Senate Special Committee on Aging, up to 2.5 million elderly Americans in need of mental care have been pushed out of budget-minded state mental hospitals — saving in 1978 an average of $21,000 per patient — into federally supported profit-making boarding houses and nursing homes; in some instances, state officials have received up to $100 per head from the homes. There the elderly live without needed therapy and without follow-up by state health officials. In no way is this exodus the consequence of progressive anti-institutional thinking; the Senate Committee uses the term "wholesale dumping."

Eighty-six percent of persons over 65 have one or more chronic diseases. With their physical infirmities the elderly are easy victims of medical quacks, and steady users of useless and unsafe drugs. By 1973 medical fraud in the United States had reached the $10 billion level; the scandals of 1978 suggest a higher figure now. The largest subset of victims are always the elderly poor.

The elderly poor cannot readily reach a clinic and when they do the hours they face in outpatient corridors are exhausting. In some areas the long clinic lines now have an added feature — for the elderly poor among the 25 million Americans who have no Medicare, Medicaid, or private health insurance, up to $21 a visit payable in advance. Similar though costlier is private medicine. 25 percent of all American doctors now demand on-the-spot payment for all visits, and over 30 percent demand immediate payment for at least the first visit. By 1977, the average per capita health cost for persons over 65 had climbed to $1,738 per annum; on the average, Medicare covers 38 percent.

In New York City, only 23 percent of doctors accept Medicaid patients, and 4 percent to 7 percent of the city's doctors — many of them practicing in its infamous "Medicaid mills" — collect up to 85 percent of all Medicaid fees; one doctor, William Triebel, received $451,156 in 1974 and $785,114 in 1975. 95 percent of New York City's Medicaid dental services are provided by 5 percent of the city's dentists. In Chicago, 73 of Cook County's 6,000 private doctors (another study puts these figures at 100 of 9,000) see over half of the county's 285,000 Medicaid recipients. This amounts to one doctor per 2,000 persons on Medicaid, and the ratio gets worse as these doctors, with their increased income from Medicaid fees, leave the poorer sections of the county. In New York City there are 280 doctors per 100,000 population, but in the impoverished South Bronx area the number has fallen to 10. In the nation's capital about 20 persons, most of them elderly poor, die each year in the process of transfer from private hospital *emergency* rooms, where they are not wanted, to the District of Columbia General

Hospital. In 1970 in Chicago, 18,000 persons, again with a disproportion of elderly poor, were turned away from private hospital emergency rooms, and more than 50 of them died in the process of dismissal or transfer to Cook County Hospital, an overloaded facility which cares for half of Chicago's Medicaid patients (and half of the county's blacks). The turnaway, known in medical circles as patient dumping, generally consists of suggested use of a car or taxi, or simply pointing out the nearest bus stop.

Some of the elderly poor are still involved in the consequences of earlier unwise installment buying; harassment is common and repossession is more than occasional. Some have discovered that not only can an item on which one default has occurred be repossessed, but other items sold on prior contracts by the same merchant and completely paid for can also be repossessed. They have learned that dealers sometimes sell the notes of cheated buyers to finance houses, thereby nullifying complaints of fraud against the dealers. The few loans available to the elderly poor are seldom from banks and always at high interest rates; up to 1,000 percent per year in the experience of Justice William Douglas. With their too-small last-ditch savings (40 percent have assets under $1,000), they are the vulnerable prey of flim-flam specialists. They are exploited in smaller stores skilled at offering inferior merchandise to the elderly and to welfare recipients and careful not to show prices; side-street merchants have discovered the optimal way to deal with the elderly poor — get all you can now.

Five and one-tenth million women — a number rapidly increasing — and 1.3 million men over 65 live alone. One-third of all elderly poor women, a very high percentage of them widows, live alone; their median income is $2,600. Many are found in declining residential hotels and tenements. With minimal experience one can describe, confidently, a typical room before seeing it — the rust-locked window, artificial flowers, slow plumbing, framed family pictures and the inevitable

two-burner hot plate. 30 percent of the residences of the elderly poor have no inside flush toilets, 40 percent no hot water bath, 54 percent have minimal winter heat. Except in seven states the tenant's obligation to pay rent is absolute (while the landlord's obligation to maintain the premises is unmentioned), and the consequence for some is eviction. Contrary to a few dramatic situations noted by the press, most rental evictions are quiet; for different reasons neither the landlord nor the tenant is eager for publicity.

Arrests of the elderly poor for shoplifting food are up sharply in the United States. A fair number of the elderly poor have discovered the greater protein value of dog food, that it is edible though bland (ketchup and onions are a standard addition), that the health hazard is probably small, that it is somewhat cheaper than the food previously bought, and they have quietly made the change. The Washington *Post* estimates that the elderly poor purchase more dog food than do dog owners. Dr. Edward Peeples, Jr. estimates that pet food forms a significant part of the diet of at least 225,000 American households — up to 1 million persons. The Senate Nutrition Committee estimates that one-third of all pet food purchased in depressed areas is for human consumption.

Except for burial policies, insurance is either not available or is outside their means; a furniture fire insurance policy is uncommon. Against even more primitive menaces like hunger, prolonged illness, and eviction, protection is slight. Protection could come from savings or income, but the savings are modest and the principal source of lifetime income — typically small earnings — have often come to an end. For the elderly poor, with their small inflation-damaged income from federal and state sources and their improved life span, insecurity is even more threatening than poverty; it saps much of their remaining vitality. As they age, we watch them draw on their children's resources, then move or be moved to the lower strata of rest and nursing homes. The latter, over 23,000 in all and three-quarters of them profit-making, have been described in detail in numerous studies, among them the report by Val Halamandaris to the Senate Special Committee and Robert Butler's *Why Survive?* These studies find the nursing home industry to be, on average, one of America's most destructive. Edith Stern describes many of these homes, housing 900,000 persons, under the title "Buried Alive."

Even final dignity is denied the elderly poor; they are cheated on funeral and cemetery arrangements.

Among these people you find no general absence of character, not even irremediable loss of initiative. Their strength is diminished but it is not negligible; it has been paralyzed by forces against which they cannot, acting separately as the elderly poor do, prevail. Researches by Dr. David Blau and others have shown the alacrity with which, given some support, the elderly poor can recover mental and physical strength. But in the common absence of such support, degradation sets in. Seeing those who are better off express by indifference their doubt of the value to the community of the elderly poor, so finally the elderly poor themselves doubt their value. For many the consequence is to turn inward, to protect what little they still have, not reaching out at all. Watching such a person, who wanted no help, get a solid block of ice out of a toilet in an apartment on Western Avenue — a street in Cambridge halfway between Harvard University and the Massachusetts Institute of Technology — one learns to respect the characteristic reaction of the elderly poor to all indignities, silence.

The tragedy of the elderly poor is unmistakable. Yet it would be difficult to find Americans in ordinary walks of life who would decline to support measures ensuring a better deal for these people; in a Harris poll in 1975, 76 percent of Americans questioned stated that a person should be able to live comfortably during retirement no matter how much was earned during his or her worklife. But nothing like this prevails and the situation improves minimally. Why? The reason is

uncomplicated. In the logic of capitalism the elderly poor are a problem simply because they are unproductive. In a society which rewards according to contribution they have no proper place. Like the sick and disabled, like all who can produce but little, the elderly poor are an externality to the theory of capitalism; they are found, if at all, in a chapter toward the end of the textbook. They have no solution within the system; Duncan Foley writes,

> Capitalism offers no systematic support to these people so that more or less effective devices outside the capitalist distribution system become necessary. Charity, welfare, public housing, socialized medicine . . . exist to support or help support persons of low productivity but they are all unnatural in a capitalist society, conflict with its basic principles, and as a result tend automatically to be controversial, badly run, inadequate and ineffective.

In his study of poverty Ben Seligman writes, "The aged are simply an embarrassment. They are poor, unable to provide medical care for themselves, they violate the canon of self-help, so we dishonor them." Seligman continues, "Perhaps in *our* society . . . give the aged poor money and let them stand aside, silent and unseen."

Liberals believe that the elderly poor may somehow, someday enjoy political influence commeasurable with their numbers; the 1978 heavy election turnout of the elderly in seven states in successful support of limits on taxation offers some credence in such an expectation. But the economics of capitalism is heavily stacked against the elderly poor. Most of these millions of men and women worked hard; they were energetic and productive for years. But not at a level which enabled them to save much for their old age. Capitalism rewards according to assets, not effort; on this scale the elderly poor do not measure up.

SOURCE: Freeman, Harold, *Toward Socialism in America,* Copyright © 1979 Schenkman Publishing, Cambridge, Mass. Reprinted by permission.

Part IV

Social Organization

If a society is to survive, it must be organized, but most of us take social organization so much for granted we are hardly aware it exists. This section deals with social organization, and we believe that when you become aware of the subtlety, the power, the consistency, the variety, and the complexity of social organization and social systems, you may better understand why sociologists are so fascinated by this topic of study.

Chapter 11 discusses the way groups are organized. Even small groups organize themselves since different people assume different statuses and perform different functions in the group. Larger groups often have a very complicated organization, as you can readily see when you look at a huge bureaucracy. The next five chapters describe how societies are organized to carry out specific functions. The chapter on families discusses how families are organized in order to care for children. The chapter on religion shows how various types of religious systems organize the beliefs of the public. We discuss how educational systems are organized to socialize children, and how political systems are organized to maintain order, make decisions, and distribute the resources of a society. The final chapter in this section explains how economic systems are organized to produce the goods and services we need. Each society, given its own history and culture, has its own way of organizing these systems.

Chapter 11
Social Groups and Social Organizations

We do not mind our not arriving anywhere nearly so much as our not having company on the way.

— Frank Moore

Humans are social animals. Even those who think of themselves as loners participate in many groups, and, for most of us, they are a major source of satisfaction. You may eat with a certain group of friends every day, belong to a drama club, or play tennis every week with your gym class. You probably depend on social groups, social organizations, and social systems for most of your psychological and physical needs. Research indicates that we are influenced not only by the groups we currently belong to and those we identify with but also by those we associated with in the past. In fact, life without groups seems impossible. Without group involvements, infants die, adolescents get depressed, middle-aged people suffer psychologically, and the elderly get lonely and lose their will to live. We learn, eat, work, and worship in groups.

Because groups play such a large role in our lives, we tend not to recognize the extent of their influence, yet they affect the structure of society as well as our personal interactions. The groups that comprise society are of many different sizes, and they have a wide range of goals. A group of two may join together to raise a child. The group that elects a president consists of many millions. Groups may be based on friendship or family. Others have a different basis. Corporations are economic groups, the Republicans and Democrats are political groups, and stamp collectors share a common interest. Although we may take their existence for granted, it is important to understand how they influence individuals and society. The first step in developing such an understanding is learning what sociologists mean when they use the word "group."

What Is a Group?

The answer to this question may seem obvious: a group is a number of people who have something in common. Like most topics in sociology, however, the problem is not that simple. Although the concept of group is one of the key elements of sociology, no single definition of it is universally accepted. The problem is not that sociologists are unable to decide what a group is; it is, rather, that there are many types, and sociologists attach different meanings to their forms, their functions, and their consequences.

In our discussion, we will focus chiefly on *social groups* — those in which people physically or socially interact. Several other types are also recognized by most sociologists, however, and deserve to be mentioned.

Statistical groups are formed not by the group members but by sociologists and statisticians. In 1980, for example, there were 58,426,000 families in the United States with an average size of 3.28 people per family (*Statistical Abstract*, 1981). The group of women between 5 feet 1 inch and 5 feet 5 inches tall would be another statistical group. Some sociologists do not consider groups of this sort to be groups at all, because the members are unaware of their membership and there is no social interaction or social organization (see Table 11-1). Many purely statistical groups have more than a statistical significance, however, and some can indicate important characteristics of societies. A society in which 5 percent of the population is illiterate is very different from one in which 90 percent of the population is illiterate, and information of this sort can be very useful in making policy decisions.

Another type of group is the *categorical group*, or *societal unit*, one in which a number of people share a common characteristic. Drivers of DeLorean automobiles, millionaires, redheads, students, women, senior citizens, and virgins are all categorical groups. Members of groups of this type are likely to be aware that they share a particular characteristic and a common identity. Drivers of DeLoreans may wave to each other as they pass on the highway.

The importance of categorical groupings is evident in the extent to which people tend to live and associate with others who share certain characteristics. Teenagers, the aged, interracial couples, unwed mothers, widows, the handicapped, the wealthy — all are aware of their similarity to other members of their own social category.

A third type of group is the *aggregate*. Some sociologists use the term group to refer to any collection of people who are together in one place. You may join a group of this sort buying an ice cream cone, watching a football game, riding a bus, or waiting to cross a street. Aggregates are basically unstructured, and the participants interact briefly and sporadically. Most members act as if they were alone, except perhaps to comment about the weather, ask the time, or complain about the service. The members of an aggregate need not converse but may do so; they need not know one another but may see familiar faces. Members are generally not concerned with the feelings and attitudes of the others. Most aggregates meet only once.

A fourth type is the *associational* or *organizational group,* which is especially important in complex industrialized societies. Associational groups consist of people who join together in some organized way to pursue a common interest, and they have a formal structure. Most of us belong to a number of them; they can be formed for almost any conceivable purpose. A university, a volleyball team, a Rotary club, the Democratic party, General Motors Corporation, Protestant churches — all are associational groups. They share the major charactristics of other types of groups, but in addition they also have a formal structure.

As you can see, a number of different kinds of groups are recognized, and their boundaries are by no means easy to state clearly. Like other classification schemes, the one we have suggested makes use of certain criteria but ignores others that may in some circumstance be equally important. Groups might also be classified on the basis of social boundaries between members and non-members, adherence to a special set of norms, awareness not only of kind, as in Table 11-1, but of membership, or a variety of other factors.

Given this range of definitions and possible classification criteria, what types of collectives can we call social groups? Although sociologists do not accept a single definition, there would be widespread agreement that membership in a social group involves (1) some type of interaction; (2) a sense of belonging or membership; (3) shared interests or agreement on values, norms, and goals; and (4) a structure, that is, a definable, recognizable arrangement of parts. According to this definition, the statistical, categorical, and aggregate classifications would not be considered social groups, but many associational groups would be. Thus a given family might be considered a social group, but the fifty-seven million families in the United States would be statistical. The League of Women Voters would be a social group, but the class of all those who consider themselves female would be categorical. A college class riding a bus on a field trip would be a social group, but a crowd of people waiting at a bus stop would be an aggregate. The sociological use of group involves a consciousness of membership, interaction, shared interests, and structure.

Social groups are important because they provide us with a social identity, serve as a key to understanding social behavior, link the self with the larger society, and help us understand social structure and societal organization. By studying the individual in a group context, the dynamic interactions within groups, and the organizational network of the larger society, we can improve our understanding of the self, of human interaction, and of the larger social order.

Types of Social Groups

Social groups vary widely in their size, purpose, and structure (see Figure 11-1). Membership in one type does not preclude membership in other types; in fact, it is not unusual for a single group to fall into several different categories. We will cover the types most often discussed in sociology, including primary and secondary groups, in-groups and out-groups, peer groups, reference groups, and small and large groups.

Primary and Secondary Groups

Perhaps the most fundamental distinction is that made between primary and secondary groups. The term *primary group*, coined by Charles H. Cooley (1909), is used to refer to such groups as the family and play group, which he believed

Table 11-1

TYPE OF GROUP	AWARENESS OF KIND	SOCIAL INTERACTION	SOCIAL ORGANIZATION	EXAMPLE
Statistical	No	No	No	Average family size
Categorical	Yes	No	No	Redheads
Aggregate	Yes	Yes	No	Football crowd
Associational	Yes	Yes	Yes	Rotary club

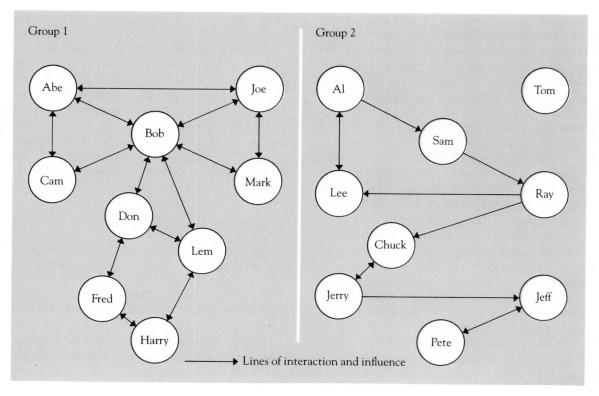

Figure 11-1

Applying sociology to group relationships: A sociogram. Sociologists often use sociograms to chart communication patterns, friendship linkages, and general interaction patterns among the members of small groups. Compare the sociograms of these two groups of nine boys. From the data provided, which group does the most interacting? What conclusions can you draw about these two groups? How might sociograms be useful in actual situations?

were the most important in shaping the human personality. Primary groups involve intimate face-to-face association and interaction, their members have a sense of "we-ness" involving mutual identification and shared feelings, and they are characteristically small and informal. Their members tend to be emotionally attached to one another and involved with other group members as whole people, not just with those aspects of a person

that pertain to work, school, or some other isolated part of one's life. Your family, close friends, and certain neighbors and work associates are likely to be members of your primary group.

Distinguished from the primary group is the *secondary group*. Like primary groups, they are usually small and involve face-to-face contacts. Although the interactions may be cordial or friendly, they are more formal and impersonal than primary group interactions, and sociologically they are just as important. Most of our time is spent in secondary groups — committees, professional groups, sales-related groups, classroom groups, or neighborhood groups. The key difference between primary and secondary groups is in the quality of the relationships and the extent of personal intimacy and involvement. Primary groups are person-oriented, whereas secondary groups tend to be goal-oriented. A primary group conversation usually focuses on personal experiences, feelings, and casual, open sharing, whereas a secondary group conversation is more apt to be impersonal, purposeful, and limited to socially relevant topics.

Primary and secondary groups are important both to individuals and to society. Primary groups are particularly important in shaping the personal-

ity, in formulating self-concepts, in developing a sense of personal worth, and in becoming an accepted member of society. They are also an important source of social control and social cohesion. Such scholars as Erich Fromm (1965) and Lewis Mumford (1962) contend that the strength and vitality of primary groups are the basis of the health of a society. In an increasingly impersonal world, they are sources of openness, trust, and intimacy. People who are not accepted members of some primary group — a marriage, friendship, or work relationship — may have difficulty coping with life (see Table 11-2).

Although primary groups are vital to the health of both individuals and society, secondary groups are also important because they tend to meet specific goals. They help societies function effectively and permit people who don't know

Table 11-2

Psychological well-being of men and women by marital status

	MEN				
	MARITAL STATUS				
HAPPINESS	MARRIED	SINGLE	SEPARATED	DIVORCED	WIDOWED
Very happy	35	18	7	12	7
Pretty happy	56	63	55	53	56
Not too happy	9	19	38	35	37
	WOMEN				
	MARITAL STATUS				
HAPPINESS	MARRIED	SINGLE	SEPARATED	DIVORCED	WIDOWED
Very happy	38	18	12	11	14
Pretty happy	55	68	45	66	54
Not too happy	7	14	44	23	32

SOURCE: Bradburn, Norman M., *The Structure of Psychological Well-Being*, Copyright © 1966 by National Opinion Research Center. Reprinted by permission.

Sociologists distinguish primary groups from secondary ones. Two teenagers, engaged in informal conversation and involved in intimate face-to-face association, are an example of a primary group. A committee or business meeting is more likely to represent a secondary group. Although a secondary group such as this one may involve friendly, face-to-face interaction, the relationships are likely to be formal and impersonal.

one another intimately to perform more effectively in their jobs. Most formal organizations such as schools, corporations, hospitals, and unions are comprised of many secondary groups and relationships. The impersonality and formality of the secondary group allows members to focus on skills and specialized interests rather than on personalities. Although pressures may exist to hire a relative or best friend from your primary group, he or she may not be the best trained or most knowledgeable person available for the job. Likewise, people usually avoid romantic involvement with their coworkers because it can disrupt or complicate progress toward a goal. Most jobs, whether they involve driving a bus or performing heart surgery, have clearly defined goals and role expectations, so the personal characteristics of the people fulfilling the roles and the public's need for emotional involvement with them are not of great importance.

It should be recognized that the difference between a primary and secondary group is one of degree. Many formal secondary group situations involve instances of informality and personal openness. In fact, many primary groups develop from secondary groups and organizations. Two students who meet in a formal lecture hall (secondary group) may later marry (primary group); coworkers in a large organization may develop an intimate friendship. Conversely, two friends who join a corporation may grow apart and ultimately have only a secondary relationship. The composition of an individual's primary and secondary groups shifts frequently.

In-Groups and Out-Groups

As mentioned earlier, one of the key characteristics of a group is the members' sense of belonging. Those who belong think of one another as forming a social unit. This unit has boundaries that separate "us" from "them," that differentiate those who are "in" from those who are "out." An *in-group* is a social category to which persons feel they belong and, in addition, is one in which the members have a consciousness or awareness of kind (as in Table 11-1). They feel that they share a common fate, adhere to a common ideology, come from a common background, or otherwise resemble the other members. In-groups may be primary groups but not necessarily. We can feel "in" with people we have never met or shared personal intimacies with — members of our alumni group, religious group, or veterans group, for example. University of California graduates, Buddhists, or Vietnam veterans may experience feelings of comradeship or a sense of togetherness.

Conversely, an *out-group* is one to which people feel they do not belong. If you are a member of the in-group, the out-group is everyone else. It is made up of those who do not share an awareness of kind. We do not identify or affiliate ourselves with them, and we feel little allegiance to them. We treat most members of out-groups with indifference, but at times we may feel hostile toward them because of our tendency toward ethnocentrism (see Chapter 4): the predisposition to perceive our own in-group as superior to others. The out-group, being inferior, does not deserve the same respect as the in-group. Thus the members of an in-group — friends, classmates, doctors, industrialists — may defend other in-group members even when it does an injustice to those who are "out."

The difference between in- and out-groups is sociologically important for several reasons. First, the in-group tends to stereotype members of the out-group. Although we may notice individual differences among members of the in-group, most of us notice only similarities in the out-group, and we label them accordingly. Americans may recognize a wide range of variations in appearance, beliefs, and behavior among our fellow citizens but fail to recognize that all Chinese do not look alike, that not all Germans love sauerkraut, that not all Iranians are revolutionaries, or that not all Russians are anticapitalistic. Within the United States, whites (in-group) may label blacks (out-group) as lazy, and blacks (in-group) may label whites (out-group) as racists. Republicans may label Democrats as spendthrifts, Democrats may label Republicans as rich and greedy. Students sometimes assume that all professors are absent-minded, but exceptions have been known to exist.

A second reason that the two groups are important is that any threat or attack, whether imaginary or real, from the out-group tends to increase the cohesion and solidarity of the in-group. Strange as it may seem, a war with a foreign enemy can have a positive effect on a divided nation. Similarly, economic hardships may bring the members of a family closer together.

Unlike primary groups, which are always small, in-groups and out-groups can vary in size. They may be as large as a nation or continent or as small as a two-person marriage.

We all have many in-group identities and loyalties, some of which overlap and some of which cause conflict. We may, for example, strongly identify with both the women's movement and the Catholic church but find that our belief that a woman should be able to choose whether to have an abortion is in direct conflict with the position of the Catholic church. Whom should you be loyal to when your employer discriminates against your ethnic group? Whom should you root for when your daughter, who plays on the Michigan tennis team, plays against your alma mater? Our affiliation with a particular in-group may provide us with an identity and a sense of belonging, but it also induces conflict and restricts our relationships and interactions with others.

Peer Groups

One type of group from which in- and out-groups draw their members is the *peer group*. In earlier chapters, we discussed the influence of peers in the socialization process, for example, age peers such as teenagers. The unique factor in peer groups is equality. In most groups, even small ones such as marriages or committees, one person or more has a higher status or a position of dominance, but peer groups are informal primary groups in which the members are roughly equal in status and importance.

Although peer groups are most often discussed in connection with young people, they are found in all age groups. Most friendships, regardless of the friends' ages, share the characteristics of a peer group: they are informal, primary relationships, and the participants are of equal rank and often of the same sex. The emphasis on teenagers in discussions of peer groups might have resulted from the post–World War II baby boom, which produced a large population that came to be associated with a unique subculture. This subculture, with its own dress, language, music, values, and goals was emphasized by the media, which focused on their large rock concerts, the student anti-war movement, and the hippies and flower children of the mid- and late 1960s. This network of age peer group provided support for its members as well as guidance in both attitude and behavior.

Reference Groups

In our earlier discussion of the looking-glass self, it was suggested that we see ourselves through the eyes of other people. We imagine how we appear to others and try, successfully or unsuccessfully, to figure out how they evaluate our appearance. In addition to other individuals, certain social groups and social categories also serve as sources of self-evaluation. These groups, known as *reference groups,* are the ones we psychologically identify with. People need not belong to a group for it to be a reference group for them, and groups we aspire to belong to may also be reference groups. Negative reference groups, those we do not want to be identified with, also serve as sources of self-evaluation. A person might, for example, try to avoid resembling members of a group composed of intellectuals or football players.

Most attention is focused on positive reference groups. These are the ones we want to be accepted by. Thus if you want to be an executive, you might carefully observe and imitate the behavior of executives. If you note that they play golf, wear conservative clothes, and read *The Wall Street Journal,* you might do the same.

Reference groups are an important source of information about our performance in a given area. Just as cultures tend to assess themselves on the basis of their own standards (see the discussion on cultural relativity in Chapter 4), individuals assess themselves in accordance with the standards of their reference group. A B grade may be a source of pride to students if their peer reference group did worse, but it may be a source of disappointment to a family reference group if they expected an A. A professor's income may be good relative to an assistant professor's income, but it may be poor relative to the income of someone employed in industry. In brief, we tend to judge our worth, accomplishments, and even our morality in comparison with groups of reference.

Reference groups serve not only as sources of current evaluation but also as sources of aspiration and goal attainment. A person who chooses to become a professional baseball player, a lawyer, or

As we develop into functioning social adults, we identify with persons and groups who are significant to us. Traditionally, at least, girls were given dolls and boys were given baseballs and footballs. This psychological identification with particular reference groups is further enhanced by dressing children in the outfits appropriate for these groups.

a teacher begins to identify with that group and becomes socialized to have certain goals and expectations.

A knowledge of people's reference groups can sometimes help us understand why they behave as they do. It may explain why a teenager who never smokes or drinks at home will do so with a school group, or why politicians may take varying stances on an issue, depending on the audience they are addressing. Our aim is to please and conform to the expectations and behaviors of the groups that are important to us.

Small Groups and Large Groups

Categorizing groups according to size is an imprecise way of differentiating them, but size has a dramatic effect on member interactions. The smallest group, called a *dyad*, consists of two people. When just two people are involved, each of them has a special responsibility to interact — if one person withdraws, the group no longer exists. With the addition of a third person, the dyad becomes a *triad* and the interactions change drastically. If one person drops out, the group can still survive. In a group of three, one person can serve as a mediator in a disagreement, or alternatively side with one person and then the other. A third person, however, can also be a source of conflict or tension. The phrase "two's company, three's a crowd" emphasizes the dramatic shift that takes place when dyads become triads. When a triad adds a fourth or fifth member, two subgroups can emerge. As size increases, it may be more difficult to choose a leader, arrive at an agreement or consensus, or decide who will perform certain tasks.

At what point does a small group become large? Is it small if it has two, ten, or twenty members? Is it large if it has 25, 250, or 25,000 members? Determinations of whether a group is large or small may be influenced by the type of group as well as its goals. In a marriage in most cultures, three would be large. In politics, 30,000 may be small. As you can see, choosing a cutoff point between large and small groups requires that we consider a number of different factors. Even so, such a designation may be largely arbitrary.

Regardless of the distinction between large and small groups, the complexity of group relations increases much more rapidly than the number of members. Two people have only one reciprocal relationship, three people have 6 reciprocal relationships, four people have 24 relation-

Groups come in all sizes, from as small as two to as large as thousands. As group size increases, so does the division of labor, the formality of interaction, and the type of leadership. This can be seen clearly in these two contrasting photos. In one a dyad engages in a leisure activity — the interaction is highly personal and informal. In the other a board meeting takes place, a meeting that is highly formal and impersonal with a clear-cut division of labor and a defined chair or leader.

ships, five people have 120 relationships, six people have 720 relationships, and seven people have 5,040 relationships. Beyond that, the number of relationships quickly becomes astronomical. Size *does* make a difference.

In addition to the number of relationships, several other characteristics change with increasing size. First, as size increases, so does the *division of labor.* If the group is small, all the members may engage in the same activities. As size increases, however, activities tend to become specialized. The father of one of the authors, for example, once taught eight grades in a one-room school. He covered the three R's and any other subjects, supervised the playground, did some personal counseling, and occasionally had some transportation responsibilities. As schools got larger, teachers were assigned not only to specific grade levels but also to specific subject areas. They were employed to teach music, art, and other specialized subjects, and a complex system was developed to provide transportation, counseling, lunches, sports, and a wide variety of clubs and other school-related activities. Similar changes in the division of labor occur as churches, families, manufacturing concerns, and other groups grow. Generally, as group size increases, so does the division of labor.

Second, as the size of a group increases, its structure becomes more rigid and formal. Whereas small groups are likely to operate informally according to unwritten rules, large groups usually conduct meetings in accordance with Robert's Rules of Order or some other standard formula. Also, small groups are more apt to emphasize personal and primary characteristics. A small grocery store run by a family, for example, may reflect the tastes of the family members. Jobs may be delegated to various people on the basis of their preferences, and work schedules may be drawn up to accommodate one person's going to college or another person's social life. Large groups, on the other hand, emphasize status and secondary characteristics. In a large supermarket chain, decisions are made by committees. Chairpersons, division heads, or managers are selected, and the problems of bureaucratic red tape begin. In contrast to small groups, employees are expected to conform to the demands of their jobs rather than changing their job to meet their personal preferences.

Third, as the size of a group increases, so does the need for a more formal type of *leadership.* With increasing size comes a complexity of problems relating to the coordination of activities and decisions, which leads to the emergence of group leaders, persons who have the authority, the power, or the potential ability to direct and/or influence the behavior of others.

In all groups, somebody or some collectivity must make the decisions. In small groups, these decisions may be made informally in a spirit of mutual sharing and agreement with no assigned leader as such. In large groups, which as indicated have more specialized activities and a more rigid and formal structure, the leadership becomes more formal as well and the decision making is more constraining. When the population of these groups bestows the right to leadership, *authority* exists. Authority is legitimized power (this subject is covered more extensively in Chapter 15 where political groups are discussed). Effective leaders must be able to make decisions, settle disputes, coordinate activities, direct communication, influence behaviors, and bring persons and diverse units together. Seldom do these abilities reside in the same individual. A leader effective in doing one thing may be ineffective in another.

In analyzing leadership in small groups, Bales (1953) found that leaders are of two types. *Instrumental* leaders organize the group around its goals by suggesting ways to achieve them and persuading the members to act appropriately. Thus the instrumental leader performs the function of directing activities and making group decisions. *Expressive* leaders, on the other hand, resolve conflict and create group harmony and social cohesion. They make sure that the members can get along with one another and are relatively satisfied and happy. For groups to function effectively, Bales concluded, both types of leaders are needed.

How are leaders selected? In some instances that person or those persons who are most efficient and resourceful in directing and moving the group in desired directions will be recognized and awarded the leadership positions. They will be looked to for direction, their suggestions will be honored, and they will have considerable influence in the group's behavior. This idea implies that groups exist independently of the larger society, which is of course not true. Suppose a neighborhood meeting is called to complain about the garbage collection. Ten men and four women show up. What would you guess are the odds that a male will be asked to take the notes or a female will be asked to chair the session or take the formal complaint to the official source? It is unlikely the group will wait to see who can write most effectively (which might be a male) or who can best serve as leader (which might be a female). Similarly, groups may assign the leadership position to the eldest, the most popular, the one with the most formal training, or the one who called the meeting.

Are there particular traits that distinguish leaders from nonleaders? For several decades psychologists and social psychologists have tried to compile lists of leadership characteristics, but most results have been disappointing. Why? One explanation is that the attempt has been to find characteristics or traits that reside within individuals rather than seeking characteristics or traits relative to a task environment or a specific interpersonal and social context. Again, leaders and leadership qualities do not exist in a vacuum. Assigned cultural and social statuses, skills for specific tasks,

and prior experience and training will influence the choice of leaders, which suggests that there is no such thing as a "born leader." The "born" status and characteristics, in combination with training, experience, skills, and social circumstances, will determine the likelihood of leadership positions. Now we can better understand why women and blacks seldom become presidents of corporations or top government officials. They may have the leadership characteristics but not the social status characteristics appropriate to the culture.

Fourth, as the size of a group increases the *communication* patterns change. In large groups the leaders tend to dominate the discussions. They talk the most and are addressed the most since the discussion and comments of other members are directed at them. Although similar patterns of communication may exist in small groups, members who never join the discussion in a large group may do so in a small one. Some teachers prefer a large or small class for this very reason. In a large class the communication is both dominated by them and directed toward them. In a small class the chances increase that most members will participate and the communication exchange may take place among the group members. Social psychologists have been especially fascinated with "small-group dynamics"; that is, what happens when two, five, or eight people get together: who sits where, who talks to whom, how are decisions made, and similar considerations. With committees, families, classes, and other small groups, controlled experiments have been conducted to determine how changes in size and composition affect the members' communication, interaction, performance of tasks, and other outcomes. The *Handbook of Small Group Research* (Hare, 1976) is a comprehensive source for the student interested in learning more about these studies.

Fifth, as size increases, *cohesion* decreases. A group is considered cohesive when members interact frequently, when they talk of "we," when they defend the group from external criticism, when they work together to achieve common goals, and when they are willing to yield personal preferences for those of the group. Membership stability is important for cohesion because a high turnover rate has a negative effect. Conformity is also important for cohesion because a failure to abide by group norms and decisions lessens cohesiveness. Groups induce conformity by formal means such as fines, not allowing participation, or assigning specific tasks as well as by informal means such as verbal chides or jokes. Although these informal means become less effective as group size increases, it is important to recognize that within the large group or complex organization there is always the small group and informal network. The importance of this small group cohesiveness operating in a large group context was evident in World War II among both American and German soldiers who admitted to fighting for their buddies, not for the glory and fame of their country.

In summary, group size does make a difference: in interaction patterns, in the division of labor, in structural formality, in leadership, in decision-making processes, in communication, in cohesion and consensus, and in norms and rules.

In this section we have covered several types of social groups: primary, secondary, in, out, peer, reference, small, and large. We have shown how size affects the division of labor, formality, leadership, communication, and cohesion. As mentioned earlier, the list is not exhaustive. We could easily have discussed many other types of groups: cliques, friendships, communes, majority and minority, long-lived and short-lived, open and closed, independent and dependent, organized and unorganized, personal and impersonal, traditional and utilitarian, and so on. Some of these labels can be applied to formal organizations, which are discussed next.

Formal Organizations

Many sociologists view the study of social organizations as the key to understanding society, groups, and personal behavior. A social organization is more than a collection of individuals. The whole is greater than the sum of its parts. In analyzing organizations, we focus not on the individual but on the group as a whole, which has structures, norms, and roles of its own. (Note the example of the structure of two organizations in Figure 11-2.)

From a social organization perspective, sociologists suggest that the organization as an entity is different from the sum of the individuals who belong to it. If, for example, all the parts of an automobile are put in one pile, we have all the ingredients necessary for a car, but we certainly do not have an operable means of transportation. Only when those parts are properly assembled and interrelated do we get a car that works. Organizations are much the same.

Used generally, social organization refers to the way in which society is organized: its norms, mores, roles, values, communication patterns, social institutions, and the like. One aspect of social organization is what is known as *formal organization*: those deliberately constructed groups and structural arrangements that are organized to achieve certain specific and clearly stated goals. The encyclopedia of national organizations in the United States (1981) provides details of more than 15,300 such professional societies, labor unions, trade associations, fraternal and patriotic organizations, and other types of structured groups consisting solely of voluntary members.

Organizations tend to be stable, often keeping the same structure and continuing to exist for many years, and those who belong to an organization generally feel a sense of membership. Formal organizations differ from smaller, less complex groups in that they are organized to achieve spe-

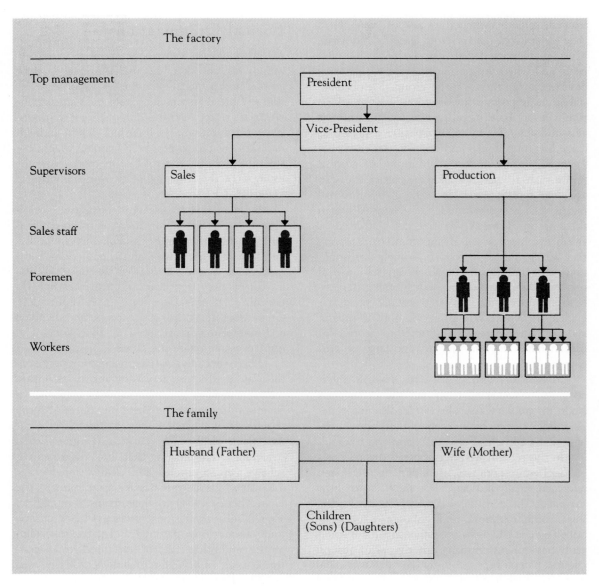

Figure 11-2
The structure of two social organizations

Professional basketball represents one type of formal organization. As sports fans you may recognize the faces of some of basketball's superstars. As students of sociology you may notice the statuses — that is, positions — of players, trainers, coaches, general managers, and owners. The success of the Boston Celtics extends beyond any given player to the nature of the organization, the positions and structural arrangements established to achieve particular goals.

cific, clearly stated goals. Industrial corporations, professional sports, country clubs, trade unions, schools, churches, prisons, hospitals, and government agencies are formal organizations created to meet specific goals. All groups have goals of some sort, but they are often latent, unstated, and general. Group members may even have conflicting goals, but in an organization, the goals are specific, clearly stated, and usually understood precisely by the members.

Consider, for example, the case of a family and a school. Both have as goals the education of

children. The parents in a family may read to the youngest children and provide the older ones with books, magazines, and newspapers. They may also encourage children to play learning games or take them to museums and concerts. In a formal organization such as a school, however, the education program is much more highly structured. The teachers, administrators, and other staff members will each have been trained to teach a particular subject to a single age group or meet some other specific goal. The overall goals of the school, although perhaps subject to disagreement, are stated and understood more clearly than those of the family. The same holds true with factories (see Figure 11-2) and all other formal organizations.

The Importance of Formal Organizations

The importance of formal organizations in modern complex societies can hardly be overestimated. Every day, we deal with some sort of formal organization in connection with work, food, travel, health care, police protection, or some other necessity of life. Organizations enable people who are often total strangers to work together toward common goals. They create levels of authority and channels of command that clarify who gives orders, who obeys them, and who does which tasks. They are also a source of continuity and permanence in a society's efforts to meet specific goals. In other words, individual members may come and go but the organization will continue to function. Thus formal organizations make it possible for highly complex industrialized societies to meet their most fundamental needs and pursue their collective aspirations.

Formalization is the process by which norms, roles, or procedures of a group or organization become established, precise, binding, and valid and whereby increasing attention is given to structure, detail, and form. The formalization of organization is the characteristic that distinguishes complex societies from small tribal societies. Herman Turk (1970) goes so far as to state that modern societies are "an aggregate of organizations, which appear, disappear, change, merge, and form networks of relations with one another" (p. 1). The United States, for example, contains many highly professional and often powerful organizations, which are involved in mutually beneficial efforts to serve their own interests and meet their own goals. The American Medical Association and the AFL-CIO are just two of the many such organizations that could be mentioned.

The Goals of Formal Organizations

As you can well imagine, the goals of different organizations vary widely. Businesses are interested chiefly in making a profit. Service organizations assist people with problems like unemployment or illness. Some organizations, such as unions or stamp collectors, exist to promote the interests of their own group; other organizations, such as governments, the military, and prisons, are established to provide services to the general public.

Given this diversity of goals, it is not surprising that certain formal organizations are in conflict with each other. The United Auto Workers, in its attempt to improve the salaries, working conditions, and fringe benefits of its members, is in conflict with the profit goals of the automobile companies. Environmental groups often conflict with the goals of government and industrial groups over the use of our natural resources. Organizations such as the Moral Majority have goals that are in conflict with those of the American Civil Liberties Union.

Conflicts appear not only between organizations but within them as well. Universities must determine whether the primary goal of their faculty is teaching or research. Medical organizations must decide whether their chief function is to aid and protect the physician or to improve the health care given to the public. Sometimes an organization's apparent primary goal (e.g., service) is used to conceal its actual primary goal (e.g., profit). A private mental institution, for example, may emphasize the quality of the care it gives in its literature, but decisions about whether or not to provide a certain service to its clients may always be made on the basis of its profitability.

There are often conflicts between the goals of an organization's administration and its employees or the clients or public it serves. In a university, for example, the main priority for the administration may be to balance the budget. The aim of the faculty may be to do research and publish papers. The students may be most concerned with receiving a good education through exceptional teaching and the use of outstanding library and laboratory facilities, which may conflict with cost-saving measures and cut into professors' research time. Finally, certain influential alumni may consider all these goals less important than having an outstanding football team, which brings the school national recognition.

Formal organizations have a certain type of administrative machinery designed to help them meet their goals. This administrative structure is known as bureaucratic organization, or, more simply, as bureaucracy.

Bureaucracy

A *bureaucracy* is a formal organizational structure that directs and coordinates the efforts of the people involved in various organizational tasks. It is simply a hierarchical arrangement of an organization's parts based on the division of labor and authority. A hierarchical structure is like a pyramid — the people at each level have authority over the larger number of people at the level below them. The authority resides in the office, position, or status, not in a particular person. In other words, the responsibilities and authority associated with a particular job in the hierarchy remain essentially the same, regardless of the person occupying the position. Merton (1968) defines bureaucracy as "a formal, rationally organized social structure involving clearly defined patterns of activity in which, ideally, every series of actions is functionally related to the purposes of the organization" (p. 195).

Bureaucracy as an Ideal Type

The classical work on bureaucracy was written by Max Weber (1864–1920), one of the pioneers in sociology. Weber dealt with bureaucracy as an *ideal type,* which is a model of a hypothetical pure form of an existing entity. In other words, he did not concern himself with describing a specific bureaucracy; he examined, rather, a great many bureaucracies in an attempt to discover the general principles that govern how they operate. An ideal type, then, is not to be thought of as a perfect entity in the usual sense of the word "ideal." As we will see later in this chapter, bureaucracies are often far from perfect. Weber (1946) found that bureaucracies typically have the following characteristics.

Division of Labor. The staff and activities of an organization are divided into units called offices or bureaus. Each bureau has certain carefully described responsibilities, and each job is designed to meet a specific need. Thus experts can be hired to meet various organizational requirements, and they can be held accountable for an effective performance in their area of responsibility.

Hierarchy of Authority. Organizations are run by a chain of command, a hierarchy of bosses and workers who are, in turn, the bosses of other workers. As indicated earlier, the hierarchy is in the form of a pyramid: all officials are accountable to those at a higher level for their own responsibilities and those of subordinates. The top of the chain of command is often a board of directors or company officers. Below this level are the middle-level managers, administrators, foremen, and department heads. The largest number of workers is at the bottom of the hierarchy (refer back to Figure 11-2).

Public Office. The office and the organization's written files are in a separate location from the employees' homes and families and are not subject to their influence. The organization's money and equipment belong to the organization, not to individuals, and its activity is separate from the activity of private life.

Merit Selection. Organizations select personnel on the basis of merit, using standardized criteria such as civil service examinations or educational training rather than personal, friendship, political, or family connections. Those who are hired are expected to have the specialized knowledge or skills necessary to perform their assigned task.

Career Pattern. Employees are expected to devote themselves completely to the business of the organization and recognize that people work their way to the top. As one moves up in the hierarchy, job security and salaries improve. Seniority is recognized, valued, and rewarded. Whether the organization is the U.S. Army, General Motors, or the Catholic church, increasing time with the organization and adequate job performance are supposed to bring promotions, higher pay and status, and stronger tenure.

Objective Rules. The operation of the organization is governed by a consistent set of rules that define the responsibilities of various positions, assure the coordination of tasks, and encourage the uniform treatment of clients. These rules are quite stable and comprehensive, and they can be readily learned and followed.

Although in any given formal organization some members are employed for personal reasons rather than merit, the rules are occasionally ignored, and some customers are not treated impartially, most bureaucracies share the characteristics we have described. A hierarchical organization, division of labor, and the other attributes of the bureaucratic ideal type are essential to efficient functioning. As we all know, however, bureaucracies have their shortcomings, especially government buraucracies. Most of us associate them with red tape, mountains of forms to complete, and endless lines. How and why do bureaucracies get so bogged down?

Dysfunctions of Bureaucracies

Weber concerned himself almost exclusively with the positive accomplishments of bureaucracies: precision, coordination, reliability, efficiency, stability, and continuity while Merton (1957) was the most important writer on the subject of the dysfunctions of bureaucracy. He observed that people in bureaucracies tend to develop what Veblen called *trained incapacity*, a condition similar to ritualism, which was discussed in Chapter 7. Trained incapacity occurs when the demands of discipline, rigidity, conformity, and adherence to rules render people unable to perceive the end for which the rules were developed. In Merton's words, "Adherence to the rules, originally conceived as a means, becomes transformed into an end-in-itself" (p. 199).

We have all had experiences where an obsessive adherence to procedures and rules has kept us from meeting goals. In corporations, for example, employees are often required to routinely send copies of memos and letters to people who don't look at them and who wouldn't know what they meant if they did. It would be much more efficient simply to stop sending them. Often, our training, habits, or traditional ways of behaving blind us to alternatives that might be far more effective than the ones we are accustomed to.

Another dysfunction of bureaucracies has come to be called the *Peter Principle*. Peter and Hull (1969) have expressed it succinctly: "In a hierarchy, every employee tends to rise to his level of incompetence" (p. 25). In other words, those who do their jobs well are promoted into new jobs. If they can't manage their new jobs well, that's where they stay. Thus many people are moved from jobs they do well to jobs they do poorly, and the whole organization suffers. The authors argue that work is accomplished by the employees who have not yet reached their level of incompetence.

A related dysfunction comes about when hiring and promotions are based on a rigid set of formal qualifications — five years' experience or a college degree, for example — rather than skill or performance. In one instance, a woman with ten years' experience in her company and an excellent work reputation was passed over for promotion to supervisor because her company's policy dictated that supervisors must have a college degree. There are also instances in which excellent college teachers are denied tenure because they do not have a sufficient number of publishing credits. In bureaucratic organizations, formal qualifications may supersede performance in hiring and promotion.

Another dysfunction of bureaucracy that we are all familiar with is the "runaround." Who among us has not called an organization and had our call transferred to two or three other departments, only to be returned to the first person we spoke to with the problem still unresolved? You will recall that bureaucracies have rules defining the duties and responsibilities of various offices. The legal department handles legal matters, the personnel office handles recruitment, rank, and salary matters, and the payroll department issues checks, withholds money for benefits, and pays taxes. Other departments handle other matters. Now which one would you get in touch with about a lawsuit concerning the payment of salary? The difficulty is that actual problems do not always fit neatly into the compartments designed to handle them. If a problem does not clearly fall

within a department's area of responsibility, or if it involves several departments, the runaround is likely to begin.

The Dehumanization and Impersonality of the Bureaucracy

The very impersonality that makes an organization efficient can create problems on the human level. Merton (1957) wrote that bureaucracies stress depersonalization of relationships, categorization, and indifference to individuals. C. Wright Mills (1951) wrote that middle-class, white-collar employees of bureaucratic organizations were en-

meshed in a vast impersonal structure of rationalized activity in which their own rationality is lost. The most logical and efficient way for an organization to operate, for example, is to have one department that does all of the billing. This system may mean, however, that some people will do nothing but put computerized bills in envelopes all day. Even though they know that they are doing necessary work, they are likely to feel as though their work is meaningless, as though they're doing nothing of any consequence. Interestingly, Webster's College Dictionary defines a bureaucrat as a member of a bureaucracy, espe-

SOCIOLOGISTS AT WORK
Studying Courts as Organizations

Carroll Seron is a research associate at the Federal Judicial Center, an agency of the judicial branch in Washington, D.C. The small staff of lawyers and social scientists at the center does research, development, and training for the federal court system. She joined the staff of the center in 1981, after working for a year as a judicial fellow at the United States Supreme Court. She was the first sociologist ever selected for a fellowship at the Court.

Seron became interested in the study of courts while she was a graduate student and research assistant in sociology at New York University. "Specifically, I became interested in the way courts as organizations are entering the twentieth century. That may sound somewhat strange given the fact that we are on the brink of the twenty-first century, but courts are amazingly antiquated compared to most of the organizations that touch our daily lives. At the same time, they seek to uphold a crucial set of political values, to protect

our most fundamental freedoms. Can they change — become more efficient, professional, managerially sophisticated — without any sacrifice to their political role in American society? In somewhat less grandiose language, I became interested in the study of court reform and its impact on the political role of the judicial branch in contemporary society. At the Federal Judicial Center I am studying court reform. I am working now on a project to examine the impact of magistrates — a new tier of judicial officers — in federal trial courts. The design of this project draws directly on my substantive training in organizations and my methodological skills as a sociologist. Substantively, I will be examining the role of a new profession in federal trial courts, with specific attention to the ways magistrates and judges are defining the parameters of their respective judicial terrain. Methodologically, I am analyzing secondary data collected by the courts on the kinds of actions reported by magistrates, and I am design-

cially a government official, following a narrow rigid formal routine. To the author, the prevalence of rigidity and formality suggests that bureaucracies will almost inevitably be dehumanized and impersonal.

Kohn (1971) questions some of these notions about the impersonality and rigidity of bureaucracies. In interviews with more than 3000 men employed in civilian occupations, he found a small but consistent tendency for men who work in bureaucratic organizations to be more intellectually flexible, more open to new experience, and more self-directed in their values than men who

worked in nonbureaucratic organizations. Kohn attributed these findings in part to the fact that bureaucracies draw on a more educated work force. He suggested, however, that the tendencies he found resulted largely from conditions associated with bureaucratization — most notably, job security, somewhat higher income, and more complex work.

Often, people find ways to get around bureaucratic dysfunctions. In the impersonal structure of bureaucracies, people develop personal relationships. Official rules frequently leave room for interpretations and exceptions that per-

ing a survey to investigate the evolution of the relations between these court officers."

Seron came to sociology by a roundabout route. Her undergraduate major was American Studies, and she began her graduate work at NYU in that field. "I went to college at the University of California at Santa Cruz from 1966 to 1970. It was a new school. I was there at its birth and had, as a result, a unique college experience. Santa Cruz is often described as a trend-setter in higher education, and in many respects that is true. A large part of that trend-setting had to do with the fact that there was a strong commitment to a solid liberal arts education at a time when that very idea was beginning to be dismantled." But after a year of graduate study she switched to sociology. "I decided that as a sociologist I was going to learn theory, method, and technique. The emphasis I placed on theory was a continuation of my interest in the study of history and the need to learn how to ask the big questions. The emphasis on method and technique was so I could learn how to make some small stabs at answering the big questions. I became interested in the study of bureaucracies and the twentieth-century preoccupation with rational administration

for its own sake. I saw the study of organizations as a study of twentieth-century American society in microcosm. So in many respects there are some rather clear links between my undergraduate concerns and my graduate training."

After completing her degree, Seron took a teaching post at the University of Texas at Dallas. Three years later she came to Washington. "The questions I ask in my research at the center are very much a piece of those that have concerned me for years," she says. "My work today is an outgrowth of my concerns about our society and the events of the years when I came of age. I went to school during the 1960s and was very much affected by the social and political forces that were converging during that period. I have always thought of the work I do as intrinsically tied to a set of political commitments. I believe that one must find personal pleasure and satisfaction in work and at the same time find ways to use one's work to think about the issues confronting us as a society. In fact, I don't think I would enjoy my work if it did not provide a setting for thinking about ways in which we can create a better, more humane, and more just world community."

mit adaptations to unique and unanticipated circumstances. The fact that an organization has been deliberately organized to achieve specific goals does not mean that all activities and interactions will conform strictly to the official blueprint. As Blau and Scott (1963) suggest, regardless of the time and effort devoted by management to the design of a rational organization chart and elaborate procedure manuals, the official plan can never completely determine the conduct and social relations of the organization members.

Social Institutions

Formal organizations are often confused with social institutions, but they are not the same thing. An organization, you will recall, is a group formed to meet a specific goal: a corporation, church, hospital, or college, for example. An *institution,* however, is not an actual group. It is a system of norms, values, positions, and activities that develops around a basic societal goal. The concept institution, like the concept social system, is abstract and is used to refer to a fundamental form of social organization that meets a broad social goal: teaching children right and wrong, providing them with needed skills, maintaining order, producing and distributing goods, or providing answers to the unknown, for example. Thus all societies have institutions such as family, education, government, and religion to meet certain goals. How do institutions differ from organizations since they both revolve around meeting social goals? Organizations are deliberately constructed groups, whereas institutions are systems of norms. Thus education is an institution; the University of Vermont is an organization. Religion is an institution; the Baptist church is an organization. In addition to education and religion, several other institutions are of such fundamental importance that they are found in virtually all societies: the family, and political and economic systems. We will devote a separate chapter to each of these five institutions.

Why are institutions so important? Because they form the foundation of society and supply the basic prerequisites of group life: the reproduction and socialization of children (family); the affirmation of values and an approach to nonempirical questions (religion); the transmission of cultural heritage, knowledge, and skills from one generation to the next (education); the production and distribution of goods and services (economics); and social leadership and the protection of individuals from one another and from forces outside the society (politics). This list is not complete, of course. Marriage, medicine, transportation, war, and entertainment are a few of the other important institutions.

The confusion between institutions and organizations stems in part from the fact that the names of institutions can often be used to describe concrete entities as well. In its abstract sense, for example, the word "family" is used to refer to an institution. Using the word in this way, we might say, "During the 1960s, the family in the United States began to undergo important changes." We can also use the word "family" to refer to an actual group of people, however. Using the word in this concrete sense, we might say, "I am going to spend my vacation with my family." The speaker is referring to an existing group of individuals — mother, father, sisters, and brothers. The two meanings of the word are closely related but nevertheless distinct. The word "institution" is an abstraction; the word "organization" refers to an existing group. The distinction should become clearer as we discuss specific institutions in the next five chapters.

Summary

Social groups are so fundamental a part of our existence that it is difficult to imagine life without them. Most social groups involve interaction, a sense of belonging or membership, shared interests and values, and some type of structure. The group concept has been used in many different ways, however. Statistical groups are formed by the social scientist and have no awareness of kind, no social interaction, and no social organization. Categories, or societal groups, differ from statistical groups only in that the members are conscious that they share a particular characteristic. In other words, their members have an awareness of kind. Aggregates are collections of people who are in physical proximity to one another. They are loosely structured, short-lived, and involve little interaction. Members of associational and organizational groups interact, are aware of their similarity, and, in addition, are organized to pursue a common goal.

Although the various types of groups have distinguishing characteristics, it is not unusual for them to overlap or to change from one type to another. Primary groups are small and informal, and they emphasize interpersonal cohesion and personal involvement. Secondary groups are less personal and intimate, and they are more goal-oriented and purposeful. In-groups are those that people feel they belong to; everyone else belongs to the out-group. The in-group shares a common allegiance and identity, tends to be ethnocentric, and stereotypes members of the out-group. In-group cohesion is intensified by out-group threats.

Peer groups generally include people of roughly the same age, status, and importance. The members influence one another's socialization and act as sources of support and guidance. Reference groups provide self-evaluation and aspiration. They are the groups we use to assess our own performance, even if we do not actually belong to them.

Groups are also differentiated by size. The smallest group possible is a dyad, which has two members. A third person makes it a triad. The addition of even a few people changes group interactions considerably, and, as size increases, there are generally changes in the division of labor, formality, leadership, communication, and cohesion.

Formal organizations are deliberately orga-nized to achieve specific goals. They are particularly important in industrialized societies where many relationships are impersonal. Formal organizations are sources of authority and of continuity in our efforts to meet basic societal and personal goals, but conflict within and between organizations is common.

Bureaucracy is a type of administrative structure found in formal organizations. It is a hierarchical arrangement of the parts of an organization based on a division of labor and authority, which are based on position or office, not on individual characteristics. Bureaucracies operate in a location separate from the homes and families of its employees. They also operate according to objective rules, hire and promote people on the basis of merit, and encourage them to rise in the hierarchy through hard work. They can have a positive influence on efficiency, precision, coordination, stability, and continuity, but they can also have negative effects. Trained incapacity, the Peter Principle, the bureaucratic runaround, dehumanization, and impersonality are dysfunctional characteristics of bureaucracies.

Like formal organizations, institutions are intended to meet basic societal goals or needs. Organizations, however, are actual groups deliberately formed to achieve specific goals, whereas institutions exist only in the abstract, as organized patterns of norms, values, and statuses designed to meet larger societal goals. The basic institutions (family, religion, education, politics, and economics) provide the basic necessities of group life. In modern industrialized societies, additional institutions have developed around medicine, war, entertainment, and transportation, to mention a few. These institutions are organized ways of meeting broad societal goals.

Key Terms

aggregate group
associational or organizational group
bureaucracy

categorical group or societal unit
dyad
formal organization
ideal type
in-group
institution
out-group
peer group
Peter Principle
primary group
reference group
secondary group
social group
statistical group
trained incapacity
triad

Suggested Readings

Corwin, Ronald H. and Ray A. Eddfelt. **Perspectives on Organizations: Viewpoints for Teachers.** *Washington, D.C.: American Association for Colleges of Teacher Education, 1976.* A series of training publications designed to develop an awareness among teachers of what organizations are, how organizations affect them, and how they can deal with organizations.

Etzioni, Amitai. **A Sociological Reader on Complex Organizations.** *New York: Rinehart & Winston, 3rd ed., 1980.* An excellent collection of readings on complex organizations, this book covers theories, models for comparing organizations, the

structure of organizations, interorganizational relations, change, problems of organizations, and methods of study.

Hall, Richard H. **Organizations: Structure and Process.** *Englewood Cliffs, NJ: Prentice-Hall, 2nd ed., 1977.* A textbook that covers most of the major theories and research relating to bureaucracies.

Hare, A. Paul. **Handbook of Small Group Research.** *New York: The Free Press, 1976.* A review of the literature on small group research covering group process and structure, six variables that affect the interaction process (personality, social characteristics, group size, task, communication networks, and leadership), and performance characteristics.

Kanter, Rosabeth Moss. **Men and Women of the Corporation.** *New York: Basic Books, 1977.* A major study of sex stratification in the corporation, showing clearly the male dominance and sex symbolism that occur at all levels.

Katz, Daniel, Robert L. Kahn, and J. Stacy Adams (eds.). **The Study of Organizations: Findings from Field and Laboratory.** *San Francisco: Jossey-Bass, 1980.* A collection of thirty-eight articles on organization covering environment, motivation, communication, leadership, work and health, conflict, and change.

Weber, Max. **From Max Weber: Essays in Sociology,** *trans. and ed. H. H. Gerth and C. Wright Mills. New York: Oxford University Press, 1946.* A classical work on power and the bureaucracy.

Wilson, Stephen. **Informal Groups: An Introduction.** *Englewood Cliffs, NJ.: Prentice-Hall, 1978.* A text covering various aspects of informal groups, this book discusses solidarity, theorists, leadership, and problem solving.

Chapter 12
Family Groups and Systems

No matter how many communes anybody invents,
the family always creeps back.

— Margaret Mead

If we want to understand society and social life, it is impossible to ignore the family. Most of us spend a major portion of our lives in one form of family or another. It is unlikely that any society has ever existed without some social arrangement that could be termed *family,* and we cannot overestimate its importance to the individual and the society as a whole.

In this chapter, we will consider the family as a group, a social system, and a social institution. For most of us, the family serves as a primary social group. It is the first agency of socialization (see Chapter 5). Sociologists consider the family a social system because it is composed of interdependent parts, it has a characteristic organization and pattern of functioning, and it has subsystems that are part of the larger system. The family is considered a social institution because it is an area of human social life that is organized in discernible patterns and because it helps meet crucial societal goals.

Families do not exist in isolation, of course. They are an interdependent unit of the larger society. If families have many children, for example, schools may become crowded and unemployment may become a problem. If, on the other hand, they have few children over several generations, Social Security, the care of the aged, and an adequate work force may become important issues. It also makes a difference whether one spouse is employed or both are. Do newlyweds live with one set of parents or establish independent residences? Is divorce frequent or infrequent? Do people select their own mates or have them selected for them? Family practices have a profound influence on many aspects of social life.

We begin our discussion by clarifying what we mean by "family." Although the answer may appear quite obvious, this issue raised a major controversy at the 1980 White House Conference on Families. The definition of "family" influences who is eligible for various benefits. Certain definitions could result in informal stigmatization and discrimination against families who did not meet the qualifications, such as a mother and her child, two men, or an unmarried man and woman.

What Is a Family?

There is usually little confusion about what we mean by "family" when we talk with friends about our own family life because we generally associate with people from our own social class and culture who share our values and norms about families. In other cultures around the world, however, there is tremendous variation in family structure.

The smallest units are called *conjugal families,* which must include a husband and wife. *Nuclear families* may or may not include a husband and wife — they consist of any two or more persons related to one another by blood, marriage, or adoption who share a common residence. Thus, a brother and sister or a single parent and child would be nuclear families but not, strictly speaking, conjugal families. These terms are sometimes used interchangeably, and some families fall under both categories.

The definition used in census reporting in the United States is the nuclear family. In 1980, there were 58.4 million families in this country. Of these, 48.1 million were husband-and-wife families, 1.7 million were headed by males with no wife present, and 8.5 million were headed by females with no husband present (U.S. Bureau of the Census, 1981b, p. 5).

Approximately 95 percent of Americans marry at some time in their lives. In so doing, they become members of two different but overlapping nuclear families. The nuclear family in which one is born and reared (consisting of oneself, brothers and sisters, and parents) is termed the *family of orientation.* This is the family in which most basic early childhood socialization occurs. When a person marries, a new nuclear (and conjugal) family is formed, which is called the *family of procreation.* This family consists of oneself and one's spouse and children. These relations are diagrammed in Figure 12-1.

In the world as a whole, conjugal and nuclear families as isolated and independent units are extremely rare. In most societies the *extended family* is the norm, which goes beyond the nuclear family unit to include other nuclear families and relatives such as grandparents, aunts, uncles, and cousins.

Is the typical family in the United States nuclear or extended? Actually, it is both. American families typically have what is called a *modified-extended family structure,* in which individual nuclear families retain considerable autonomy and yet maintain connections with other nuclear families to exchange goods and services. This type of family differs from the extended family in that its members may live in different parts of the country and choose their occupations independently rather than following the parent's occupation.

Generally, we may say that the family arises out of marriage and includes people who are united by blood, marriage, or adoption. Its members share a common residence for some part of their lives and assume reciprocal rights and obligations with regard to one another. Since the family is the principal source of socialization, especially of the infant, factors such as these tend to differentiate the family from other social groups.

Family groups and systems are only one type of kinship association. *Kinship* is the web of relationships among family units or people with family linkages. All societies have general norms for defining family and kin groups and how these relationships are organized. These norms concern such matters as who lives together, who is the head of the group, who marries whom, how mates are selected, which relatives in family and

Figure 12-1
Families of orientation and procreation

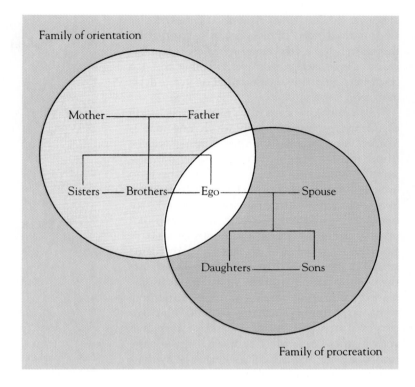

Family of orientation

Mother———————Father

Sisters——Brothers—Ego————Spouse

Daughters————Sons

Family of procreation

kin groups are most important, and how children are to be raised and by whom. Although these norms and the kinship systems they govern vary greatly, certain general norms tend to determine the statuses and roles of family members. These variations are discussed in the next section.

Variations in Kinship and Family Organization

Each society defines certain patterns of marriage, family, and kinship as correct and proper. Because we tend to be ethnocentric and favor the family structure found in our own society, we may overlook the wide range of variations that exist. We may also tend to assume that if our current family forms change too drastically, the institution of the family will collapse. It is important to recognize that a tremendous variety of marriage, family, and kinship patterns exist and that any of these patterns may be both appropriate and workable in a particular social context. One fundamental variation concerns marriage and the number of spouses considered acceptable.

Marriage and Number of Spouses

Marital status (single, married, separated, widowed, divorced) and number of spouses (none, one, more than one) are two major variations in family organization. Every society permits some form of marriage, although certain groups believe that the single life is the ultimate form of perfection. Nuns in the Catholic church, for example, are regarded as being symbolically married to God. In the United States today, it seems that remaining single may be emerging as an acceptable lifestyle. It is unclear, however, whether this is a permanent alternative to marriage or just a delay in marriage.

To most Americans, the "most proper" form of marriage is *monogamy*, in which one man is married to one woman at a time. Throughout the world, this form of marriage is the only one universally recognized; it is the predominant form even in societies where other forms exist. However, only about 20 percent of the world's societies are strictly monogamous, considering monogamy the only acceptable form of marriage.

Although the United States is considered strictly monogamous, it is possible to have more than one husband or one wife. An increasing number of married people end their relationship with one spouse and remarry another. This pattern of marrying is called *serial monogamy*. It is both legally and socially approved to have more than one wife or husband as long as it is done sequentially and not simultaneously.

There are a variety of alternatives to monogamy, however. Murdock (1957) investigated the frequency of *polygamy*, marriage to more than one spouse, in a sample of 554 societies from around the world. He found that *polygyny*, in which a man has more than one wife, was the norm in 77 percent of these societies, whereas *polyandry*, in which a woman has more than one husband, was culturally favored in less than 1 percent. *Group marriage*, in which several or many men are married to several or many women, is practiced in some societies, but it is nowhere the dominant marriage form.

In dealing with polygamy, several words of caution are in order. First, a distinction must be made between ideology and actual occurrence. The fact that a society advocates or permits several spouses does not necessarily mean that a large proportion of all marriages will be polygamous.

Many societies include norms of polygyny, the practice of having more than one wife. Frequently, this is a mark of high prestige, distinction, and status. This Iranian family consists of a Bakhtiari chief with his three wives and several children. The eldest wife is probably his first wife and is likely to occupy a privileged position among the women of the family.

Second, except for group marriage, multiple spouses are possible on a large scale only when the ratio of the sexes is unbalanced. Third, when polygamy is practiced, it is controlled by societal norms, like any other form of marriage. Rather than resulting from strictly personal or psychological motives, it is supported by the values and norms of both sexes and is closely linked to the economic conditions and belief systems of the wider society. Fourth, polygamy itself may take a variety of forms. The multiple husbands may all be brothers or the multiple wives may all be sisters, for example.

The most common form of polygamy is polygyny. In many societies, having several wives is a mark of prestige, distinction, and high status. The wealthy, the leaders, and the best hunters may get a second or third wife. Multiple wives may also be desired as a source of children, especially sons. Polygyny is very common in Africa, among Muslim groups in the Middle East and Asia, and in many tribal groups in South America and throughout the world. In Ibadan, Nigeria, for example, in a study of more than 6,600 women (Ware, 1979) nearly one wife in two was living in a polygynous marriage, a proportion that rose to two out of three for wives aged forty and above. The Muslim religion permits men to have up to four wives. In the United States, the most frequently cited source of polygyny is that of certain Mormon fundamentalists living in underground polygynous family units in Utah and neighboring states.

Polyandry is quite rare. Where it is practiced, the co-husbands are usually brothers, either blood brothers or clan brothers who belong to the same clan and are of the same generation. Among the Todas, for example, a non-Hindu tribe in India, it is understood that when a woman marries a man she becomes the wife of his brothers at the same time.

Norms of Residence

When people marry, they must decide where to live. Decisions about place of residence are typically dictated by societal norms and conform to one of three patterns.

In Western societies, the residence norm is *neolocal* — the couple lives alone wherever they wish — but this pattern is rare in the rest of the world. Of the societies Murdock (1949) examined, only about 10 percent considered it appropriate for newlywed couples to move to a place of residence separate from both the husband's and the

wife's families. This type of residence pattern seems to be linked most closely with norms of monogamy and individualism. Nearly three-fourths of the societies studied by Murdock were *patrilocal* — the newlywed couple lived not just in the groom's community, but usually in his parents' home or compound. This type of residence is most common in polygynous hunting and gathering societies throughout Asia, Africa, and Latin America. In the United States, the Amish communities represent one example of a patrilocal system. A *matrilocal* residence pattern was the norm in about 15 percent of the societies Murdock studied and was generally found where women held title to the land.

Norms of Descent and Inheritance

Children inherit two separate bloodlines at birth, the mother's and the father's. Most societies place more importance on one lineage or the other. In much of the Western world, particularly in the United States, lineage is of small importance. It determines surname but little else. In most societies, however, explicit rules indicate that one blood line is more important than the other. These rules are known as the norms of descent and inheritance.

The most common norms of descent are *patrilineal*. Kinship is represented through the male kin, the father's lineage. In this type of descent system, offspring owe a special allegiance and loyalty to the father and his kin who in turn protect and socialize the children and eventually pass to the sons their authority, property, and wealth. Under this system, the key ties are those among father, sons, and grandsons. The wife may maintain ties to her kin, and she contributes her genes to her children, but she and her children are considered members of her husband's family.

In a *matrilineal* system of descent, the mother's kin assume the important role among offspring. Matrilineal norms of descent are un-

The Trobriand Islanders, about 200 miles off the northeast coast of New Guinea, have a matrilineal descent system. While some powers and functions, such as that of village chief, are vested in the male, these hereditary offices or social positions are passed on exclusively through the mother line. The Trobriand Islanders do not consider a child to be biologically related to its father, for they believe the father has no procreative function. Thus the important males for children are not their fathers but their mothers' brothers.

common, but they do exist. Among the Trobriand Islanders, for example, kinship, wealth, and responsibility for support are traced through the female line.

In the United States, the norm is to assign influence, wealth, and power to both sides of the family. This system is referred to as *bilateral*. Kinship lines are traced equally through the biological relatives of both the mother and the father and inheritance is passed on in equal proportions to all children regardless of sex. One consequence of this descent system is that, although the kin of both parents are equally recognized and respected, neither kin group exerts much power and influence over the children, which has a significant effect on social change: a newlywed couple coming from families with different values and lifestyles may choose to conform to neither and establish a lifestyle of their own. In addition, the likelihood of marrying someone with different values increases, since the parents and kin groups in bilateral systems have relatively little influence over who their sons or daughters marry.

Norms of Authority

All families and kinship systems have norms concerning who makes important decisions. These norms follow the pattern of other norm variations in that they are aligned with gender. Most societies are *patriarchal* — the men have the power and authority and are dominant. In Iran, Thailand, and Japan, the male position of dominance is even reflected in the law. In *matriarchal* societies, the authority rests with the females, especially wives and mothers. Matriarchal systems are rare, even in a matrilineal society such as that of the Trobriand Islanders where the wives do not have authority over their husbands.

It is important to recognize that although authority in most families rests with the males, other family members have a strong influence on the decision-making process. Male family members are generally most influential, but wives and mothers often have a strong impact on decisions as well.

The least common pattern of authority is the *egalitarian* model in which decisions are equally divided between husband and wife. Some have argued that the United States is egalitarian because husbands and wives either make decisions jointly or assume responsibility for different areas of concern. The husband might make decisions related to his job, the automobile, or home repairs, whereas the wife might make decisions related to her job, the home, food, clothing, or the children. Many would argue that the family system in the United States is more patriarchal than egalitarian, however, since males generally control income and other family resources.

Norms for Choice of Marriage Partner

Every society, including the United States, has norms concerning the appropriateness or unacceptability of certain types of marriage partners. These norms can be divided into two categories: *exogamy,* where people must marry outside of their own group or sex and *endogamy,* which requires that people considering marriage share certain group characteristics.

Certain exogamous norms are almost universal. *Incest,* for example, is forbidden in almost every society. One cannot marry one's mother, father, brother, sister, son, or daughter. Isolated exceptions to this taboo are said to have existed among Egyptian and Inca royalty. Most societies also forbid marriage between first cousins and between members of the same sex.

Endogamous norms of one sort or another are also very widespread, although they vary greatly from one society to another. In this country, for example, marriages between members of different racial groups were considered improper or even forbidden by law at different times.

Why have norms concerning endogamy and exogamy evolved? It seems clear from their universality that they perform an important social function, but the nature of that function is widely debated. A number of authorities have suggested that the incest taboo, for instance, is a result of the dangers of inbreeding. Others contend that the taboo is instinctive, that prolonged associations with people during childhood precludes viewing them as a marriage partner, or that marriage within a kinship group would lead to intense conflicts and jealousy. Each of these explanations has its shortcomings, however. Murdock (1949) suggests that a complete explanation of the incest taboo must synthesize theories from the different disciplines that deal with human behavior.

There are also a number of explanations for endogamy. It is widely believed that members of similar groups share similar values, role expectations, and attitudes, which result in fewer marital or kinship conflicts. Other explanations suggest that people from similar age groups share similar developmental tasks and interests or that marriage within one's own race maintains "pure" genetic traits. It has also been suggested that marriages between people of the same socioeconomic status keep the wealth and power within the social class and that those of the same religious orientation are likely to agree on child-rearing practices, family rituals, and beliefs relating to the sacred. Although the norms of endogamy vary among and within societies such as the United States, all societies foster suspicion and dislike of groups whose values, behaviors, and customs are unfamiliar or seem strange. Both exogamy and endogamy, therefore, restrict the eligibility of available marriage partners for both sexes.

A Functionalist Perspective on the Family

The functionalist perspective, which was introduced in Chapter 2, emphasizes the parts and structures of social systems and the functions of these parts in maintaining the society. Despite the many variations that exist in family structure around the world, families everywhere perform many of the same functions. Among the more important are socialization, affection and emotional support, sexual regulation, reproduction, and social placement.

Socialization

As discussed in Chapter 5, the family is one of the most important agents of socialization because it teaches its members the rules and expec-

One of the universal functions of families is that of nurturant socialization. The primary group interaction between parent and child has proven to be indispensable to the development of mentally and physically healthy human beings. It appears that an increasing number of fathers are becoming more intimately involved in the child rearing process.

tations for behavior in the society. Reiss (1965) argues that although families perform many functions, only the function of *nurturant socialization* is universal. It is doubtful whether infants could even survive, much less develop into mentally, physically, and socially healthy human beings, outside of the intimate network of the family. The family is not only more permanent than other social institutions but also provides the care, protection, and love best suited to teaching children the knowledge, skills, values, and norms of the society and subculture. However excellent hospitals, day care centers, and nursery or elementary schools may be, none seems to perform the socialization and learning functions as well as the family (Spitz, 1945; Elkin and Handel, 1978). This emphasis on the infant and young child should not cause us to overlook the socialization function of the family on adults, however. Parents learn from each other, from their children, and from other kin as they interact in the intimate network bound by blood and marriage ties. This affective support is a second function provided by the family.

Affection and Emotional Support

More than twenty-five years ago, Parsons and Bales (1955) suggested that the family has two essential functions: (1) the primary socialization of children so that they can become true members of the society they were born in and (2) the stabilization of the adult personalities of the society. This second function, while often ignored, seems to be just as important as the first. Although some individuals enjoy living alone, most people need others who care, show affection, share joys and sorrows, and give support in times of need. Humans are social animals who depend on their families at every stage of the life cycle, and while social support is also provided by friends, neighbors, coworkers, and government agencies, none is as effective as the family at providing warm, supportive relationships.

The importance of this family function is evidenced in many different ways. Aging persons often indicate that good relationships with their children are a major source of gratification. In fact, people who have a network of family connections live longer than those who are single, widowed, or divorced.

Sexual Regulation

All societies grant approval to some sexual behaviors and disapproval to others. As mentioned earlier there is an almost universal taboo against incest, whereas marriage is the most universally approved outlet for sexual behavior. Both are linked to the family system.

Societies control sexual activity in a number of different ways. The chief means is by socializing sexual norms and attempting to enforce them. The norm of chastity, for example, might be enforced by secluding single women. Society also differentiates sexual rights in accord with various roles and statuses (male, female, single, married, priest, teacher) and places taboos on intercourse at certain times in the reproductive cycle such as during menstruation, pregnancy, or following childbirth. The norms of most societies discourage practices such as rape, child molesting, voyeurism, and the like. Sexual norms are concerned with more than just sexual intercourse; they also cover such behaviors as kissing and touching as well as appropriate attitudes and values.

In the United States, the most pervasive socially approved sexual interest is in heterosexual behavior and relationships. Sexual relationships are generally defined in terms of the family and marriage, as premarital or extramarital relationships, for example. Other institutions — religion, education, economics, or politics — may also regulate sexual behaviors and attitudes, but it is not one of their primary tasks. Families have the chief responsibility in this area, and since they regulate sexual activity, it seems logical that they also control the function of reproduction.

Reproduction

The family is the most widely approved social context for having children. Children are sometimes born outside the family, of course, but if it becomes a common occurrence it is considered a social problem. According to the functionalist perspective, a society's reproductive practices should conform to institutional patterns and be integrated with other societal functions such as sexual regulation, physical and emotional support, and socialization. This view reflects the *principle of legitimacy* formulated by Bronislaw Malinowski (1930) more than fifty years ago. The principle states that every society has a rule that every child should have a legitimate father to act as the child's protector, guardian, and representative in the society.

Those who are not functionalists may be disturbed at this explanation of the role of the family. It suggests that children born outside of the family are stigmatized in some way, that they are illegitimate. Even functionalists would concede that there are functional alternatives to a biological father; father substitutes can fulfill the essential social tasks and roles of a father. Interactionists would also argue that the biological link between parent and child is less significant than the social links — what is important to the child are role models, social support, and patterns of interaction that will enable the child to develop adequately and function effectively in society. Although it is true that children born outside the family can develop into functioning members of society, it is undeniably the family that universally fulfills the function of giving legal status and social approval to parenthood and reproduction. This function is related to another family function, that of social placement.

Social Placement

The *social placement* of children is a family function closely associated with socialization and reproduction. Social placement involves determin-

ing what roles and statuses the child will occupy in society. As discussed in Chapter 2, some of the statuses that a person will occupy are *ascribed* at birth, such as age, sex, and social class position. Children generally assume the legal, religious, and political status of their family as well. Even statuses that are *achieved* such as marriage, occupation, and education are greatly influenced by one's

One function of the family is social placement: influencing and determining the many roles and statuses children will occupy in society. Here, young children, most likely as a result of their parents' influence and Catholic religious status, prepare to receive their first Communion.

Changing Functions of the American Family

Many critics of the American family have included in their argument for the "breakdown" of the family the loss of functions which has taken place. Throughout written history, the family has been the major social institution. With changes that have occurred, particularly within the functions that a family has performed, the increasing specialization and complexity of modern society has led to a dehumanizing and fragmentizing process.

This issue is by no means a recent one. William Ogburn (1938) argued that the dilemma of the modern family was due to its loss of function. It was his belief that prior to modern times the power and prestige of the family was due to the seven functions it performed.

1. Foremost was the economic function. The family was a self-sufficient unit in which the members of the family consumed primarily that which they produced. Thus banks, stores, and factories were not needed.

2. The family served the basic function of giving prestige and status to its members. The family name was important, and a member of the family was less an individual and more a member of the family.

3. The family performed the basic function of education, not only of infants and children, but also of youths for their vocational education, physical education, domestic science, and so on.

4. The family provided the function of protecting its members. Not only did the father provide physical protection for his family, but children provided social and economic protection against economic and psychological needs in old age.

5. The family exercised a religious function, as was evidenced by grace at meals, family prayers, and the reading together of passages in the Bible.

6. The recreation function was performed at the homestead of some family or within the family rather than at recreation centers outside the home, provided by the school, community, or industry.

7. The final function was that of providing affection between mates and the procreation of children.

Many people in our society today are committed to the idea that these traditional functions of the family should be maintained. That is, families should be relatively sufficient, familism should have priority over individualism, education should be centered in the home, children should care for their aging parents, prayer and religious rituals should be a basic part of the daily life of the family, recreation should be engaged in by the family as a unit, and affection should be received relatively exclusively within the family unit.

The emerging norms suggest that many of these traditional family functions are being performed by other agencies. The economic function has gone to the factory, store, and office. The prestige and status function is increasingly centering around a family member rather than the family name. Teachers have become substitute parents and are basically responsible for the education of the child. Police, reform schools, social security, medicare and medicaid, unemployment compensation, and other types of social legislation provided by the state have replaced the traditional protective function. The professional priest, rabbi, or clergyman has assumed the responsibility for fulfilling the religious function. Little league baseball, industrial bowling teams, TV watching, or women's tennis groups have replaced the family as a source of recreation. And, although many would argue that the family still remains the center of the affectional life and is the only recognized place for producing children, one does not have to engage in an intensive investigation to discover the extent to which these two are sought and found outside the boundaries of the family and its members.

SOURCE: Eshleman, J. Ross, *The Family: An Introduction*, 3rd ed., Boston: Allyn & Bacon, 1981, pp. 10–11. Copyright © 1981 by Allyn and Bacon, Inc. Reprinted by permission.

membership in a particular family or kin network. Although it is often overlooked as a basic function of the family, a person's social placement, statuses (positions) occupied, and life chances are greatly influenced by his or her family and kin network.

The family performs functions other than the five mentioned. It fulfills basic economic, protective, educational, recreational, and religious functions as well.

A Conflict Perspective on the Family

Conflict theorists, like functionalists, recognize variations in family structure and accept the idea that the family provides basic social needs and goals. The two approaches are fundamentally very different, however. Conflict theorists contend that social systems, including the family, are not static structures that maintain equilibrium and harmony among the parts. They argue, rather, that social systems are constantly in a state of conflict and change. They contend that conflict is natural and inevitable in all human interactions including those between male and female, husband and wife, parent and child and that these conflicts are the result of a continual struggle for power and control. Marriage is one of many contexts in which each person seeks his or her rights. The struggles of parenthood involve not just rivalries between siblings but between parents and children as well.

Conflict stems from the unequal distribution of scarce resources. In all systems, some have greater resources than others, which gives them dominance and power over others. These inequalities exist not only in the economic and occupational realm but also in the family. Fredrick Engels (1902) claimed that the family, the basic unit in a capitalist society, serves as the chief means of oppressing women. The husband is the bourgeois and the wife the proletariat. As general Marxist theory suggests, when women become aware of their collective interests, they will question the legitimacy of the existing patterns of inequality and join together against men to bring about changes and the redistribution of resources: power, money, education, job opportunities, and the like. Conflict is as inevitable in the family as it is in society, and it leads to change.

As indicated in Chapters 2 and 8, for example, conflict theory assumes that economic organization, especially the ownership of property, generates revolutionary class conflict. In families, property ownership involves not just one's home and possessions but people as well. Collins (1971) argues that the basic institution of sexual stratification is the notion of sexual property, the belief that one has permanent exclusive sexual rights to a particular person. In societies dominated by males, the principal form of sexual property is male ownership of females, husband ownership of wives. This pattern of male ownership and male dominance has a long history, stemming from the laws in ancient Hebrew society and continuing through the twentieth century. The Hebrew laws stated, among other things, that if a man had sexual intercourse with an unbetrothed (not contracted for marriage) virgin, he was required to marry her and pay her father the bride price. In many societies, women are closely guarded so they will not attract other men and lose their market value. These practices are reflected in such customs as wearing a veil and strict chaperonage. Even in the United States, women could not legally make contracts or obtain credit until recently, and women are still not guaranteed equal rights under the Constitution. The status of women is also evident in wedding ceremonies, in which the father "gives away" some of his property — the bride — and the bride vows not just to love but to honor and obey her new owner (the groom).

How can this inequality and prevalence of male domination be explained? The most common theory relates power and domination to available resources. Men gain power over women by their physical strength and their freedom from the biological limitations of childbirth. The traditional resource of women, on the other hand, is their sexuality. Before and during marriage, women traditionally control men by withholding sexual "favors."

Conflict theory suggests that the structure of domination shifts as resources shift. Thus women today have a better bargaining position because they hold jobs and are economically independent and because they are free from unwanted pregnancies and childbirth. As Collins (1971) states, "Women become at least potentially free to negotiate their own sexual relationships" (p. 13). The changes involve much more than just sexual relationships, however. There seems to be a major trend, at least in the more industrialized nations, toward greater equality between the sexes both within and outside of marriage and the family.

Conflict in families also occurs over issues other than inequality between men and women. It can arise over a variety of issues: place of residence, inheritance rights, decison making, selection of mates, violence (especially rape), sexual relationships, and marital adjustment, to mention a few. In every instance, the issue is likely to involve an inequality of power, authority, or resources, which will lead to conflict.

Other Perspectives on the Family

An Exchange Perspective

All human interactions, including those between husbands and wives or parents and children, can be viewed in terms of social exchange. Social exchange theory assumes that people weigh rewards and costs in their social interactions. If the exchange is unequal or perceived as unequal, one person will be at a disadvantage and the other will control the relationship. In this regard, exchange theory parallels the conflict perspective. If people in a relationship give a great deal and receive little in return, they will perceive the relationship as highly unsatisfactory. These ideas can be illustrated by using mate selection as an example of social exchanges.

Everywhere in the world, selecting a mate involves trying to get the best spouse for what one has to offer. As you know from our earlier discussion of the endogamous and exogamous rules of marriage, selecting a mate is never a matter of completely free and independent choice. One must conform to societal norms.

Marriages may be arranged in several ways. At one extreme, they may be organized by the families of the people to be married; the prospective spouses may have no say in the matter at all. When this practice is followed, the criteria of the exchange involve such factors as money, prestige, family position, or power. When, on the other hand, the people to be married choose their mates themselves, the exchange criteria involve factors like love, beauty, fulfillment of needs, prestige, or personality. The latter procedure is rare in the world as a whole, the United States being one of the few countries that practices it.

One of the most widely researched exchange theories of mate selection is the theory of *complementary needs*. Robert Winch (1954, 1958) believed that although mates tend to resemble each other in terms of such social characteristics as age, race, religion, ethnic origin, socioeconomic status, and education, they are usually complementary rather than similar in respect to needs, psychic fulfillment, and individual motivation. Rather than seeking a mate with a similar personality, one seeks a person who will satisfy one's needs. If both people are dominant, for example, the relationship won't succeed, but if one is dominant and the other submissive, the relationship is complementary and the needs of both parties are met. A great deal of research was instigated by this theory of complementary needs, but the results did not provide empirical support for the notion that people choose mates whose needs complement their own.

An earlier exchange theory of mate selection was Willard Waller's (1938) analysis of courtship conduct as a process of bargaining, exploitation, or both. In his words, "When one marries he makes a number of different bargains. Everyone knows this and this knowledge affects the sentiment of love and the process of falling in love" (p. 239). While it is doubtful that "everyone knows this," the fact that bargaining and exchanges take place in the mate selection process is today widely recognized and accepted. In dating, for example, the male may consider sexual intercourse a desirable goal. To achieve this reward, he may offer in exchange flattery ("My, how beautiful you look"), commitment ("You are the only one I love"), goods ("I thought you might enjoy these flowers"), or services ("Let me buy you a drink"). In mate selection as in other interaction processes, people rarely get something for nothing although each person, either consciously or unconsciously, tries to maximize gains and minimize costs. Over the long run, however, actual exchanges tend to be about equal, and if they are not they are likely to end.

An Interactionist Perspective

An interactionist perspective on the family uses a social-psychological approach to examine interaction patterns, socialization processes, role expectations and behaviors, and the definitions or meanings given to various family issues. As noted in earlier chapters, this approach considers not just structural variations but the interactional patterns and covert definitions associated with structural arrangements.

Few relationships are more enduring or more intense than marriage, and few reflect the principles of interactionism so comprehensively. Mar-

Few relationships are more enduring and intimate than marriage, and few reflect the significance of interaction and communication so intensely. Marriage is a dynamic and changing relationship, and since it involves at least two people, a change in one without change or understanding in the other increases the probability of conflict. Thus successful relationships require shared perceptions and meanings.

riage exemplifies all the ideas central to symbolic interaction: shared meanings, significant others, role expectations, role taking, definitions of situations, symbolic communication, and so on.

Marriage is dynamic — the needs of the married individuals and their role relationships change frequently. According to the interactionist perspective, husband and wife have a reciprocal influence on each other. Each partner continually affects the other and thus adjustment is a process, not an end result. Good adjustment means that "the individual or the pair has a good working arrangement with reality, adulthood, and expectations of others" (Waller and Hill, 1951, p. 362).

Everyone brings to a marriage certain ideas about what is proper behavior for oneself and one's spouse. Inevitably, people find as they interact that some behaviors do not fit their preconceived definitions. Unless the definitions or the behaviors change, one spouse or both may be frustrated in attempting to fulfill their roles. Some argue that these frustrations are increasing, since the roles of husband and wife are more flexible and diverse than they were in the past. Others maintain that today's increased flexibility and diversity decrease marital strain by allowing partners a greater range of options. In either case, what the interactionist considers important is that the couple share definitions, perceptions, and meanings. Also, disagreements may not lead to conflict if they involve issues considered unimportant. Suppose, for example, that a husband likes football but his wife neither understands nor enjoys the game. The situation will not lead to conflict if the wife defines football as important to her husband and accepts his behavior. In the same way, a wife's desire for full-time employment or her wish to avoid cooking is a source of conflict only if the husband has different expectations. Adjustment is a result of shared expectations.

To maintain a satisfactory relationship, married couples must continually redefine themselves in relation to each other, which is often an unconscious process. When problems arise, marriage counseling may help by bringing unconscious definitions into consciousness, thus allowing the couple to examine how they influence the relationship.

The interactionist perspective stresses the importance of analyzing marriages and other relationships in the context in which they occur. A definition, role expectation, or behavior that is appropriate in one setting may be inappropriate in another. This perspective also emphasizes the notion that successful marriage involves a process of adjustment, of continual adaptation to shifts in shared meaning.

The American Family System

As indicated earlier in the chapter, the American family system emphasizes monogamy, neolocal residence, a modified-extended kinship linkage, bilateral descent and inheritance, egalitarian decision making, endogamous marriage, and relatively free choice of mate. A number of other structural characteristics have also been described: American families tend to be small and, compared with other countries, rather isolated; marital and family roles for women and men are becoming increasingly ambiguous; we tend to emphasize love in mate selection; we are often sexually permissive prior to or outside of marriage; and divorce is granted easily.

Table 12-1 shows the marital status of the population by sex and age. You can see that as of 1980, the population of the United States included 74 million males and 82 million females age 18 and over. Approximately 69 percent of the men and 63 percent of the women were married. Nearly one-fourth (23.5 percent) of the men and one-sixth (17 percent) of the women were single. A relatively small percentage (2.7 percent) of the men were widowers compared to 12.8 percent of the women who were widows. While much publicity is given to the frequency of divorce, you can see that only 5 percent of the men and 7 percent of the women were divorced. Note how these figures vary by age. Very few older people are single and very few young and middle-age people are widowed. In contrast the divorced population is concentrated most heavily in the 30 to 50 age group.

Broad profiles of the sort given in the two previous paragraphs, however, do not indicate the

Table 12-1
Marital status of the population, by sex and age: 1980

SEX AND AGE	TOTAL	SINGLE	MARRIED	WIDOWED	DIVORCED	PERCENT DISTRIBUTION				
						TOTAL	SINGLE	MARRIED	WIDOWED	DIVORCED
Male	74,101	17,434	50,825	1,972	3,871	100.0	23.5	68.6	2.7	5.2
18–19 years	4,042	3,808	232	–	2	100.0	94.2	5.7	–	–
20–24 years	9,801	6,721	2,924	2	154	100.0	68.6	29.8	–	1.6
25–29 years	9,076	2,940	5,650	8	479	100.0	32.4	62.3	.1	5.3
30–34 years	8,270	1,298	6,310	11	651	100.0	15.7	76.3	.1	7.9
35–44 years	12,297	904	10,358	45	989	100.0	7.4	84.2	.4	8.0
45–54 years	10,962	699	9,347	176	740	100.0	6.4	85.3	1.6	6.8
55–64 years	9,870	565	8,414	397	495	100.0	5.7	85.2	4.0	5.0
65–74 years	6,549	357	5,346	557	290	100.0	5.5	81.6	8.5	4.4
75 years and over	3,234	142	2,244	776	71	100.0	4.4	69.4	24.0	2.2
Female	82,054	13,977	51,767	10,479	5,831	100.0	17.0	63.1	12.8	7.1
18–19 years	4,184	3,465	689	3	26	100.0	82.8	16.5	.1	.6
20–24 years	10,246	5,148	4,705	23	370	100.0	50.2	45.9	.2	3.6
25–29 years	9,357	1,947	6,584	33	792	100.0	20.8	70.4	.4	8.5
30–34 years	8,561	810	6,695	102	954	100.0	9.5	78.2	1.2	11.1
35–44 years	13,042	728	10,612	292	1,411	100.0	5.6	81.4	2.2	10.8
45–54 years	11,670	552	9,222	821	1,074	100.0	4.7	79.0	7.0	9.2
55–64 years	11,034	504	7,713	2,082	735	100.0	4.6	69.9	18.9	6.7
65–74 years	8,549	480	4,282	3,444	342	100.0	5.6	50.1	40.3	4.0
75 years and over	5,411	344	1,264	3,677	126	100.0	6.4	23.4	68.0	2.3

– Represents zero or rounds to zero.

Note: In thousands of persons 18 years old and over, except percent. As of March. Based on Current Population Survey, which includes members of Armed Forces living off post or with their families on post, but excludes all other members of the Armed Forces.

SOURCE: U.S. Bureau of the Census, *Statistical Abstract of the United States: 1981*, (102nd ed.) Washington, D.C., 1980, No. 49, p. 38.

frequency or range of specific trends in the evolution of the family. In the following sections, we will examine some of these trends in more detail.

Marriage Rates and Age at Marriage

Rates of marriage are influenced by a variety of factors. The rate characteristically falls during periods of economic recession and rises during periods of prosperity. The rate also tends to rise at the beginning of a war and after a war has ended. Variations in the age of the population are also influential.

In the United States prior to 1900, the rate was relatively stable, varying between 8.6 and 9.6 marriages per 1,000 population. Shortly after the turn of the century, the rate rose until the depression of the early 1930s, when it dropped to a low of 7.9. As can be seen in Figure 12-2, it rose dramatically at the outset of World War II as young men sought to avail themselves of the deferred status granted to married men or simply wanted to marry before going overseas. The end of the war and the return of men to civilian life precipitated another upsurge in marriages. In 1946, the marriage rate reached 16.4, an unprecedented and to date unsurpassed peak. Subsequently, it dropped. Over the past thirty years, the rate has fluctuated between 8.5 and 11.0 per thousand (see Figure 12-2).

In the United States, marriage rates have distinct seasonal and geographic variations. More marriages take place in June than in any other

Figure 12-2
Marriage rate: United States, 1925–1980

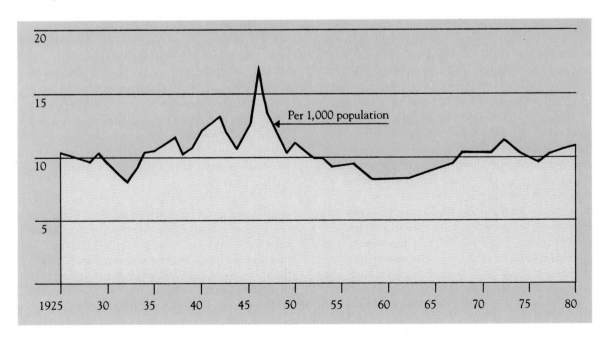

month, followed by August and September. The fewest marriages are in January, February, and March. Interestingly, the favorite month for marriage varies by age group: teenage brides and grooms prefer June; brides aged thirty to thirty-four and grooms aged forty-five to fifty-four most often choose December; and brides thirty-five to fifty-four and grooms fifty-five to sixty-four tend to select July. Most marriages take place on Saturday. Friday is next in popularity, and Tuesdays, Wednesdays, and Thursdays are the least popular. Marriage rates also vary from state to state. The extremes in 1979 were 147 per 1,000 population in Nevada and 7.5 per 1,000 in Delaware and New Jersey (*Statistical Abstract*, 1981, p. 81).

Most marriages in the United States are between people of roughly the same age, although people are free to marry someone considerably older or younger within the legal limits determined by each state. The *Current Population Reports* (March 1980) published by the U.S. Bureau of the Census shows the median age at first marriage to be 24.6 for men and 22.1 for women, an age difference of 2.5 years.

The median age at first marriage and the age difference between males and females have changed considerably since the turn of the century. In 1900, these figures were 25.9 for males and 21.9 for females, a difference of four years. Recently, people have been postponing marriage until they are older, which reflects a decision on the part of young people to live independently as they pursue higher education or job opportunities. In the past ten years, there has been a rapid increase in the percent of men and women who have never married. In 1970, one in every ten women aged twenty-five to twenty-nine years had never married, but by 1980 this proportion had doubled to one in every five. For men it was one in three in 1980, a 70 percent increase over the one-in-five rate of singlehood in 1970.

Teenage marriages are an issue of special concern in the United States. Married teenagers have a high high school dropout rate and a high unemployment rate. The divorce rate for teenagers is estimated to be from two to four times the rate for marriages that begin after age twenty. Many teenage marriages involve a pregnancy at the time of marriage, and data consistently show a higher divorce rate among marriages begun with a pregnancy. Some studies indicate that people who marry young are unprepared for the process of selecting a mate and assuming a marital role, so they derive little satisfaction from marriage and are disproportionately represented in divorce statistics (Lee, 1977).

Family Size and Parent-Child Norms

In this country, as in the rest of the world, most married couples have or want to have children. Voluntarily childless marriages are uncommon, although as we will discuss in the next section, a pattern of childless marriages is beginning to emerge. In the United States in 1980, there were 3.6 million births, a rate of 16.2 per 1,000 population (*Statistical Abstract*, 1981, p. 58). Like marriage rates, birth rates fluctuate with wars, socioeconomic conditions, and other variables, as was most evident in the "baby boom" following World War II. At the turn of the century, the birth rate was over 30 per 1,000 population. Decreasing to 19.4 in 1940, it had increased to 25 by the mid-1950s. It subsequently declined until it reached a rate of 14.8 in 1975. Since then there has been a slight increase to the current rate of slightly over 16.

Women who are now in their twenties express a desire to have fewer children than older women often had. Over one-third of the women between forty and forty-nine years old in 1975 had already borne four or more children, but less than one woman in ten who was in her twenties in 1975 expected to have four or more children (U.S. Bureau of the Census, 1976). Although this is a comparison of actual number of children born

Throughout the world, most couples have or want to have children. Only a small proportion of married women voluntarily remain childless, although women in their thirties, like this one, are expressing a wish to have fewer children than their older counterparts. The widespread availability of reliable contraceptive methods make it increasingly possible for all pregnancies to be planned and desired.

with expected number of children, the younger women may well fulfill their expectations. Improved methods of birth control, liberalized abortion laws, and increased acceptance of birth planning by Catholics are likely to decrease the number of unplanned and unwanted births.

Does family size make a difference in interactions between siblings or between children and their parents? Since families are groups and the number of people in a group influences the behavior of its members, the answer is yes. But specifically how does family size make a difference? Perhaps the greatest difference in family interaction patterns comes with the birth of the first child because the transition to parenthood involves a major shift in parental role expectations and behaviors. A number of writers have called the early stages of parenthood a crisis, a traumatic change that forces couples to drastically reorganize their lives (Hobbs, 1965; LeMasters, 1957). Later studies concluded, however, that for most couples, beginning parenthood is a period of transition but not a period of change so dramatic that a crisis results.

With the birth of the first child, a general expectation exists that a second and third child should follow. One-child families have generally been viewed as unhealthy for parents and child alike. The "only child" has been described as spoiled, selfish, overly dependent, maladjusted, and lonely, and the parents of a single child have been described as selfish, self-centered, immature, cold, and abnormal (Hawke and Knox, 1977). Many of these notions, though, have been dispelled because inflation, overpopulation, dual-career marriages, and changing lifestyles have called for a new look at this "small" family.

While agreement may exist that a one-child family is small, less agreement exists as to the number of children required to make a family "large." Perceptions of a family as "small" or "large" are relative. A family with four children in the United States at the turn of the century would not have been perceived as large. However, today it often is. The more central issue in reference to family size, however, is the identification of factors related to increased family size and the consequences that result from an increasing number of children in a given family.

It is known that family size increases with factors such as younger ages at marriage, lower

educational and socioeconomic levels, rural residence, and particular religious groups such as the
Amish or Mormons who place a major value on
children. It is known that as families increase in
size, the chances increase that some children are
unplanned and unwanted. And finally, an increased family size appears to affect the level of
health of its members. In a review of studies concerning the relationship between family size and
factors relevant to health, Wray (1971) found no
evidence of significant health benefits associated
with large families. It is not family size per se,
however, that creates health problems or family
difficulties. Large families heighten the complexity
of intragroup relations, pose problems in fulfilling
family needs, and influence how much money and
attention can be devoted to each child.

Divorce

Whenever any two people interact, conflicts
may arise and one person or both may want to
end the relationship. This is true not only of marriage but of other relationships as well. Unlike
most relationships, however, marriage involves
civil, legal, or religious ties that specify if and how
the relationship can end. In countries such as
Spain, Brazil, and Peru, in conformity with the
doctrine of the Roman Catholic church, marriage
is indissoluble except by death. In Switzerland,
the Scandinavian countries, the U.S.S.R., and Poland, a divorce is granted if it is shown that
the marriage has failed. The laws of Islam and
Judaism give a husband the power to terminate
his marriage by simply renouncing his wife or
wives. In this country most states, traditionally at
least, grant a divorce if it is shown that one party
has gravely violated his or her marital obligations.
Since 1970, however, many states have moved to
a *no-fault divorce* system in which marriages can be
ended on the basis of "irreconcilable differences."

The United States has one of the highest divorce rates in the world. According to the United

Nations *Demographic Yearbook* (1979), the U.S.
rate of divorce per 1,000 persons per year was 5.3,
compared with 3.5 in the U.S.S.R., 3.2 in Australia, 2.4 in Sweden and Canada, 1.2 in Japan,
1.1 in Israel, and 0.3 in Mexico, but this high divorce rate can be misleading. It means that only
ten people get divorced per 1,000 population.

Why, then, do we so often hear that one
marriage in two ends in divorce? Because the divorce rate is figured by dividing the number of divorces in a given year by the number of marriages
in the same year. Thus if your state had fifty divorces and one hundred marriages in 1982, the
divorce rate would be 50 percent. This is the rate
used to illustrate the "breakdown in the American
family." It does not, however, mean that half of
all marriages end in divorce, any more than the
finding that a given state had one hundred marriages and one hundred divorces in a certain year
would mean that every marriage ended in divorce.
There is, nevertheless, a great deal of concern
about the frequency of divorce in the United
States.

In 1980, there were approximately 1,182,000
divorces in this country, a rate of 5.3 divorces per
1,000 population, about half the rate of 10.9 marriages per 1,000 population. This figure is the
highest ever for the United States (see Figure
12-3).

Like marriage rates, divorce rates tend to decline in times of economic depression and rise
during periods of prosperity. They also vary by
geographic and social characteristics. Geographically, the general trend in the United States is for
divorce rates to increase as one moves from east
to west. Demographic figures show that approximately one-half of all divorces are among persons
in their twenties, and the rate is exceptionally
high among teenagers. Divorce is also most frequent in the first three years after marriage, and
the incidence is higher among the lower socioeconomic levels. Whether education, occupation, or

Figure 12-3
Divorce rates in the United States: 1920–1980

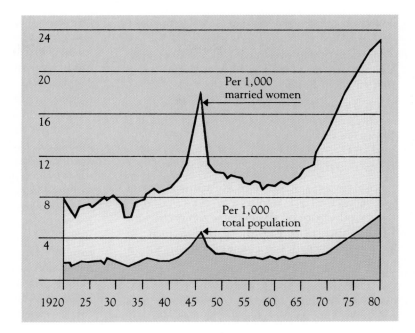

income is used as an index of socioeconomic level, the divorce rate goes up as the socioeconomic level goes down.

These variations in rate of divorce give us clues about its causes. The fact that rates are higher in the West indicates that divorce may be related to the liberality of the laws and the degree of cultural mixing. Financial problems and emotional immaturity may be factors in the high rates found among teenagers. Difficulties in adjusting to new relationships or discrepancies in role expectations may contribute to the divorce rates in the first three years after marriage. Money problems, lack of education, and working at a low-status job may account for the rates found in the lower socioeconomic levels. Although other factors are involved and some exceptions exist to these general patterns, divorce is not merely a result of personal characteristics. These variations in rates illustrate how social and cultural factors can influence the chances that a marriage will end in divorce.

Emerging Marital and Family Lifestyles

In the United States today, the diversity of families is greater than ever before, and changes are occurring rapidly. Consider the following statistics derived from the 1980 census (U.S. Bureau of the Census, 1981a):

□ More than 1.5 million unmarried couples were living together, triple the number in 1970.

□ More than 50 percent of all women and 67 percent of all men aged twenty to twenty-four had not married for the first time, compared with

36 percent of the women and 55 percent of the men in 1970.

□ One out of every five children lived with just one parent, compared with one in nine in 1970.

□ Twenty-three percent of all households consisted of one person living alone, which was a 94 percent increase for men (from 3.5 to 6.8 million) and a 51 percent increase for women (from 7.3 to 11.0 million) since 1970.

□ The ratio of divorced to married persons was higher for black women (257 per 1,000) than for any other race or sex group as compared with 151 for black men, 133 for Spanish women, 59 for Spanish men, 110 for white women, and 74 for white men.

These statements illustrate some of the dramatic shifts taking place in family life in this country. Three emerging marital and family patterns are discussed in more detail below.

Nonmarital Heterosexual Cohabitation

As stated above, more than 1.5 million unmarried couples lived together in 1980, triple the number in 1970. *Nonmarital heterosexual cohabitation,* or living together, is an emerging lifestyle in which a man and a woman who are not married to each other by ceremony or common law occupy the same dwelling. Contrary to a widely held assumption, nonmarital heterosexual cohabitation is not just a college student phenomenon, nor is it confined to the generation under age twenty-five. In fact, more than one-fourth of all unmarried couples living together in 1980 were between twenty-five and thirty-four years old, and an additional 19 percent were forty-five and over. Of this latter group, 7.4 percent or 116,000 people were sixty-five years of age and over (U.S. Bureau of the Census, 1981a, p. 5).

Despite these findings, most research on co-habitation has involved college student populations. In a review of this research, Macklin (1978) found that nonmarried cohabitants are significantly less committed to each other than married couples. With regard to the division of labor, cohabiting couples tended to mirror the society around them and accept gender roles characteristic of other couples their age. The same was true for sexual exclusivity. Most believed in sexual freedom within their nonmarried relationship, but most voluntarily restrained their sexual activity with outsiders.

Nonmarital heterosexual cohabitation does not appear to be a substitute for marriage, a cure-all for marital problems, or a solution to the problem of frequent divorce. Most cohabiting relationships are short-term and last only a few months, but the longer couples cohabit, the more likely they are to eventually marry. Unmarried couples experience problems quite similar to those of married couples: concern over financial matters, the division of labor, and relationships with extended family members. In cohabiting couples, as in married couples, women do most of the housework. Although unmarried cohabitation does not fall within acceptable value limits for everyone, it does appear to have functional value for an increasing number of adults of all ages. For many couples, it provides a financially practical situation (two together can live more cheaply than two separately), a warm, homelike atmosphere, ready access to a sexual partner, an intimate interpersonal relationship, a nonlegal, nonbinding union, and a form of trial marriage.

Childless Marriage

Most unmarried couples are childless. Among these couples, a desire for children, a pregnancy, or the birth of a child often leads to marriage. But what of the legally married couples who have no children and desire none? In recent years, the subject of the voluntarily childless marriage as an acceptable marital lifestyle has gained increased attention for a number of reasons. First, it is inconsistent with myths about the existence of a maternal instinct, the notion that all women want to have, love, and care for a child or children. Second, it changes the functions of marriage and the family that deal with reproduction, nurturant socialization, and social placement. Third, the availability and reliability of contraceptives and abortion make it possible for women and couples to have no children if they so choose.

Census data show that in 1979, 6.7 percent of all married or previously married women aged forty to forty-four were childless (*Statistical Abstract*, 1981, p. 64). This figure increases to 26.2 percent among the twenty-five to twenty-nine-year-old married women, 40.5 among those twenty to twenty-four, and 48.5 among those fifteen to nineteen years of age. These younger age groups had not completed their childbearing years, however, and most expected to have children at some time in their lives. Approximately 11 percent of all women aged eighteen to thirty-four did not expect to have any children in their lifetime. This figure was higher (14 percent) for women with one or more years of college and lower (8 percent) for women who were not high school graduates.

Veevers (1975) conducted in-depth interviews with childless wives living with their husbands and found that they held a number of unusual beliefs about parenting. Most of these women were married to husbands who agreed that children were not desirable. The wives defined parenthood in negative rather than positive terms and denied the existence of a maternal instinct. They dismissed the accusation that childlessness was abnormal. Pregnancy and childbirth were perceived to be at best unpleasant and at worst difficult and dangerous. They regarded child care as excessively burdensome and unrewarding and as having a deleterious effect on a woman's life chances. Finally, they defined parenthood as a trap that interfered with personal happiness.

The child-free alternative may be an acceptable family form and lifestyle for a small proportion of families (6 to 8 percent). Under certain conditions, as in the dual-career marriages discussed next, childlessness may be conducive to both personal and marital satisfaction and adjustment.

Dual-Career Marriages

One of the important social changes since World War II has been the increase of women in the labor force. In 1940, despite a sharp increase in the number of working wives during the depression of the 1930s, only 15 percent of all married women living with their husbands held an

Dual-career marriages have received growing attention over the past decade. Employment of women in a career sense, which is increasingly the case, designates a level of commitment and a developmental employment sequence. Evidence suggests that wives in dual-career marriages accommodate more to their husbands' careers than vice versa.

For Middle-Aged Man, a Wife's New Career Upsets Old Balances

Herbert Gleason's wife tried to warn him, but he was too busy to pay much mind. "I kept thinking nothing was going to change," the Boston attorney recalls.

He was dead wrong. From a comfortable life in which Mr. Gleason's career success was balanced neatly by his wife's full-time support as homemaker, the Gleason family abruptly changed course. At age 39, after a 10-year hiatus, Nancy Gleason resumed her career as a psychiatric counselor. Quite unexpectedly, the emotional sands beneath the marriage shifted.

"I really didn't anticipate how it would affect our attitudes toward each other," Herb Gleason says of his wife's return to her career eight years ago. "I thought she'd always be there just like before — supportive, adjusting to my needs."

For middle-aged men like Mr. Gleason, trying to accommodate to a wife's new career can be a confusing, bruising experience. These men are of a generation in which marriage was typically a one-provider, one-homemaker ef-fort, not a professional joint venture. They are of an age when change tends to come gradually and predictably, not suddenly. And although the problems of younger two-career couples have been well-chronicled, these men of a different generation are left to flounder on their own.

"Difficult Transition"

"People talk about women's prob-lems all the time, but the adaptive stress men undergo when their wives take on a career has been virtually lost sight of," says Pres-ton Munter, a psychiatric consul-tant to Itek Corp. "Even if you could postulate an ideal man and an ideal marriage, this would be a difficult transition to make."

Although it may be cold comfort, an increasing number of men are attempting to negotiate such transitions. Today 24.5 mil-lion wives, or roughly 50% of the nation's married women, are working or looking for work. Some 6.2 million of them are be-tween 35 and 44 years old, and a large portion of these are house-wives who have only recently started new careers or revived old ones.

As these homemakers seek out their professional fortunes, their husbands are left behind to struggle with a welter of conflict-ing emotions. They are proud of their wives' work accomplish-ments, yet are impatient with the demands of their wives' new jobs. They are grateful that their wives are financially self-sufficient, yet resent their new-found independence. . . .

Expressing Pain

Just how successfully an older man adjusts to his wife's pursuit of a career depends on such variables as the underlying strength of the marriage, each spouse's personality and the nature of the two careers. Yet the metamorphosis of home-maker into breadwinner sends tremors through every relationship.

"The marriage for the man provided his one big outlet for ex-pressing dependency, emotion and vulnerability," says Elizabeth Dou-van, the director of the University of Michigan's Family and Sex Roles Program. "The wife, how-ever, isn't as available for him." Mrs. Douvan, who has conducted national surveys on Americans' at-titudes and concerns, adds: "What we're seeing is men expressing a lot more unhappiness and pain." . . .

Sense of Alienation

"The problem starts when her job isn't a job but a career," says Fred Shotz, a Plantation, Fla., psychotherapist. As the secure breadwinner-and-helpmate relationship topples, men in their 40s are apt to feel that their wives value their careers more highly than their marriages. According to Mr. Shotz, this feeling surfaces in the common complaint: "What am I getting out of this relationship? I might as well have a roommate."

Ironically, it is this same sense of alienation that prompts many women to pursue a career in the first place. Yet nowadays, the emotional insecurities tip the other way. "I've heard men say, 'What scares me is that she is crossing over a bridge and I am going to be left behind,'" says Lillian Rubin, a sociologist and psychologist at the University of California.

Those who manage to overcome such fears often find their marriages strengthened. Family income swells. New career interests add excitement and vibrancy to relationships. Frequently, a wife's financial independence gives her husband a renewed sense of security.

"I know now that she is staying with me out of choice rather than because she couldn't make a better deal," says David Dorosin, whose wife embarked on an urban-planning career after 17 years as a homemaker. "Here I am pulling the responsibility wagon through life," he adds, "and it's nice to know there is another strong horse beside you."

Still, problems inevitably arise. Husbands must adjust to their wives' new preoccupation with office problems — and to their own loneliness when wives travel on business. Wives are no longer free to drop everything to accompany their spouses on business trips or extended vacations. Now, each spouse arrives home after a demanding day at the office, each vying for soothing attention from the other. Friction often arises over whose needs come first.

Many husbands are relieved that they no longer must provide their wives with vicarious career excitement by sharing every tidbit of office gossip. But that relief often gives way to the notion that nobody cares. Attorney Herb Gleason began to notice that when he would recount the latest installment of a case, his wife would distractedly interrupt with, "What is this about? Who is he?"

Similarly, Bruce Merrin, a Los Angeles public-relations man, feels that his wife is indifferent to his work now that she has her own real-estate career. Recently, he asked for her opinion of a press kit that he had spent many hours preparing for a client. "I asked her the next morning if she had looked at it, and she said, 'No,'" Mr. Merrin says. "I was extremely hurt. She had plenty of time if she had wanted to."

In a household where two careers jostle for room, bruised feelings are often brushed aside amid the tumult of other domestic changes. Suddenly, the intrusive evening and weekend phone calls from the office are for her. Vacation plans are postponed because of her job pressures. Responsibility for household chores shifts. In the Merrin household, for example, Bruce cooks breakfasts and scrubs toilets.

Most disconcerting of all, many husbands are no longer sure they know the women they married. New facets of their wives' personalities emerge. Meticulous housekeepers become more tolerant of sloppiness. Easygoing mothers flare up over the children's balkiness or dawdling — infractions they might once have overlooked. David Dorosin's wife began to exhibit a new — and sometimes intimidating — professional assurance and polish.

"She is no longer the never-judging homemaker," says Dr. Dorosin, a psychiatrist. "She is a forceful, critical intelligence...."

outside job. By 1960, the proportion had risen to 32 percent and by 1980 to about 50 percent. Today, more than half of all married women aged thirty-five years or younger hold jobs.

Women who have children are less likely to hold jobs than those who do not. The proportion of married women in the labor force is highest among those who have no small children to take care of at home. Among these women under age thirty-five, 80 percent hold jobs. Even among the women in this age group who have one or more children under the age of six, 40 percent are employed. Most of these employed women are in clerical or service work with earnings well below that of their male counterparts. Arrangements of this type are called dual-employed marriages. (It is assumed, sometimes incorrectly, that the husband is also employed.)

Although women have been taking jobs in increasing numbers, the *dual-career* marriage is a relatively recent development. The word "career" is used to designate jobs taken, not primarily to produce additional income, but for the satisfaction involved. Careers typically involve a higher level of commitment than "paid employment," and they progress through a developmental se-

SOCIOLOGISTS AT WORK
Family Counseling

Marie Witkin Kargman is a family disputes mediator in Boston. In addition, she practices marriage counseling, divorce counseling, and family counseling. She brings unique qualifications to this work: She is both a lawyer and a sociologist.

How do these different backgrounds and trainings fit together in her work? Kargman tells of a realization that she came to early in her career. "Before I trained in sociology at graduate school (Department of Social Relations, Harvard University), I was a practicing lawyer in the juvenile and family courts of Chicago. I discovered that the law is in a very real sense applied sociology: It deals with institutionalized patterns of behavior legitimized by the legal system, and with the sanctions applied when people deviate. I felt I needed to know more about the family, its structure, and its functions to be a better lawyer. Most

lawyers rearrange the family, writing divorce and separation agreements that create new family structures, without knowing much about the sociology of the family. I was not comfortable rearranging family relationships when I knew so little about the theory in the field. But by the time I got my sociology degree I knew that I wanted to be a marriage counselor who worked with lawyers, helping them do a better job."

She explains how she is able to apply the sociological theory she has learned: "In my family disputes mediation, and particularly in child custody disputes, I am apt to say to the divorced parents who have a child custody problem, 'What we are trying to do here is to get two parents and their children to come together to carry out family functions without the foundation of living in a joint household. Each household is

quence of increasing responsibility. One study (Burke and Weir, 1976) of one- and two-career families found that women in two-career families reported fewer pressures and worries, more communication with husbands, more happiness with their marriages, and better physical and mental health. In contrast, the men in the two-career families were in poorer health and less content with marriage, work, and life in general. It seems that the husband of a career wife loses part of his support system when his wife no longer functions as a servant, homemaker, and mother. Wives who have careers, on the other hand, are able to expand into roles that have a more positive value for them.

Most studies of dual-career marriages suggest that they involve certain strains. Wives usually accommodate more to the husband's career than vice versa, and husbands and wives have differential gains and losses when both have a career. Although the professional employment of women is gaining increasing acceptance, sexual equality in marriage has not yet been achieved. Wives are generally expected to give up their own jobs for the sake of their husbands and to consider their families their first duty.

a family group with a political system, an economic system, and a kinship system. The child must now live in two households, juggle two different sets of systems, integrate them, or deal with them as unrelated parts of his or her life.' We then look at the similarities of expectation of the child's two separate households, and try to decide what is in the best interests of the child."

Marie Kargman offers the following example of a case where she has relied on her sociological training. "The judge in a child custody dispute appointed me guardian ad litem." (*Ad litem* is Latin for, "for the course of the suit." The mother and the father could arrange for their own representation and choose their own lawyers; it was Kargman's job to see that the third party in the dispute — the child — was fairly represented.) "When I read the record, I discovered that two different psychiatrists and one social worker had been appointed guardians ad litem before me. When I asked the judge why he appointed me, all he said was, 'Please come up with a decision!' In this particular case, the mother had asked the court for permission to take the child out of Massachusetts. She had remarried in Massachusetts, and there were two children by the second marriage. The mother and stepfather wanted to relocate to the Midwest, where both had good job offers. After a delay of one year, the judge permitted the mother to move. Her husband had gone ahead, and she stayed behind with the children, fighting the court battle. Now the question of reasonable visitation was in dispute.

"Before I got into the dispute, the only persons discussed by the lawyers were the natural father, the natural mother, and the child. That the child was part of many different family relationships was never discussed. From a legal point of view the family before the court was the original family of procreation. But this child was a member of his original family and an additional two families, the step-family and the family of his half-sisters. The child wanted to spend holidays with 'his family' and the natural father wanted the holidays on a strict two-parent division. All of the child's social systems were described in my report to the judge, whose decision was made based on the child's multifamily expectations."

Summary

The family serves a number of different purposes. It is the primary social group, a system of interdependent statuses and structures, and a social institution organized to meet certain essential societal goals. The smallest family units, the nuclear and conjugal families, consist of persons related by blood, marriage, or adoption who share a common residence. Sociologists also distinguish families of orientation, families of procreation, extended families, and modified-extended families.

Families throughout the world vary in many different ways. First, they may vary in number of spouses. A person may have one spouse (monogamy) or two or more (polygamy). In group marriages, there are several people of each sex. Sequential monogamy involves having several wives or husbands in succession but just one at any given time. Polygyny, in which one man is married to more than one woman, is the most common form of polygamy; polyandry, in which one woman has several husbands, is very rare.

Second, families vary in their norms of residence. Most cultures adhere to one of three patterns: neolocal, in which the couple is free to choose its own place of residence; patrilocal, in which the couple lives in the groom's community; and matrilocal, in which the couple lives in the bride's community. Worldwide, the patrilocal pattern is the most common.

Third, families have different norms of descent and inheritance. The patrilineal pattern, in which lineage is traced through the father's kin, is the most common, but there are also matrilineal and bilateral patterns.

Fourth, there are variations in the norms of authority and decision making. Sociologists recognize systems of three types: patriarchal, matriarchal, and egalitarian. The patriarchal pattern of male dominance, power, and authority is the most widespread.

Fifth, norms vary with regard to the marriage partner considered appropriate. Endogamous rules state that a marriage partner should be from a similar group. Exogamous rules state that marriage partners should be from a different group. Incest and same-sex marriages are almost universally forbidden, whereas marriage to a person of the same race, religion, and socioeconomic status is widely encouraged.

Several theoretical perspectives are widely used to explain family structures, interaction patterns, and behaviors. Functionalists examine variations in family structures such as those just described in terms of the functions they perform. According to this perspective, the family has many major functions: socialization, affection and emotional support, sexual regulation, reproduction, and social placement. Socialization, especially of young infants, is one of the few universal family functions. Affection and emotional support from families are important not just for infants and children but for adults as well. In its capacity as a sexual regulator the family defines socially approved and disapproved sexual outlets while its reproductive function assures that children will be born and raised in a context in which their needs will be met. Finally, the social placement function helps family members make the transition from the family to the wider society.

According to the conflict perspective, family members continually struggle for power and control. Conflict, which stems from the unequal distribution of scarce resources, is a major force behind social change. The exchange perspective assumes that there are rewards and costs in all relationships, including those in marriage and the family. This view suggests that when selecting a spouse, people try to get the best they can with what they have to offer. The complementary needs theory proposes that people seek mates who will meet their needs without causing conflicts. The interactionist perspective emphasizes the influence of role expectations and how people define situations. In this view, marriage, like other relationships, is a dynamic process of reciprocal interactions.

The American family system emphasizes norms of monogamy, neolocal residence, modified-extended kinship, bilateral descent and inheritance, egalitarian decision making, endogamous marriage, and relatively free choice of mate. In a number of respects, however, the American family is quite variable. Rates of marriage vary widely in terms of time period, geographical location, economic conditions, and other factors. The number of marriages also vary by season and day of the week. The age at marriage in the United States, which declined from the turn of the century until the mid-1950s, has since increased, and teenage marriages are unlikely to last. Norms concerning family size and parent-child relations are influenced by such variables as socioeconomic status, religion, education, urbanization, and female participation in the labor force. Although most married couples have or want to have children, younger women today generally plan to have small families compared with earlier generations. The United States has one of the highest divorce rates in the world. Like birth rates, rates of divorce vary with time period, geographical location, and socioeconomic level, and differing techniques of computing the divorce rate yield different figures about the rate of divorce. Variations in these rates illustrate how social and cultural factors influence the chances of marital dissolution.

Several trends in marital and family lifestyles are emerging in this country. The number of unmarried couples of all ages who live together is increasing dramatically. Childless marriages are increasingly common, in part because of the availability and reliability of contraceptives and abortion. Marriages in which both spouses work have been common for a long time, but the dual-career marriage is a relatively recent development. There are many strains in these marriages, but women who have careers report fewer life pressures and

worries and more happiness in their marriages. The men involved in two-career marriages tend to be relatively discontent, however.

Key Terms

conjugal families
endogamy
exogamy
extended family
family
family of orientation
family of procreation
incest
kinship
matriarchal
matrilineal
matrilocal
modified-extended family structure
monogamy
neolocal
no-fault divorce
nonmarital heterosexual cohabitation
nuclear families
nurturant socialization
patriarchal
patrilineal
patrilocal
polygamy
polyandry
polygyny
principle of legitimacy

Suggested Readings

Albin, Mel and Dominick Cavallo. **Family Life in America, 1620–2000.** *St. James, N.Y.: Revisionary Press, 1981.* A look at the history of the family in America.

Bane, Mary Jo. **Here to Stay: American Families in the Twentieth Century.** *New York: Basic*

Books, 1976. A look at Americans' deep commitment to the family, with a discussion of how disruptive social policies contribute to family conflicts.

Burr, Wesley R., Reuben Hill, Ivan F. Nye, and Ira L. Reiss. **Contemporary Theories About the Family, vols. I and II.** *New York: The Free Press, 1979.* A two-volume work that attempts to systematically develop interrelated propositions on a wide variety of family topics. Volume II has chapters dealing with exchange theory, symbolic interaction theory, general systems theory, conflict theory, and phenomenological approaches to the family.

Eshleman, J. Ross, **The Family: An Introduction.** *Boston: Allyn & Bacon, 1981.* A sociological examination of families in the United States and around the world, this book discusses changes in the family, structural and subcultural variations, patterns of interaction throughout the life cycle, marital crises, and divorce.

Levitan, Sar A. and Richard S. Belous. **What's Happening to the American Family?** *Baltimore: Johns Hopkins University Press, 1981.* An examination of the changing American family, including four chapters on government policies that influence the family.

Mindle, Charles H. and Robert W. Habenstein. **Ethnic Families in America: Patterns and Variations, 2nd ed.** *New York: Elsevier, 1981.* An excellent overview of the family lifestyles of sixteen ethnic minorities in America.

Rubin, Lillian Breslow. **Worlds of Pain: Life in the Working-Class Family.** *New York: Basic Books, 1976.* A subjective analysis of fifty working-class families and a comparison group of twenty-five professional middle-class families.

Straus, Murray A., Richard J. Gelles, and Suzanne K. Steinmetz. **Behind Closed Doors: Violence in the American Family.** *New York: Anchor Books, 1980.* A report on the extent and meaning of violence in 2,143 families in the United States.

Willie, Charles V. **A New Look at Black Families, 2nd ed.** *Bayside, N.Y.: General Hall, 1981.* The stories of eighteen black families, combining a descriptive analysis and a theoretical explanation of behavior patterns.

Chapter 13
Religious Groups and Systems

Religion is a candle inside a multicolored lantern.
Everyone looks through a particular color, but the
candle is always there.

— Mohammed Naguib

Young American students of college age have a
bewildering array of belief systems and religious
groups to choose from. James takes a class in Tai
Chi offered by the local Tai Chi club. His roommate, Sara, takes yoga classes at the local branch
of the Sikhs. A friend of theirs seldom makes a
decision without consulting the I Ching. Another
can never attend Friday night ball games because
that is when her prayer group meets. James and
Sara themselves decided in high school to join a
commune rather than attend college. The members of the commune rise at 3 A.M. every morning
and meditate for two hours before going to work
in the vegetarian restaurant they run.

Throughout the world, people meditate,
pray, join communes, worry about "being saved,"
partake in rituals, bow to statues, burn incense,
chant, offer sacrifices, torture themselves, and pro-
claim their allegiance to many gods or to a particular god. Anthropologists suggest that events,
acts, or beliefs such as these are part of every society, both today and throughout history. Together, these behaviors comprise the religious
system of a society.

Religion has always been the anchor of identity for human beings. Religious beliefs give
meaning to life, and the experiences associated
with them provide personal gratification as well as
a release from the frustrations and anxieties of
daily life. Ceremonies, formal acts, or rituals are
essential for both personal identity and social cohesion. We have ceremonies to rejoice about the
birth of an infant, to initiate a young person into
adult society, to celebrate a new marriage, to bury
the dead, and to fortify our belief that life goes
on. Most of these ceremonies are linked to
religion.

It may make you uneasy to examine these events and rituals objectively, but the goal of sociological investigations of religion is not to criticize anyone's faith or compare the validity of different religions. Sociologists are interested, rather, in studying how religion is organized and how it affects the members of a given society. They study how people organize in groups around religious beliefs and how these belief systems affect their behavior in other areas such as family life and economic achievement. Sociologists also examine the kinds of belief systems developed by people in different circumstances and how religious beliefs change over time as external circumstances change.

A Sociological Approach to Religion

What Is Religion?

One of the earliest writers on the sociology of religion was the French sociologist, Emile Durkheim. In *The Elementary Forms of the Religious Life* (1926) Durkheim defined religion as "a unified system of beliefs and practices relative to sacred things, that is to say, things set apart and forbidden — beliefs and practices which unite into one single moral community called a Church, all those who adhere to them" (p. 47).

In this definition, Durkheim identified several elements that he believed to be common to all religions. The first element, a system of beliefs and practices, he saw as the cultural component of religion. The beliefs are states of opinion and the practices, which Durkheim termed rites, are determined modes of action. These beliefs and practices exist within a social context, consistent with the values and norms of the culture.

The second element, a community or church, he saw as the social organizational component. He claimed that in all history, we do not find a single religion without a church. Sometimes the church is strictly national, sometimes directed by a corps of priests, and sometimes devoid of any official directing body, but always with a definite group at its foundation. Even the so-called private cults satisfy this condition, for they are always celebrated by a group, the family, or a corporation. What the community or church does is translate the beliefs and practices into something shared or common, which led Durkheim to think of these first two elements as inseparable — the cultural and social components of religion are linked. Contemporary sociologists of religion do recognize a functional difference between the two, in that a person may accept a set of religious beliefs without being affiliated with a particular church.

The third element, sacred things, he saw as understood only in relation to something intrinsic to it, namely, the profane. The profane is viewed as unspiritual and treated with irreverence. As profanity may refer to an irreverent use of a sacred name, so does the profane show an unconcern with the sacred. The profane is the realm of the everyday world: food, clothes, work, play, or anything generally considered mundane and unspiritual. In contrast, the sacred consists of spirits, mythological personalities, or special objects, all of which are treated with reverence and awe. An altar, bible, prayer, or rosary is sacred. A hamburger, rock song, football, or sociology text is profane, although these too can become sacred.

Durkheim believed that anything can be sacred. Sacredness is not a property that is inherent in an object. It exists in the mind of the beholder. Thus a tree, a spring, a pebble, a piece of wood, or a house may be considered sacred. In Durkheim's view, the world is divided into two distinct categories: (1) the sacred, supernatural, divine, and spiritual, and (2) the profane, natural, human, and material. Since the idea of sacredness exists in the beholder's mind, however, sacred qualities may be attributed to profane elements.

Durkheim hypothesized that religion developed out of group experiences as primitive tribes came to believe that feelings about sacredness were derived from some supernatural power. As people perform certain rituals, they develop feelings of awe, which reinforce the moral norms of society. When they no longer feel in awe of moral norms, society is in a state of anomie or normlessness. Informal social control is possible largely because people have strong feelings that they should or should not do certain things. When they no longer have such feelings, social control breaks down. We see an example of this in some of our cities, where church doors are locked to prevent robberies. In many societies, nobody steals from churches because they believe they will be punished or suffer some form of retribution.

Other sociologists present somewhat different views of religion, but most would agree that religions have the following elements:

1. *Things considered sacred* such as gods, spirits, special persons, or any object or thought defined as sacred.

2. *A group or community of believers* who make religion a social experience as well as a personal experience or belief, since members of a religion share goals, norms, and beliefs.

Religious practices and beliefs take many forms. Here, members of a cargo cult in the South Pacific worship a cross in the belief that this will bring a return of the ancestors and give members access to the material goods of Western civilization. Cargo cults are so named because their adherents believe that European goods or cargo are made by their ancestors, but intercepted by Europeans for their own selfish purposes. In the future the Europeans will be destroyed, the ancestors will return, and the cargo will arrive. To prepare for this cargo, some cults build docks, runways, and warehouses.

3. *A set of rituals, ceremonies, or behaviors* that take on religious meaning when they express a relationship to the sacred. In Christian ceremonies, for example, wine is considered a sacred symbol of the blood of Christ.

4. *A set of beliefs* such as a creed, doctrine, or holy book. These beliefs define what is to be emphasized, how people should relate to society, or what life after death is like.

5. *A form of organization* that reinforces the sacred, unites the community of believers, carries out the rituals, teaches the creeds and doctrines, recruits new members, and so on.

The Organization of Religion

People have tried to understand the world around them throughout history, and yet we do not know exactly how or why they began to believe in supernatural beings or powers. Societies such as the Tasaday of the Philippines or the Bushmen of Africa, who rely on hunting and gathering as their primary means of subsistence, often explain things in naturalistic terms, which is a type of religion known as *animism*. Central to animism is the belief that spirits inhabit virtually everything in nature: rocks, trees, lakes, animals, and humans alike. These spirits influence and control all aspects of life and destiny. Sometimes they help, perhaps causing an arrow to strike and kill the wild pig for food to eat. At other times, they are harmful, as when they make a child get sick and die. These spirits can sometimes be influenced by specific rituals or behaviors, however, and pleasing them results in favorable treatment.

In some tribal societies, certain persons, usually men, were believed to have special charm, skill, or knowledge in influencing spirits. These people, known as *shamans*, were called upon to heal the sick and wounded, to make hunting expeditions successful, to protect the group against evil spirits, and to generally ensure the group's well-being. Shamans received their power through ecstatic experiences, which might originate from a psychotic episode, the use of a hallucinogen, or deprivation such as fasting or lack of sleep. The American Indians of the northwestern United States held that ancestral spirits worked for the good or ill of the tribe solely through shamans. Belief in a tribal wizard, medicine man, or shaman is a type of religion known as *shamanism*.

A third form of religion among primitive peoples is *totemism*. Totemism is the worship of plants, animals, and other natural objects both as gods and ancestors. The totem itself is the belief that a plant or animal is ancestrally related to a person, tribe, or clan. Totems usually represent something important to the community such as a food source or dangerous predator, and the people often wear costumes and perform dances to mimic the totem object. Most readers are probably familiar with the totem pole used by North American Indians, which is a tall post carved or painted with totemic symbols that is erected as a memorial to the dead. The symbols on the pole portray a particular plant, animal, or other object as both an ancestor and a god. This form of religion is still practiced today by some New Guinea tribes and by Australian aborigines. Durkheim believed that totemism was one of the earliest forms of religion and that other forms of religious organization evolved from it.

Religions may be organized in terms of the number of gods their adherents worship. *Polytheism* is the belief in and worship of more than one god. Hinduism, which is practiced mainly in India, has a special god for each village and caste. People believe that these gods have special powers or control a significant life event such as harvest or childbirth. *Monotheism*, on the other hand, is the belief in only one god. Monotheism is familiar to most Americans because the three major religious groups in this country, Protestants, Catholics, and Jews, all believe in one god.

Most Westerners are less familiar with such major religions as Buddhism, Confucianism, Shintoism, and Taoism. These religions are neither monotheistic nor polytheistic, because they do not involve a god figure. They are based, rather, on sets of moral, ethical, or philosophical principles. Most are dedicated to achieving some form of moral or spiritual excellence. Some groups, such as the Confucianists, have no priesthood. Shintoism and Confucianism both place heavy emphasis on honoring one's ancestors, particularly one's parents, who gave the greatest of all gifts, life itself.

Churches, Sects, and Cults

Religious systems differ in many ways and sociologists have devised numerous ways for classifying them. We have already seen how Durkheim divided the world into the sacred and the profane. We have noted how the religious practices of hunting and tribal societies were described in terms of animism, shamanism, and totemism. But can Christianity be understood in terms of the profane or of shamanism? Most contemporary religious scholars would think not. Thus another scheme of classification used is that of *churches, sects,* and *cults.* This scheme focuses directly on the relationship between the type of religious organization and the world surrounding it.

Max Weber (1905) was one of the first sociologists to clarify the interrelationships between people's beliefs and their surroundings. In his classic essay, *The Protestant Ethic and the Spirit of Capitalism,* he argued that capitalism would not have been possible without Protestantism because Protestantism stressed the importance of work as an end in itself, personal frugality, and worldly success as a means of earning salvation and as evidence of God's favor. In dealing with this relationship between religion and the economy, he identified two major types of religious leaders.

One, the *priest,* owes authority to the power of the office. By contrast, the *prophet* holds authority on the basis of charismatic qualities. These qualities include exceptional abilities, superhuman gifts, and divine characteristics granted to individuals for the benefit of others. The priestly and prophetic leaders are often in conflict, for the priest defends and represents the institution or society in question and supports the status quo. The prophet, not bound to a given institution, is more likely to criticize both the institutions and the general society.

This contrast led Weber to suggest that different sectors of society would develop and need different types of organizations to accompany different types of belief systems. The ruling class or leaders, the better educated, and the more wealthy would need a more formalized type of religion that accepts modern science and the existing social world. The laboring class or followers, the less educated, and the poor would need a type of religion that emphasizes another world or life and an emotional, spontaneous experience to console them for the deprivation in this life. Weber drew a distinction between two types of religious institutions: the church and the sect.

A German theologian and student of Weber, Ernst Troeltsch (1931), continued this line of thinking. Troeltsch divided religions into three categories: mysticism, churches, and sects. Mysticism is a belief that spiritual or divine truths come through intuition and meditation apart from the use of reason or the ordinary range of human experience and senses. *Mystics,* persons who believe in mysticism, are outside organized religion. They often pose problems for churches and sects because they purport to be in direct contact with divine power — occult power, power that is mysterious, secret, and hidden from human understanding.

The church and the sect, as Weber argued, are differentiated by their relationships with the world around them. A church is an institutionalized organization of people who share common religious beliefs. The membership of churches is fairly stable, most of them have formal bureaucratic structures with trained clergy and other officials, and they are closely linked to the larger society and seek to work within it. The majority of the religious organizations in the United States shown in Table 13-1 would be considered churches. As you can see, the Roman Catholic church is the largest religious group in the United States with 49.8 million members, but approximately two-thirds of church members in this country are Protestants. Protestants belong to such churches as the National and Southern Baptist conventions, the Assemblies of God, the United Methodist church, and the Lutheran church, to mention just a few. The Church of Jesus Christ of Latter-Day Saints (Mormons) with 2.71 million members, the Greek Orthodox church with 1.95 million members, and the Jewish congregations with 5.86 million members are the largest non-Protestant churches.

Two categories of churches that are sometimes differentiated are the ecclesia and the denomination. An *ecclesia* is an official state religion

Different religious organizations evolve to accommodate different belief systems. The Russian Orthodox Church has a highly formal bureaucracy and elaborate ceremonies. The Baptist Church is more informal. The church building may be a converted home, and the service may include much singing and congregational participation.

that includes all or most of the members of the society. As a state church, it accepts state support and sanctions the basic cultural values and norms of the society. Sometimes it administers the educational system as well. The Church of England in Great Britain and the Lutheran churches in the Scandinavian countries are two contemporary examples of national churches. The power of these churches, however, is not as great as the power of the Roman Catholic church in Western Europe in the Middle Ages and today in Spain, Italy, and many Latin American countries.

Churches in the United States are termed *denominations* rather than ecclesia because they are not officially linked to state or national governments. In fact, various denominations may be at odds with state positions on war, abortion, taxes, pornography, alcohol, equal rights, and other issues, and no nation has more denominations than the United States. Table 13-1 lists approximately eighty churches (denominations) with memberships of 50,000 or more, but the list would be considerably longer if all of the small or independent denominations were added.

Whereas churches (ecclesia and denominations) are well established and highly institutionalized, sects are small groups that have broken away from a parent church and call for a return to the old ways. They follow rigid doctrines and emphasize fundamentalist teachings. Fundamentalism is the belief that the Bible is the divine word of God and all statements within it are to be taken literally. The creation controversy, for example, stems from the fundamentalist position that the world was literally created in six days. Sect groups follow this type of literal interpretation of the Bible, although different groups focus their attention on different scriptures. Their religious services often involve extensive member participation with an emphasis on emotional expression. The clergy of sects, who frequently preach part time, often have little or no professional training or seminary degrees. Members of sects tend to emphasize "other-worldly" rewards and are more likely to be of lower occupational and educational status than members of churches. They are often dissatisfied with their position in life and believe the world is evil and sinful. As a result, their degree of commitment to the sect is often far greater than the commitment found among church members. Unwilling to compromise their beliefs, they are often in conflict with the government, the schools, and other social institutions. Although most sects are short-lived, some acquire a stable membership and a formal organizational structure and gradually become denominations. There are many sects in the United States today, including the Jehovah's Witnesses, Jews for Jesus, and a number of fundamentalist, evangelical, and Pentecostal groups. While evangelical groups, like fundamentalist groups, maintain that the Bible is the only rule of faith, they focus their attention on preaching that salvation comes through faith as described in the four New Testament Gospels: Matthew, Mark, Luke, and John. Pentecostal groups, though usually both evangelical and fundamentalist, are Christian sects with a highly emotional form of worship experience.

The final form of religious organization is the cult, the most loosely organized and most temporary of all religious groups. Unlike sects, cults call for a totally new and unique lifestyle. Often the new way is revealed in the form of a revelation to a new prophet. Jim Jones and Father Divine, for example, believed that they were divinely chosen to lead humanity as does the Reverend Sun Myung Moon today. In cults, the emphasis is on the individual rather than society. Because cults operate outside the mainstream of society and are focused around one leader or prophet, their existence depends on the life and health of their leader. In some cases, they have given up their more radical teachings and, accepting more mainstream beliefs, have become churches. The Seventh-Day Adventists, for example, began as a cult group that proclaimed the end of the world

Table 13-1
Religious bodies in the United States — selected data

RELIGIOUS BODY	YEAR	CHURCHES REPORTED	MEMBERSHIP (1,000)
Total	(x)	331,065	133,469
Bodies with membership of 50,000 or more	(x)	317,273	131,879
Current data	(x)	253,989	115,575
Noncurrent data	(x)	63,284	16,304
African Methodist Episcopal Church	1979	3,050	1,970
American Baptist Association	1980	5,000	1,500
American Baptist Churches in the U.S.A.	1978	5,897	1,272
American Carpatho-Russian Orthodox Greek Catholic Church	1976	70	100
American Lutheran Church, The	1979	4,849	2,363
Antiochian Orthodox Christian Archdiocese of North America, The	1977	110	152
Apostolic Overcoming Holy Church of God	1956	300	75
Armenian Church of America, Diocese of the (incl. Diocese of California)	1979	66	450
Assemblies of God	1979	9,562	1,629
Baptist General Conference	1979	701	127
Baptist Missionary Association of America	1979	1,439	226
Buddhist Churches of America	1975	60	60
Bulgarian Eastern Orthodox Church (Diocese of N. and S. America and Australia)	1971	13	86
Christian and Missionary Alliance	1979	1,319	174
Christian Church (Disciples of Christ)	1979	4,324	1,231
Christian Churches and Churches of Christ	1979	5,535	1,054
Christian Methodist Episcopal Church	1965	2,598	467
Christian Reformed Church in North America	1979	632	213
Church of God, The	1978	2,035	76
Church of God (Anderson, Ind.)	1979	2,259	175
Church of God (Cleveland, Tenn.)	1979	5,018	411
Church of God in Christ, The	1965	4,500	425
Church of God in Christ, International, The	1971	1,041	501
Church of God of Prophecy, The	1979	1,930	228
Church of Jesus Christ of Latter-day Saints, The	1979	6,738	2,706
Church of the Nazarene	1979	4,831	475
Churches of Christ	1979	12,700	1,600
Community Churches, National Council of	1979	185	190
Congregational Christian Churches, National Association of	1980	393	100
Conservative Baptist Association of America	1979	1,125	225
Coptic Orthodox Church	1980	25	100
Cumberland Presbyterian Church	1979	854	95
Episcopal Church, The	1979	7,022	2,841
Evangelical Convenant Church of America	1979	529	76
Evangelical Free Church of America	1979	732	78
Evangelical Lutheran Churches, The Association of	1979	283	114
Free Methodist Church of North America	1979	1,013	67
Free Will Baptists	1979	2,437	231

RELIGIOUS BODY	YEAR	CHURCHES REPORTED	MEMBERSHIP (1,000)
Friends United Meeting	1979	530	61
Full Gospel Fellowship of Churches and Ministers, International	1980	394	59
General Association of Regular Baptist Churches	1980	1,577	244
General Baptist (General Association of)	1979	866	73
Greek Orthodox Archdiocese of North and South America	1977	535	1,950
Independent Fundamental Churches of America	1980	1,019	120
International Church of the Foursquare Gospel	1963	714	89
Jehovah's Witnesses	1979	7,545	527
Jews	1979	3,500	5,861
Lutheran Church in America	1979	5,788	2,921
Mennonite Church	1979	1,107	98
Moravian Church in America (Unitas Fratrum)	1979	148	54
National Baptist Convention of America	1956	11,398	2,689
National Baptist Convention, U.S.A., Inc.	1958	26,000	5,500
National Primitive Baptist Convention, Inc.	1975	606	250
North American Old Roman Catholic Church	1979	121	69
Old Order Amish Church	1979	535	80
Open Bible Standard Churches, Inc.	1980	283	60
Orthodox Church in America	1978	440	1,000
Pentecostal Holiness Church	1977	2,340	86
Plymouth Brethren	1980	850	79
Polish National Catholic Church of America	1960	162	282
Presbyterian Church in the U.S.	1979	4,067	853
Primitive Baptists	1960	1,000	72
Progressive National Baptist Convention, Inc.	1967	655	522
Reformed Church in America	1979	904	348
Reorganized Church of Jesus Christ of Latter-day Saints	1979	1,045	189
Roman Catholic Church, The	1979	24,161	49,812
Russian Orthodox Church Outside Russia, The	1955	81	55
Salvation Army, The	1979	1,067	415
Serbian Eastern Orthodox Church of the U.S.A. and Canada	1967	52	65
Seventh-day Adventists	1979	3,672	553
Southern Baptist Convention	1979	35,552	13,373
Triumph the Church and Kingdom of God in Christ (International)	1972	475	54
Ukrainian Orthodox Church in the U.S.A.	1966	107	88
Unitarian Universalist Association	1979	988	139
United Church of Christ	1979	6,467	1,746
United Free Will Baptist Church	1952	836	100
United Methodist Church, The	1979	38,576	9,654
United Pentecostal Church, International	1980	2,829	465
United Presbyterian Church in the U.S.A., The	1979	8,633	2,477
Wesleyan Church, The	1979	1,717	101
Wisconsin Evangelical Lutheran Synod	1979	1,128	405
Bodies with membership of less than 50,000	(x)	13,792	1,590

NA Not available   (x) Not applicable.
SOURCE: U.S. Bureau of the Census, Statistical Abstract of the United States: 1981, (102nd ed.), Washington, D.C., 1981, No. 79, pp. 52–53.

When Prophecy Fails: Cult Behavior

During the week before Christmas, 1954, in a midwestern college town, a small band of students were waiting for a flying saucer to pick them up and take them to the planet Clarion, on the other side of the moon, where they would be safe from an anticipated cataclysm on earth.

Originating as a study group of students interested in flying saucers, the cult met every Sunday evening under the leadership of a physician, Dr. Armstrong, who was employed by the university health service. After six months of meeting, the belief system developed by this group became increasingly exotic, borrowing heavily from the belief system of the so-called "flying saucer cult." These people believe that flying saucers or UFOs from outer space visit earth and that some humans have gone for rides in a flying saucer.

Early in the fall of 1954, Dr. Armstrong met a woman named Mrs. Keech at a convention on flying saucers. Mrs. Keech was a medium who believed she could conduct power from a higher plane. During that fall, the Armstrongs visited Mrs. Keech in her home in Chicago, and she visited the Armstrongs in Collegeville. Messages written by Mrs. Keech were studied at the Sunday evening prayer meetings. One message said that Jesus had lived on earth in many incarnations, and that one of his names was Sananda. The study group believed that Sananda had visited them one Sunday afternoon in the form of a humming bird hovering near the patio of the Armstrongs' house. By this time, the more skeptical members had stopped attending the study group, and only the most devout believers remained.

In October, Mrs. Keech began receiving messages about an impending cataclysm. It was predicted that Atlantis would rise from the floor of the Atlantic, and Mu from the Pacific, thereby flooding the continent of North America. She also wrote that the faithful would be transported by flying saucer to Clarion for leadership training. The night before the cataclysm, this "mother ship" would hover over the earth while

on a specific date, but when that date passed, it maintained many of its other beliefs. Today, it is a church with trained clergy, a stable membership, and a formal organizational structure.

Theories of Religion

A Functionalist Approach

The university of religion suggests to the functionalist that religion is a requirement of group life and that it serves both manifest and latent functions. Durkheim's (1915) classic study of religion, *The Elementary Forms of the Religious Life,* posed two basic questions: What is religion? and What are the functions of religion for human society? In answering the first question, he noted that religion is a unified system of beliefs and practices relative to sacred things. He answered the second question by focusing on religion's social function of promoting solidarity within a society.

Unlike most people today, who view religion as primarily a private and personal experience, Durkheim believed that the primary function of religion was to *preserve and solidify society.* Noting that worship, God, and society are inseparable, he paid little attention to the other functions of religion.

little "peapod saucers" would pick up the believers. After the flooding and physical devastation had subsided following the cataclysm, the faithful would be returned to earth to repopulate it.

On the night of the expected cataclysm, Dr. and Mrs. Armstrong and their older daughter drove to Chicago with several student group members to join Mrs. Keech and her group there. The peapod saucer was due to arrive at midnight. Midnight came and went, but no peapod saucer arrived. The group waited as minute after minute, then hour after hour passed. At long last, at 4 A.M., Mrs. Keech received a message. The cataclysm had been averted. God, in his infinite mercy, had spared the earth because the group had met and prayed.

As a consequence of the nationwide publicity about the end of the world, Dr. Armstrong was

asked to resign his job with the university. He moved to Arizona, followed by some members of the faithful. Three years later they emigrated to Peru, where they proposed to found a model farm.

The cult that formed around Mrs. Keech and her beliefs was studied by some social psychologists who joined the group as participant observers. The social psychologists were testing the hypothesis that cults and sects grow as a consequence of failed prophecy. Many cults and sects are built around a belief system which includes a prophecy that the world is coming to an end; such groups are called messianic or millenarian movements. The researchers wondered what happens to these groups when the prophecied end of the world never comes.

Research into cults shows that the prophet develops a rationalization about why the world

did not end. Sometimes he or she changes the date. Eventually, the group develops a new belief system. To reinforce their belief in this new system, cult members become evangelical and go forth to convert others to the new belief: if others can be persuaded to believe, the belief must have some truth in it.

Another example of this phenomenon is the Unification Church of Rev. Sun Myung Moon. This group was studied in the early 1960s when it contained forty-five members who believed that the world would end in 1969. After this prophecy failed, and perhaps because it failed, the group grew by the thousands.

SOURCE: Festinger, Leon, Stanley Schachter, and Henry W. Reicken, *When Prophecy Fails: A Social and Psychological Study of a Modern Group that Predicted the Destruction of the World*, New York, Harper, 1956.

This perspective assumes that religion is the central focus for integrating the social system. By developing the awe that members of society feel for moral norms, religion functions to hold society together. This social solidarity is developed through rituals such as church or synagogue services, baptisms, bar mitzvahs, Christmas caroling and gift giving, and the multitude of observances and ceremonies practiced by specific religious groups.

Another function, one related to promoting social solidarity, is that of creating a *community of believers*. A religion provides a system of beliefs around which people may gather to belong to something greater than themselves in order to

have their personal beliefs reinforced by the group and its rituals. Those who share a common ideology develop a collective identity and a sense of fellowship.

A third function is *social control*. Religion reinforces social norms, providing sanctions for violations of norms and reinforcing basic values such as property rights and respect for others. Society's existence depends on its members' willingness to abide by the folkways and mores and to interact with one another in a spirit of cooperation and trust.

Religion also serves the function of *providing answers to ultimate questions*. Why are we here? Is there a Supreme Being? What happens after death? Religions provide systems of belief based on the faith that life has a purpose, that someone or something is in control of the universe. They make the world seem comprehensible, often by attributing familiar, human motives to supernatural forces.

According to Weber (in Fischoff, 1963), one of the questions that religions must address is *theodicy*: Why does God allow evil to exist? In attempting to answer this question, theologians develop complex systems to explain the meaning of life, which among other things deal with values — what is good and what is evil? These values provide the basis for ethical systems, rules of behavior by which people may find favor in the sight of God. Buddhism and some other religions involve no belief in a supernatural power because they have developed into an ethical system altogether.

Religion also provides us with *rites of passage*, ceremonies and rituals designed to give sacred meaning and a social significance to birth, the attainment of adulthood, marriage, death, and other momentous events.

Religion helps *reconcile people to hardship*. All societies have inequality, poverty, and oppression, and everyone experiences pain, crisis, prejudice, and sorrow. By belonging to a religion, people may come to feel that they are special in some way, that they will be rewarded in the future. Many religions call for caring, mercy, charity, kindness, and other prosocial behaviors. They may provide moral, ethical, social, and even financial support to those in need.

Religion can *cultivate social change*. Many religious groups criticize social injustice, existing social morality, and community or government actions. Some take action to change unfavorable conditions. The churches have been a major force in the civil rights movement, for example. Many protests against the Vietnam war were a result of

Religion performs many functions. Some religious groups advocate social justice and specific government action. During the Vietnam War, for example, Quakers demonstrated in front of the White House for peace in Vietnam. The Quakers (Friends), the Church of the Brethren, and the Mennonites are three of the historic peace churches in the United States.

religious teachings about love and peace. Other major protests have been mounted by religious groups against the right to have an abortion, equal rights for homosexuals, and the women's rights movement.

This list of manifest functions performed by religion could be continued. Some latent functions of religion concern mate selection, experience in public speaking, and psychic reward for donating funds or labor to worthy causes. While other groups and systems may be able to fulfill some of these manifest or latent functions, many social scientists argue that the functions provided by religion cannot be adequately met by other means.

A functionalist approach to religion reminds us that while it performs many basic functions for society and individuals, it is likely to have dysfunctions as well. If it serves to preserve and solidify society, to create a community of believers, to reinforce social norms, and reconcile people to hardship, it also can serve to divide society, denounce the nonbeliever, create guilt in the nonconformist, exclude nongroup members, and maintain the status quo. Religion can be dysfunctional in forcing people to accept inequities and inhibiting its members from acting to change them. It can be dysfunctional in convincing its followers to reject this world for a future life in which rewards are guaranteed, and it can often inhibit the search for new truths, new ideas, and additional knowledge.

Examples of religion as both a source of integration and conflict are evident throughout the world. In Iran, the religious teachings of Islam formed the basis for the revolution against the Shah and the creation of a religious state that attacked nonbelievers within the country. In Northern Ireland, protests abound between Catholics and Protestants. In the Middle East, the conflicts between Jews and Moslems are intense. In India and Pakistan, caste and class conflicts linked to religious traditions cause death and destruction. In many countries, Jews are persecuted. Overpopula-

tion and wars can be defended and justified in the name of religion. As seen in Chapter 11, to have in-groups is to have out-groups. To believe there is one Truth is to reject ideas that challenge all truth. Thus religion has both functional and dysfunctional aspects for societies and individuals within these societies.

A Conflict Approach

As discussed in previous chapters, the conflict approach suggests that inequality is a major source of alienation and social change. Marx felt that religion was a profound form of alienation, as indicated by the fact that people create gods and remain unaware that the gods are their own creation. He also believed that the dominant religion in a society is used by the ruling class to set standards for and oppress the lower classes. Sometimes religion is even summoned to lend supernatural support to this power elite, as is evident in the idea of the "divine right" of kings. According to this notion, kings have been granted the "right" to rule from a divine source and thus their rule cannot be challenged.

Conflict theorists also contend that church ideology is used to defend the belief of the dominant classes that God has given them stewardship over the land. In addition, Marxists feel that religious beliefs and practices are used to keep the lower classes in their place by distracting them from efforts to find immediate political solutions to their problems. Rather than fighting against the unequal distribution of wealth, religion creates the illusion that everything is in accordance with a divine plan. In the words of Karl Marx, religion "is the opium of the people." It drugs the poor into submission by offering them rewards in heaven for accepting their harsh lives on earth.

Because of the nature of their approach, conflict theorists have contributed little research to the sociology of religion. They say that religion serves only to distract people from efforts to obtain their just rewards on earth.

Religions of the World

It is difficult to obtain accurate counts of the number of adherents to the world's religions. The procedures used by different countries and groups to measure religious membership vary widely. Some assessments include only adults, others include everyone who attends services. Some people may be included in several different religious groups, such as Confucianism, Taoism, and Shintoism. Some religions forbid counts of their members. In countries where a certain religion has prevailed for many centuries (such as Christianity in Europe and Hinduism in India), the entire population may be reported as adherents.

Because of these and other variables, the figures in Table 13-2 are only rough estimates. According to the table, the world population is 4.288 billion and the total membership of all religious groups is 2.578 billion. Simple subtraction shows that 1.710 billion people are not included, either because they did not belong to one of the major religions or because they were not included in the tallying procedure.

Christianity and Judaism

There are approximately 1 billion Christians and more than 14 million Jews in the world today (see Table 13-2). *Christians* profess faith in the teachings of Jesus Christ, as found in the New Testament of the Bible, while adherents to *Judaism* find the source of their beliefs in the Hebrew Bible (called the Old Testament by Christians) especially in its first five books called the *Torah*. The Torah was traditionally regarded as the primary revelation of God, originally passed on orally and eventually written.

Judaism is the oldest religion in the Western world. It comprises both a religious and an ethnic community (see Chapter 9). It was the first religion to teach monotheism and was based on the Old Testament verse "Hear O Israel, the Lord our God, the Lord is one" (Deut. 6:4). Jews, the people

who identify with and practice Judaism, believe that God's providence extends into a special covenant with the ancient Israelites: to bring God's message to humanity by their example. As a result, stress is on conduct rather than on doctrinal correctness. Adherents to Judaism have a considerable measure of latitude in matters of belief since their beliefs have never been formulated in an official creed. This lack of an official creed meant, as well, that Judaism did not stop developing after the Bible was completed. One result of this development was the traditional Jewish prayer book that reflects the basic beliefs of Judaism as well as changes in emphasis in response to changing conditions.

Judaism has a system of law that regulates civil and criminal justice, family relationships, personal ethics and manners, and social responsibilities to the community as well as worship and other religious observances. Individual practices of these laws vary widely. Some widely observed ones include a strict adherence to Kosher foods, daily prayer and study, the laws concerning the marital relationship, and those dealing with the meaning of the Yarmulka (skull cap) and Tefillin (worn on the forehead and left arm during morning prayers).

The Jewish religious calendar, which is of Babylonian origin, consists of twelve lunar months amounting to approximately 354 days. Six times over a nineteen-year cycle a thirteenth month is added to adjust the calendar to the solar year. A day goes from sunset to sunset, thus the Sabbath is from sunset Friday to sunset Saturday.

Male children are circumcised on the eighth day after birth as a sign of the covenant with Abraham. At age thirteen, a *bar mitzvah* is given to Jewish boys to signify adult status and a responsibility for performing the commandments. A similar ceremony for girls, the *bat mitzvah*, is a more recent innovation.

Christianity diverged from Judaism in ancient Israel. Christians considered Jesus to be the Jewish

Table 13-2

Estimated membership of the principal religions of the world

RELIGIONS	NORTH AMERICA[a]	SOUTH AMERICA	EUROPE[b]	ASIA[c]	AFRICA	OCEANIA[d]	WORLD
Total Christian	235,109,500	177,266,000	342,630,400	95,987,240	129,717,000	18,063,500	998,773,640
Roman Catholic	132,489,000	165,640,000	176,087,300	55,077,000	47,224,500	4,395,500	580,913,300
Eastern Orthodox	4,763,000	517,000	57,035,600	2,428,000	14,306,000[e]	414,000	79,463,600
Protestant[f]	97,857,500	11,109,000	109,507,500	38,482,240	68,186,500[g]	13,254,000	338,396,740
Jewish	6,155,340	635,800	4,061,620	3,212,860	176,400	76,000	14,318,020
Muslim[h]	371,200	251,500	14,145,000	427,266,000	145,214,700	87,000	587,335,400
Zoroastrian	250	2,100	7,000	254,000	650	–	264,000
Shinto[i]	60,000	92,000	–	57,003,000	200	–	57,155,200
Taoist	16,000	10,000	–	31,261,000	–	–	31,287,000
Confucian	97,100	70,150	–	157,887,500	1,500	80,300	158,136,550
Buddhist[j]	171,250	192,300	192,000	254,241,000	14,000	30,000	254,840,550
Hindu[k]	88,500	849,300	350,000	473,073,000	1,079,800	499,000	475,939,600
Totals	242,069,140	179,369,150	361,386,020	1,500,185,600	276,204,250	18,835,800	2,578,049,960
Population[l]	365,314,000	242,560,000	749,373,000	2,460,380,000	447,905,000	23,035,000	4,288,567,000

[a] Includes Central America and the West Indies.

[b] Includes the U.S.S.R. and other countries with established Marxist ideology where religious adherence is difficult to estimate.

[c] Includes areas in which persons have traditionally enrolled in several religions, as well as China with an official Marxist establishment.

[d] Includes Australia and New Zealand as well as islands of the South Pacific.

[e] Includes Coptic Christians.

[f] Protestant statistics usually count "full members," that is adults, rather than all family members or baptized infants and are therefore not comparable with the statistics of ethnic religions or churches counting all constituents of all ages.

[g] Including many new sects and cults among African Christians.

[h] The chief base of Islam is still ethnic, although some missionary work is now carried on in Europe and America (viz. "Black Muslims"). In countries where Islam is established, minority religions are frequently persecuted and their statistics are hard to come by.

[i] A Japanese ethnic religion, Shinto has declined since the Japanese emperor gave up his claim to divinity (1947). Neither does it survive well outside the homeland.

[j] Buddhism has produced several modern renewal movements which have gained adherents in Europe and America and other areas not formerly ethnic-Buddhist. In Asia it has made rapid gains in recent years in some areas, and under persecution it has shown greater staying power than Taoism or Confucianism. It transplants better.

[k] Hinduism's strength in India has been enhanced by nationalism, a phenomenon also observable in Islam. Modern Hinduism has also developed renewal movements that have won converts in Europe and America.

[l] United Nations, Department of Economic and Social Affairs; data refer to midyear 1979.

SOURCE: Reprinted with permission from the *1980 Britannica Book of the Year*, copyright 1980. Encyclopaedia Britannica, Inc., Chicago, Ill. p. 605.

savior, or Messiah, and incorporated the Hebrew writings of Christ's followers into the canon of their faith, the Bible. After his death (and, as Christians believe, his resurrection) Christ's teachings spread to Rome and many other centers of the Roman Empire. When the Roman Empire split in 1054 A.D., so did the Christian church; it came to be called the Orthodox church in the East and the Roman Catholic church in the West. The Roman Catholic church was united under Popes until the sixteenth century. Today, of the estimated 1 billion Christians nearly sixty percent are Roman Catholic. Slightly more than one-third are Protestant and the rest are Eastern Orthodox.

Christians, like Jews, believe in one god (monotheism) but their God takes the form of a Holy Trinity: Father, Son, and Holy Spirit. Christians experience God as the Father, Jesus Christ as the son of God, and the Holy Spirit as the continuing presence of God. Most Christians worship on Sunday instead of Saturday, which is the Jewish Sabbath. They also practice baptism by water when they become adherents or give a public testimony of their acceptance of Christ. Christians also take the Eucharist, a sacred meal recalling the last supper that Jesus had with his disciples. The breaking of bread, symbolizing the body of Christ, and the drinking of wine, symbolizing the blood of Christ, are sacred acts (sacraments) to most Christians. Prayer and preaching are also important Christian functions.

Islam

There are more than half a billion Islamic adherents in the world. *Islam* means "surrender," "resignation," and "submission." A person who submits to the will of Allah, the one and only God, is called Muslim (sometimes spelled Moslem). This surrender involves a total commitment in faith, obedience, and trust to this one God. The insistence that no one but God be wor-

shipped has led many Muslims to object to the term "Muhammadanism," a designation widely used in the West but thought to suggest that Muhammad, a great prophet to the Muslim, is worshipped in a manner that parallels the worship of Christ by Christians.

It is sometimes assumed that Islam originated during the lifetime of Muhammad (570–630), specifically during the years in which he received the divine revelations recorded in the Muslim sacred book, the Koran. Many Muslims, however, believe that the prophet Muhammad simply restored the original religion of Abraham.

Islam encompasses a code of ethics, a distinctive culture, a system of laws, and guidelines and rules for other aspects of life. The Muslim place of worship is the mosque, and the chief gathering of the congregation takes place on Fridays. Muslims profess their faith by repeating that "there is no God but God, and Muhammad is the messenger of God." The Muslims also have a deep awareness of the importance of a fellowship of faith and a community of believers.

The Koran includes rules for ordering social relationships. It is especially explicit about matters pertaining to the family, marriage, divorce, and inheritance. The family is basically authoritarian, patriarchal, polygamous, patrilineal, and largely patrilocal. Women are clearly subordinate to men and receive only half the inheritance that male heirs receive. Muslim males may marry non-Muslim women, but except in countries where the holy law has been abolished, Muslim women may not marry outside their faith. A Muslim male may take up to four wives (polygyny) and traditionally can divorce a wife by simple pronouncement and repayment of the dowry. Children, especially sons, are perceived as desirable.

Although laws are changing in many Islamic countries and the education of women has increased dramatically, there are still fewer females than males who attend school and even less with

Muslim women are often identified by the chador *(veil). At approximately age nine, according to Islamic belief, women become adults and must wear this type of garb in public. Departing from past tradition, many women today do not cover the entire face or all the hair. Thus the chador no longer provides anonymity but nonetheless serves as modest and nonprovocative dress, as a source of status identification, and as religious-political symbolism.*

a higher education. Marriage and housekeeping are considered the proper occupations of women. It is not surprising, therefore, that Islam is finding it difficult to come to terms with the scientific ideas and the technology of the Western world.

Hinduism

The great majority of the 400 million Hindus in the world live in India and Pakistan. In India, approximately 85 percent of the population is Hindu. *Hinduism* has evolved over about 4,000 years and comprises an enormous variety of beliefs and practices. It hardly corresponds to most Western conceptions of religion since organization is minimal and there is no religious hierarchy.

Hinduism is so closely intertwined with other aspects of the society that it is difficult to describe it clearly, especially in the case of castes (described in Chapter 8). Hindus sometimes refer to the ideal way of life as fulfilling the duties of one's class and station, which means obeying the rules of the four great castes of India: the Brahmins, or priests; the Ksatriyas, warriors and rulers; the Vaisyas, merchants and farmers; and the Sudras, peasants and laborers. A fifth class, the Untouchables, includes those whose occupations require them to handle "unclean" objects.

These classes encompass males only. The position of women is ambiguous. In some respects they are treated as symbols of the divine, yet in other ways they are considered inferior beings. Traditionally, women have been expected to serve their husbands and to have no independent interests but this is rapidly changing.

Although caste is a powerful influence in Hindu religious behavior, one's village community and family are important as well. Every village has gods and goddesses who ward off epidemics and drought. Hindu belief holds that the universe is populated by a multitude of gods (polytheism) who behave much as humans do, and worship of these gods takes many forms. Some are thought to require sacrifices, others are worshipped at shrines or temples, and shrines devoted to several gods associated with a family deity are often erected in private homes.

To Hindus, the word "dharma" means the cosmos, or the social order. Hindus practice rituals that uphold the great cosmic order. They believe that, to be righteous, one must strive to behave in accordance with the way things are. In a sense, the Hindu sees life as ritual. The world is regarded as a great dance determined by one's Karma, or personal destiny, and the final goal of the believer is liberation from this cosmic dance. Hindus also believe in transmigration of souls. One is born again in another form, as either a higher or lower being, depending on whether the person was righteous or evil in the previous life. If one becomes righteous enough, one will cease to be reborn.

A fundamental principle of Hinduism is that our perceptions of the external world are limitations. When we think about one thing, we are cut off from the infinite number of things we are not thinking about but could be. If we think of nothing, we become in tune with the universe and freed of limitations. One means of doing this is through meditation.

The actual belief systems of India are extremely confusing to Westerners, because so many different tribal religions have been assimilated into Hinduism, but the basic nature of polytheism in general and Hinduism in particular permits new gods to be admitted.

Buddhism

Buddhism, another of the major religions of the world, has about 250 million adherents. It is impossible to precisely determine the Buddhist population because many people accept Buddhist beliefs and engage in Buddhist rites while practicing other religions such as Shintoism, Confucianism, Taoism, or Hinduism.

Buddhism is thought to have originated as a reaction against the Brahminic tradition of Hinduism in the fifth century B.C.

At this time, a prince named Siddhartha Gautama was born in northern India to a prosperous ruling family. As he grew older, he was distressed by the suffering he witnessed among the people. At the age of 29, he left his wife and family to go on a religious quest. One day, sitting under a giant fig tree, he passed through several stages of awareness and became the Buddha, the enlightened one. He decided to share his experience with others and became a wandering teacher, preaching his doctrine of the "Four Noble Truths": (1) this life is suffering and pain; (2) the source of suffering is desire and craving; (3) suffering can cease; and (4) the practice of an "eightfold path" can end suffering. The eightfold path consisted of right views, right intentions, right speech, right conduct, right livelihood, right effort, right mindfulness, and right concentration. It combined ethical and disciplinary practices, training in concentration and meditation, and the development of enlightened wisdom. This doctrine was Buddha's message until the age of eighty, when he passed into final *Nirvana,* a state of transcendence forever free from the cycle of suffering and rebirth.

After Buddha's death, legends of his great deeds and supernatural powers emerged. Stories were told of his heroism in past lives, and speculations arose about his true nature. Some groups viewed him as a historical figure while others placed him in a succession of several Buddhas of the past and a Buddha yet to come. Differing views eventually led to a diversity of Buddhist sects in different countries. Some remained householders who set up Buddha images and established many holy sites that became centers of pilgrimage. Others became monks, living in monastic communities and depending on the laity for food and material support. Many monks became beggars, and in several Southeast Asian countries, they still go on daily alms rounds. They spend their days in rituals, devotions, meditation, study, and preaching. Flowers, incense, and praise are offered to the image of the Buddha. These acts are thought to ensure that the monks will be reborn in one of the heavens or in a better place in life from which they may be able to attain the goal of enlightenment.

In every society where Buddhism is widespread, people combine Buddhist thought with a native religion, supporting the monks and paying for rituals in the temples. These societies are organized around other religions, however.

Today, Buddhism is divided into two major traditions, but its integration into many cultures has resulted in many different interpretations of the way to Buddhahood. Yet we can all achieve Nirvana by seeing with complete detachment, by seeing things as they really are without being attached to any theoretical concept or doctrine.

Confucianism

Confucianism, which has about 160 million adherents, is associated primarily with China, but it has influenced the civilizations of Korea, Japan, and Vietnam as well. Confucianism is the philosophical and religious system based on the teachings of Confucius. Confucius, born to a poor family in 551 B.C. in what is today Shantung

Buddhism is practiced throughout most of East and Southeast Asia. Many of the Buddhist clergy live in monastic communities. Others serve like pastors in Christian communities, offering prayers, counseling, and instruction, and maintaining close contact with the people.

Province in China, was orphaned at an early age. As a young man, he held several minor government positions, but he became best known as a teacher, philosopher, and scholar. Distressed by the misery and oppression that surrounded him, he dedicated his life to attempting to relieve the suffering of the people.

By talking with younger men about his ideas to reform government to serve the people rather than the rulers, Confucius attracted many disciples. He emphasized the total person, sincerity, ethics, and the right of individuals to make decisions for themselves. Although Confucius was not a religious leader in the usual sense of the word, he believed that there was a righteous force in the universe, and yet his philosophy was founded not on supernaturalism but on humanity. Virtue, he said, is to love people, and wisdom is to understand them.

The basic philosophy of Confucius is found in his many sayings. All people are brothers. Sincerity and reciprocity should be one's guiding principles. The truly virtuous person, desiring to be established personally, seeks to establish others; desiring success for self, strives to help others succeed. The superior person stands in awe of three things: the ordinances of Heaven, great persons, and the words of sages. The ideals of Confucius were motivated not by the desire for rewards or an afterlife but simply by the satisfaction of acting in accordance with the divine order.

Confucius had a pervasive influence on all aspects of Chinese life, so much so that every county in China built a temple to him. Everyone tried to live in accordance with the Confucian code of conduct. His values guided human relations at all levels — among individuals, communities, and nations. His thought guided one's conduct in work and in the family. Even today, the Chinese who profess to be Taoists, Buddhists, or Christians generally act in accordance with Confucian ideals.

One of the books in the classical literature of Confucius is the *Book of Change,* or the I Ching. This book is familiar to many Americans and is used to guide one's behavior and attitude toward the future.

Religion in the United States

The United States, which has no state church, has more than 200 denominations and is greatly influenced by a variety of religious groups and belief systems. In addition to churches and denominations, revivalists preach on TV and radio and religious leaders such as Billy Graham give spiritual advice. Bumper stickers tell us that "Jesus Saves" or to "Honk if you love Jesus."

Williams (1980) conceptualizes American religion as an interplay between two forces, the structured and the unstructured, the major religious communities and the informal groups that he calls "popular religions." These two trends developed, he says, in response to the demands of life in a new country. Faced with a diverse population, a new political system, and rapid technological change, Americans sometimes found organized religions too limited, and in response to the demands of a new nation, they developed new religious movements.

The Development of Religious Movements

Religion in American society has become increasingly rationalized and centralized. Some "liberal" religious groups have downplayed the supernatural aspects of Christianity and emphasized neoorthodoxy, which is a theological movement emphasizing the importance of ethical conduct and a remote, depersonalized God. Others worship a personal god and express their beliefs emotionally. Those who worship in this way seek signs of divine intervention in their daily lives.

Amish Must Pay Social Security Tax

Washington, Feb. 23 — The Supreme Court ruled unanimously today that members of the Old Order Amish Church who operate businesses must pay the Social Security and unemployment taxes required of all employers, despite their religious belief that paying the taxes is a sin.

The decision, written by Chief Justice Warren E. Burger, reversed a ruling by a federal district court in Pennsylvania. That court held that the Amish could not be forced to pay the taxes without violating their constitutional right to the free exercise of their religion.

The 80,000 members of the Old Order Amish Church believe they have a religious duty to provide for all members of the community from birth to death. They regard the acceptance of Social Security benefits, and the payment of taxes to support the Social Security system, as a sin.

Congress has exempted the Amish who are self-employed, a majority in a community that consists primarily of small farmers, from paying Social Security taxes. But it has not relieved Amish employers of the obligation to withhold Social Security taxes from their employees or to pay the employer share of Social Security and federal unemployment taxes.

Edwin D. Lee, an Amish farmer and carpenter who employed several workers in his carpentry shop, sued the federal government after he was assessed $27,000 for seven years of unpaid taxes. He argued that he was constitutionally entitled not to pay, and the trial court agreed. The government appealed directly to the Supreme Court.

Faith and Obligation

Writing for the court, Chief Justice Burger said that the "conclusion that there is a conflict between the Amish faith and the obligation imposed by the Social Security system is only the beginning and not the end of the inquiry."

He continued: "The state may justify a limitation on religious liberty by showing that it is essential to accomplish an overriding governmental interest," and concluded that a strong Social Security System was such an interest. "Mandatory participation is indispensable to the fiscal vitality" of the system, he said.

The Amish, he noted, were not required either to "enter into commercial activity" by becoming employers, or to accept Social Security benefits.

Chief Justice Burger wrote: "To maintain an organized society that guarantees religious freedom to a great variety of faiths requires that some religious practices yield to the common good."

The Amish were the subject of a Supreme Court decision 10 years ago that also required a balancing of public policy and religious belief. In that decision, *Wisconsin* v. *Yoder,* the court exempted the Amish from compulsory school-attendance laws.

While agreeing with the outcome of today's decision, *U.S.* v. *Lee,* No. 80-767, Associate Justice John Paul Stevens did not join in the court's opinion but wrote a concurring opinion of his own.

SOURCE: Linda Greenhouse, *The New York Times,* Feb. 24, 1982, p. 11. © 1982 by The New York Times Company. Reprinted by permission.

Another religious movement is the development of sect groups. The proliferation of these groups accompanied the breakdown of the feudal structure and the development of industrialization. One wave of groups known as the pietist sects rejected worldliness in favor of pacifism, communal living, and aspiration toward perfection. The Amish and the Hutterites are American groups descended from these sects.

One of the pietist sects was the Quakers who

came to Pennsylvania from England. Quakers believe in an "Inner Light," that people mystically partake of the nature of God. Thus they see no need for a religious structure interceding between God and human beings.

Another persistent theme in American religious life is *millennialism,* the belief that a dramatic transformation of the earth will occur and that Christ will rule the world for a thousand years of prosperity and happiness. One millennial movement took place among the Millerites in the 1830s. William Miller, the founder, was convinced that the Second Coming of Christ would happen in 1843. When it did not, he changed the date to 1844. Again nothing happened. Some of his followers, who believed that the Second Coming had occurred invisibly and spiritually, founded the Seventh-Day Adventists.

Other religious movements have been based on *divine revelation.* One American prophet who received a divine revelation was Joseph Smith, who founded the Church of Jesus Christ of Latter-Day Saints (Mormons) in 1830. His following was recruited from the rural people of upstate New York. About thirty years later, Mary Baker Eddy began a movement in the urban middle class that came to be known as the Christian Science movement. Mrs. Eddy's revelation was that illness could be controlled by the mind. This sect developed into a denomination when people of wealth and status became adherents.

Pentecostalism involves a practice similar to divine revelation. Pentecostal Christians hold highly emotional services that resemble revivals, and they "speak in tongues." Participants go into an ecstatic seizure during which they utter a rapid flow of meaningless syllables.

An offshoot of pentecostalism is *faith healing,* which experienced a rapid growth after World War II. In faith healing, the fundamentalist preacher asks members of the congregation who are sick or disabled to come forward. The preacher asks the disabled person and the rest of the congregation to call upon the power of the Lord to heal: "In the name of Jesus, Heal." If their faith in Christ is strong enough, the blind will see, the lame can throw away their crutches, and so on. The clientele of faith healers comes primarily from the poor who do not have the resources for adequate medical treatment.

A recent manifestation of the interplay between churches or denominations and fundamentalist groups of the sect type concerns the teaching of evolution in the public schools. Most educated people in the United States accept Darwin's theory of biological evolution. Many fundamentalist Christians, however, interpret the Bible literally and believe that God created heaven and earth in six days. The highly vocal creationists are urging that creationism be given "equal time" with evolution in school science classes. The basic assumptions of scientists and religious fundamentalists are in direct conflict: science is based on deductions drawn from empirical reality, whereas creationism is based on divine revelation. The issue of whether creationism should be taught in the public schools was temporarily muted in January of 1982 when Federal District Judge William Overton of Little Rock, Arkansas, ruled that the two-model approach of the creationists is simply a contrived dualism that has no scientific factual basis or legitimate educational purpose. The ruling contended that since creation is not science, the conclusion is inescapable that the only real effect of teaching creation theory is the advancement of religion. What the creation law does, in effect, is make the teaching of creationism in the public schools unconstitutional.

Current Trends in Religion

The use of computers and sophisticated statistical techniques have brought about significant changes in social science research in general and the scientific study of religion in particular. Researchers can now deal efficiently with large samples of the population and test some of the theories developed by Durkheim and Weber.

One such study was published in 1961 by Gerhard Lenski whose book, *The Religious Factor,* is now considered a pioneering quantitative study of religion. Using survey techniques on a probability sample of males in the Detroit area, Lenski tried to test Weber's notions about the Protestant ethic. Lenski reasoned that if Protestants were more oriented toward the Protestant ethic than Catholics, they should show more upward mobility. He found that more white Protestant men than Catholic men rose into the upper middle class or retained that status and that Catholic men were more likely to move into or remain in the lower half of the working class.

Subsequent studies (reviewed by Riccio, 1979) have contradicted Lenski's findings and show no direct relationship between Protestant or Catholic religious beliefs and socioeconomic status. Nevertheless, quantitative research on religion became much more popular following Lenski's publication. We now have a profile of American religious beliefs and their relation to social class, race, age, and other factors. One important finding of this research has been that a sizable part of the population has no conventional religious commitment, although they are concerned with religious belief. This movement away from the church is known as *secularization.*

Secularization

It is widely accepted by social scientists that the dominant trend in modern religion is secularization. Not only are fewer people attending church, but the churches themselves are moving away from supernaturalism. Stark and Bainbridge (1981), however, dispute the dominant view that secularization is an irreversible trend that will eventually bring about the end of religion and its influence.

Although Stark and Bainbridge agree that liberal Protestantism is in a state of decline, they note several signs that human commitment to supernaturalism will remain. One is that those who claim no religious affiliation are likely to accept a whole range of supernaturalism—from Astrology to Zen. A second sign is the fact that most Americans who grew up in an irreligious home enter a Christian denomination as adults. Third, the evangelical denominations are growing. Fourth, they claim it is myopic to note the weakening of once potent religious organizations but dismiss the significance of the formation of new religions.

For these reasons, Stark and Bainbridge argue that secularization is a self-limiting process that prompts religious revival and innovation. In other words, the secularization of the long-dominant religions is a source of the energy pouring into new religious channels. Their central thesis is that cults will flourish where the conventional churches are weakest. They provide evidence that in America there are very robust *negative* correlations between church membership rates and cult activity rates. The states and cities that have low church membership rates have the highest rates of membership in cults. Centuries ago, Christianity, Judaism, Islam, and Buddhism began as cults that rose to power because of the weaknesses in the dominant religions of their time. Stark and Bainbridge argue that the same process is happening today.

Religiosity and Church Attendance

Is religion important to Americans? *Religiosity,* intensity of religious feeling, is a qualitative factor that is difficult to accurately assess. Church attendance figures may provide some indication of religiosity, however. Beginning in the late 1950s, weekly church attendance declined steadily for fifteen years (see Figure 13–1), but since the early 1970s it has remained stable at about 40 percent

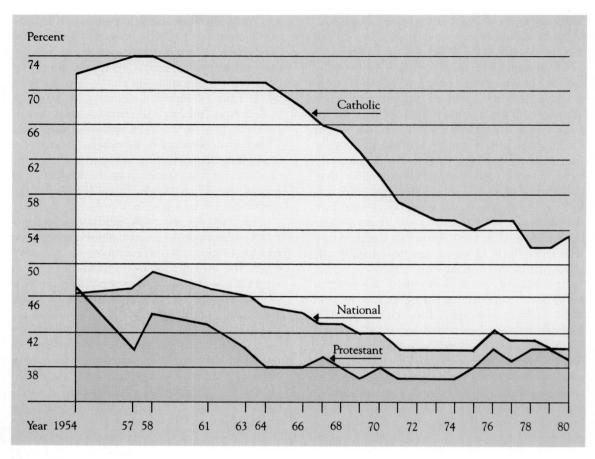

Figure 13-1
Church attendance: 1954–1980

(Jacquet, 1979). Yet church attendance may not be an accurate measure of religiosity because people go to church for many reasons: to worship God, see friends, enjoy music, meet social expectations, and so on. Public opinion polls consistently indicate that a high percentage of people believe in God (more than 90 percent) and a life after death (about 75 percent) and overwhelmingly want their children to have religious training. The discrepancy between church attendance figures and religious beliefs indicates that factors other than formal religious organizations influence religious thought.

The Electronic Church

Through the medium of television many people in the United States "attend church" without ever leaving their homes. Although the impact of religious programming is not fully understood, its influence should not be underestimated. The *electronic church,* as it has been called, apparently fulfills some religious functions. It may provide answers to ultimate questions, reconcile people to hardship, and promote social change. The extent to which it facilitates social integration, creates a community of believers, and provides rituals is questionable, however. It is unlikely that many people kneel for prayer or join hands with others in front of a TV set. On the other hand, the millions of dollars sent to television preachers, most of whom are conservative, fundamentalist, and anticommunist, indicate that they are important to many Americans.

Ecumenism

One response to the current trend toward secularization has been for different denominations to join together in pursuit of common interests. This trend, known as *ecumenism,* or the ecumenical movement, calls for worldwide Christian unity. Interdenominational organizations such as the National Council of Churches are attempting to reconcile the beliefs and practices of different religious groups.

A New Religious Consciousness

A number of new religious groups have sprung up in the United States over the last few decades. Many of them emphasize the personal religious experience rather than a rational, bureaucratic religious organization. The ideas of many of these new groups, such as the Moral Majority, Jews for Jesus, and the Christian World Liberation Front, are rooted in the Christian tradition. Others, like Synanon, EST, and Silva Mind Control, grew out of the "human potential" movement of the 1960s and 1970s. Still others are rooted in Eastern religions such as Buddhism, Hinduism, and Confucianism.

Jerry Falwell is a television preacher who, in the early 1980s, has become heavily involved in political issues. As the leader of the Moral Majority he argued for legislative action against abortion, homosexuals, sex education in the schools, and the Equal Rights Amendment, and action in favor of prayer in the public schools. This conservative right wing movement raised millions of dollars to defeat political candidates who did not support these positions.

SOCIOLOGISTS AT WORK
Helping Religious Refugees Adjust

Baila Miller is assistant director of research at the Jewish Federation of Metropolitan Chicago. She joined the federation in 1982 after two years as a program consultant with the United Way of Metropolitan Chicago. Before that she spent six years lecturing, researching, and completing a doctorate in sociology at the University of Illinois at Chicago Circle.

How does Baila Miller use her sociological training in her work at the Jewish Federation? "The federation raises charitable funds and allocates them to Jewish causes in Israel and overseas and to local Jewish social welfare, health, and educational institutions. The office of research and planning is a small department — just three people. We are responsible for analyzing the budgets of some of the agencies we support, for preparing service statistics for submission to the United

Way, for collecting and analyzing data needed by our volunteer committees, and for carrying out special research projects."

It is in these special research projects that Miller finds the fullest application of her training. "We recently completed a survey of the Jewish population of greater Chicago," she says — a survey that presents unique problems among population studies because the U.S. Bureau of the Census does not collect data on religious affiliations in its decennial census. "We did a lot of random-digit dialing," she admits. "We were trying to determine many things about the Jewish community: How many people are there? Where do they live? How are they maintaining their Jewish identity? Are they participating in religious observances and in Jewish education? What are their service needs and how can a Jewish agency meet

---

Why have these groups and religious movements arisen? A number of factors may be responsible. Durkheim believed that as societies become more complex and diversified, so do the forms of religious belief and practice. Hans Mol (1976) suggests that the new religious consciousness is a search for identity and meaning. Some see these movements as a reaction against the militaristic and capitalistic values that are emphasized by contemporary American society. Others contend that the new religions have arisen in response to the climate of moral ambiguity in the United States. The decline of the established churches has undoubtedly been influential as well. In all probability, each of these factors has had an effect.

Religion and Other Institutions

The relationship between the church and other institutions is a complex one. The institutions and the functions they perform are not always easy to differentiate. Durkheim made this point most clearly when he stated that anything can be made sacred. Political rituals such as those that accompany the election of a president, family behaviors such as dinner together, economic goods such as automobiles, or educational events such as a graduation, all can be considered sacred. These interrelationships and religious influences extend beyond the basic institutions. Note, for

them? Should we be concentrating on services for the elderly or on day care for two-career families? Where are the Jewish poor?"

Another research project that Miller will be involved in at the Jewish Federation of Chicago is a study of the adjustment of Soviet Jewish emigrés to life in various communities in the United States. "We will be working with a data set collected at the University of Illinois, where Rita and Julian Simon, a sociologist and an economist, have done pioneering research in this field. We will approach the data four ways. On an individual level, we will study four adjustment outcomes: occupational achievement, language acquisition, social and cultural involvement in the Jewish community, and maintenance of Jewish identity. We'll be looking for the relative effects of *background characteristics* — social and economic status and place of origin in the Soviet Union — and of *mediating factors* — the type of early resettlement services that are offered in various communities in this country. Then we will analyze our data on a community level, looking for *aggregate measures* of differences in adjust-

ment in various cities in the United States. We will be looking at comparable studies that have been done or are being done in thirteen cities, including Denver, Houston, and New York. We will do a cross-cultural analysis, looking for similarities and differences in adjustment in other large refugee or emigré groups — Indochinese and Mexican, for example. Then we plan to do a policy analysis, with implications for Jewish agencies and national refugee organizations. We will examine the relative advantages and disadvantages of different service patterns: Is it better to provide many services intensively for the new immigrant, at greater short-term cost, or sequential services, such as language training, then vocational training and job placement? We will try to determine the relative effectiveness of different approaches."

"Gathering information like this on the characteristics of a religious group is a challenging task," Baila Miller says. "I use my sociological background in many ways. Research methodology, statistics, and organizational theory — I hope to put all of these to use in my projects at the Jewish Federation of Chicago."

example, how religious principles have served as the foundation for opposition to war, restrictions on alcohol, or exclusion from taxes. In today's society, while the church as a social institution has come under attack, religion and religious values continue to exert a major influence on societies and on the lives of individuals throughout the world.

Summary

A religion is a ritualized system of beliefs and practices related to things defined as sacred by an organized community of believers. People have believed in supernatural powers throughout his-

tory. Some societies have believed that supernatural powers inhabit objects such as rocks and trees, which is known as animism. Others have assumed that supernatural powers reside in a medicine man or shaman who could be called upon to protect the group or to bring success. A third form of belief is totemism, in which a plant or animal is thought to be ancestrally related to a person or tribe. There are monotheistic religions that believe in one god and polytheistic religions that believe in a number of gods.

Religion may take a variety of forms. Mysticism is based on the belief in powers that are mysterious, secret, and hidden from human understanding. Churches are institutional organizations with formal bureaucratic structures. They are sometimes differentiated into ecclesia, which are official state religions, and denominations, which are independent of the state. Sects are small separatist groups that follow rigid doctrines and emphasize fundamentalist teachings. Cults are loosely organized religious organizations whose members adopt a new and unique lifestyle. Rather than attempting to change society, cults generally focus on the spiritual lives of the individual participants.

There are a number of theories about religion. The functionalist perspective examines what religion does for society. Religion is generally perceived as fulfilling social functions such as preserving and solidifying society, creating a community of believers, cultivating social change, and providing a means of social control. It also fulfills personal functions such as answering ultimate questions, providing rites of passage, and reconciling people to hardship. The conflict perspective views religion as a tool used by the dominant forces to justify their position and to keep the less privileged in subordinate positions.

More than 2.5 billion people are believed to have an affiliation with one of the world's major religions. About one billion are Christians, who profess faith in the teachings of Jesus Christ. Another half billion believe in Islam, surrendering their wills to Allah and following the teachings of the prophet Muhammad. The third largest group, followers of Hinduism, is closely linked to the traditional caste system of India. Hindus have a vast array of religious practices and beliefs. Followers of Buddhism believe that they can avoid human suffering by following an eightfold path of appropriate behavior. Confucianism, based on the life and teachings of Confucius, is both a philosophy and a religion and is closely linked to Taoism and Shintoism.

The United States has no state church, but a wide variety of religious groups exist in this country. There are two contrasting trends in contemporary religious practice. One type of group emphasizes formal religious organization, whereas the other emphasizes an informal, personalized, emotional belief system. Throughout our history, religious life has been influenced by folk religions, sects, Pentecostal groups, and groups that believe in millennialism, divine revelation, and faith healing.

Currently, religion is being studied in new ways as a result of developments in qualitative and quantitative research techniques and computer technology. The use of these and other techniques has revealed a trend toward secularization, which is believed to contribute to the emergence of cult activities. While church attendance has leveled off at an estimated 40 percent, a large majority of the population professes a belief in God and life after death, and televised religious programs reach millions of persons in their homes. Along with these developments have come increased ecumenicalism and a new religious consciousness. This new consciousness is professed by many new religious sects and movements, some derived from the Christian tradition, others from the human potential movement and Eastern religions. Several explanations for the creation of these groups have been offered. It has been suggested that they have arisen in response to our diverse culture, our search for identity, our need for precise, simplistic answers, or as a protest against secularization and materialism. The religious system in America and around the world is closely linked with the family as well as economic, political, and educational institutions.

Key Terms

animism
Buddhism
Christianity and Judaism
churches
Confucianism
cults

denominations
divine revelation
ecclesia
ecumenism
electronic church
faith healing
Hinduism
Islam
millennialism
monotheism
mystics
Pentecostalism
polytheism
priests and prophets
religion
religiosity
sacred and profane
sect
secularization
shamanism
theodicy
totemism

Suggested Readings

Berger, Peter L. **A Rumor of Angels: Modern Society and the Rediscovery of the Supernatural.** *Garden City, N.Y.: Doubleday, 1970.* A sociologist's explanation of the role of religion in the modern world.

Demerath, M. J. and Phillip E. Hammon. **Religion in Social Context.** *New York: Random House, 1969.* An advanced text for students interested in further study of religion as a social institution.

Greeley, Andrew. **Unsecular Man. The Persistence of Religion.** *New York: Schocken Books, 1972.* A Catholic priest's declaration that because human needs are timeless, people need religion.

Lofland, John. **Doomsday Cult.** *Englewood Cliffs, N.J.: Prentice-Hall, 1966.* A study of the beginning of a millenarian movement.

Mol, Hans. **Identity and the Sacred.** *New York: The Free Press, 1976.* An attempt to integrate anthropological, historical, psychological, and sociological approaches to religion into a general, social-scientific theory of religion.

Neihardt, John G. **Black Elk Speaks.** *Lincoln: University of Nebraska Press, 1961.* An American Indian recounts in his own words the religious beliefs of his people.

Williams, Peter. **Popular Religion in America.** *Englewood Cliffs, N.J.: Prentice-Hall, 1980.* A fresh approach to religion in America. The author describes the varied religious activities practiced by Americans.

Wilson, John. **Religion in American Society: The Effective Presence.** *Englewood Cliffs, N.J.: Prentice-Hall, 1978.* A text providing comprehensive coverage of recent literature on the sociology of religion.

Wuthnow, Robert (ed.). **The Religious Dimension: New Directions in Quantitative Research.** *New York: Academic Press, 1979.* The application of systematic, quantitative research techniques to the study of modern religion.

Chapter 14
Educational Groups and Systems

Education makes a people easy to lead, but difficult to drive; easy to govern, but impossible to enslave.

— Henry Peter, Lord Brougham

Children in the United States are required to go to school. They sometimes begin at age two or three, long before the required age of six or seven, and often stay in school long past age sixteen, when they could legally drop out. While education dominates the lives of children, it also plays an important role in adult life, as adult students, parents, taxpayers, school employees, government officials, and voters participate in the school system.

Why is education so important? We all know some of the reasons we believe in education. We learn science, the arts, skills for employment, and we learn to make informed judgments about our leisure activities, our political involvement, and our everyday lives.

But is this all that we get from education? What else does it accomplish for society? What part does our education system play in creating a literate population and selecting people for occupations that match their talents, and what part does it play in maintaining the stratification system and justifying the unequal distribution of wealth in society? Much of the debate about whether schools are doing the job they are supposed to do is really a debate about the proper function of schools. The goal of this chapter is to help you understand how education functions in society today.

Structural-Functional Theory of Education

Structural-functional theory recognizes the family as an important agency of socialization. It is in the family that the child learns the culture's values, norms, and language — how to be a social person.

By the age of five or six, the child has developed a unique social personality, and in a properly functioning family the child is socialized to adjust to the routines and disciplines of the school system. But how does education in the schools differ from education in the home?

The Manifest Functions of Schools

The intended function of the educational system, according to structural functionalists, is to supplement family socialization. The schools use experts (teachers) to teach children the knowledge, skills, and values necessary to function in the world outside the family (Parsons, 1959).

The most obvious teaching in school is the teaching of skills. Currently students are expected to learn to read, write, and do arithmetic, which are taught by specially trained experts. Schools also teach students about the larger world through such courses as history, geography, and science. In addition, students learn the values of the larger society, including those that pertain to large organizations. They learn to tell time and be punctual, to cooperate with others to achieve group goals, and to obey the rules necessary for a smooth-running organization.

Another function of education is to select and develop, through evaluation and testing, those young people who have especially useful talents so that each individual will be as productive as his or her abilities permit. Schools give I.Q. tests to determine how capable the students are, and they give grades and achievement tests to find out how much students have learned. They also give psychological tests to help determine which occupations suit the students so that they can then guide them into vocational lines appropriate to their abilities. Some students are guided into vocational courses and the work force; others go to academic high schools and then into junior or four-year colleges. A few of the most talented go to elite colleges and then on to the professions.

A third function of the education system is to transmit new behaviors, skills, ideas, discoveries, and inventions resulting from research. Today, for example, schools teach typing and place less emphasis on penmanship. In some school systems, elementary school students are taught to use a computer terminal before they've mastered their multiplication tables.

The creation of new knowledge is another function of education. Our medical technology is one outstanding example of the knowledge developed in universities. Attempts have also been made to use the educational system to decrease poverty. Education develops the skills necessary to earn income, and special programs have been devised to help the poor develop these skills. Some high schools and colleges, for example, offer students training in specific skills such as car repair, computer programming, or restaurant management. Programs like Head Start are designed to teach disadvantaged children the skills they need to keep up with their peers.

The Latent Functions of Education

The functions so far discussed are the manifest functions, but the educational system also operates in ways that are latent or unintentional, and these functions are also influential. Two latent functions are prolonged adolescence and age segregation.

Prolonged adolescence is a unique feature of modern industrial society. In other societies, the transition from childhood to adulthood is clearly marked. The Kpelle of Liberia in West Africa, for example, mark the passage of boy to man by a circumcision ritual. After this ceremony, the young man is regarded as having the same responsibilities as the other men of his tribe. In our society, children have been relieved of work roles for increasingly longer periods so that they acquire an education. Since the age of mandatory school attendance has been raised from twelve to fourteen and then to sixteen, students today have to remain in school longer than they did. Another factor that has increased the number of years they spend in school is that many jobs require a high school or college diploma. Students stay in school longer when unemployment rates are high and jobs are not available, and parents have to continue to support and assume responsibility for their children during this extended education. As a result, childhood and adolescence sometimes continue for almost two decades in the United States, and maybe even longer for upper-middle-class children — longer than in any other society.

Our education system has also developed other latent functions such as baby sitting for siblings. This function has become increasingly important in American society because in many families both parents must work simply to make ends meet. Although the hours that children are in school — 9 A.M. to 3 P.M. — are often not convenient for working parents, they could not even consider working if their children weren't in school. Some school systems are so attuned to their baby-sitting function that they offer after-school playgroup — at a nominal fee — to take care of children until a parent gets off work and can bring the child home.

Age segregation is the separation of certain age groups from the larger population. Children in schools spend their time with children of the same age, their peers, and, as discussed in Chapter 5, the peer group is an important agency of socialization. Peer groups sometimes develop into distinct subcultures, whose members dress alike, listen to the same music, eat the same foods, wear similar hairstyles and makeup, and develop code

Our educational system segregates adolescents by age and postpones their entry into the work force. Students have free time to spend with one another, and as they talk and laugh together they develop their own set of values, creating a peer culture different from the cultural expectations of family and school. Adolescents value their equality and independence in the peer group, often to the consternation of their parents.

words and slang — a language of their own. One such age-segregated subculture evolved in the late 1960s. During that decade, adolescents and college students were often in conflict with families, schools, and businesses. Fathers and sons stopped speaking over the length of the sons' hair, and students were expelled from schools and colleges and denied jobs because they wore long hair and blue jeans. Signs appeared on storefronts announcing "Shirts and shoes required." Students in the late 1960s learned values of equality and individual worth in school but found that the larger society did not reflect these values (Clark, 1964).

In sum, structural functionalists believe the educational system fulfills both manifest and latent functions. It reinforces the socialization process that started with the family. It prepares children for work in a complex industrial society and guides them into the occupations most appropriate to their abilities and society's needs. Certain latent functions of education, the segregation of age groups and the extension of adolescence, give peer groups an important role in society.

Conflict Theory of Education

Conflict theorists believe that the educational system is used by the elite to maintain their social position (Collins, 1979). The "elite" is the group that controls the wealth and power, the group that has the kinds of jobs affording wealth and prestige to those who hold them. Since such jobs are a scarce resource and since so many people want them and compete for them, the people who control the jobs can require qualifications of their applicants that have little to do with the skills needed for the job but serve to weed out the nonelite. The school system is controlled by the elite, who use their control to select elite children for elite jobs.

Conflict theorists also contend that the elite use the school system to teach the population that inequality is justified. They legitimize their own position by teaching their values and norms to the population so that everyone will believe they deserve their position. Conflict theorists say that education functions not for the good of society but for the good of the elite. It legitimizes their hold on the power, privilege, and wealth and maintains a structure that enables them to continue in their privileged position. Some documentation of this perspective has been provided by Litt (1963), who found in a study of high school civics courses that children in upper-class schools were taught a sense of civic duty. They learned to vote and otherwise participate in politics. They were also taught about the importance of group struggles in settling political issues. The civics courses in lower-class schools, on the other hand, emphasized the smooth working of an invisible hand of government. Lower-class students were not taught the importance of power and group conflict in the political process.

Teaching Values

Conflict theorists believe that schools teach children the values of the group in power. Children are taught patriotism by saying the pledge of allegiance and by studying the history and geography of the United States and of their state and community. They learn that the United States is a great country founded by great leaders who believed in freedom for all. Indians are portrayed as cruel warriors who had to be conquered, and the British as foes who would not permit us to have our freedom. Students learn about the democratic system of government, the fairness of representation, and the importance of the vote. They are taught to value the capitalist system, in which everyone has the right to accumulate as much private property as possible and pass it on to one's children.

The importance of teaching values can be appreciated by looking at the conflicts that sometimes arise in schools. Teachers may be fired if they teach high school students the advantages of communism or the disadvantages of capitalism. The topics omitted from school curricula also shed light on the teaching of values. Students are not instructed on the family systems or sexual practices of people in other cultures. They are not taught about great philosophers who have criticized the United States's political or economic systems, and they are not made aware of the people who have suffered under these systems. Students who reach a college sociology course that attempts to analyze both strengths and weaknesses of social systems are often shocked by what they learn.

Learning Norms

Students learn to conform to elite standards of behavior through the educational process. They conform to rules by being required to conform to them. They are told when to stand in line, when to take turns, when to talk, when to be quiet, when to read, when to listen, when to hang up their coats — the list goes on and on. Rules are an important part of the complex organization of a school, and acceptance of rules is vital to the maintenance of the social order.

Students also learn to compete with other students in school. They are taught that they must do better than others to receive attention, grades, and privileges. Those who do not compete, who pursue the activities they enjoy, will fail, be separated from their peer group, and be labeled slow, hyperactive, disabled, or otherwise deviant. In short, they are punished.

The competition, however, is unfair because it is based on the norms of the middle class, not those of the working-class ethnics or the inner-city blacks. Most teachers come from the middle class and teach students their own values and

Children are assumed to receive equal education and equal evaluation through testing, but education in American schools is based on the middle-class culture. Children from other racial, ethnic, or class groups do not have the same cultural background and often have a more difficult time achieving the expected performance levels in the middle-class environment.

norms, their own level of literature, not literature that might be more germane, and even their own perspective on sports is stressed in gym. Middle-class children are given a superior academic education and do better on tests while the working class are given working-class vocational training and the poor fail completely. Conflict theorists argue that the competitive school system is used to justify keeping the poor in poverty.

Credentialism

Conflict theorists argue that the credentials, diplomas, and degrees given by schools represent learning that is not essential to doing most jobs (Collins, 1979). Everyone from physicians to assembly line workers learns much more than is necessary to do their work. Physicians must take four years of college, four years of medical school, and a one-year internship to become general practitioners. Those who want to specialize need an additional three or more years of training. Communist societies such as China and Cuba successfully train people in a much shorter time to take care of most of the health needs of the society. The system in the United States perpetuates the prestige of physicians by demanding *credentials* that can be obtained only by those who have the time and money to enter this elite profession. In addition, physicians come to form their own subculture of shared values and beliefs during their years of training.

Collins also argues that the jobs requiring a great deal of education do not necessarily require the skills people learn in school, but the jobs do require the cultural norms learned in school. When college-educated people enter management positions, the elite can rest assured that managers will make decisions consistent with the cultural norms.

In sum, conflict theorists believe that the educational system is run by the group in power to legitimize their position. They teach values and norms useful in maintaining their position, use an unfair competitive system to legitimize upper-middle class winners, and insist on certification of skills beyond those necessary to do a job. The upper-middle class has the competitive advantage, but everyone learns the values and norms that maintain the system.

Historical Perspectives on Education

When sociologists study education, they ask whether it functions to teach a body of knowledge to students, to select students most capable to perform work in society, or to generate new knowledge as the structural-functional theorists describe some of its functions. They also ask if education reflects the conflicts in society by maintaining the stratification system. When we look at historical evidence to analyze how the system functions, we find that at the beginning education was only minimally related to occupational training.

The Puritans, who considered education important, founded Harvard College in Massachusetts in 1636. Modeled after Cambridge and Oxford in England, it was created to educate ministers, and, initially, only male students between the ages of twelve and twenty were accepted. The subject matter was morals and ethics, and learning was accomplished through rote memorization. William and Mary (1693), Yale (1701), and Princeton (1746) were founded in quick succession and for the same purpose as Harvard.

The University of Virginia, founded by Thomas Jefferson in 1819, had a somewhat broader goal than many earlier universities. Aware of the need to train national leaders, Jefferson wanted to form an institution to educate all capable people, a "natural aristocracy," in a wide range of subjects including modern languages, science, and mathematics. This curriculum was widely adopted later in the century (Seely, 1970).

After about 1850, the federal government began to encourage states to begin colleges that would teach agriculture and mechanics. They were provided with land grants to build the colleges. These land-grant colleges developed into today's public state universities.

During the same period, universities such as

Johns Hopkins (1876), which emphasized a scientific curriculum, were founded. Johns Hopkins was also one of the first to systematically support advanced research and the publishing of research findings. Prior to the founding of schools with advanced scientific programs, professions such as medicine, law, and dentistry were learned through the apprenticeship system or practiced without formal education.

Today, most colleges admit only students who have graduated from high school, and most graduate schools admit only students who have graduated from a four-year college program and earned a bachelor's degree. Schools that offer graduate degrees are known as universities, which award master's degrees, doctorate degrees, and professional degrees in such fields as law (LL.D.), medicine (M.D.), veterinary medicine (D.V.M.), and dentistry (D.D.S.). The trend in the development of colleges, then, has been a move away from classical studies and a move toward more and more professional training.

The Founding Fathers believed that citizens in a democracy should be able to read, write, and make intelligent decisions at election time. They also believed that a nation that promised to provide equal opportunity for all had to educate the population to take advantage of their opportunities. They therefore began a system of *compulsory public education.*

Compulsory public education grew quickly during the eighteenth and nineteenth centuries to accommodate the influx of immigrants. *Elementary schools,* for the teaching of basic reading and writing skills, were used to socialize these foreigners to the American way of life because they had to learn to speak English and become familiar with American customs. The immigrant children who attended school were assimilated into American society, but some were ashamed of their parents, who often did not learn the new culture (Novak, 1972).

Public schools met with resistance from a variety of groups. Religious leaders believed that education should include training in morals and ethics. Catholic religious leaders were afraid that public education would be Protestant education. Landowners did not want to pay taxes for other people's education because they felt that this was socialism. Farmers did not want to lose the labor of their sons to the schoolroom. In spite of the objections of these groups, however, local educational systems were developed and run by local leaders, which reflected the strong commitment to local governance in the United States.

Secondary schools (high schools) developed in the last two decades of the nineteenth century. They were initially designed to guide students through the period between elementary school and college. The subjects taught were intended to provide students with standards for making judgments about art, literature, music, economics, and politics. According to Seely (1970), taxpayers in this period were told that the subject matter taught was less important than the development of standards, taste, judgment, discipline, and a sense of justice and decency.

At first, secondary education began when elementary education ended. In the United States, however, school systems have developed transitional schools called middle or junior high schools. Middle schools begin as early as the sixth grade, and junior high schools begin in seventh or eighth grade. Enrollment in the senior high school, which takes place in ninth or tenth grade, now marks the beginning of secondary education.

Secondary schools traditionally prepared students for college, but as education became compulsory for fourteen-, fifteen-, and then sixteen-year-olds, they began to offer courses in vocational training or career development for students not planning to go to college. Again we see the movement away from a moral education and a move toward occupational education.

The development of junior and community colleges began relatively recently. Like junior high schools, they were created to provide a transition, in this case from high school to college. Junior colleges offer an associate's degree after two years of study and provide an opportunity for advanced education to the increasing number of students who graduate from high school. A great many junior colleges have been founded in the last few decades and have placed heavy emphasis on occupational training.

The goals and structure of an education system also shape and are shaped by the society's views of the nature and role of children. Are children good or evil, impulsive or rational? Are they fundamentally different from adults in some ways? Are they naturally curious or naturally passive and indolent? The answers a society provides to questions such as these are manifested in the structure of its education system.

During the Middle Ages, society was considered corrupt and children were believed to be innocent. Children were thought to need protec-

tion from the adult realm of sin and worldliness. Accordingly, the Jesuits who started the first schools for children were careful to guard them from influences considered immoral. Vestiges of this view can still be found in our education system today, in which children are generally forbidden access to books dealing with sex, different political systems, and other potentially "corrupting" influences.

The Puritans believed that children were possessed by the devil. Their education involved memorizing parts of the Bible, catechisms, and other pieces of moral wisdom until the evil nature of children was overcome. This process was hurried along by the schoolmaster's liberal use of the switch. Rather than being isolated from adults, children were encouraged to emulate their good example, since it was assumed that adults had already learned right from wrong.

Early in this century, it was thought that children were impulsive, controlled not by the devil

Two centuries ago children of all ages attended school together, where reading, writing, and arithmetic were the subjects emphasized. Lessons were memorized and reciting for the teacher was an important part of classwork. Notice the absence of books in the classroom — children who are not reciting work on their slates. In spite of the strict discipline in these schools, children relaxed when the teacher's back was turned.

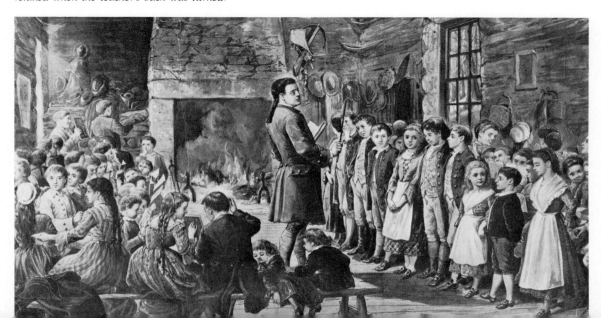

but by their biological drives, and thus strict discipline was necessary. Children were required to sit in rows, memorize their spelling and mathematics, and raise their hands to recite.

Since 1960, some important changes have taken place. The moral issue of whether children are good or evil has lost importance, but it has come to be believed that children have a natural curiosity — they want to learn. In schools based on this belief, discipline has decreased, rows of chairs have been rearranged to allow freedom of movement, and "learning centers" have been developed and placed around the room so that children can move from center to center as their interest dictates. This view has not been adopted by most parents, who think that children need to be controlled. They would like to see a return to an emphasis on basic skills and strict discipline. They believe that an education is necessary in order to acquire a good job, and they want to be sure their children learn the necessary skills rather than relying on their natural curiosity. While parents may not approve of the way schools are run, their power to bring about changes is limited, however.

Who Rules the Schools?

Most American education is public — the schools are open to everyone. They are funded by local and federal government, so there are strong ties between the educational system and the political system. Education is paid for by tax dollars, and although it is controlled locally, it complies with all the laws of the land.

The Bureaucratic Structure of Public Schools

The bureaucracy of a local school system is headed by a school board, which adopts a budget, sets policies, and directs the supervisor of schools. The supervisor develops guidelines based on the policies of the school board and directs the principals of the schools in the area. The principals make rules for the local schools based on the guidelines of the supervisor and directs the teachers to carry out the rules. The teacher establishes rules for the classroom in accordance with the principal's direction and teaches the students.

Although the United States emphasizes local control of schools, it is somewhat misleading to suggest that school boards operate independently because the federal government passes many laws that affect the educational system. Schools must respect the rights protected by the Constitution; they must allow religious freedom and offer equal opportunity. The federal government influences such consideration as prayer in school, the teaching of evolution, equal opportunity for minorities, and the education of the handicapped. School boards must comply with federal laws regarding these and other concerns.

States also have constitutions, which cannot contradict federal law. Within the restrictions of federal law and the state constitution, the states pass laws that set standards for the schools. They certify teachers, set the number of days students must attend school, determine holidays, and establish minimum requirements for the curriculum and for graduation. Any school board policies, therefore, must comply with these laws.

Compare the bureaucratic system of modern schools to the informal organization of private tutors and craftsmen who taught in the Middle Ages. Boys and men sought out a tutor who agreed to teach or to take them on as an apprentice in a trade. There were no rules about who could teach, who could learn, what subject matter would be covered, what the fees would be, how often lessons would take place, or how long the teaching-learning relationship would continue. Unlike what is practiced in present-day school systems, decisions about each of these considerations were made by the individual pupil and teacher and therefore could be tailored to the individual's needs.

The Public Schools Are Failing

In the urban slums where some thirty million Americans now live, the public schools have been doing a terrible job. They prepare almost none of their students for college, and this means that almost none will be able to get a good job or live a comfortable life. More than half the students in these schools are made so miserable that they drop out at the first legal opportunity, filled with despair and rebellion against society.

Many educators claim that these students come from such wretched homes that the schools cannot do much to educate them. Yet while slum children are clearly difficult to educate, experiments have repeatedly shown that with the right kind of school the job can be done.

Why haven't the people who run our big-city schools been able to find solutions to their problems? The reason, I think, is that effective remedies would require basic changes in the character of the public school system itself. After several years of studying the problem, I have concluded that we cannot hope to establish good schools in the slums so long as we cling to the tradition of direct public management of public schools.

Public management means public accountability — not just for long-term educational results but for every penny, every minute, and every word of every educator on the public payroll. In such a system, the fate of a school's alumni inevitably seems less important than avoiding overt conflict and "staying out of trouble." If nobody is found with his hand in the till, if no "subversives" are alleged to be in the classrooms, if no serious discipline problems arise, if no unfavorable news stories appear, if taxes don't have to be raised, public officials seem to feel that all is well.

The working assumption of those in charge seems to be that everyone in the system is incompetent, irresponsible, and potentially dishonest. Everyone is therefore told to follow detailed procedures laid down by someone "higher up" and is held accountable for his conformity to the rules. State legislators assume that if local school boards are left to their own devices they will hire incompetents, so the legislature imposes elaborate (and largely irrelevant) state certification requirements for teachers. The school board assumes that the superintendent assumes the principals have questionable judgment, and insists on prior approval of their budgets, personnel, curriculum, and even teaching materials. The principals, in turn, assume that teachers are inherently self-indulgent, and give them little control over the school or even over their own syllabi. Some principals go so far as to install intercom systems with which they can monitor classes. The teachers are also infected by the pervasive deference to authority and tradition and try to impose it on their pupils by placing innumerable restrictions on social and academic behavior. Everywhere there is an atmosphere of suspicion more appropriate to a prison.

SOURCE: From Christopher Jencks, "The Public Schools are Failing." Reprinted by permission from *The Saturday Evening Post*, April 23, 1966. © 1966 The Curtis Publishing Company.

Financing the Schools

Public elementary and secondary schools are financed entirely by taxes — local real estate taxes are the largest source of support for schools, but funds from the federal and state governments have played an increasingly important role in funding schools, as shown in Table 14-1. Public colleges and universities likewise receive much of their support from taxes, but they also charge tuition to help pay the costs of running the colleges and raise money from alumni and charitable foundations. Private schools at every level rely on tuition and private donations for support, which

Table 14-1
Percent of public school revenue by source

	1920	1940	1960	1980 EST.
Local	83.2	68.0	52.2	36.5
State	16.5	30.3	38.7	49.6
Federal	.3	1.8	9.1	13.9

SOURCES: U.S. Bureau of the Census, *Statistical Abstract of the United States, 1980* (101st ed.), Washington, D.C., 1980, No. 222, p. 141, and *Historical Statistics of the United States,* Washington, D.C., 1973.

come from alumni, charitable foundations, and sponsoring churches, but they also receive state and federal tax dollars to support special programs such as research projects, experimental programs, and the training of scarce professionals such as physicians or scientists. Wealthy private colleges rely heavily on endowments, the money the college has to invest. Income from these investments is used to help pay yearly expenses.

Stratification in the School System

Like other social systems, schools reflect stratification and can be a cause of it, and the school that children attend can have an enormous influence on their life chances. Those who attend first-rate elementary and high schools usually go on to prestigious colleges and land high-paying jobs. Those who receive a poor education may become so frustrated that they quit without graduating. Some critics contend that schools are biased in favor of middle- and upper-class students at all levels, from the federal education bureaucracy to the local school board.

School Boards

Local school boards are usually elected by the people of the school district, although in about 10 percent of the districts they are appointed by the mayor. They consist primarily of white, male business or professional people, even in predominantly black or working-class schools. Sometimes board members come into conflict with the minority groups in their school districts. Disagreements have ranged from hair styles to vocational training, from teaching the basics of reading, writing, and arithmetic to discipline.

Eighty-five percent of the college regents or trustees in the United States are male. One-third are in administrative or executive positions in business or industry and one-fourth are in a profession, but only one in seven is employed in education. Some critics argue that school boards would represent their communities better if they consisted of a greater variety of intelligent people, including members from minority groups, ethnic groups, labor, faculty, and the student body.

The Faculty

The majority of the faculty in elementary schools are women, 74 percent of whom are from the middle class. In high schools, there are more male faculty, many of whom are from the lower class. In colleges and universities, the majority of faculty members are white males, although the number of females increased between 1969 and 1975 from 15 to 20 percent. They are found mostly in the lower ranks and are often paid less than their male colleagues of equal rank, in spite of laws requiring equal pay for equal work. Women in some schools, however, have successfully filed complaints to raise their salaries to the level of the men on the faculty. Also significant is the fact that in 1976 only 4 percent of all college and university faculty were black (Stadtman, 1980).

Students

Traditionally, schools have been segregated by socioeconomic class in the United States, because children go to neighborhood schools and neighborhoods are segregated. Students of different races often attend different schools for the same reason. Many blacks and Hispanics live in inner-city neighborhoods and go to predominantly black and Hispanic schools. They have also traditionally finished fewer years of school (see Table 14-2).

Achievement in school has been related to social class and to race. Compared with working-class students, upper-middle-class white students have higher grades and higher achievement and I.Q. test scores. They are more likely to go to college, they more frequently attend four-year colleges, and they complete more years of education. Working-class students, in turn, have higher achievement than blacks. Why have our schools so often failed to educate black students properly? To answer this question, James Coleman and a team of sociologists (1966) compared the facilities of schools in black and white neighborhoods. He found that the schools were the same age, spent the same amount of money per pupil, and had equivalent library and laboratory facilities. Teacher qualifications and class size were also the same. He concluded that the differences in achievement were related to the students' socioeconomic backgrounds, not to differences in the schools themselves.

Coleman also found that black students performed better in white schools and recommended busing students to promote integration. Busing was carried out in many localities, but few people, black or white, liked busing children to schools in other neighborhoods. Many argued that it interfered with the concept of neighborhood schools and local control.

Although Coleman found no differences between predominantly black and predominantly white schools, researchers who have studied other features of the educational process argue that blacks are in inferior schools.

One of the tools used in schools that may be biased in favor of the middle class is the I.Q. test, which was designed by Lewis M. Terman in 1916 to test skills used in upper-middle-class occupations that involved manipulating numbers and words. The purpose of the test was to select students who might benefit from advanced training. Terman and others believed that it measured an inherited genetic trait called intelligence. They assumed that those who scored low on the test lacked intelligence and were less capable of learning than those who did well. It was argued that those who did poorly should be assigned to lower-class jobs.

Table 14-2

Comparative levels of education of the population age twenty-five and over, 1979

	PERCENT SPANISH ORIGIN	PERCENT BLACK	PERCENT WHITE
Less than four years of high school	58.0	50.6	30.3
High school, four years	25.6	30.0	37.6
College, one to three years	9.7	11.5	15.0
College, four or more years	6.7	7.9	17.2

SOURCE: *The World Almanac and Book of Facts, 1982* edition, copyright © Newspaper Enterprise Association, 1981, New York, New York 10166. By permission.

Children from a black neighborhood in Boston are bussed to another neighborhood where they will be able to attend school with white children. There is some evidence that children perform better in integrated schools, but black children must often face discrimination from teachers, from white children, and from educational and testing procedures that were not designed to teach children with their cultural background.

Critics have argued that I.Q. tests measure not an inherited characteristic but a person's knowledge of upper-middle-class American culture, which is why immigrants, the working class, the poor, and blacks score low while upper-middle-class Americans score high. These critics say the test serves the stratification system by creating a myth that convinces the lower classes that their station in life is part of the natural order of things (Karier, 1976).

Can a low score on an I.Q. test hurt even a bright student in the classroom? Rosenthal and Jacobson (1968) believe it can. As discussed in Chapter 5, "Socialization as a Lifelong Process," these investigators found that students do not learn as well when their teachers believe they are not very bright. If teachers have learned that lower-class and minority students did not perform well on I.Q. and achievement tests, they will have lower expectations of them in class. Even if they do perform well, teachers may not recognize their talents, give them lower grades, and confuse and frustrate them.

In one study of pupil-teacher interaction, it was found that teachers asked black students simpler questions than they asked white students. If a black pupil could not answer a question the teacher asked somebody else. If a white pupil could not answer a question, however, the teacher gave an explanation. Teachers also praised and complimented white students more than black students when they gave correct answers (Weinberg, 1977, p. 232). Notice in Table 14-2 how much less education blacks and people of Spanish origin have than whites.

Education and Mobility

Contest and Sponsored Mobility

In the United States, students can get as much education as they are willing and able to pay for as long as they maintain the grades necessary for acceptance at the next higher level. This system has been labeled *contest mobility* (Turner,

1960), because students can continue as long as they meet the standards of each level. The high school graduate can apply to college, the junior college graduate can apply to a four-year institution, and the college graduate can apply to a graduate school.

By contrast, Japan and most European countries have a system known as *sponsored mobility*. In these countries, students must pass qualifying examinations to gain admittance into different types of high schools and colleges. They may receive a classical education leading to a university degree, a business education, or engineering and technical training. Once they enter a particular track, they rarely change to another type of education. A student in business school, for example, is unlikely to switch to a university.

Education in Britain is typical of the sponsored-mobility system. The British have a long tradition of formal education. Oxford and Cambridge, both founded in the Middle Ages, emphasized Latin and the classics. Members of the elite class were selected to attend the university and become educated gentlemen. In time, private

A student who attends Eton, a prestigious British prep school, entertains his parents while other students look on. The opportunity to attend an elite school such as Eton assures these students of an education in one of Great Britain's finer universities and continued membership in the British upper class.

grammar schools (called public schools) developed to prepare the young of the upper classes for their university education. This system of upper-class education continues in Great Britain today.

Tax-supported schools for British children were slow to develop. At the turn of the twentieth century, education for all children became mandatory until age twelve. This law, however, was resisted by farmers who would lose the help of their sons and country squires who would lose their source of cheap labor. The Boy Scouts and Girl Scouts, a very popular movement in Great Britain, filled the educational gap for older children by teaching them to lead the good life in the open air.

The British fought two world wars during the first half of this century, which drained the population of its resources, but they realized that to keep up with advanced technology, they had to have technical education, so they gradually developed a system of secondary schools. Under this system, the grammar schools taught the traditional college preparatory subjects, technical schools taught engineering and sciences, and other schools were designed to provide a more general education. Children were selected for one of these types of schools at age thirteen on the basis of tests and teacher evaluations. Only 20 percent of the schools were grammar schools, and these were attended almost exclusively by members of the elite classes.

In the 1960s, publicly financed secondary schools were changed to offer a comprehensive education, so the elite fled to privately funded schools where they could continue to receive the grammar school preparatory education. At about the same time, a crash program was begun to build public colleges, but financing for the program ran out. The cost of building a system of higher education and class differences in access to higher education remain major problems in the British educational system.

Mobility Through Education in the United States

In this country, most people have great faith in education as a means to upward mobility. It is this faith that is largely responsible for the phenomenal growth of our educational institutions, especially public institutions. Community and junior colleges have been built, and loan programs have been established to assist those who could not otherwise afford a college education. The women's movement has stressed education as a means of upward mobility for women, and poverty programs have focused on training and educating the poor to help them rise out of poverty. Underlying all these steps is the assumption that education leads to upward mobility.

In the past, most sociologists supported this view. Blau and Duncan (1967), for example, argued that if children from large families could get as much education as children from small families, their existing occupational disadvantages would largely disappear. The belief among sociologists that education leads to upward mobility was so widespread that the presidential address of the annual meeting of the American Sociological Association in 1971 (Sewell, 1971) was essentially a call for political action to increase opportunities for the less privileged to acquire an education so that they too might become upwardly mobile.

There is, however, reason to doubt that education has much impact on social mobility. One critic (Collins, 1979) has argued that increasing educational opportunities for the disadvantaged creates a hardship for them. They are encouraged to spend more money on education, but when they complete their education, they do not have additional earning power.

The fact that increased education does not necessarily lead to better jobs may come as a surprise. The truth is, however, that factors other than education have a powerful influence on what jobs people take and what salaries they earn. Family background, for example, is more closely related to future occupation than level of education (Jencks, 1979). A son from a working-class family is more likely to enter a working-class occupation than a son from a middle-class family, even if they have the same amount of education (Lipset and Bendix, 1967; Jencks, 1979). Children who grow up on welfare are hampered more by their poverty than their lack of education (Schiller, 1970). At the opposite end of the spectrum, an increasing proportion of business executives come from families of high economic status (Keller, 1968).

It seems that as the level of education for everyone in the society increases the upper class gets more education than others, they go to the elite schools, and they use their influential family and friends to help them find the best jobs. On the other hand, the children of the working class, although they get more education than their parents had, find that working-class jobs now require at least a high school diploma, and many

jobs in corporations that used to require only a high school diploma now require a college degree.

Another factor affecting upward mobility is that the size of the educated work force has been increasing faster than the need for educated workers. Between 1950 and 1960, the labor force gained one-half million more college graduates than it needed (Berg, 1970). We have a much more highly educated population than other countries (see Table 14-3) and certainly many more educated people than we had at the turn of the century (see Table 14-4). As a result, college graduates began to take white-collar jobs that had previously gone to high school graduates. High school graduates, no longer able to get white-collar jobs, moved into blue-collar work. The middle-class father with a high school education and a white-collar job who sent his son through college often found that the son had to settle for a white-collar job at the same level of prestige as himself. The excess of college graduates has continued to increase, so the benefits of having a college degree are also decreasing.

Table 14-3

Educational attainment in selected countries during the decade of the 1960s

COUNTRY	PERCENT COMPLETING SECONDARY SCHOOL	PERCENT ATTENDING COLLEGE	PERCENT OF COLLEGE STUDENTS GRADUATING FROM COLLEGE
U.S.	75	39	18
U.S.S.R.	47	19	9
Japan	57	11	12
France	30	11	NA
England	12	6	5
West Germany	11	6	NA

NA = not available.

SOURCE: Collins, Randall. *The Credential Society: An Historical Sociology of Education and Stratification.* New York: Academic Press, 1979, p. 92. Reprinted by permission of the publisher and the author.

Table 14-4

Educational attainment in the United States, 1900 and 1970

YEAR	HIGH SCHOOL GRADUATES POPULATION: 17 YEARS OLD (%)	COLLEGE STUDENTS POPULATION: 18–21 YEARS OLD (%)	BACHELORS DEGREES POPULATION: 21 YEARS OLD (%)	PH.D.s POPULATION: 30 YEARS OLD (%)
1900	6.4	4.0	1.7	.03
1970	76.5	52.8	21.1	1.04

SOURCE: Collins, Randall. *The Credential Society: An Historical Sociology of Education and Stratification.* New York: Academic Press, 1979, p. 4. Reprinted by permission of the publisher and the author.

The excess of college graduates has also affected blue-collar workers. When it became apparent that blue-collar jobs were growing scarce, students from blue-collar families began finishing high school in increasing numbers, hoping to move into white-collar jobs. Today, however, many blue-collar jobs require a high school diploma, and much white-collar work requires at least some college. Thus, despite their increase in education, the sons and daughters of blue-collar families tend to remain in blue-collar work. The existence of this obstacle to upward mobility is substantiated by statistics: in 1960, 26 percent of all blue-collar workers were high school graduates; in 1970, the proportion was 41 percent.

The costs of remaining in school are enormous because students are dependent on their families longer and they lose additional years of income. It is not surprising that those who make sacrifices to stay in school and then can't get better jobs are disappointed in the work they do.

Education, Employment, and Income

In the United States, the more education people get, the more likely they are to be employed and the more income they will receive. Even if education does not bring upward mobility, that is, does not move the children into a higher

class than their parents, education is rewarded by jobs and income. As a rule, companies prefer to hire educated people. We assume that this system is rational, yet men in Canada have an easier time finding a job if they do not go to college. Men who are college graduates are more likely to be unemployed (Martin and Macdonnell, 1978).

Education is not as rewarding to women and blacks as it is to white men, however. In this country, men earn more than women who have the same level of education, and white men earn more than equally educated black men. In 1966, the average lifetime earnings for men with a high school education working full time was $341,000; for women the figure was $249,000. With a college education, men earned an average of $508,000 and women earned $436,000. Black men with a high school education earned only three-fourths of the salary of white male high school graduates. Even black men with a college education did not earn as much as white men with a high school education (Miller, 1971).

The status of one's college also increases earnings. Jencks (1979) found that men who attended a highly selective college earned 28 percent more than men of similar family background who graduated from other colleges.

The evidence we have presented on education and mobility suggests that increasing amounts

A student is congratulated by her father at graduation. Education will be an advantage to her when she seeks work because educational requirements for jobs have steadily increased. But because she is a woman and a member of a minority group, she may not earn as much as a white male with equivalent education.

of education are necessary just to maintain one's class position. It is true that people with a college degree earn more money. Among college graduates, poor people may not do as well as members of the middle class, but they earn more than those who do not attend college at all. Jencks (1979) suggests that in the future college may improve equality — as more people go to college, their earnings will increase. On the other hand, if everyone gets a college education, it may lose its value, and the social class of one's family may come to have the most important influence in determining who gets ahead.

Collins (1979) argues that educational credentials should not be used to determine who advances in jobs. Secretaries should be allowed to move into management jobs, as they did before the turn of the century when many secretaries were men. Collins further states that medical professionals should all start as orderlies and work their way through the ranks of nurse to become physicians through a combination of work experience and special training. This system would make it possible for people who could not pay for long years of education to reach rewarding positions in society.

Education and Change in the 1980s

Americans take great pride in education and the public school system. At the same time, we speak of a crisis in American education, which is reflected in lowering achievement test scores, discipline problems, the persistent lack of upward mobility for the poor, and the decreasing worth of a college degree. Although debates about these crises tend to focus on the schools, many of these problems are caused by changes in the larger society. One major change that has altered education in the past two decades and will continue to affect it is the size of the school-age population.

The number of young children in this country grew dramatically with the onset of the baby boom in the late 1940s. Many children were born to people who had postponed childbearing during the depression of the 1930s and during World War II. These babies were born in addition to those being born to people who were just reaching the age of marriage and childbearing. More will be said about the reasons for this population increase in a later chapter.

The baby boom children entered the public school system in the 1950s, and an enormous building program had to be undertaken to construct schools for them. Classrooms were crowded, children went to classes in shifts, and there was a shortage of teachers. When these same students went on to college in the affluent 1960s, public colleges grew rapidly, and new com-

munity and state colleges were built. Some classes in large universities were enormous, and there was a severe shortage of teachers at this level as well.

The baby boom children began to enter the job market in the 1970s. Just as there were not enough schools for them, there were not enough jobs for them. College graduates were absorbed into the job market, but high school graduates had to struggle for low-paying jobs, and the poor, especially black youths, often could not find any jobs. A college education seemed less worthwhile unless one studied for a career, and the number of students in the liberal arts decreased while the number in engineering and business increased.

By the beginning of the 1980s, the last of the baby boom generation had entered college —

Students mark the closing of their high school in Alpena, Michigan, by draping the doorway with a black banner. There has been a decrease in the number of children in the school-age population in some areas, especially in neighborhoods where the children have grown up and moved away from home.

the baby boom was over. Today school enrollments are decreasing. Elementary schools and secondary schools began closing in the 1970s, and there is an overabundance of teachers. College enrollments will drop in the mid-1980s, and by 1997, there will be 23 percent fewer eighteen- to twenty-four-year-olds than there were in 1977 (Stradtman, 1980). Public colleges, which grew so rapidly for two decades, may become smaller, but because they are financed by tax dollars and relatively inexpensive to attend, they should continue to recruit students. Private colleges, however, are in serious trouble. Since they must charge more tuition, they can't compete with the public colleges, and many are closing. In 1955, 45 percent of students attended private colleges. In 1977, that figure had dropped to 24 percent (see Figure 14-1). There may be empty college buildings and unemployed professors unless a larger percentage of today's high school graduates go to college.

These figures suggest that, in the future, colleges will be less diverse. Most students will probably attend public institutions that emphasize education for careers. Public colleges have also been attempting to attract students with evening programs, work-study programs, weekend programs, and other options for working students. The diversity provided by small liberal arts colleges may all but disappear from the American scene.

In the mid-1980s, there will be fewer young people entering the work force. Employers may be willing to start college-educated people in better jobs, and they may be more willing to hire high school graduates. If the high school diploma becomes more valuable, high school students may be more motivated to compete for jobs, and high school achievement scores and discipline may improve. Also, the competition found in college career-line programs may be reduced. Whether

Figure 14-1
Enrollment in private institutions as a percentage of enrollment in all U.S. institutions of higher education, 1955, 1965, and 1977

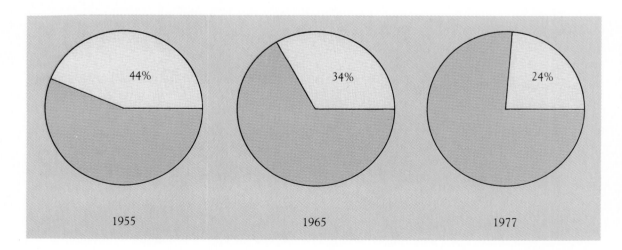

1955   1965   1977

The Kibbutz: Collective Education

When the state of Israel was founded after World War II, the settlers formed communal settlements known as kibbutzim. In these settlements, people built homes and began farms, sharing the work and the rewards for their labor. As Israel developed, the kibbutz changed to include industry in its labor, but its communal nature remained the same.

The kibbutz developed its communal style of child care and education to be compatible with the social structure. Infants are not raised at home, but in the community Babies' Homes. Parents and grandparents can visit at any time. The mother visits often enough to breast-feed the infant during its first six months. At age one, infants move to the Toddlers' House, then into kindergarten and first grade. The Junior Children's Community is the home of children aged eight to twelve. Until age eighteen, children live in the much larger Youth Society. At each level, they are under the care of adults on the permanent staff,

so the children have a variety of adults who are a dependable and consistent part of their lives. The adults are trained to guide the emotional and intellectual development of the children and to teach patriotism and the kibbutz way of life.

Teaching is done through projects such as gardening, the study of the locality, or the study of roads. Language, literature, and mathematics are taught not as separate subjects but as a part of each project. As the students garden, for example, they learn botany, zoology, general economics, and the economics of Israel. If a butterfly appears in the garden, the butterfly is studied. If a comet appears in the sky, the children study comets, including mathematics and astronomy, and since the children live together in the community, they can all get together to watch the comet at night.

The children are encouraged to achieve in their projects to the best of their abilities, just as those who work in the kibbutz achieve

according to their abilities. There is no competition for grades. The goal of the educational system is to foster concern for the group, not the individual.

Each evening for three hours the children gather in the homes of their parents and other members of their extended families. Tea may be served, and the family exchanges the news of the day. The parents play with the children or take walks with them. These are relaxing times for everyone. Because the parents have no responsibility for training or discipline, close emotional relationships develop easily.

The educational system in the kibbutz has been criticized by some American educators because the young children are reared by someone other than their parents. Other Americans have praised the kibbutz system because the parents, the educational system, and the larger society are in harmony, children are not divided by the expectations of parents, schools, and peer groups, and parents can provide total emotional support to their children.

SOURCE: Rabin and Hazan eds. *Collective Education in the Kibbutz from Infancy to Maturity.* New York: Springer, 1973.

these events will in fact develop, however, depends on many variables that cannot be predicted, especially political and economic variables that could affect employment in the next decade.

Rabin and Hazan (1973) described the ideal of the kibbutzim (see box above). They present a rather idyllic portrait, but it serves to provide a view of an alternative educational philosophy.

SOCIOLOGISTS AT WORK
Assessing Educational Opportunity

James C. Hearn is a principal analyst at Advanced Technology, Inc., a private consulting firm in McLean, Virginia, near the nation's capital. He is also deputy program director for one of the three parts of that company's Social Science Operations Center. "I coordinate research projects here, produce reports, coordinate our publications programs, do marketing, write on proposal teams, recruit, and do some analytic work in my areas of knowledge." One of those areas of knowledge is sociology: Hearn has earned two graduate degrees in sociology from Stanford University.

How has Jim Hearn been able to apply this knowledge? "When I left Stanford, I wanted to take a position that would allow full-time research. I went to work for the American College Testing Program (ACT). I did some research into the factors involved in students' decision-making about postsecondary education: whether to go, where to go, how many years to go. One of the big factors in postsecondary attendance and attainment levels is financial aid. ACT has a number of financial aid services and products, so I became something of an expert in the field. I put together a successful proposal to get internal funding for a study of the social, economic, and educational factors involved in students' decisions about college attendance. I modeled the effects of race, income, status, sex, ability, achievement, and other characteristics, much as other sociologists have done to examine other aspects of educational attainment."

Hearn eventually presented the results of part of this analysis at an annual meeting of the American Educational Research Association. He reviewed the evidence from other researchers

Summary

Why is education so important? Structural-functional theory argues that education in a complex industrial society supplements what families can teach their children, that it helps children acquire complex skills and the knowledge necessary to function in the world. The educational system also selects students on the basis of their talents and abilities to meet the needs of society, directing the most talented into advanced education and training for positions of leadership and directing those with less talent to the positions in which they will serve society best. Educational institutions also create new knowledge and new technology, which they teach to the next generation. They create innovation and change so that society can advance.

Conflict theory argues that education is a means by which powerful groups prevent change. The elites use the educational system to teach children elite values and norms so that everyone will believe that the position of the elites is justified. Elite groups promote children and give diplomas and degrees on the basis of how well they know the elite culture. Elite children usually receive high credentials and move into elite jobs,

that minority students, female students, and students with lower socioeconomic status were enrolling in educational institutions with limited resources, low prestige, and less thorough preparation for future advancement opportunities. Analyzing data collected by the Higher Education Research Institute, he found that "black and female students, students whose parents had lower incomes and lower educational attainments, and students who had a larger number of brothers and sisters all were less likely to go to highly selective institutions, even when other educationally relevant characteristics such as ability and achievement were controlled." The results suggested that inequities in college choices sprang more from class-related factors than from the "ascriptive factors" of race or sex. "The words 'fair choice' do not yet fully describe the matching of students and colleges in the United States," Hearn concluded. "There seem to exist mechanisms that work to ease the paths of the socioeconomically advantaged into the colleges that can help assure the maintenance of those advantages. These mechanisms may also work to make the entry of

college-bound members of other groups into the outstanding colleges less likely."*

What implications does this finding have for government and educational policymakers? This is one of the questions Hearn can confront at Advanced Techology. "I work on evaluation and survey contracts studying the federal role in postsecondary education, with a particular focus on federal financial aid for postsecondary students. I use the quantitative methods I learned in graduate school, and I also use — extensively — the styles of thinking and writing I learned there." Jim Hearn once asked of the findings of his study of college choices, "Are we to regard such a situation as trivial, as merely unfortunate, or as grounds for serious policy action?" As a sociologist who advises educational policymakers, he is in a unique position to influence the answer to that question.

*Quotations in this paragraph are from James C. Hearn, "The relative roles of academic, ascribed, and socioeconomic characteristics in college destinations" (working draft, April 1982). Reprinted by permission of the author.

whereas those from the lower classes tend to remain in lower-class jobs.

The American educational system was begun by the Puritans and later developed by American political leaders into our modern system of elementary schools, secondary schools, colleges, and universities. These schools are complicated bureaucracies, directed and financed by local, state, and federal boards who determine curriculums, testing procedures, and other requirements for certification. Supervisors, principals, and teachers implement the various rules and standards, and students, upon meeting the standards, receive the appropriate diplomas and degrees.

Whether students are from the upper or lower classes, family background is the single most accurate predictor of the school attended, years of schooling, type of occupation, and income. Race and sex also influence future earnings.

The British school system is similar to the American system, but the process of selecting who will receive a higher education and an advanced job and who will enter working-class vocational schools and jobs takes place much earlier, at age thirteen. Family background is an important predictor of which type of education a student will receive.

The baby boom of the late 1940s dramatically

increased the number of students attending school during the 1950s and 1960s. This burst of population is over now, and the number of students is decreasing, which has led to declining college enrollments, especially in private colleges. A larger proportion of students will probably attend local and state public colleges. Whether more working-class and poor students will attend college and whether a college education will become more or less valuable in the job market depends on the political decisions and economic hiring policies of the next decade.

Key Terms

age segregation
compulsory public education
contest mobility
credentials
sponsored mobility

Suggested Readings

Chesler, Mark A. and William M. Cave. **A Sociology of Education: Access to Power and Privilege.** *New York: Macmillan, 1981.* A basic text that emphasizes how the social structure influences education.

Clark, Burton R. **"The Cooling-Out Function in Higher Education,"** American Journal of Sociology *(May 1960): 569–576.* A discussion of the role of counseling in junior colleges in placing students in working-class jobs.

Collins, Randall. **The Credential Society: An Historical Sociology of Education and Stratification.** *New York: Academic Press, 1979.* This book argues strongly that education maintains the current stratification system and the status quo rather than encouraging upward mobility.

Jencks, Christopher and David Riesman. **The Academic Revolution.** *Garden City, N.Y.: Doubleday, 1968.* A classic sociological analysis of universities.

Mandell, Richard D. **The Professor Game.** *New York: Doubleday, 1977.* A good description, sometimes critical, sometimes sympathetic, often funny, of why professors act as they do.

Schrag, Peter and Diane Divoky. **The Myth of the Hyperactive Child.** *N.Y.: Pantheon Books, 1975.* This book argues that children are drugged to keep control in the classroom, not because the children are ill.

Stadtman, Verne A. **Academic Adaptations: Higher Education Prepares for the 1980s and 1990s.** *San Francisco: Jossey-Bass, 1980.* A Carnegie report on education containing articles on recent studies and statistics.

Chapter 15
Political Groups and Systems

Man by nature is a political animal.

— Aristotle

There are numerous laws in the United States. We register our births, go to school, marry, and often divorce according to the law. We paint our houses, mow our grass, shovel our sidewalks, take our driving test, drive on the right side of the road, park our cars when and where we are supposed to, and refrain from spitting in public places. We may get a summons if we do not behave in these ways, but often we are not even aware that there are laws dictating these activities.

Some laws are not obeyed, however. Prohibition of liquor did not stop people from drinking, banning abortions does not stop people from having them, and making marijuana illegal does not stop people from smoking it.

In large, complex societies, many decisions must be made about the duties and responsibilities of citizens and also about their rights and privileges. If the society is to be orderly, people must obey the rules that are made.

Politics is the use of power to determine who gets what in society. The political institution determines and enforces the laws and punishes those who disobey them. It can levy taxes, distribute scarce resources, sponsor education, plan the economy, encourage or ban religion, determine who can marry and who is responsible for children, and otherwise influence behavior. The study of political groups and systems is, therefore, the study of power.

Types of Power

Weber (1958) pointed out that there are several types of power. *Physical force* is one obvious type. An individual or an army can be captured and put in handcuffs or prison by force if those who capture are stronger than those captured. Often, however, sheer force accomplishes little. Although people can be physically restrained, they cannot be made to perform complicated tasks by force alone.

Latent force, or the threat of force, is more powerful than force alone. A kidnapper can get what he wants from a victim by demanding ransom in exchange for the victim's life. The kidnapper wants the money and hopes the threat of murder will produce it because a dead victim doesn't do the kidnapper any good. Similarly, a ruler can say, "Either perform your duty or you will go to jail," hoping that the threat of jail will make the citizen perform the desired duty. Putting the citizen in jail, however, does not really help the ruler. Thus latent force can sometimes produce results in situations in which direct force would not.

Controlling a society through force, whether actual or latent, is expensive and inefficient. It does not bring about the cooperation necessary for society to function productively. A group that relies on force to maintain its power faces a constant threat of being overthrown by its citizens whereas more reliable types of power do not rely on force for their effectiveness. Legitimate power, for example, is accepted by the people in a society as being necessary and beneficial because they recognize the right of the ruling power both to make and enforce rules.

Authority is a form of legitimate power. The people give to the ruler the authority to rule, and they obey willingly without the need or threat of force.

Weber, who was a master at classifying the abstract concepts needed to understand society, identified three types of authority. In traditional authority, the leader of the group leads by tradition or custom. In a patriarchal society, the father is the ruler and is obeyed because it is the accepted practice. When the father dies, his eldest son becomes ruler and has authority based on the

nation's customs. Rulers who have traditional authority are usually born into their positions and their competence to rule is not usually at issue. Also, the bounds of authority for traditional rulers are fairly broad — their power can range from settling minor disagreements to dictating who can marry whom.

The second type, legal authority, is based on a system of rules and regulations that determine how the society will be governed. In the United States, the Constitution sets down the bases for the government's authority, the congress enacts the laws, and the president carries them out. He directs the military when it is needed to enforce the law and brings before the courts or pardons those who break it. The courts interpret the laws and make judgments about whether they have been broken.

The third type of authority is charismatic. Charismatic authority is based on the personal attributes of the leader. Sometimes a person can win the confidence, support, and trust of a group of people who then give the leader the authority to make decisions and set down rules. A charismatic leader attracts followers because they judge him or her to be particularly wise or capable.

Martin Luther King was this kind of leader. He led black people to fight for their civil rights and against segregation. King was a minister and as such had the respect of his followers, but he had no legal authority to lead a political fight to improve the position of blacks in the United States. He gained followers because he was a moving speaker who addressed people with sincerity and a sense of mission and won their respect.

Another charismatic leader is the Reverend Sun Myung Moon of the Unification Church. Moon has built a following on the basis of his own conviction that he was chosen by God to spread the word of Christianity throughout the world and to rebuild God's kingdom on earth. Moon, who has gained followers in his native

Martin Luther King speaks to demonstrators who marched on Washington in August of 1963. King was leader of the Southern Christian Leadership Conference, a group with no legal power to rule in this country. King's charismatic leadership, however, enabled him to lead great masses of people in peaceful demonstrations and to press those with legal authority for equal treatment of blacks.

Korea and in Japan, Europe, and America, instructs his people to work hard and live a simple life of poverty. When they join the church, they sacrifice the worldly goods and pleasures they consider evil, such as alcohol, tobacco, and drugs.

Because charismatic leaders have no legal right to their authority, they are often viewed with suspicion by those who do have legal authority. Since the responsibilities and duties of charismatic leaders are not defined by law, they may pursue a wide choice of activities as long as they have the support of followers. If they do not have it, a charismatic movement usually deteriorates.

Charismatic leaders often try to gain legal authority, which is a more permanent and powerful form of authority in our society. They may run for Congress or other public office, or they may lobby for laws that will permanently protect and uphold their beliefs. The Reverend Moon has held protests and prayer rallies on several political issues, and many believe that he will seek legal authority at some point in his career.

The Development of Political Systems

As societies become wealthier and more complex, political systems develop and grow more powerful. In the chapter on stratification, we discussed an example of a very primitive and simple society, the Tasaday, who had no ruler and made decisions as a group. As societies evolved from similar uncomplicated bands, they grew wealthier and their rulers were able to control larger areas with their armies. At first the controlled areas were small, but later whole cities and surrounding areas came under the power of individual rulers. These territories were called *city-states*. In most modern societies, the territories are vast and are referred to as *nation-states*. Nation-states developed in Europe several centuries ago, but they developed in Africa only during the last century.

When does a nation-state become a cohesive society? How does a country develop laws that will unite the population, create an orderly society, give authority to the governed, and eliminate the need for force? This is one of the oldest questions in political history, but the modern ideas of particular concern to sociologists fall within the basic theoretical approaches discussed throughout this text.

Structural-Functional Theory

Structural functionalists believe that a society is built on a common set of values. As discussed in Chapter 4, our society believes in work, achievement, equal opportunity, and the freedom to run our own lives, to name just a few of our predominant values. These values are learned by young children in the family and passed on to subsequent generations.

Normally, the values of a society shape its laws and political policies. If people value achievement, the law will protect the right to achieve and social policy will develop to encourage equal opportunity in education and jobs. If people value freedom, the law will protect freedom and social policy will encourage freedom — no one will be forced to practice a particular religion, for example, and marriage will be a matter of personal choice. It is the political institutions that pass the laws and develop the policies necessary to enhance the values of the population. Often, the political institution must extend itself into international affairs to protect the society's values. It may limit imports of foreign goods to protect its own workers, and it may negotiate with other nations to allow trade for the benefit of its own citizens. It protects its citizens from aggressive acts and maintains armed forces to carry out its international functions.

Sometimes, however, the values of a society are not mutually consistent. Our view about work and achievement may come into conflict with our view about the freedom to run our own lives: if some people do not want to work, forcing them to do so would impinge on their freedom. Even with a shared set of values, it is not always easy to determine which ones will be translated into laws and which laws will be obeyed. The abortion issue involves two basically conflicting values, one involving the rights of the fetus and one involving the rights of the mother. Legislatures must decide which rights to protect and individuals must choose whether to abide by the law or act according to their own values if they conflict with the law. Predicting which laws will be obeyed becomes even more difficult when different subcultures have conflicting values. Youth groups who use drugs and religious groups who practice polygamy are subcultures whose values are in conflict with the dominant culture.

Structural functionalists believe that the political institution holds the values of the dominant society and arbitrates conflicts when they arise. One person may act on a value of freedom by marrying more than one spouse, or members of a subculture may feel free to use drugs. It is the political system that decides which values must be upheld and which must be limited to maintain social order. In the United States, where freedom is a value, constant arbitration is necessary to protect the freedoms of the individual without impinging on the other values of society.

Conflict Theory

Conflict theory differs radically from structural-functional theory. It does not assume that societies are based on a set of values, but, rather, that they are drawn together by people's need for resources: food, shelter, and other necessities. Some groups get a larger share of the resources, and they use these resources to gain power. Just as they hire people to work for them in the economic sphere, they use their resources to hire people to protect their interests in the political sphere. They use their wealth to influence political leaders to support their economic interests and bring about the downfall of individuals or governments who do not support their interests.

The history of Europe provides many examples of how economic groups have used political power to protect their own interests (Pirenne, 1914). European merchants in the Middle Ages at

During the Middle Ages merchants settled in towns to carry on their trade, as shown in this French engraving of an apothecary, a barber, a furrier, and a tailor. Merchants developed their political power by forming organizations called guilds. Only members of a guild were permitted to trade in the town, and the merchants were able to reduce the competition from vagabond traders.

first sold their goods at strategic points along heavily traveled highways. Eventually, however, they built towns at those points and passed laws restricting others from trading, thus using their political power to create a monopoly of trade. These merchants dominated the cities of Europe for several centuries by passing laws to protect their interests.

In the fifteenth and sixteenth centuries, as worldwide shipping increased, nations became powerful and used their political power to protect their shippers. Later, when machinery came into use and manufacturing grew, the manufacturers initially required no political support. They preferred laissez-faire, a free, competitive market. Workers were plentiful and industry could hire them for very low wages and fire them at will. The workers, who suffered greatly under this system, eventually caused serious civil disturbances, and the industrialists had to develop a political system to protect their interests. Conflict theorists believe that in every age, the wealthy have used political laws and political force to protect their wealth.

Why, then, do the great majority of people support the laws of the wealthy? According to the conflict theorists, it is because the rich use their wealth and power to control the mass media. They teach their values to the majority of people by controlling the schools, the press, radio, television, and other means of communication. They try to convince the population that the rich have a right to their wealth, that they should have the power to restrict trade, hire and fire workers, and otherwise restrict the behavior of the majority to maintain their own position. Unlike the structural functionalists, who believe that the values of the society shape the political system, conflict theorists believe political systems are run by elites who shape the values of society.

Legal Structures in Modern Societies

There are two types of legal political rule in modern societies. Neither type is found in a pure form, and many countries have a mixed power structure. In analyzing modern societies, however, it is useful to describe power structures in terms of their ideal types — whether they are democratic or totalitarian.

The Democratic State

In its ideal form, *democracy* is a power structure in which people govern themselves. Philosophers such as Jean Jacques Rousseau, John Locke, John Stuart Mill, and John Dewey believed that people knew what was in their own best interest and could learn how to protect these interests within the political system. They also believed that the experience of being politically involved would develop better citizens (Orum, 1978).

In large, complex societies, however, it is impossible for every citizen to be involved in the political process. Thus when we refer to "democratic" power structures, we mean those in which people are allowed to vote for elected representatives. It is assumed that the elected representatives will be removed from office if they are not responsive to the desires of the people. These representative governments have laws to limit the power of officials and protect the rights of individuals, especially their equality and their right to dissent.

To organize the individuals in a democracy, *political parties* and other groups develop, which provide candidates and debatable issues so that people can express their opinions and preferences.

Democracies have typically developed in societies like the United States where there is an abundance of natural resources. Wealth gives people the freedom to be involved in politics, and the abundance of resources permits the economy to grow without regulation. Some poor countries, however, such as India have also developed democratic political systems despite their poverty.

Democratic states will be covered more thoroughly in our discussion of the American political system later in this chapter.

France: A Bureaucratic State. France is a democracy, but because its bureaucrats wield such enormous power, it has been described as "a state within a state" (Ridley, 1979, p. 105). The government is headed by a president elected by popular vote. The president appoints a prime minister to be "in general charge of the work of the government" (Ridley, 1979, p. 75). Thus it is not clear whether the president or the prime minister runs the government. In practice, the president has been the more powerful official, although many presidential acts such as decrees, appointments of senior officials, pardons, and foreign treaties also require the signature of the prime minister. The prime minister selects the ministers of justice, defense, budget, education, and so on, and directs their activity, but the president must approve the prime minister's choices. The two legislative houses, the Parliament and the National Assembly, are elected, but the National Assembly can be dissolved by the president.

The French government is a strong, central government, but there are extensive conflicts among the various ministers, their staffs, and the legislative bodies. The state's stability rests in its huge civil service, especially in the elite corps who are "the state within the state."

To qualify for an elite position in the French civil service, candidates must pass through a special school that trains government officials, the Ecole National d'Administration (ENA). Selection for the ENA is based on a competitive examination. Students usually study for these exams after they have completed college, and after completing the two-year ENA program, they must again take competitive examinations.

The elite civil servants selected through this process serve in the top jobs in government and industry. While serving in government posts, they are allowed to participate in labor or political organizations and can leave the civil service to run for an elected office. They head the government-owned industries: coal, gas, the railways, aviation, the largest banks, and the Renault car firm. They are recruited for key posts in private corporations and often move back and forth between the civil

service and private industry. According to some critics, they are an elite ruling class that controls government and industry.

The Totalitarian State

Totalitarianism is a system of rule in which the government has total control. Unlike democracies, where a variety of groups struggle for a voice in government, the government dictates the society's values, ideology, rules, and form of government. It also controls the economic development, which is planned in advance, and production is based on the needs of the society, as determined by the dictator.

Totalitarian societies do not permit dissent. Their goal is to develop a unified population, one that is not divided by differing religious loyalties or political views. They eliminate dissenters either through violence, imprisonment, or expulsion, especially when the societies are just developing. Totalitarian states are ruled by one political party that organizes the citizens into a unified group by educating them on party policies and by providing an organization through which supporters can express their support.

The Soviet Union: A Totalitarian State. The Soviet Union's political system is based on the ideas of Karl Marx and Freidrich Engels. Marx believed that a society's first responsibility is to meet the economic needs of its people. Communism, he argued, could meet those needs. He did not describe how a communist system would work, but after Marx's death Engels spoke

Delegates elected by Communists throughout the Soviet Union meet in Moscow under an image of Lenin to decide who will lead the Communist party. The party does not officially rule the Soviet Union, but it is the only political party in that country and extremely powerful in determining Soviet policy.

of the "withering away of the state" (Hazard, 1980, p. 6), which would happen when the people were prosperous and knew the rules of social living necessary to maintain prosperity. At that time, there would be no need for a state or police to enforce laws. People would live cooperatively, and only administrators would be needed to achieve efficient production and direct the flow of goods to the people.

The Soviet Union's goal is very clear: a communist nation run by administrators. Communism is not yet possible, however, partly because the economy is not yet efficient enough and partly because the people have not yet learned how to live in a communist society. Until they learn to function in such a society, strong leadership will be necessary to reach the goals of communism.

This leadership is provided by the Communist party, which is open to any citizen who understands the goals of communism and is committed to work for them. Membership is gained when two members of the party recommend the applicant. Currently, about 10 percent of the population of the Soviet Union belong to the party.

Members meet in local groups called *primary party organizations*. All members are allowed to speak at meetings, but they are not allowed to create factions or rival groups. They may not discuss their views with other party members outside of meetings, nor may they try to win support from other members before they speak to the group as a whole. In short, they cannot organize coalitions (Hazard, 1980).

The primary party organization elects a secretary as a leader and delegates to represent the organization at local conferences. At these local conferences, the delegates elect a committee which, in turn, elects a secretary to run regional affairs. They also elect delegates to the larger provincial conferences. The process continues on a larger scale; ultimately, about 5,000 delegates meet in Moscow to elect the Central Committee, which elects the Political Bureau, a steering committee of thirteen members and nine alternates. This committee determines policy and elects the leader of the Communist party.

Because members are carefully selected and vote only at the local level and because factions cannot get started, there is little chance of great upheaval within the Communist party. The secretaries at each level normally place only their own names on the ballot to elect secretaries, so it would take an enormous wave of discontent to disturb the election process.

The Communist party determines Soviet government policy, but it is not itself the government. The government is the Soviet, a system of committees begun in 1905 before the Russian Revolution. This system parallels the party system.

The Supreme Soviet is the highest committee, dealing with the budget, foreign affairs, new legislation, and other important matters. The members of the Supreme Soviet and the various local Soviets do not have to belong to the Communist party, but party members are well represented in the Soviets, especially in those at higher levels.

From time to time the Communist party has tried to ignore the Soviet committees, but they have been more successful when they work with the Soviets. Cooperation enables them to radiate party influence to citizens outside of the party, and they benefit from the expertise of members of Soviets who are not party members.

The Soviet Union considers itself a democracy. All citizens are equal under the law regardless of race, sex, or nationality, and all have the right to vote, but these freedoms may be used only to further the socialist cause. Thus people may speak or publish statements to further the cause of communism, but they may not oppose it. The Communists control the press and censor statements that do not promote communism. They welcome letters to the editor, but they publish only those that support major policies or help promote efficiency in the lower echelons of the bureaucracy.

The state owns all industry, and most people work for the state. It is possible to have a private business, but taxes are very high, while pensions and payments for disability are very low. Consequently, career-minded people strive for a state position. The better positions are obtained by successfully completing a university education, and students enter the university after the tenth grade. The vast majority of people, who are not selected to attend the university, never get management-level jobs. Those who do receive higher education are assigned a job in their field for three years, after which they are free to seek employment where they wish.

The major political difference, then, between the political systems of the United States and the

Soviet Union is that the Soviet system does not allow dissent from its one stated goal. Individuals, groups, churches, and the press need not work for the system, but they are not permitted to work against it. The major economic difference between the two countries is that the Soviet government owns the industry and employs most of the citizens.

Democratic and totalitarian societies also have several characteristics in common. They often have similar ideologies. Both types may believe in freedom and equality, yet inequality exists in societies of both types. Another similarity is that each considers its own system superior to the other. The most conspicuous similarity, however, is their bureaucratic organization. The political parties, governments, and economic systems of modern societies are so highly bureaucratized that some believe it is the bureaucracy, not the political leader, the party, or the people, that runs the government (Orum, 1978).

The Political System in the United States

The United States has a democratic political system. Citizens are expected to participate in the political process by voting, debating issues, joining one of the two political parties or remaining "independent," and expressing their views to their elected officials. To participate fully, citizens must both understand and trust their political system, and in this country the political socialization of citizens begins very early in childhood (Orum, 1978).

Political Socialization

In most American communities, many children watch the mayor lead the Fourth of July parade, and the very young ones assume that the mayor is a good and benevolent leader. Most youngsters find that other leaders also give time and money to make the community a better place to live. During elections, children often learn about political parties from their families, and frequently they identify with a political party on an emotional level long before they can understand political issues. To a child, the President of the United States is to the country what the father is to the family: a leader, provider, and protector. This *political socialization* continues when children enter school. Through formal courses in history, literature, and government, they learn to respect the society's norms and political system. From their relationships with teachers, they learn that leadership is acquired through achievement. The principal, they discover, has achieved more than the teacher, and team captains, class officers, and other school leaders have attained their posts through their achievements.

Not all children emerge from their family and school socialization with the idea that political leaders are benevolent, caring, achieving people, of course. They may accumulate contradictory evidence along the way, perhaps having experiences with parents, teachers, or other leaders that indicate their leaders are not to be trusted. They may also acquire a distrust of the political system by listening to parental complaints about lack of jobs or other conditions that result from political decisions and cause family hardship. Schools teaching middle-class values may fail to convince a child living in poverty that the political system is fair and benevolent; environmental realities may provide harsh evidence that not everyone can move from log cabin to president. Children from Appalachia and urban ghettos are much less apt to support the American political system than are middle-class Americans (Dowse and Hughes, 1972).

By the time children finish school, they have developed political attitudes that will shape their political behavior in adult life, but political socialization still continues, especially through the mass media, which reinforces childhood socialization. Much mass media socialization presents political issues in emotional terms. Slogans that promise a better America without offering factual data about how this is to be done are seeking an emotional response from voters, a response resembling the one a child feels for the mayor leading the Fourth of July parade. Although these emotional appeals for voter support are routinely criticized as "flag waving," emotion is believed to play a very large role in voter choice.

The most effective way for the mass media to influence people is to present information in such a way that there is only one obvious conclusion (Goodin, 1980). The media often give only one side of an issue, and if the "obvious" solution is heard frequently enough, it will seem to make sense to most people. Often, for a year or two before an election, we hear a candidate mentioned as the "obvious" choice for the party. If people don't have jobs, it is "obviously" because they don't want them. If people don't vote, they are "obviously" not interested. These statements are not obvious at all, but unless information is provided they may seem obvious enough and will probably be accepted by the majority of the public.

In the United States, there is concern that the mass media express only the views of the large corporations that generally own them. Few newspapers, for example, are still locally owned and compete with other locally owned newspapers. In 1977, only thirty-seven cities had competing newspapers (Reasons and Perdue, 1981), and many of these were owned by large publishing syndicates that controlled the press in several cities. There are only three major television networks: ABC, NBC, and CBS. Thus information about politics may be severely limited, and the information presented may represent only the viewpoint of the mass media owners.

The federal government also provides information to its citizens on health, agriculture, education, labor, housing, and population statistics. This information is dispensed in a variety of ways, through county agricultural agents, public health centers, libraries, newspapers, radio, and television. Many of the statistics used by sociologists are collected and published by government agencies. Sociologists are well aware, however, that the government also attempts to shape public opinion, and sometimes reports provide information that presents a misleading description of a problem. Government unemployment figures, for example, count only those unemployed who are actively seeking work but do not report the number of people who have given up the search for a job — which minimizes the problem of unemployment in the country.

Political Participation

American voters traditionally remain very loyal to their political party. They tend to consistently vote for Republican or Democratic candidates, although in recent years the number of voters who remain independent of party ties has been increasing. It seems that party loyalty is based primarily on emotional ties (Dowse and Hughes, 1972). Most people are not well informed about political issues and do not choose a party on the basis of political opinions. Rather, they support a party for traditional or emotional reasons — perhaps because their families have always supported that party — and they are then guided by the party's stand on the issues. In other words, voters are socialized by their political parties to view political issues in a certain way.

The so-called moral issues such as race, sexual behavior, and religion are an exception to this general rule. People usually have a strong opinion on moral issues, and they will leave their party and not vote or else vote for the other party if they disagree with their party's stand. As a result,

Ku Klux Klansmen march to a rally in Salisbury, North Carolina in 1957 to protest Supreme Court actions that aided black citizens. Weathermen march in protest in downtown Chicago in 1969 to protest the war in Vietnam. The Klan is typical of right wing groups, who protest changes in social policy that advance the cause of others, and the Weathermen are typical of left wing groups, who desire change in the status quo.

political parties generally try to avoid moral issues altogether and take a middle-of-the-road stand on other issues to attract the largest number of voters.

Certain groups outside of the major political parties have attempted to bring moral issues into politics. They recognize that people can be easily influenced by emotional issues and have used these issues successfully to attract followers. If the majority of the voters agreed, for example, that abortions should be outlawed, the major political parties would also express that belief and the issue would cease to exist.

The *right wing* in American politics consists

of conservative people who want to conserve the traditional ways of life. They often support moral issues because they fear the decay of traditional American values. Most of them come from middle-class families in which they or their parents were small shop owners, farmers, garage owners, small business owners, or members of middle management in larger organizations.

One hypothesis about the extreme right suggests that its members are frustrated by their inability to acquire status, either in small communities or large ones. Due to social changes, it has become more difficult to succeed in small business and in small towns. In addition, the attainment of status is not easy to recognize when so many people live in large cities, work in large organizations, and are unknown to most of their neighbors. Under these conditions, people feel insecure about their status. They want recognizable success, theorists argue, and believe that they would achieve it if society would return to what it was in the past. The more extreme groups in the right wing are the Ku Klux Klan and the John Birch Society.

The *left wing* of American politics is also motivated by political or religious moral issues, but its followers are more likely to be deprived economically. They want to change certain aspects of American life in order to create a society with more equality, less poverty, more jobs, better housing for all, and other improvements. To reach these goals, they argue, a radical redistribution of wealth and power is necessary. They are therefore sometimes considered enemies of the American political system.

One such group is the Black Muslim church, which has attracted poor blacks who have been utterly frustrated with their living conditions. They believe that American society will never integrate blacks and want to develop a culture within the nation, but separate and distinct so that blacks can have the self-respect and economic security not available to them in a racist

society. They are therefore viewed by some to be dangerous enemies even though the United States is a nation of many groups of people.

Who Rules America?

The American system of government was designed to include many diverse groups in a decentralized system of federal, state, and local governments. Each level of government has a system of checks and balances: the legislative branches make the law, the executive branches carry out the law, and the judicial branches interpret the law. Officials are elected for short terms, and at first these representatives were elected only by white male property owners, who comprised perhaps one-sixth of the white male population. Over the years, the vote has been extended to all men and women aged twenty-one and over.

Our system of government is decentralized and representative, but the questions remain: Who holds the power? Which groups influence government the most? There are three major perspectives on power in America.

David Riesman et al. (1953) described the power system of the United States as one of *political pluralism* — rule by many different groups. A variety of special interest groups try to influence legislation by forming lobbies that represent various industries, labor groups, religions, educational groups, and other special interests. No single group has absolute power, but many groups can protect their own interests by pressuring politicians for favorable legislation or by fighting against legislation that would damage their interests.

Mills (1958) argued that the country is run by a *power elite*: heads of large corporations, military leaders, a few important senators, members of congress, and federal officials. These groups, although they may differ about some things, cooperate with one another to gain their major goal, power. To preserve their status, they socialize the

Bending the Facts: Reagan's Press Talk

In his first press conference of the new year, President Reagan displayed one of those skills necessary to get past embarrassing moments in any administration — selective use and interpretation of facts.

The press conference is replete with examples:

Unemployment. The president said he had great sympathy for those who are out of work. But he added, "Comparing this to the beginning of our term, there are a million people more working than there were in 1980 . . ."

Actually, there are fewer

Americans working today than there were when Reagan took office, and there are also far more Americans unemployed. The unemployment rate is now at 8.9 percent.

According to the Bureau of Labor Statistics, about 100,000 fewer Americans were working in December 1981 than had jobs in December 1980. About 1.6 million more Americans were unemployed at the end of 1981 than were unemployed when President Carter left office.

Tax breaks for schools that discriminate against blacks. The ad-

ministration announced on Jan. 8 that it would reverse 12 years of government policy and begin giving tax exemptions to non-profit private schools that practice racial discrimination. The White House said it was trying to keep the Internal Revenue Service from making social policy that should be made by Congress. Following a public outcry, the president this week asked Congress to ban such tax breaks by law.

Asked about these reversals, Reagan said he was dealing with a "procedural matter," not a "policy matter," and that "there was no basis in the law for what they (the IRS) were doing" in denying tax exemptions.

In fact, there is a basis in the law for denying tax breaks to schools that discriminate. Most administration officials concede that the IRS was not acting on

---

public through the mass media by using advertising, news broadcasts, and political reports to convince citizens that each individual has a voice in government and that the elite rulers act as the people's servants. If necessary, however, the elite will sometimes make concessions to gain the people's support, but ideally, from the perspective of the elite, the people will passively support the rulers and not try to actively influence government.

The third viewpoint, derived from Marx, suggests that economic powers dominate America. Big business supports the candidates who will represent their interests, regardless of their political party affiliation. Big business also sends representa-

tives to Washington to influence legislation, to lobby for special privileges, and to hold key positions in government. In other words, big business ensures that the friends of big business will be elected. These officials then appoint representatives of big business to office and promote legislation designed to meet the needs of big business.

Much of the power of big business is attained through its *lobbies*. Business lobbies, staffed by business people and lawyers, devote a great deal of time, effort, and money to winning favorable legislation from government. The example below of the battle between the auto safety lobby and the auto industry lobby offers an interesting look at how lobbies operate.

whim. The Supreme Court has ruled that the IRS was required to deny such exemptions, based on the 1964 Civil Rights Act.

Richard Allen. "We did not dismiss Richard Allen," the president said of his former national security adviser. "He is still a part of this administration."

In fact, Allen was replaced by William Clark as national security adviser, and given a job as a day-by-day consultant to the Presidential Foreign Intelligence Advisory Board. White House officials, from top to bottom, made it clear they were unhappy with Allen's performance, and that he had embarrassed the president sufficiently to be removed from any substantive job.

Steel industry expansion. As proof that his economic program is stimulating industry to invest, Reagan, as he has done on several other occasions, said the steel industry has a multibillion-dollar expansion program in the works and is ready to go with it.

In fact, a spokesman for the steel industry conceded that most of the $6.4 billion in capital improvements, essentially modernization, was being planned before Reagan took office, and would probably have gone ahead even if Jimmy Carter were still in office. Foreign steelmakers, with more modern plants and equipment, are making steel more cheaply than U.S. plants, and the industry "had to modernize to keep up," an official said. He added that because of the recession and high interest rates, some of those expansion plans are now being reconsidered and may be "stretched out" over a longer number of years.

Social program cuts. Reagan said most of what his administration has done in social programs "has not been a cut. There has not been a cut in overall spending on human resources."

The president is correct in saying that the government, overall, spent more for human resources in 1981 than it did in 1980. But it was in fact cut in specific programs. Thousands of individuals lost benefits or got reduced benefits.

One example is block grant programs, which were reduced by as much as 27 percent. Maternal and child health programs, which received $475 million in the fiscal year that ended in October, will get $347 million in the current fiscal year.

SOURCE: Devroy, Ann, *The Prince George's Journal*, Jan. 21, 1982, p. A2. Reprinted by permission of Gannett News Service.

During the early 1960s, Ralph Nader launched an attack on the faulty design of American automobiles with his book *Unsafe at Any Speed.* After the book was published, Nader continued to lobby for improved auto safety. Congress considered passing legislation to set safety standards for cars, but the auto lobby, led by Henry Ford, moved in to stop the legislation (Dowie, 1977). Ford went to Washington and spoke to the Business Council, an organization of one hundred executives of large organizations who come to Washington from time to time to advise government. He visited members of Congress, held press conferences, and recruited business support, but he failed to stop the passage of the Motor Vehicle Safety Act, which was signed into law in 1966.

A regulatory agency was then made responsible for setting guidelines for auto safety, but the Ford Motor Company sent representatives to the agency to argue that poor drivers, unsafe guardrail designs, poor visibility, and a variety of other highway and driving hazards were responsible for accidents. Not only was the automobile safe, they contended, but regulations requiring improvements would increase the cost of cars while saving few lives.

Nevertheless, in 1968 the regulatory agency issued new safety standards designed to reduce the risk of fire in automobiles after a rear-end crash.

Ralph Nader is a lawyer who holds no legal position in government, but he lives in Washington, D.C. and lobbies for consumer protection legislation. His charisma stems from his commitment to his cause, and his followers have been nicknamed "Nader's Raiders." He and his group have lobbied for consumer protection in the sale of many products and services, but they are most noted for their fight for auto safety.

As required by law, the agency scheduled hearings on the regulation. Ford responded with a report stating that automobile fires were not a problem. The agency then had to do several studies to determine if fire was a problem. It found that 400,000 cars burned up every year and that 3,000 people burned to death. It again proposed safety standards, and Ford again responded, arguing that although burning accidents do happen, rear-end collisions were not the cause. The agency re-searched this question and found that rear-end collisions were in fact the cause in most cases. Again regulations were proposed, again Ford responded, and again research was conducted. The total delay in developing regulations was eight years. The regulations eventually did pass, giving a victory to Ralph Nader and consumer groups and a defeat of sorts to Ford Motor Company. During those eight years, however, the company killed regulations requiring other safety measures, and it cost taxpayers a great deal to finance the eight-year battle to improve automobiles. The improvements ultimately cost the auto manufacturers approximately $11 per car.

This account of one corporation's reluctance to comply with an auto safety regulation shows that big business has enormous but not absolute power over government. It also shows how time-consuming and expensive the business of lobbying is. It is a procedure that can be practiced only by organizations with much wealth and power.

Politics and the Distribution of Wealth

Although economics will be covered in the next chapter, politics has a strong impact on economics. Both are very much intertwined in all societies. The economic system produces the wealth, but it is the political system that determines how the wealth is distributed.

In the United States, the government can levy taxes and use its funds to support programs for its citizens. In recent years, debate has centered on whether government should support business or the less privileged in society. Opponents in the debate tend to favor either supply-side or demand-side economic policies.

Demand-side Economy

During the decade called the Roaring Twenties, the rich became very rich and the poor became poorer. By 1929, the richest 15,000 families in the United States made as much money as the five to six million families at the bottom of the pay scale combined (Heilbroner, 1980). These top-earning families did not spend all or even most of their money on consumer goods — they saved it. The six million people at the bottom of the pay scale could not buy consumer goods because they did not have enough money. A

demand-side economy requires consumers who buy goods, but businesses could not find buyers.

The so-called New Deal programs were developed by President Franklin D. Roosevelt in the 1930s. The country was in a severe depression, and manufacturers could not sell their products because so many unemployed people could not afford to buy products. New Deal programs were designed to put more spending money into the hands of millions of these poorer Americans. Income taxes were developed to tax the rich, and programs such as the Emergency Farm Mortgages Act and the Civilian Conservation Corps were initiated to put unemployed workers back to work. As mentioned in Chapter 9, the distribution of wealth has remained essentially the same from the 1940s to the present. When the amount of money available to the poor increased, their purchasing power improved and demand was created in the marketplace.

World War II caused a demand for the goods needed to fight a war, and it was this demand that pulled the United States out of the Great Depression. After World War II, the returning military forces created a demand for homes, cars, furnishings, and the other amenities of a middle-class lifestyle. That generation had large families whose needs continued to increase demand throughout the middle part of this century.

Supply-side Economy

While the demand for goods and services was strong, American industries made large profits selling consumer products. At the same time, however, factories were growing old and the United States was falling behind other nations in its ability to produce such vital products as steel and automobiles. Products like railroad passenger cars and ball bearings did not bring as much profit, and production of these items stopped. The United States was then no longer able to supply the manufactured goods consumers de-

Mea Culpa, Mea Culpa, I'm Part of a Tax Rip-Off

I have to confess that a lot of the time I eat lunch for free. I take someone to lunch and I discuss business a bit and then I pay for him or her, put the tab on my expense account and then have the company pay for it. Then the company deducts it from its taxes so we all wind up paying for my lunch — you, me and the very poor, assuming you are not the very poor.

I have more to confess. I know of worse outrages than the poor who cheat on welfare and the kids who don't deserve food stamps and the people who take advantage of government and don't do any work. I know people who take their girlfriends or their mistresses to lunch, put it on their expense accounts and wind up having the government pay for some of it. I know people who work for themselves and then just deduct almost every meal from their taxes.

I have even more to confess. I know someone who bought a yacht that he uses just part of the time. The rest of the time he rents it out to a company that charters it to still other people. It's a tax dodge. It's perfectly legal and probably the people who rent the yacht from the company that charters it deduct the cost from their taxes. It's legal for them, too. This is called smart business. When the poor do it, it's called cheating.

Oh I have even more to confess. I deduct the interest on my mortgage. I am entitled to do it and so I do it and it was this deduction that forced me to stop being a renter and become an owner. If you are poor, you cannot become an owner and so you cannot take this deduction.

If the poor were getting away with what the rich are getting away with, someone in Congress would introduce a bill to stop it all from happening. They would say something about how it's ruining the fabric of society. *Time* magazine would make it the cover story. I would buy it and believe it — and deduct the cost of the

manded as efficiently as other nations. Thus, while demand in the marketplace remained strong, the *supply-side economy* had weakened.

Current supply-side economists suggest that this problem can be corrected by making it profitable to invest in upgrading means of production. Accordingly, the Reagan Administration, which advocated supply-side economics, reduced the taxes of the rich so that they had more money to invest in businesses. It also reduced taxes on money made from investments as a further incentive. As a result, the rich saved money on taxes, and the earnings they made if they invested their savings were taxed at a lower rate. Under supply-side economics, the government, therefore, receives fewer tax dollars and cuts programs designed to aid the poor such as welfare, Medicaid, food stamps, and school lunches.

Some critics of supply-side economics have argued that the country must not drop programs that aid those unable to work because they are too young, too old, ill, or because no jobs are available. Critics of the capitalist system argue that a fundamental change in the profit system is required. As long as the needs of society are met only when they provide profits to capitalists, the society will continue to have unemployment and poverty, and human needs will go unmet simply

magazine. This is something else I confess.

I confess also that I deduct the newspapers I might buy anyway and the books that I cherish. I do not belong to any clubs, but if one would have me and I did belong, I probably would deduct the cost of that also. Either that, or my company would pay for it and it would deduct it from its taxes. It's okay. It's always okay when the rich do it. Only the poor rip off the government. Those are the rules.

I confess that I sometimes do not understand why I am allowed to deduct for things that I would buy anyway. I confess that I do not think it's fair that some guy has to buy his lunch and I can get mine free and I confess that a good deal of the time I think I have all this coming — that I am entitled to it. I lose sight, I think, of what is really fair and really

right and I start to think that if it benefits me, it has to be right and fair. I know lots of people like that. By and large, they won the last election.

I know, of course, that there is more to tax law than just what is fair and equitable. There is the little matter of making policy, of encouraging the housing industry, say, or wanting to help people who will take some financial risks — like drilling for oil. I understand all that and I suppose it is a good idea, but I have to confess that I feel a bit guilty when I get worked up over something like welfare fraud and discuss it, say, over a swell lunch that the government has just helped me buy.

There is more for me to confess. I confess that I know a man who earns more than $100,000 a year and paid something like $4,000 in taxes. He deducts almost everything. I know people who

have summer homes, rent them most of the year, stay in them something like two weeks, and save a bundle on taxes. They deduct, they depreciate, they finagle and they fib a little and when all is said and done the government pays for their house. So nice of us to do that for them.

I confess I have yet to hear anyone in the Reagan Administration talk of saving money by closing these loopholes. I confess I take advantage of these loopholes and I confess, further, that if it were not for the government, I might not be able to afford my house or, for that matter, my lunches.

I'll repent. I'll take a poor person to lunch.

SOURCE: Cohen, Richard, *The Washington Post*, Feb. 24, 1981, p. B1. © 1981, The Washington Post Company, reprinted with permission.

because it is not profitable to meet them. Whether profit is made by manufacturing consumer goods or building modern factories, the contention of critics is that today's profit system will maintain inequality and the problems associated with it. They argue that a more equitable redistribution of money would permit everyone to benefit from the wealth generated by society. They would also prefer an economy designed to meet the needs of society even when those needs do not yield great profit. Today, the government's efforts to help those who cannot manage financially take the form of some type of welfare payment.

Welfare

Welfare consists of payments made by the government to people who have an inadequate income. Welfare programs include:

1. Aid to Families with Dependent Children (AFDC), the largest program, aids families with children under eighteen years of age if there is no adult capable of supporting them. This program does not provide payments when there is an able-bodied male in the household.
2. Medicaid is the medical insurance program for the poor.

3. Supplemental Security Income (SSI) is part of the Social Security system designed to aid the poorest of the aged, blind, and disabled.
4. General Assistance is a program to help poor people not covered by other programs.

Because there are so many poor people in this country, benefits are very meager. The program that provides support for children when parents cannot work (AFDC) cost over 1 billion dollars but paid only an average of $99.68 per month per recipient in 1980 (World Almanac, 1982).

Critics of the present welfare system argue that it exploits poor people. Gans (1972) scathingly lists some advantages to a society for keeping people on welfare:

SOCIOLOGISTS AT WORK
Policymaking in City Government

Mel Ravitz is a member of Detroit's city council, the only sociologist ever to serve on that body. He is a graduate of Detroit's Wayne State University and has a doctorate in sociology from the University of Michigan. For thirty years he has been combining political activity and community organizing with a teaching career at Wayne State.

What insights can a sociologist bring to the role of urban policymaker? "The sociologist," Mel Ravitz says, "should be expected to contribute a comprehensive way of looking at social problems; to point out that nothing exists apart from other things and that, to be understood, a proposal, plan, or ordinance must be analyzed in relation to other proposals, plans, or ordinances; and to emphasize that any response to any issue must be seen in terms of its real consequences rather than in terms of its author's intentions." As a sociologist, he feels that he is especially well prepared to understand the social dimensions of community life — a welcome balance to the preoccupation of most people in government with things physical and fiscal. "Other policymakers," he says, "at both the legislative and the administrative levels are often people whose experience is in working with material things rather than with social or cultural ones." His city council colleagues during his first term were an accountant, a civil engineer, a former union leader, a former major league baseball player, and four lawyers. "Of course they were more familiar with, and therefore more trusting of, such things as neighborhood design, facility location, and budgeting than they were with the concepts of cultural difference, social stratification, social mobility, assimilation, and relative deprivation. There was only the barest beginning perception of the human effects of urban renewal."

In his first campaign, in 1961, Ravitz had his eyes opened to the power of various groups in the city politic. As he told a meeting of sociologists, "It should come as no surprise that there are countless groups meeting simultaneously around the city. The firsthand experience of visiting fifteen meetings in one day makes you realize that all these diverse groups — unions, church groups, house parties, block clubs, political associations — are functioning side by side around the city, busily and narrowly focused on their respective problems, each unaware of the existence of the others. One has a thrilling insight into the complex social organization of a vast urban community."

Ultimately, it was the strength of such

1. They are a source of cheap labor.
2. They can be sold goods of inferior quality that otherwise could not be sold at all.
3. They serve as examples of deviance, thereby motivating others to support the norms of the dominant group.
4. They make mobility easier for others, because they are out of the competition.

5. They do the most unpleasant jobs.
6. They absorb the costs of change, since they suffer the unemployment when technological advances are made by industry.
7. They create jobs in social work and related fields for the middle class.
8. They create distinctive cultural forms in music and art, which the middle class adopts.

groups that swept Ravitz into office in 1961. "In my role as a community organizer I had built a political constituency," he says, and that constituency — made up of, among others, well-organized groups of the elderly and teenagers — worked tirelessly on his campaign. Then an unforeseeable sequence of events mobilized other important groups. Several astonishing incidents of police brutality took place in the black community. An ordinance that would have increased the power of the city's Commission on Community Relations to deal with such incidents was defeated in the city council. After this, a coalition of black church and community groups, white liberals, and labor union members endorsed a slate of reform candidates, including Ravitz. All four of the incumbents endorsed by the coalition were re-elected, Ravitz and two other new council members were chosen, and the incumbent mayor was ousted. It was the biggest political upset in Detroit history.

After his election, Ravitz had to make adjustments in his way of looking at the world and at himself. The need for the first such adjustment became apparent immediately: "My change of status from professor to council member brought about a significant change in social perception and behavior. Before the election I was simply a liberal or even radical sociology professor. Only my friends paid any attention to what I said. After the election, the manager of the city's best hotel

extended his best wishes; the police officers and fire fighters associations wired their congratulations and a dozen roses; and a large home-owners organization hoped I would be guided by 'good will' during my tenure in office. If ever one doubted the significance of status change, here was ample proof."

More important, he saw a need for change in his approach to his work. "The sociologist by academic preparation and professional experience is an analyst of and adviser on decisions rather than a decision-maker. I had to be willing to accept a shift of role. No longer could I afford the luxury of never-ending analysis; no longer was I able to qualify issues and categorize them into infinite shades of grey. Time is always short for legislators, and decisions are constantly demanded by both colleagues and constituents. Any one who cannot make decisions on the basis of available and always limited information cannot long survive in this public role."

Mel Ravitz was re-elected to four-year terms in 1965 and 1969. In 1973 he ran for mayor, lost, and became director of the Detroit–Wayne County Community Mental Health Board. But in 1981 the political bug bit him again, and he ran for and won his old seat on the city council. That's where you'll find him today, as he says, "legislating, advocating, serving as an ombudsman, performing a ministerial function, attending political events, speaking — and campaigning."

Welfare payments also tend to keep the unemployed from expressing their discontentment. Piven and Cloward (1971) have shown that welfare payments increase when unemployment is high and discontent is widespread but decrease when workers are scarce and unemployment is low.

Other "Welfare" Programs

Welfare payments to the poor comprise only a small part of the federal government's efforts to improve living conditions. Actually there are many programs designed to assist classes other than the poor:

1. veterans benefits such as life insurance, health care, educational support, housing loans, and burial grounds
2. housing loans, which are available to higher-income groups, offering lower interest rates and reduced down payments
3. business loans, on favorable terms, which are available to owners of both small and large businesses
4. farming subsidies to landowners who agree not to farm certain of their lands
5. social security, which is not available to the unemployed or to those who work in jobs the program does not cover
6. medical care in hospitals built with government funds, staffed by doctors educated with government support, who use treatments developed with the help of government grants
7. college classrooms and dormitories built with government funds and financial assistance for college students

In fact, there are more government programs to help the middle and upper classes than the poor. Government support for the poor and for business will be discussed further in the next chapter, which deals with our economic institutions.

Summary

A political institution has the power to rule in a society. Power is the ability to make others follow the rules or dictates set down by those in control, which can be done by force, but force is an inefficient way to control a society. Latent force, making people comply by threatening them with punishment, is more effective.

Authority is a still more powerful means of control and is considered legitimate because the people believe the ruler has a right to rule and they comply voluntarily. Traditional authority is derived from accepted practices or customs. Legal authority is based on a system of legislated rules and regulations. Charismatic authority comes from the personal traits of the leader.

Modern societies have two types of legal power structures. Democratic systems allow citizens to participate in their own governance. Totalitarian systems provide a consistent form of government in which different groups do not cause dissent as they compete for power. The Soviet Union is a totalitarian society. Both power systems are based on legal authority and have similar values. Both profess a belief in freedom and equality for their citizens and are organized bureaucratically. The bureaucracies may be the real seats of power in both countries.

Structural functionalists believe that political systems reflect societal values. If a society values freedom, monogamy, hard work, and achievement, laws will be passed to enforce these values, and members of the society will comply with the law because it reflects their own beliefs. Structural functionalists also believe that the political system must try to resolve conflicts in values. The value of freedom, for example, may come in conflict with the value of hard work, and the government must arbitrate to ensure that behavior does not infringe on either value. Some subcultures teach values that conflict with those of the larger society, but the government must protect the values of the dominant society.

Conflict theorists believe that certain groups gain power because they possess a large share of society's resources. They use these resources to acquire power and use the law and the political system to protect their own wealth. The rich teach the population through the schools and the mass media that their wealth, power, and laws are legitimate. In other words, they shape the values of the society to serve their own interests.

In the United States, political socialization begins early. Youngsters learn about political leaders and political parties at home and in the community. Socialization continues in school, and most children learn to respect the political system, although poor children are more likely to question government and its practices.

Most Americans remain loyal to one political party and permit it to guide them on important issues. On moral issues, however, voters tend to act more independently.

Debate about how power is distributed in the United States has been continuing for many years. Theorists have argued variously that there are many powerful groups that all try to protect their own interests, that a power elite made up of business and government officials controls the power, and that big business runs the country. Regardless of the explanation one accepts, clearly power requires resources that many groups do not have.

The political system has the power to tax and the power to distribute resources to citizens. American policy has varied, sometimes distributing wealth to business, sometimes to the consumer. The poorest citizens in the United States receive very small welfare payments and other benefits from the government.

Key Terms

authority
charismatic authority
city-states
demand-side economy
democracy

left wing
legal authority
legitimate power
lobbies
nation-states
political pluralism
power elite
right wing
supply-side economy
totalitarianism
traditional authority

Suggested Readings

Goodin, Robert E. **Manipulatory Politics.** *New Haven: Yale University Press, 1980.* If you believe that you are sometimes manipulated by politicians' use of the information they control, you should read this book.

Janeway, Elizabeth. **Powers of the Weak.** *New York: Knopf, 1980.* This book suggests that the weak in a stratified society — women, blacks, and the poor — have power because they do not have to meet the expectations of the powerful. They cannot be ruled if they do not consent to it.

Mills, C. Wright. **The Power Elite.** *New York: Oxford University Press, 1958.* This classic, which is still being debated, describes how supposedly diverse powerful people and groups are really interrelated to form one power elite.

Orum, Anthony M. **Introduction to Political Sociology: The Social Anatomy of the Body Politic.** *Englewood Cliffs, N.J.: Prentice-Hall, 1978.* A well-documented text that could serve as a handbook for anyone interested in pursuing the topic of political sociology.

Piven, Frances Fox and Richard A. Cloward. **Regulating the Poor: The Functions of Public Welfare.** *New York: Vintage Books, 1971.* A history of public welfare that discusses the many social variables and complicated political processes that shape our welfare system.

Szymanski, Albert. **The Capitalist State and the Politics of Class.** *Cambridge, Mass.: Winthrop Publishers, 1978.* This basic text is especially useful for understanding how the elite control power.

Chapter 16
Economic Groups and Systems

The love of money is the root of all evil.

      — I Timothy 6:10

Lack of money is the root of all evil.

      — George Bernard Shaw

To survive, people need food, shelter, and health care. Except for those who live in the tropics, people also need clothing and a source of heat. To be accepted in modern American society, however, we need a great deal more — soap, deodorant, toothpaste, shoes, and various types of clothes for different occasions. We also like the luxuries our society provides: plates, knives, forks, furniture, cars, sporting equipment, radios, televisions, and so on. All these things, from the most basic necessities to the most expensive luxuries, are produced by our economic system.

The *economic system* is defined as the social system that provides for the production, distribution, and consumption of goods and services. It is thus a very important social institution. It influences our lives from before we are born until we die; as you will see, it even influences how we are buried.

Sociologists study the economic system because it is a major social institution, one that interacts with all segments of society. Sociologists are not economists, however. Economists study the internal workings of the economic system: supply and demand, how much industry is producing, how much consumers are buying, how much government is taxing, borrowing, and spending, and so on. Sociologists, on the other hand, study how the economic system interacts with other social institutions. They study types of economic systems, the size and power of corporations, the occupations in economic systems, how work affects the rest of our lives, and similar issues.

Although sociologists and economists do not study the same subjects, they actually cover much of the same material. Economists cannot understand the success or failure of an economic system without considering how it interacts with the rest of society. Sociologists cannot understand how systems interact unless they understand the internal functioning of each system. Nevertheless, the disciplines have different goals. Economists specialize in studying the economic system, which is just one of society's important interacting parts, whereas sociologists study the whole of society, including the economic system.

Types of Economic Systems

To produce goods and services for a society, an economic system requires land on which to produce food and build factories. It also needs raw materials, tools and machinery to process them, and labor. Economic systems in modern societies vary according to who owns the land, the factories, the raw materials, and the equipment. These means of production may be privately owned, that is, owned by individuals, or they may be owned publicly by the state. Systems based on private ownership practice *capitalism,* and systems based on state ownership practice *socialism.* Once again we are dealing with ideal types. In capitalist societies, some property is owned by the state, and in socialist societies, some property is privately owned, perhaps just small plots of land used to grow food. No society is purely capitalist or purely socialist. Mixed economies in which private and public ownership are both practiced extensively have a system called *democratic socialism.* A society's economic system has a powerful influence on how it produces and distributes goods.

Capitalism

The United States has a capitalist economic system. The means of production, the land and the factories, are owned by one or more individuals. Most large corporations are owned by the many groups and individuals who own stock,

stock being shares of the corporation. Many small businesses are owned by one person, a family, or a few individuals.

Capitalism is a *market economy.* The goods sold and the price they are sold at are determined by the people who buy them and the people who sell them. Products no one wants to buy or sell are not traded. If everyone needs a product — fuel, for example — the product will be sold for as much money as people will pay for it. In a free market system, all people are free to buy, sell, and make a profit if they can, which is why capitalism is so strongly associated with freedom.

Socialism

Socialism differs from capitalism in that the means of production are owned by all the people through the state. Socialist systems are designed to ensure that all members of the society have some share of its wealth. Ownership is social rather than private. So-called communist systems such as the Soviet Union are actually socialist systems because the government owns all of the industries in the country.

Socialism also differs from capitalism in that it is not controlled by the marketplace — it has a planned economy. The government controls what will be produced and consumed. It sets prices for goods, decides what goods the society needs, what are luxuries, and what can be done without altogether. Thus there are no free markets. The Soviet Union, for example, faced with a severe housing shortage after World War II, gave high priority to building low-cost housing for its population. Poland, with its large debts to other countries, makes decisions about how much to pay farmers for food, how much to allow the Polish people to buy, and how much to export in order to pay its international debts. The decisions to pay farmers low prices for food and to export food, which caused shortages within the country, created much of the unrest and worker strikes that began in 1981.

Democratic Socialism

Democratic socialism, sometimes called welfare capitalism in the United States, is found in most West European countries. In Sweden and Great Britain, some industries are privately owned and others are state owned. Generally, the state owns the industries most vital to the country's well-being such as the railroads and communications industry. The most crucial needs — housing, medical care, education, and old age benefits — are paid for by the government with tax dollars. The taxes in democratic socialist countries are quite high in order to pay for these benefits and to prevent a few people from accumulating all the wealth. Whether a country is more capitalist or socialist can be determined by comparing the taxes collected to the *Gross National Product* (GNP), the total value of the goods and services the country produces in a year. The greater the proportion of the GNP that goes to taxes, the more socialistic the country is. The GNP includes all necessities, luxuries, and military supplies produced for a price. It does not include anything not produced for profit. The worth of the work of housewives, for example, is the largest item not included in the GNP. As you can see from Table 16-1, taxes in the United States are low compared with those of most West European countries.

The GNP does not indicate what the various countries produce, nor does it show what the tax dollars are spent for. The United States, which spends much of its tax money on the armed forces, includes military spending in its GNP. Sweden, on the other hand, spends little of its tax revenue on the military and a great deal on health, social planning, and the reduction of poverty. As a result, Sweden has the lowest infant mortality rate of all nations, the most hospital beds per capita, and the fifth highest life expectancy. The United States ranks seventeenth in infant mortality, twenty-ninth in hospital beds per capita, and twentieth in life expectancy (Heil-

Table 16-1
Total tax revenues expressed as a percentage of gross national product

COUNTRY	PERCENT
Sweden	49.6
Norway	47.3
Netherlands	46.2
Luxembourg	45.8
Denmark	45.7
Britain	36.1
Canada	32.9
United States	30.7
Japan	26.1
Spain	24.5

SOURCE: Revenue statistics from the Organisation for Economic Co-operation and Development, Paris. Reprinted by permission.

broner, 1980). Sweden has clearly combined social programs with capitalism through taxation and government spending programs.

The American Economic System

Most American citizens believe that the capitalist system is good and cherish the freedom of the marketplace, the freedom to buy, sell, and earn a living any way one can. We value these freedoms as much as we value our religious freedom. In fact, our economic system has its roots in our religious heritage.

In *The Protestant Ethic and the Spirit of Capitalism* (1958), Weber pointed out the Puritans' influence on the American desire for profit. He noted that capitalism, the exchange of goods for profit, has occurred at one time or another in all societies but that in the United States profit became a major goal. Profit was desired not simply to provide for one's daily needs but to accumulate wealth.

The Puritans were Protestant Calvinists. Their doctrine stated that most people lived in sin but that a few had been predestined for everlasting life by the grace of God. No one on this earth could affect that predestination; people's fates were sealed by God. The chosen were on earth to build God's kingdom as God intended.

How did people know if they were among the elect? They couldn't know, but it was believed that those who were involved in the work of the world, who appeared to be building God's kingdom, must be among the elect. Those who spent their lives in idleness, carousing, drinking, and card playing were obviously not doing God's work and obviously not among the chosen. The Calvinists sought confirmation that they were among the chosen, so overwhelming was their fear of everlasting death. They worked and produced goods, taking this as a sign that they were among the chosen. They did not spend time or money on comforts, play, or anything else that might indicate they were not chosen, nor did they associate with people believed to be outside the elect. They worked and they accumulated wealth. Wealth was an indication of self-worth. This viewpoint we now know as *the Protestant ethic.*

Although religious factors no longer play a strong role in the accumulation of wealth, our religious heritage has had a strong influence on our economic values (Chesler and Cave, 1981). Several of these values are described below.

1. We value the individual rather than the group. We believe everyone should have an opportunity to accumulate wealth, and we will protect the individual's rights even if it makes the group suffer. Building office buildings for profit is considered acceptable even when there is a housing shortage.

2. We value the economic well-being of the individual. The rich are considered successful, the poor are not. We do not judge people on the basis of how much they love or are loved by their family or friends, how much fun they have, how long they live, or whether they understand themselves and others. When we talk about success, we mean economic success.

3. We value private property. That people should own property seems natural, a God-given right. People who own and conquer the land, harvest timber, or drill for oil have a right to the profit, just as if they were the elect building God's kingdom. How different we are from the American Indians, who believe the land is not theirs to own or conquer but to live with in harmony.

4. We value growth, the ever-increasing accumulation of wealth. We do not make a profit to subsist or even to live comfortably. We value profit for the sake of profit, and the more the better.

The Growth of Large Corporations

The quest for ever-increasing profits in the capitalist system has contributed to the growth of large corporations. Building one car by hand is very expensive. Obviously, workers on an assembly line using machinery can assemble many identical parts and produce many cars in less time, at a lower cost per car. The cars can then be sold at a much greater profit than could be earned from building cars by hand one at a time. Factories and mass production have replaced the shoemaker, the spinner, the weaver, the dressmaker, the furniture maker, the cigar maker, the glass blower, the potter, the butcher, the baker, and the candlestick maker. Factories and the specialized division of labor were the basis of the industrial revolution. These innovations made it possible to mass produce goods that could be sold at low cost and still bring profit to the manufacturer.

More recently, profits have been increased by vertical expansion of businesses. If a business owns not only the factory that produces the

A man works at a forge while his helper works behind him. Men in the eighteenth and nineteenth centuries manufactured products by hand, carrying out the various processes necessary to achieve the final product. Workers learned their skills by serving an apprenticeship until they had learned each stage of the manufacturing process. Production was slow and products lacked uniformity, but exceptional craftmanship was highly valued.

goods but also the source of raw material purchased by the factory, the trucks that take the goods to market, and the stores that sell the products, the business can cut its costs at every step of the operation. It doesn't have to pay part of its profits to the owner of the raw material, the trucker, and the store owner. A business that owns all related businesses from the raw material to the retailer can increase its profits at every stage of its operation.

American corporations have expanded their operations to control the entire process from raw material to retail sales (Zwerdling, 1976). Safeway, for example, owns thousands of food stores and over a hundred manufacturing and processing plants, including bakeries, milk plants, ice cream plants, soft drink plants, meat processors, and coffee roasting plants. It manufactures its own soap, peanut butter, and salad oil, and owns a fleet of thousands of trucks to ship these products to its stores. Members of the board of directors of Safeway also sit on the boards of banks and corporations involved in agriculture, food production, food processing, food packaging, gas and electric power, and fuel oil. By owning or influencing every stage of production from the land food is grown on to retail sales, Safeway has become a very large corporation.

Another form of expansion that assures continued profits is *diversification*. Investors might buy a variety of stocks so that if one went down, another might remain stable or go up and they would be protected from losing their entire investment. In the same way, corporations buy a variety of businesses so that those which are not highly profitable can be supported by those that are. Great Western United reportedly owns sugar companies, Shaky's Pizza, and large real estate holdings. The real estate is extremely valuable, but it does not provide income. By diversifying, however, Great Western United can support its real estate holdings with income from other sources.

Between 1950 and 1960, 20 percent of this country's largest 100 firms merged with other large, healthy firms, because they could increase their profits by working together (Chesler and Cave, 1981). In 1980, another round of mergers by major corporations took place, and corporations grew larger still.

The size of corporations as they are legally structured tells only half the story of their tremendous power. *Corporate links* may join corporations that appear to be unrelated. A large bank or investment company, for example, may own controlling stock in a variety of corporations and control their business such that each will be able to maintain optimum profits. Family wealth is also used to control large corporations that are other-

wise unrelated. Families such as the Fords, Gettys, Dows, DuPonts, Rockefellers, and Mellons hold large blocks of stock in many corporations. Numerous other firms and families that own large blocks of stock in United States corporations are not even Americans — they are from foreign countries.

Multinational Corporations

As corporations grow, they do not confine their operations to their own country. They also own companies in foreign nations, where they employ workers and produce and sell their products. One-third of the assets of Ford Motor Company are invested in foreign countries, and one-third of Ford's employees are foreigners working in these countries (Heilbroner, 1980).

Most *multinational corporations* are owned by Americans. These companies often become involved in political arrangements made between the United States and other countries. They affect the economies of this country and those in which they have holdings in several ways. They can buy foreign companies even when the United States would like to reduce overseas spending and have us "Buy American." They can also play one country against another, offering to build a plant in the one that gives them the greatest advantages in taxes, cheap labor, and freedom from regulation. By closing unprofitable plants, they can create unemployment problems. In a sense, multinational corporations are above the laws of any nation because they can use their vast wealth and power to dominate a nation's economy. The annual sales of either General Motors or Exxon is greater than the GNP of countries such as Austria, Denmark, Norway, Greece, Portugal, and the smaller nations of the world. Corporations can borrow vast amounts of money on the basis of their sales; countries can tax only their GNP. As corporations increase in size, they gain progressively more power to dominate the economies of entire nations.

The major increase in multinational business has been in the developed nations of the world. Canada has been affected especially strongly by multinational corporations. Canadians own only about 15 percent of their own industry. Almost half of Canadian industry is owned by United States corporations and individuals, and most of the rest is owned by Europeans, which makes it extremely difficult for the Canadian government to control its own economy.

Third World nations have also been powerfully influenced by multinationals. Large agricultural corporations, for example, have converted large tracts of farmland into huge plantations cultivated by modern machinery to produce cash crops for worldwide shipment. Ralston-Purina has built a large feedmill in Colombia to process corn for feed — corn that had previously been consumed by people (George, 1967). Del Monte and Dole grow pineapples in the Philippines and Thailand, where there is an abundance of cheap labor, and ship the pineapples to United States and Japanese markets. Gulf and Western controls land in the Dominican Republic, which is used to grow sugar for Gulf and Western's sugar mill. The large corporations often do not own the land but enter into agreements with local landowners to grow what they need for their processing plants, and the local landowners and governments cooperate even when the nutrition of the local people will suffer.

Multinational corporations have such a great impact on the nations in which they do business and are so influential in international relations that some observers believe that nations as we know them today will eventually vanish and that affairs of state will be run by the boards of directors of huge corporations. Whether this will happen and if it does, whether it will create a more peaceful and orderly world or more poverty for the workers is for now a matter of speculation. In any case, as corporations change and grow, the nature of work also changes.

American multinational corporations do business throughout the world, producing a great deal of food for export. Some foodstuffs are produced for local consumption, however, and these are advertised widely to create a demand for the product. This worker in Kenya earns his living working for an American multinational familiar to us all.

Inequality and Land Ownership

A mere 2.5 percent of the world's landowners control nearly three-quarters of the land in the world (George, 1977). Using farming techniques developed in modern industrial society, these landowners are increasing food production on this land to sell to large food corporations, and as they increase production, they are removing tenant farmers who grow food for their families. We find this situation throughout India, Africa, and Central and South America.

George has written a dialogue that illustrates the social effects of modern technological food production on an agrarian society. The characters are a landlord and tenant at harvest time.

LANDLORD: You owe me a third more rent this year — I'll take it in wheat or in cash.

TENANT: But I can't pay you any more — I didn't even feed my family all year on the last harvest.

LANDLORD: Just look at what my land has produced. You see that it can be done and you ought to be growing more yourself. Your land belongs to me and it isn't bringing in enough profit.

TENANT: It's easy enough for you to talk. I know how you did it — you spread a hundred stacks of fertilizer on the soil and the well is on your property. How am I supposed to buy fertilizer when I already have to buy food? I can't even use the water when I want to.

LANDLORD: Tell you what. I'll give you this money right now and you get off that land. In the bargain, I'll even hire you next year at sowing and harvest time and maybe in between. That's more than you would have got last year, but the land's valuable and I'm generous.

TENANT: But I don't want to get off the land. My father and his father farmed it before me, for your father and his father.

LANDLORD: In that case, I'll loan you the money to buy fertilizer and seeds. That way you can pay me a higher rent when the new crop comes in. The loan will only cost you 5 percent a month. (Aside: Heh heh, I get the money at 8 percent a *year* from the bank in town.)

TENANT: But I could never pay you back. I already owe money for my daughter's wedding and for the money I had to borrow to buy food last year.

LANDLORD: In that case, consider yourself evicted. I'll farm the land myself. By the way, I still may be needing your services, so stay around. Of course, I won't be able to pay you much. Times aren't *that* good, and if you don't like your wages, there are plenty of others around who'll be glad of a job. Besides, I plan to buy a tractor.

TENANT: But what about my wife and children? What are we to do? In your father's time this could not have happened. He even gave food to tide us over the bad times.

LANDLORD: Sorry about that. Business is business. You might try the city.

SOURCE: George, Susan, *How the Other Half Dies: The Real Reason for World Hunger,* Totowa, N.J.: Allanheld, Osmund & Company, 1977. Reprinted by permission.

The Changing Nature of Work

In simple rural societies, most people are primary workers. Those who grow food, fish, mine, or otherwise produce raw materials are referred to as *primary workers* because their work is so essential to their country. In an industrial society such as our own where most farming is done by machine, only a small portion of the population farms for a living. Most of the population works to produce manufactured goods; these workers are called *secondary workers.* They are the wage earners, the people on the assembly line, the construction workers, the laborers in industry. The fastest growing segment of the labor force consists of *tertiary* (or service) *workers*. They include such people as police officers, doctors, lawyers, maids, and plumbers. In the following section we will describe the nature of secondary and tertiary work in modern society.

The Factory Worker and Alienation

In an earlier era, the cobbler or the candlestick maker developed a product from start to finish, sold it to the customer, took pride in the finished goods, and stood by his or her reputation as a skillful producer. The factory worker has none of these satisfactions, which has been a continuous problem for worker and management alike.

Alienation is a term Marx used in describing the working conditions of the factory worker. Factory workers are alienated from their work because they have no control over it and derive no satisfaction from it. Their work involves only a part of the finished product, and they see neither the beginning nor the end of the process. They have no satisfaction in creating a product and no pride in selling it to the customer. They perform one routine task over and over again, and in return they receive money, which may or may not be enough to provide them with a satisfactory lifestyle.

Factory workers have been studied extensively since the turn of the century, often as part of an effort to improve worker efficiency. In fact, the earliest approach to the study of work, *scientific management,* had no other goal. Later, the *human relations school* of management realized that efficiency could be improved by increasing worker satisfaction, and alienation became a concern of factory managers. Recently, there has been a major renewal of interest in this area, and the history of the study of workers illustrates the dramatic change in attitudes toward labor in America.

Scientific Management. Scientific management is a term coined by Frederick W. Taylor (1911) to describe the type of management required on an assembly line. In an entrepreneurial setting, the workers own the business and are responsible for knowing the best way to do their own job, but in scientific management, the manager is the one who knows how to accomplish a task efficiently. The manager, through record keeping and the use of a stopwatch, establishes rules for the most efficient work routine and then selects and trains workers to follow directions. The division of labor requires the manager to do the thinking and the worker to do the labor.

Taylor developed his program at Bethlehem Steel Company to improve the efficient use of workers loading pig iron into railroad cars. A pig of iron weighed 92 pounds; workers lifted a pig, carried it up a plank, and dropped it into a car. Before Taylor designed his scientific management plan, each worker loaded an average of 12½ tons of pig iron a day. By carefully controlling the pace at which the workers lifted, walked up the plank, rested, and lifted again, Taylor found that he could get the workers to load 47 tons of pig iron a day, almost four times as much as they had been loading. The workers were rewarded with a pay increase of 60 percent, and the profit to the company was enormous.

Taylor (1911) described the best type of worker to handle pig iron as follows: "that he shall be so stupid and so phlegmatic that he more nearly resembles in his mental make-up the ox than any other type" (p. 51). A man who was alert and intelligent would quickly be dissatisfied and bored with routine labor and the way it was scientifically managed. Nevertheless, scientific management played an important role in increasing the efficient use of workers, although the fact that most workers were not as dumb as an ox was overlooked. The intelligence of human workers, however, eventually had to be considered, and it was at that point that the human relations school of management developed.

The Human Relations School. A scientific management study discovered the importance of human relations in the workplace by accident. In the now famous Hawthorne studies, experiments were done to improve the productivity of assembly line workers making telephone equipment. As you may recall from the discussion of the Hawthorne effect in Chapter 3, worker productivity did not increase as scientific management had expected — the workers responded to the attention they received from the researchers. More important, the study found that worker productivity depended on the informal group structure of the workers. When they were allowed to form their own working relationships and develop some of their own rules, they were much more cooperative with management, and their productivity increased. When they felt uneasy about changes handed down by management, they resisted these changes and productivity did not increase. The findings of the Hawthorne studies made management aware of the importance of informal groups, their attitudes toward management, and the effect these factors could have on productivity.

The human relations school of worker management developed to probe these issues further. Its researchers studied the formal organization of the workplace, company rules and working conditions, and informal organization among the workers themselves, including their customs, traditions, routines, values, and beliefs (Roethlisberger and Dickson, 1939). The goal of these studies was to find the best type of person for the job and the best type of environment for maintaining and improving worker attitudes.

A classic study of employee values and their effect on productivity was done in a gypsum factory by Gouldner (1954). Initially, the workers had been quite happy with their management and management had been flexible with the workers. They were allowed to leave early occasionally for personal reasons, and they were sometimes allowed to take supplies for their personal use. They were also encouraged to discuss work problems with management and make suggestions for improving working conditions. Managers and workers cooperated well together, and neither took advantage of the other.

Then, however, a new management team came to the company. To increase production, they strictly adhered to the rules. Workers were not allowed to leave early or take supplies, nor were they given a chance to discuss problems with management. The workers, who valued the flexibility of the earlier managers, resented the enforcement of the rules. They believed they were being treated with less respect, and they no longer cooperated with and supported the company.

After decades of research in human relations, workers in the United States are still frustrated in their jobs, and management continues to be frustrated with low productivity. In recent years, American managers have turned their attention to Japanese workers to try to understand why they are more productive than Americans.

Modern Trends in Management

The Japanese work force has proven itself to be exceptional in producing automobiles, and American employers have been studying their productivity with increasing interest (Ouchi, 1981). Their efficiency is attributed to two Japanese employee policies — lifetime jobs and quality control circles.

Lifetime jobs are held by only a third of Japanese men and no women, and they are held only until age fifty-five or sixty, which creates a hardship for these workers when they are older. Nevertheless, a guarantee of even this short a "lifetime" job creates security for the Japanese man — a security most American workers do not have because they can be fired or laid off at any time. The Japanese man is also encouraged to have close personal relationships with other workers, to care about those in his work group just as he cares

Workers in a Nikon factory in Japan take a break from making cameras to exercise at their stations. The Japanese have developed a variety of practices to reduce workers' fatigue and increase efficiency and morale.

about his family. The group takes pride in its work and its members do not need to compete as individuals. They are paid a low base pay and then receive a bonus, often 50 percent of base pay, on the basis of their productivity. The arrangement of a lifetime job, commitment to the group, and high productivity are to everyone's advantage.

Quality control circles are meetings held by the group to improve its productivity. Orders do not come down from the manager, as they do in American bureaucracies; instead, the groups meet regularly to decide how their work can best be accomplished and then make recommendations to management. If management approves the recommendations, the work group is allowed to change its procedures.

Although these management techniques seem quite revolutionary to American managers, who still value scientific management, efficiency experts, and stopwatches, quality control groups are being tried in a few American companies, and with reported success.

Unionization

Workers have for years tried to improve their own working conditions and economic benefits through *unionization*. Unions can be traced back to the guilds of the Middle Ages, which protected skilled workers in the arts and crafts. As factories developed, workers formed unions to improve their working conditions. In the United States, skilled craftsmen were unionized before 1800, and women textile workers united in the early 1800s to protest working conditions in factories.

The latter part of the nineteenth century was a period of intense labor union struggle and conflict, and the results of this struggle continue to shape labor unions today. The more conservative unions of the period worked to protect their jobs through legislation. Tariff laws were passed to prevent competition from cheap imported goods, and immigration laws prevented cheap foreign labor from entering the country. Protective labor laws kept women and children out of the labor force, thereby eliminating another source of cheap labor. In addition, the unions maintained a cooperative relationship with their employers. They wanted work contracts and preferred to settle disputes by mediation and compromise. Strikes were used only as a last resort.

There was also a strong and popular socialist movement in the United States during this period, which was influenced by Marx's theory and his conception of alienation. Workers in various industries saw that they had much in common with one another and wanted to build a strong union

At Staley, Management Loves Worker Takeover

LAFAYETTE, IND. Out here on the prairie, almost within earshot of the consumptive rattles of the big steel and automobile centers, one view of the future of American industry is taking shape, and it is not without a sweeter side, no pun intended.

This future involves computers and people, but here at the A. E. Staley Manufacturing Co.'s plant, where corn is converted to high-powered syrup, the story really is about people.

Workers have taken over the Staley plant — not by force, but by management fiat, from the home offices in Decatur, Ill. To no one's real surprise, it's working like a charm.

The sudden rise of the high fructose corn syrup (HFCS) industry in itself is fascinating enough, but there's more to it than that. Staley is pioneering management techniques that are as compelling as the automation making the plant one of the most modern in the sweetener industry.

Some examples:

Since it opened in 1977, the $120-million plant has been expanded twice — in part because demand for HFCS has grown by quantum leaps, in part because workers keep exceeding production goals that Staley regularly sets for them.

All 240 employees, management or not, are on salary. There are no time clocks. Plant workers, set up as teams, decide who is hired, who is fired; who gets a raise, who doesn't; who works when, who needs disciplining for not doing his or her share.

In keeping with their added responsibilities, the nonunion plant workers here are paid more and have heftier benefits than their brethren in other unionized Staley corn and soybean processing plants in the Midwest.

Involvement of workers in some of the basic decisions that rule their lives is not that revolutionary in American industry. Such household names as DuPont, Alcoa, Procter and Gamble, and Texas Instruments, among others, have moved in that direction.

But here in Lafayette, it is being taken farther, faster than elsewhere and the results — steadily increasing production, notable efficiency, pride in work and team spirit — are laden with implications for the troubled U.S. industrial machine.

SOURCE: *The Washington Post*, April 26, 1981, p. G1. © 1981 The Washington Post. Reprinted by permission.

covering all workers. They did not expect to co-operate with industry. They wanted, rather, to fight for collective ownership of industry so that they would own the companies they worked in and reap the profits of their own labor. Removing industry from private ownership and placing it in collective ownership would cause a radical redistribution of wealth, of course. The owners of American business, with the aid of federal, state, and local police and military power, forced these more radical labor unions out of existence, deported their foreign-born members, tried citizens for treason, and passed laws preventing such unions from forming in the future.

The more conservative type of union that accepts the private ownership of business is the kind representing labor in America today. Increasingly, this type of union covers the lower-paid workers in a newer set of occupations, the service workers.

Service Workers

The increase in the size of corporations has increased the number of tertiary, or service, workers, who are not directly involved in producing goods. These are the employees who answer the telephones, keep the records, file the papers, pay the taxes, clean the buildings, and do a host of other jobs necessary to keep large corporations functioning. Another class of service workers meets community rather than corporate needs, and this class has also been growing. As people have moved to urban areas to work, more police officers, firefighters, teachers, doctors, lawyers, and accountants have been needed to serve them.

Service workers are an expense to a corporation, part of its fixed overhead costs. They increase the cost of products, but they do not directly increase the production of products. Similarly, in a community they are a necessary expense to taxpayers, but they do not produce any tangible wealth. Service workers such as filing clerks, typists, police officers, and teachers typically have

more education and training than blue-collar workers, but they do not necessarily receive more pay. Most lower-paid service workers are joining unions whereas the higher-paid ones are professionals who can control their work environment and demand high fees.

Professionalization

The professions are widely regarded as rewarding service occupations. Professional jobs share five characteristics that set them apart from other types of work:

1. *A body of knowledge.* The professions are based on knowledge not generally available to the public. Because only professionals fully understand this knowledge, they can control how the knowledge is applied.

2. *A code of ethics.* Professionals gain the confidence of the public by adhering to a code of ethics promising a certain level of service.

3. *Licensing.* Licensing demonstrates to the community that the licensed individuals have in fact mastered the body of knowledge associated with their profession.

4. *Peer control.* Because the body of knowledge is specialized, only professionals can judge one another's work. Outsiders do not have the knowledge necessary to make such judgments.

5. *A professional association.* The association devises and maintains the profession's educational standards, licensing requirements, peer review procedures, and code of ethics.

The most respected area of *professionalization* in the United States is the practice of medicine, which has developed slowly over the past two centuries. Before that time, the ill were cared for in the home, especially in the United States. Sick people were looked after by relatives or experienced individuals from the community, usually older women. By colonial times, however, there were doctors in America. Some were educated, others were not. Some learned medicine as an apprentice to another doctor. Many practiced "heroic" medicine, performing dramatic bleeding or blistering treatments or giving patients poisonous laxatives. Most people went to doctors only when they were desperate, and most patients died. Doctors were often poor and had little work to do and sometimes had to beg in the streets to survive (Rothstein, 1970).

In about 1800, educated physicians were able to get state legislatures to pass laws forbidding healers without formal education from practicing medicine, but the laws were unpopular and soon repealed. In 1847, physicians formed the American Medical Association (AMA) and adopted the Hippocratic oath and a code of ethics. They lobbied states to ban abortion, something widely practiced until that time and an important source of income to women healers who were not physicians. These healers also cared for the sick and delivered babies. The AMA again succeeded in getting state legislatures to limit the practice of medicine to the educated, which was a major step in developing the profession.

In 1910, Abraham Flexner published the Flexner report, which stated that most existing medical schools were inadequate. Congress responded to the Flexner report by giving the AMA the right to determine which schools were qualified to train physicians, an important power in controlling the profession. All seven medical schools for women and most medical schools for blacks were closed, eliminating women and most blacks from the profession. Part-time schools were closed, eliminating those who could not afford full-time study. The profession remained open to white males of the upper classes, and a shortage of physicians developed, which made medicine a very lucrative profession.

Today, medical care has become a huge industry in the United States, with 350,000 physicians supported by the pharmaceutical industry, the medical technology industry, the health insurance industry, and over 7,000 hospitals. The AMA controls hospitals, medical education, prescription drugs, the use of medical technology, and the qualifications for receiving insurance payments.

The Economy and Everyday Life

The economy affects a great deal more than our work. We have made frequent references throughout this book to the economic factors that influence our daily lives. We obviously play a role in the economy when we work, but we also participate in the economy in our leisure time, as consumers. By leisure time we mean the time when we are not at work. In this section, we will discuss leisure time and two other examples of how economics affects everyday life: child care and funerals.

Leisure

Some of the ways the economy shapes leisure activity are obvious, but others are not so obvious. Workers in modern industrial societies work fewer hours a week than they did formerly. Whereas a six-day week was common at one time, most full-time employees now work five days a week and some even work a four-day week. Much of the time not spent at work — leisure time — is spent preparing for work, traveling to and from work, keeping the car in good repair, buying and cleaning clothes to work in, dressing for work, and otherwise maintaining an appropriate appearance. Other time is spent shopping for food, preparing meals, maintaining one's house and possessions, and taking care of self, family, and home in other ways.

The most popular leisure-time activity is watching television. Over 90 percent of families in the United States own a television set. Buying a TV set is an economic activity, of course, and while watching television, viewers are bombarded with many advertisements suggesting that they buy certain consumer goods. Television may also induce us to follow other leisure time activities, such as sports.

Americans spend many leisure hours participating in sports and in buying sporting equipment such as boats, recreational vehicles, skis, balls, racquets, and other paraphernalia. Even as simple a leisure-time activity as jogging created a boom in the athletic shoe industry. Those who prefer spectator sports buy tickets to sporting events. Sports is a very big industry in the United States. When people have a longer period of leisure such as a weekend or a vacation, they often go somewhere: to the beach, the mountains, the city, or a foreign country. Travel agencies arrange transportation, hotel rooms, meals, sightseeing trips, and other activities. Both sports and travel are very important to the American economy.

Child Care

Although the type of child care societies provide would appear to be unrelated to the economy, unemployment rates have a direct effect on its availability. In countries where workers are scarce, systems of child care centers are provided to mothers to enter the labor market. Nations in which there are more workers than jobs have high unemployment rates and do not provide child care (Kamerman and Kahn, 1981).

In East Germany, Hungary, Sweden, and France, there is a labor shortage. As a result, these countries want to increase the number of women in the work force and at the same time increase the birth rate so that there will be workers for the next generation. These nations offer a variety of programs to families such as day care centers, allowances to supplement family incomes, and work

In Sweden, birth rates are low, unemployment rates are low, and workers are valued. Excellent programs exist to support parents in their efforts to both work and raise a family. This day care center in Stockholm is an example of the excellent facilities available for child care while parents are at work.

leaves for parents to care for infants. In the United States, where the unemployment rate is high, day care centers are scarce, leaves of absence from work are given for only brief periods at the time of childbirth, and allowances to working families with children are nonexistent.

Funerals

Even after death, funerals and the way people mourn the dead are influenced by the economy (Pratt, 1981). Funeral practices have changed dramatically as a result of the growth of large bureaucracies. Funerals used to be very elaborate affairs attended by relatives from far and near. They included processions, lying in state, ornamental caskets and tombstones, and elaborate mourning clothes. Widows and widowers were expected to wear black or dark subdued colors for a year after the death of a spouse. These practices were not based on religious beliefs, however. They developed in the nineteenth century in response to industrial expansion and the efforts of entrepreneurs. Elaborate funerals were highly profitable to those who arranged them.

During the twentieth century, more people began to work for large bureaucracies, which give three days' paid leave for bereavement as a fringe benefit. They specify that employees can take three days off for the death of a spouse, parent, or child; most also include parents-in-law and siblings but exclude siblings-in-law, grandparents, grandchildren, aunts, uncles, friends, and roommates. These benefits specify that leave begins with the death of a relative, not when the relative is ill and dying. The employee is expected to return to work after three days, and some plans even specify that if the relative dies on a Saturday, the employee will receive only two days' leave. Some employees must bring obituaries or other proof of death when they return to work.

These employee benefits have greatly changed the behavior of the bereaved. Only the immediate family is involved in the mourning, except for brief visits or attendance at the funeral.

The wake, an all-night gathering of the clan that was often a celebration of the life of the deceased, has been eliminated in recent years. Fewer people attend funerals, and funerals are simpler, shorter, and more private. The practice of viewing the body is on the verge of disappearing, and caskets are simpler. Instead of being buried in a pastoral setting, the deceased are now often placed in high-rise mausoleums modeled after the office filing cabinet, or else they are cremated. The bereaved return to work the next day ready for business, and mourning clothes are considered inappropriate.

These practices reflect the time management and efficiency of the business world, as well as the decrease in family unity, which formerly brought support to the family, acknowledged the importance of the life of each family member, and bonded family members to one another.

Economic Systems in Other Countries

The variety of economic systems in the world today cannot be discussed adequately in this chapter. We can, however, describe a socialist system, that of the Chinese, and a social democratic system, that of the British, to demonstrate the various ways an economy can develop to meet the needs of a society.

A Socialist System: The Chinese

In 1920, China was a nation ruled by local warlords and populated by millions of poor peasants. More than half the peasants owned no land whatsoever, and many who did have land owned so little that they could not support themselves. Chinese workers in the cities were equally poor. Women and children who worked in the silk mills labored 15 hours a day and earned 12 cents a day. The average wage for male workers was $10 a month (Freeman, 1979).

Two groups of Chinese organized to fight the warlords and modernize the Chinese nation. One group, the Kuomintang, was made up of middle-class people, merchants, nationalists, and intellectuals. This group had the support of the United States in their efforts to organize labor and make China a modern industrial nation. The other group, the Chinese Communist party, developed around a small number of radicals from the middle class. This group had the support of the Soviet Union.

For almost thirty years, these two groups fought the warlords, Japanese invaders, and each other. The Japanese invasion of China did much to turn peasant support to the Communist party. The Kuomintang leaders treated the peasants cruelly, forcibly drafting them into their army and bringing them to training camps in chains. When the Kuomintang fought the Japanese in open battle, they generally lost and then they taxed the peasants heavily to rebuild their army. Inflation and corruption were rampant. When World War II ended, the Kuomintang controlled most of Chinese industry and had the support of most of the world's nations. The United States sent them $1.1 billion in aid in 1945 alone, they had no social programs; they specialized in graft and corruption and treated the peasants with contempt.

The peasants, unhappy under Kuomintang rule, turned to the Communist party, where they were well treated. The Communists gave the peasants guns, fought the Japanese in guerrilla warfare, and were better able to protect themselves and the peasants. They preached mutual love and assistance and instructed their army to behave as follows (Freeman, 1979 p. 210):

1. Obey orders in all your actions.
2. Do not take a single needle or piece of thread from the masses.
3. Turn in everything captured.
4. Speak politely.
5. Pay fairly for what you buy.
6. Return everything you borrow.
7. Pay for anything you damage.
8. Do not hit or swear at people.
9. Do not damage crops.
10. Do not take liberties with women.
11. Do not ill-treat captives.

The Communists gained the support of the peasants, two million in the army and ten million in village self-defense squads. They eventually won the civil war and created the People's Republic of China on October 1, 1949.

In a matter of months, the Communists made dramatic changes in support of their theme of mutual love and assistance. They outlawed opium growing, gambling, female infanticide (the killing of girl infants), dowries, arranged marriages, the selling of wives and concubines, and many other practices that had existed for centuries. The benefits were great to everyone except the wealthy landowners.

The primary workers were formed into thousands of agricultural communes. The communes today average 15,000 members, each divided into brigades averaging 1,000 members each. Brigades are divided into teams of 150 persons. The peasants were slow to adapt to communes after centuries of working their own plots, but the Communists brought much new land under cultivation by terracing hillsides, digging wells for irrigation, improving the soil, and using new seed strains. They also introduced modern farming equipment such as machines for planting and transplanting rice. As improvements in farming developed, crop yields increased enormously. The life of the peasants improved, and they have now adapted to communal living.

The Chinese Communists developed successful industries rather quickly. Industries such as iron, steel, machinery, coal, petroleum, electric power, and chemicals were developed in moderate-size factories and plants spread about the country. An effort was made to keep industry in small-scale plants so the secondary workers would not feel lost or alienated. In addition, workers were encouraged to feel pride in their individual contribution to the functioning of the plant and the commune it served.

The Communists have also made remarkable strides in tertiary or service areas such as education and health care. To educate people, the language was simplified, schools and colleges were opened, and teachers were trained. In the ten years after the Communist takeover, enrollment in middle schools, comparable to our junior high and high schools, jumped from one million to 12 million students. The schools emphasize the teaching of Communist doctrine, equality, mutual love and assistance, and pride in the ability to contribute to the good of society.

Perhaps Communist doctrine is exemplified best by the development of medical care for the population. When the Communists came into power, disease and starvation were rampant (Denton, 1978). There was a shortage of doctors, and the few doctors available were divided between Eastern and Western medical practices. It was necessary first to increase the number of doctors and second to make use of what was available, whether it was Eastern herbs and acupuncture or Western drugs and technology. The Communists trained enormous numbers of so-called *barefoot doctors* in both Eastern and Western medical techniques to serve the peasants. The barefoot doctors are selected by the peasants in their communes to serve as health workers without pay. They receive three to eighteen months' training in medicine and then serve their communes, emphasizing not only preventive medicine but also treating simple problems and emergencies. They direct the more seriously ill to better-trained doctors and nurses.

Not so well trained as the barefoot doctors are the Red Guard doctors, who work in urban areas, and the worker doctors, who work in factories. These doctors receive less training because highly trained full-time doctors and nurses are available in urban areas. The Red Guard and worker doctors serve the same grass roots function as the barefoot doctors, serving without pay, stressing preventive

medicine such as sanitation and inoculations, and generally looking after the health of members of their communes.

When hospitalization is necessary for an illness, individuals must pay for it. A variety of insurance plans are available to cover the costs of hospital care, but in any case the costs are not high. Open heart surgery, the most expensive procedure, costs about two weeks' wages, far less than in the United States.

Like the peasants and factory workers, the service workers emphasize equality. Doctors are moved to rural areas when they are needed. They also help nurses care for patients, and any class differentiation among the various types of doctors and nurses is discouraged.

One problem facing the Chinese Communists is how to motivate people to be more productive and accumulate more wealth for the society without at the same time motivating them to want more wealth for themselves. Although higher wages have been used to motivate factory workers from time to time, this practice is contrary to Chinese ideology. There is, therefore, a continuing effort to teach the Communist doctrine of equality, love, and service as the motivating spirit in Chinese society, but such a doctrine may become increasingly difficult to maintain when China grows wealthier.

Democratic Socialism: Great Britain

Most European countries are basically capitalist societies, but as the need has arisen, they have nationalized vital industries and services to meet social needs. Although Great Britain was at one point in its history a capitalist nation with a strong bias against government interference, it now has socialized its railroads, telephones, broadcasting, education (through the college level), and medical system. The history of the British Public Health Service demonstrates both the nationalization of an industry to meet needs not otherwise being

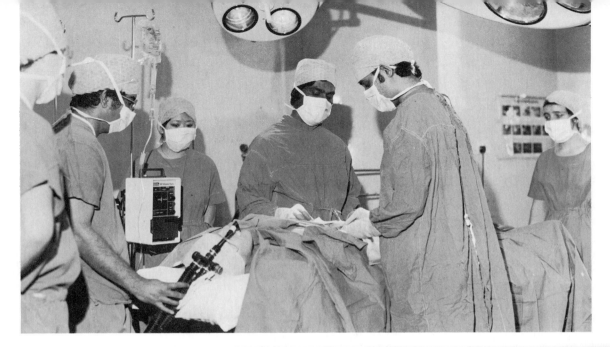

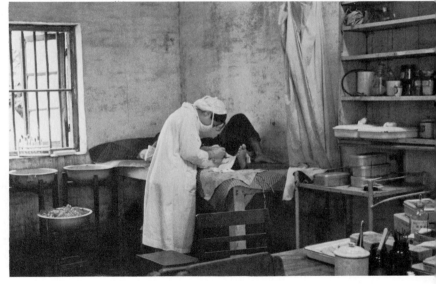

Compare here the modern British hospital with the rural Chinese commune hospital. The rural hospital is certainly crude, but the Chinese, like the British, have a system of socialized medicine. All Chinese citizens have access to health care in their own areas as well as access to modern medical centers in the cities if an illness requires more extensive treatment.

met and the pragmatic development of a nationalized industry in a capitalist society.

Since 1911, Great Britain has had national health insurance, which covered the medical expenses of workers. Their wives and children and the elderly were not insured, however, and they either never went to doctors or else postponed health care until it was too late. After World War II, the poor health of the people and the large number of elderly in the population created a serious problem, and Great Britain developed the National Health Service, which is funded by tax revenue.

The health service has three branches: hospitals and "consultants," the physician specialists who work in hospitals; general practitioners, who

SOCIOLOGISTS AT WORK
Societal Analysis in the Auto Industry

Carroll DeWeese is a staff research scientist in the Societal Analysis Department of General Motors Research Laboratories. The objectives of GM Research Laboratories are to generate new technical knowledge of commercial interest to GM, to evaluate outside technical advances for possible application to GM products and processes, to anticipate future technological needs and develop the expertise to meet those needs, and to assist in the analysis of corporate priorities, policies, and programs. About 1,500 people work at GM Research Laboratories. More than a third of them are research and development professionals; of this number, about thirty come from backgrounds in the social sciences, including four with doctorates in sociology.

The Societal Analysis Department is an interdisciplinary department whose mission is to study the impact of GM on society and vice versa. DeWeese leads a group with degrees in applied mathematics, economics, operations research, psychology, and sociology.

Research in the department is generally interdisciplinary, problem-oriented, and quantitative. Researchers have worked on a variety of topics, including air pollution, auto safety, auto service, customer satisfaction, energy, product quality, diesel odor, and other areas of public concern.

Carroll DeWeese studied sociology at the University of Houston and at Purdue. He joined GM Research Laboratories immediately on completing his work at Purdue. One of his first jobs there was to develop a computerized system for identifying and studying public concerns as they emerge and grow. This valuable information could then be put to good use by GM's management. After this solid start, he was soon put in charge of all the department's sociologists, and a few years later he was promoted to his current position as leader of an interdisciplinary research group.

The thing that most appeals to DeWeese about his work at GM Research Laboratories is his independence. "I have picked all the projects I work on. No one tells me what I have to do or how I have to do it. My superiors are primarily concerned with providing the resources for me to

treat the sick in their community; and nursing homes, home nursing services, vaccinations, health inspections, and other community health services.

Any citizen can go to a general practitioner without paying a fee, and if hospitalization is required, the general practitioner refers the patient to a hospital consultant, again without charge. To control the costs of such a system, patients who

do not have serious problems may have to wait for weeks or months for a consultation. Those who do have serious problems are seen first. The citizens of Great Britain have nevertheless been very happy with the system, but physicians, especially specialists who were not appointed to hospital consulting positions, were dissatisfied because their incomes and practices were severely limited. To satisfy the physicians, the health service pays

accomplish my objectives, and with helping me get my results across to others. Time and resources are made available for researchers to explore and test ideas at an early stage of development without having to justify them. I am not tied down to what management or my colleagues tell me I have to work on, although their suggestions are important inputs. I have more freedom to do research than the academic sociologists I know."

DeWeese has done a lot of thinking about what makes researchers successful in this challenging environment. He has been able to identify several characteristics: "They must be pragmatic, not ideological — interested in doing whatever is necessary to solve a problem. They are persons looking for tools to solve problems, not persons with some particular tool trying to find problems to solve. They must be able to communicate, to excite and convince others about their ideas. Brevity is a virtue here. After a year's work, they should be able to convince a decision-maker of the importance of the problem studied and the results found on a single sheet of paper or in five minutes of conversation. They must know how to identify critical problems — the more critical the problem, the more attention any actionable results will receive. They must know how to work as part of a team, to secure the cooperation and support of their colleagues. And they must have quantitative ability combined with qualitative flexibility. That's where the interdisciplinary arrangement, the variety of perspectives, pays off.

"But perhaps most of all, successful people in this job are persistent. They can go a long time without positive feedback. They are self-starters who know how to keep a project alive until it bears fruit. Some of the most successful research projects I know of were only minimally supported by management at first and were kept alive by researchers who believed in their importance. These researchers knew how to overcome all obstacles until the usefulness of their ideas became clear to others. They took risks to provide what was really needed, not just what other people thought was needed."

It is no accident that DeWeese's list of characteristics of the successful researcher in his department does not include specific substantive knowledge. "People are expected to acquire whatever substantive knowledge is needed to solve the problem they are working on," he explains. "On the other hand, use of the sociological imagination is critical for identifying, studying, and solving problems. The strength of sociology is the perspective it gives a person. I am not saying substantive knowledge is unimportant. When we hire people, we have problem areas in mind and we look for people with substantive backgrounds in those problem areas. But that substantive knowledge is a given. It is not a characteristic of success."

---

the doctors for each patient they see rather than giving them a salary; thus they can make more money by seeing more patients. They are also allowed to have private patients. Critics have argued that this provision of the service has created a dual health care system, one for the rich and one for the poor. The public, however, has no desire to do away with the free medical care they receive from the service.

Summary

A society's economic system provides for the production and distribution of all the necessities and luxuries the society uses. Sociologists study economic systems to better understand how the production of goods influences social life.

There are currently two basic types of economic systems. One is capitalism, in which the property needed to produce resources and goods is privately owned. The United States is the most capitalist of modern nations, but even in this country some property is not privately owned. In the other type of system, socialism, the property needed to produce goods and resources is owned by the state. In countries such as Great Britain and Sweden, some property is private and some is owned by the state. This system is called democratic socialism.

Capitalism is a market economy in which the emphasis is on products that provide a profit to manufacturers. In contrast, socialism is a planned economy. The state decides what will be manufactured and sold, and at what price.

The American economic system reflects values held by its people. These values were strongly influenced by the Puritans, who believed that those who accumulated wealth were chosen by God. Americans value the individual right to accumulate property and confer status on the rich. They also value growth and increasing profits.

American corporations have grown from large factories to giant corporations that control every step in the manufacturing process from raw materials to retail sales. Some corporations own a number of different types of businesses, and apparently unrelated business may also be linked through being owned or controlled by the same bank or wealthy individual. Many very large corporations do business in many countries. These are called multinational corporations.

Marx believed that work in large factories was alienating. Employees who could not control their work or create a product from start to finish could take no pride in their work, and a great deal of research has been done to increase productivity. Two schools of thought, the scientific management and human relations perspectives, offer different views on how to improve efficiency. The Japanese, who emphasize lifetime jobs and quality control circles, have been more successful than Americans in this respect.

Employees have formed unions to improve their working conditions. American unions have been conservative, choosing to bar workers from other fields and to cooperate with management, striking only as a last resort. More radical labor unions, who want workers to own the means of production, are outlawed in America.

Large corporations and urban areas need many service workers. Most of them are poorly paid, and many are joining unions. Professionals are an exception, however. Professionals are familiar with certain bodies of knowledge and have codes of ethics, licensing procedures, peer controls, and professional organizations. Through legislation, they can limit the practice of their profession and demand high fees.

The economic system affects our everyday lives in countless ways. Three areas that we rarely think of as influenced by the economic system were discussed: leisure, child care, and funerals and mourning.

China has a socialist economic system. Through their planned economy, the Chinese have been able to improve the standard of living of a very poor nation. The Chinese Communist party organized workers into communes, built industries, and provided for the country's other basic needs by teaching group support and training volunteers in health care and other basic services.

The British economic system was a capitalist state strongly opposed to government interference in the early days of industrialization, but it has evolved into a democratic socialist state, and the state provides many services that were not provided adequately by the private sector. The British medical system of general practitioners, hospitals, and community health services developed from a system of private physicians. In the private system, many people could not afford health care. Although the physicians have not been entirely satisfied, most British people prefer the new system. Whether by revolution or gradual change, economic systems can adapt to meet the changing needs of societies.

Key Terms

barefoot doctors
capitalism
democratic socialism
diversification
Gross National Product (GNP)
human relations school
lifetime jobs
market economy
multinational corporations
planned economy
primary workers
professionalization
Protestant ethic
quality control circles
scientific management
secondary workers
socialism
tertiary workers
unionization

Suggested Readings

Anderson, Arthur L. **Divided We Stand.** *Dubuque, Iowa: Kendall/Hunt, 1978.* In this study of churches, Anderson argues that churches are more in agreement about our fundamental economic beliefs than they are about Christianity.

Anthony, P. D. **The Ideology of Work.** *London: Javistock Publications, 1977.* The work ethic is deeply ingrained in industrial society. Anthony philosophically analyzes why this is so and challenges managers of workers to take a realistic look at their own work.

Freeman, Harold. **Toward Socialism in America.** *Cambridge, Mass.: Schenkman, 1979.* Freeman describes the strengths and weaknesses of both capitalism and socialism and suggests that this country make certain knowledgeable adjustments in its economy.

Gouldner, Alvin W. **Patterns of Industrial Bureaucracy.** *New York: The Free Press, 1954.* This is a classic case study in industrial sociology which shows that cooperation decreases when rules are strictly enforced.

Heilbroner, Robert L. **The Making of Economic Society.** *Englewood Cliffs, N.J.: Prentice-Hall, 1980.* This book, referred to several times throughout the chapter, is a good, brief, readable introduction to economics. It is written by an economist.

Skolnick, Jerome H. and Elliot Curie. **Crisis in American Institutions.** *Boston: Little, Brown, 1976.* This is a good collection of articles on the social problems caused by our economic system.

Weber, Max. **The Protestant Ethic and the Spirit of Capitalism.** *New York: Scribner's, 1958.* Weber's brilliant thinking is evident in his discussion of the relationship between religion and the economy. This is one of Weber's more readable works.

The Benefits of Bureaucracy

by Melvin L. Kohn

How would you like to work in a bureaucracy? Before you answer, read the results of Melvin H. Kohn's study, which challenges many popular misconceptions about the nature of bureaucratic organizations and their effects on the people who work for them.

In *Ikiru,* Japanese film director Akira Kurosawa sketches in beautifully harrowing detail the life of a bureaucrat. One of the early scenes shows a stoop-shouldered elderly man sitting behind a desk in a drab, gray office. On the desk are two slightly disordered stacks of paper. As the day passes, the man methodically takes a sheet from one stack, examines it, stamps it, signs it, and deposits it on the other stack.

This view of the paper-shuffling bureaucrat is so ingrained in popular imagination that *Webster's Third New International Dictionary* presents, as one definition of bureaucracy, "a system marked by . . . lack of initiative and flexibility, by indifference to human needs or public opinion, and by a tendency to defer decisions to superiors or to impede action with red tape." The widespread view of bureaucrats as rigid people who have found their proper niches in the world affects even social scientists. Impressed by the way in which bureaucracies function to coordinate the activities of many people, most of them assume that bureaucracies suppress or destroy individuality.

That assumption is wrong. Working in a bureaucracy does not turn people into automatons. Our data indicate that bureaucracies often encourage the development of intellectual flexibility, a tolerance for nonconformity, and a willingness to accept change and innovation among their employees. Bureaucrats often operate at high levels of creativity, performing complex tasks and working under demanding conditions. They also engage in intellectually demanding leisure-time activities. All levels of bureaucratic employees, blue-collar as well as white-collar, enjoy richer lives than nonbureaucrats — both on and off the job.

These findings are based on interviews conducted with a large group of men representative of all civilian job holders in the United States, from bricklayers to board chairmen. With the help of the National Opinion Research Center, a University of Chicago based research group, my colleagues and I collected information about each man's background, current job, past career, values, attitudes toward nonconformity and change, and intellectual flexibility. The first interviews were conducted in 1964 with 3,101 men; in 1974 we reinterviewed a representative sample of these men and, this time, their wives as well. The findings reported here are based on the original group of 3,101 men, but preliminary analyses indicate that the conclusions are just as applicable to employed women.

Bureaucracies, according to Columbia University sociologist Robert K. Merton, are characterized by four elements: a clear-cut division of labor; a system of controls that are stated in regulations; an assignment of roles based on technical qualifications that are determined by formal, impersonal procedures (such as examinations); and a carefully structured hierarchy of authority. Of these, the hierarchy of authority is the central dimension of bureaucracies. A bureaucracy can operate with greater or lesser specialization, with more or less impersonality, and with or without a variety of preestablished rules and procedures — but unless there is a hierarchy of authority, an organization cannot be a bureaucracy. To establish the degree of bureaucratization of the firm in which each of these men was employed, we focused on the structure of authority.

In each interview we asked the employee to count the formal levels of supervision in his firm. A man who sells clothing in a small retail shop, for instance, works for a nonbureaucratic organization because he has only one supervisor — the owner — over him. But a man who sells clothes in a department store is surrounded by floor managers, assistant buyers, department heads, and company executives. His world is highly bureaucratic. Although many employees do not have a clear view of the authority structure in their organizations, even the man at the bottom knows whether or not his boss has a boss, and whether or not that man has ultimate responsibility for the company.

We could thus divide organizations into those with one, two, and three or more levels of supervision. Firms in the third category were further broken down into those with fewer than 100 employees, 100 to 999 employees, and 1,000 employees or more, on the rationale that the number of levels of authority is roughly proportional to size of organization.

Once we had established the degree of bureaucracy of each man's organization, we determined several aspects of his personality, including his intellectual performance; the extent to which

he valued self-direction, tolerated nonconformity, and held himself responsible for his standards of morality; and the way he responded to change. We used two measures of intellectual performance: one an appraisal of the man's performance during the interview, the other an index of the intellectual demands of his leisure activities.

The first measure, which we call intellectual flexibility, used as wide an array of tests of intellectual performance as possible in a demanding two-and-a-half-hour home interview. We gave the men a simple perceptual task, the Embedded Figures Test, in which they had to distinguish between figure and background in complex color designs. We also asked them to draw recognizable human figures. These tests, developed by psychologist H. A. Witkin, demonstrate a fairly strong relationship between perceptual and analytic abilities.

Next we gave the men two apparently simple but highly revealing intellectual problems designed to see if they could weigh both sides of an economic or social issue. They were asked, "Suppose you wanted to open a hamburger stand and there were two locations available. What questions would you consider in deciding which of the two locations offers a better business opportunity?" We wanted to know whether they were aware that profitability is a ratio of income to expenses. Next the men were asked to supply all the arguments they could think of for and against banning cigarette commercials on television.

The second measure of intellectual functioning was the demand that workers put on themselves during leisure-time activities — such as watching television; reading books and magazines; attending plays, concerts, and museums; and working on hobbies.

We gauged the extent to which a man valued self-direction or preferred working under clear-cut rules imposed by external authority by the personal characteristics he considered most desirable for himself. Preferring such characteristics as "curiosity," "good sense and sound judgment," and the "ability to face facts squarely" indicated a belief in self-direction; giving priority to "respectability," "an ability to keep out of trouble," and "law-abidingness" reflected a belief in the value of conforming to external authority.

To measure a man's tolerance of nonconformity, we asked him whether he agreed or disagreed with such statements as: "The most important thing to teach children is absolute obedience to their parents"; "Young people should not be allowed to read books that are likely to confuse them"; and "People who question the old and accepted ways of doing things usually just end up causing trouble."

To determine whether the men believed that morality consisted simply of conformity to the letter of the law, or whether they took personal responsibility for their moral standards, we asked such questions as, "Do you believe that it's all right to do whatever the law allows, or are there some things that are wrong even if they are legal?" We also asked whether they agreed or disagreed with statements like, "It's all right to do anything you want as long as you stay out of trouble," and "If something works, it doesn't matter whether it's right or wrong."

A man's attitude toward change — his receptiveness or resistance to innovation — was revealed by his answers to questions like: "Are you generally one of the first people to try out something new, or do you wait until you see how it's worked out for other people?" and "Are you the sort of person who takes life as it comes, or are you working toward some definite goal?"

The next step for us was to examine the relationship between psychological characteristics and bureaucratic or nonbureaucratic employment. We did this by looking at correlations — the extent to which two things, such as working for a bureaucracy and tolerance of nonconformity, are linked in predictable ways. A positive correlation runs from 0 to 1; the higher the number, the stronger the

association between the two factors. A negative correlation runs from 0 to −1; it means that a *high* score in one factor is reliably associated with a *low* score in another.

The correlations we found were relatively small, ranging from 0.05 to 0.17. But they were always positive and they consistently contradicted most preconceptions of bureaucracy. Men who worked in bureaucratic firms valued self-direction, not conformity; they were more open-minded, were more likely to take personal responsibility for their moral standards, and were more receptive to change than men who worked in nonbureaucratic organizations (whether business, government, or nonprofit associations). Bureaucrats showed greater intellectual flexibility and spent their leisure time in more intellectually demanding pursuits.

A typical bureaucrat is likely to prefer to go his own way both on and off the job and to take responsibility for his own actions; he is likely to welcome changes in the organization of work; he can see many sides of an issue and compare arguments before choosing his own position; and he probably spends more of his free time reading, going to concerts, museums, or plays, or engaging in a hobby that requires thought and interest — anything from stamp collecting to furniture refinishing.

The antithesis of the bureaucrat is considered by many people to be the entrepreneur, who by virtue of business activities must be innovative and flexible. But bureaucrats and entrepreneurs were remarkably similar in their responses to our questions; and on our measure of intellectual flexibility, bureaucrats did better than entrepreneurs. The owner of a small company that manufactures leather goods, according to our data, is likely to be similar to a manager in a major corporation and unlike his own nonbureaucratic employees. The strongest contrast is not between bureaucrats and entrepreneurs, but between both of these groups and nonbureaucratic employees.

Just as the entrepreneur is usually thought of as the antithesis of the bureaucrat, the government official is seen as the prototype. In a sense this is true, for government employees certainly do share the characteristics we found to be typical of bureaucrats. But government employees are not much different from the employees of bureaucratically organized profit-making and nonprofit organizations. Bureaucratic organization, not sector of the economy, matters most.

There could be three possible reasons that employees of bureaucratic organizations are more intellectually flexible, open-minded, and receptive to change than are employees of nonbureaucratic organizations. First, the social origins of bureaucrats might make them more flexible and more tolerant of nonconformity and change. Employees of bureaucratic organizations tend to come from urban backgrounds, generally live in large cities, and have more education than employees of nonbureaucratic firms. Of these factors, education seems to be the strongest potential influence. But when we controlled statistically for the effect of education, the overall correlation was reduced by only 30 percent. Moreover, all but one of the correlations of bureaucracy with values and intellectual functioning remained significant. (Open-mindedness was no longer significantly related to working in a bureaucracy.) Education explains some but not all of the results.

The second possibility is that bureaucracies hold a special attraction for people who are already intellectually flexible and receptive to change. But this possibility seems unlikely since most people are not aware of the working conditions in bureaucracies — if anything, they have the wrong idea. In addition, many occupations can be pursued only in specifically bureaucratic or nonbureaucratic settings. It is as difficult to be an actuary in a nonbureaucratic setting as it is to be a sculptor in a bureaucracy.

The third and strongest possible reason for the relationship between bureaucratic employment and personality is that the working conditions of bureaucracies encourage the development of these characteristics among employees. The common assumption is that people fit into and perhaps mold their jobs, and that jobs have little effect on the personality. But our data, particularly the results from the second survey, show that job conditions do affect psychological functioning. We find, for example, that the complexity of men's work substantially affects their intellectual flexibility.

Employees of bureaucracies tend to have more complex jobs than do other men with a comparable education. They work a shorter week under greater time pressure, work in the company of colleagues but not necessarily in harness with them, face more competition, enjoy greater job security and higher salaries. If we hold education constant, we find that three of these job conditions — the complexity of the work, job security, and income — largely account for the correlation of bureaucracy with values, attitudes, and intellectual ability.

The white-collar bureaucrat has highly diversified responsibilities; unlike Kurosawa's Japanese gentleman, he is not a mechanical paper stamper. Managers in any factory constantly evaluate information, make decisions for which there are a multitude of alternatives, juggle competing interests, and move back and forth between meetings and solitary office work. School officials, principals, and assistant principals face continually changing conditions. The typical blue-collar bureaucrat is not strapped to a production line to tighten the fourth screw on the left side of the flipscan, but carries out a variety of tasks, enjoys the possibility of reorganizing his work, and deals with many different situations throughout the workday.

Our index of the complexity of work included the intricacy of a man's work with data, things, and people, and the amount of time he spent working with each of these. Job security consists of such basic job protection as tenure, seniority, the existence of formal grievance procedures, and sick pay. As a result of unionization, job security is stronger for blue-collar than for white-collar workers. Nevertheless, white-collar bureaucrats are protected by bureaucratic regulations. Supervisors cannot dismiss white-collar employees unless they can show their superiors sufficient cause. Tradition, severance pay, a paid period in which to search for alternative employment — all provide a level of security unavailable in nonbureaucratic employment, where hiring and firing is often arbitrary. And bureaucrats work within organizational structures that pay higher salaries than firms that employ nonbureaucrats; bureaucrats can also depend on regular pay increases based on established schedules.

We examined each job condition separately to see how it helps explain the psychological impact of working in a bureaucracy. The complexity of work is particularly pertinent to bureaucratic employees' intellectual flexibility and to their making intellectually demanding use of their leisure time. These correlations suggest a direct carryover to off-the-job activities. Job protection helps account for the correlation between bureaucratic employment and moral codes, attitudes toward change, and even intellectual flexibility. Men who are protected from the hazards of change, it seems, are less fearful of innovation and more willing to accept personal responsibility for their acts. Income, in turn, helps determine what a man can spend on leisure hobbies and pleasures, and it also affects a man's sense of self-direction. High-income employees apparently feel enough control over their lives to value self-direction and to view it as an attainable goal.

Although both blue-collar and white-collar workers are subject to the influences of the job conditions we measured, job protection has a stronger effect on employees in blue-collar jobs, and the complexity of work has a greater impact on employees in white-collar jobs. Thus the welder who works for General Motors is likely to be more flexible and open to change than the welder who works for the owner of a small, local auto body shop. Similarly, the accountant who works for General Motors — and whose job calls for flexibility and initiative, and demands much of his talents and knowledge — is more likely to read and less likely to watch television in his spare time than the accountant who balances the books for the local body shop.

The relationships between bureaucracy and personality would be even stronger, we believe, were it not for one other attribute of bureaucracy: The bureaucrats we studied, even though they did more complex work, were more closely supervised, and supervised by people further removed from them in the hierarchy, than nonbureaucrats. Bureaucracies hire educated workers, provide them with complex tasks (especially white-collar workers), but fail to give them freedom to direct themselves. In this one respect, the stereotype that bureaucracies limit flexibility and initiative is confirmed. Overall, though, the tendency of bureaucracies to supervise their employees too closely is more than offset by the advantages they provide in work complexity, income, and — especially — job protection.

Bureaucracies are usually seen as occupational dead ends. Upon entering a large organization, a person's career is supposed to come to a halt, or at least slow down. Ability no longer matters, for advancement depends on the retirement or death of the person who is next higher in the structure of authority. This constraint on his career is supposed to limit an individual's social mobility.

But the facts of bureaucratic life belie the picture of bureaucracy as a dead end. Because they provide job security and freedom from arbitrary authority, bureaucracies actually stimulate the individual initiative that leads to successful careers. In the end, the much maligned bureaucracy exerts a positive influence that is reflected in people's work performance, personalities, and psychological functioning.

Bureaucracies ensure that officials are limited in the facets of their subordinates' behavior they control and how they may exercise that control; they cannot dismiss subordinates at will, and questionable actions can sometimes be appealed. The power of nonbureaucratic organizations over their employees is more complete and may be more capricious. The alternative to bureaucracy's circumscribed authority is not less authority, but personal authority, subject to a boss's whims.

The Japanese bureaucrat in *Ikiru*, dying of cancer and disgusted by his meaningless career, revolts against the bureaucracy of the Parks De-partment and forces "the system" to build a play-ground for children. After a quarter century of working in the organization, he has learned how to manipulate it toward his own ends. But Kuro-sawa's bureaucrat is motivated by bitterness and despair. The bureaucrats we studied do not find their careers meaningless and are seldom forced to revolt against the system. Bureaucracies allow their employees much more opportunity to exercise their ingenuity and their skills than is commonly understood.

SOURCE: Kohn, Melvin L., "The Benefits of Bureau-cracy," *Human Nature*, August 1978, pp. 60–66.

Three Who Aren't Making It

by Terry P. Brown

This is the story of three hardworking, skilled, and experienced men who feel unfairly treated by the companies they work for and are fighting the systems that allow such treatment.

Marvin E. Walden

In only five years at GM, Marvin E. Walden was promoted to senior mathematician at the company's technical center, receiving several merit pay increases and extensive training at company expense. He felt, however, that his chances of en-tering management would be better at a company with "less technical depth" in personnel and facili-ties. "I was young and ambitious, so I sent out resumes to Ford and Chrysler," he says. In mid-1969, he joined Chrysler for a "substantial pay increase."

Within a few months, Mr. Walden became head of a thirty-two-man department assigned to computerize the process of turning clay models of car designs into precisely measured body compo-nents. For nearly a year and a half, he ran the department and developed facilities which, he claims, now save Chrysler about $1 million an-nually. During that time, Mr. Walden says he re-ceived a "favorable" oral performance review from the head of Chrysler's technical computer center. He says this was the only performance appraisal he has had in eight years with the company.

With a managerial position that paid about $24,000 a year, Mr. Walden's career seemed "on track." In addition, he was completing his doctor-ate in mathematics at Detroit's Wayne State University, where he had graduated Phi Beta Kappa with a physics degree and earned a master's degree in math.

His job prospects changed dramatically, however, when his boss was promoted and, according to Mr. Walden, a "personality clash" developed with the new man. In May 1971, Mr. Walden's department was disbanded without warning, and he was demoted to a supervisor without any cut in pay. Chrysler says the move was necessary to eliminate duplication of work with another department; Mr. Walden thinks he was "set up" as part of an inter-departmental political struggle.

"At first, I was angry and wanted to quit," says forty-one-year-old Mr. Walden, "but after sending out hundreds of resumes, I quickly learned I'd have to take a substantial cut in pay." He decided to stay on at Chrysler, hoping that he might eventually be promoted back to his former level. Instead, Mr. Walden says he has been given a series of "make-work, letter-writing assignments, leading nowhere."

In 1975, Mr. Walden was laid off, along with about 20,000 other Chrysler salaried workers, due to the recession. When he returned he found that several younger men had been promoted to positions he thought himself qualified to fill. So, Mr. Walden sued his employer, seeking reinstatement to his former management position and $500,000 in damages. "My demotion was without cause, but if they had treated me like a gentleman, I would have saluted and waited for a promotion back to a manager's level," he says. "But there was no internal due process, no mediation procedure."

As part of his suit, Mr. Walden is demanding to see Chrysler's list of "exceptional" employees. Chrysler admits that it centrally compiles such lists to assist it in selecting candidates for internal openings, but the company denies that it uses the list in a discriminatory manner. "One's name on such a list doesn't guarantee advancement," company lawyers say. "There are many, many employ-ees whose names haven't been on such a list who have been advanced much further than most of the employees so listed." Chrysler has been ordered by Wayne County Circuit Court to produce certain details of the list for inspection.

"Usually in Chrysler," contends Mr. Walden, "you get on the list, and you get promoted if you know a director (a management level one step below vice president). It's a 100 percent sponsor- or godfather-type system and has nothing to do with any kind of scientific management system."

"What results," he feels, "is that many people are underutilized; yet they continue to pay us high salaries, wasting millions." He says his total economic package, including such benefits as medical insurance, is about $35,000 a year. He lives in a comfortable brick ranch house in the affluent Detroit suburb of Bloomfield Hills, has two cars, and sends his three children to private schools. "I've lost a lot of sleep over this," he says. "I started grinding my teeth so much I had to buy a teeth protector." He adds: "It won't be possible for me to take less money and change my life style now."

Richard E. Mathews

"If they thought they were clearing out some deadwood, they picked the wrong man," declares Richard E. Mathews, who has worked for Ford for nearly thirty-eight years. "No one ever told me I didn't do a good job, and I certainly never felt I was ready to retire." But Mr. Mathews asserts that in rough times Ford "makes the mistake of assuming that young is good, older is bad, or now is our chance to weed out the older employees." Mr. Mathews never thought he would be one of those "eased out the door."

In 1939 at the age of nineteen, Mr. Mathews joined Ford as an assembly-line worker. He left in 1942 to fly B29s during World War II, rising to the rank of captain. He returned to Ford in 1947, and was assigned to testing Ford's German-made trucks. Except for three years on the assembly line, Mr. Mathews's entire career has been in testing and developing products for Ford's foreign affiliates and export markets.

Despite the lack of a college degree, Mr. Mathews rose to the post of supervisor, with as many as twenty-two engineers and technicians under him. After eight years, he was asked to take a lateral transfer to become supervisor of another department's Latin American section. "I thought the move was made to train younger supervisors and to expand my overall experience," says Mr. Mathews. Two years later, in 1974, however, the department was eliminated, and Mr. Mathews, then 53 years old, was demoted and transferred back to his old department as an engineer.

An indignant Mr. Mathews fired off a letter to chairman Henry Ford II. But the only response was a call from the personnel department saying his complaint wasn't "valid." Mr. Mathews sued, asking for reinstatement to his former position. Ford argues that Mr. Mathews was demoted without any cut in pay at a time when "thousands of employees were being released outright" due to the recession. Mr. Mathews claims that in his department there was a net gain in personnel of about 15 percent during the recession.

Although his salary wasn't cut (last year, he earned about $45,000, including $10,000 of overtime), he says he "lost prestige, a private office, a secretary and any right to a bonus, which probably would have amounted to about $4,500 last year." He declares: "I didn't have any illusions that I could go much higher than one more notch, but the demotion put me further back in the pack for any future advancement."

Sitting in the living room of his Dearborn Heights, Mich., home, not far from Ford's world headquarters, Mr. Mathews says: "I don't disagree with the idea of bringing fresh blood into an organization, but you have to try to hit a happy medium between the young world-beaters and your loyal, experienced people. A lot of the stars burn themselves out at an early age."

Edward B. Mazzotta

In 1953, Edward B. Mazzotta joined Ford as a project engineer designing vehicle components. Eight years later, he left to work for two smaller Detroit-area engineering firms, but rejoined Ford in 1971. Within fifteen months he was promoted two pay grades to resident engineer of the Dearborn engine plant, a $30,000-a-year management job.

"In any corporation, nine times out of ten, you need an angel to watch over you if you're going to get ahead," says the fifty-six-year-old Mr. Mazzotta. "I had an angel, but when a new regime came in to head up the resident engineering staff, my angel got his wings clipped and was forced into early retirement."

What resulted, in Mr. Mazzotta's view, was a "humiliating, systematic step-by-step discrediting" by his new supervisors. Within about three months, Mr. Mazzotta received two poor performance reviews. "These were unwarranted and based on a lack of facts," he claims. "When the reviews were presented to me, I was told to read them and then sign them, but I had no opportunity to discuss them." In March 1974, Mr. Mazzotta, then fifty-three, was demoted two pay grades without a cut in pay and transferred to another department. Now, he says, he's "a paper shuffler, doing nothing that any high school graduate couldn't do," at a salary of about $35,000 a year.

"Some people will tolerate a lot of abuse before they do anything: they'll sit there and take the money. But the desire to feel useful and constructive was too great for me," he says. Mr. Mazzotta says he tried to appeal his case through Ford's personnel department, asking for a promotional transfer, but "it was like going to a priest for confession. Once you've been demoted, it's unlikely you'll ever shake the stigma and be promoted again."

In a lawsuit filed last year in Wayne County Circuit Court, seeking reinstatement and $500,000 in damages, Mr. Mazzotta charges that younger men "with far less experience" have been promoted within the department, while several older men "in my age range" have been either demoted or forced into early retirement. Ford says that Mr. Mazzotta's lack of promotion is a function of "few position openings" and of his performance "in relation to others seeking the positions."

The demotion and the decision to sue Ford haven't been easy on Mr. Mazzotta. Eight months after his demotion, he required medical treatment for a duodenal ulcer. At his request, he was interviewed for this story in his hospital room after

suffering a heart attack while on the job. Mr. Mazzotta blames his health problems on the way he was treated at Ford.

"You can't eliminate politics from a corporation, but you can try to minimize it," he reasons. "In my case, the performance review was used as a weapon, and I had no way to refute or rebut what was happening to me.

"I don't agree with the idea that a man slows down as he gets older," he says. "If a man is slow at fifty-five, he was slow at thirty-five, and the company has an obligation to tell him of his limited potential then — and not wait twenty years to shelve him or sweep him out the door."

SOURCE: Brown, Terry P., "Three Who Aren't Making It." Reprinted by permission of *The Wall Street Journal,* © Dow Jones & Company, Inc. 1977. All Rights Reserved.

Part V

Human Ecology and Change

No matter how well we understand sociology, we all know that it is difficult to predict the future because societies change. At this point in history they are changing very rapidly. Even now groups of people are acting together to gain power, to gain equal rights, to create a better lifestyle for themselves or to protect a lifestyle they now enjoy. The size of the population is increasing dramatically, the health of the population has improved, and we are living longer. The ever-increasing numbers of people make our earth more crowded, and many now live in congested urban areas. Our cities strain under the weight of this population increase. All these issues are examined in the first three chapters of this section.

How can we possibly understand what our future will be like? The last chapter in this book summarizes theories of social change and analyzes the kinds of events that could have a great impact on modern societies. While we cannot know which events will occur in the future, we can better understand what impact certain types of events might have. As you read through these final chapters, we hope you find that you have gained a new perspective, a sociological perspective, which gives you a new understanding of the world about you. We trust this new perspective will be useful as you prepare for your own future in this rapidly changing world.

Chapter 17

Collective Behavior and Social Movements

Clapping with the right hand only will not produce a noise.

— Malay proverb

Most facets of social life follow patterns of rules and norms. People generally have a daily routine and conform to the roles expected of them. In the same way, such organizations as schools, churches, factories, and governments are highly structured institutions that tend to be stable and relatively static. In these organizations, decisions are made through some semblance of logical, rational discussion.

There is, however, another dimension of social life in which the activities are relatively spontaneous, unstructured, and unstable. This category includes such collective actions as panics, demonstrations, riots, fads and fashions, disasters, and social movements. These actions, which may also follow certain patterns and established norms and rules, are instances of what sociologists call *collective behavior*.

What Is Collective Behavior?

Sociologists use the term collective behavior to refer to spontaneous, unstructured, and transitory behavior of a group of people to a specific event. If the term were taken literally, it would incorporate all behaviors involving more than one person, that is, all of sociology, but sociologists use it in a more restrictive sense. The difference between the literal and the sociological definition can be clarified with an example. Take an event like automobile crashes. To conduct safety tests, car manufacturers have a group of employees perform tests repeatedly and collect data in an organized fashion on what happens when a car moving 35 mph hits something. Compare this with the behavior of a group of people gathered at the site of a highway accident. Although both groups gathered to observe car crashes and are thus behaving collectively in the literal sense, only the second group is engaged in collective behavior in the sociological sense. The car company employees are reacting to a carefully controlled event in which the action is both expected and repeated. The group observing the highway accident reacts to a spontaneous, unstructured, unexpected, nonrecurring event. Panics, riots, crowds, fads, and fashions can all be viewed as spontaneous collective responses to transitory and loosely structured circumstances.

Collective behavior can be contrasted with *institutionalized behavior,* which is recurrent and follows an orderly pattern with a relatively stable set of goals, expectations, and values. In the example above, the auto workers are involved in stitutionalized behavior. Other examples of routine, predictable behavior would be going to class, commuting on a train, and going to church. If some unusual event takes place — an earthquake, train wreck, or fire, for example — collective behavior takes over. When people are confronted with an unfamiliar event, for which no norms or rules have been established, they may behave in ways that differ radically from their normal conduct. People generally leave a theater in a calm, orderly fashion without pushing or shouting. If a fire breaks out, however, their conventional behavior would change to screams, shoving, and a rush for the exits. The ordinary norms break down and are replaced by new ones. Such actions occur infrequently, however, and only under certain conditions.

Preconditions of Collective Behavior

Certain conditions in contemporary societies tend to increase the likelihood of collective behavior. Rapid social change creates tensions and conflicts that sometimes lead to collective actions and violence. Social diversity and the associated in-

equalities in the distribution of wealth and opportunities have produced many social movements — the women's movement, the Gray Panthers, the civil rights movement, and the labor movement. The mass media also play an important role in the dissemination of information of all types, from the pet rock and hula hoop fads to prison riots. Some critics have suggested that the ghetto riots of the 1960s occurred in part because information on riots in other cities was transmitted through the media.

In addition to rapid social change, social diversity, and mass communications, certain other preconditions encourage collective behavior. Neil Smelser, in his *Theory of Collective Behavior* (1962), identified six factors that, when they exist simultaneously, will produce collective behavior: (1) structural conduciveness, (2) structural strain, (3) a generalized belief, (4) precipitating factors, (5) mobilization for action, and (6) operation of social control.

Structural conduciveness, the most general precondition, is the extent to which a society's organization makes collective behavior possible. A society that has no stock market cannot have a stock market crash. A country that has only one race or religion will not have race or religious riots. Note that structural conduciveness — the existence of banks, stock markets, or different religious or racial groups, for example — does not cause collective behavior. Rather, it is a measure of the existence of conditions in which it can happen. The fact that a society is structurally conducive does not mean that collective behavior *will* happen; it means that, given certain other conditions, it *can.*

A *structural strain* is any kind of conflict or ambiguity that causes frustration and stress. Structural strains may be caused by conflicts between real and ideal norms, by conflicts between goals and available means to reaching them (anomie), or by the gap between the social ideals (full employment, wealth, equality) and social realities (unem-

Collective behavior is the spontaneous and unstructured response of a group of people to a specific event. At a rock concert in Cincinnati, hundreds of fans rushed forward when the doors were opened. Eleven people were trampled to death and countless others were knocked down and crushed. Shown here are the covered body of one known dead and a group of firefighters working to revive other young people who were victims of the collective response.

ployment, poverty, and discrimination by age, race, and sex). Widespread unemployment among teenage blacks is an example of a structural strain.

A third determinant of collective behavior is a *generalized belief*. Given structural conduciveness and structural strain, people must identify a problem and share a common interpretation of it for collective action to occur. People develop generalized beliefs about the conditions causing the strain. The women's movement, for example, began to grow only after the belief became widespread that women were discriminated against in employment, education, and other areas. Mobs form and riots take place only when people share a belief in some injustice or unfair treatment. Generalized beliefs may be based on known facts, shared attitudes, or a common ideology. The truth or accuracy of the beliefs is unimportant — the important thing is that they are shared.

Precipitating factors are the fourth determinant. Structural conduciveness, structural strain, and generalized belief alone do not inevitably cause collective behavior. A precipitating event

must trigger a collective response. The precipitating event itself is sometimes fairly insignificant. An unwarranted search may start a collective protest in an overcrowded prison. Commodity trading may proceed quietly until a rumor arises that frost has severely damaged the expected orange harvest. The precipitating event can also be a more serious incident, of course. News that a policeman has shot a black youth can inflame a tense racial situation. As was true of generalized beliefs, a precipitating event need not be true or accurately communicated to exert an influence. Even an unfounded rumor can lend focus and support to a belief and increase the likelihood of a collective response.

Mobilization for action is the fifth determinant of collective behavior. Once a precipitating event has taken place, people have to be persuaded to join the movement. Sometimes an event mobilizes a group spontaneously, as when the crowd boos the umpire for making a bad call, or when a crowd panics if someone yells fire. Sometimes leaders emerge from within the group to encourage participation, which is what occurred during the formation of the Solidarity labor movement in Poland in 1980, when Lech Walesa, an unemployed electrician, quickly became the leader and spokesman for the group. In other cases, outside leadership steps in to organize the people and push them into action, which is what often happened during the era when labor unions were being formed in this country. Collective behavior begins when mobilization for action takes place.

The operation of social control is the sixth and final determinant of collective behavior. Social control consists of the actions of the mass media, government, and other groups when they try to suppress or influence collective behavior (Smelser, 1969). In the case of a potential strike, management might agree to listen to grievances, make a few changes, or raise wages slightly. If the strike takes place, it might fire striking workers and hire new ones. If social control cannot prevent collective action before it starts or halt it once it has begun, the collective behavior continues.

Smelser's approach, then, suggests that a series of six preconditions is necessary to produce collective action. The preconditions are closely interrelated — structural strains will not appear unless the society is structurally conducive to them, for example. This approach has been widely criticized, but it remains the most systematic and important theory of collective behavior.

Smelser's model was applied by Lewis (1972) in an attempt to explain events at Kent State University on May 4, 1970, when four students were killed and nine others wounded by National Guardsmen. The incident happened during a period of widespread student antiwar rallies and protests, and the Kent State rally was a reaction to President Nixon's announcement that troops had been sent into Cambodia. The situation was extremely tense, and ultimately the National Guard fired at the taunting students. In evaluating Smelser's general theory as applied to this incident, Lewis found that all six conditions were present:

(1) the circumstances were structurally conducive to a hostile outburst; (2) structural strain was produced by the National Guard's presence on the students' turf, by illegal student rallies, and by the use of tear gas; (3) a generalized hostile belief about the Guard developed; (4) the use of force and the actions of the Guard in making a stand in front of a burned ROTC building served as precipitating events; (5) the events themselves as well as the announcement that the rally was illegal, tended to mobilize the Guard as well as the students for action; (6) attempts to exert social control were made by the Guard, but these efforts were unsuccessful. The theory was found to be extremely useful in organizing the large body of information generated by the Kent State episode.

Now that we have considered preconditions to collective behavior, we will direct our attention to specific types of collective behavior.

Spatially Proximate Collective Behaviors: Crowds

A *spatially proximate collective* is one in which people are geographically close and physically visible to one another. The most common type of a spatially proximate collective is the *crowd*.

Crowds are temporary or transitory groups of people in face-to-face contact who share a common interest or focus of attention. This common interest may be unexpected and unusual but not necessarily. Although people in crowds interact considerably, the crowd as a whole is organized poorly if at all. According to Turner (1978), crowds have certain features that make them a unique area for study, including anonymity, suggestibility, contagion, and emotional arousability.

Most types of collective behavior involve *anonymity*. People who do not know those around them may behave in ways that they would consider unacceptable if they were alone or with their family or neighbors. During a riot, the anonymity of crowd members makes it easier for people to loot and steal. In a lynch mob, brutal and atrocious acts can be committed without feelings of shame or responsibility. Whatever the type of crowd, the anonymity of the individuals involved shifts the responsibility to the crowd as a whole.

Because crowds are relatively unstructured and often unpredictable, crowd members are often highly *suggestible*. People who are seeking direction in an uncertain situation are highly responsive to the suggestions of others and become very willing to do what a leader or group of individuals suggests, especially given the crowd's anonymity.

The characteristic of *contagion* is closely linked to anonymity and suggestibility. Turner (1978) defines this aspect of crowd behavior as "interactional amplification" (p. 284). As people interact, the crowd's response to the common event or situation increases in intensity. If they are clapping or screaming, their behavior is likely to move others to clap or scream, and contagion increases when people are packed close together. An alert evangelist, comedian, or rock singer will try to get the audience to move close to one another to increase the likelihood of contagion and encourage the listeners to get caught up in the mood, spirit, and activity of the crowd.

A fourth characteristic is *emotional arousal*. Anonymity, suggestibility, and contagion tend to arouse emotions. Inhibitions are forgotten, and people become "charged" to act. In some cases, their emotional involvement encourages them to act in uncharacteristic ways. During the Beatles concerts in the early 1960s, for example, teenage girls who were presumably quite conventional most of the time tried to rush on stage and had to be carried away by police. The combination of the four characteristics of crowds makes their behavior extremely volatile and sometimes frightening.

Although these four aspects of crowd behavior may be seen in any crowd, their intensity varies. Some crowds permit greater anonymity than others, some have higher levels of suggestibility and contagion, and yet one or more of these characteristics may not appear at all. The presence or absence of certain crowd features has been used to organize crowds into different categories.

Types of Crowds

All crowds are spatially proximate and temporary, and they all share a common focus. The most complete classification, advanced more than forty years ago by Herbert Blumer (1939), identified crowds of four types: (1) casual, (2) conventional, (3) expressive, and (4) acting.

A *casual crowd* is high in anonymity but low in suggestibility, contagion, and emotional arousal. A group of people gathered to listen to a street musician, to observe a person who has fainted, or to look at an animated holiday display would be a casual crowd. Casual crowds have little unity and a very loose organization. The participants interact little with one another; they are drawn together to observe an event out of simple curiosity or a common interest. Blumer notes that although the chief mechanisms of crowd formation occur in the casual crowd, their influence is not very strong.

A *conventional crowd* resembles the casual crowd except that it is more highly structured and participants express themselves in established ways. The spectators at a baseball game, the audience at a concert, students listening to a lecture, or the passengers on an airplane are conventional crowds. Although the participants are generally unknown to one another (anonymous), they have a specific goal or common purpose. This type of crowd is conventional in that the members are expected to follow established social norms and rules. Running up and down the aisles and shouting, for example, would be disapproved behaviors in a theater or airplane.

All crowds share a common focus. Some groups, such as those that form to listen to street performers (left), have little unity and organization. They are drawn together to listen to the musicians but remain anonymous to one another. Other groups, such as those at a religious revival (right), have a greater degree of unity and organization and less anonymity. In this religious service, snakes serve as a test of faith and as a source of emotional expression.

Conventional crowds may not seem like crowds at all since they generally follow established rules and procedures. Concerts and baseball games are scheduled at preestablished times and places, and crowd members sit in designated areas. People applaud at the end of the music or when an outstanding play has been made. Nevertheless, a conventional crowd has all of the characteristics of our definition: it is spatially proximate, temporary, and focused on a single event.

The distinguishing feature of the *expressive crowd*, which Blumer also terms the "dancing" crowd, is the physical movement of its members as a form of release. Unlike the other types, the expressive crowd's attention is not directed toward an external object or goal. Rather, "It is introverted in that its impulses and feelings are spent in mere expressive actions, usually in unrestrained physical movements, which give release to tension without having any other purpose" (Blumer, 1939, p. 182). Expressive crowds can be found at street carnivals and festivals, at discos, at evangelical religious revivals, and elsewhere. The expressive activities may include singing, shouting, drinking, and competitive actions as well as dancing. At events of this sort, people "let loose," become emotionally involved, and in extreme instances become completely uninhibited. Although this expressive behavior may appear wild and unrestrained, social rules and norms are operating: people know what kinds of behavior are acceptable within the boundaries of the ceremony or festivity. For this reason, most expressive crowd events, including very large gatherings such as the Mardi Gras or rock festivals, are quite orderly and peaceful. Anthropologists point out that expressive events are especially important in cultures with a high level of emotional repression. The dances and festivals provide an outlet for tensions and emotions.

The *acting crowd* exhibits all the features of crowds mentioned earlier: anonymity, suggestibility, contagion, and emotional arousal. Like the casual or conventional crowd, the acting crowd focuses on some external goal or object. Acting crowds, however, may be aggressive, hostile, volatile, and sometimes dangerous. Rather than following rules and acting within the confines of a structured organization, they act on the basis of aroused impulse. Participants have rapport with other crowd members and are drawn into the excitement of the event. They respond immediately and directly to the remarks and actions of others without thinking about them or trying to weigh alternative courses of action. The two most dramatic forms of acting crowds are mobs and riots.

Mobs are groups that are emotionally aroused and ready to engage in violent behavior. They are generally short-lived and highly unstable. Their violent actions often stem from strong dissatisfaction with existing government policies or social circumstances, and extreme discontentment with prevailing conditions is used as justification for immediate and direct action. Disdainful of regular institutional channels and legal approaches, mobs take matters into their own hands.

Most mobs are predisposed to violence before their actions are triggered by a specific event. Widespread feelings of frustration and hostility enable leaders to recruit members and make them obey their commands. With aggressive leadership, an angry, frustrated mob in an atmosphere of hostility can be readily motivated to riot, commit lynchings, throw firebombs, hang people in effigy, or engage in destructive orgies.

Mob violence has erupted in many different circumstances. During the French Revolution of the 1780s and 1790s, angry mobs stormed through Paris, breaking into the Bastille prison for arms and calling for the execution of Louis XVI. In nineteenth-century England, enraged workers burned the factories they worked in. Lynchings of blacks in the United States for real or imagined offenses continued into the twentieth century, often with little or no opposition from the formal agencies of control — police, courts, and other public officials. Although lynch mobs are uncommon today, occasional instances of mob behavior take place over civil rights issues such as busing or housing, during political conventions and rallies, and among student or labor groups angry about perceived injustices.

Riots resemble mobs except that the targets of their hostility and violence are less specific and the groups involved are more diffuse. Riots often involve mob actions — the destruction of a particular building, for example — but most actions result from an intense hatred of a particular group with no specific person or property in mind. Destruction, burning, or looting may be indiscriminate, and unfocused anger can lead to violent acts against any object or person who happens to be in the wrong area at the wrong time. Like mobs, rioters take actions into their own hands when they feel that institutional reactions to their concerns about war, poverty, racial injustices, or other problems are inadequate.

The race riots of the 1960s in Watts in Los Angeles, Harlem in New York, and many other cities are the most commonly cited examples of rioting. These riots, which generally occurred in black ghettos, involved widespread destruction of property followed by extensive looting. The National Advisory Commission on Civil Disorders (Kerner, 1968) found that riots are associated with a number of factors, including discrimination, prejudice, disadvantaged living conditions, and frustration over the inability to bring about change. The incident that triggers a riot can be relatively trivial. In Detroit, for example, riots began after police raided social clubs suspected of permitting illegal gambling and the sale of liquor after hours. The riots of the 1960s, however, took place almost without exception in communities long frustrated by high unemployment, poverty, police harassment, and other factors. In the riots of the summer of 1967, tensions were increased by the sweltering weather.

These findings are highly consistent with those of Lieberson and Silverman (1965), who studied conditions underlying seventy-six race riots in the United States between 1913 and 1963. They found that only four of them started without a precipitating event such as a rape, murder, arrest, or holdup. They also found that riots are most probable in communities with a history of being unable to resolve racial problems. The characteristics of crowd behavior — anonymity, suggestibility, contagion, and emotional arousal — were present in all the riots studied by Lieberson and Silverman.

Theories of Acting Crowd Behavior

Students of crowd behavior have historically focused on acting crowds. How do acting crowds diminish individualism and encourage people to accept the attitudes and behaviors of the group? We have already examined Smelser's theory about the preconditions of collective behavior. Four additional perspectives are representative of the various other interpretations prevalent today. These include Le Bon's *classical* perspective, Blumer's *interactionist* perspective, Turner and Killian's *emergent norm* perspective, and Berk's *game* perspective.

The Classical Perspective

Probably the most influential single book ever written on collective behavior is *The Crowd* (1895), by the French sociologist Gustave Le Bon (1841–1931). During Le Bon's life, France was experiencing rapid social change, and, earlier, mobs and riots had brought about the French Revolution. Le Bon, who considered crowds pathological, violent, threatening groups, believed that their destructive potential stemmed from "the psychological law of the mental unity of the crowd." According to Le Bon (1968),

> The sentiments and ideas of all the persons in the gathering take one and the same direction, and their conscious personality vanishes. A collective mind is formed, doubtless transitory, but presenting very clearly defined characteristics. The gathering has thus become what, in the absence of a better expression, I will call an organised crowd, or, if the term is considered preferable, a psychological crowd. It forms a single being, and is subjected to the *law of the mental unity of crowds.* (p.2)

This quote mentions two key concepts in the classical view of crowds: *collective mind* and *mental unity.* Le Bon, the originator of the "group mind" concept, believed that crowds cause people to regress. According to this view, crowds are guided by instinct, not by rational decisions. Under the influence of crowds, even conventional, law-abiding citizens may act impulsively and be guided by unconscious influences. Crowds do not reason, they respond instantly to the immediate situation. Why? (1) The anonymity of the collective gives each person in a crowd a feeling of power. (2) A contagion sweeps through the crowd like a virus that passes from one person to another. (3) The participants become as suggestible as if they had been hypnotized. The result is the unquestioned acceptance of and obedience to the leaders.

The Interactionist Perspective

Herbert Blumer (1939), like Le Bon, believed that crowd behavior is often irrational and emotional, but he rejected the idea that it stems from a group or collective mind. Rather, he believed that crowd behavior results from *circular reactions* operating in a situation of *social unrest*. In Blumer's words, circular reaction

> ... refers to a type of interstimulation wherein the response of one individual reproduces the stimulation that has come from another individual and in being reflected back to this individual reinforces the stimulation. Thus the interstimulation assumes a circular form in which individuals reflect one another's states of feeling and in so doing intensify this feeling. (p. 170)

In other words, in a situation of social unrest, interactions reinforce and heighten the unrest. If one group, for example, shouts "Let's get him," others model this behavior and usually adopt the same feelings and ways of expressing them. The reactions of these others increase the fervor of the original group, which in turn excites the rest of the crowd even further. In the absence of widespread unrest, such a reaction would never begin. Three types of circular reactions are milling, collective excitement, and social contagion.

In a *milling* crowd, people move about aimlessly. Milling tends to make people preoccupied with one another and less responsive to the usual sources of stimulation. Like hypnotic subjects who become increasingly preoccupied with the hypnotist, milling individuals grow more preoccupied with others in the crowd and become increasingly inclined to respond quickly, directly, and without thinking.

Collective excitement takes place when milling reaches a high level of agitation. People in the grip of collective excitement are emotionally aroused. They respond on the basis of their impulses, they are likely to feel little personal responsibility for their actions, and under the influence of collective excitement they may behave in an uncharacteristic manner (Blumer, 1939).

Social contagion comes about wherever milling and collective excitement are intense and widespread. What is fascinating about social contagion is that it can attract people who were initially just indifferent spectators. They get caught up in the excitement and become more inclined to become involved. Unlike Le Bon's theory, this theory does not suggest the existence of a group mind. Rather, people's interactions tend to heighten in intensity until the group is capable of spontaneous behavior.

The Emergent Norm Perspective

The emergent norm perspective, first proposed by Turner and Killian (1957), emphasizes how norms influence crowd behavior and how new norms emerge and are maintained. Whereas Le Bon and Blumer stress similarities in the behavior of crowd members, the emergent norm perspective focuses on differences in crowd member behavior. As Turner and Killian (1972) state,

> An emergent norm approach reflects the empirical observation that the crowd is characterized not by unanimity but by differential expression, with different individuals in the crowd feeling differently, participating because of diverse motives, and even acting differently. (p. 22)

According to this view, crowds do not behave as a homogeneous unit. Observers may think they act as a unit, but divergent views and behaviors may go unrecognized or be dismissed as unimportant. When attention is focused on the acting crowd, people frequently overlook those who remain silently on the sidelines, those who passively lend their support, and those who express little excitement. People behave differently because they act in accordance with different norms.

Norms influence all social conduct, and new norms arise during novel situations such as mob actions or riots. Some may accept norms that make violence and looting acceptable. Others may define the situation differently and choose to leave or remain uninvolved.

The process by which norms emerge occurs daily in any context of human social interaction and communication. All of us are dependent on those around us to define and determine what a given event means. When others in the group shout, run, express fear, or whatever, we are likely to feel tremendous pressure to conform to their behavior. An untrained observer may note the one dominant behavior and describe the group members as unanimous in their definition, mood, and behavior. More careful observation, as an emergent norm theory would suggest, is that unanimity is an illusion and that differential expression does take place. The problem of accounting for differential expression is illuminated by Turner (1980) who cites the following example, which is a first-hand account of an adult male with his young son and daughter in a toy department of a store:

> Suddenly there was a loud and continuous hissing noise from the center of the room, a few cries of fear, and in an instant the entire basement room was cleared of shoppers and clerks alike. I was astonished and even amused at the panicky flight of women shoppers and clerks. I felt no fear — it sounded to me as if one of the automatic sprinkler heads had been broken, which was nothing to be afraid of. I looked down at my daughter, who was holding my hand and looking rather wide-eyed, but giving no sign of fear. I looked across the room for my son, but could see no one in the room. I felt quite concerned lest he be hurt or frightened, being alone in the crowd. I looked for the broken sprinkler so that I could cross the room to find him without getting drenched. There was no sign of water, so I walked with my daughter toward the center of the room where the hissing was still coming from. Then I

> saw the gas escaping from the hydrogen container used to inflate toy balloons.

> As I started to walk out across the room, I felt a sudden strangeness — was there something wrong with me? Why did I feel no fear when a hundred or so people had run in panic from the room? Still I felt no fear, but I began to reexamine the situation. No, the amount of gas in the one container could not possibly be dangerous in a room so large, with a high ceiling. Furthermore, both doors leading upstairs were wide open, and they were wide doors. There would be plenty of natural air circulation. And yet, there I was with my daughter who simply mirrored my confidence, the only ones left in the basement. Could my reasoning really be right — could everyone else's fear be unjustified? I could find no flaw in my reasoning — but I began to wish that I did feel some fear. Then I felt the responsibility for my daughter. There was no danger — but if anything *did* happen to hurt my daughter, all these other people would be around to say that I brazenly carried her into danger.

> I turned back, walked quickly to the nearest exit, told my daughter to walk to the first landing (half a flight up), and wait right there while I went and found her brother. Then I hurried across the room toward the other exit, feeling immensely relieved. When I was halfway across the room the hissing stopped; and then I saw Santa Claus, who had also not left the room. Suddenly I felt normal again — someone else had seen the situation the same way I had. ... The violence of my sense of relief at this moment has been paralleled by few other experiences in my lifetime. As people began filing back in, I met my son at the door, listened to him assure me spontaneously that he just ran because everyone else did, as we walked back to the other exit, where my daughter waited obediently. (pp. 31–41)

The Game Perspective

The game interpretation of crowd behavior suggests that crowd members think about their actions and consciously try to act in ways that will produce rewards (Berk, 1974). Unlike other theories, which assume that crowds behave irrationally, game theory stresses the importance of rational decisions. People weigh the rewards and costs of various actions and choose the course that is most likely to lead to a desired end. Looting, for example, may yield a reward such as a television set. If few people are looting, the chances of arrest may be fairly great, and a potential looter may choose not to take the risk. If, on the other hand, there are thousands of people looting stores, the chances of arrest are quite low and the person may decide to join in. Milling about before engaging in violent action may be

Myths About Disasters

The term *disaster* is used to refer both to events — earthquakes, floods, tornadoes, explosions — and to the social disruptions caused by these events. They are discussed here because they generally happen in a limited geographical area and involve a group of individuals in close association with one another — a spatially proximate collective.

Most of us have a number of misconceptions about disasters and their aftermath, which are often created and reinforced by the mass media. We have all seen movies of people fleeing in panic from a nuclear holocaust, fires, or flying saucers, for example, but studies indicate that panic flight following a disaster is rare. Even after a catastrophe as terrible as the bombing of Hiroshima, "the rate of extreme nonadaptive behavior . . . is generally very low" (Barton, 1970, p. 146). In the same way, we assume that looters descend on the sites of disasters and steal everything they can lay their hands on from the homes and businesses of the victims. Once again, however, studies show that looting is uncommon following disasters. Victims themselves have been found to believe that looting is a widespread occurrence. The prevalence of this belief is probably due to the publicity given to looting during civil disturbances.

Below are listed some other common myths about disasters:

Martial law must be established following a disaster to control both the victims and the exploiters. In most situations, martial law is neither necessary nor desirable, and it has never been declared in a disaster area in the United States (Quarantelli and Dynes, 1972).

Crime rates rise during a disaster. Crime rates actually drop during disasters. The reduction in arrests, however, may be due more to changes in law enforcement than to lower rates of crime.

When residents are warned of an impending disaster they get out of the disaster area. The evidence suggests that most inhabitants will not leave until forced to do so by the effects of the disaster or by legal authorities.

Disaster victims go into a state of shock and are unable to care for themselves. The few shock reactions that do occur are generally short-lived. The initial search and rescue activity, casualty care, and provision of essential services are usually undertaken by the victims themselves.

The Red Cross, the disaster relief organization, is on the scene immediately, and it is welcomed by the disaster victims. The Red Cross does provide valuable assistance to disaster victims, but many studies indicate that victims express resentment and hostility toward this agency, noting its tendency to overstate its accomplishments, its reliance on outsiders, its imperialistic stance, its failure to convey sympathy, and its insensitivity to local problems.

Most of those who evacuate their homes use shelters established by the authorities. Most people actually find shelter with their friends, relatives, or neighbors, or else they provide for their own lodging.

used as a time for assessing various courses of action and evaluating the strength of support. According to this perspective, violence is not necessarily irrational. It may be the result of a conscious decision that it will be useful in acquiring a desired end: civil rights, jobs, housing, new leaders, or something else. When many people desire the same goal, collective action can increase their chances of achieving it.

Spatially Diffuse Collective Behaviors

Spatially diffuse collectives are those that form among people spread over a wide geographical area. The most common types are known as masses and publics.

Masses and Mass Behavior

A *mass* is a collective of geographically dispersed individuals who react to or focus on some common event. We often hear the term "mass" in speech: mass media, mass communication, mass hysteria. The millions of people who watch the Super Bowl or World Series on television or listen on radio constitute a mass. The thousands of people who rush to their local store to buy an item rumored to be in short supply constitute a mass. Although dispersed over a large geographical area, they are reacting to a common event.

Members of a mass come from all educational and socioeconomic levels. They are anonymous, and they interact little or not at all. A mass has no established rules or rituals, no shared or common ideology, no hierarchy of statuses or roles, and no established leadership (Blumer, 1939).

Fads and *fashions* are specific types of diffuse collective mass behaviors. Generally, they arrive suddenly and disappear quickly, but they may attract great interest from large numbers of people during their tenure. Some examples of fads are flagpole sitting, crowding into telephone booths, hula hoops, dancing the jitterbug, twist or frug, swallowing goldfish, streaking, and more recently, Rubik's cube and Pac-man. Most of these fads were harmless and had no long-range social consequences.

Fashions are similar to fads but tend to be more cyclical. They are generally thought of as influencing styles of dress and behavior, but there are also fashions in music, art, literature, and even sociological theories. To be "in fashion" is to wear the style of hair and the types of clothes that advertisers are pushing and that are currently in vogue. At any given time, hemlines may be long or short, neckties may be wide or narrow, and hair styles may be straight or curly.

Fads and fashions provide many people with a sense of excitement, feelings of belonging, or a source of identification and self-esteem. Fads and fashions, however, are also big business. Packaging pet rocks, opening a disco club, and selling the latest clothes are ways of making money. Although fads and fashions may seem trivial to the average consumer, they can bring large profits to those who take advantage of them.

Mass hysteria and panic are two other types of diffuse collective mass behaviors. *Mass hysteria* is a widespread, highly emotional fear of a potentially threatening situation. It is sometimes accompanied by *panic* when people try to escape from the perceived danger. A recent example of mass hysteria and panic took place at Three Mile Island beginning on Wednesday, March 28, 1979, and continued for several weeks. The incident involved a series of events at the nuclear power plant at Middletown, Pennsylvania. It began when control rods rammed into the core of Unit 2, stopping the fission reaction and immediately dropping the thermal power of the reactor from 2,700 megawatts to 180 megawatts. The fear was that a total meltdown of the unit would cause serious radiation contamination of all people in the area and

Fads and fashions are two forms of mass behavior that people enthusiastically pursue. Fads are usually short-lived variations in behavior or activities whereas fashions, although similar to fads, change less rapidly, are less trivial, and tend to be more cyclical. Fashion may involve the arts and literature, but it most often affects clothing and adornment. Some fads and fashions enjoyed by Americans over the past three decades are: 3-D glasses, worn by moviegoers in the fifties and apparently making a comeback in the eighties; the punk look, a style of dress adopted by fans of "new wave" music; and Rubik's cube, a brain-teasing toy named after its creator, Erno Rubik.

the destruction of all plant life covering a vast land area. When news of the event first broke, commercial telephone lines were jammed with calls to and from people living near the Three Mile Island area. Newspapers around the country carried maps of the area that showed 5-, 10-, and 20-mile concentric circles of danger and reported that evacuation would be the only hope of avoiding contamination. By noon Friday, just two days after the event, the governor of Pennsylvania recommended the immediate evacuation of all pregnant women and preschool children living within 5 miles of the area. By evening that plan was expanded to include everyone within a 20-mile radius. By this time, vast numbers (actual percents and numbers unknown) had already departed, many going to stay with relatives and friends in neighboring states or other areas. To lessen the extent of mass hysteria and panic and convey an impression that all was "safe and under control," President Carter visited the reactor site on Saturday, March 31.

How serious was this event to the residents of the area? *Science News* reported in November of 1979 that according to the President's Commission on the accident at Three Mile Island, there was immediate short-lived mental distress produced among certain groups of the general population living within 20 miles. The results of a representative sample of interviewees showed that a substantial minority, perhaps 10 percent, experienced "severe demoralization" at the time of and in the two or three weeks following the accident.

Publics and Public Opinion

A *public* is another type of spatially diffuse collective. Blumer (1939) defines a public as a group of people who are confronted with an issue, who do not agree on how to address the issue, and who discuss the issue. Publics have no culture and no consciousness of themselves as a group. Voters, consumers, magazine subscribers, and stockholders are separate publics. Although

these people are geographically dispersed, they share a concern about an issue. As they discuss the issue in order to resolve their differences about it, certain attitudes, or *public opinion*, begin to prevail.

Public opinion is defined variously as any opinion held by a substantial number of people or as the dominant opinion in a given population. Public opinion is especially complex in mass cultures where many publics have differing viewpoints. Some publics want their tax money to go to defense, others would prefer to see it spent on social programs. Some publics favor abortion, others oppose it. These conflicts of interest multiply as cultures become more complex, while in simpler cultures most decisions about new issues can be made on the basis of traditional folkways and mores.

The formation of public opinion is influenced by a wide range of factors. Organizations such as the political parties, the National Organization of Women, and the National Rifle Association have a profound effect on public opinion. The mass media are also influential. They do not merely report the news, they can also create it. By choosing to discuss a certain issue, the media focus people's attention on it. If their reporting tends to favor one side of the issue, they may succeed in shifting public opinion in that direction. Opinion is further influenced by a population's cultural values and ethnic and social makeup. Leaders from business, government, or religion also shape public opinion, and it is interesting that elected leaders, who were put in office by the public, often try to use their office to influence those who elected them. Because public opinion is so important in contemporary social life, there is considerable interest in how it is measured.

Knowledge of public opinion is generally obtained through the use of polls, which are a form of survey research (see Chapter 2). A public opinion poll is a sampling of a population representative of a geographical area, a specific public of

Seventy-six Percent in Poll Say War Is Likely in a Few Years

Three of four Americans say it is likely that the United States will become involved in a war in the next few years, according to the latest Associated Press/NBC poll.

Yet 59 percent said they were not worried that President Reagan would get this country involved in a war.

Seventy-six percent said it was either very likely or somewhat likely that the United States would become involved in a war in the next few years, an increase from 68 percent in the September and October polls conducted by the two news organizations and 57 percent in the August poll.

There were 1,602 scientifically selected respondents in the Dec. 14–15 nationwide poll, conducted by telephone.

Respondents split 48 to 44 in saying that Mr. Reagan and his Administration were talking too much about the possibility of using nuclear weapons and 48 to 46 in saying that such talk increased the danger of nuclear war. The remainder said they were not sure.

A slight majority said that the United States should move toward nuclear disarmament but only if the Soviet Union agreed to disarm. Yet only about ⅓ favored a freeze on the production of nuclear weapons in this country.

Respondents split 52 to 38 in favor of reinstatement of the draft for the armed forces, marking a continuing decline in support for the draft. Reinstatement was favored by 59 percent in the July poll and 65 percent in the January poll.

There was no significant change, however, on three other questions: Forty-three percent said Mr. Reagan was doing a good or excellent job in handling foreign affairs; 66 percent said he had set the right tone in his dealings with the Soviet; and 38 percent said the United States and Soviet Union were equal in military strength, while 39 percent said the Soviet Union was stronger, 13 percent said the United States was stronger and 10 percent were not sure.

The results are subject to a margin of error of 3 percentage points either way. Thus, if one could have talked this past week to all Americans with telephones, there is only one chance in 20 that the findings would vary by more than 3 percentage points.

SOURCE: "76% in Poll Say War Is Likely in a Few Years," *The New York Times*, December 22, 1981. 1981 by The New York Times Company. Reprinted by permission.

---

interest to the pollster, or of the society as a whole. The pollster asks the sample population a series of questions about the issue of concern. In most polls, the responses are provided in advance, and the respondents simply state whether they agree or disagree with a statement or answer a yes-no question. These responses are then tabulated and reported to the sponsoring agency.

In recent elections, pollsters have been criticized for announcing results before the voting is completed, but in most cases increasingly refined polling techniques enable pollsters to make very accurate predictions. There are a number of potential problems in taking accurate polls, however. The sample to be polled and the questions to be asked must be carefully selected because answers to ambiguous or loaded questions may not reflect true opinions. Even those who support a woman's right to abortion might find it difficult to answer yes to a question such as "Do you favor the murder of helpless unborn children?" A question phrased in this way will not yield representative responses. Polls may also force people to express opinions on subjects they know nothing about.

"FRANKLY, I DON'T CARE ONE WAY OR THE OTHER ABOUT VOTER APATHY"

Another problem is that they do not attempt to assess a person's reasons for giving a yes or no response.

Those who sponsor polls often use the results to influence public opinion, which may be done through the use of *propaganda,* attempts to manipulate ideas or opinions by presenting limited, selective, or false information. The purpose is to induce the public to accept a particular view. Propagandists rarely present opposing or alternative views, and when they are presented, they are usually distorted. Propaganda tries to influence people by playing on their emotions rather than by discussing the merits of the various positions, but if it diverges too far from known facts or personal beliefs, the public may simply dismiss it as nonsense.

An example of the use of propaganda in the early 1980s was evident in the controversy over requiring the biblical as well as the evolutionary version of creation to be taught in the public schools. Each side issued statements that played on emotions, that diverged from known facts, and that contained limited and selected information. Each side had the goal of inducing people to accept its own point of view. Those who believe in the literal biblical interpretation that God created all matter and energy in six days, probably only a few thousand years ago, are not swayed by those who present fossil evidence of evolution covering a time period of millions of years. And those who believe in the separation of church and state are not swayed by the argument that evolution is as much a religion or religious belief as the creation theory. If propaganda is to be successful, therefore, it must not conflict too strongly with a person's existing values and beliefs.

Another way to manipulate public opinion is through *censorship*, which prohibits the dissemination of some type of information. A community may try to prohibit sex education, X-rated movies, or the sale of pornographic magazines. A car manufacturer may refuse to release information on a potential danger in a car's construction. Government officials may withhold controversial information, as the United States government did when it kept secret the bombing of Cambodia during the Vietnam war. Censorship manipulates public opinion not by presenting distorted or incomplete information, as in propaganda, but by withholding information that might influence public opinion.

Social Movements

Social movements represent a collective effort to bring about social change and establish a new order of social thought and action. They involve more than a single event or community, they begin during periods of unrest and dissatisfaction with some aspect of society, and they are motivated by the hope that the society can be changed. Initially, social movements are poorly organized. They have no identity, and their actions are often spontaneous. As they develop, however, they acquire an established leadership, a body of customs and traditions, divisions of labor, social rules and values, and new ways of thinking. This process of institutionalization leads to the development of formal organizations and, ultimately, new social systems.

In the United States, a number of new movements have developed in the last few decades, including the civil rights movement, the peace movement, the women's liberation movement, the ecology movement, and the gay liberation movement. Each one involves a collective effort to bring about social change and establish a new social order. Although movements may involve crowds, publics, riots, or masses, they differ from these forms of collective behavior in that they devote continuous efforts over a long period to attain a particular goal.

The Development of Social Movements

Social movements develop most frequently in complex, nontotalitarian societies. They evolve from a series of stages that closely parallel those suggested by Smelser as preconditions of the development of any type of collective behavior. Blumer (1939) divided the development of movements into four steps: social unrest, popular excitement, formalization, and institutionalization. These stages are idealized types, of course, because development varies considerably from one movement to another.

The stage of *social unrest* parallels Smelser's stages of conduciveness and structural strain. This stage is characterized by unfocused restlessness and increasing disorder (Turner and Killian, 1972). Often, we are unaware that others share the same feelings and concerns. Rumors abound, and we become increasingly susceptible to the appeals of agitators. These agitators do not advocate any particular ideology or course of action; rather, they make people more aware of their discontentment and raise issues and questions to get them thinking.

Social unrest is followed by the stage of *popular excitement*. During this period, unrest is brought into the open. People with similar concerns begin to establish a rapport with one another and openly express their anger and restlessness. Then the group begins to acquire a collective identity, and more definite ideas emerge about the causes of the group's condition and how the situation can be changed. Leaders help define and justify feelings, identify the opposition, and point out obstacles that must be overcome.

Lech Walesa, leader of the Gdansk Solidarity Union in Poland, speaks to some of his followers prior to his imprisonment. Solidarity came to symbolize the social movement in Poland for self-government, independence, and democracy. The major conflict between the Solidarity movement and the Polish Communist Party centered around questions of economic policy; the Party wanted a centralized, controlled economy, and Solidarity fought for decentralization and a greater voice for the workers themselves.

They also offer a vision of what things could be like after the movement succeeds. In the past, movements like these have fallen to social reformers such as a Martin Luther King, charismatic leaders such as Gandhi, and prophets such as Christ. In other instances, it is a group of individuals that clarifies the issues, provides direction, and stirs up excitement. In these cases, the movement becomes increasingly better organized.

During the third stage, *formalization,* a formal structure is developed, and rules, policies, and tactics are laid out. The movement becomes a disciplined organization capable of securing member commitment to stable goals and strategies. At this stage, movements make concerted efforts to influence centers of power (Turner and Killian, 1972). The stable organization of the movement and the establishment of various programs and committees serve to keep members involved after the initial urgency has died down. The leadership shifts from agitators, reformers, or prophets to statesmen or intellectual leaders and administrators. The statesmen develop the ideology, symbols, and slogans that keep the movement alive. The administrators work on procedures, tactics, and organization. It is at this stage that movements often split into factions or break down completely due to differences of opinion over such questions as how the movement should proceed, how radical its tactics should be, and what type of concessions can be granted.

In the final stage, *institutionalization,* the movement becomes integrated into society. It may have a permanent office and personnel hired to continue its efforts. At this point, it may have accomplished its primary purpose and disappear into the network of institutions that already exists. In other instances, the success of a movement leads to the development of new social movements. Some movements never reach this stage — they are suppressed by formal or informal powers and disappear or go underground. At the institutional stage, unrest, discontent, and popular excitement have largely ceased and are replaced by formal offices, organized groups, and structured activities.

Articles on the origins of the women's liberation movement indicate that this group passed through the four stages typical of movement development. According to Jo Freeman (1973), four factors were essential to the emergence of this movement in the mid-1960s. (1) There was an established network for communication about women's issues. (2) This network could be used to convey the ideas of the new movement. (3) A

series of crises galvanized people using this network into action. (4) Subsequent organizing efforts formed the groups into a movement. These four elements reflect the stages of development we have discussed.

Social unrest, stage one, began during the nineteenth century, when organizations such as the Women's Trade Union League, the Federation of Women's Clubs, and the Women's Suffrage Association worked to obtain equal rights. By the 1960s, most of these organizations were relatively small, but the National Women's Party, started in 1916, and other groups remained dedicated to feminist concerns. These organizations served as a lobbying group for the Equal Rights Amendment and helped bring the unrest into the open (the popular excitement stage). During the 1960s, existing and newly formed groups, composed of women who shared similar perceptions and concerns and faced similar crisis situations, began to organize nationally (the formalization stage). Leadership came, not from an individual, as in some social movements, but from a number of sources, and the National Organization of Women (NOW) and its sister organizations were formed. These national organizations began to make use of the media and legal and political means to express their views and developed formal rules, policies, tactics, and discipline. Like many social movements, NOW split into several factions in the late 1960s. Today, there is evidence of institutionalization, and in many ways the movement has become an integral part of society. There is widespread sensitivity toward sexist language in textbooks and the media. Affirmative action programs encourage the employment of women, and they are moving into roles formerly considered the province of men. This is not to say that the movement has met all its goals. Many would argue that institutionalization will not be achieved until an equal rights amendment is added to the Constitution.

Types of Social Movements

Various authorities have used different schemes for the classification of movements. Turner and Killian (1972) organize them in terms of their orientation. *Value-oriented movements* advocate social changes concerning various groups that result in broader adherence to the central values of the larger society. The civil rights, gay liberation, and women's movements, for example, are efforts to fulfill the American values of equality, freedom, and justice. *Power-oriented movements* aim to achieve power, recognition, or status. The Nazi movement in Germany and the

---

SOCIOLOGISTS AT WORK
Public Opinion Research

A. Emerson Smith is the founder, director of research, and one of the major stockholders of Metromark Market Research Inc. in Columbia, South Carolina. This firm gathers information on public opinions and preferences for companies with products to sell to the public. Smith is also a sociologist.

How did Emerson Smith become a marketing researcher? "I did not make a real decision to go into this area," he says. "It just happened that way." In 1974 Smith was an assistant professor at the University of South Carolina, in Columbia. He and another sociology professor, Frank K. Brown, began talking about possible applications for their extensive background in sociology. They wanted something new. So they started a nonprofit research organization called Sociology Research Associates. "Our goal was to do contract work for local and state government agencies. We rented an office, got a phone, had some letterhead printed up, and made arrangements to share a secretary with an architect we knew. We chose nonprofit status because of our training in sociology. We didn't know of one sociologist who worked *as a sociologist* for a profit-making organization.

"Nearly all the work we did in those days was survey research for state agencies and city governments. In 1977 we did some research for a department store chain as part of a survey for the state of South Carolina. This department store asked us to do some surveys in other cities in the southeast, and suddenly we found ourselves doing marketing research. This prompted us to list ourselves in the Yellow Pages as marketing researchers.

"Before 1978 we were listed under the heading *Public Opinion Analysts.* This was the only heading we could find where sociologists would fit, and we were the first ones to use this heading in South Carolina. But we found that we were not getting any calls based on this listing. When we decided to list ourselves under the heading *Marketing Research and Analysis,* we felt that we were not really trained for marketing research, so we went to the university library and looked at all the marketing research periodicals. We discovered that marketing researchers were using many of the methods of sociology and social psychology. In fact, we saw areas where the methods of sociology could be used but weren't. We found that many people in marketing research had business and marketing backgrounds but little training in research methods or statistics."

In 1979, Smith and his colleagues incorporated their business as Metromark Market Re-

Bolshevik revolution in Russia are extreme examples of this type of movement. *Participant-oriented movements* focus on personal rewards and fulfillment for their participants. Back-to-nature and evangelical movements are of this type.

Actually, there are as many different kinds of movements as there are goals. *Reactionary movements* advocate the restoration of the values and behaviors of previous times. *Conservative movements* attempt to protect the status quo and resist change. *Resistance movements* are aimed at preventing or reversing changes that have already occurred. *Reformist movements* try to modify some aspect of society without destroying or changing

---

search Inc. and dissolved Sociology Research Associates.

Smith's job is to plan, conduct, and analyze surveys for companies that have a problem marketing a product or service or are thinking of marketing a new product. "The bulk of my time," he says, "is spent reviewing data and writing summary reports for clients.

"All of our work involves applications of our training in sociology. The marketing director of a department store chain came to us with this problem: Several other downtown stores in a city in Tennessee had decided to close their doors and move to a proposed mall in a fast-growing residential suburb. What proportion of the department store's customers would transfer their business to the new mall? How many new customers could the store expect to attract if *it* moved to the mall? Many of the downtown store's customers were elderly and poor, and many of the mall's customers would be younger and more affluent. How should the store's current merchandise selection change if it moved to the mall? What changes in advertising and marketing would the store have to make? How far would customers travel to come to the mall store? How much of the family clothing business could a store in the mall have after the first year there?

"First we looked at Census data to see the population changes in this city from 1970 to 1980. This involved application of our training in demography. Then we sent interviewers into the downtown store to ask customers about their shopping habits, and we did telephone interviews of adults within a ten-mile radius of the mall. Here we used our training in survey research. We asked about shopping habits, driving habits, preferences in clothing, and what forms of advertising they paid most attention to in making shopping decisions. We needed to know who made the decision to go to a specific store to shop, so advertising could be directed at these decision-makers. Our background in sociology helped us understand family decision-making."

They also needed to advise their client on possible problems in closing the downtown store. Energy issues and possible downtown revitalization would affect this decision, and their training in urban development and social change found an application here. But perhaps the most important application Smith found for his training as a sociologist, in this and in all his projects, was in the area of statistical techniques. "While I was sitting through six undergraduate and graduate courses in social statistics, I wondered how in the world this was going to be useful to me. Now those statistics courses and textbooks (which I kept) are invaluable."

"We don't try to sell ourselves as sociologists," Smith sums up. "We try to sell the skills we have acquired in our sociological training. Our clients don't care that we have Ph.D. degrees or that we have published in academic journals. Our clients just want to know if we can apply our skills to help them create and sell a product that will make them money."

the entire system. *Revolutionary movements* believe in the overthrow of the existing social order as a means of creating a new one. *Nationalistic movements* hope to instill national pride and a sense of identity with one's country. The goal of *utopian movements* is to create the perfect community. *Religious movements* want to convert or modify the existing belief system in accordance with a religious principle. *Expressive movements* would like to change people's emotional reactions to help them cope with prevailing social conditions. Some movements have several purposes or combine the features of several types of movements. Regardless of the way they are categorized, they all involve collective efforts to initiate (or sometimes resist) a new order of social thought and action.

Summary

Collective behavior is spontaneous, loosely structured, and transitory. Institutionalized behavior, by contrast, is more orderly and has stable goals, expectations, and values. There are two types of collective behavior: spatially proximate, in which people are in face-to-face contact or geographical proximity, and spatially diffuse, in which people are dispersed over a wide geographical area.

Certain conditions increase the likelihood of collective behavior. Smelser described six of them: (1) structural conduciveness, the existence of conditions or situations in which collective behavior is possible; (2) structural strain, some type of frustration, stress, conflict, or dissatisfaction in society; (3) generalized belief, a shared understanding of the reasons for the strain and stress; (4) precipitating factors, events that trigger a collective response; (5) mobilization for action, in which individuals or groups encourage participation in collective behavior; and (6) the initiation of social controls to counter the conditions just listed.

The most common type of spatially proximate collective behavior is the crowd. The characteristics of crowds are anonymity, suggestibility, contagion, and emotional arousability. There are four types of crowds. A casual crowd such as a street gathering has a momentary existence and little unity. The participants are simply drawn to an event by a common interest. A conventional crowd, such as spectators at a baseball game, follows established social norms and rules. An expressive crowd, like a religious revival or festival dance, is distinguished by physical movement as a form of release. Finally, acting crowds such as mobs or rioters are often aggressive and hostile. In acting crowds, the four characteristics of crowd behavior occur in an extreme form.

There are four major theories of acting crowd behavior. The classical theory of Le Bon posited the existence of a collective or group mind that has a regressive influence on behavior, which tends to be irrational, irritable, and impulsive. Blumer's interactionist theory focused on social interactions and a circular reaction process that generates milling, collective excitement, and social contagion. The emergent norm theory of Turner and Killian emphasized how norms influence crowd behavior and how the emergence of new norms causes a divergence of crowd views and behaviors. Berk's game theory stressed the rational decision-making processes involved in crowd behavior and suggested that people consciously weigh the rewards and costs associated with various kinds of collective activity.

In spatially diffuse collectives, people who are widely dispersed focus on a common event. The groups who watch a certain television show or buy a given item are considered masses — although they are geographically separate, they participate in a common behavior. Fads and fashions are mass behaviors that large numbers of people participate in for a brief period. Mass hysteria takes place when a potentially destructive or threatening event causes a widespread, highly emotional fear. Sometimes these fears are accompanied by panic, mass flight, or attempts to escape.

A public is a spatially dispersed group confronted with a common issue but divided about how to address it. As the issue is debated or discussed, a variety of public opinions develop, which vary from one public to another. Opinions are influenced by such factors as dominant cultural values, the mass media, group affiliations, and social backgrounds. They can be measured by a type of survey research known as polling. Propaganda and censorship are two ways of manipulating public opinion.

Social movements, which are collective efforts to bring about social change and establish a new order of social thought and action, consist of elements of both spatially proximate and spatially diffuse behavior. As they develop, they generally go through four distinct stages: social unrest, popular excitement, formalization, and institutionalization. Although all social movements grow through roughly the same process, the goals of different movements can vary considerably. Turner and Killian classify movements in terms of their orientation, while other authorities use different classification schemes.

Key Terms

acting crowd
casual crowd
censorship
collective behavior
collective mind
conventional crowd
crowd
emergent norm perspective
expressive crowd
fads
fashions
game perspective

generalized belief
institutionalized behavior
mass
mass hysteria
mental unity
milling
mobs
panic
participant-oriented movements
power-oriented movements
propaganda
public
public opinion
riots
social contagion
social movements
spatially diffuse collectives
spatially proximate collective
structural conduciveness
structural strain
value-oriented movements

Suggested Readings

Deckard, Barbara Sinclair. **The Women's Movement: Political, Socioeconomic and Psychological Issues, 2nd ed.** *New York: Harper & Row, 1979.* A book about changes in the social, economic, and political status of women during the past and present in their struggle for liberation.

Evans, Robert R. **Readings in Collective Behavior.** *Chicago: Rand McNally, 1975.* A collection of readings covering theories of collective behavior as well as research, studies of disaster, contagion, riots, protest, and fashion.

Le Bon, Gustave. **The Crowd: A Study of the Popular Mind.** *London: Ernest Benn, 1895; Dunwoody, Georgia: Norman S. Berg, 1968.* An early classic on collective behavior.

Perry, Joseph B., Jr. and M. D. Pugh. **Collective Behavior: Response to Social Stress.** *New York: West Publishing, 1978.* An introduction to the field of collective behavior covering theoretical developments and research results.

Piven, Frances Fox and Richard A. Cloward. **Poor People's Movements: Why They Succeed and How They Fail.** *New York: Pantheon Books, 1977.* A book about protest movements among the poor in the United States, including the civil rights and welfare rights movements, industrial workers, and the unemployed.

Pugh, Meredith D. **Collective Behavior: A Sourcebook.** *New York: West Publishing, 1980.* A collection of twenty-four articles on collective behavior covering theory, disaster research, collective violence, and social movements.

Smelser, Neil J. **Theory of Collective Behavior.** *New York: The Free Press, 1962.* An important, systematic theoretical work on collective behavior that attempts to explain the conditions under which it occurs and the forms it takes.

Turner, Ralph and Lewis M. Killian. **Collective Behavior, 2nd ed.** *Englewood Cliffs, N.J.: Prentice-Hall, 1972.* A textbook that covers the nature and emergence of collective behavior and the organization and functioning of crowds, the public, and social movements. It also contains a section of selected readings.

Wright, Sam. **Crowds and Riots: A Study in Social Organization.** *Beverly Hills, Calif.: Sage, 1978.* The results of a three-year study of crowds and riots.

Zald, Mayer M. and John D. McCarthy. **The Dynamics of Social Movements.** *Cambridge, Mass.: Winthrop, 1979.* Papers delivered at a 1977 symposium at Vanderbilt University on tactics, resource mobilization, and the social control of movements.

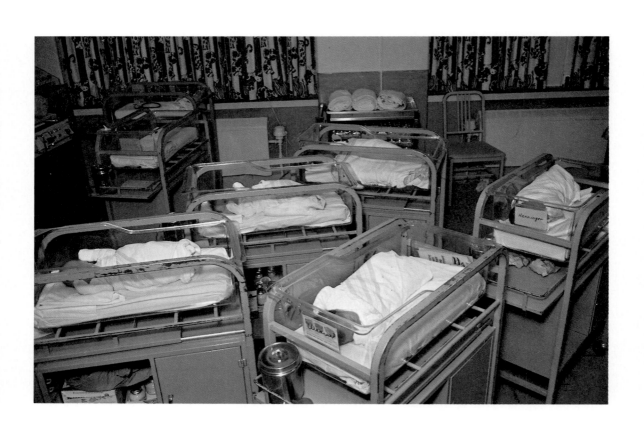

Chapter 18
Population and Health

Population, when unchecked, increases in a geometrical ratio. Subsistence increases only in an arithmetical ratio. A slight acquaintance with numbers will show the immensity of the first power in comparison with the second.

— Thomas Robert Malthus

If you are like most people, you worry about the population a great deal, even though you may not realize it. By *population* we mean the number of people in a society. The population affects your chances of finding a job and a spouse. If you do marry, it is likely to influence the age of your spouse, whether you have children, and if so how many you will have. It may also affect your chances of being promoted, your taxes, the age at which you will retire, and your income after retirement. Sometimes we also worry about population problems in the larger world. Poverty, disease, accident and death rates, world hunger, the problems of crowded cities, vanishing farmlands — all are population problems. Lest this all sound too gloomy, we should point out that some of the most practical things we can do to resolve problems involve studying the population in hopes of influencing it. By understanding the size, age, sex ratios, and movements of the population, we may be able to better understand our own lives and plan sensible social policies to shape the world's future.

Figure 18-1 is a population pyramid, a graph that shows how many males and females from each age category there are in the United States today. Find in the left-hand column the category containing the year you were born, noting that the bars extending to the left and right represent the males and females born in those years. By looking at the bottom of the graph, you can determine the percentage of people of your age and sex in the population. If you were born between 1960 and 1964, the bottom line tells you that more than 4 percent of the population consist of females your age and that about 5 percent are males your age. Notice also how the pyramid bulges out for the years between 1955 and 1964

Figure 18-1
Age-sex population pyramid, United States

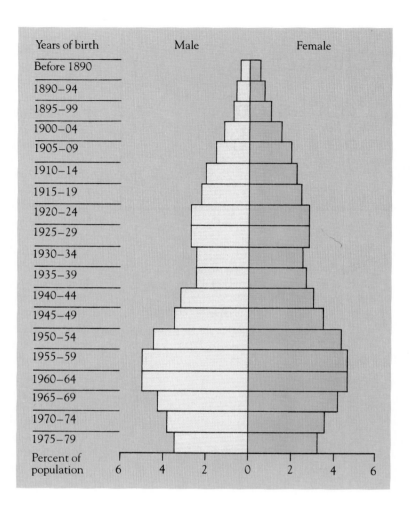

Years of birth	Male	Female
Before 1890		
1890–94		
1895–99		
1900–04		
1905–09		
1910–14		
1915–19		
1920–24		
1925–29		
1930–34		
1935–39		
1940–44		
1945–49		
1950–54		
1955–59		
1960–64		
1965–69		
1970–74		
1975–79		

Percent of population   6   4   2   0   2   4   6

and how it becomes smaller again in later years. The bulge represents the people born during the baby boom.

Why were so many people born in the middle of this century? During the depression of the 1930s and World War II in the 1940s, many people postponed having children. After the war, the country was both peaceful and affluent. Those who had postponed having children began families, and those who were just entering their twen-

ties began having children too. Because the times were so affluent, some people decided to have three or four children instead of just two.

How has the baby boom affected your life? If you were born when it began, you may not have gone to nursery school because they were full. Schools were crowded, and you may have gone to elementary school in a temporary classroom building. If you went to school at the end of the baby boom, your school may have closed shortly after you left it. Some students, especially those in suburban areas, watched their elementary schools close, went to a junior high school that was closed while they were there, moved to a second junior high, and saw that one close before they had finished senior high school.

Baby boom children have had to compete for space in college and then compete for jobs when they completed their education. The scarcity of jobs has been increased by the fact that only a small percentage of the population is of retirement age. By looking at the top of the pyramid, you will see that people born before 1920, who will have retired before 1985, comprise only a small part of the work force and thus their retirement will not create a large number of openings. Jobs may be more plentiful when individuals born between 1920 and 1930 begin to retire in 1985. They will leave vacancies that may be filled by those born during the baby boom, but they are more likely to be filled by people born after the baby boom because industry prefers to hire younger workers at lower wages.

The baby boom generation caused great changes in fashion. Miniskirts became the vogue because manufacturers began to design clothes for this age group when they were very young, and only the very young look good in miniskirts. Youngsters born during the baby boom represented a big market, and manufacturers catered to them. It became stylish to be thin because adolescents tend to be thin during their period of rapid growth, and a whole nation dieted to look like adolescents, whereas previously the mark of beauty was to have a more well-developed figure like Marilyn Monroe or Betty Grable. As the baby boom generation grows older, clothing manufacturers are changing styles to meet the market for clothes for more mature figures, and the miniskirt has been replaced by stretch blue jeans with a fuller-cut thigh and an elastic waist. The fuller figure may soon be back in style if it isn't already by the time this book is published.

Women born during the baby boom are more likely to marry at an older age or to stay single than was true in earlier generations. Why? Because women traditionally marry older men, and a look at the population pyramid shows that there is a shortage of older men for these women. Women born late in the baby boom or after it have many older men to marry, so they may marry at a younger age.

Men born late in the baby boom who want to follow the normative practice of marrying younger women face a shortage. They may set a new trend by marrying slightly older women.

Imagine that bulge in the population pyramid when the baby boom reaches age sixty-five or seventy. Think of how many people will be on Social Security! By the time they reach that age, they will have held and may still hold powerful positions in business and government. Moreover, because they will be a large voting bloc, they may be able to control votes about continuing the support of Social Security benefits. Since the smaller population just younger than the baby boom may have a large tax burden to help support all the people in retirement, it is to be hoped that the younger population will be fully employed. By studying population and predicting how it will affect our lives, we are at least able to plan for these shifts in population trends, which is essential to the planning of public policies.

Demography and the Study of Population

Demography is the study of the size and makeup of the human population and how it changes. Demographers want to know how many babies are being born, what diseases there are in the population, how long people live, whether they stay in the same place or move about, and whether they live in remote regions or crowded urban areas. This information makes it possible to recognize changing trends in the population and help plan social policies. Where will new houses and jobs be needed? What diseases should be cared for most? How many elderly will require care in 1995? It is questions such as these that are addressed by demographers.

Collecting the Data

Demographers use many statistics in their work. After all, their main concern is counting people. In fact, the word "demography" is often used to refer to the study of population statistics. The statistics demographers use are fortunately rather straightforward and easy to understand, and they are also readily available.

Societies have always realized how important it is to know about their members. Records of births and deaths have been kept since ancient times, and from such records estimates of early populations can be made and studied. Since the time of Abraham, family lineages have been recorded and passed on orally so as to keep track of who was born to whom. Records of deaths can be found in early Greek and Egyptian accounts. The Bible says that Mary and Joseph were on their way to be counted in a Roman census when Jesus was born. A *census* is a count of the population in which people's sex and age are recorded.

Modern nations keep much more reliable records of their populations. The first census in the United States was carried out in 1790, and censuses are still carried out once every ten years with questionnaires mailed to all known households. In addition, interviewers search door to door for those who are not contacted or do not respond by mail. A smaller census is made every year, which may be more accurate than the ten-year census because it is based on a carefully chosen random sample of the population and it is done by expert interviewers who use every available method to ensure its accuracy.

In addition to population counts, *vital statis-* tics — records of all births, deaths and their causes, marriages, divorces, certain diseases, etc. — are recorded in each state and reported to the National Center for Health Statistics. Most modern nations keep records as accurate as those of the United States. Underdeveloped nations also attempt to record their populations, and although data from these countries may be relatively inaccurate, they provide enough information to study world population trends.

Three variables can cause the size of the population in a given region to change: (1) births, (2) deaths, and (3) migrations. Demographers measure these factors in terms of their rates. *Fertility* is a measure of the rate at which people are born. *Mortality* is a measure of the rate at which people die. To measure *migration*, the people moving into or out of a geographical area are counted. In order to understand how populations change, it is necessary to understand how demographers measure these factors.

Fertility

Fertility data indicate the rate at which babies are born. The crude birth rate is simply the number of births per 1,000 population, but if we want to predict how many babies will actually be born, more information is needed. We must know the *age-sex composition* of the society, which involves determining how many women are in the population — a population with few women will have few children. We must also know how old the women are, because young girls and older women do not have babies.

In most societies, the number of men and women is about equal. More men are born than women, about 105 males for each 100 women, but women live longer than men. Thus there may be more men at younger ages, but there are more women in older groups. During the childbearing years, the number of men and women is usually about equal except in societies suffering from wars

Francis W. Edmunds' painting The Census Taker *(1854) depicts such a person as he visits a home to record the names and ages of everyone in the family. Often family members could not read, write, or accurately spell their names; sometimes they were not sure how old they were. Even though these older records are not entirely accurate, they have been used by many American families to trace their family history.*

in which large numbers of men are killed or in societies experiencing a great deal of migration. Areas that men move out of have a surplus of women, whereas the areas they move into have a surplus of men, and a society with unequal numbers of men and women will have a low birth rate. There was an imbalance of this sort in the Soviet Union because so many men were killed during World War I, the Civil War of 1917–

1921, World War II, and the repressive era following World War II. As a result, many women were left without husbands and did not have children, and the birth rate dropped dramatically. For years the Soviets kept secret their great loss of manpower and low birth rates, but the latest available information indicates that they are now comparable to the United States in birth rates and population size.

Demographers generally assume that women are fertile from age fifteen to age forty-nine. They also know that more children are born to women in the middle of their childbearing years, but some women in their childbearing years choose not to have children, and few have as many as they potentially could. A woman's potential for bearing children is called her *fecundity*. Although women can potentially have twenty to twenty-five children, very few have this many.

Fertility varies greatly among societies and among subcultures within societies. The Hutterites, a religious group in the northwestern United States, apparently have the most children of any American subculture. The mean number of children reported by women between forty-five and fifty-four years old was 10.6 (Eaton and Mayer, 1953). Swedish women have the fewest children, fewer even than women in the United States, who have one of the lowest birth rates in the world (Heer, 1975).

The number of children born in a society is affected by three major factors: wealth, environment, and societal norms about marriage and children. Generally, richer nations have lower birth rates and poorer nations have higher birth rates. The same relationship between wealth and birth rates holds within nations. The upper classes usually have lower birth rates than the poor classes.

Fertility rates are also different in rural and urban areas. Women in rural areas usually have more children than those in cities. In rural areas, children are needed to help with farm labor, but in modern urban areas, children are not productive. Rather, they are an expense to house, feed, clothe, and educate. They may also decrease a family's income because a parent may have to stay home to care for them. Many demographers believe that the birth rate of the world will decline and maybe drop sharply as underdeveloped nations become more industrialized and urban.

The birth rate is higher in rural areas and in poorer classes. This large North Carolina family is both rural and poor. A large number of children is often considered an asset, as they can help a great deal with family chores and, as they grow older, provide security to their parents.

A society's norms regarding the value of children and the age at which marriage is considered acceptable have a strong effect on fertility rates. In countries where women marry young the birth rates are higher than those where they marry when they are older, because of differences in the number of childbearing years. Norms about the number of children a family should have and about the acceptability of birth control and abortion also affect the birth rate. Separation by war, working away from home, and conflicts between spouses reduce the birth rate, whereas abstaining from intercourse during the menstrual cycle may make intercourse more likely during fertile periods and result in an increased birth rate.

A low or high fertility rate will of course affect the number of people born into the population, but this is only one of several factors that influence population size. Mortality and migration rates are also influential.

Mortality

Mortality, the rate of death in a population, can be measured very simply. The *crude death rate* is the number of deaths in a given year per 1,000 population. Like the crude birth rate, however, the crude death rate does not provide enough information to predict how many people will die or to compare death rates among populations. For a more accurate estimate of the death rate, demographers consider age and sex. A population with many old people will have a higher death rate than a comparatively young population, and because women live longer than men, a population with many women will have a lower death rate. Thus demographers often use an *age-adjusted death rate*, which calculates the number of deaths at each age for each sex, usually per hundred thousand living at that age. Demographers can also compute *life expectancy* by predicting how many of each *cohort*, or age group, will die at each age.

Mortality, like fertility, varies with wealth. When people have adequate food, housing, and medical care, they are less likely to die of disease, especially infants. The rate of infant mortality, death in the first year of life, was very high in the Middle Ages, but now it is such that the average life expectancy has been greatly increased. Infant mortality is low and life expectancy high in more developed nations like the United States, Canada, and European countries. People in Norway, Sweden, and the Netherlands have the longest life expectancy. An infant boy in these countries can expect to live seventy-two years, an infant girl seventy-eight years. The death rate is higher and the life expectancy shorter in India, Africa, South America, and Southeast Asia, where poverty is widespread. Death rates also vary by class within nations. In the United States, poor people have a higher rate of infant mortality and a shorter life expectancy than the rich, and blacks, a larger proportion of whom are poor, have more infant mortality and a shorter life expectancy than whites, as shown in Figure 18-2.

Migration

Migration includes both *immigration,* movement into an area, and *emigration,* movement out of an area. Migration is harder to define and measure than either births or deaths. How far must one move to be considered a migrant, and how long should one remain in a place to be considered a migrant? In the United States, moving within a county is not considered migration, but moving from one county to another is. *Migrant workers* who travel about the country doing farm labor are not technically considered migrants because rather than remaining in a new location after the work season is over, they return to their original starting point and take up jobs in that area.

Why do people move? Demographers speak in terms of *push factors* and *pull factors.* Push factors are those that push people away from their homes: famines, wars, political oppression, loss of jobs, or bad climate. Austria, for example, reported that the number of emigrants from Poland increased dramatically during the recent labor and

Figure 18-2

Life expectancy at birth, by sex and race, 1900–1978

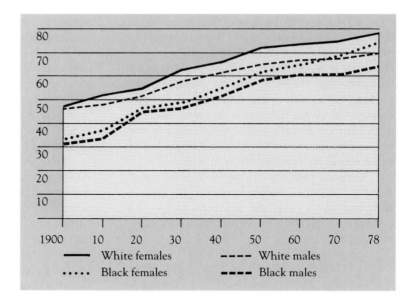

economic troubles. Pull factors are those that make a new place seem more inviting: the chance to acquire land or jobs, the discovery of riches such as gold or oil, or the chance to live in a more desirable climate. Discoveries of gold in California, for example, drew fortune seekers from all over the world.

There have been migrations since early in history when waves of migrants moved out of Asia into the Middle East and eastern Europe. Later, tribes moved further into Europe, spreading their culture as they moved. It is assumed that these waves of migration were caused by push factors such as changes in climate, changes in food supply, or pressure from increasing populations in Asia, and pull factors such as Europe's warmer climate.

The population of Europe increased slowly throughout the Middle Ages. When Columbus discovered America, a new wave of migration began. It started slowly, but it is estimated that over 60 million Europeans eventually left Europe.

Many later returned, so the net migration, the actual population change, was much lower (Heer, 1975).

Between 1820 and 1970, 46 million migrants entered the United States (Thomlinson, 1976). In a single peak year, 1854, a total of 428,000 immigrants came to this country. This group consisted mainly of Irish leaving their country because of the potato famine and Germans leaving as political refugees. A second peak was reached around the turn of the century, when immigrants averaged a million a year. Most of the Europeans who entered the United States at that time were from Italy or other southern and eastern European countries.

Another great migration was of a different sort. Between 1619 and 1808 400,000 Africans were forced to migrate to the United States. Between 10 and 20 million Africans were brought to the entire Western Hemisphere (Thomlinson, 1976).

Immigration restrictions were first imposed in

the United States in 1921 and again in 1924 to slow the rate of immigration. During this period, most immigrants were from Canada, Mexico, Germany, the United Kingdom, or Italy. After 1965, immigration quotas were relaxed and a new wave of immigrants, many from Southeast Asia, entered the country.

Migration within the United States has also been extensive. Throughout this country's history, people have moved from the East to the West and from rural to urban areas. After World War I, for example, when immigration was restricted and the supply of laborers entering the country was limited, northern cities recruited southern blacks to fill labor jobs, but many more blacks moved to northern cities than there were available jobs. Most recently, people have been migrating from northern to southern (or Sunbelt) cities such as Houston, Phoenix, and Charlotte, North Carolina.

Rate of Population Change

The rate of population change is determined by all the factors discussed above. If the birth rate is high and the mortality rate is low, the popula-

The recent wave of immigrants to the United States led to this mass naturalization ceremony, when 9,700 immigrants were sworn in as citizens at the Los Angeles Coliseum. U.S. Immigration and Naturalization officials processed the documents of each new citizen as they all waited their turn in the hot sun.

tion increases. If the mortality rate is high compared with the birth rate, the population will decline. As shown in Figure 18-3, countries in which the population is very young, such as Mexico, can be expected to grow rapidly as children mature and have children of their own, and the ratio of adults to children in such countries is quite small. In Sweden, where there are more older people, the population will grow slowly, but the large number of elderly who need to be cared for may be a cause for concern. The overall population of the world is expected to grow rapidly because of overall high birth rates and low death rates.

Figure 18-3

Population pyramids of a young population (Mexico) and an older population (Sweden)

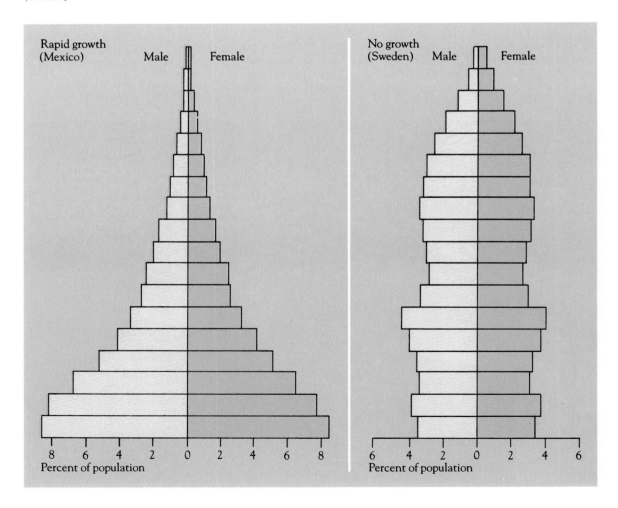

Health and the World Population Explosion

Until about 200 years ago, both birth rates and death rates were very high. As a result, the size of the world population remained stable (see Figure 18-4) For every person who was born, someone died. In most parts of the world today, the birth rate has not declined dramatically, but the death rate has dropped sharply. This is what created today's population explosion, depicted in the graph in Figure 18-5. People who are born now live longer and add to the numbers in the population.

Figure 18-4
World birth and death rates (estimated)

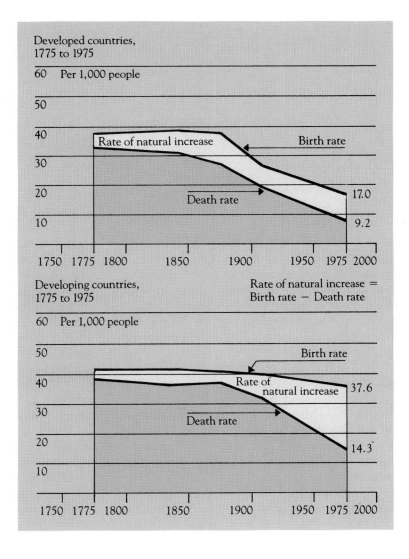

Developed countries, 1775 to 1975

60   Per 1,000 people

50

40   Rate of natural increase   Birth rate

30

20   Death rate   17.0

10   9.2

1750 1775 1800   1850   1900   1950 1975 2000

Developing countries, 1775 to 1975

Rate of natural increase = Birth rate − Death rate

60   Per 1,000 people

50   Birth rate

40   Rate of natural increase   37.6

30   Death rate

20   14.3

10

1750 1775 1800   1850   1900   1950 1975 2000

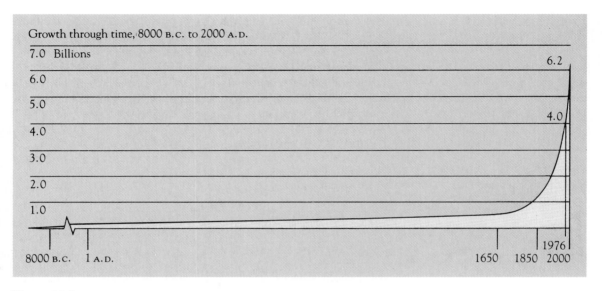

Growth through time, 8000 B.C. to 2000 A.D.

Figure 18-5
World population growth

Why Has the Death Rate Dropped?

Death rates were high throughout most of human history because of poor nutrition and the prevalence of infectious diseases. Whenever crops failed, there would be a food shortage. Transportation was not good enough to bring in large supplies of food, so the population would become undernourished, weak, and increasingly susceptible to infection, and when infection strikes a person weak from malnourishment, it can often be fatal. It is believed that nutrition improved in Europe when the potato came into widespread use in about the middle of the eighteenth century. Until then, infections had been rampant, and the average life expectancy was probably less than forty years.

Devastating plagues swept Europe from 1370 on. In some areas, one-third to one-half the population died. Often, when the plague hit a city, people fled to the countryside, dying on the way or carrying the plague deep into rural areas.

In the Middle Ages, the causes of the plague and other diseases were not understood. In the cities, human waste was thrown into the streets. People did not concern themselves with cleanliness and did not use soap and water. It was considered immoral to concern oneself with the flesh and immodest to wash below the waist (Thomlinson, 1976).

When it came to be understood that rats carry the plague and that germs cause infections, urban sanitation systems were developed. Supplies of water were brought to cities and sewage systems were built. The improvement of sanitation may have added more to the average life expectancy than all the medical advances.

Modern medicine may have helped reduce the death rate from infectious disease in two important ways. Penicillin and other drugs were developed to cure infections, and vaccines were

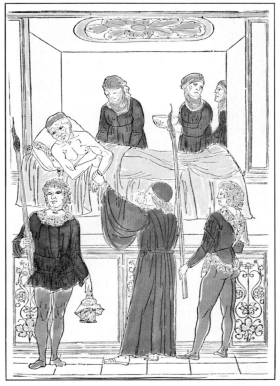

A physician attends a patient suffering from the plague while servants burn perfume. The plague and other infectious diseases killed so many people that the size of the population decreased markedly. When cities developed better sanitation and a better food supply, the number of deaths from infectious diseases went down and the size of the population began to increase rapidly.

developed to prevent disease. Researchers McKinlay and McKinlay (1981) argue, however, that these measures actually affected the death rate only slightly, reducing it by 3.5 percent at most. The infectious diseases that were the major causes of death in 1900 — influenza, pneumonia, tuberculosis, diphtheria, typhoid, scarlet fever, measles, whooping cough, and poliomyelitis — were declining steadily as causes of death long before penicillin and other modern drugs were discovered. They continued to decline after the drugs were introduced, but the drugs did not appreciably increase the rate of decline. Vaccines apparently did not reduce death rates either, except for poliomyelitis, which showed a very noticeable decline soon after the vaccine came into widespread use. Thus, although medicines and vaccines may improve our health and comfort, they do not appear to have contributed greatly to our greater life expectancy. As far as we know, the reduction in infectious disease was a result of better nutrition, better sanitation, and better housing.

A child is vaccinated against an infectious disease while her mother obviously prefers not to watch. Better nutrition, better sanitation, and modern vaccines and medications all contribute to the reduction of death from infectious diseases.

Current Causes of Death

Poor nutrition is still a widespread problem for the poor of most nations, but with improved transportation, food can be delivered to populations threatened with starvation.

Since 1950, the major causes of mortality in the United States and most other industrial nations have been heart disease, cancer, stroke, and accidents (see Table 18-1). Heart disease and strokes have been declining, especially in younger people and women. Cancer, the second leading cause of death, is increasing. Cancer caused 129 deaths per 100,000 population in 1968 and 133 deaths per 100,000 in 1978 (U.S. Dept. of Health and Human Services, 1980). Accidents, the fourth most common cause of death, are the leading cause of death for persons under age thirty-five. Motor vehicle accidents, which account for half of these deaths, have increased steadily since 1976, at which time it declined briefly when speed limits were reduced to 55 mph. White males between the ages of fifteen and twenty-five have the highest death rate from automobile accidents. Among black males in this age category, the leading cause of death is homicide.

The death rate in the United States has not changed significantly since 1950 because the leading causes of death have not been reduced significantly. It has remained at about 9.4 per 1,000 population, but it could increase as the cancer rate increases, and although it is now slightly higher than in many European nations, it is much lower than in previous centuries.

Health Care and the Death Rate

The United States has higher death and infant mortality rates than many western European countries, most notably the democratic socialist states. Infant mortality is low in these countries in part because they have social programs to ensure that even the poorest mothers get good nutrition. The countries with the lowest infant mortality rates, such as Sweden, Switzerland, and the Netherlands, have very little poverty. In the United

Table 18-1
Major causes of death in the United States

1900	1975
Infancy diseases 3.6%	Influenza and pneumonia 3.0%
Cancer 3.7%	Accidents 5.3%
Accidents 4.2%	Stroke 10.2%
Kidney disease 4.7%	Cancer 19.5%
Stroke 6.2%	Heart disease 37.8%
Heart disease 8.0%	All other[a] 24.2%
Gastroenteritis 8.3%	
Tuberculosis 11.3%	
Influenza and pneumonia 11.8%	
All other[a] 38.2%	

[a] No disease in this category represents more than 3 percent of all deaths.
SOURCE: Adapted from Population Reference Bureau, Washington, D.C., no date.

States, blacks suffer disproportionately from poverty and have a relatively high rate of infant mortality.

Cuba is an outstanding example of a country that reduced its infant mortality and increased life expectancy by instituting social programs. Before its revolution, Cuba had a very poor population, and infectious diseases were a major cause of death. After the revolution, Castro began social programs to provide housing, adequate nutrition, and medical care for the entire population. The Cuban people are still relatively poor by United States standards, but through these programs the life expectancy of Cubans has risen as high as that of Americans, and infectious diseases are no longer the major cause of death.

Modern medicine emphasizes the *medical model of illness,* in which sickness is viewed as an individual problem requiring individual treatment. Through the use of modern drugs many infectious diseases can be prevented or cured. Today, medical researchers are looking for cures for heart disease and cancer. Some observers, however, believe that heart disease and cancer could be conquered sooner by using a *social model of illness,* in which the disease is considered in a social rather than an individual context. Perhaps the United States could eliminate these diseases by doing more research on their social causes, just as Cuba and other countries have solved certain medical problems through social programs.

Heart disease, for example, is related to stress. Many things could be done to reduce the stresses of modern life — getting good grades, getting to work, competing for promotions, and so on. Cancer is sometimes related to pollution — from cigarette smoke, industry, and internal combustion engines. We may find that we can reduce cancer deaths better by preventing the disease through social programs than by treating people after they have contracted it. In the future, medical research and health care may be very different from what they are today.

Population Density

The *population explosion* has dramatically increased the number of people in the world, but migrations have not distributed people evenly over the face of the earth. While the population is sparse in many areas of the world, in some regions it is extremely dense and the region cannot provide the natural resources needed to maintain itself.

The United States, although it has absorbed millions of immigrants, has a relatively low population density. In some remote areas, the density is only five people per square mile. In major cities during the business day, on the other hand, the population density is as high as 100,000 people per square mile. For the whole country, the density is sixty people per square mile, which is very low compared with Bangladesh, where there are approximately 1,500 people per square mile.

Land farmed very intensively to provide food for a large population is sometimes ruined. Even the United States with its comparatively low population density has lost 10 to 15 percent of its farmland through soil erosion since the time of the European settlement (Humphrey and Buttel, 1982). In parts of Asia, Latin America, and Africa, the problem is much worse. In these areas, overuse of the land is causing it to deteriorate very rapidly. In Africa, the size of the Sahara desert is increasing by thirty miles a year because the land cannot sustain the population using it.

Population, Politics, and the Economy

How large a population can survive on earth? Theories about population were initially developed during a period when it was feared that there were too few people to produce what society needed. Between 1450 and 1750, European traders were exporting Europe's products in exchange for gold and silver. In some areas, however, one-third to one-half of the population had been killed by the plague. Many writers argued that if the population were larger, more products could be produced and exported, which would bring more gold and silver to the merchants. It was reasoned that this would be profitable if imports for the larger population could be limited. If the population were large enough, labor would be cheap, wages could be kept low, the people would have little to spend, and increases in imports would not be needed. Thus all increased production could be traded for gold, silver, or merchandise valuable to the traders, rather than basic supplies needed by the population as a whole.

The political activity of this period was designed to encourage a high birth rate. The birth rate did increase, and by 1750, writers had begun to worry about overpopulation. The most famous of these writers was Thomas Malthus.

Malthus's Theory of Population

Thomas Robert Malthus (1766–1834) argued in his *Essay on the Principle of Population* that because of the strong attraction of the two sexes, the population could increase by multiples, doubling every twenty-five years. According to *Malthusian theory*, if two parents had four children, who then had four children each, the size of the population would increase much more rapidly than the food supply. Furthermore, Malthus believed that the more intensively land was farmed, the less the land would produce and that even by expanding farmlands, food production would not keep up with population growth. Malthus contended that the population would eventually grow so large that food production would be insufficient, and famine and crowding would cause widespread suffering and increase the death rate, which is nature's check on overpopulation. Malthus suggested as an alternative that the birth rate be decreased, especially through postponing marriage until a later age.

The debate about Malthusian theory has continued down to the present. Writers such as John Stuart Mill and the economist John Maynard Keynes supported his theory. Others have argued against it. Karl Marx, for example, contended that starvation was caused by the unequal distribution of the wealth and its accumulation by capitalists.

Malthus's contention that food production could not increase rapidly was debated when new technology began to give farmers much greater yields. In fact, the French sociologist Dupreel (1977) argued that an increasing population would spur rapid innovation and development to solve problems, whereas a stable population would be complacent and less likely to progress.

During the depression of the 1930s, the debate changed somewhat because the birth rate fell sharply in industrial nations. Some predicted that the human species would die out, first the Caucasians, then other races. Schemes were proposed to encourage families to have more children by giving them allowances for each child born. Many economists, however, believed that even in societies with smaller populations, people could prosper and industry could grow if the wealth were redistributed to increase consumption by poor families. Government spending on programs for the poor and unemployed could be increased, and low interest rates could be used to encourage spending on houses, cars, and other consumer goods. These demand-side economic programs were widely adopted during the depression years.

The birth rate rose sharply after World War II, especially in the underdeveloped nations; people starved in Bangladesh, Africa, and India. Birth control programs were instituted, and it was argued that the only way to eliminate starvation was to reduce the birth rate.

World Food Distribution Today

Before World War II, Africa, India, and Asia exported grain to other nations, primarily to the industrial nations of Europe (George, 1977). Why,

The distribution of food in the world is an enormous problem. As sharecroppers are removed from the land to make room for modern agriculture and local fishermen are replaced by modern fisheries, more and more of the rural poor are left without a source of food. These people await food distribution at Sagar Island, India.

then, are people in these underdeveloped nations starving today?

Observers of the world food situation have criticized American corporations for creating the world food shortage. They contend that because we had a surplus of grain, we encouraged underdeveloped nations to grow nonfood *cash crops* such as cotton and rubber or nonnutritious foods such as coffee, tea, and sugar. The United States would lend money and supply fertilizer and farm equipment only to nations who agreed to grow products it needed. In Brazil, for example, the United States encouraged soybean production, but American corporations own all the soybean processing plants and receive most of the profit from soybean production.

In the last few decades, many underdeveloped nations have become increasingly dependent on American grain imports because they use their land for nonfood products. In the 1970s, the price of grains rose dramatically, and critics argue that

the United States, having acquired a monopoly of the food supply, increased prices to make enormous profits. Today, the cash crops grown by other nations cannot be sold at prices high enough to buy all the grain needed from the United States. Thus poor people everywhere starve because they do not have land on which to grow food, even though enough food is produced in the world to feed all its people.

Political Policies on Population

Regardless of whether starvation could be prevented with better food distribution, current government policies encourage reducing the birth rate to improve the standard of living. After World War II, Japan initiated a program legalizing abortion and encouraging contraception. Soon afterward, India and most other Asian nations began such programs. In the 1960s, the United States began to offer millions of dollars' worth of contraceptive aids, especially intrauterine devices

SOCIOLOGISTS AT WORK
Helping Disabled Drug Addicts

Alexander Boros is the director of Addiction Intervention with the Disabled (AID) in Cleveland, Ohio. He started that program in 1974 when a group of deaf people in Cleveland asked him to do something about the lack of alcohol- and drug-abuse programs for the deaf community. Boros was the right person for the job: In more than twenty years as an applied sociologist at Kent State University, he has been involved in numerous applied projects in the area of rehabilitation of the physically disabled. And in 1969 he organized the first graduate program in applied sociology.

How does Alex Boros use his sociological perspective in his work at AID? "Human services people tend to have a very individualistic orientation," he says. "Whether they're doctors or therapists or counselors, they deal with the problem as an individual's problem. Sociologists try to understand the social and cultural conditions in which the problem arises. Most deaf people, for example, live out their lives as members of a closed community. They have their own language and their own culture. They read at, on the average, a third-grade level. The rate of intermarriage within the group is about 90 percent. Deaf people represent a different community with different needs. As a sociologist, I am able to see the social context in which members of this group act out their problems through alcohol and drug abuse."

The deaf leaders who approached Boros had one immediate short-term goal: They wanted sign-language interpreters at local meetings of Alcoholics Anonymous. AID organized a national conference on treating deaf alcoholics. It also

and birth control pills, to underdeveloped countries requesting help in controlling their populations. The federal government also provided funds to states to open family planning clinics and disseminate information about contraceptives in this country. These programs have succeeded in reducing birth rates in many nations, but they have also been severely criticized, for several reasons.

First, some of the contraceptive methods used in underdeveloped nations are those considered unsafe and banned in the United States. Users in other countries, not warned of the dangers, unknowingly risk infection, heart attacks, stroke, and death when they use these contraceptives. Second, lowering the birth rate in underdeveloped nations deprives parents of children, who are an asset in rural areas. They can help carry water and grow food on family plots and care for their parents in illness and old age. Thus we see that policies used to reduce poverty in Japan could well increase poverty in underdeveloped countries. When planning policy, it is crucially important to consider all the factors at work in the countries that will be affected by the policy.

Zero Population Growth

The goal of current world population policy is *zero population growth,* which is achieved when parents have only two children, just enough to replace themselves. If this practice were followed, the population would remain the same generation after generation. In reality, of course, some people do not have children and some children die be-

conducted workshops for people already involved in the treatment of alcohol and drug addiction on the unique needs of the deaf. But Boros began to perceive a larger need. "About 16 percent of the population is disabled — deaf, blind, retarded, spinal cord–injured, and so on. We have been able to determine that the rate of alcohol and drug addiction among the deaf is about the same as among the general population. But the other disabled lack the kind of cohesive community the deaf have developed. They probably experience a much higher rate — some of us estimate twice as high. But in the standard treatment programs, the rate of participation by the disabled is about 1 percent. So it's not just that the need was being met badly. It wasn't being met at all."

The solution: Set up special services for the deaf and multidisabled, find the alcohol and drug abusers in that population, and refer them to those services. "The rehabilitation agencies for the disabled tend not to understand alcohol and drug addiction. They see it as a self-inflicted problem. They prefer to work with what they call the 'true disabled.' The people who work in alcohol addiction treatment, on the other hand, are people whose expertise is life experience: They tend to be recovering alcoholics themselves. Many do not have the time or the desire to learn about the special needs of the deaf or the disabled. So we needed something new."

Something new is what they got. Boros, his staff of three, and their volunteer assistants train alcohol- and drug-abuse counselors to work with the deaf and the disabled. They use publicity to create an awareness of their activities among the disabled, and they conduct educational programs. They get referrals from individuals and from rehabilitation agencies. Once they have located a disabled person with a problem, they help him or her obtain the necessary services. "We started out in Cleveland, and we are still based in Cleveland," Alex Boros says. "But we soon started getting referrals from other communities. By now we are getting referrals from six or seven states. Once the word got out, we started hearing from people all over."

fore reaching adulthood, so zero population growth could be attained if couples averaged slightly more than two children each. Given current rates of infant mortality and the number of women who actually have children, the population would remain stable if couples averaged 2.1 children.

The 2.1 zero growth rate is maintained in Japan and many European countries. In the United States the rate has been dropping; in 1980, it was 2.2, just a bit above the zero growth rate. Many underdeveloped nations have much higher birth rates, however, so the world population explosion is continuing.

The size of the world population and the associated problem of world hunger will surely continue to be crucial issues in the years to come. A more equal distribution of resources is essential to prevent starvation, and if hunger is caused by the practices of capitalists, reducing the population will not prevent the world's poor from starving. This relationship between population and the economy illustrates the need for a sociological understanding of the interrelationships between population size and social institutions.

Summary

The size of the population affects each of us quite personally. Whether we are born into a growing or a shrinking population has a bearing on our education, the age at which we marry, our ability to get a job, the taxes we pay, and many other factors.

Demography is the study of population statistics. Demographers study census data on the number of people in the population and records of births and deaths to compute the birth and death rates. Their goal is to understand how the population is changing.

The crude birth and death rates are computed by determining the number of births and deaths per 1,000 people. Neither of these measures takes age or sex into account, but these factors also influence numbers of births and deaths.

Populations remain stable when people are born at the same rate that they die. They increase when the birth rate exceeds the death rate and decrease when the death rate exceeds the birth rate. They may also change through migration. Push factors are conditions that encourage people to move out of an area, while pull factors encourage people to move into an area.

The population explosion of the last two hundred years occurred because the death rate dropped. People today live longer now that malnutrition has been reduced, especially in industrial nations, which in turn has decreased the frequency and severity of infectious diseases. The average life expectancy in industrial countries has increased from forty to over seventy years. Currently, the major causes of death in industrial nations are heart disease, cancer, stroke, and accidents. Heart disease and cancer might be conquered more rapidly if we adopted a social model of illness in addition to our current medical model.

Malnutrition and starvation are still common among the world's poor. Malthus argued that because the population grows faster than the food supply, starvation is inevitable if population growth is not controlled. His arguments have received much support through the years, although critics contend that the world produces enough food to feed everyone but that food is distributed unequally.

Some underdeveloped nations raise cash crops that neither feed the people nor bring in enough money to buy food for them. Some observers believe that the United States, which is the world's largest food exporter, encouraged other countries to grow nonfood cash crops and then, having cornered the grain market, raised prices to increase profits.

Most nations are now attempting to reduce their birth rates, and contraceptives have been distributed throughout the world for this purpose. It is expected that the size of the population will decrease as the world becomes urbanized, and it is hoped that eventually the world will reach zero population growth, calculated to be an average of 2.1 children per family. Until this goal is reached, the size of the population and the distribution of food will continue to be major problems.

Key Terms

age-adjusted death rate
age-sex composition
cash crops
census
cohort
demography
emigration
fecundity
fertility
immigration
Malthusian theory
migration
mortality
pull factors
push factors
vital statistics
zero population growth

Suggested Readings

Heer, David M. **Society and Population.** *Englewood Cliffs, N.J.: Prentice-Hall, 1975.* A concise overview of the study of population and demography.

Jones, Landon. **Great Expectations. America and the Baby Boom Generation.** *New York: Ballan-*

tine Books, 1981. A detailed description of the impact of the baby boom on American society.

Overbeek, Johannes (ed.). **The Evolution of Population Theory.** *Westport, Conn.: Greenwood Press, 1977.* A collection of articles on population, beginning with Malthus's theory and including a sampling of later writers who agreed or disagreed with him. It is interesting to note how long the population debate has continued with few new twists in the arguments.

Thomlinson, Ralph. **Population Dynamics. Causes and Consequences of World Demographic Change.** *New York: Random House, 1976.* A comprehensive text on population.

Valentey, D. I. (ed.). **The Theory of Population. Essays in Marxist Research.** *Moscow: Progress Publishers, 1978.* The Soviets are serious students of population. This collection of essays translated into English will help you understand their point of view.

Chapter 19

The Changing Community

The only credential the city asked was the boldness to dream. For those who did it, it unlocked its gates and its treasures, not caring who they were or where they came from.

— Moss Hart

The towns and cities of the United States and the rest of the world have been changing rapidly for many years. The communities in which many of you were brought up have probably undergone dramatic changes during your lifetime, or even since you entered college. Some of these changes are readily apparent: one of your favorite old buildings may have been razed to make way for a new office complex, or perhaps a new park has been created near your home. Other changes, although less tangible, are equally important. The streets you played on as a child may now be considered unsafe after dark. You may have trouble finding a summer job because several large businesses have left your city.

The reasons for changes such as these are many. We touched on a number of them in earlier chapters. Form of government, the family, changing gender roles, bureaucracies, ethnicity — the list of factors that influence the communities we live in is endless. Past and present trends in community living, their causes, and the problems they have brought are the subject of this chapter.

The Origin and Development of Communities

A *community* is a collection of people within a geographic area among whom there is some degree of mutual identification, interdependence, or organization of activities. This term is applied by sociologists to a variety of social groups, including small North American Indian tribes, towns, communes, and large urban centers. As we will show, urban communities have become larger and more diverse through the course of human history.

Early Community Development

The first communities, which originated over 35,000 years ago, were small bands that hunted and foraged for food. Their means of subsistence dictated the size and activity of the group: they were nomadic, moving frequently to new areas as food ran out. There were few status distinctions among members of these communities, although males and older persons had somewhat higher status and more power than others. Apparently there was little conflict between hunting and gathering bands. There is little evidence of war-making tools or group attacks (Lenski, 1966). This rather idyllic form of community predominated for about 25,000 years.

Roughly ten thousand years ago, humans learned to *produce* and to *store* their food. This "Neolithic revolution," as it was called, ushered in the era of horticultural communities. *Horticulture* was essentially small-scale farming that relied on tools such as the hoe to till the soil. Though horticulture was tedious, back-breaking work, it doubled the number of people the land could support — from one to nearly two persons per square mile (Davis, 1973). Stable communities developed around fertile agricultural regions, and in the more fertile areas a surplus of food was produced, which freed some members of the community from agricultural activities. As agricultural techniques improved, horticultural communities became larger and more diverse. Craftsmen who produced the tools and implements necessary for survival were the first specialists in history (Childe, 1951). It was during this era, which lasted about seven thousand years, that the first urban communities emerged.

An *urban community* is one in which a number of people are not engaged in the collection or production of food (Ucko et al., 1972). The earliest cities, which developed along the fertile banks of the Tigris and Euphrates rivers, were small by modern standards. Cities could grow only as large as the food surplus allowed; that is, the release of a number of people from agriculture required that the remaining members produce more than before. Ancient Babylon, for example, had a population of 25,000 and covered roughly three square miles; Ur, one of the oldest known cities, had about 5,000 people and covered less than a square mile (Davis, 1970; Cook, 1969). Urban communities grew slowly for the next several thousand years because of the inefficiency of horticultural techniques — it took about fifty horticulturalists to produce enough surplus to support one urban resident — and also because of the primitive political and social organization (Davis, 1973).

Preindustrial Urban Communities

The introduction of metals, the invention of the plow, the use of animals for transportation and farming, and the refinement of irrigation techniques helped usher in a new era in human history around 3000 B.C. — the Agrarian Age (Lenski, 1966). The development of writing and counting and the evolution of political and social organizations were also essential to the spread of agrarian society. These technological advances increased surpluses, so more people were freed from agriculture. Cities grew larger and their activities became more diverse. Around 1600 B.C., Thebes, the capital of Egypt, had a population of over 200,000. Athens had a population of 150,000 or so during the same period (Childe, 1951). Later, during the first century A.D., Rome had an estimated population of over half a million.

This trend of urban growth was not to continue, however. The fall of Rome in the fifth century, subsequent wars, and plagues changed the face of what had been the Roman Empire to a proliferation of self-sufficient cities that were economically separate from one another by the fif-

Nineveh, the ancient capital of Assyria, was a preindustrial urban community. Located on the Tigris River, it was the leading city of the ancient world until its fall in 612 B.C.

teenth century (Weber, 1958). After the fall of Rome, cities declined in size. The rate of agricultural innovations was slow because human energies were directed toward the technology of war. The social system became more rigid: status and occupations were determined on the basis of heredity rather than achievement or ability.

In the eleventh century, cities, especially those along natural routes and junctures, began to flourish after feudal wars subsided. As the food surplus increased, the population in the cities became more specialized. In fourteenth-century Paris, for example, tax rolls listed 157 different trades (Russell, 1972). In addition to craftsmen, cities also had specialists in other areas such as government, military service, education, and religion. Each major urban activity led to the development of an institution devoted to its performance, and churches, shops, marketplaces, city halls, and palaces became the prominent features of medieval cities.

Community Development in the Industrial Era

It was not until the end of the eighteenth century that cities began to grow rapidly, due largely to the effects of the industrial revolution. The social and economic forces that converged at this time eventually changed western Europe and later the United States from rural to urban societies. The growth of the number of people who live in urban rather than rural areas and the subsequent development of different values and lifestyles are referred to as *urbanization*. Agricultural innovations — crop rotation, soil fertilization, and the selective breeding of animals — brought larger and larger surpluses. At the same time, the development of manufacturing in the cities attracted many people. As the nineteenth century progressed, cities became much larger and grew into centers of commerce and production, but they were at the same time the locus of poverty and disease. Also, as migration from rural areas increased, the city population became more heterogeneous. The variety of occupations, ethnic backgrounds, dialects, and lifestyles in these urban areas stood in sharp contrast to the relatively homogeneous populations of small towns and rural communities. Population diversity, poverty, cramped living quarters, inadequate garbage disposal and sewage facilities, and other social and economic problems placed a tremendous strain on the urban political order. Cities became centers of unrest. Riots and revolutions, strikes by workers, and numerous clashes among members of different social groups were a significant part of nineteenth-century urban history. Many of the problems that arose in European cities during this era persist to some degree in Western nations and in a differing way in Third World nations.

Third World Urbanization

Prior to 1900, urbanization outside of western Europe and North America was limited in both scale and extent to colonial expansion. Throughout this century, however, the situation has been changing dramatically. During the last fifty years, the urban population of the developed regions increased by a factor of 2.75 while in the Third World countries it increased by a factor of 6.75 (Berry, 1973). Urbanization was fastest in the least developed countries. In Latin America and Africa, the urban population increased eightfold.

By the end of World War II, the colonial powers had relinquished control to the governments they had created. In each developing nation, one city became the focus of change and progress. Because these cities had improved health conditions and facilities, more jobs, and better education, they drew masses of people. The newly created governments, usually controlled by military juntas or totalitarian regimes, were unable to keep pace with this rapid growth, however, and those who had moved from the country found that they had exchanged lives of rural poverty for lives of urban poverty.

Much of this Third World urban growth became concentrated in "squatter" settlements. People would settle temporarily — squat — along railways, highways, the banks of streams, or on vacant government land. Most major cities in developing countries have squatter areas: Manila in the Philippines; Calcutta, India; Lima, Peru; Saigon, Viet Nam. Although these areas lacked all the basic amenities, were physically decrepit and highly disorganized, and became centers of squalor, poverty, illiteracy, sickness, and human depravity, they played an important role in solving the housing shortage problem and the other complex problems associated with migration from rural to urban centers. On closer examination, they were found to provide access to the jobs and services of the central city. Many squatter areas developed highly organized self-help efforts over a period of a few years. The residents gave shelter, security, and assistance to one another, and many of these settlements provided opportunities to continue rural values and ways of living, thereby easing the transition to the density and fast pace of the city.

To Western observers the solution to these "problem" areas was to relocate them and provide housing, usually outside the central city limits. These solutions rarely solved the problems of most squatters, however, for they involved heavy interest, maintenance, and transportation costs and did not originate in the self-help efforts of the squatters themselves. Often funded by developed nations, these efforts tended to follow patterns established in the Western world, ignoring the values and priorities of the Third World residents themselves. They also tended to overlook the importance of urban community services and failed to follow through on a long-term basis with a commitment to the residents themselves. In most Third World countries, one of the residents' high priorities is to own or have a secure right to the land they occupy. These problems, which have existed in most Third World countries throughout this century, are more severe today than ever before because of rapid population growth.

Urbanization in the United States

The industrial revolution began approximately half a century later in the United States than it did in Western Europe. The major population shift from rural to urban areas did not begin here until the Civil War. An *urban area*, according to the United States Census, is a city or town that has at least 2,500 inhabitants. In 1800, 6 percent of the population of the United States lived in urban areas (see Table 19-1). This figure rose to 20 percent by 1860. The period of greatest urban development took place during the sixty-year period between 1860 and 1920; by the latter date, slightly more than half the population lived in urban areas. This figure has continued to increase until today about three of every four Americans live in an urban area.

Why do people live in cities? The answer is that an increasing number of jobs in our society are nonagricultural. Thus the shift of the population from rural to urban areas has paralleled the growth of jobs and opportunities in the industrial and service sectors. Because of their early industrial and commercial development, northeastern states such as New York and Pennsylvania were among the first to urbanize. A few years later,

Table 19-1

Urban population: 1800–present

YEAR	URBAN POPULATION[a]	PERCENT URBAN
1800	322,000	6
1820	693,000	7
1840	1,845,000	11
1860	6,217,000	20
1880	14,130,000	28
1900	30,160,000	40
1910	41,999,000	46
1920	54,158,000	51
1930	68,955,000	56
1940	74,424,000	57
1950	96,468,000	64
1960	124,899,000	70
1970	149,325,000	74
1980	166,965,000	74

[a] All numbers and percentages are rounded.

SOURCE: U.S. Bureau of the Census, *Statistical Abstract of the United States: 1981.* 102nd ed., Washington, D.C., 1981, no. 26, p. 25.

midwestern cities such as Chicago and Detroit became large urban centers. The western states experienced an urban thrust only after World War II as a result of the growth of the defense industries. Today the South and Southwest are our fastest growing regions. In the last decade, the population of the "Sunbelt" states has increased significantly, from 61 million in 1970 to over 85 million at the end of the last decade (Biggar, 1979), mainly as a result of increased job opportunities. A number of businesses have relocated in the Sunbelt because of the economic advantages this area offers: primarily low wage scales, few problems with unions, cheap land and energy, and low taxes. As history demonstrates, people want to move to areas that provide, or at least are *perceived* as providing, good employment opportunities. Recently, a number of Sunbelt businesses have been advertising their job openings in city newspapers in the "Snowbelt" states, attracting skilled specialists to Sunbelt areas. This loss of industry and commerce in Snowbelt cities has magnified their social and economic problems.

The Metropolitan Community

The large, densely populated cities of the 1900s have given way to the growth of *metropolitan areas*. These are areas consisting of one or more large cities and the surrounding suburbs. The metropolitan community is the organization of people and institutions that perform the routine functions necessary to sustain the existence of both the city and the area around it.

The growth of metropolitan areas has been rapid and dramatic (see Table 19-2). Las Vegas, Phoenix, and Tucson, for example, had more than a 50 percent increase in the past decade. Developments in technology, in transportation, and in social structure resulting from immigration (e.g., population composition or sex ratios) have made the concentration of large numbers of people possible. These same developments have enabled a

Metropolitan communities are often perceived in terms of high buildings, crowded streets, and impersonal relationships. These areas have few children or elderly persons but contain businesspeople, shoppers, and persons who migrate daily from areas surrounding the central city to places of employment.

population dispersed over a wide area to become part of a larger, integrated community.

Metropolitan growth was caused initially by a shortage of space for industrial development, new housing, and new highways. Businesses were forced to design their facilities to fit the space that was available. Because streets were narrow and heavily congested, the transportation of goods was tedious and costly. Room for storage and loading was scarce. The land adjacent to the cities was ideal: it was inexpensive, taxes were low, and businesses could design their facilities to suit their needs. The development of the steam engine and, later, the electric trolley facilitated the transportation of goods and employees over a wider area (Hawley, 1971). After the 1920s, the increase in motor vehicles and the accompanying growth of highway systems stimulated unprecedented metropolitan development. Trucking became an impor-

tant method of moving goods and supplies (Dobriner, 1970). As manufacturing and industry moved to the suburbs, so did the people and a variety of small businesses and stores. After World War II, hundreds of suburbs developed, each of which had its own government, school system, and public services. The suburban growth paralleled a slower growth, and recently a decline, in the population of central cities.

Two terms can be used to conceptualize the dispersion of population in metropolitan communities: standard metropolitan statistical area and

Table 19-2

Population growth in metropolitan areas and the western states, in millions

	1970	1980	GROWTH, %
High growth metropolitan areas			
Dallas–Ft. Worth	2,378	2,964	24.6
Houston	1,999	2,891	44.6
Denver–Boulder	1,240	1,620	30.7
Phoenix	971	1,508	55.3
San Antonio	888	1,070	20.5
Salt Lake City	705	936	32.7
Austin	360	533	48.1
Tucson	352	531	51.1
El Paso	359	479	33.4
Las Vegas	273	462	69.0
Albuquerque	333	454	36.3
Colorado Springs	239	317	32.7
State populations			
Arizona	1,775	2,718	53.1
Colorado	2,210	2,889	30.7
Idaho	713	944	32.4
Montana	694	787	13.4
Nevada	489	799	63.4
New Mexico	1,017	1,300	27.8
Oklahoma	2,559	3,025	18.2
Texas	11,199	14,228	27.0
Utah	1,059	1,461	38.0
Wyoming	332	471	41.9

SOURCE: Blonston, Gary, "Boom!" *The Detroit Free Press*, January 10, 1982, pp. 1, 4B. Reprinted by permission.

megalopolis. According to the Bureau of the Census, a *Standard Metropolitan Statistical Area* (SMSA) is a county or group of counties that has three characteristics: a central city with a population of at least 50,000, a density of at least 1,000 persons per square mile, and outlying areas that are socially and economically integrated with the central city. There are 318 SMSAs today, and the number has been growing — 74 have been added since 1970. The size of existing SMSAs is also increasing. The size of Houston, for example, increased by 5,071 square miles in two decades (Barry and Kasarda, 1977). The sizes of the largest SMSAs today and their growth rates over the past two decades are shown in Table 19–3. Two changes are noteworthy. The growth rate of our largest metropolitan areas slowed considerably during the last decade; note that the population change percentage figures in the 1970–1980 column are significantly lower than those in the adjacent column. Also, while a number of Sunbelt cities grew during both decades, several northern cities such as Boston, Cleveland, Detroit, Philadelphia, New York, Pittsburgh, and Newark declined in population during the last decade.

The second term relating to metropolitan expansion is *megalopolis*, which is a continuous strip of urban and suburban development that may

Table 19-3

Size and population change of largest U.S. metropolitan areas: 1960–1980

	1980 POPULATION	POPULATION CHANGE: 1970–1980, %	POPULATION CHANGE: 1960–1980, %
1. New York, N.Y.–N.J.	9,120,000	−8.6	4.5
2. Los Angeles–Long Beach, Calif.	7,478,000	6.2	16.6
3. Chicago, Ill.	7,102,000	1.8	12.2
4. Philadelphia, Pa.	4,717,000	−2.2	11.1
5. Detroit, Mich.	4,353,000	−1.9	12.3
6. San Francisco–Oakland, Calif.	3,253,000	4.6	17.4
7. Washington, D.C.	3,060,000	5.2	38.8
8. Dallas–Fort Worth, Texas	2,975,000	25.1	36.8
9. Houston, Texas	2,905,000	45.3	39.8
10. Boston, Mass.	2,763,000	−4.7	11.3
11. Nassau–Suffolk, N.Y.	2,606,000	2.0	29.9
12. St. Louis, Mo.	2,355,000	−2.3	12.4
13. Pittsburgh, Pa.	2,264,000	−5.7	−.2
14. Baltimore, Md.	2,174,000	5.0	14.8
15. Minneapolis–St. Paul, Minn.	2,114,000	7.6	23.0
16. Atlanta, Ga.	2,030,000	27.2	36.5
17. Newark, N.J.	1,965,000	−4.5	12.2
18. Anaheim–Santa Ana, Calif.	1,932,000	35.9	101.9
19. Cleveland, Ohio	1,899,000	−8.0	8.1
20. San Diego, Calif.	1,862,000	37.1	31.4

SOURCE: U.S. Bureau of the Census, *Statistical Abstract of the United States: 1980*, 101st ed., Washington, D.C., 1980, No. 27, pp. 21–23; *Statistical Abstract of the United States: 1981*, 102nd ed., Washington, D.C., 1981, No. 23, pp. 19–21.

stretch for hundreds of miles. One example exists between Boston and Washington, D.C. on the East Coast. This megalopolis covers ten states, includes hundreds of local governments, and has a population of nearly 50 million. Other megalopolis areas are forming between San Francisco and San Diego on the West Coast and between Chicago and Pittsburgh in the Midwest. Sometime in the next fifty years, half the United States population may live in one of these three enormous population conglomerations.

Nonmetropolitan Growth

During the first seventy years of this century, metropolitan populations grew far more rapidly than nonmetropolitan ones. As recently as the decade from 1960–1970, while the U.S. population increased by 24 million persons, only 4.1 million of that growth (a 6.8 percent change) was in nonmetropolitan areas. Between 1970 and 1980, however, while the population increased by 23.2 million, 7.5 million of that growth (a 15.1 percent change) was in nonmetropolitan areas (Statistical Abstract, 1981, p. 16). Virtually all metropolitan areas grew significantly less and nonmetropolitan areas grew significantly more during the 1970s than they had previously. Why are these changes taking place?

In some ways, the same factors that stimulated the development of the suburbs (cheap land, low taxes, ease in commuting) are responsible for the growth of rural areas. Manufacturing development is one factor, although more important is the growth of specialized areas of recreation and retirement. Scenic areas and those with hospitable climates have grown considerably in recent years, and a number of "retirement communities" have sprung up in Florida, Arizona, and other states. Finally, the growth of rural areas is the outcome of a traditional "antiurban" mentality. The move to the suburbs resulted in part from negative attitudes toward city living because of crime, decay, pollution, and other problems. At the same time,

people have a positive attitude toward suburban living because of the clean air, low crime rate, and open space. As suburbs become more congested and experience some of the same problems as large cities, however, the entire metropolitan area comes to be regarded as an area to escape from. Also, nonmetropolitan growth is limited by job and time constraints. Many people cannot leave the metropolitan area because they are tied to their jobs and many cannot move farther from the city because commuting would become too costly and time-consuming. The nonmetropolitan population of the 1980s will probably consist mainly of the affluent who can afford to move, those who have flexible work schedules that permit long travel times, and those who are not tied to jobs, such as the elderly.

Urban Ecology

In recent years, "ecology" has come to be associated with the biological and "natural" world of plants and animals and how they are affected by pollution and other environmental influences, but it is also concerned with populations and communities. In this context, it is the study of the interrelationships of people and the environment they live in. *Urban ecology* is concerned not only with urban spatial arrangements but also with the processes that create and reinforce these arrangements.

Urban Processes

Urban areas are not static; they change continually. The urban environment is formed and transformed by three processes: (1) concentration and deconcentration, (2) ecological specialization, and (3) invasion and succession.

The term *concentration* refers to increasing density of population, services, and institutions in a region. As people migrate to the city to find jobs, living quarters become scarce and the institutions that serve the people become strained. The increase in land values and taxes and the decline of services and public facilities create an outward movement: *deconcentration*. As a result, the core of the city — the central business district — eventually comes to consist of businesses that use space intensively and can afford to pay the economic costs, usually prestigious department and retail stores, financial institutions, high-rise luxury apartments, and other profitable ventures.

People, institutions, and services are not randomly distributed in the city. Different groups and activities tend to be concentrated in different areas. This phenomenon is called *ecological specialization*. Commercial and retail trade concerns are generally found in a different part of the city than manufacturing and production. Similarly, public housing and low-rent tenements are not located near suburban residences. The basic principle at work is that people and institutions usually sort themselves into spatially homogeneous groups. As we have indicated, this homogeneity may result from economic factors: people gravitate toward places they can afford. Personal preference is also influential, as is evident from the existence of ethnic communities and areas that attract people with a particular lifestyle such as Greenwich Village and Chicago's Gold Coast.

Changes in community membership or land use result from *invasion* by other social groups or land users, which leads to *succession* as the old occupants and institutions are replaced by the new. We can give a number of examples of this process. As cities increased in size, areas that consisted originally of single-family dwellings were converted to commercial or industrial use. A recent example is the displacement of residents in an ethnic community called "Poletown" in metropolitan Detroit by a huge automobile assembly complex. Perhaps the most notable case of invasion and succession is that which is reflected in

the changing racial composition of central cities. The "white flight" of the 1960s and 1970s changed the racial composition of large cities such as Detroit, Atlanta, and Washington, D.C. from predominantly white to predominantly black. A related development is the "ghettoization" of inner cities, which occurs as minorities become trapped in central cities that have diminishing tax bases, deteriorating housing, and inefficient public services.

Urban Structure

The three ecological processes just discussed are the basis for different models of urban structure. One of the most influential models during the early development of ecological theory was the *concentric zone model*, developed by Ernest W. Burgess (Burgess, 1925) in the 1920s (see Figure 19-1). According to this theory, a city spreads out equally in all directions from its original center to produce uniform circles of growth. Each zone has its own characteristic land use, population, activities, and institutions. At the center of the city is the business district, which consists of retail stores, civil activity centers, banks, hotels, and institutional administrative offices. Zone 2, the transitional zone, contains older factories, wholesale and light manufacturing businesses, and low-rent tenements. It is in this zone that immigrants or migrants are likely to live when they first arrive in the city. At the turn of the century, first-generation European immigrants made their home in this zone, but today it is populated by minorities: blacks, Hispanics, and other ethnic groups. Zone 3 marks the edge of the residential areas and consists of progressively more expensive houses and apartments, ending finally with the commuter zone.

Since its formulation, Burgess's zone theory has come under considerable attack. Many cities do not fit the concentric zone pattern, which is more characteristic of commercial-industrial cities

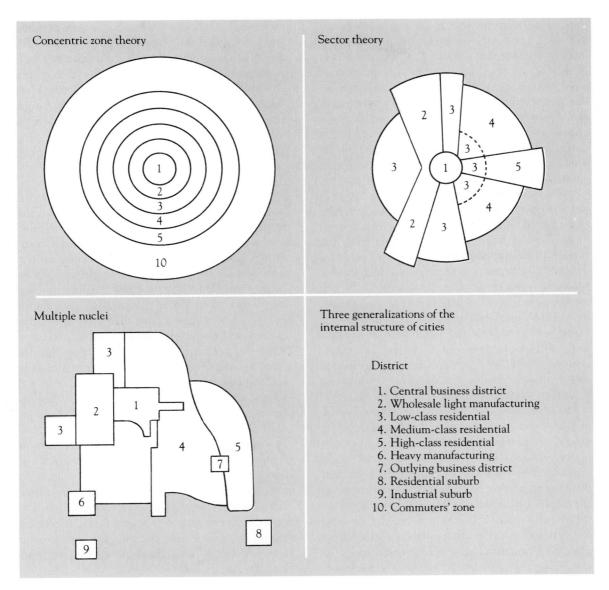

Figure 19-1
Ecological models of urban structure

than of administrative cities. Commercial-industrial cities are those built around industry, for example, Detroit, Cleveland, Pittsburgh, and so forth. These cities have a high proportion of blue-collar workers. Administrative cities such as Washington, D.C. or New York City rely heavily on government, education, and nonindustrial businesses. Also, it seems to more accurately describe cities like Chicago that developed at the turn of the century than cities like Houston that are developing today (Schnore, 1965).

There are two major alternatives to Burgess's theory. One is the *sector model* formulated by Hoyt (1939). According to Hoyt, the city is organized into pie-shaped wedges radiating from the central business district. Patterns of land use — industrial, high-income residential, and low-income tenement — tend to extend outward from the city core in internally consistent sectors or wedges. An industrial zone might radiate from the core in one wedge and spread into the suburbs, whereas high-income housing might push from the core in another wedge. Hoyt noticed this pattern in several large cities, notably Minneapolis and San Francisco.

The third theory of spatial growth rejects the idea of a single urban core or center, maintaining instead that areas of different land use have different centers. This is the *multiple nuclei model* formulated by Harris and Ullman (1945). In their view, each area expands from its center, and the form of expansion may fit either the concentric or sector zone models. In many ways, the multiple nuclei model describes the growth of metropolitan areas better than the growth of central cities.

These three models do not reflect every possible variety or pattern of growth. Urban expansion is influenced by a variety of factors, including rate of migration into the city, cultural and historical precedents for urban development, and the physical characteristics of the land. As a result of these and other factors, Latin American cities, for example, do not fit American growth patterns, and cities built near major waterways grow differently from other cities (Thomlinson, 1969). Sociologists today are developing more complex models of urban development that take into account a wide variety of factors, including social, economic, and cultural variables.

Life in Cities and Suburbs

The emergence of urban communities has altered human lifestyles and values. The size, complexity, and density of urban communities have given rise to new forms of social organization, new behaviors, and new attitudes. One of the major questions sociologists have grappled with is why urban communities are different from rural areas in so many ways, rather than just the fact that they are larger and more densely populated. Sociologists have long recognized that there are qualitative differences between urban and rural life, and Ferdinand Tönnies (1887), a German sociologist, made a distinction in this regard nearly a century ago. He called small, rural villages of his boyhood *gemeinschaft* (communities); the centers of activity he called *gesellschaft* (associations).

A gemeinschaft community is characterized by a sense of solidarity and a common identity. It is a primary community rooted in tradition. Relationships between neighbors are intimate and personal, and there is a strong emphasis on shared values and sentiments, a "we" feeling. People frequently interact with one another and tend to establish deep, long-term relationships. Small towns and communes generally have many of these characteristics.

A gesellschaft community, in contrast, is based on diverse economic, political, and social interrelationships. It is characterized by individualism, mobility, impersonality, the pursuit of self-interest, and an emphasis on progress rather than tradition. Shared values and total personal

Tönnies described two contrasting orientations to social and community life. One orientation, termed gesellshaft, he saw as relationships that occur contractually and are based on formal, impersonal, and legal terms. The other, gemeinshaft, referred to relationships that occur "naturally" and are based on informal, personal, and nonlegal terms. Gesellschaft is more typical of large cities, whereas gemeinshaft is more typical of small villages.

involvement become secondary. People live and work together because it is necessary or convenient, and people are viewed more in terms of their roles than as unique individuals. In a large city, for example, one is likely to interact with a policeman as a public servant or authority figure who has certain stereotyped characteristics and obligations. In a small town, on the other hand, one would be likely to know a policeman personally. Rather

than viewing him as a manifestation of a certain form of authority, one would know him as an individual with certain unique character traits. Historically, there has been a shift from gemeinshaft to gesellschaft relationships as a result of role specialization and, more generally, of bureaucratization. In the nineteenth century, Weber labeled this as a change from a traditional to a rational society. In the twentieth century, American sociologists have used these ideas as a springboard for their own theories. In the next two sections, we will examine some of these theories about the quality of life in cities and suburbs.

City Life

One American sociologist, Robert Redfield (1941), developed a typology similar to those formulated by nineteenth-century scholars. He distinguished a *folk society*, which is small, isolated, homogeneous, and kin-oriented, from an urban society, which is large, impersonal, heterogeneous, and fast-paced. Around the same time, Louis Wirth, a colleague of Redfield's at the University of Chicago, described the effects of large numbers, density, and heterogeneity on urban life. In "Urbanism as a Way of Life" (1938), Wirth argued that as the population in an area becomes denser, lifestyles diversify, new opportunities arise, and institutions develop. At the same time, density increases the number of short-term, impersonal, and utilitarian social relationships a person is likely to have.

According to Wirth, these three factors — large numbers, density, and heterogeneity — create a distinct way of life called *urbanism*. The distinctive characteristics of urbanism are: an extensive and complex division of labor; an emphasis on success, achievement, and social mobility, along with a behavioral orientation that includes rationality and utilitarianism; a decline of the family and kinship bonds and a concurrent rise of specialized agencies that assume roles previously taken by kin; a breakdown of primary relationships and the substitution of secondary group control mechanisms; a replacement of deep, long-term relationships with superficial, short-term relationships; a decline of shared values and homogeneity and an increase in diversity; and finally, segregation on the basis of achieved and ascribed status characteristics.

Recently, Milgram (1970) has focused on the effects of urbanism. In midtown Manhattan, for example, someone can meet 220,000 people within a ten-minute walking radius of his or her office and not recognize a single person! Such an experience, says Milgram, may cause "pyschic overload" and result in the detached, "don't get involved" attitude that is frequently cited as a part of big city life. There have been a number of recorded incidents, for instance, in which people have been mugged, raped, or beaten in plain view of pedestrians who refused to help the victim.

These views of urban life give the impression that it is cold, violent, and alienating. City living conditions have been blamed by scholars as the cause of crime, mental illness, aggresssion, and other serious problems, but recent studies by sociologists have questioned the validity of this assessment. Certainly these negative aspects of city life do exist; the real question is how typical or widespread they are. Several studies have found that there is considerable cohesion and solidarity in the city, particularly in neighborhoods where the residents are relatively homogeneous in terms of social or demographic characteristics. The findings of early sociologists may have accurately described the central core of American cities such as Chicago during periods of rapid growth. Contemporary research illustrates that a variety of lifestyles and adaptations can be found in cities.

A fine example of research on the diversity of urban lifestyles has been presented by Herbert Gans (1962). He argues that there are at least five types of residents in the city: cosmopolites, singles, ethnic villagers, the deprived, and the trapped.

Cosmopolites usually choose to remain in the city because of its convenience and cultural benefits. This group includes artists, intellectuals, and professionals who are drawn by the opportunities and activities generally found only in large urban centers. They are typically young, married, and involved in upper-middle-class occupations.

Singles like to live in the city because it is close to their jobs and permits a suitable lifestyle. The central city, with its nightclubs and "singles only" apartments, offers a basis for social interaction. It gives singles opportunities to make friends, develop a social identity, and eventually find a mate (Starr and Carns, 1973). Many of these people are not permanent urban residents; they live in the city only until they marry, at which time they move to the suburbs.

The third group identified by Gans, *ethnic villagers*, generally consists of working-class people who have chosen to reside in specific areas of the city. Their neighborhoods often develop a distinctive ethnic color as shops, restaurants, and organizations spring up. The Chinatowns in New York and San Francisco and the Polish communities of Chicago and Detroit are neighborhoods of this type. Because of their strong ethnic ties, they usually do not identify strongly with the city, nor do they engage in many of the cultural, social, or political activities. Their identity and allegiance are tied to the ethnic group and local community to a far greater extent than to the city. A strong emphasis is placed on kinship and primary group relationships, and members of other groups are often perceived as intruders or outsiders.

The fourth group, the *deprived*, is composed of the poor, the handicapped, and racial minorities who have fallen victim to class inequality, prejudice, or personal misfortune. They live in the city because it offers inexpensive housing and holds the promise of future job opportunities that will enable them to move to a better environment. Finally, the *trapped* are those who cannot afford to move to a newer community and must remain in their deteriorating neighborhoods. The elderly who live on pensions make up most of this group, and since many have lived in the city all their lives, they tend to identify strongly with their neighborhoods. The deprived and the trapped are the most frequent victims of the problems of the city. They are more likely to be the targets of assault, mugging, extortion, and other crimes than other city residents. In high crime areas, many of these people live isolated lives and are terrified by the ongoing violence in their neighborhoods.

Suburban Life

The dominance of *suburbs* in metropolitan areas is a recent phenomenon, although the population movement to the suburbs began at the end of the last century. Suburbs grew as a result of both push and pull factors. The problems of the city drove residents to the suburbs, while the positive aspects of suburban life — clean air, low taxes, large lots, and a chance to own a home — attracted people. Since the move involved a substantial capital investment, this transition was made primarily by the affluent.

The growth of the suburbs was also influenced by technological developments, especially those in transportation. Before the 1920s, trains and electric trolleys were the major means of mass transportation to and from the central city. Accordingly, the first pattern of suburban growth was star-shaped as communities sprung up along the railway and trolley corridors radiating from the center of the city. The automobile gave the suburban movement a significant boost by permitting the development of land not located near a railway or a trolley corridor.

After World War II, the suburbs took on a different appearance. The increased affluence of American workers and the mass production of relatively inexpensive housing enabled many lower-middle-class and blue-collar families to become suburbanites. The type of housing that emerged in the post–World War II suburbs, called *tract housing,* was based on mass production techniques. Neighborhoods and sometimes whole communities of similar houses were constructed.

As the population began to shift to the suburbs, so did the retail trade and small businesses. The result was an unprecedented growth of suburban shopping centers.

The rapid growth of suburbs in the 1950s and early 1960s caused a great deal of concern

Suburbs have been said to offer the best of both urban and rural life: the varied activities and events of the city and the quiet, open spaces of the country. To lower costs and thus make suburban home owner-ship available to an increasing number of moderate-income persons, housing developers in the sixties and seventies often used mass produc-tion technology. Today a large number of housing tracts bear wit-ness to this residential cloning.

among many social commentators. Suburban life was characterized as a "rat race" dominated by a preoccupation with "keeping up with the Jones's." Suburbanites were seen as anxious, child-oriented, status-seeking people who lead empty, frustrating lives (Bell, 1958; Gordon, et al., 1961; Mills, 1951). The typical suburbanites were viewed as more concerned with household gadgets, status symbols, and getting into the "right" organizations than with understanding the world around them or achieving individuality. These views generated what sociologists call the "myth of suburbia." Recent research has given us reason to doubt that the patterns of behavior found in the suburbs are due to suburban residence and even that there is a distinctly suburban way of life.

The suburbs and the people who live there (sometimes called "suburbanites") are actually quite diverse. Harris (1971) captured some of this diversity in his categorization of suburbs on the basis of income levels and growth rates. He found four types: the affluent bedroom, the affluent settled, the low-income growing, and the low-income stagnant. The first two types are populated by upper-middle-class residents who are typically white, Protestant, and Republican. They tend to find suburban living quite satisfactory, although boring in some respects. The latter two categories are dominated by blue-collar workers. One finds a larger proportion of nonwhites, Democrats, and Catholics in these communities. People in all categories gave as their primary reason for moving to the suburbs the desire to own a home. The second most important reason was to find a suitable environment in which to raise children. Other factors common to all suburbanites were a desire for open spaces and for a less hectic pace.

Do people change when they move from the city to the suburbs? Is there evidence of a *conversion effect*, a radical shift of interest and lifestyle? Berger (1960) and Cohen and Hodges (1963) found that blue-collar families had similar values, behavior patterns, and psychological orientations whether they lived in the city or in the suburbs. Similarly, Gans (1967) found that middle-class suburbanites in Levittown were not plagued by the stereotypical problems of boredom, unhappiness, and frustrated status seeking. He found instead that they were generally happy, well adjusted, and involved in family and social activities. In short, there is little evidence of a conversion effect.

The differences in the lifestyles of the city and the suburbs should be thought of as differences of degree, not of kind. Suburban residents tend to be more family-oriented and more concerned about the quality of education their children receive than city dwellers (Bell, 1958). On the other hand, because the suburbs consist largely of single-family homes, most young and single people prefer city life. Suburbanites are usually more affluent than city residents and more apt to have stable career or occupational patterns. As a result, they seem to be more hardworking and achievement-oriented than city residents. They may also seem to be unduly concerned with consumption, since they often buy goods and services that offer visible evidence of their financial success. The career involvement and the consumption patterns, however, are related more to social class position than to a mythical "suburban mentality" (Seeley et al., 1972). Suburbanites are also more involved than city residents in local social activities (Marshall, 1973; Tallman and Morgner, 1970), which is probably due partly to the demographic homogeneity of suburbs and partly to suburbanites' concern for their neighborhoods and schools.

In recent years, the number of blacks who live in the suburbs has increased sharply. In the last decade, the rate of black suburbanization increased by over 33 percent compared with a 10 percent increase for whites (Current Population Reports, Special Studies P-23 no. 75, 1978, Table F). There is little evidence, however, that the suburbs are becoming racially integrated. Since the median income of blacks is still considerably lower than that of whites, most blacks cannot afford to move into the suburbs where most whites reside. Instead they are moving into the older suburbs with lower property values that whites are leaving behind in their search for better suburban communities. Though whites often react strongly to blacks who move into their suburban communities because they are perceived as being different, there is research evidence that blacks who move to the suburbs have values and lifestyles similar to those of their white neighbors (Austin, 1976).

Urban Problems

The most severe problems in urban areas are found in the central cities: poverty, unemployment, crime, noise and air pollution, waste disposal, water purity, transportation, housing, population congestion, and so on. Although the suburbs are by no means immune to these problems, they generally do not experience them to the same degree as central cities. The central cities are beset by a number of crises, some of which are becoming worse. In this section, we will discuss three problems: poverty and unemployment, crime, and schooling.

Among the most serious issues facing cities today are the related problems of poverty and unemployment. The economic vitality of central cities has diminished over the years as industry, affluent taxpayers, and jobs have moved out. The result has been a steady deterioration of housing and public services and the loss of high-paying jobs. The least fortunate of city residents are forced to live in slums. *Slums* are overcrowded streets or sections of a city marked by poverty and poor living conditions, which result from the dirt, disease, rodents, and other health hazards that accompany concentrations of housing with poor plumbing, garbage disposal, and sanitation facilities (National Commission on Urban Problems, 1972). Slum residents are often victims of social injustice and personal misfortune: racial minorities, the elderly, women who head large families, and addicts. Slum living has a number of detrimental effects on health: residents of slums are more likely than other city dwellers to contract diseases and to become seriously ill; they have poorer overall health and shorter life spans as well (Schorr, 1970; Ways, 1971); and they are also more apt to have poor self-images and experience psychological problems such as depression and alienation (Polk, 1967; Lander, 1971).

The term *ghetto* is relevant to an understanding of urban poverty and unemployment. A ghetto is an area, usually a deteriorating one, in which members of a racial or ethnic minority are forcibly segregated. Urban areas that are no longer of interest to the more affluent majority tend to become ghettos. A ghetto is a social and economic trap that keeps members of the minority group within a controllable geographic area. In a sense, an urban ghetto is the counterpart of an Indian reservation, and there is evidence that black ghettoization is increasing today. During the last decade, the number of whites in central cities declined by 8 percent while the number of blacks increased by nearly 4 percent (Current Population Reports, Special Studies P-23, no. 75, Table F). As a result of this change, blacks, many of whom are poor, constitute a numerical majority in several large cities, including Washington, D.C., Atlanta, and Detroit.

The jobs that the less affluent central city residents are qualified for are usually low-paying and scarce, and the unemployment rate is twice as high as the rate in the suburbs. The departure of industry and manufacturing jobs has left inner-city residents with jobs characterized by high turnover, low wages, and few opportunities for advancement. It is not unusual to find a person who heads a family and works fulltime but barely earns enough to stay above the poverty line. With recent cuts in federal aid to job-training programs, it is unlikely that the situation of these city residents will improve in the near future.

Crime is another serious urban problem. In the 1970s, crime was ranked as the nation's number one social problem, especially by residents of cities of more than a million (Nelson, 1977), and there is evidence that it is increasing. A comparison of burglary rates in the mid-1960s and mid-1970s, for example, found an increase of nearly 200 percent (Wilson and Boland, 1976). Crime has often been viewed as essentially an *urban* problem, one that is especially common in large cities. There are several justifications for this view. Illegal vice activities like prostitution, gambling, and the use and sale of narcotics are found more generally in large cities where there is greater anonymity (Wolfgang, 1970). In addition, the methods of control are different in large cities and small towns. While towns rely on internalized values and primary group pressure for enforcement, cities depend on abstract laws and impersonal, bureaucratic agencies such as the police (Dinitz, 1973). When high density, heterogeneity, and anonymity are combined with poverty, a physically decayed environment, and other characteristics of inner-city living, there is great potential for deviance and violence.

Not all areas of a city experience the same crime rate or the same types of crimes. The highest crime rates are found in the inner-city sectors, while the rate decreases as one moves toward the fringes of the urban area. Zonal differences in crime tend to persist, however, even when the physical characteristics and the occupants of a zone change.

Using sociological research as a guide, one might argue that there are several ways of reducing urban crime. Increased police surveillance is often an important political issue in cities, but there is some evidence that it has little if any effect on the crime rate. Since high crime areas are located in similar areas in different cities — generally the most poverty-stricken areas — one might argue that providing the people in these areas decent living conditions and meaningful jobs would have a greater impact on crime than increasing the size of the police force. One could also argue that voluntary neighborhood organizations in high crime areas might not only provide role models of lawful behavior but also create a sense of community that is frequently lacking in these areas (Wilson, 1968).

A third urban problem area is schooling. City schools are faced with two major problems today: inadequate financing and disorder and violence. The cost of a public school education rose by over 150 percent in the last decade (Coleman and Kelly, 1976), and many cities have had a very difficult time keeping pace with the accelerating costs. This difficulty is accentuated by inequalities in school funding: urban schools have a much lower per student expenditure allowance than schools in the suburbs (Berlowitz, 1974). City schools have reacted to this funding problem in several ways. In some areas, school bond increases have been used to retain financial solvency. In recent years, however, an increasing percentage of school bond proposals are being rejected by irate taxpayers (Coleman and Kelly, 1976). As a result of the fiscal crisis, many schools are forced to use outdated or damaged curricular material. It was recently discovered that one Detroit school was using history books that made reference to Lyndon Johnson as president! Reductions in staff and salary are another means of dealing with the financial woes. This "solution" has been a factor in recent teacher strikes and walkouts, which are becoming more frequent (Browne, 1976). Staff and salary cutbacks also seem to be related to the morale problems found in many inner-city schools.

School disorder, especially violence, is increasing. Incidents that rarely occurred a generation ago happen today on a fairly routine basis in many city schools: theft, extortion, physical attacks on fellow students and teachers, and vandalism (U.S. Department of Health, Education, and Welfare, 1978). In some schools, the halls are routinely patrolled by police officers; in others, the doors of classrooms are locked during class hours to prevent intruders from entering; still other schools have unannounced locker checks to confiscate drugs and weapons. One explanation for the increase in school crime is that schools are no longer immune to the day-to-day problems of the city. Solving some of the problems that cause crime on the streets would therefore probably reduce crime in the schools. Another explanation is that the schools themselves are responsible for disorder. Deteriorating buildings, prejudiced teachers, curricular tracking, and pessimism about the future may all produce an atmosphere of despair and anger (Rist, 1970). Without adequate funds to buy better equipment and hire more qualified teachers, this problem is likely to persist.

Urban Rejuvenation: Problems and Prospects

What can be done to our cities to help them survive? Has the central city outlived its use? These are a couple of the serious questions addressed by scholars concerned about the future of our cities. Some feel that the future is not very bright. Hauser (1977) thinks that the present crises many cities are experiencing will worsen as the tax base continues to erode, buildings and homes continue to deteriorate, and "tax rebellions" become more frequent. Sternlieb (1977) has compared the function of the central city of the future to that of a sandbox: as the city loses its economic functions, it becomes a place to keep the American poor in check by periodically giving them new "toys" — welfare and relief programs. Other scholars are less pessimistic. Banfield (1974) argues that the urban crisis is not becoming more severe but that cities are simply not recovering at the rate we expected them to. He suggests that the financial drain in large cities could be alleviated by redrawing city boundary lines to include all metropolitan residents for tax purposes or by charging nonresidents for their use of city services. He admits that although these ideas are economically feasible, they are politically explosive.

Downtown Revitalization

One's view of the problems and prospects of the city depends greatly on whether the central business district or residential areas are being considered. Many business districts are being revitalized. Most cities, even those in the Northeast and Midwest, are experiencing significant new business construction. In Chicago, over a billion dollars of construction is planned before 1985. Detroit recently built a new sports arena as well as a "Renaissance Center," a huge complex including a hotel, offices, and a variety of retail shops. Since the downtown areas of our cities are a major center of white-collar employment, financial firms, insurance companies, and private and government services, the future of these areas is relatively secure.

Downtown revitalization programs tend to have a greater impact on white-collar jobs than blue-collar ones, however. The number of white-collar jobs in cities is increasing, but the number of blue-collar jobs continues to decline (Kasarda, 1976). Since the revitalization of the central business district creates a need for well-educated, highly skilled employees, many inner city residents who have weaker credentials do not directly benefit from these types of economic programs. This has made many city residents angry because they feel that their problems and concerns are secondary to the plans of affluent city and suburban residents. Citizen groups such as ACORN (The Association of Community Organizations for Reform Now) have voiced the concerns of many people, stressing that urban rejuvenation must include residential neighborhoods as well as the business district and must create jobs for all city residents regardless of their levels of skill or education (see box on page 521).

Urban Renewal

Urban renewal is, at least in theory, the residential counterpart of downtown revitalization. According to the Urban Renewal Act of 1954, the major goal is to rebuild and renovate the ghettos and slums of American cities, but urban renewal projects have had several shortcomings. First, local urban renewal agencies were given the power by the federal government to define which areas were "blighted" and therefore qualified for renewal. Generally, the better areas of the slums were developed while the worst were allowed to remain. Sometimes the reason for this selection was the perception that one area was more likely to produce income than the other. Shopping centers and high-rise apartments for the middle class, for example, often replaced low-income housing. Ironically, many of the residents whose homes were razed did not benefit at all from the structures that were erected (Greer, 1965). Second, the act specified that the people displaced by urban renewal should be relocated in "decent, safe, and sanitary" housing in other areas of the city. In a number of instances, the new neighborhoods were just as bad as the old ones, and the relocation often destroyed an existing sense of community with friends and neighbors (Ryan, 1973).

The case of the Pruitt-Igoe Housing Project in St. Louis exemplifies some of the problems associated with urban renewal projects (Newman, 1972). The project, which had cleared some of the city's slum dwellings by 1955, consisted of thirty-three buildings, each eleven stories high. It was lauded as a model for all future public housing projects because of its design and use of innovative structures. By 1970, however, the project had become a symbol of all the negative aspects of public housing. The physical deterioration and destruction of elevators, laundry rooms, and stairways was considerable. Residents were

ACORN

Their detractors portray them as carpetbaggers and chronic malcontents. Their boosters claim they provide the lone avenue to some measure of political power for Detroit's low- and middle-income neighborhood residents.

They are members of ACORN – the Association of Community Organizations for Reform Now. And in conversation, they make a point of saying it just that way: that ACORN is the people in it and vice versa.

ACORN is relatively new as Detroit neighborhood groups go, having established itself with help from out-of-town organizers in 1978. But in the 3½ years since, it has managed to win over – and alienate – a remarkable number of people through its concentration on neighborhood issues and its confrontation tactics.

While ACORN is a national organization with 40,000 members and chapters in 23 states, there are 17 separate branches and 2,000 members in Detroit alone. ACORN also has chapters in Grand Rapids, Adrian and Lansing and is seen by some political observers as a growing force to be reckoned with.

The group came to the spotlight most recently when a member, 24-year-old Detroiter Lisa Redd, moved illegally into an abandoned, city-owned house on Ohio Avenue with her 22-month-old son. The move was highly publicized. It became highly emotional when the woman's financial support was revealed to be more than first indicated – and when she and her son were evicted from the home.

Late last week, six officers and members of several Detroit-area ACORN branches discussed ACORN and its motives in an interview.

"We have a lot of small victories and quiet meetings with city officials that never make the paper," said Ella Stulz of Detroit, a delegate to ACORN's national board. "But sometimes it takes big numbers to get the support and the attention we need."

George Montgomery, co-chairman of the Clark Park segment of ACORN, added, "Sometimes we make a lot of noise, but the squeaking axle gets the grease. Don't you people (the Free Press) use headlines to get attention for a story you want to tell? Well, we just do the same thing.

"Anything we have ever done, we have been very sincere about. Our purpose is betterment of people in Detroit's neighborhoods."

ACORN's view of what is in the best interests of Detroit's neighborhoods often clashes spectacularly with Mayor Young's view of what will benefit the whole city.

ACORN has opposed all or part of such projects as the General Motors revitalization of the New Center area . . . the Republican National Convention . . . construction of Joe Louis Arena . . . construction of GM's new Poletown plant.

ACORN maintained in each case that the money would be better spent on Detroit's residential neighborhoods.

SOURCE: Craig, Charlotte W. and Judy Diebolt, "ACORN: A Thorn in the Side of City Hall," *The Detroit Free Press,* Oct. 11, 1981, p. 3–A. Reprinted by permission.

---

afraid to leave their apartments because of the frequency of robbery and rape. The absence of public bathrooms on the ground floors resulted in foul-smelling hallways. Gradually, most of the occupants fled the project, and even the most desperate welfare recipients were unwilling to tolerate the living conditions. The government finally closed down the entire project and later razed it. The basic problem was that human values and lifestyles were not fully considered in the project's

During the past decade many American cities have undergone downtown revitalization. Detroit, for example, has demolished many of its old downtown structures. In their place the city has built apartment complexes and malls, planted trees and shrubs, and along the Detroit River erected a "Renaissance Center." The Center, which appears in the background of this photo, consists of a major hotel surrounded by six office towers, a plaza often used for ethnic festivals, an auditorium for concerts, a hall for major auto/home/industrial shows, and a sports complex for professional hockey.

design. The high-rise construction isolated residents from one another; the architectural design left too much open space (halls, elevators, laundry rooms) that no one felt responsible for and that made surveillance of children and adolescents very difficult.

Other means of housing the poor were legislated after the problems with urban renewal projects were publicized in the 1960s. Most of them received mixed reviews. Title 235 and Title 236 of the Housing and Urban Redevelopment Act provided direct subsidies to low-income families so that they could either buy their own homes or else rent apartments of their choice. Section 8 and the Experimental Housing Allowance Program were implemented in the early 1970s to help low-income tenants pay their rent. In both cases part of the rent was paid by the government, either to the tenant or directly to the landlord.

A recent federal plan that is becoming increasingly popular is *urban homesteading*. Homesteading programs sell abandoned and foreclosed homes to private families for between one and 100 dollars if they agree to live in the house for at least three years and to bring the house up to code standards within eighteen months. Though the program is less than a decade old and has limited funds, it has had a significant effect on a number of cities, but there have been pitfalls. Individuals and lending institutions are reluctant to invest in houses surrounded by vandalized, rundown buildings, and despite the low purchase price, repairs may be quite expensive. Recently, the Department of Housing and Urban Development has acted to alleviate these problems by buying up and making modest repairs on entire neighborhoods. If the federal government were to continue its commitment to urban homesteading in the 1980s, some of our deteriorating neighborhoods could probably be transformed. At the time of this writing, however, this type of commitment by the federal government appears highly unlikely.

A growing number of urban neighborhoods are being rejuvenated by *gentrification*. Since the mid-1970s, middle-class people have been moving into and repairing old rundown homes at their own expense. Notable examples of this are found in Chicago's Newtown, the Mission District of San Francisco, and Atlanta's Ansley Park. These people are generally young, white, childless couples who work in the city. They tend to have different values than their suburban counterparts. Many do not want to have families and most are turned off by the sameness and the lack of charm of suburban housing (Bradley, 1977). This trend may continue in the future with the increasing costs of transportation and suburban housing.

Urban Planning

Most of our urban development has occurred without a long-term commitment to community living or a strong theoretical understanding of it.

Urban planning is a field of study concerned with urban physical structures and spatial configurations and their effects on human attitudes and behavior. Two traditional goals of this field are the reduction of population density and the creation of appealing community structures.

Urban planning became a concern in the nineteenth century when many large cities in Europe and the United States were experiencing severe problems because of rapid industrial and population growth. One early influential figure was Ebenezer Howard. Howard, in *Garden Cities of Tomorrow* (1902), argued that the ideal was to develop cities that combined the benefits of both rural and urban living. All new towns, or "garden cities" as he called them, would be built on undeveloped land in accordance with scientific principles. Population density, a factor he felt was responsible for urban blight, would be carefully controlled. Cities were also to be surrounded by a *greenbelt,* an area preserved for farming and recreation, thus limiting the outward growth of the city. Howard's ideas have had a significant impact on the theoretical orientations of several generations of urban planners whose major focus has been the construction of "new towns" that have a careful mixture of houses, entertainment areas, businesses and industries.

One of the most popular critics of this view is Jane Jacobs (1961). She feels that urban planners who are trying to create "garden cities" are actually eliminating some of the characteristics that make urban life unique. Cities are naturally diverse and innovative, and attempts to zone various activities into distinct areas and to establish routine patterns of behavior will only create a dull, stagnant, social and economic environment. She suggests four ways to create a healthy, diverse urban environment:

1. Urban districts should serve several functions, and different parts of a district should be active at different times. This diversity and activ-

Picture the city of the future. Will it resemble this city of the future, from the movie Metropolis? Will our living environment be totally controlled by artificial lighting, cooling, and heating? Will millions of people live on confined geographical areas? Will personal relationships in urban areas be increasingly impersonal and contractual? Urban planners, including sociologists, will need to design the types of communities that combine the available resources with societal values and group preferences.

ity will attract people and make the streets safe at all hours of the day.

2. Most blocks should be short; there should be frequent opportunities to turn corners. This will prevent residents from walking the same, long monotonous streets. This would also encourage shops and small businesses to open up on previously untraveled streets, adding to the diversity of the area.

3. Old and new buildings should be mingled in the district. This intermingling is necessary so

that high and low yield economic enterprises can coexist in the same area. Low-profit businesses, such as art shops and foreign restaurants, can rarely afford the costs of large, modern buildings whereas high-profit enterprises such as banks or chain supermarkets can.

4. The district must have a sufficiently dense concentration of residences and people. In constructing residences, extremes should be avoided. Too much density creates turmoil and reduces the ability of residents to enjoy the diversity; too much open space, on the other hand, makes surveillance difficult. This may lead to inappropriate or deviant behavior. (pp. 143–151)

A number of modern new towns have been carefully designed and monitored. Columbia, Maryland, located between Washington D.C., and Baltimore, is an example of a city developed with human needs and lifestyles in mind. When it is fully developed, it will house 110,000 people in ten "villages," each containing four neighborhoods. Each neighborhood has its own elementary school and recreational facilities, and the villages form a circle around a plaza with a shopping center, office buildings, and medical facilities. The community has also made a conscious attempt to achieve racial balance: a little less than a quarter of the residents are black (Rouse, 1971).

Other, more recent new towns have not been as successful as Columbia, and federal cutbacks in funding for development have led to the demise of more than half a dozen new towns. Soul City, North Carolina, is one of the latest to be foreclosed by HUD. The lesson to be learned from these recent experiences is that the successful development of planned communities requires a long-term investment of money, perhaps as long as fifteen or twenty years, by the federal government. With its present economic woes, our government is unlikely to make such a commitment in the near future.

Diversity of Values

Although urban planners should be sensitive to the diverse values and lifestyles of the people who live in urban communities if they are to achieve their goals, they have not been completely successful in this area, and they have been criticized as having a distinct middle-class bias (Gans, 1968). This point can be illustrated with findings about the design and use of space.

Most planners assume that people like a considerable amount of open public space and clearly demarcated areas of private space. Among many blue-collar and minority groups, however, the distinction between public and private space is blurred, and social interactions tend to flow more freely across private and public regions than they do in middle-class environments (Freid and Gleicher, 1961). The effects of spatial arrangements on behavior are also class-related, as was illustrated in a study by Newman (1972). He found that two adjacent housing projects in New York with similar population densities and residents had significantly different rates of crime and maintenance problems. The only difference was that the one with few crime and maintenance problems was smaller than the other; it had six-story rather than mostly thirteen-story buildings. The reader might generalize these findings to our earlier discussion of the Pruitt-Igoe Project.

That urban planners and the less affluent have different spatial preferences has also been noted with regard to the structure of individual apartments. An experiment in which Hispanic residents of a New York tenement conferred with an architect about the redesign of their apartments revealed that the residents did not like the large areas of open space in an apartment that middle-class couples prefer; that they wanted an apartment entrance that did not open directly into the living room; and that they liked an apartment in which the kitchen was isolated from the rest of the house by a wall or door (Zeisel, 1973).

Sensitive design of new urban places can greatly enhance the satisfaction city residents derive from their surroundings. Newman (1972) offers five guidelines for achieving this end:

1. Design buildings of no more than six stories in which not more than a dozen families share the same stairwell.

2. Acknowledge definitions of space that reflect the values of the inhabitants and the community to which they belong.

3. Position apartment windows so that residents can easily survey the interior and exterior public areas of their environment.

SOCIOLOGISTS AT WORK
City Planning

Arthur B. Shostak is an urban sociologist, a futurist, and a Philadelphian. He was able to put all of those perspectives to work when he co-chaired a volunteer task force that wrote a report called *Seven Scenarios for Philadelphia's Next Twenty-Five Years.*

Art Shostak has been teaching sociology since 1961, first at the University of Pennsylvania and now at Drexel University. A consultant with the nation's largest companies and labor unions on reforms in blue-collar life, personnel advances, and family life, he has paid special attention to the future and the ways our present actions can shape it. As part of his futurist research he has studied "New Towns" (planned communities) such as Reston, Virginia, and Columbia, Maryland, as well as comparable small cities in England, France, and Israel. So when the University of Pennsylvania's Center for Philadelphia Studies decided to have a task force explore Philadelphia's future options, Shostak was a logical choice to play a leading role.

A group of twenty-five concerned citizens met throughout 1981 for lengthy focused discussions of city prospects. Shostak presented various possible scenarios to them, based on his years of

sociological research and study, and the group — whose members included an architect, a graduate student, a city planner, an internationally known artist, a film maker, a retired public relations expert, a free-lance writer, and a drummer in a rock band — eventually ruled out five as unlikely. They ranked the remaining seven in order of probability, and Shostak proceeded to write up their findings, complete with a set of policy recommendations for city government, business, and community activists who wanted to promote any particular outcome. The seven scenarios were:

□ *Conflict City* — a desperate, troubled struggle to make do. (Shostak says all the city needs to do to reach this outcome is to follow its present course.)

□ *Wired City* — a thoroughgoing reliance on telecommunications advances.

□ *Neighborhood City* — a well-coordinated configuration of viable neighborhoods, with food and worker-owned cooperatives.

□ *Conservation City* — a drive to save energy in every way, including new reliance on mass transit and building redesign.

4. Construct buildings in a manner that does not stigmatize the inhabitants and allow others to perceive their vulnerability and isolation.

5. Increase the safety of residents by locating residential developments in functionally sympathetic areas away from areas that would provide a continual threat. (p. 9)

The development of attractive, functional physical surroundings cannot be accomplished without a long-term commitment by the government to aid our ailing cities. The rejuvenation of the city also requires the creation of jobs and opportunities for inner-city residents. In the last two decades major steps have been taken toward the realization of these goals.

□ *International City* — a worldwide center for new job-offering factories, offices, and markets based on overseas sources.

□ *Regional City* — a substantial collaborative arrangement with surrounding counties and nearby cities.

□ *Leisure City* — oriented around recreation, culture, and the pursuit of happiness, with work reduced in its lifelong role.

The report was published late in 1981, at the beginning of a year-long celebration of Philadelphia's 300th birthday. It immediately earned considerable citizen attention and sparked dialogue around the city.

But the task force's work was not done. In the months that followed, Shostak supervised volunteers who interviewed Philadelphians about their vision of a desirable future and any actions they might be taking to shape that future. They conducted nearly 2,000 telephone interviews and about 150 more detailed "living room" interviews, testing citizen reactions to the seven scenarios with a wide range of questions.

The next job for the task force was to prepare a synthesis of the scenarios. A major complaint heard about their initial report was that, while it presented seven scenarios (none of which the task force advocated in particular), Philadelphia only had *one* future within which to "mix and match" elements of the seven scenarios. So

they drew up a report that fit the most likely features of each scenario into one over-arching vision of the most desirable future for the city.

The task force hopes its deliberations will have a long-lasting and deep-reaching impact on the city's and region's future. "We've had close contact with the city council through all this," Shostak said while in the middle of the project, "and we've had a good pipeline into the mayor's office — some of his younger staff members have been heavily involved in our research and discussion groups. As the 300th anniversary celebration draws to a close in 1983, we will conduct a series of monthly seminars for community leaders from both the public and the private sector. We're working on a list of distinguished speakers who will help us sustain interest in the idea of future-shaping planning for our collective urban lives."

Comparable studies, of course, have been done in other cities, notably Chicago, Dallas, and Atlanta. But those were generally done by city government staffers or by hired consultants. "Never before have we seen this kind of volunteer citizen participation," Shostak says, "and *sustained* citizen participation." Its effects over the next few decades on Philadelphia-area life should be interesting to watch. The 300th anniversary celebration of which the study is a part is called "Century IV" — a forward-looking title that naturally appeals to an applied futurist like Art Shostak.

Summary

Urban communities can exist only when there is a group of people to grow and process food for the urbanites. A degree of social organization is also necessary to transform overcrowded people into a social group that behaves in an orderly and predictable manner. The first urban communities developed approximately 10,000 years ago during the horticultural era. This development was possible because of increased food production and the creation of regular surpluses. Several thousand years later, technological advances — the plow, the use of animals, counting, and writing — and the increasing complexity of social and political organization enabled cities to grow to unprecedented sizes. The fall of Rome in the fifth century A.D. marked the beginning of a precipitous decline in city size and complexity that lasted for nearly six hundred years. Urban communities did not begin to grow substantially again until the late eighteenth century with the dawn of the Industrial Age. Urban populations increased dramatically, and within a few decades more people lived in cities than in rural areas. In the United States, this population shift took place between 1860 and 1920.

Today, three-quarters of our population live in urban areas, which have increased in size as well as in number. The rapid industrial and population growth in large cities during the early part of this century caused people and industry to move from central cities to the sparsely populated areas outside of them. This process resulted in the modern metropolis. A Standard Metropolitan Statistical Area (SMSA) is a county or a group of counties with a large central city, a dense population, and complex social and economic interrelationships among the people and localities. A megalopolis results from the overlap of two or more metropolitan areas. Since the mid-1970s, nonmetropolitan areas have been growing at a faster rate than metropolitan areas.

Urban ecology is the study of the spatial configurations of communities and their effects on social life. Three models of spatial growth — the concentric zone, the sector zone, and the multiple nuclei zone models — have been used to describe structural changes in the urban environment.

Cities and suburbs, in contrast to popular stereotypes, have quite diverse populations. Early sociologists believed that city living was unhealthy and encouraged family breakdown, violence, and depersonalization. Recent research, however, shows that a variety of people and lifestyles are found in the city. A number of people prefer the city because of its social and economic advantages. Suburban life is also quite diverse, and sub-

urbanites do not differ in lifestyle or values from city residents with similar demographic and social characteristics.

Our cities face a number of problems today, notably poverty and unemployment, crime, and inadequate schools. Attempts to remedy these problems are not likely to succeed without a considerable influx of money and the creation of social and economic opportunities. The downtown areas of many cities are being revitalized, and a number of residental neighborhoods are being given a new appearance as a result of urban renewal, urban recovery, and urban homesteading projects. The field of urban planning may play an important role in the future of our cities and can have a significant impact on the quality of urban social and cultural life if it is sensitive to the needs and values of different groups of city residents.

Key Terms

community
concentration
concentric zone model
conversion effect
cosmopolites
deconcentration
ecological specialization
ethnic villagers
folk society
Gemeinschaft
gentrification
Gesellschaft
ghetto
greenbelt
horticulture
megalopolis
multiple nuclei model
sector model
slums
Standard Metropolitan Statistical Area
suburbs

succession
urban ecology
urban homesteading
urbanization

Suggested Readings

Abrahamson, Mark. **Urban Sociology, 2nd ed.** *Englewood Cliffs, N.J.: Prentice-Hall, 1980.* An introduction to urban sociology.

Banfield, Edward. **The Unheavenly City Revisited.** *Boston: Little, Brown, 1974.* This controversial book examines the problems of American cities. The author contends that the sort of programs undertaken in the last decade will not solve these problems.

Clark, Kenneth. **Dark Ghetto.** *New York: Harper & Row, 1965.* An anaylsis of the problems of the ghetto in relation to the educational, political, religious, and economic institutions of our society.

Glaab, Charles and Theodore Brown. **The History of Urban America.** *New York: Macmillan, 1967.* An overview of the development and growth of American cities from colonial times to the present, this book discusses some of the major problems that have been encountered and how they have been approached.

Hawley, Amos. **Urban Society.** *New York: Ronald Press, 1971.* An analysis of the structural and demographic forces that influence the city. The author takes an urban ecological approach.

Jacobs, Jane. **The Death and Life of Great American Cities.** *New York: Random House, 1961.* An innovative analysis of why urban decay is occurring, and why urban renewal is failing. The author criticizes traditional theories of urban planning.

Karp, David A., Gregory P. Stone, and William C. Yoels. **Being Urban: A Social Psychological View of City Life.** *Lexington, Mass.: D. C. Heath, 1977.* A look at some neglected aspects of the urban scene from a symbolic interaction perspective.

Liebow, Elliot. **Tally's Corner.** *Boston: Little, Brown, 1967.* A descriptive study of black men in the inner city of Washington, D.C. and how they adjust to urban life.

Lottman, Herbert. **How Cities Are Saved.** *New York: Universe Books, 1976.* An analysis of the sources of the present urban crises and the author's prescription for solving them.

Mumford, Lewis. **The City in History.** *New York: Harcourt Brace Jovanovich, 1961.* An analysis of the conditions that led to the development of Western cities. The author traces the history of a number of urban problems.

Palen, J. John. **City Scenes: Problems and Prospects, 2nd ed.** *Boston: Little, Brown, 1981.* An integrated collection of provocative essays on urban problems and issues.

Walton, John and Donald E. Carns (eds.). **Cities in Change: Studies on the Urban Condition.** *Boston: Allyn & Bacon, 1973.* An interesting collection of articles on topics concerning the urban environment: lifestyles, politics, structural change, and class relationships.

Wirth, Louis. **"Urbanism as a Way of Life,"** **American Journal of Sociology.** *44 July 1938:1–24.* This article outlines the major ideas of one of the early American theorists about urban life.

Chapter 20
The Nature of Social Change

When society requires to be rebuilt, there is no use in attempting to rebuild it on the old plans.

— John Stuart Mill

In our rapidly changing society, sociology is largely the study of *social change,* which we have discussed throughout the text. This chapter is devoted to a discussion of the approaches that are used to understand social change, with an emphasis on changes in social structures and social institutions.

Sociologists have tried to answer three basic questions about social change. The earlier sociologists wanted to know whether social change was good or bad. As societies change, do they get better or do they deteriorate? Writing at the beginning of the industrial revolution, they saw their traditional family-oriented society vanish and watched it being replaced by urbanization and factory work.

Today, we are more likely to accept social change, but we are still interested in the reasons for it. Thus the second basic question is: What causes the change? And, like the early sociologists, we are still concerned with the third question: What happens to the people in a society when their society changes?

Theories of Social Change

The Evolutionary
Theory of Change

During more optimistic periods of our history, social change was regarded as *progress.* When society changed, it was assumed to be getting better. Herbert Spencer, a classic evolutionary theorist, lived in England at a time when Great Britain was a powerful, progressive nation. As discussed in Chapter 2, he believed that societies evolved from the simple and primitive to the more complex and advanced, just as animal life progressed from the simplest one-celled organisms to the most complex animal, the human being. He believed that Great Britain was the most advanced of societies and that eventually all nations on earth would evolve to the level of his society. Spencer believed that as a society grows, the functions of its members will become more specialized and coordinated into the larger system, just as when animals increase in size, they develop millions of body cells to serve specific complex functions, all of which are interrelated.

Spencer was very influential for many years, especially in the United States where growth was equated with progress. It was assumed that growth would unquestionably lead to a better society and that a lack of growth would lead to deterioration.

Evolutionary theory is less popular today. Growth may create social problems rather than social progress, and Spencer's optimistic theory is regarded with some skepticism. Conflict theorists are among those who do not believe in the continuous evolution of progress.

Conflict Theory of Social Change

Conflict theorists are in many ways as optimistic as evolutionary theorists, but they do not assume that societies smoothly evolve to higher levels. Instead, they believe that conflict is necessary and that conflicting groups must struggle to ensure progress (Coser, 1956). They contend that societies progress to a higher order only if oppressed groups improve their lot.

Karl Marx was a conflict theorist who predicted the revolt of the masses under capitalist economic systems, but Marx was by no means a pessimist. He saw the upcoming conflict as a stage of development that would lead to a higher order. Although social change was not synonymous with social progress, progress could eventually be hoped for. Marx was very optimistic compared with some cyclical theorists of his own day and of ours.

Cyclical Theories of Change

The most pessimistic cyclical theorists think that decay is inevitable. One such theorist was the historian Oswald Spengler, who believed that civilizations go through a *cyclical change* similar to that of humans. According to Spengler (1918), every society is born, matures, decays, and eventually dies. The Roman Empire rose to power and then gradually collapsed, just as the British Empire grew strong and then deteriorated. Spengler contended that social change may take the form of progress or of decay but that no society lives forever.

Most sociologists believe this view is too rigid and that although societies may have cycles of change, the cycles are not preordained. Pitirim Sorokin (1889–1968), a Russian social theorist who lived through the Russian Revolution of 1917, did not equate change with progress, but neither did he believe that all societies are inevitably destined to decay. He noted, rather, that societies go through various stages. At different stages, he suggested, they emphasize religious beliefs, scientific beliefs, or the pleasures of art, music and the beauty of nature, which contribute to sense experiences. They shift from one cycle to another, moving first in one direction, then in another as the needs of the society demand. The fact that a society is changing does not necessarily mean that it is progressing or decaying; change may simply be change. Sorokin is still respected for these ideas and has greatly influenced the attempts of structural-functionalists to explain social change.

Structural Functionalism and Social Change

As you know, structural-functionalists believe that society, like the human body, is a balanced system of institutions, each of which serves a function in maintaining society. When events outside or inside the society disrupt the equilibrium, social institutions make adjustments to re-

The Roman Empire was once powerful and wealthy. Many people believe that wealthy nations inevitably decline because they spend their wealth and energy in frivolous ways, on extravagant parties, meals, and entertainments. Such an explanation, however, is too simple a theory to explain social change.

store stability. An influx of immigrants, a natural disaster, a famine, or a war may disrupt the social order and force the social institutions to make adjustments. Like Sorokin, the structural-functionalists do not necessarily consider social change per se to be good or bad as long as a society maintains equilibrium.

The term *cultural lag* is often used to describe the state of disequilibrium. When an event such as an increase in population or a depletion of natural resources causes a strain in a society, it takes some time for the society to understand the strain and alter its values and institutions to adapt to the change. Just as the human body must adjust its functioning to adapt to changes, societies adjust to maintain and restore themselves.

Social Change Theory: A Synthesis

Few theorists today are so optimistic that they believe societies inevitably improve, and few are so pessimistic that they believe societies inevitably decay. Most integrate the ideas of Sorokin, the structural functionalists, and the conflict theorists. Societies do change, but the changes are not necessarily good or bad. Societies attempt to remain stable, and although a stable one is usually better than a chaotic one, stability sometimes incurs harsh conditions, injustice, and oppression. When this happens, conflict will arise and society will be forced to change, perhaps for the better.

Change and stability, then, are processes that

can take place simultaneously in any society. At any given time, one or the other will dominate, depending on the society's needs, and although change is inevitable, it is often beneficial.

What Causes Social Change?

Sociologists believe that social systems change when powerful internal or external forces influence them such that the previous social order can no longer be maintained, but societies are complex, interdependent systems of values, norms, and institutions. They are often amazingly resistant to change and rarely transformed by the ideas or behavior of a single person, yet when a major change does occur, it influences the entire society and each social institution must adapt to the new order.

Sociologists have determined that *ecological changes* — variations in the relationship between population and geography — are the most powerful sources of social change, although social innovations and conflicts may also cause major changes in societies.

Population, Geography, and Ecology

A *population change* can bring dramatic social changes. The decreasing death rate over the past two hundred years, for example, has caused an enormous increase in the size of the population. The average age of the population has also increased. While the size of the population has grown, the birth rate has been decreasing, which means that there are relatively few children in many societies and that social programs will be oriented more toward the older population than toward children.

Societies that were once sparsely populated are now crowded, so people have been migrating to new areas with more space. When they migrate, they bring with them the ideas and customs of their old culture, which are often new to the society they enter. The migrants not only increase the size of the population but also influence it culturally. The spread of one culture to another as populations migrate is termed *cultural diffusion*.

A *geographic change* may also cause migrations. In the preceding chapter, we noted that great waves of Asians migrated to the Middle East and Europe long before written history began. It is assumed that this migration was largely the result of changes in the Asian climate, perhaps increasing cold weather or severe droughts. Geographic changes have been a major source of social change: volcanic eruptions ended the society at Pompeii, an earthquake and fire destroyed San Francisco in 1906, and the drought in the southern United States during the 1930s caused migrations to Southern California. These migrations were movingly portrayed by John Steinbeck in *The Grapes of Wrath*.

Natural disasters can cause both environmental and social changes. Although small fires and floods may not affect the larger society, they have a great impact on the local community. People caught in a natural disaster may be left without friends, relatives, or resources. They may have to abandon their community or completely rebuild it.

Today, many geographic changes and natural disasters are induced by the inhabitants of a region — for example, the size of the population using a geographic area and the way it uses natural resources. An *ecological change* of this sort is now a far greater source of social change than migrations or natural disasters.

The growing population of the United States has dramatically changed this country's geography. Consider, for example, the history of the small town of Williamsport, Pennsylvania (Humphrey and Buttel, 1982). In the mid-nineteenth century, the increasing population of the East Coast needed lumber for houses, and the Susquehanna Boom Company began to harvest timber in Williamsport, which was located in a wilderness re-

Destruction of a city changes the lives of its people, whether the destruction is caused by a natural disaster or a man-made disaster. These photos show the results of an earthquake in Algeria and war in Lebanon, where a soldier stands guard over the ruins. Such disasters would have to be extremely widespread to change the nature of the larger society.

gion of the Appalachian mountains on the west branch of the Susquehanna River. The company built a boom one-quarter mile wide and seven miles long in the middle of the river to hold lumber for transport to eastern cities. Thirty-five mills were started, and thousands of immigrants came to the area to find work. The mill owners got wealthy, but the workers, who labored fourteen hours a day for very poor pay, were discontented. Union leaders entered the area, strikes broke out, and the state militia was called in to subdue the strikers. Williamsport became a violent town. Although the timber was soon cleared from the mountains, the branches left behind made excellent tinder, and when lightning struck the mountains, they burned. When it rained on the bare mountains, the soil washed away and ruined the area for agriculture. The region could no longer support a large population, and people began to move out at the end of the century.

The resources of Williamsport attracted its population, but the ecological relationships between the population and the environment led to dramatic social changes. The population grew stratified and violent as resources were used up, and the society changed again when the resources were depleted. The area has continued ever since to decline in population.

A more recent ecological disaster, described by Kai Erikson (1976), took place at Buffalo Creek in West Virginia. Waste material from mining operations had been piled on a mountainside, and behind it the mining company had created a vast pond of waste water, which accumulated from mining operations. The heap of slag collapsed, and the slag and water, churned together, crashed down the side of the mountain in a twenty-foot wave. As Erikson describes it,

> It did not crush the village into mounds of rubble, but carried everything away with it — houses, cars, trailers, a church whose white spire had pointed to the slag pile for years — and scraped the ground as cleanly as if a thousand bulldozers had been at work. (p. 29)

Those who survived were left without family, friends, or community; they were dazed, angered, isolated, and apathetic. Those who could created new lives; their old lives had been destroyed forever.

Discoveries and Inventions

Discoveries and *inventions* have caused far-reaching changes in modern societies, which are becoming increasingly technological. Discoveries and inventions are called *innovations,* changes that alter society. Discovery is the act of finding something that has always existed but that no one previously knew about. The discovery of America led to the great migrations from Europe and the creation of a new country. The discovery of gold and other scarce resources in the West led Americans to continue their migration. Infection is no longer a leading cause of death since the discovery of penicillin. The discovery of oil today leads to great social changes in the areas where it is found.

An invention is a device constructed by putting two or more things together in a new way. Henry Ford invented the automobile by putting together materials already known using knowledge that was already available. This particular invention has caused widespread social change.

The Automobile and Social Change

The automobile has brought about a number of social changes and has altered individual lifestyles. Because the automobile was developed hand-in-hand with the assembly line, it changed the nature of work. Since assembly lines were more economical when large quantities were produced, companies had to create public demand — that is, socialize people into buying their automobiles.

The automobile has also affected international relationships because it requires oil, and our demand for oil has far outstripped the supply available within the United States. As our discussion will show, each change creates other changes, and today our society is very different from what it was at the turn of the century.

The Automobile and Social Control

When cars became common in the 1920s, the nature of the American family began to change rapidly. Cars provided people with a measure of privacy and anonymity never before possible and removed them from the social control of the community. Young people could escape the watchful eyes of family and community by leaving town and pursuing recreation in other towns. Dating became commonplace and beyond the control of the family. There was less emphasis on proper introductions to suitable people and evenings spent chaperoned by family members. As a result, there was a dramatic increase in premarital sex, and the twenties marked the first major sexual revolution in this country.

Adults likewise began to travel more and change their lifestyles. While previously the church had been the center of both religious and social life for many people, adults with automobiles began to take Sunday drives instead of going to church, and they were able to travel to more distant places for recreation. They were also free to live a distance from work if they had a car for transportation. Where once it had been considered suspect for a family to live outside of town — people would question what suspicious kind of activity a family might pursue in a remote area — the automobile made it possible for families to work in town while living in the country. The move to the country grew rapidly and removed people further from the watchful eyes of neighbors and the social control small towns provided.

(Above) courtesy, Museum of Fine Arts, Boston

Scenes of Tremont Street in Boston show changes since 1843, when families with children and dogs lived in the city and congregated in the street. Now families live in the suburbs and bring their cars to the city where office buildings have replaced homes.

The Assembly Line and the Nature of Work

An automobile assembly line is a noisy, exhausting, tedious place to work. To produce cars efficiently, manufacturers have tried to make assembly lines as fast and as automatic as possible. The more efficiently and predictably space, time, and workers are used, the more economically automobiles can be produced.

One assembly plant, built at Lordstown by General Motors in 1970, was designed to provide three remarkable improvements in efficiency (Rothschild, 1976). First, the assembly line made use of the most modern automated equipment to perform some routine tasks. Robots were used to weld steel parts together and worked far more rapidly than humans. Second, the assembly-line process was made more efficient through computers, which carefully analyzed every stage in the assembly-line process. Each step was measured to the second, every second of time was planned, and every movement of the workers was timed. The assembly line itself moved up and down so that workers did not have to reach up or bend down, which increased the workers' speed because they did not need time to move. The third innovation was computer control of the work process. Computers controlled the assembly line, scanned the work area, detected problems instantly, and otherwise supervised the work.

This great efficiency in assembly-line production made the job intolerable for workers. They no longer worked in teams for the satisfaction of producing a product. Instead, they worked for computers, which controlled their every move and reported every move not prescribed. If workers saw a problem on the assembly line such as a tool not functioning properly or a machine spraying paint in the wrong direction, they reported it to the computer, not to a human boss. Many employees felt that they too were expected to perform like robots.

Creating Demand

Mass production becomes more economical as larger quantities of goods are produced. Cars are made more cheaply when constructed in large numbers, which increases the industry's profit margin. Once produced, of course, the cars must be sold — a market must be found for them.

General Motors has long been in the business of creating a market for its automobile products. By the 1920s, most people who wanted and could afford a car had bought one, and General Motors needed new markets (Snell, 1976), so they began to produce buses. They bought interurban electric railways and urban trolley systems, dismantled them, and replaced them with buses. By 1949, General Motors, working with companies such as Greyhound, Standard Oil of California, and Firestone Tire, had replaced more than one hundred electric transit systems with buses.

Buses were slow, inefficient, dirty, and expensive to operate. People did not enjoy riding in them, and, furthermore, they were bombarded with advertisements encouraging them to buy cars not just as a means of transportation but as a status symbol. They turned, therefore, from using public transportation and bought automobiles. In the meantime, the automotive industry lobbied to have the federal interstate highway system constructed. Between 1945 and 1970, state and local governments spent $156 billion to build hundreds of thousands of miles of roads. Only 16 miles of subway were built during the same period. Thus the automobile became a necessity as a means of transportation, and Americans bought them in ever-increasing numbers. As a result, the auto business became the major U.S. industry.

The Automobile and the Environment

The heavy use of automobiles and diesel buses causes pollution, and smog from automobile emissions has become a serious problem in American cities. The bad urban air burns the eyes, damages lung tissues, and increases the levels of lead and other poisons in the human body and in food products. It has been estimated that 500 Los Angeles residents die every year of diseases caused by auto-produced smog (Snell, 1976). It is not known how many deaths occur nationally because of pollution.

The automobile has also vastly increased our need for oil. The United States, even though it has huge supplies of oil, uses so much that it must import more.

Oil is the major pollutant of the sea (Mostert, 1976), and huge tankers routinely dump oil into the sea. It is not known how much oil tankers dump, but the most conservative estimate is that the total is well over a million tons a year. When oil leaks, spills, or is purposely dumped from tankers, it poisons, smothers, burns, or coats sea plants and animals and kills them. The oceans of the world from the Arctic to the Antarctic are slowly being covered with oil slicks, and to date there is no effective way to clean them up.

In addition to the oil dumped during routine operations, hundreds of accidents involving tankers take place at sea each year, and they cause far more serious problems than dumping. In one accident, in May of 1970, a Norwegian tanker carrying a full cargo of oil ran aground and burst into flames off the Spanish coast. The oil burned with such intensity that the flames started a fire storm. Winds created by the heat reached hurricane force, lifted the oil into the air, and carried it to high altitudes. A few days later the oil rained down on coastal farmlands as a fine mist, damaging homes, gardens, crops, and pastures. Grazing cattle died from eating the oil-covered grasses. Fortunately, much of the oil fell in uninhabited areas, and the ship involved was only a small tanker. An accident of this type would be much worse if it involved a larger ship near a populated area.

Our need for oil as a fuel is so great that the

THE WALL STREET JOURNAL

"The program, 'Alternative Energy Sources' will not be shown tonight, thanks to a grant from a major oil company."

United States is willing to go to war to protect its supply from foreign oil fields. Since World War II, this country has built up a vast military force, and the government has vowed to use it to protect oil-producing nations that sell to the United States. It has also sold billions of dollars' worth of arms to these nations, including Iran under the Shah and Saudi Arabia.

Thus we see that the United States has become so economically dependent on the automobile and on oil that it is willing to pollute land and sea, further the arms race, and threaten to go to war to prevent economic disaster. It is obvious that these factors have serious sociological consequences.

Other Energy Sources

Because the automobile uses such great quantities of oil, it is not available for other uses, and new sources of fuel must be found to heat our homes and run our industries. Some people believe that nuclear power should be used to solve our energy problems. Others do not, and its advantages and disadvantages have been hotly debated. The debate centers around two basic problems.

The first problem is the current safety of nuclear energy plants. Those who believe they are safe argue that although a nuclear reactor accident could be dangerous, the probability of an accident is very small. A person is more likely to die from an earthquake, hurricane, tornado, or from being hit by a meteorite than as a result of a nuclear accident, proponents contend. Even if an accident did happen, it would be contained within the power plant. In the very unlikely case that the accident was not contained and radioactive steam did escape, there would be enough warning to evacuate the population and minimize deaths and illnesses.

Those who believe that nuclear reactors are unsafe argue that the chance of an accident is very great and cite the many accidents that have already taken place in power plants. They also argue that an accident could have catastrophic consequences. A reactor not operating normally could become so hot that it would explode, filling the air with enormous quantities of radioactive dust that would rain down on large areas as it was carried by the wind. Critics believe that both the number of immediate deaths and the illnesses leading to cancer and premature death would be enormous.

The second problem is the disposal of nuclear waste. Reactors create waste that remains dangerous to human life for hundreds of years, and everyone agrees that there is no good way to dispose of it. Proponents argue that a way will be found to dispose of the wastes; opponents say that we may not find a way. If we don't, we may kill or injure the next generation of the earth's population.

The Uses of Sociology

Although we do not usually think of the disposal of nuclear waste as related to the invention of the automobile, the mass production of cars created the need to sell them, which in turn gave rise to fuel and pollution problems that technology has not been able to solve. Sociologists who study society from a historical perspective, observing the relationship between increasing automobile use and today's energy problems, are likely to be frustrated by our practice of solving problems as they arise rather than trying to find long-range solutions. These solutions might require better technology — to control auto emissions, clean up oil spills, or dispose of nuclear wastes — but more effective solutions can be developed if we understand the social basis of the problems and change our system of transportation.

Our transportation problems are caused in part by a cultural lag in our awareness of the need for safe public transportation. Social planning could help us change our social systems and improve the situation. Those who have a vested interest in our current system might resist change, which would create a certain amount of conflict, but such conflict might be beneficial to society. Sociologists, by helping us understand social change, can help us direct it.

Modernization in Underdeveloped Nations

Evolutionary theorists tend to assume that today's underdeveloped nations in Africa, South America, and other areas that do not have modern industry, such as is found in Europe and North America, will pass through the same stages that industrialized nations passed through in their quest for *modernization*. Eventually, they believe, these preindustrial countries will emerge as urban societies with lower birth rates, more goods and services, better nutrition and health care, improved housing, and a share of some of the luxuries enjoyed in industrial nations.

A closer comparison, however, suggests that contemporary nations may not be able to take the same course as those that are already industrialized. When the United States developed into an industrial society, it had a vast supply of natural resources, including land, coal, iron, and an unlimited supply of immigrants to serve as a work force. It also had little competition.

The Third World, however, lacks many resources. Tropical forests and deserts cannot easily be developed to produce grain. Oil, coal, iron, and lumber are unavailable in many countries, and even when resources are available, industries just developing have to sell their goods in a highly competitive world market. These countries must therefore be able to produce goods at lower prices than those offered by nations rich in resources and experienced through years of product development.

Even when a newly developing nation can produce goods that are competitive on the market, they may find markets closed to them. Textiles and clothing, for example, can be produced very inexpensively in many underdeveloped nations because they have many workers who will work for extremely low wages. As a result, their clothing is cheaper than any produced in the United States. In an effort to protect its own industry, however, the United States limits the amount of foreign clothing that can be imported.

The assumption that underdeveloped nations will develop into industrial nations is overly optimistic. Given the very different circumstances existing today, the Third World will probably have a different pattern of development.

Social Change and the Individual

How does social change affect the individual? This question is a major concern of all sociologists.

Most early sociologists believed that industrial society alienates individuals from their work and from one another. Durkheim was one of the few who believed that complex industrial societies would have a positive effect on human relationships. Noting that peasants were moving to European cities in large numbers, he recognized that this changed the nature of their labor. Peasants had been self-sufficient and performed all of the work necessary to meet their personal needs, while in the city, work was specialized and workers were not self-sufficient. Each person specialized in a particular product and then traded that product for money to meet personal needs. Thus the cobbler sold shoes and bought food and clothing. In *The Division of Labor* (1893), Durkheim endorsed the move toward specialization, arguing that this interdependence would create a more integrated society.

Marx, on the other hand, was concerned that the move from agrarian to industrial societies would alienate people from their work. The goods produced would be owned by the factory owner, not the worker. Marx believed this arrangement was so unfair that it would not survive. Workers would rebel and a more equitable system of work would be developed.

Tönnies (1887), whose theories we discussed in Chapter 19, was also concerned that interpersonal relationships would suffer in industrial society. Peasant society, he contended, was characterized by Gemeinschaft relationships in which people knew one another totally, while in urban society they would be strangers. Those who worked together would know nothing about their coworkers' families or religious or political views, for example. Tönnies referred to these impersonal relationships as Gesellschaft.

Weber was concerned about the increasing rationalization of society. The traditional beliefs of the family were rapidly disappearing, and in Weber's day society was becoming more bureaucratic. Decisions were no longer being based on traditional family concerns. The system in which people performed tasks according to their capabilities and were taken care of when they were unable to be productive gave way to one in which decisions about employment were made on the basis of the employer's needs. Employees were hired or fired regardless of their own needs for work, income, or self-respect.

Sociologists realize that modern socialization encourages individuals to behave in a fashion compatible with industrial society. In the nineteenth century, when frontiers were being conquered and industries were being built, people were encouraged to be highly innovative, and even those who were the most ruthless were needed to tame the frontier and build the new industries. Also, people on the frontier far from neighbors did not have to worry about being popular, getting along with others, cooperating, or making a good impression. They did, however, need the skill and wit to stay alive.

The same skills were needed in the business world. Businesses were small, and whether one owned a store or began a small factory, survival depended on one's own skill and hard work. The most successful industrial leaders of the nineteenth century, the so-called robber barons, were noted for their extreme ruthlessness.

Today, the nature of work has changed dramatically. Most people work in corporations with many other individuals. In a large corporation, a competitive person who lives by skill and wit and is concerned exclusively with his or her own survival makes many enemies and can create chaos rather than cooperation.

The type of manager corporations seek today, according to Maccoby (1977), is the *gamesman*, the person who is highly competitive and innovative but who prefers to function as the leader of a team. The gamesman thus occupies a position similar to that of a quarterback on a football team. Interestingly, football surpassed baseball as the most popular American sport in the mid-1960s. The more individualistic sport of baseball has given way to a type of sport requiring a team effort and cooperation. It seems that changes in the way we spend our leisure correspond to changes in the types of managers sought in the job market.

Television and the other mass media have also affected individual lifestyles. The media encourage us to buy cosmetics and designer clothes, and we watch programs depicting middle-class lifestyles. We listen to news broadcasts that tell us what is important in the world. As a result of the mass media, there are probably fewer eccentric individualists in society — most of us have learned the ideal of the middle-class lifestyle.

The Future

Futurists, people who attempt to describe what the future will be like, range from the most pessimistic doomsayers to the greatest optimists. The doomsayers predict an economic depression far worse than the depression of the 1930s. The wisest investment, they say, is to buy a piece of land in a very remote part of the country, build a substantial shelter that will be well hidden from the hordes of the poor and starving who will be roaming the countryside when the economy collapses, and bury near the shelter a supply of dehydrated food, guns, and other basic equipment needed to survive alone in the wilderness.

The optimists predict an end to poverty and drudgery and believe that human innovation will solve our problems. Alvin Toffler (1981), in his book *The Third Wave,* suggests that computers may make a more individualistic society possible. People will be able to remain at home and earn their livings by telecommunications, creating for themselves and their children a more unique and creative individual lifestyle.

Sociologists are more hesitant to make predictions. One realistic method of determining what the future will be like is to analyze the possibilities and problems that it might hold and use social planning to strive for future goals and avoid future disasters.

Writers and filmmakers have often fantasized about the future. Woody Allen's movie Sleeper *offered a satirical view of the future, in which elements of present-day society exist side by side with futuristic elements. No one really can predict the future, but most likely it will fall somewhere between the visions of the pessimists and those of the optimists.*

Etzioni (1980) followed this course in making his predictions. He argues that society should make choices and plan for a future that will provide a satisfactory lifestyle to its members. Our economy is currently based on the consumption of vast amounts of goods, and we are using up our natural and economic resources. Meanwhile, our factories, transportation systems, roads, railroads, and bridges are deteriorating rapidly. We must choose either to continue to spend money on goods or to spend hundreds of billions of dollars to modernize our factories and build an efficient transportation system. This rebuilding would reduce the hazards of pollution and improve the quality of life for all, but it might mean we would have to cut back on our consumption of goods.

Etzioni used the typical approach of sociologists in his study of social change, which is to try to understand the social system. Our social system is based on a profit-oriented economy, and we manufacture products that can be sold for a profit. Our system functions to support a cycle of production and consumption, but it does not support modernization of factories or an efficient use of resources unless such actions provide a profit. By understanding that our system now functions only when profits are made, it is possible to predict what will happen if we continue to function as we have in the past. We will use up all our resources. Yet innovations can be made, institutions can be changed, and values and goals can be altered: a society can change its course and move in a new direction. We cannot today optimistically assume that progress will inevitably be made and that we do not have to plan to reach our goals. Neither is there reason to be so pessimistic that we resign ourselves to becoming victims of a social system in decline. Furthermore, we cannot blithely assume that society will run its course from good times to bad and then bounce back to good times again; we could in the meantime destroy all life on earth. By understanding how soci-

SOCIOLOGISTS AT WORK
Planning and Social Change

Cynthia Cook is a staff sociologist with the World Bank. She came to that position with a varied background that includes an advanced degree in sociology.

How did Cynthia Cook get where she is today? "I was turned on to the problems of developing countries by an outstanding high school social science teacher," she explains. "As an undergraduate, I majored in Latin American studies with a disciplinary focus on history. After graduation I received a Fulbright fellowship to study "intellectual history" in Chile for a year. In the course of this project, I became interested in the current curriculum reform as a vehicle for implementing the social change objectives of the Christian Democratic government. I returned to Harvard for a master's degree in teaching social science, a program that allowed me to pursue my interdisciplinary interests while providing a marketable credential.

"At about this time, I married an engineer/economist who was also interested in the problems of development. Together we joined a U.S.-based planning firm that does development work both in the U.S. and overseas. For several years I worked as a paraprofessional for this firm, gaining valuable experience in the analytic methods used as well as in the more practical aspects of the consulting business. I also did research for other organizations on a free-lance basis.

"With this experience, I felt well qualified to assume professional level responsibilities. However, it became clear to me that one could not make this leap without acquiring some kind of additional credential. Thus, in 1977 I took a second master's in the field of sociology and became a practitioner of applied social change. I worked on environmental impact analysis, social analysis of development projects, and program evaluation for about five years and had assumed major management responsibilities for my firm before receiving a job offer from the World Bank.

"There are relatively few sociologists on the Bank Staff, and each has a sectoral specialty. Mine is in rural infrastructure. I do basically three things: research coordination (our research program is carried out by institutions in developing countries); policy analysis of Bank experience and that of other assistance agencies; and operational support to the regions. This offers me occasional opportunities to travel and to conduct field work.

"The sociology courses that have proved most helpful to me in my work are those in modernization and social change, urban and rural sociology, and methods of social research. Work on organizations has proved especially helpful as we try to address the problems of building local institutions capable of designing and implementing development projects."

eties function, we can make choices, alter our social institutions, and develop lifestyles that will reduce conflict, avoid ecological devastation, and support human life in the ever-increasing numbers that seem to be inevitable. We can plan to use our resources wisely. The authors hope that this introduction to the study of sociology has sparked your own sociological imagination so that you can think about "the good life" in terms of social as well as individual accomplishments.

Summary

Society is changing so rapidly that sociologists must always consider the influence of social change. Evolutionary theory has the optimistic view that change is progress, that growth is always good, and that stagnation leads to decay.

Conflict theorists are also optimistic about social change, but they believe that conflict will occasionally arise to correct adverse social developments. The outcome of such conflict, they say, will be better social systems.

Cyclical theories can be very pessimistic. They assume that societies grow, reach a peak, and then inevitably decay. Some cyclical theories, however, do not assume that change is always for the better or the worse. Societies move back and forth, they contend, emphasizing first one value, then another as the needs of the society demand.

Structural functionalists have been concerned primarily with stability, but they recognize that society changes occasionally. Often, a change that affects one social institution will be followed by a cultural lag, a disruption in the functioning of society until other institutions adjust to the change.

Most sociologists agree that society is orderly and that social institutions function to maintain order. They also agree that conflicts may arise when the existing social order causes hardship for the members of a society but that such conflicts can be beneficial.

Some major causes of social change and conflict are population changes, geographic changes, changes in the ecology, discoveries, and inventions. Population changes that have altered modern society include a decrease in the death rate, which has caused a population explosion and increased the number of older people; a decrease in the birth rate, which has decreased the number of young people; and migration, which has brought different cultures into contact with one another, spreading the ideas of one culture to another — we call this overlapping cultural diffusion.

Geographic changes such as droughts or increasing cold weather may cause people to migrate. Natural disasters such as floods, tornados, hurricanes, or fires can also precipitate sudden changes in the societies they affect. Today, many geographic changes are caused by the human population and its activities. Ecology is the study of the relationship between the population and the environment. Populations that strip an area of natural resources must often undergo dramatic social changes.

Discoveries and inventions, which are human innovations, also change society. The discovery of resources not previously known and inventions that used resources in new ways brought about the industrial revolution. The invention of the automobile changed American lifestyles, relationships to family and community, the nature of work, the size of corporations, the use of fuels, ecology, and our willingness to go to war. Even with the diffusion of modern technology, it is unlikely that today's Third World nations will develop as industrial nations did because they lack important natural resources and must compete with the well-established industries of the industrial nations.

Changes in modern industry have changed the nature of human relationships. From the peasant's concern for family and community we moved to a period of competitive individualism, and we are now moving into an era of competitive team play. In the future, it is hoped that we will be able to plan innovations that will improve our ecology and our ways of relating to one another.

Key Terms

cultural diffusion
cyclical change
discoveries
ecological change
gamesman
geographic change

innovations
inventions
modernization
progress
population change
social change

Suggested Readings

Critchfield, Richard. **Villages.** *New York: Doubleday, 1981.* Advances in agriculture and contraceptive techniques have brought progress to some underdeveloped villages, but this book suggests further reforms to improve life in underdeveloped countries.

DiRenzo, Gordon J. **We, The People: American Character and Social Change.** *Westport, Conn.: Greenwood Press, 1977.* This collection of essays discusses how social changes affect the changing American character.

Erikson, Kai T. **Everything in Its Path: Destruction of Community in the Buffalo Creek Flood.** *New York: Simon & Schuster, 1976.* A moving story of what happened to the people in one community after a disaster.

Humphrey, Craig R. and Frederick R. Buttel. **Environment, Energy and Society.** *Belmont, Calif.: Wadsworth, 1982.* Two sociologists review the problems of environment and energy and discuss social changes needed to overcome them.

Ward, Barbara. **Progress for a Small Planet.** *New York: Norton, 1979.* This book optimistically argues that the world can progress and solve its present problems of pollution, nutrition, and economic inequality.

Wright, James D. and Peter Rossi. **Social Science and Natural Hazards.** *Cambridge, Mass.: Abt Books, 1981.* These authors, who studied natural disasters over a period of a decade, concluded that disasters do not cause social change.

The Promise

by C. Wright Mills

In this classic of sociological literature C. Wright Mills discusses "the promise and the task" of the sociological imagination: to guide us to an understanding of the life of the individual, the history of society, and the relations between the two.

Nowadays men often feel that their private lives are a series of traps. They sense that within their everyday worlds, they cannot overcome their troubles, and in this feeling, they are often quite correct: What ordinary men are directly aware of and what they try to do are bounded by the private orbits in which they live; their visions and their powers are limited to the close-up scenes of job, family, neighborhood; in other milieux, they move vicariously and remain spectators. And the more aware they become, however vaguely, of ambitions and of threats which transcend their immediate locales, the more trapped they seem to feel.

Underlying this sense of being trapped are seemingly impersonal changes in the very structure of continent-wide societies. The facts of contemporary history are also facts about the success and the failure of individual men and women. When a society is industrialized, a peasant becomes a worker; a feudal lord is liquidated or becomes a businessman. When classes rise or fall, a man is employed or unemployed; when the rate of investment goes up or down, a man takes new heart or goes broke. When wars happen, an insurance salesman becomes a rocket launcher; a store clerk, a radar man; a wife lives alone; a child grows up without a father. Neither the life of an individual nor the history of a society can be understood without understanding both.

Yet men do not usually define the troubles they endure in terms of historical change and institutional contradiction. The well-being they enjoy, they do not usually impute to the big ups and downs of the societies in which they live. Seldom aware of the intricate connection between the patterns of their own lives and the course of world history, ordinary men do not usually know what this connection means for the kinds of men they are becoming and for the kinds of history-making in which they might take part. They do not possess the quality of mind essential to grasp the interplay of man and society, of biography and history, of self and world. They cannot cope with their personal troubles in such ways as to control the structural transformations that usually lie behind them.

Surely it is no wonder. In what period have so many men been so totally exposed at so fast a pace to such earthquakes of change? That Americans have not known such catastrophic changes as have the men and women of other societies is due to historical facts that are now quickly becoming "merely history." The history that now affects every man is world history. Within this scene and this period, in the course of a single generation, one sixth of mankind is transformed from all that is feudal and backward into all that is modern, advanced, and fearful. Political colonies are freed; new and less visible forms of imperialism installed. Revolutions occur; men feel the intimate grip of new kinds of authority. Totalitarian societies rise, and are smashed to bits — or succeed fabulously. After two centuries of ascendancy, capitalism is shown up as only one way to make society into an industrial apparatus. After two centuries of hope, even formal democracy is restricted to a quite small portion of mankind. Everywhere in the underdeveloped world, ancient ways of life are broken up and vague expectations become urgent demands. Everywhere in the overdeveloped world, the means of authority and of violence become total in scope and bureaucratic in form. Humanity itself now lies before us, the super-nation at either pole concentrating its most co-ordinated and massive efforts upon the preparation of World War Three.

The very shaping of history now outpaces the ability of men to orient themselves in accordance with cherished values. And which values? Even when they do not panic, men often sense that older ways of feeling and thinking have collapsed and that newer beginnings are ambiguous to the point of moral stasis. Is it any wonder that ordinary men feel they cannot cope with the larger worlds with which they are so suddenly confronted? That they cannot understand the meaning of their epoch for their own lives? That — in defense of selfhood — they become morally insensible, trying to remain altogether private men? Is it any wonder that they come to be possessed by a sense of the trap?

It is not only information that they need — in this Age of Fact, information often dominates their attention and overwhelms their capacities to assimilate it. It is not only the skills of reason that they need — although their struggles to acquire these often exhaust their limited moral energy.

What they need, and what they feel they need, is a quality of mind that will help them to use information and to develop reason in order to achieve lucid summations of what is going on in the world and of what may be happening within

themselves. It is this quality, I am going to contend, that journalists and scholars, artists and publics, scientists and editors are coming to expect of what may be called the sociological imagination.

1

The sociological imagination enables its possessor to understand the larger historical scene in terms of its meaning for the inner life and the external career of a variety of individuals. It enables him to take into account how individuals, in the welter of their daily experience, often become falsely conscious of their social positions. Within that welter, the framework of modern society is sought, and within that framework the psychologies of a variety of men and women are formulated. By such means the personal uneasiness of individuals is focused upon explicit troubles and the indifference of publics is transformed into involvement with public issues.

The first fruit of this imagination — and the first lesson of the social science that embodies it — is the idea that the individual can understand his own experience and gauge his own fate only by locating himself within his period, that he can know his own chances in life only by becoming aware of those of all individuals in his circumstances. In many ways it is a terrible lesson; in many ways a magnificent one. We do not know the limits of man's capacities for supreme effort or willing degradation, for agony or glee, for pleasurable brutality or the sweetness of reason. But in our time we have come to know that the limits of "human nature" are frighteningly broad. We have come to know that every individual lives, from one generation to the next, in some society; that he lives out a biography, and that he lives it out within some historical sequence. By the fact of his living he contributes, however minutely, to the shaping of this society and to the course of its history, even as he is made by society and by its historical push and shove.

The sociological imagination enables us to

grasp history and biography and the relations between the two within society. That is its task and
its promise. To recognize this task and this promise is the mark of the classic social analyst. It is
characteristic of Herbert Spencer — turgid, poly-
syllabic, comprehensive; of E. A. Ross — graceful,
muckraking, upright; of Auguste Comte and
Emile Durkheim; of the intricate and subtle Karl
Mannheim. It is the quality of all that is intellectually excellent in Karl Marx; it is the clue to
Thorstein Veblen's brilliant and ironic insight, to
Joseph Schumpeter's many-sided constructions of
reality; it is the basis of the psychological sweep of
W. E. H. Lecky no less than of the profundity
and clarity of Max Weber. And it is the signal of
what is best in contemporary studies of man and
society.

No social study that does not come back to
the problems of biography, of history and of their
intersections within a society has completed its intellectual journey. Whatever the specific problems
of the classic social analysts, however limited or
however broad the features of social reality they
have examined, those who have been imaginatively aware of the promise of their work have
consistently asked three sorts of questions:

1. What is the structure of this particular society as a whole? What are its essential components, and how are they related to one another?
How does it differ from other varieties of social
order? Within it, what is the meaning of any particular feature for its continuance and for its
change?

2. Where does this society stand in human
history? What are the mechanics by which it is
changing? What is its place within and its meaning
for the development of humanity as a whole?
How does any particular feature we are examining
affect, and how is it affected by, the historical
period in which it moves? And this period —
what are its essential features? How does it differ
from other periods? What are its characteristic
ways of history-making?

3. What varieties of men and women now
prevail in this society and in this period? And
what varieties are coming to prevail? In what ways
are they selected and formed, liberated and re-
pressed, made sensitive and blunted? What kinds
of "human nature" are revealed in the conduct
and character we observe in this society in this
period? And what is the meaning for "human nature" of each and every feature of the society we
are examining?

Whether the point of interest is a great
power state or a minor literary mood, a family, a
prison, a creed — these are the kinds of questions
the best social analysts have asked. They are the
intellectual pivots of classic studies of man in society — and they are the questions inevitably raised
by any mind possessing the sociological imagination. For that imagination is the capacity to shift
from one perspective to another — from the political to the psychological; from examination of a
single family to comparative assessment of the national budgets of the world; from the theological
school to the military establishment; from considerations of an oil industry to studies of contemporary poetry. It is the capacity to range from the
most impersonal and remote transformations to
the most intimate features of the human self —
and to see the relations between the two. Back of
its use there is always the urge to know the social
and historical meaning of the individual in the society and in the period in which he has his quality
and his being.

That, in brief, is why it is by means of the
sociological imagination that men now hope to
grasp what is going on in the world, and to understand what is happening in themselves as minute
points of the intersections of biography and history within society. In large part, contemporary
man's self-conscious view of himself as at least an
outsider, if not a permanent stranger, rests upon
an absorbed realization of social relativity and of
the transformative power of history. The sociological imagination is the most fruitful form of

this self-consciousness. By its use men whose mentalities have swept only a series of limited orbits often come to feel as if suddenly awakened in a house with which they had only supposed themselves to be familiar. Correctly or incorrectly, they often come to feel that they can now provide themselves with adequate summations, cohesive assessments, comprehensive orientations. Older decisions that once appeared sound now seem to them products of a mind unaccountably dense. Their capacity for astonishment is made lively again. They acquire a new way of thinking, they experience a transvaluation of values: in a word, by their reflection and by their sensibility, they realize the cultural meaning of the social sciences.

2

Perhaps the most fruitful distinction with which the sociological imagination works is between "the personal troubles of milieu" and "the public issues of social structure." This distinction is an essential tool of the sociological imagination and a feature of all classic work in social science.

Troubles occur within the character of the individual and within the range of his immediate relations with others; they have to do with his self and with those limited areas of social life of which he is directly and personally aware. Accordingly, the statement and the resolution of troubles properly lie within the individual as a biographical entity and within the scope of his immediate milieu — the social setting that is directly open to his personal experience and to some extent his willful activity. A trouble is a private matter: values cherished by an individual are felt by him to be threatened.

Issues have to do with matters that transcend these local environments of the individual and the range of his inner life. They have to do with the organization of many such milieux into the institutions of an historical society as a whole, with the ways in which various milieux overlap and in-

terpenetrate to form the larger structure of social and historical life. An issue is a public matter: some value cherished by publics is felt to be threatened. Often there is a debate about what that value really is and about what it is that really threatens it. This debate is often without focus if only because it is the very nature of an issue, unlike even widespread trouble, that it cannot very well be defined in terms of the immediate and everyday environments of ordinary men. An issue, in fact, often involves a crisis in institutional arrangements, and often too it involves what Marxists call "contradictions" or "antagonisms."

In these terms, consider unemployment. When, in a city of 100,000, only one man is unemployed, that is his personal trouble, and for its relief we properly look to the character of the man, his skills, and his immediate opportunities. But when in a nation of 50 million employees, 15 million men are unemployed, that is an issue, and we may not hope to find its solution within the range of opportunities open to any one individual. The very structure of opportunities has collapsed. Both the correct statement of the problem and the range of possible solutions require us to consider the economic and political institutions of the society, and not merely the personal situation and character of a scatter of individuals.

Consider war. The personal problem of war, when it occurs, may be how to survive it or how to die in it with honor; how to make money out of it; how to climb into the higher safety of the military apparatus; or how to contribute to the war's termination. In short, according to one's values, to find a set of milieux and within it to survive the war or make one's death in it meaningful. But the structural issues of war have to do with its causes; with what types of men it throws up into command; with its effects upon economic and political, family and religious institutions; with the unorganized irresponsibility of a world of nation-states.

Consider marriage. Inside a marriage a man and a woman may experience personal troubles, but when the divorce rate during the first four years of marriage is 250 out of every 1,000 attempts, this is an indication of a structural issue having to do with the institutions of marriage and the family and other institutions that bear upon them.

Or consider the metropolis — the horrible, beautiful, ugly, magnificent sprawl of the great city. For many upper-class people, the personal solution to "the problem of the city" is to have an apartment with private garage under it in the heart of the city, and forty miles out, a house by Henry Hill, garden by Garrett Eckbo, on a hundred acres of private land. In these two controlled environments — with a small staff at each end and a private helicopter connection — most people could solve many of the problems of personal milieux caused by the facts of the city. But all this, however splendid, does not solve the public issues that the structural fact of the city poses. What should be done with this wonderful monstrosity? Break it all up into scattered units, combining residence and work? Refurbish it as it stands? Or, after evacuation, dynamite it and build new cities according to new plans in new places? What should those plans be? And who is to decide and to accomplish whatever choice is made? These are structural issues; to confront them and to solve them requires us to consider political and economic issues that affect innumerable milieux.

In so far as an economy is so arranged that slumps occur, the problem of unemployment becomes incapable of personal solution. In so far as war is inherent in the nation-state system and in the uneven industrialization of the world, the ordinary individual in his restricted milieu will be powerless — with or without psychiatric aid — to solve the troubles this system or lack of system imposes upon him. In so far as the family as an institution turns women into darling little slaves and men into their chief providers and unweaned dependents, the problem of a satisfactory marriage remains incapable of purely private solution. In so far as the overdeveloped megalopolis and the overdeveloped automobile are built-in features of the overdeveloped society, the issues of urban living will not be solved by personal ingenuity and private wealth.

What we experience in various and specific milieux, I have noted, is often caused by structural changes. Accordingly, to understand the changes of many personal milieux we are required to look beyond them. And the number and variety of such structural changes increase as the institutions within which we live become more embracing and more intricately connected with one another. To be aware of the idea of social structure and to use it with sensibility is to be capable of tracing such linkages among a great variety of milieux. To be able to do that is to possess the sociological imagination.

SOURCE: Mills, C. Wright, "The Promise," in C. Wright Mills, ed., *The Sociological Imagination*, New York, Oxford University Press, 1959, pp. 3–11. Copyright © 1959 by Oxford University Press, Inc. Reprinted by permission.

Appendix: Exploring A Career in Sociology

We hope that the twenty profiles of "Sociologists at Work" in the preceding chapters have stimulated your interest in sociology and broadened your awareness of the wide variety of careers now open in this field. Although they are but a small sampling, the sociologists clearly represent some of the many areas in which their knowledge, perspective, and methodologies can be applied. Traditionally, the vast majority of sociologists have chosen to teach and conduct their research in an academic setting. Although most sociologists continue to do so, an increasing number are electing to apply their skills to the government, business and industry, health services, and welfare and other nonprofit agencies. According to the American Sociological Association's 1977 publication *Careers in Sociology*, "sociology's career potential is just beginning to be tapped," and "many sociologists predict that the next quarter century will be the most exciting and most critical period in the field's 150-year history."

Over nine hundred colleges and universities in the United States offer bachelor's degree programs in sociology; the master's degree is the highest offered in 150 schools; and 140 schools offer both the master's and doctoral degrees (Bureau of Labor Statistics, *Occupational Outlook Handbook*, 1980). The National Center of Education reports that 19,164 bachelor's degrees, 1,341 master's degrees, and 583 doctorates were awarded in sociology in the United States in 1980.

What career opportunities are available in the 1980's to graduates with varying levels of training? What options might you consider if you choose to pursue your studies? This appendix provides a brief overview, followed by a list of sources — both organizations and publications — from which you can learn more about what sociologists

553

are doing today and how you might make the best use of your training.

Degrees in Sociology: How Far Will You Go?

Once you decide to major in sociology, how far will you go? A B.A.? An M.A.? A Ph.D.? We hope the following information, drawn from conversations with other sociologists and from publications of professional sociological associations, will help you make this decision.

If you are thinking about beginning your career after four years of college, you might consider the following positions for which you would be qualified with a bachelor's degree. They are drawn from a list in the American Sociological Association brochure *Majoring in Sociology*.

- □ interviewer
- □ research assistant
- □ recreation worker
- □ group worker
- □ teacher (if certified)
- □ probation and parole worker
- □ career counselor
- □ community planner
- □ statistical assistant
- □ social worker (not certified)

Several of these positions and others like them begin as entry-level jobs but may lead to positions of increasing responsibility through on-the-job training and advancement. These types of jobs are available in a wide variety of settings — public and private welfare agencies, hospitals, research institutes, consulting firms, retail stores, corporations, schools, and residential treatment centers, and federal, state, and local government departments. You would do well to investigate these different settings to determine which environment you would prefer to work in. Taking full advantage of school internships, volunteer work, and summer

and part-time jobs can help you make this choice while allowing you to gain valuable practical experience and establish contacts during your undergraduate years. Once you have chosen to major in sociology, visits to your school career placement office, state and local employment agencies, federal job information centers, and the personnel departments of businesses and corporations can provide you with specific job descriptions as well as general information in areas that interest you. As you plan your course work, discuss your interests and goals with your professors. They can help you select the courses that will best prepare you for your chosen career. Whether you begin work after four years of college, seek advanced training, or pursue professional training in some other field, your undergraduate studies in sociology can be a valuable asset: They can provide you with a greater understanding of people and organizations — both of which you will deal with in almost every aspect of your life.

If you decide to go on to graduate studies, you have a broad spectrum of subjects from which to choose a particular area of expertise. Your special interest may lie, for example, in the sociology of the family, urban or rural life, education, health, gerontology, occupations, environmental issues, racial issues, stratification, religion, sports, government, the military, or law enforcement. Your approach to your specialty may involve concentrating on social organization, human ecology, demography, or methodology.

The 290 graduate programs in the United States offering master's degrees in sociology vary considerably in strengths and weaknesses, requirements for a degree, settings, and orientations. Review school catalogs carefully, talk with your instructors, visit as many schools as you can, and talk to alumni, if possible. You should find the graduate program that is strongest in your area of special interest and the one best suited to your career objectives.

Would you like to research population trends

for the Census Bureau in Washington? Would you like to evaluate the effects of treatment programs in a rehabilitation center? Would you like to teach? Some graduate programs emphasize preparation for an academic career, and others are designed specifically to prepare students for careers in applied sociology in government or business.

According to Dr. Alexander Boros of Kent State University, the first program offering a master's degree in applied sociology was developed at Kent State in 1969. Similar programs are now offered in over a third of the nation's graduate schools. They place major emphasis on the application of sociological skills in a variety of settings. Many universities provide in addition to core courses in theory, research, and statistics, training in (1) research for the practitioner, including evaluation research, (2) program designing/planning, (3) grant writing, (4) in-service training, and (5) clinical roles (counseling). At Kent State, students apply their training by doing an internship in an agency, where they work on a specific project and complete it within a forty-day time limit. Instead of a thesis, students write an "applied monograph," which consists of a log of their daily activities, a report on their project to the agency, and a report on the project from a sociological perspective. In addition to this close involvement with one agency, students spend one day a week visiting the sites of other internships, where they observe and evaluate activities and programs. Seventy-six students graduated from the Kent State program between 1970 and 1981. Just a few examples of their current jobs from a list by Dr. Boros, will give you an idea of some of the career options open to you with a master's degree in sociology.

- vocational rehabilitation specialist with the Veterans Administration
- coordinator, deaf-blind services, with a city society for the blind
- educational consultant for a regional council on alcoholism
- Affirmative Action officer at a state university
- administrator at a state home for the deaf
- urban planning consultant, self-employed
- researcher with the state Department of Health
- research assistant at a private interviewing service
- teaching associate at a state university
- marketing administration coordinator at a banking equipment company

Many of our "Sociologists at Work" decided to continue their studies and earn a doctoral degree. As you can see from their career paths, they play rich and varied roles in today's society. As consultants, researchers, policy planners, administrators, clinical counselors, teachers, social critics, and program evaluators, they work in areas as broad and diverse as the discipline they have chosen.

Finding a Job

Once you've earned your degree, find the best job for which it qualifies you. You'll be using many of your skills — interviewing, writing, researching, and evaluating — before you start working. You've probably heard a lot of people complain that job hunting is harder work than working, but tracking down the right job for you will be well worth the effort.

How do people find out about their jobs? Talk with a few successful job hunters and the answer will be "in every way imaginable. . . ." Consider some of our "Sociologists at Work," for example. Henry Lewis found out about his job as a group leader and counselor at New Horizons Ranch and Center from a friend in the criminal justice system who knew Henry had a B.A. in sociology and wanted to work with people. Carroll De Weese learned about his position with General Motors from a posting on a sociology department bulletin board. Lana Leggett read about her job with NECOEMS in a local newspaper ad. Joanne Willette got her job with a management and government consulting firm by finding a company she was interested in working for and writing to the president of the company.

Plan your job hunting strategies around your three main resources: people, job listings, and referral agencies.

One of the most successful strategies is developing a network of contacts whom you can call to ask about openings and who may call you when they hear about a job which might interest you. Building up such a network may involve several kinds of activity. Many leads arise out of social contacts — conversations with friends, friends of friends, and even strangers. You may want to establish a file of the names and phone numbers of whoever does the hiring at companies and agencies where you'd like to work (and use the file *often*). It is almost always worthwhile to attend meetings of professional organizations where you can meet people already working in the field.

Let your professors know you are looking for a job — a referral and recommendation from a professor helped secure the jobs of three of our "Sociologists at Work." Get in touch with anyone you've previously worked for during summer internships, on summer and part-time jobs, or while doing volunteer work. Never underestimate the power of word-of-mouth in your job search.

While you're keeping your ears open and staying in touch with your contacts, watch for job listings and postings. Most sociology departments have bulletin boards set aside for job postings. Check these as well as postings in departments of education, theology, and social work, which often list social service jobs for which a degree in sociology can be an advantage. Visit your school's career placement office where you'll find counseling as well as lists of available positions. Don't ignore the most obvious and current list available — the newspaper want ads. If you don't see the particu-

lar job you're looking for, you can use the ads to build up your contact network by obtaining the names and addresses of agencies, businesses, and organizations where you might want to look in the future. Check the phone book and the local Chamber of Commerce for additional possibilities. Since many companies issue weekly listings of job openings, find out how to get hold of them. Professional organizations (see some below) often list jobs in newsletters or distribute employment bulletins.

Make the best use you can of public and private employment agencies. Register with the best agency in town — preferably one to whom the employer, and not you, pays the fee — and contact it on a regular basis. Register with state and local employment agencies and hound them for results. Don't forget the federal job information center in your area, where you can find out about federal jobs for which your degree qualifies you.

Job hunting requires energy, imagination, endurance, and the most complete and current information you can obtain. Give yourself the best chance to find the career that will most fulfill you by determining your goals and planning your strategies early. If sociology is your field, take a look at the sources below for more information about educational opportunities, job prospects, and career potential.

Organizations

Among the best sources of information about any field and its career potential are its professional organizations. In the United States, sociologists are organized on the national, regional, and state level, as well as by special interests. These groups provide a variety of services and activities directed toward the furthering of sociology. Career prospects and opportunities are a frequent topic of discussions and reports at annual meetings and workshops and in newsletters and journals. Most of these organizations welcome student members.

Below are some of the groups you can contact for additional information.

The American Sociological Association (ASA)
1722 N Street NW
Washington, D.C. 20036

The American Sociological Association represents sociologists on the national level and comprises the largest sociological organization in the United States, with a total membership of almost 14,000 in 1982. Founded in 1905, it is "an organization of persons interested in the research, teaching, and application of sociology; the Association seeks to stimulate and improve research, instruction, and discussion, and to encourage cooperative relations among persons engaged in the scientific study of society" (ASA brochure). Within ASA are several "sections" organized by special interest, such as the Practice Section, the Medical Section, and the Social Psychology Section. ASA also provides a Teaching Resources Center and conducts an annual meeting, attended by thousands of people. Hundreds of research papers and reports are read at the meetings, and sociologists have the opportunity to share new ideas, make important contacts, and discuss new developments in the field. In addition, the association provides an employment service at the annual meetings. At other times during the year, members of ASA organize workshops devoted to specific concerns, such as one held in December 1981 on "Directions in Applied Sociology." The ASA newsletter, *ASA Footnotes,* is distributed to members nine times a year and contains career information, reports on the activities of ASA, departmental news, and organizational reports and proceedings. The association also publishes a monthly employment bulletin, several professional journals, a teaching newsletter, and a series of studies on areas of sociological concern. As the largest network of sociologists in the United States, ASA provides the most comprehensive clearinghouse for information about the field.

The Society for Applied Sociology (SAS)
c/o Dr. Alexander Boros
Department of Sociology
Kent State University
Kent, Ohio 44242

Founded in 1979, the Society for Applied Sociology was formed primarily to give an organizational role to sociologists employed outside academia and to promote interest in applied sociology. According to one of its founders, Dr. Alexander Boros, members "seek to promote social and cultural change with the sociological perspective." SAS publishes the quarterly *Applied Sociology Bulletin,* which provides conference updates, reports on activities in the field, presents position papers, and lists job openings in applied settings. A journal and annual conferences are being planned for the future.

The Clinical Sociology Association (CSA)
c/o Dr. Jonathan Freedman
Hutchings Psychiatric Center
P.O. Box 27
Syracuse, N.Y. 13210

The Clinical Sociology Association was founded in 1978 to promote the establishment of a profession of clinical sociology. According to CSA's Fall 1979 newsletter, *Clinical Sociology,* the group's goals are "(1) to promote the application of sociological knowledge to intervention for individual and social change; (2) to develop opportunities for the employment and utilization of clinical sociologists; (3) to provide a meeting ground for sociological practitioners, allied professionals, scholars, and students; (4) to develop training, internship, certification, and other activities to further clinical sociological practice; and (5) to advance theory, research, and methods for sociological interventions in the widest range of professional settings." In addition to many other features, each issue of the quarterly *Clinical Sociology Newsletter* highlights the career path and work of a practicing clinical sociologist.

Other Special Interest Organizations

There are several other sociological organizations with activities and services similar to those mentioned above and directed to areas of special interest and concern. Among these are the Rural Sociological Association, the Association of the Study of Religion, the Society for the Study of Social Problems, the Gerontological Society of America, the National Council on Family Relations, and the American Criminological Association. Current addresses for these groups may be obtained through the ASA.

Regional and State Organizations

There are several regional organizations (for example, the North Central Sociological Association, the Eastern Sociological Association, the Midwestern Sociological Association, the Pacific Sociological Association, and the Southern Sociological Association) as well as approximately twenty-five state associations, such as the D.C. Sociological Association. These groups generally hold annual meetings, conduct workshops in areas of special concern, and publish journals or newsletters. Some provide employment services and career information. For the past several years the D.C. Sociological Association, for example, has conducted an annual workshop devoted to employment opportunities for undergraduate sociology majors. Potential employers talk to students about where and how they would employ a person with a bachelor's degree in sociology. Current addresses for these groups may be, obtained from ASA or your sociology professors.

Publications

The following publications may be ordered through ASA at the address listed above.

◻ *Majoring in Sociology: A Guide for Students.* Contains information on how to apply to a college and secure a degree in sociology, what programs are offered in sociology departments, how and where to seek employment information, and what areas a sociology student might choose to specialize in. (Single copies are free.)

◻ *Careers in Sociology.* Provides a description of the various careers in sociology and an understanding of the scope of the field. (Single copies are free.)

◻ *Embarking on a Career: The Role of the Undergraduate Sociology Major.* Provides job-hunting strategies for the undergraduate sociology major. (Single copies are free.)

◻ Reprints from *ASA Footnotes.* The following articles provide career information and are available for a nominal fee.

◻ Hollin, Albert E. "ASA Committee Makes Recommendations for Expanding Employment Opportunities," *ASA Footnotes* 5(7) (October 1977):1, 8.

◻ Jacobs, Ruth. "Job Hunting Hints Given to Undergraduate Majors," *ASA Footnotes* 3(1) (January 1975):1, 12.

◻ Manderscheid, Ronald W. "Training for Federal Careers," *ASA Footnotes,* January 1978.

◻ Orzack, Louis H. "Rutgers Searches for Non-Academic Jobs for Sociologists," *ASA Footnotes* 2(9) (December 1974):4.

◻ Wilkinson, Doris. "Employment Projections, Job Seeking Tips for Undergraduate, Graduate Sociology Trainees," *ASA Footnotes* 6 (August 1978):6–7.

◻ Wilkinson, Doris. "A Synopsis: Projections for the profession in the 1980's," *ASA Footnotes,* April 1980.

◻ *Directory of Departments of Sociology.* A reference book listing departments of sociology in 1,936 institutions in the United States and Canada. Information includes name and address of departments, chairperson, telephone number, number of members of sociology faculty, number of undergraduate majors, and number of graduate students. Try the Department of Sociology for this. ($10.00)

□ *Guide to Graduate Departments of Sociology, 1982.* Listing of 258 departments of sociology offering master's and/or doctoral degrees in sociology. Includes information on faculty as well as special programs, tuition costs, and student enrollment statistics, along with a listing of recent Ph.D. dissertations and current positions. ($4 for students)

□ *Federal Funding Programs for Social Scientists.* A guide to federal funding opportunities; contains a description of more than fifty programs that support social science research.

□ *ASA Employment Bulletin.* Monthly listing of positions available in academic and applied settings; sent free of charge to all sociology departments. While positions listed generally call for graduate training, reading several issues can give you a sense of specific job descriptions of openings available to sociologists.

The following articles have appeared in professional sociological journals as noted and should be available in your school library:

Teaching Sociology

□ Lutz, Gene M. "Employment and a Liberal Arts Undergraduate Degree in Sociology," *Teaching Sociology* 6(4) (July 1979):373-390.
□ Schultz, C. C. "The Occupation of the Undergraduate Sociology Major," *Teaching Sociology* 2 (October 1974):91-100.
□ Vaughan, Charlotte A. "Career Information for Sociology Undergraduates," *Teaching Sociology* 7 (October 1979):55-64.
□ Watson, J. Mark. "Would You Employ Sociology Majors: A Survey of Employers," *Teaching Sociology* 9(2) (January 1982): 127-135.

The American Sociologist

□ Foote, N. N. "Putting Sociologists to Work," *American Sociologist* 9 (1974): 125-134.

□ Gelfund, D. E. "The Challenge of Applied Sociology," *American Sociologist* 10 (February 1975): 13-18.
□ Street, D. P. and E. A. Weinstein. "Problems and Prospects of Applied Sociology," *American Sociologist* 10 (May 1975):65-72.

The following publications of the Federal Bureau of Labor Statistics are available at your regional office of the Bureau of Labor Statistics by writing to Superintendant of Documents, Dept. 34, U.S. Government Printing Office, Washington, D.C. 20402.

□ *Federal Career Directory: A Guide for College Students.* Lists federal careers by type and agency and includes qualifications, descriptions, and projected openings for federal jobs.

□ *Occupational Outlook Handbook.* Provides information under the following categories for several hundred professions: nature of work, working conditions, places of employment, training, other qualifications, advancement, employment outlook, earnings, related occupations, sources of additional information.

Additional Sources of Information

□ "Working with People: Careers in Sociology." Contact the Department of Sociology and Philosophy, Tennessee Technical University, Cookville, TN 38501.

□ *NELS Bulletin.* Monthly listing of positions available in the criminal justice system and social services. Write to the National Employment Listing Service, Criminal Justice Center, Sam Houston State University, Huntsville, TX 77341. Lists job descriptions, qualifications, salaries, and persons to contact.

□ "Clinical Sociology," a special issue of *The American Behavioural Scientist,* (March–April 1979). Several articles describing aims and practice of clinical sociology. May be ordered through Sage Publications, P.O. Box 5024, Beverly Hills, CA 90210.

Glossary

absolutist view The perspective that assumes that social rules are clear and obvious to most members of society and that certain behaviors are deviant regardless of the social context in which they occur.

achieved status A social position that is obtained through one's own efforts, such as teacher, graduate, or wife.

acting crowd A crowd that acts on the basis of aroused impulse and thus may be aggressive, hostile, and potentially dangerous, as a mob or riot.

age-adjusted death rate The number of deaths occurring at each age for each sex, per 100,000 living of that age.

age segregation Separation of people into groups of the same age such as occurs in schools and in retirement communities.

age-sex composition Refers to the number of men, the number of women, and the ages of people in any population.

aggregate group Any collection of people who are together in one place. This "group" is basically unstructured and the participants interact briefly and sporadically.

Anglo-conformity A form of assimilation whereby the minority loses its identity completely to the dominant WASP culture; equated with "Americanization."

animism A religious belief that spirits inhabit virtually everything in nature and influence and control all aspects of life and destiny.

anomie A condition of social normlessness or normative confusion brought about by a lack of integration between the cultural goals of society and the institutionalized means to achieve them.

anthropology The study of the physical, biological, social, and cultural development of human forms, often on a comparative basis.

applied sciences Those areas of study and practice that put to use, that is, apply, the principles of knowledge gained from the basic or pure sciences.

artifacts Physical productions or objects resulting from human action.

ascribed status A social position that is assigned to persons by society or by birth such as age, sex, or race.

assimilation The process by which minority groups acquire the sociocultural patterns of the dominant group and which involves both cultural assimilation — the learning of the day to day norms of a dominant group by minority group members and their internalization of the dominant group's values, beliefs, and ideas — and structural assimilation — developing patterns of intimate contact between the "guest" group and the "host" group in the clubs, organizations, and institutions of the host society.

associational group A group of people who join together to pursue a common interest in an organized, formally structured way.

authority Power and leadership accepted as legitimate by those affected.

barefoot doctors Health care workers who served the peasants in rural areas of post-revolutionary China after receiving 3 to 18 months training in Eastern and Western medical techniques.

beguines During the Middle Ages, communes of peasant women who did not choose to marry and who took vows of celibacy upon entering the communes.

behavior modification The process of changing behavior by changing the response to the behavior. Behavior that has been rewarded in the past will cease to occur if the rewards for it cease.

behaviorism The study of observable behavior in humans and animals, so-called to distinguish it from the study of conscious or unconscious motivation that presumably leads to certain behaviors.

bourgeoisie The "class" or grouping of people who control the means of production and use capitol, natural resources and labor for profit.

Buddhism One of the principle religions of the world, adherents of whom follow the teachings of Buddha, the enlightened one who preached a doctrine of "Four Noble Truths."

bureaucracy A hierarchical, formally organized, structural arrangement of an organization based on the division of labor and authority.

capitalism An economic system where all of the means of production, the land and factories, are owned by individuals or groups of individuals.

561

case study A detailed record of observation of a single individual, group, community, or activity.

cash crops Crops grown to be sold rather than used by the farmer.

caste system A system of stratification where class is ascribed at birth, worth is based on religious or traditional beliefs, and there is no possible upward social mobility.

casual crowd A crowd that is high in anonymity but low in suggestibility, contagion, emotional arousal, and unity.

categorical group A group of people who share a common characteristic but do not interact or have any social organization.

censorship Dissemination or prohibiting the availability of some type of information.

census The official process of counting the number of people in a given area.

charismatic authority The right to rule granted to someone who wins the confidence of a group of people on the basis of personality characteristics, such as by appearing to be wise and trustworthy.

The Chicago School An approach, developed by scholars including Charles Horton Cooley, George Herbert Mead, and W. I. Thomas during the 1920's, that emphasized the importance of social interactions in the development of human thought and action.

Christianity One of the principle religions in the world, followers of whom profess faith in the teaching of Jesus Christ.

churches Institutionalized organizations of people who share common religious beliefs.

city-state A city and its surrounding area which is ruled independently of other areas.

class consciousness Awareness among the members of the society that the society is stratified.

class system A system of stratification found in industrial society that is defined by the amount of wealth ascribed or acquired, and in which vertical social mobility is possible.

classical conditioning A response to an occurrence which has been associated with another occurrence. The classical example is of a dog who will salivate at the sound of a bell, if the bell has been rung consistently when food is presented to the dog.

closed system A system of stratification where there is no movement from one rank to another.

cohort A particular age group in the population.

collective behavior Spontaneous, unstructured, and transitory behavior of a group of people to a specific event.

community A collection of people within a geographic area among whom there is some degree of mutual identification, interdependence, or organization of activities.

compulsory public education Education until a particular age, mandatory by law and provided for by publicly funded schools.

Comte's law of progress Idea proposed by Auguste Comte that all knowledge passes through three successive theoretical conditions: the theological, the metaphysical, and the scientific.

concentration An ecological urban process of an increasing density of population, services, and institutions in the areas where conditions are advantageous.

concentric zone model An explanation of the ecology of cities as a series of zones (uniform circles) spreading from the original center, each with its own characteristic land use, population, activities, and institutions.

concept Tools or symbols by which one can share meanings and enable a phenomenon to be perceived in a certain way.

conceptual framework A cluster of interrelated concepts used to describe and classify phenomena.

conflict theory A set of propositions that views conflict as natural, permanent, and inevitable and as a significant source of social change.

Confucianism A principle religion of the world found predominately in China, adherents of whom follow the teachings of Confucius who founded his philosophy upon humanity rather than supernaturalism.

conjugal family A nuclear family that always has a husband and wife (the conjugal unit) and may or may not include children.

construction of reality A phrase used to denote the process of interpreting meanings learned about the world in order to give meaning to a particular phenomenon.

contest mobility A competitive system of education, where advanced education is available to those who excel at each previous level.

control group In an experimental design, this group is not exposed to the independent variable that is introduced to the experimental group.

conventional crowd A crowd in which members, although unknown to each other, share a common purpose and are expected to follow established social norms and rules.

convents Religious communities made up of women who wish to devote their lives to the religious order.

conversion effect A radical shift of interest and life-style that occurs when people move from one type of area to another.

cosmopolites According to Herbert Gans, an urban lifestyle that includes artists, intellectuals, and professionals who remain in the city for the conveniences and cultural benefits urban life offers.

counterculture A subculture that adheres to a set of beliefs and values that radically rejects the society's dominant culture and prescribes an alternative one.

credentials Educational certificates such as diplomas and degrees.

crowd A temporary and transitory group of people in face to face contact who share a common interest or focus of attention.

cults An extreme form of sect that calls for a totally new and unique life style often under the direction of a charismatic leader.

cultural diffusion The spread of the ideas and customs of one culture to another as populations migrate.

cultural lag The time discrepancy that occurs when changes in technology and material culture come more rapidly than changes in the nonmaterial culture.

cultural pluralism The situation in which the various ethnic groups in a society maintain their distinctive cultural patterns, subsystems, and institutions.

cultural relativism The idea that cultures must be judged on their own terms rather than by the standards of another culture.

cultural traits The smallest meaningful units of culture.

cultural transmission (or subculture theory) Theory that when deviance is part of a community's (or subculture's) cultural pattern, it is transmitted to newcomers through learning and socialization.

cultural universals Those aspects of culture such as symbols, language, shelter, etc. that are shared by and are basic concerns of all people.

culture All the human components of a society including all learned behavior as well as material and nonmaterial aspects such as symbols, language, values, norms, and technology.

cyclical change Change that moves back and forth between change for the better and a deterioration of conditions.

deconcentration A movement outward from the city because of increases in land values and taxes and decline in services and public facilities.

demand-side economics Political and economic policies which are designed to put more money into the hands of consumers so that they will be able to spur the economy by buying more goods and services.

democracy A power structure in which people govern themselves, ideally, or one in which people elect representatives who will govern them according to their wishes.

democratic socialism An economic system in which much of the means of production is owned by individuals or groups of individuals, but in which the production of goods and services vital to the society, such as transportation systems or medical care, are owned and run by the state.

demography The statistical study of populations regarding their birth rates, death rates, marriage rates, health and migration.

denominations Well established and highly institutionalized churches.

dependent variable A variable that is changed or influenced by the effect of another variable (termed the independent variable).

descriptive research Research findings that describe or summarize reality or provide facts about the world.

developmental theory Any theory which explains the process of development through the chronological stages of a person's life.

deviance Variation from a set of norms or shared social expectations.

differential association Sutherland's explanation of variations in deviant behavior due to the learning process that results from greater contact with groups that define deviance favorably than with groups that define it unfavorably.

differential reinforcement The reward or punishment of particular behaviors resulting in the acquisition or persistence of either deviant or conforming behavior.

direct relationship Two variables that change in the same direction. That is, as one variable increases, the other increases as well (in contrast to an inverse relationship where as one increases the other decreases).

directional hypotheses Hypotheses that involve direct or inverse relationships between the variables of interest.

disclaimers Statements made by a person to convey to others that what the person says or does is not to be taken as a claim to a particular status, but rather is to be ignored when defining the person.

discoveries Finding things which have always been but no one knew about, such as oil.

discrimination Overt unequal and unfair treatment of people based on their group membership.

disengagement The withdrawal of people from active participation in social life.

diversification The practice of corporations to enter business in a variety of areas of manufacture in order to assure profits.

divine revelation Something that is revealed to an individual or group by God.

downward mobility A move to a position of lower rank in the stratification system.

dramaturgical approach Studying interaction as if it were a drama on stage, noting the importance of the setting, the appearance and the manner of self, all of which shapes the interaction.

dyad A group of two people.

dysfunctions As related to structural-functional theory, refers to those consequences that lead to the disruption or breakdown of the system.

ecclesia An official state religion that includes all or most members of the society.

ecological change Change brought about by the way a given population uses the natural resources available to them.

ecological specialization The concentration of groups and activities into spatially homogenous areas in urban areas.

economic determinism The idea that social conditions, activities, and institutions have economic origins and that changes are brought about by economic factors.

economics The study of how goods, services, and wealth are produced, consumed, and distributed within societies.

ecumenism The joining together of different religious denominations with a call for worldwide Christian unity.

ego In Freudian theory, the part of the personality which reconciles the desires of the person and the demands of society in order to allow appropriate behavior.

electronic church Religious services presented through the medium of television.

elementary schools Schools that teach the elementary subjects of reading, writing and arithmetic.

emergent norm perspective A perspective of collective behavior that emphasizes how norms influence crowd behavior and how new norms emerge and are maintained.

emigration Movement of people out of an area.

endogamy A marriage pattern requiring persons to marry someone within their own social group.

endomorph, mesomorph, ectomorph The three types of physique according to which William Sheldon classified people and with which he associated certain temperamental and behavioral tendencies.

Equal Rights Amendment A proposed amendment to the Constitution of the United States giving equal rights to women. It was not ratified by a sufficient number of states to become part of the Constitution.

estate system A system of stratification determined by the family's relation to the land — either noble, serf or slave. This system was practiced in Europe during the Middle Ages.

ethnic groups Group membership based on national origin, religion, language or region, that is, people who perceive themselves or are perceived by others as sharing common origins or important parts of a common culture.

ethnic villagers According to Herbert Gans, an urban lifestyle of working class city dwellers who live in specific areas of a city and whose allegiance and identity are more closely tied to their ethnic group and community than to the city.

ethnocentrism The attitude that one's own culture is superior to others, that one's own beliefs, values, and behavior are more correct than others, and that other people and cultures can be evaluated in terms of one's own culture.

ethnomethodology The study of the ways people construct, maintain, and share their definitions of reality in everyday interaction.

euthanasia Mercy killing, where a patient is suffering and dying. Also used to describe the withholding of extraordinary measures to keep alive a hopelessly ill person.

evolutionary theory A set of propositions that suggest that societies, like biological organisms, process through stages of increasing complexity.

exchange theory A set of propositions that seeks to explain personal and social behaviors based on reciprocity of rewards and costs.

exogamy A marriage pattern requiring individuals to marry outside their own group.

experimental design A classic scientific procedure in which at least two matched groups, differing only in the one variable being studied, are used to collect data.

experimental group In an experimental design, this group is the one to which an independent variable is introduced that is not present in the control group.

explanatory research   Research findings that are aimed at explaining why things happen or don't happen (as contrasted with descriptive research).

expressive role   A role which requires understanding and creating good human relationships. It is usually associated with the female status in the early stages of industrialization.

extended family   A family in which two or more generations of the same kin live together (extension beyond the nuclear family).

fads   A form of diffuse collective mass behavior that is popular for a brief time period and usually involves rather superficial activities such as hula hoops or goldfish swallowing.

faith healing   Process by which fundamentalist preachers invoke the name of Christ to cure the ill and crippled in the belief that those who have sufficient faith in Christ will be made well.

false consciousness   A lack of awareness that there is a stratification system in a society and the inability to realize that one is in the same position in the stratification system as others like oneself.

family   A kinship-structured group of persons related by blood, marriage, or adoption.

family of orientation   The nuclear family into which one was born and reared (consists of self, siblings, and parents).

family of procreation   The nuclear family formed by marriage (consists of self, spouse, and children).

fashions   A form of diffuse collective behavior much like fads but more cyclical and invoking a currently accepted style of appearance or behavior.

fecundity   The biological potential of a woman to bear children (in contrast to fertility, the actual number of births).

field observation   The use of natural, on location settings to observe social processes.

folk society   Communities described by Redfield as those which are small, isolated, homogenous, and kin-oriented.

folkways   Norms of conduct of everyday life that bring only mild censure or punishment if violated.

formal external controls   Systems external to the individual such as courts, police, or prisons created specifically to control deviance.

formal organization   A large social group, deliberately constructed and organized to achieve certain specific and clearly stated goals.

Freudian theory   A body of theory first developed by Sigmund Freud which emphasizes unconscious biological drives as the source of human behavior.

frustration-aggression theory   A set of propositions that suggest prejudice is based on seeking outlets for personal frustrations by displacing their aggressive behavior to a socially approved racial or ethnic target.

functions   As related to structural-functional theory refers to what a system does (the functions it performs) or the consequences of a given form of structure.

game perspective   A view of crowd behavior that suggests that members think about their actions and consciously try to act in ways that will produce rewards.

gamesman   A person who practices the types of skills used by corporate managers when they manage workers in large corporations in a way similar to inspiring a team to play a cooperative, winning game.

gemeinschaft   A type of community characterized by a sense of solidarity, a common identity, rooted in tradition, and intimate and personal relationships.

gender roles   The cultural concepts of masculinity and femininity that society creates around sex (the biological fact of being male or female).

generalized belief   The common identification and shared interpretation of a problem based on known facts, shared attitudes, or a common ideology. One of the determinants of collective behavior.

generalized other   The assumption that other people have similar attitudes, values, beliefs and expectations. It is therefore not necessary to know a specific individual in order to know how to behave toward that individual.

genocide   The practice of deliberately destroying an entire racial or ethnic group.

gentrification   The rejuvenation of urban neighborhoods by middle-class people who move into and repair old run-down houses.

geographical change   Change in the climate, earth, and natural life of an area that causes social change.

geographical mobility   Movement from one geographical area to another, such as to a new community or to a new nation.

geography   The study of the physical environment and the distribution of plants and animals, including humans.

gesellschaft   A type of community characterized by individualism, mobility, impersonality, and an emphasis on progress rather than tradition.

ghetto   An area within a city, usually a deteriorating one, in which members of a racial or ethnic minority are forcibly segregated.

greenbelt   According to Ebenezer Howard's concept of urban planning, an area to surround cities which would be preserved for farming and recreation and which would limit the outgrowth of cities.

gross national product (GNP)   The total value of the goods and services a nation produces each year.

Hinduism   One of the principle polytheistic religions of the world, found predominately in India and Pakistan, with no religious hierarchy but closely intertwined with society and the cosmic order.

history   The study of past events. Social history is concerned with the past that involves human life and social events.

horizontal mobility   A move from one job to another that does not raise or lower one's position in the stratification system.

horticulture communities   Those early communities organized around and dependent upon small-scale farming that rely upon tools such as the hoe to till the soil.

hospice   Homes for dying patients where emphasis is on positive attitudes toward the last days of life and inevitable death.

human relations school   A type of management which considers the psychological makeup of workers, such as their attitudes toward management and peer group pressures.

hypothesis   A statement of a relationship between variables that can be put to an empirical test.

id   In Freudian theory, the collection of biological drives that motivate behavior.

ideal culture   The norms and values that people are supposed to follow (which may or may not be the same as what they actually follow).

ideal-type   A hypothetical model of polar extremes that provide contrasting (opposite) points with which to compare social phenomenon.

idioculture   The cultural system of knowledge, beliefs, behaviors and customs created through human interaction that is unique to a given group.

immigration   Movement of people into an area.

incest   Socially forbidden sexual relationships or marriage with certain close relatives.

independent variable   A variable that causes a change or variation in another variable (termed the dependent variable).

inequality   A word used by sociologists to denote differences between groups in their share of wealth, status or power.

informal external controls   Pressures applied by peers, friends, parents, and other people with whom one associates regularly to encourage an individual to obey rules and conform to social expectations.

in-group   A social group to which persons feel they belong and share a consciousness of kind.

institution   A stable cluster of values, norms, statuses, and roles that develop around a basic goal of society.

institutionalized behavior   Behavior that is recurrent and follows an orderly pattern with a relatively stable set of goals, expectations, and values.

instrumental role   A role which requires the accomplishment of tasks such as earning a living to provide food and shelter necessary for survival, a role usually associated with the male status in the early stages of industrialization.

integration   When racial and ethnic characteristics become insignificant and everyone can participate freely in the social, economic, and political mainstream.

internal controls   Learned patterns of control that exist in the minds of individuals that make them want to conform to the norms of society.

interpretation   A key process in symbolic interaction, whereby people interpret those meanings they have learned in order to evaluate any situation.

inventions   Devices created by putting two or more things together in a new way.

inverse relationship   Two variables that change in opposite directions. That is, as one variable increases, the other decreases.

Islam   One of the principle religions in the world, the followers who are known as Muslims and follow the teachings of the Koran and of Muhammad, one of their prophets.

Judaism   The oldest religion in the western world, the first to teach monotheism, and today viewed as both an ethnic and religious community.

kinship   The web of relationships among family units or people with linkages of common ancestry (birth), adoption, or marriage.

labeling theory   A set of propositions explaining how definitions of deviance are created by society and applied to individuals as well as the processes and consequences of being designated with a deviant label.

laboratory observation   The use of a controlled environment to observe social processes.

language   The systematized usage of speech and hearing to convey, communicate, or express feelings and ideas.

latent force   Using threats of violence in order to make a person do something they do not want to do.

latent functions   Those social consequences of a system that are neither intended nor recognized.

laws   Formal, standardized expressions of norms enacted by legislative bodies to regulate certain types of behaviors.

left-wing   Political groups motivated by religious or moral issues who desire radical changes in society so that the society can reach certain goals such as equality for all.

legitimate power   Power given to a person by others because it is seen as necessary and beneficial, such as the power to make and enforce laws beneficial to all.

life chances   The opportunity a person has to improve his or her income and acquire a better style of life.

lifetime jobs   An employment practice whereby workers are guaranteed a job, if not for life, at least for a lengthy period of time.

lobbies   Groups of people who devote their time and effort to winning favorable legislation in order to further their own particular interests.

Lombroso's body types   Cesare Lombroso believed that the major determinants of crime were biological and hereditary and that potential criminals could be recognized by certain physical characteristics.

looking-glass self   The reflection of ourselves as we imagine others see us.

macrosociology   A level of sociological analysis that deals with large-scale units such as institutions, social categories, and social systems.

Malthusian theory   A classic theory proposed by Thomas Robert Malthus that population expands much faster than the food supply, resulting in famine and death for much of the population when it grows too large.

manifest functions   Those social consequences of a system that are both intended and recognized.

Marx and social conflict   Karl Marx believed that social conflict — class struggles due to economic inequality — was at the core of society and the source of all social change.

market economy   An economy in which the production and the price of goods is determined in the marketplace, depending on whether people want to buy goods and how much they are willing to pay for them.

mass   A spatially diffuse form of collective that involves geographically dispersed persons who react to or focus upon some common event.

mass expulsion   The practice of expelling racial or ethnic groups from one's homeland.

mass hysteria   A form of diffuse collective behavior involving a widespread, highly emotional fear of a potentially threatening situation.

mass media   Communication which reaches the masses of people, especially television, radio and popular magazines.

matriarchal   A family structure in which the wife rules or has dominance over the husband.

matrilineal   A family structure that traces descent and inheritance through the mother's line.

matrilocal   A family structure where a newly married couple is expected to live with the wife's family.

mean   A descriptive measure of central tendency best known as the average and computed by taking the sum of the values and dividing by the number of cases.

median   A descriptive measure of central tendency, often referred to as the mid-point, where one half of the respondents fall below and one half are above.

megalopolis   A continuous strip of urban and suburban development that may stretch for hundreds of miles.

melting pot   A form of assimilation where each group contributes a bit of its own culture and absorbs aspects of other cultures such that the whole is a combination of all the groups.

mental unity   Term used in the classical perspective of crowds that describes the sentiments and ideas of all people taking the same direction and forming a collective mind.

microsociology   A level of sociological analysis that deals with small-scale units such as individuals in small group interaction.

middle range theory   Sets of propositions that are concerned with linking abstract propositions with empirical testing.

migration   Movement of people into or out of an area.

millennialism   A sect belief that a dramatic transformation of the earth will occur and that Christ will rule the world for a thousand years of prosperity and happiness.

milling That stage in crowd behavior when people are moving about aimlessly, are growing increasingly preoccupied with others, and are increasingly inclined to respond without thinking.

minority groups Those groups, usually but not always smaller in size than the dominant group, who are subordinate with regard to the distribution of social power based on physical or cultural characteristics.

mobs Groups that are emotionally aroused and ready to engage in violent behavior.

mode A descriptive statistic that refers to the most frequent response.

modernization The process by which societies develop into industrial societies.

modified-extended family Nuclear families that retain considerable autonomy and yet maintain a coalition with other nuclear families where they exchange goods and services.

monogamy The marriage of one female to one male.

monotheism The belief in only one god.

mores Norms of conduct associated with strong feelings of right or wrong, violations of which inspire intense reaction and some type of punishment.

mortification of self The stripping of the self of all characteristics of a past identity, including clothing, personal possessions, old friends and relationships, old roles and routines, and anything else that creates a sense of identity.

multinational corporations Corporations which do business in a number of nations.

multiple nuclei model An explanation of the ecology of cities as areas of different land use with different centers.

mystics Those who believe that spiritual or divine truths come through intuition and meditation apart from the use of reason or the ordinary range of human experience and senses.

nation-state A vast territory ruled by a single political institution.

nature-nurture debate An age-old debate over whether behavior results from predetermined biological characteristics or from socialization.

neolocal A family structure in which a newly married couple is expected to establish a new place of residence separate from either parent.

no-fault divorce The dissolution of marriage based on irreconcilable differences where neither party is "at fault."

nonmarital heterosexual cohabitation An arrangement where an unmarried male and female share a common dwelling.

norms Formal and informal rules of conduct or social expectations for behavior.

nuclear family Any two or more persons of the same or adjoining generations related by blood, marriage, or adoption sharing a common residence.

null hypothesis An hypothesis that states no relationship exists between variables.

nurturant socialization A universal family function of caring for and teaching the newborn infant the norms, values, and behaviors appropriate to the culture.

objectivity A standard of scientific inquiry that asserts that the personal biases and values of the researchers must never influence the data reported or the interpretation of results.

open system A system of stratification where it is possible to move from a lower to a higher or a higher to a lower rank in the system.

operant conditioning The condition where one repeats a behavior because that behavior has been rewarded in the past.

operational definition Defining a concept or variable in a way it can be measured in the conduct of research.

operationalization The process of arriving at a means of measuring a concept or variable.

organic solidarity A term used by Durkheim to describe the integration of society as a result of the division of labor. As each person specializes in one phase of production, he or she becomes dependent on others to produce other products, thus the society is made up of interdependent individuals.

organizational group (See Associational Group)

out-group A social group in which persons feel they do not belong, do not share a consciousness of kind, and to whom they feel little allegiance or identity.

panic A form of collective behavior where people react in fear and seek a rapid exit or departure from a threatening situation.

participant observation A technique of data gathering and observation in which the researcher is an active participant in the event being studied.

participant-oriented movements Social movements which focus on personal rewards and fulfillment for those taking part.

parties   Any organization in which decisions are made to reach certain goals and where the achievement of those goals affects the society.

patriarchal family   A family in which the husband rules or has dominance over the wife.

patrilineal   A family system that traces descent and inheritance through the father's line.

patrilocal   A family structure where a newly married couple is expected to make their home with the husband's family.

peer group   An informal primary group of people who share a similar or equal status and usually are of similar age.

Pentecostalism   A segment of Christianity that holds highly emotional services where the participants speak in "tongues" and go into ecstatic seizures and utter meaningless syllables.

Peter Principle   The idea that in a hierarchy, employees tend to rise to their level of incompetence.

Piagetian theory   A body of theory first developed by Jean Piaget which emphasizes the development of the mind, or cognitive development, that is assumed to be associated with biological development.

planned economy   An economy in which the production and the price of goods are planned by the government.

play   A word used by Mead to describe the process of learning to role-take by playing house or school, as children take the role of parent or teacher.

political pluralism   A political system in which many diversified groups have a share of the power.

political science   The study of power, governments, and political processes.

political socialization   Any process of socialization that teaches the values and norms of the political system.

polyandry   The marriage of one woman to more than one husband at the same time.

polygamy   The marriage of one man or one woman to more than one wife or more than one husband at the same time.

polygyny   The marriage of one man to more than one wife at the same time.

polytheism   The belief in and worship of more than one god.

population   In research, the group or unit from which a sample is drawn. In society, the number of people living within a particular geographical or social area.

population change   A change in the number of people in a society, or the characteristics of the population such as age or sex.

power   The ability to control or influence the behavior of others, even in the absence of their consent.

power elite   A political system in which a small group of people hold all the powerful positions and work cooperatively with each other to maintain their powerful positions.

precision of measurement   A standard of scientific inquiry that asserts that phenomenon being studied should be measured in precise, reliable, and valid ways.

prejudice   A preconceived attitude or judgment, either good or bad, about another group. It usually involves negative stereotyped beliefs.

presentation of self   The appearance, the manner, the gestures, the body language of self as they intentionally or unintentionally give messages to others which influence interaction.

priests and prophets   Two major types of religious leaders as identified by Max Weber: priests owe their authority to the power of the office; prophets hold their authority on the basis of charismatic qualities.

primary group   A small informal group of people who interact in a personal, direct, and intimate way.

primary workers   Workers who produce raw materials such as food or minerals.

principle of legitimacy   Malinowski's idea that every society has a rule that every child should have a legitimate father to act as the child's protector, guardian, and representative in society.

profane   In religious terms, anything that is unspiritual and treated with irreverence. According to Durkheim, the profane is the realm of the everyday world.

professionalization   The process of developing a service occupation which is licensed by government, has a body of knowledge, a code of ethics, peer control and an association of members.

progress   To move forward to a condition that is better.

projection   A psychological explanation of prejudice that suggests that people transfer responsibility for their own failures to a vulnerable group, usually a racial or ethnic one.

proletariat   The "class" or grouping of people who labor and serve as the instrument of production for the bourgeoisie.

propaganda   Attempts at the manipulation of ideas or opinions of a public by presenting limited, selective, or false information.

proposition   A statement of the relationship between two or more concepts or variables.

protestant ethic   An ethic associated with the Puritans which valued hard work and shunned frivolous play, an ethic which Weber claimed led to the high value placed on the capitalist system in America.

psychology   The study of human mental processes and individual human behavior.

public   A spatially diffuse form of collective behavior where a group of people are confronted with a controversial issue of common interest or concern.

public opinion   Attitudes, decisions, or viewpoints about an issue held by the members of a public.

pull factors   Natural or social events which cause people to immigrate, or move into an area.

pure science   Those areas of study that seek to gain knowledge for its own sake with little thought or concern for how it may be used or applied.

push factors   Natural or social events which cause people to emigrate, or move out of an area.

qualitative methods   Research methods used to study conditions or processes that are hard to measure with numbers.

quantitative methods   Research methods designed to study variables that can be measured in numbers.

quality control circles   A type of management in which workers meet together to discuss ways of improving production and set policy to reach their goals.

racial group   A group of people who are socially defined and set apart by some combination of inherited physical characteristics.

racism   A form of discrimination based on characteristics of race and existing either as individual racism, which originates in the racist beliefs of a single person or institutional racism, which occurs when racist ideas and practices are embodied in the folkways, mores, or legal structures of various institutions.

random sample   A selection of persons in a way that every member of the population has an equal chance of being chosen.

range   The distance between the largest and smallest amount of the variable.

real culture   The norms and values that people actually follow and practice (which may or may not be the same as what they are supposed to follow).

reification   The process of giving a particular meaning to something, and then assuming that it in fact has the meaning given to it. This is often done, for example, when we assume that life is fair and then expect life to be fair.

reference group   A group with which persons psychologically identify and to which people refer when making evaluations of themselves and their behavior.

reliability   The extent to which repeated observations of the same phenomena yield similar results.

religion   A system of beliefs and behaviors by a group or community of believers, oriented toward the supernatural and sacred.

religiosity   The degree to which a person holds religious beliefs, takes part in religious rituals, and professes religious feelings.

replication   A standard of scientific inquiry that asserts that research should be conducted and reported in such a way that someone else can duplicate it.

resocialization   Socialization to a new role or position in life which requires a dramatic shift in attitudes, values, behaviors, and expectations learned in the past.

right-wing   Political groups motivated by religious or moral issues who believe society is deteriorating and wish to return society to a condition or position it held in the past.

riots   A form of collective behavior involving mass violence and mob action.

role   The social expectations or behaviors that accompany a particular status.

roleless role   A position in society not associated with any expectations of performance, used to describe the condition of the elderly in modern industrial society.

role taking   The ability to assume the status of persons with whom one interacts and see the world from their perspective.

sacred   Objects and ideas treated with reverence and awe.

sample   A number of individuals or cases drawn from a larger population.

Sapir-Whorf Hypothesis   The hypothesis that societies with different languages perceive the world differently because people see and interpret the world through the grammatical forms, labels, and categories provided by their language.

scapegoating   A psychological explanation of prejudice that involves blaming another person or group for one's own problems.

scientific management   A method of managing assembly-line workers so that their every movement is efficient.

scientific method   The established procedures of science that include objectivity, replication and precise measurements to gather accurate and verifiable knowledge about the world in which we live.

secondary group   A group whose members interact in an impersonal manner, have few emotional ties, and come together for a specific, practical purpose.

secondary workers   Workers who produce manufactured goods from raw materials.

sector model   An explanation of the ecology of cities as a series of pie-shaped wedges radiating from the central business district and each with its own characteristics and uses.

sect   A religious group that has broken away from a parent church, follows rigid doctrines and fundamentalist teachings, and emphasizes "other-worldly" rewards thus rejecting or deemphasizing contemporary society.

secularization   The process whereby beliefs concerning the supernatural and religious institutions lose social influence.

self-image   The idea, or image, we have of ourselves as male or female, old or young, literate, athletic, tall, short, or any other characteristics we attribute to self.

self-esteem   The evaluation of ourselves as good or bad, capable or incompetent, talented or not, skilled or inept, or any other evaluation of the self.

segregation   The spacial or social separation of groups from one another. Usually involves separating a minority group from the dominant ones.

sexual harassment   Unwelcome sexual advances, requests for sexual favors, and other sexually suggestive physical or verbal behaviors of coworkers or superiors that causes the recipient discomfort and which, in addition, if denied, can result in the loss of a job or promotion.

shamanism   The religious belief that certain persons (shamans) have special charm, skill, or knowledge in influencing spirits.

significant others   Persons with whom one psychologically identifies and whose opinions are important. These persons, such as parents, assume a major role in teaching the person about self and others.

slums   Sections of a city marked by poverty, overcrowding, substandard housing, and poor living conditions.

social change   Changes in the structure of a society or in its social institutions.

social class   A category of people who have approximately the same amount of wealth, the same amount of power derived from wealth, and the same life chance to acquire wealth.

social contagion   An aspect of crowd behavior in which the crowd's response to a common event or situation increases in intensity as the behavior of the crowd moves others to similar behavior.

social control   Internal and external sanctions and processes used to maintain conformity to social norms.

social dynamics   Comte's perception of societal processes and forms of change (in contrast to his social statics — the structure of society).

social group   A number of people who physically and socially interact in a patterned way on the basis of shared expectations about each other's behavior.

socialism   An economic system where all the means of production, the land, and the factories are owned by all of the people through the state.

socialization   The process of creating a social self, that is, learning or internalizing the rules of and expectations for behavior for a given society.

social facts   Those social phenomena that, according to Emile Durkheim, are external to the individual, are distinctively social in their characteristics and determinants, and exercise constraint on individuals. In general, social facts are reliable and valid items of information.

social group   A number of people who physically and socially interact in a patterned way on the basis of shared expectations about each other's behavior.

social learning theory   A set of propositions about learning that are based on behavioral principles of conditioning and rewards or punishments.

social movement   A collective noninstitutionalized effort to bring about social change and establish a new order of social thought and action.

social psychology   The study of how an individual influences his or her social interactions with other individuals or groups, and of how these groups influence the individual.

social science   The empirical body of knowledge about human behavior, social organization and society that has been accumulated by methods subject to verification.

social statics   Comet's idea that society, like plants and animals, had a structure consisting of many interrelated parts (in contrast to his social dynamics — the processes and forms of change).

social status   As structure, a socially defined position that a person occupies that may be ascribed (age, race, sex) or achieved (husband, father, teacher). In stratification, the amount of honor and prestige a person receives from members of the community and from the larger society.

social system   A set of interrelated social statuses (positions) and the expectations that accompany these positions.

social work   An applied field involving clinical, social, or recreational services aimed at the improvement of human and community welfare.

societal unit   (See Categorical Group.)

society   A group of interacting people living in a specific geographical area, organized in a cooperative manner, and sharing a common culture.

sociobiology   The study of social behavior to learn if it is determined biologically, especially genetically.

sociocultural learning theories   Theories that deal with processes through which acts are learned and the conditions under which learning takes place.

socioeconomic status   A measure that combines a person's education, occupation, and income in order to derive that person's ranking in the stratification system.

sociological perspective   A way of looking at society and social behavior that involves questioning the obvious, seeking patterns and regularities, and looking beyond individuals to social interactions and group processes.

sociology   The study of human society and social life and the social causes and consequences of human behavior.

spatially diffuse collectives   Collectives that form among people spread over a wide geographical area (as masses and publics).

spatially proximate collectives   Collectives in which people are geographically close and physically visible to one another (as a crowd).

Spencer's evolutionary scheme   Herbert Spencer's belief that human societies evolve according to the principals of natural selection from relative homogeneity and simplicity to heterogeneity and complexity.

split labor market   A labor market which assigns career paths to some jobs so that higher ranking jobs can be attained through promotion, while other jobs have no career path and no promotion is possible.

sponsored mobility   A system of education where students are selected early to receive advanced education and training.

standard deviation   A statistical measure that indicates the proportion of cases that fall within a standard unit of measurement from the mean.

standard metropolitan statistical area (SMSA)   A county or group of counties with a central city with a population of at least 50,000 a density of at least 1000 persons per square mile, and outlying areas that are socially and economically integrated with the central city.

statistical group   A group formed by sociologists and statisticians. Members are unaware of belonging and there is no social interaction or social organization.

stereotypes   Widely held beliefs about the character and behavior of all members of a group.

stratification   The ranking within the social structure of groups and categories of people according to the amount of wealth, status and power they have, and according to the life chances they have to acquire wealth, status and power.

stratified sampling   A sample obtained by dividing a population into various categories and then proportionately selecting units or cases from each category.

structural conduciveness   The extent to which a society's organization has the conditions that make a particular form of collective behavior possible.

structural strain   Any kind of conflict or ambiguity in a society's organization that causes frustration and stress. Is often seen as a precondition for collective behavior.

structural-functional theory   A set of propositions that emphasizes the interdependence of units or organization plus the consequences of a given structured arrangement.

subculture   A group of persons who share in the overall culture of a society but also have their own distinctive values, norms, and lifestyles.

suburbs   Communities surrounding and dependent on a central city.

succession   An urban process of replacing old occupants and institutions with the new. The completion of the invasion process.

superego   In Freudian theory, that part of the personality that has learned the rules of society and is concerned with acting according to those rules.

supply side economics   Political and economic policies which are designed to put money and incentives in the hands of the rich so they will spur the economy by investing in better and more competitive manufacturing systems.

survey research   A quantitative research technique involving systematically asking people about their attitudes, feelings ideas, behavior or anything else.

symbol   Something used to represent something else, that is signs such as words, gestures or objects used to represent some aspect of the world.

symbolic interaction theory   A set of propositions that stress interaction between people as well as the social processes that occur within individuals made possible by language and internalized meanings.

systematic sampling   Obtaining a sample from a population by following a specific pattern of selection such as every tenth case.

taboos   Mores that prohibit something.

technology   The practical production and application of nonmaterial and material aspects of societies to maintain their standards of living and lifestyles.

temporocentrism   The belief that one's own time, the present, or the contemporary are more important than the past or future.

tertiary workers   Workers who provide a service, such as doctors, lawyers, politicians, police officers, and secretaries.

theodicy   That which deals with the question of why an omnipotent and good God allows evil to exist in the world.

theories   Sets of logically and systematically interrelated propositions that explain some particular process or phenomenon.

totalitarianism   A power structure in which the government has total power to dictate the values, rules, ideology, and economic development of the society.

totemism   The worship of plants, animals, and other natural objects both as gods and ancestors.

tract housing   Housing that emerged in the post-World War II suburbs based on mass production techniques.

traditional authority   The right to rule granted to someone on the basis of tradition, such as a patriarch or king.

trained incapacity   Veblen's concept to refer to a rigid adherence to rules, originally concerned as a means, becomes transformed into an end-in-itself.

triad   A group of three people.

unionization   Organizations of workers who form unions to protect and improve their wages and working conditions.

universe   (See Population.)

upward mobility   A move up in the stratification system to a position of more wealth, status or power.

urban ecology   The study of the interrelationships of people in urban settings and the social and physical environment in which they live.

urban homesteading   A federal plan where abandoned and foreclosed homes are sold to private families at extremely low price if they agree to live in the house and bring it up to code standards.

urbanization   The growth of the number of people who live in urban rather than rural areas and the process of taking on organizational patterns and lifestyles characteristic of urban areas.

validity   the extent to which observations actually yield measures of what they are supposed to measure.

value-oriented movements   Social movements which advocate social changes concerning various groups that result in broader adherence to the central values of the larger society.

values   Ideals and beliefs shared by people in a society on what is important and worthwhile.

variables   Characteristics such as age, class, or income that can vary from one person to another.

variance   The extent to which the results or cases are distributed, that is, the extent to which scores, ages, or results differ or vary from one another.

verstehen   A term used by Max Weber for understanding human action by examining the subjective meanings that people attach to their own behavior and to the behavior of others.

women's movement   The collection of social movements led by women to gain political and economic equality.

xenocentrism   The belief that what is foreign is best and that one's own lifestyles, products, or ideas are inferior to those of others.

XYY chromosomes   A specific genetic condition — an extra Y chromosome — believed to be associated with crimes of physical violence.

zero population growth   Population policy which encourages parents to have only two children to replace themselves so as to limit the growth of the population.

References

Aberle, David and Kasper Naegele. "Middle-Class Father's Occupational Role and Attitudes Toward Children," *American Journal of Orthopsychiatry* 22 (1952): 366–378.

Adorno, T. W., Else Frenkel-Brunswik, Daniel J. Levinson, and R. Nevitt Sanford. *The Authoritarian Personality.* New York: Wiley, 1950.

Akers, Ronald L. *Deviant Behavior: A Social Learning Approach.* 2nd ed. Belmont, Calif.: Wadsworth, 1977.

Akers, R. L., M. D. Krohn, L. Lonza-Kaduce, and M. Radosevich. "Social Learning and Deviant Behavior: A Specific Test of a General Theory," *American Sociological Review* 44 (August 1979):636–655.

Albrecht, Stanley L., Darwin L. Thomas, and Bruce A. Chadwick. *Social Psychology.* Englewood Cliffs: N.J.: Prentice-Hall, 1980.

Allport, Gordon, *The Nature of Prejudice.* Boston: Beacon Press, 1954.

Asch, Solomon E. "Opinions and Social Pressure," *Scientific American,* 193(5) (1955):31–35.

Austin, Sarah. "Crisis in New York City," *The New York Times,* Jan. 4, 1976, p. 40.

Bales, Robert F. "The Equilibrium Problem in Small Groups," in Talcott Parsons, et al., eds., *Working Papers in the Theory of Action.* Glencoe, Ill.: The Free Press, 1953.

Bandura, A. "Vicarious Processes: A Case of No-Trial Learning," in L. Berkowitz, ed., *Advances in Society Psychology,* vol 2. New York: Academic Press, 1965, pp. 1–55.

Banfield, Edward. *The Unheavenly City Revisited.* Boston: Little, Brown, 1974.

Barry, Brian and John D. Kasarda. *Contemporary Urban Ecology.* New York: Macmillan, 1977.

Becker, Howard S. "The Labeling Theory Reconsidered," in *Deviance and Social Control.* Edited by Paul Rock and Mary McIntosh. London: Tavistock, 1974.

Becker, Howard S. *Outsiders: Studies in the Sociology of Deviance.* New York: The Free Press, 1963.

Bell, Wendell. "Social Choice, Life Styles, and Suburban Residences," in W. Dobriner, ed., *The Suburban Community.* New York: Putnam, 1958.

Bem, S. and D. Bem. "Training the Woman to Know Her Place: The Power of a Nonconscious Ideology," In S. Cox, ed., *Female Psychology: The Emerging Self.* Chicago: SRA, 1976, pp. 180–191.

Berg, Ivar. *Education and Jobs: the Great Training Robbery.* New York: Praeger Publishers, 1970.

Berger, Bennett. *Working Class Suburbs.* Berkeley, Calif.: University of California Press, 1960.

Berger, Peter L. and Thomas Luckmann. *The Social Construction of Reality. A Treatise in the Sociology of Knowledge.* Doubleday, 1966.

Berlowitz, Marvin S. "Institutional Racism and School Staffing in an Urban Area," *Journal of Negro Education* 43 (Winter 1974):25–29.

Bernard, Jesse. *The Female World.* New York: The Free Press, 1981.

Berry, Brewton and Henry L. Tischler. *Race and Ethnic Relations.* Boston: Houghton Mifflin, 1978.

Berry, Brian, J. L. *The Human Consequences of Urbanization,* New York: St. Martin's Press, 1973.

Bierstedt, Robert. *The Social Order.* 3rd ed. New York: McGraw-Hill, 1970.

Biggar, Jeanne. "The Sunning of America: Migration to the Sunbelt," *Population Bulletin* 34 (March 1979):128–144.

Billingsley, Andrew. *Black Families in White America.* Englewood Cliffs, N.J.: Prentice-Hall, 1968.

Blau, Peter M. and Otis Dudley Duncan. *The American Occupational Structure.* New York: Wiley, 1967.

Blau, Peter M. and Richard C. Scott. *Formal Organizations.* San Francisco: Chandler, 1963.

Blumer, Herbert. "Collective Behavior," in Alfred McClung Lee, ed., *Principles of Sociology.* New York: Barnes & Noble, 1939.

Bradley, Donald. "Neighborhood Transition: Middle Class Home Buying in an Inner-City, Deteriorating Neighborhood." Paper presented at the annual meeting of the American Sociological Association, Chicago, Sept. 1977.

Broverman, I. K., S. R. Vogel, D. M. Broverman. F. E. Clarkson and P. S. Rosenkrantz. "Sex-Role Stereotypes: A Current Appraisal," *Journal of Social Issues* 28 (1972):59–78.

Browne, James. "Power Politics for Teachers, Modern Style," *Phi Delta Kappan* 58 (1976):158–164.

Burgess, Ernest W. "The Growth of the City," in Robert E. Park and Ernest W. Burgess, eds., *The City.* Chicago: University of Chicago Press, 1925, pp. 47–62.

Burke, Ronald J. and Tamara Weir. "Relationship of Wives' Employment Status to Husband, Wife and Pair Satisfaction and Performance." *Journal of Marriage and the Family* 38 (May 1976):279–287.

Burstein, Paul. "Equal Employment Opportunity Legislation and the Income of Women and Non-Whites," *American Sociological Review* 44 (June 1979):367–391.

Caplovitz, David. *The Poor Pay More.* New York: The Free Press, 1963.

Careers in Sociology. Washington, D.C. American Sociological Association, 1977.

Chambliss, William J. *Crime and the Legal Process.* New York: McGraw-Hill, 1969.

Chambliss, William J. and Robert Seidman. *Law, Order and Power.* Reading Mass.: Addison-Wesley, 1971.

Charon, Joel M. *The Meaning of Sociology*. Sherman Oaks, Calif.: Alfred Publishing, 1980.

Chesler, Mark A. and William M. Cave. *A Sociology of Education: Access to Power and Privilege*. New York: Macmillan, 1981.

Childe, V. Gordon. "The Urban Revolution," *Town Planning Review* 21 (April 1951):3–17

Cicourel, Aaron. *Social Organization of Juvenile Justice*. New York: Wiley. 1968.

Cohen, Albert K. and Harold M. Hodges, Jr. "Characteristics of Lower Blue-Collar Class," *Social Problems* 10 (Winter 1963):307–321.

Coleman, James and S. D. Kelly. "Education," in W. Gorham and N. Glazer, eds., *The Urban Situation*. Washington, D.C.: The Urban Institute, 1976.

Coleman, James S. et al. *Equality of Educational Opportunity*. Washington, D.C.: U.S. Government Printing Office, 1966.

Coleman, James S. et al. *Youth: Transition to Adulthood*. Report of the Panel on Youth of the President's Science Advisory Committee. Chicago: The University of Chicago Press, 1974.

Collins, Randall. "A Conflict Theory of Sexual Satisfaction," *Social Problems* 19 (Summer 1971):3–21.

Collins, Randall. *The Credential Society An Historical Sociology of Education and Stratification*. New York: Academic Press, 1979.

Cook, Robert. "The World's Great Cities: Evolution or Devolution?" in P. Meadows and E. Mizruchi, eds, *Urbanism, Urbanization and Change*. Reading, Mass.: Addison-Wesley, 1969.

Cooley, Charles H. *Human Nature and the Social Order*. New York: Schocken, 1964 (Scribner, 1902).

Cooley, Charles H. *Social Organization*. New York: Scribner's, 1909.

Coser, Lewis. *The Functions of Social Conflict*. New York: The Free Press, 1956.

Cumming, E. and W. Henry. *Growing Old: The Process of Disengagement*. New York: Basic Books, 1961.

Dahrendorf, Ralph. *Class and Class Conflict in Industrial Society*. Stanford, Calif.: Stanford University Press, 1951.

Davis, Kingsley. "Extreme Social Isolation of a Child," *American Journal of Sociology* 45 (1940):554–565.

Davis Kingsley. "The First Cities: How and Why Did They Arise?" in K. Davis, ed., *Cities: Their Origin, Growth, and Human Impact*. San Francisco: W. H. Freeman, 1973.

Davis, Kingsley and Wilbert E. Moore. "Some Principles of Stratification," *American Sociological Review* 10 April (1945):242–249.

Davis, Wayne H. "Overpopulated America," *The New Republic*, Jan. 10, 1970, pp. 13–15.

Denton, John A. *Medical Sociology*. Boston: Houghton Mifflin, 1978.

Derber, Charles. *The Pursuit of Attention, Power and Individualism in Everyday Life*. Cambridge, Mass.: Schenkman, 1979.

Dinitz, Simon. "Progress, Crime, and the Folk Ethic," *Criminology* 11 (May 1973):3–21.

Dinnerstein, Leonard and David M. Reimers. *Ethnic Americans: A History of Immigration and Assimilation*. New York: Harper and Row, 1975.

Dobriner, William. "The Growth and Structure of Metropolitan Areas," in Robert Gutman and David Poponoe, eds., *Neighborhood, City and Metropolis*, New York: Random House, 1970, pp. 190–205.

Dollard, John, et al. *Frustration and Aggression*. New Haven: Yale University Press, 1939.

Dowse, Robert E. and John A. Hughes. *Political Sociology*. New York: Wiley, 1972.

Duberman, Lucile. *Social Inequality: Class and Caste in America*. Philadelphia: Lippincott, 1976.

Dupreel, Eugene G. "Demographic Change and Progress." Pp. 80–85 in *The Evolution of Population Theory*. Johannes Overbeek Ed. Westport, Conn: Greenwood Press, 1977. Originally published in 1922.

Durkheim, Emile. *The Division of Labor in Society*. New York: The Free Press, 1947. Originally published in 1893.

Durkheim, Emile. *The Elementary Forms of the Religious Life*. New York: The Free Press, 1926 (originally published in 1915).

Eaton, Joseph and Albert J. Mayer. "The Social Biology of Very High Fertility Among the Hutterites: The Demography of a Unique Population," *Human Biology* September 25(3) (1953):206–264.

Elkin, Frederick and Gerald Handel. *The Child and Society: The Process of Socialization*, 3rd ed. New York: Random House, 1978.

Encyclopedia of Associations, vol. 1, 16th ed. "National Organizations of the U.S." Detroit: Gale Research Co., 1981.

Engels, Frederich. *The Origin of the Family, Private Property and the State*. Chicago: Charles H. Kerr, 1902.

Erikson, Kai J. *Everything in Its Path: Destruction of Community in the Buffalo Creek Flood*. New York: Simon & Schuster, 1976.

Eshleman, J. Ross. *The Family: An Introduction*, 3d. ed. Boston: Allyn & Bacon, 1981.

Etzioni, Amitai. *A Sociological Reader on Complex Organizations*, 3rd ed. New York: Holt, Rinehart & Winston, 1980.

Farley, Lin. *Sexual Shakedown*. New York: Warner Books, 1978.

Feagin, Joe. *Racial and Ethnic Relations*. Englewood Cliffs, N.J. Prentice-Hall, 1978.

Featherman, David L. and Robert M. Hauser. "Changes in the Socioeconomic Stratification of the Races, 1962–1973," *American Journal of Sociology* 82 (November 1976): 621–651.

Fine, Gary Alan. "Small Groups and Culture Creation: The Ideoculture of Little League Baseball Teams," *American Sociological Review* 44 (October 1979):733–745.

Flacks, Richard. *Youth and Social Change*. Chicago: Markham, 1971.

Form, William H. and Joan Rytina Huber. "Ideological Beliefs on the Distribution of Power in the United States," *American Sociological Review* 34 (February 1969):19–36.

Freeman, Harold. *Toward Socialism in America.* Cambridge, Mass: Schenkman, 1979.

Freeman, Jo. "The Origins of the Women's Liberation Movement," *American Journal of Sociology* 78 (January 1973):792–811.

Fried, Marc and Peggy Gleicher. "Some Sources of Residential Satisfaction in an Urban Slum," *Journal of the American Institute of Planners* 27 (November 1961):305–315.

Fromm, Erich. *The Sane Society.* New York: Holt, Rinehart & Winston, 1965.

Gardner, R. A., and B. T. Gardner. "Teaching Sign Language to a Chimpanzee," *Science* 165 (1969):664–672.

Garfinkel, H. *Studies in Ethnomethodology.* Englewood Cliffs, N.J.: Prentice-Hall, 1967.

George, Susan. *How the Other Half Dies. The Real Reasons for World Hunger.* Montclair, N.J.: Allanheld, Osmun, 1977.

Georgetown Law Weekly. Washington, D.C.: Georgetown University Law Center, vol. 16, no. 17, January 26, 1981.

Glassner, Barry and Bruce Berg. "How Jews Avoid Alcohol Problems," *American Sociological Review* 45 (August 1980): 647–664.

Glazer, Nathan and Daniel P. Moynihan. *Beyond the Melting Pot,* 2nd ed. Cambridge, Mass.: Mass. Institute of Technology Press, 1970.

Goering, John M. "The Emergence of Ethnic Interests: A Case of Serendipity," *Social Forces* 48 (March 1971):379–384.

Goffman, Erving. *Asylums: Essays on the Situation of Mental Patients and Other Inmates.* Garden City, N.Y.: Anchor/Doubleday, 1961.

Goffman, Erving. *Encounters.* Indianapolis: Bobbs-Merrill, 1961.

Goffman, Erving. *Interaction Ritual. Essays on Face-to-Face Behavior.* Garden City, N.Y.: Doubleday/Anchor, 1967.

Goffman, Erving. *The Presentation of Self in Everyday Life.* Garden City, N.Y.: Doubleday/Anchor, 1959.

Goldberg, S. and M. Lewis. "Play Behavior in the Year-Old Infant: Early Sex Differences," *Child Development* 40 (1969):21–30.

Goode, William J. *World Revolution and Family Patterns.* New York: The Free Press, 1970.

Goodin, Robert E. *Manipulatory Politics.* New Haven: Yale University Press, 1980.

Gordon, Milton. *Assimilation in American Life.* New York: Oxford University Press, 1964.

Gordon, Milton M. *Human Nature, Class and Ethnicity.* New York: Oxford University Press, 1978.

Gordon, Richard, Katherine Gordon, and Max Gunther. *The Split Level Trap.* New York: Bernard Geis Associates, 1961.

Gouldner, Alvin W. *Patterns of Industrial Bureaucracy.* New York: The Free Press, 1954.

Greeley, Andrew M. and Paul B. Sheatsley. "Attitudes Toward Racial Integration," *Scientic American* 225 (December 1971):13–19.

Greer, Scott. *Urban Renewal and American Cities.* Indianapolis, Ind.: Bobbs-Merrill, 1965.

Griandjean, Berke D. "History and Career in a Bureaucratic Labor Market," *American Journal of Sociology* 86 (5), March 1981:1057–1092.

Hall, Edward Twitchell. *The Silent Language.* Garden City, New York: Doubleday Books, 1959

Hare, A. Paul. *Handbook of Small Group Research.* New York: The Free Press, 1976.

Harris, Chauncey. "Suburbs and Suburban Life-Styles," *Time,* June 13, 1971, p. 78.

Harris, Chauncy and Edward L. Ullman. "The Nature of Cities," *Annals of the American Academy of Political and Social Science* 242 (November 1945):7–17.

Hartmann, Heidi. "Capitalism, Patriarchy, and Job Segregation by Sex." in Nona Glazer and Helen Youngelson Waehrer eds., *Woman in a Man-Made World,* Second Edition. Chicago: Rand McNally, 1977, pp. 71–84.

Hauser, Phillip. "Chicago — Urban Crisis Exemplar," in J. John Palen, ed., *City Scenes.* Boston: Little, Brown 1977, pp. 15–25.

Hawke, Sharryl and David Knox. *One Child by Choice.* Englewood Cliffs, N.J.: Prentice-Hall, 1977.

Hawley, Amos. *Urban Society: An Ecological Approach.* New York: Ronald Press, 1971.

Hayes, C. *The Ape in Our House.* New York: Harper & Row, 1951.

Hazard, John N. *The Soviet System of Government,* 5th ed. Chicago: The University of Chicago Press, 1980.

Heer, David M. *Society and Population.* Englewood Cliffs, N.J.: Prentice-Hall, 1975.

Heilbroner, Robert L. *The Making of Economic Society.* Englewood Cliffs, N.J.: Prentice-Hall, 1980.

Hobbs, Daniel F., Jr. "Parenthood as Crisis: A Third Study," *Journal of Marriage and the Family* 27 (August 1965):367–372.

Hochschild, Arlie Russell. "The Sociology of Feeling and Emotion: Selected Possibilities," in Marcia Millmav and Rosabeth Moss Kantor, eds., *Another Voice.* Garden City, N.Y.: Doubleday/Anchor, 1975, pp. 280–307.

Hogan, Dennis P. and David L. Featherman. "Racial Stratification and Socioeconomic Change in the American North and South," *American Journal of Sociology* 83 (July 1977):100–126.

Howard, Ebenezer. *Garden Cities of Tomorrow.* London: Faber & Faber, 1902.

Hoyt, Homer. *The Structure of Residential Neighborhoods in American Cities.* Washington, D.C. Federal Housing Administration, 1939.

Humphrey, Craig, R. and Frederick R. Buttel. *Environment, Energy and Society.* Belmont, Calif.: Wadsworth, 1982.

Jacobs, Jane. *The Death and Life of Great American Cities.* New York: Random House, 1961.

Jacquet, Constant H., Jr. ed. *Yearbook of American and Canadian Churches.* Nashville: Abingdon, 1979.

Jencks, Christopher. *Who Gets Ahead? The Determinant of Economic Success in America.* New York: Basic Books, 1979.

Jones, James M. *Prejudice and Racism.* Reading, Mass.: Addison-Wesley, 1972.

Kamerman, Sheila B. and Alfred J. Kahn. *Child Care, Family Benefits and Working Parents.* New York: Columbia University Press, 1981.

Kantor, Rosabeth M. *Men and Women of the Corporation.* New York: Basic Books, 1979.

Karier, Clarence J. "Testing for Order and Control in the Corporate Liberal State." In N. J. Block and Gerald Dworkin, eds., *The I.Q. Controversy, Critical Readings.* New York: Pantheon Books, 1976, pp. 339–373.

Kasarda, John. "The Changing Occupational Structure of the American Metropolis," in Barry Schwartz, ed., *The Changing Face of the Suburbs.* Chicago: University of Chicago Press, 1976, pp. 113–136.

Keller, Suzanne. *Beyond the Ruling Class, Strategic Elites in Modern Society.* New York: Random House, 1968.

Kellogg, W. N. and L. A. Kellogg. *The Ape and the Child.* New York: McGraw-Hill, 1933.

Kelly, Delos H. *Deviant Behavior: Readings in the Sociology of Deviance.* New York: St. Martin's Press, 1979.

Kerner Report. *National Advisory Commission on Civil Disorders.* New York: Bantam Books, 1968.

Kinloch, Graham C. *The Dynamics of Race Relations: A Sociological Analysis.* New York: McGraw-Hill, 1974.

Kitano, Harry H. L. *Race Relations,* 2nd ed. Englewood Cliffs, N.J.: Prentice-Hall, 1980.

Kitsuse, John I. "Societal Reaction to Deviant Behavior: Problems of Theory and Method," *Social Problems* 9 (Winter 1962):247–256.

Kohn, Melvin L. "Bureaucratic Man: A Portrait and an Interpretation," *American Sociological Review* 36 (June 1971):461–474.

Kohn, Melvin L. "Social Class and Parental Values," *American Journal of Sociology* 64 (January 1959):337–351.

Kraut, Robert E. "Deterrent and Definitional Influences on Shoplifting," *Social Problems* 23 (February 1976): 358–368.

La Barre, Weston. "The Cultural Basis of Emotions and Gestures," in *Social Structure and Social Personality.* Jerold M. Starr, ed. Boston: Little, Brown, 1974, pp. 74–80.

Labovitz, Sanford and Robert Hagedorn. *Introduction to Social Research.* 3rd ed. New York: McGraw-Hill, 1981.

Lander, Bernard. "Towards an Understanding of Juvenile Delinquency," In H. Voss and D. Petersen, eds., *Ecology, Crime, and Delinquency.* New York:Appleton-Century-Crofts,1971.

Leavitt, Ruby R. "Women of Other Cultures." In *Women in Sexist Society Studies in Power and Powerlessness.* Vivian Gornick and Barbara K. Moran New York: New American Library, 1971.

Le Bon, Gustave. *The Crowd: A Study of the Popular Mind.* London: Ernest Benn, 1895 2nd ed., Dunwoody, Ga.: Norman S. Berg, 1968.

Lee, Gary R. "Age of Marriage and Marital Satisfaction: A Multivariate Analysis with Implications for Marital Stability," *Journal of Marriage and the Family* 39 (August 1977):493–503.

LeMasters, E. E. "Parenthood as Crisis," *Marriage and Family Living* 19 (November 1957):352–355.

Lemert, Edwin. *Social Pathology.* New York: McGraw-Hill, 1951.

Lengermann, Patricia M. "The Founding of the American Sociological Review: The Anatomy of a Rebellion," *American Sociological Review* 44 (April 1979):185–198.

Lenski, Gerhard. *Power and Privilege.* New York: McGraw-Hill, 1966.

Levison, Andrew. *The Working-Class Majority.* New York: Coward, McCann and Geoghegan, 1974.

Lewis, Jerry M. "A Study of the Kent State Incident Using Smelor's Theory of Collective Behavior," *Sociological Inquiry* 42 (1972):87–96.

Lieberson, Stanley and Arnold R. Silverman. "The Precipitants and Underlying Conditions of Race Riots," *American Sociological Review* 30 (December 1965):887–898.

Lipset, S. M. and Bendix, Reinhard. *Social Mobility in Industrial Society.* Berkeley: University of California Press, 1967.

Litt, Edgar. "Civic Education, Community Norms, and Political Indoctrination," *American Sociological Review* 28 (February 1963):69–75.

Lopata, Helena Z. *Polish Americans: Status Competition in an Ethnic Community.* Englewood Cliffs, N.J.: Prentice-Hall, 1976.

Maccoby, Michael. "The Changing Corporate Character," in Gordon J. Di Renzo, ed., *We, The People: American Character and Social Change.* Westport, Conn.: Greenwood Press, 1977.

Madsen, William. *The Mexican-Americans of South Texas.* New York: Holt, Rinehart & Winston, 1964.

Malinowski, Bronislaw. "Parenthood, The Basis of Social Structure," in V. F. Calverton and Samuel D. Schmalhausen, eds., *The New Generation.* New York: Macaulay, 1930.

Manion, O. V. *Aging: Old Myths versus New Facts.* Eugene, Oregon: Retirement Services, Inc., 1972.

Margolis, Diane Rothbard. *The Managers: Corporate Life in America.* New York: Morrow, 1979.

Markle, Gerald E. and Ronald J. Troyer. "Smoke Gets in Your Eyes: Cigarette Smoking as Deviant Behavior," *Social Problems* 26 (June 1979):611–625.

Marshall, Harvey. "Suburban Life Styles: A Contribution to the Debate," in L. Masotti and J. Hadden, eds., *The Urbanization of the Suburbs.* Beverly Hills, Calif.: Sage Publications, 1973.

Martin, Wilfred B. W. and Allan J. Macdonell. *Canadian Education. A Sociological Analysis.* Scarborough, Ont.: Prentice-Hall of Canada, 1978.

Marx, Karl and Friedrich Engels. *Communist Manifesto.* Baltimore: Penguin Books, 1969 (originally published 1848).

McKinlay, John B. and Sonja M. McKinlay. "Medical Measures and the Decline of Mortality, in Peter

Conrad and Rochelle Kern, eds., *The Sociology of Health and Illness. Critical Perspectives*. New York: St. Martin's Press, 1981, pp. 12–30.

Mead, George Herbert. *Mind, Self and Society from the Standpoint of a Social Behaviorist*, Charles Morris, ed., Chicago: University of Chicago Press, 1934.

Mead, Margaret. *Sex and Temperament in Three Primitive Societies*. New York: Morrow, 1935.

Merton, Robert K. *Social Theory and Social Structure*. New York: The Free Press, 1949 (rev. ed., 1957 and 1968).

Merton, Robert K. *Sociological Ambivalence and Other Essays*. New York: The Free Press, 1976.

Milgram, Stanley. "The Experience of Living in Cities," *Science* 167 (March 13, 1970):1461–1468.

Milgram, Stanley. "Behavioral Study of Obedience," *The Journal of Abnormal and Social Psychology* 67 (4) (Oct. 1963):pp. 371–378.

Miller, Herman P. *Rich Man, Poor Man*. New York: Thomas Y. Crowell, 1971.

Mills, C. Wright. *The Power Elite*. New York: Oxford University Press, 1958.

Mills, Charles W. *White Collar: American Middle Classes*. New York: Oxford University Press, 1951.

Mol, Hans. *Identity and the Sacred*. New York: The Free Press, 1976.

Money, John. *Love and Love Sickness: The Science of Sex, Gender Difference, and Pair-Bonding*. Baltimore: The Johns Hopkins University Press, 1980.

Money, J. and Ehrhardt, Anke A. *Man and Woman, Boy and Girl: The Differentiation and Dimorphism of Gender Identity from Conception to Maturity*. Baltimore: Johns Hopkins University Press, 1972.

Moss, H. "Sex, Age and State as Determinants of Mother-Infant Interaction," *Merrill-Palmer Quarterly* 13 (1967):19–36.

Mostert, Noel. "Supership," in Jerome H. Skolnick and Elliott Currie, eds., *Crisis in American Institutions*, 3rd ed. Boston: Little, Brown, 1976, pp. 286–304.

Mumford, Lewis. *The Transformation of Man*. New York: Collier, 1962.

Murdock, George P. *Social Structure*. New York: Macmillan, 1949.

Murdock, George P. "World Ethnographic Sample," *American Anthropologist* 59 (August 1957):664–687.

National Commission on Urban Problems. *Building the American City*. Washington, D.C.: U.S. Government Printing Office, 1972.

Nelson, Mary. "Why Witches Were Women." in Jo Freeman, ed., *Women. A Feminist Perspective*. Palo Alto, California: Mayfield Publishers, 1975, pp. 335–350.

Newman, Oscar. *Defensible Space*. New York: Macmillan, 1972.

Newman, William M. *American Pluralism: A Study of Social Groups and Social Theory*. New York: Harper & Row, 1973.

Noel, Donald L. "A Theory of the Origin of Ethnic Stratification," in Norman R. Yetman and C. Hoy Steele, eds., *Majority and Minority: The Dynamics of Racial and Ethnic Relations*. Boston: Allyn & Bacon, 1975, chap. 2.

Novak, M. *The Rise of the Unmeltable Ethnics*. New York: Macmillan, 1972.

Novak, Michael. "White Ethnic," in Norman R. Yetman and C. Hoy Steele, eds., *Majority and Minority: The Dynamics of Racial and Ethnic Relations*. Boston: Allyn & Bacon, 1975.

Ogburn, William F. *Social Change*. New York: Viking, 1950.

Orcutt, James D. "Deviance as a Situated Phenomenon: Variations in the Social Interpretation of Marijuana and Alcohol Use," *Social Problems* 22 (February 1975):346–356.

Orum, Anthony M. *Introduction to Political Sociology: The Social Anatomy of the Body Politic*. Englewood Cliffs, N.J.: Prentice-Hall, 1978.

Ouchi, William G. *Theory Z: How American Business Can Meet the Japanese Challenge*. Reading, Mass.: Addison-Wesley, 1981.

Park, Robert E. and Ernest W. Burgess. *Introduction to the Science of Sociology*. Chicago: University of Chicago Press, 1921.

Parsons, Talcott. "The School Class as Social System: Some of Its Functions in American Society," *Harvard Educational Review* 29(4) (1959):297–318.

Parsons, Talcott and Edward A. Shils eds. *Toward a General Theory of Action*. New York: Harper & Row, 1951.

Parsons, Talcott and Robert F. Bales. *Family, Socialization and Interaction Process*. New York: The Free Press, 1955.

Patterson, Orlando. "Context and Choice in Ethnic Allegiance," in Nathan Glazer and Daniel Moynihan, eds. *Ethnicity*. Cambridge: Harvard University Press, 1975, pp. 305–345.

Peter, Lawrence J. and Raymond Hull. *The Peter Principle*. New York: Morrow, 1969.

Pirenne, Henri. "Stages in the Social History of Capitalism," *American Historical Review* Vol. XIX, July (1914):494–515.

Piven, Frances Fox and Richard A. Cloward. *Regulating the Poor: The Functions of Public Welfare*. New York: Vintage Books, a Division of Random House, 1971.

Polk, Kenneth. "Urban Social Areas and Delinquency," *Social Problems* 14 (Winter 1967):320–325.

Pratt, Lois. "Business Temporal Norms and Bereavement Behavior," *American Sociological Review* 46(31) (June 1981):317–333.

Quarantelli, E. L. and Russell R. Dynes, "When Disaster Strikes: It Isn't Much Like What You've Heard and Read About," *Psychology Today*, February 1972:67–70.

Queen, Stuart A. and Robert W. Habenstein. *The Family in Various Cultures*, 4th ed. Philadelphia: Lippincott, 1974.

Quinney, Richard. *Criminology*. Boston: Little, Brown, 1979.

Radke, Marian J. and Helen G. Trager. "Children's Perceptions of the Social Roles of Negroes and Whites," *The Journal of Psychology* 29 (1950):3–33.

Riccio, James. "Religious Affiliation and Socioeconomic Achievement," in Robert Wuthnow, ed., *The Religious Dimension: New Directions in Quantitative Research*. New York: Academic Press, 1979, pp. 199–231.

Ridley, F. F. ed. *Government and Administration in Western Europe*. New York: St. Martin's Press, 1979.

Riesman, David, Nathan Glazer and Reuel Denny. *The Lonely Crowd. A Study of the Changing American Character*. Garden City, N.Y.: Anchor Books, Doubleday, 1953.

Riley, Matilda White, Anne Foner, Beth Hess, and Marcia L. Toby. "Socialization for the Middle and Later Years," in David A. Goslin, ed., *Handbook of Socialization Theory and Research*. Chicago: Rand McNally, 1969, pp. 951–982.

Rist, Ray. "Student Social Class and Teacher Expectations: The Self-Fulfilling Prophecy in Ghetto Education," *Harvard Educational Review* 40 (August 1970):411–451.

Roethlisberger, Fritz J. and William J. Dickson. *Management and the Worker*. Cambridge, Mass.: Harvard University Press, 1939.

Rokeach, Milton, Patricia W. Smith, and Richard I. Evans. "Two Kinds of Prejudice or One?" in Milton Rokeach, ed., *The Open and Closed Mind*. New York: Basic Books, 1960, pp. 132–168.

Rosenkrantz, P., S. Vogel, H. Bee, I. Broverman, and D. M. Broverman. "Sex-Role Stereotypes and Self-Concepts in College Students," *Journal of Consulting and Clinical Psychology* 3 (1968):287–295.

Rosenthal, R. and L. Jacobson. *Pygmalion in the Classroom: Teacher Expectation and Pupil's Intellectual Development*. New York: Holt, Rinehart & Winston, 1968.

Rossides, Daniel W. *The American Class System: An Introduction to Social Stratification*. Boston: Houghton Mifflin, 1976.

Rothman, Robert A. *Inequality and Stratification in the United States*. Englewood Cliffs, N.J.: Prentice-Hall, 1978.

Rothstein, William G. *American Physicians in the Nineteenth Century: From Sects to Science*. Baltimore: Johns Hopkins Press, 1970.

Rouse, James. "The City of Columbia," in Victor Fisher and Herbert Graves, eds., *Social Science and Urban Crises*. New York: Macmillan, 1971.

Rubin, J., F. Provenzano, and Z. Luria. "The Eye of the Beholder: Parents' Views on Sex of Newborns," *American Journal of Orthopyschiatry* 44 (1974):512–519.

Russell, John. *British Medieval Population*. Albuquerque: University of New Mexico Press, 1972.

Ryan, Edward. Cited in Marc Fried and Peggy Gleicher, "Some Sources of Residential Satisfaction in an Urban Slum," in Sandor Halebsky, ed., *The Sociology of the City*. New York: Charles Scribner, 1973.

Schaefer, Richard T. *Racial and Ethnic Groups*. Boston: Little, Brown, 1979.

Schiller, Bradley R. "Stratified Opportunities: The Essence of the 'vicious circle'," *American Journal of Sociology* 76 (November 1970):426–442.

Schnore, Leo. "The Socioeconomic Status of Cities and Suburbs," in L. Schnore, ed., *The Urban Scene*. New York: The Free Press, 1965.

Schorr, Alvin. "Housing and Its Effects," in D. Gutman and R. Popenoe, eds., *Neighborhood, City and Metropolis*. New York: Random House, 1970.

Schur, Edwin M. *Interpreting Deviance: A Sociological Introduction*. New York: Harper & Row, 1979.

Scott, Marvin and Stanford Lyman. "Accounts," *The American Sociological Review* 33 (December 1968): 46–62.

Sears, R. R., Eleanor E. Maccoby, and H. Levin. *Patterns of Child Rearing*. Evanston, Ill.: Row, Peterson, 1957.

Second, P. F. and C. W. Backman. *Social Psychology*. New York: McGraw-Hill, 1964.

Seely, Gordon M. *Education and Opportunity: For What and For Whom?* Englewood Cliffs, N.J.: Prentice-Hall, 1970.

Seeley, John, R. Sim, and E. Loosley. "The Home in Crestwood Heights," in J. Kramer, ed., *North American Suburbs: Politics, Diversity, and Change*. Berkeley, Calif.: Glendessary, 1972.

Serbin, L. and K. O'Leary. "How Nursery Schools Teach Girls to Shut Up," *Psychology Today* 9 (December 1975):56–58.

Sewell, William H. "Inequality of Opportunity for Higher Education," *American Sociological Review* 36 (October, 1971):793–809.

Shackley, Pamela and Constance Staley. "Women in Management Training Programs: What They Think About Key Issues." *Public Personnel Management Journal*, 9 (3), 1980.

Shattuck, Roger. *The Forbidden Experiment: The Story of the Wild Boy of Aveyron*. New York: Farrar, Straus, Giroux, 1980.

Shortridge, Kathleen. "Working Poor Women." in Jo Freeman, ed., *Women. A Feminist Perspective*. Palo Alto, California: Mayfield Publishers, 1975, pp. 242–253.

Simmons, Roberta G., Leslie Brown, Diane M. Bush, and Dale A. Blyth. "Self-Esteem and Achievement of Black and White Adolescents," *Social Problems* 26 (October 1978):86–96.

Simpson, George Eaton and J. Milton Yinger. *Racial and Cultural Minorities: An Analysis of Prejudice and Discrimination*. New York: Harper & Row, 1972.

Smelser, Neil J. "Theoretical Issues of Scope and Problems," in Robert R. Evans, ed., *Readings in Collective Behavior*. Chicago: Rand McNally, 1969, pp. 89–94.

Smelser, Neil J. *Theory of Collective Behavior*. New York: The Free Press, 1962.

Smirlock, Michael L. "Working Women in America: Factors which Influence Their Participation and Attachment to the Labor Force." *American Economist*, 24 (Fall 1980) (2):47–52.

Smith, Douglas A. and Christy A. Visher. "Sex and Involvement in Deviance/Crime: A Quantitative Review of the Empirical Literature," *American Sociological Review* 45 (August 1980):691–701.

Snell, Bradford. "American Ground Transport," in Jerome H. Skolnick and Elliott Currue, Boston: Little, Brown, 1976, pp. 304–326.

Sorokin, Pitirim A. *Social and Cultural Dynamics*. Englewood Cliffs, N.J.: Bedminster Press, 1962.

Spates, James L. "Counterculture and Dominant Culture Values: A Cross-National Analysis of the Underground Press and Dominant Culture Magazines," *American Sociological Review* 41 (October 1976):868–883.

Spengler, Oswald. *The Decline of the West*. New York: Knopf. 1962. Originally published in 1918.

Spitz, Rene A. "Hospitalism," *The Psychoanalytic Study of the Child* 1 (1945):53–72; and "Hospitalism: A Follow-Up Report," *ibid.* 2 (1946): 113–117.

Spitzer, Steven. "Toward a Marxist Theory of Deviance," *Social Problems* 22 (June 1975):638–651.

Spradley, James P. and Brenda J. Mann. *The Cocktail Waitress. Woman's Work in a Man's World*. New York: Wiley, 1975.

Stadtman, Verne A. *Academic Adaptations: Higher Education Prepares for the 1980s and 1990s*. San Francisco: Jossey-Bass, 1980.

Stark, Rodney and William Sims Bainbridge. "Secularization and Cult Formation in the Jazz Age," *Journal for the Scientific Study of Religion* 20 (December 1981):360–373.

Starr, Joyce and Donald Carns. "Singles and the City: Notes on Urban Adaptation," in J. Walton and D. Carns, eds., *Cities in Change*. Boston: Allyn & Bacon, 1973.

Sternglanz, S. and L. Serbin. "Sex-Role Stereotyping in Children's Television Programs," *Developmental Psychology* 10 (1974):710–715.

Sternlieb, George. "The City as Sandbox," in J. John Palen, ed., *City Scenes*. Boston: Little, Brown, 1977, pp. 73–91.

Suchar, Charles S. *Social Deviance: Perspectives and Prospects*. New York: Holt, Rinehart & Winston, 1978.

Sumner, William G. *Folkways*. New York: New American Library, reprint ed., 1980 (originally published in 1906).

Sung, Betty Lee. *Mountain of Gold*. New York: Macmillan, 1967.

Sutherland, Edwin H. *Principles of Criminology*. Philadelphia: Lippincott, 1939.

Sutherland, Edwin H. and Donald R. Cressey. *Criminology*. Philadelphia: Lippincott, 1970.

Szymanski, Albert. *The Capitalist State and the Politics of Class*. Cambridge, Mass.: Winthrop Publishers, 1978.

Tallman, Irvin and Ramona Morgner. "Life-Style Differences Among Urban and Suburban Blue-Collar Families," *Social Forces* 48 (March 1970): 334–348.

Taylor, Frederick Winslow. *Scientific Management*. New York: Harper & Row, 1911.

Terkel, Studs. *Working People Talk About What They Do All Day and How They Feel About What They Do*. New York: Pantheon Books, 1974.

Thio, Alex. *Deviant Behavior*. Boston: Houghton Mifflin, 1978.

Thomlinson, Ralph. *Population Dynamics. Causes and Consequences of World Demographic Change*. New York: Random House, 1976.

Thomlinson, Ralph. *Urban Structure*. New York: Random House, 1969.

Toffler, Alvin. *The Third Wave*. New York: Bantam Books, 1981.

Tönnies, Ferdinand. *Community and Society*, trans. C. P. Loomis, New York: Harper & Row, 1963 (originally published in 1887).

Troeltsch, Ernst. *The Social Teachings of the Christian Churches*. New York: Macmillan, 1931.

Tumin, Melvin. "On Social Inequality," *American Sociological Review* 28 February (1963):19–26.

Turk, Herman. "Interorganizational Networks in Urban Society: Initial Perspectives and Comparative Research," *American Sociological Review* 35 (February 1970):1–19.

Turner, Jonathan A. *Sociology: Studying the Human System*. Santa Monica, Calif.: Goodyear, 1978.

Turner, Jonathan H. *The Structure of Sociological Theory*. Homewood, Ill.: The Dorsey Press, rev. ed., 1978.

Turner, R. H. "Sponsored and Contest Mobility and the School System,"

American Sociological Review 25 December (1960):855–867.

Turner, Ralph and Lewis M. Killian. *Collective Behavior*, 2nd ed. Englewood Cliffs, N.J.: Prentice-Hall, 1972.

Ucko, Peter, Ruth Tringham, and G. W. Dimbleby (eds.) *Man, Settlement, and Urbanism*. London: Duckworth, 1972.

United Nations. *Demographic Yearbook*, 1977.

U.S. Bureau of the Census. *Current Population Reports*, Series P-20, No. 288, "Fertility History and Prospects of American Women: June 1975." Washington, D.C.: U.S. Government Printing Office, 1976.

U.S. Bureau of the Census. *Current Population Reports*, Series P-20, No. 341, "Fertility of American Women: June 1978." Washington, D.C.: U.S. Government Printing Office, 1979.

U.S. Bureau of the Census. *Current Population Reports*, Series P-20, No. 365, "Marital Status and Living Arrangements: March 1980." Washington, D.C.: U.S. Government Printing Office, 1981a.

U.S. Bureau of the Census. *Current Population Reports*, Series P-20, No. 366, "Household and Family Characteristics: March 1980." Washington, D.C.: U.S. Government Printing Office, 1981b.

U.S. Bureau of the Census, "Social and Economic Characteristics of the Metropolitan and Nonmetropolitan Population: 1977 and 1970," *Current Population Reports*. Special Studies P-23 No. 75, Washington, D.C.: November 1978.

U.S. Bureau of the Census. *Statistical Abstract of the United States: 1980*, 101st ed., Washington, D.C., 1980.

U.S. Department of Commerce, Bureau of the Census. *Current Population Reports*, Series P-60, 127. Washington, D.C.: U.S. Government Printing Office, 1981.

U.S. Dept. of Health and Human Services. *Health United States: 1980*. Washington, D.C.: U.S. Government Printing Office, 1981.

U.S. Department of Health, Education and Welfare, *Violent Schools — Safe*

Schools. U.S. Government Printing Office, Washington, D.C., 1978.

Van den Berghe, Pierre L. *Human Family Systems. An Evolutionary View.* New York: Elsevier, 1979.

Van Den Berghe, Pierre L. *Man in Society: A Biosocial View.* 2nd ed. New York: Elsevier, 1978.

Veevers, J. E. "The Moral Careers of Voluntary Childless Wives: Notes on the Defense of a Variant World View," *The Family Coordinator* 24 (October 1975):473–487.

Vitarello, James. "The Red Lining Route to Urban Decay," *Focus* 3(10), (1975):4–5.

Vold, George B. *Theoretical Criminology.* New York: Oxford University Press, 1958.

Waller, Willard. *The Family: A Dynamic Interpretation.* New York: Cordon, 1938.

Waller, Willard and Reuben Hill. *The Family.* New York: The Dryden Press, 1951.

Ware, Helen. "Polygyny: Women's Views in a Traditional Society, Nigeria, 1975," *Journal of Marriage and the Family* 41 (February 1979): 185–195.

Warner, W. Lloyd and Paul S. Lunt. *The Status System of a Modern Community.* New Haven: Yale University Press, 1942.

Ways, Max. "How to Think About the Environment," in J. Hadden et al., eds., *Metropolis in Crisis.* Itasca, Ill.: F. E. Peacock, 1971.

Weber, Max. *The City.* New York: The Free Press, 1958.

Weber, Max. *From Max Weber: Essays in Sociology,* trans. and eds., H. Gerth and C. Wright Mills. New York: Oxford University Press, 1946.

Weber, Max. *The Protestant Ethic and the Spirit of Capitalism.* Translated by Talcott Parsons. New York:

Scribner's, 1930. (originally published in 1905).

Weber, Max. *The Protestant Ethic and the Spirit of Capitalism,* trans. Talcott Parsons. New York: Scribner's, 1958.

Weinberg, M. *Minority Students: A Research Appraisal.* Washington, D.C.: U.S. Government Printing Office, 1977.

Weitzman, L. J., D. Eifler, E. Hokada, and C. Ross. "Sex Role Socialization in Picture Books for Preschool Children. *American Journal of Sociology* 77 (1972):1125–1130.

Westhues, Kenneth. *Society's Shadow: Studies in the Sociology of Countercultures.* Toronto: McGraw-Hill Ryerson, 1972.

Westoff, Charles F. and Elise F. Jones. "The Secularization of U.S. Catholic Birth Control Practices," *Family Planning Perspectives* 9 (September–October, 1977):203–206.

Whorf, Benjamin L. "The Relation of Habitual Thought and Behavior to Language," in *Language, Culture and Personality.* Menasha, Wisc.: Sapir Memorial Publication, 1941.

Williams, Peter. *Popular Religion in America; Symbolic Change and the Modernization Process in Historical Perspective.* Englewood Cliffs, N.J.: Prentice-Hall, 1980.

Williams, Robin M. Jr. *American Society: A Sociological Interpretation.* 3rd ed. New York: Alfred Knopf, 1970.

Williamson, John B., David A. Karp, and John R. Dalphin. *The Research Craft: An Introduction to Social Science Methods.* Boston: Little, Brown, 1977.

Wilson, E. O. *Sociobiology.* Cambridge, Mass: Harvard University Press, 1975.

Wilson, James Q. "The Urban Unease: Community vs. City," *The Public Interest* 12 (Summer 1968):25–39.

Wilson, James W. and Barbara Boland. "Crime," in W. Gorham and N.

Glazer, eds., *The Urban Situation.* Washington, D.C.: The Urban Institute, 1976.

Winch, Robert F. *Mate Selection.* New York: Harper, 1958.

Winch, Robert F., Thomas Ktsanes, and Virginia Ktsanes. "The Theory of Complementary Needs in Mate Selection: An Analytic and Descriptive Study," *American Sociological Review* 19 (June 1954):241–249.

Wolfgang, Marvin. "Urban Crime," in J. Wilson, ed., *The Metropolitan Enigma.* Garden City, N.Y.: Doubleday, 1970.

World Almanac and Book of Facts, 1982. New York: Newspaper Enterprise Association, 1981:251.

Wray, Joe D. "Population Pressure on Families: Family Size and Child Spacing," *Reports on Population Family Planning* 9 (August 1971):403–461. Published by The Population Council, New York.

Yinger, J. Milton. "Countercultures and Social Change," *American Sociological Review* 42 (December 1977):833–853.

Zeisel, John. *Sociology and Architectural Design.* New York: Russell Sage Foundation, 1973.

Zelditch, M. Jr. "Role Differentiation in the Nuclear Family," in Parsons, Bales et al., eds., *Family, Socialization and Interaction Process.* New York: The Free Press of Glencoe, 1955.

Zirkel, P. A. "Self-Concept and the Disadvantage of Ethnic Group Membership and Mixture," *Review of Educational Research* 41 (1971): 211–225.

Zwerdling, Daniel. "The Food Monopolies," in Jerome H. Skolnick and Elliott Curie, eds., *Crisis in American Institutions,* 3rd ed. pp. 43–51. Boston: Little, Brown, 1976.

Text Credits

(continued from page iv)

Wallace, "Significa," *Parade,* May 16, 1981, p. 16. Reprinted by permission.

Chapter 16. p. 433: From Harold Freeman, *Toward Socialism in America.* Copyright © 1979 by Schenkman Publishing Company, Inc. Reprinted by permission.

Chapter 17. p. 462: From Ralph H. Turner, "Collective Behavior and Conflict: New Theoretical Frameworks," *The Sociological Quarterly,* vol. 5, no. 2 (Spring 1964). Reprinted by permission.

Chapter 19. p. 525–526: Adapted by permission of Macmillan Publishing Co., Inc. from *Defensible Space* by Oscar Newman. Copyright © 1972, 1973 by Oscar Newman.

Appendix. From *Clinical Sociology Newsletter,* Fall 1979. Reprinted by permission.

Figure Credits

Chapter 4. Figure 4-1, p. 89: From *New Rules: Searching for Self-Fulfillment in a World Turned Upside Down,* by Daniel Yankelovich. Copyright © 1981 by Daniel Yankelovich. Reprinted by permission of Random House, Inc.

Chapter 10. Figure 10-1, p. 249: U.S. Department of Commerce, Bureau of the Census, *Current Population Reports.* Series P-60. No. 127. "Money Income and Poverty Status of Families and Persons in the United States: 1980." Washington, D.C.: U.S. Government Printing Office, 1981.

Chapter 12. Figure 12-2, p. 321: National Center for Health Statistics, "Advance Report of Final Marriage Statistics, 1979," *Monthly Vital Statistics Report,* no. 30 (July 31, 1981), p. 2; *Figure 12-3, p. 325:* U.S. Department of Health, Education and Welfare, *Increases in Divorces: United States, 1967,* Public Health Service publication no. 1000, Series 21, no. 20 Washington, D.C.: Government Printing Office, 1970, p. 1.

Chapter 13. Figure 13-1, p. 360: "The Gallup Opinion Index," *Religion in America: 1981.* Princeton, N.J. The Gallup Organization, Inc. and the Princeton Religion Research Center, Inc.,

Report no. 184, January 1981, p. 36. Reprinted by permission.

Chapter 14. Figure 14-1, p. 386: American Council on Education, *A Fact Book on Higher Education,* 2nd ed., Washington, D.C.: U.S. Government Printing Office, 1977. Used by permission.

Chapter 18. Figure 18-1, p. 480: Population Reference Bureau, no date. *Statistical Abstract of the United States:* 1980, Washington, D.C.: U.S. Government Printing Office, 1980, p. 29; *Figure 18-2, p. 486: Historical Statistics of the U.S. Colonial Times to 1970.* U.S. Bureau of the Census, Washington, D.C.: U.S. Government Printing Office, 1973. Statistical Abstract of the U.S., 1980; *Figure 18-3, p. 488:* Population Reference Bureau, Washington, D.C.; *Figure 18-4, p. 489:* Population Reference Bureau, Washington, D.C.; *Figure 18-5, p. 490:* Population Reference Bureau, Washington, D.C.

Chapter 19. Figure 19-1, p. 511: Reprinted from "The Nature of Cities" by Chauncy D. Harris and Edward L. Ullman in volume 242 of *The Annals* of the American Academy of Political and Social Science.

Photo Credits

Chapter 1. p. 4: Hugh Rogers/Monkmeyer Press Photo Service; *p. 7 (top):* Nicholas Sapieha/Stock, Boston; *p. 7 (bottom):* Julie O'Neil/Stock, Boston; *p. 9 (left):* © John Lei/Stock, Boston; *p. 9 (right):* Owen Franken/Stock, Boston; *p. 16:* © Arthur Grace/Stock, Boston; *p. 17:* Crime Prevention Section, Department of Police, Detroit, Michigan.

Chapter 2. p. 24: Culver Pictures, Inc.; *p. 27:* The Granger Collection; *p. 29:* The Bettmann Archive, Inc.; *p. 30:* Culver Pictures, Inc.; *p. 32:* United Press International; *p. 33 (top):* Harvard University News Office; *p. 33 (bottom):* American Philosophical Society; *p. 37:* Eric Roth/The Picture Cube; *p. 39:* Rhoda Sidney/Monkmeyer.

Chapter 3. p. 46: Owen Franken/Stock, Boston; *p. 49:* Jean-Claude Lejeune/Stock, Boston; *p. 53:* Jay Godwin/Dallas Morning News/Sygma; *p. 55:* The Granger Collection; *p. 56:*

Traver/Liaison Photo Agency; *p. 60:* Mimi Forsyth/Monkmeyer Press Photo Service; *p. 62:* Richard Wood/The Picture Cube.

Chapter 4. p. 80: The Granger Collection; *p. 83 (top):* Hugh Rogers/Monkmeyer Press Photo Service; *p. 83 (bottom):* © Frank Siteman 1980/The Picture Cube; *p. 86:* Rank/Anglo Enterprise/Vineyard/The Museum of Modern Art, Film Stills Archive; *p. 92:* W. Campbell/Sygma; *p. 93:* Ira Kirschenbaum/Stock, Boston; *p. 94:* David A. Burnett/Stock, Boston; *p. 98:* Cartoon by William Hamilton. Reprinted by permission of Chronicle Features, San Francisco.

Chapter 5. p. 104: David Maybury-Lewis/Anthro-Photo File; *p. 107:* United Artists/Museum of Modern Art, Film Stills Archive; *p. 110:* Peter Vandermark/Stock, Boston; *p. 112:* Jamie Cope; *p. 114:* David S. Strickler/The Picture Cube; *p. 116:* Sybil Shackman/Monkmeyer Press Photo Service; *p. 120:* David S. Strickler/The Picture Cube; *p. 121:* Photo courtesy of The National Broadcasting Company, Inc.

Chapter 6. p. 128: Daniel S. Brody/Stock, Boston; *p. 131 (top and bottom):* Copyright © 1972 Metro-Goldwyn-Mayer, Inc./Museum of Modern Art, Film Stills Archive; *p. 135 (top):* Charles Leavitt/The Picture Cube; *p. 135 (bottom):* Peter Menzel/Stock, Boston; *p. 136:* Rick Friedman/The Picture Cube; *p. 139:* © Susan Lapides 1980; *p. 140:* © Bill Owens/Archive Pictures; *p. 141:* © Cecile Brunswick/Peter Arnold, Inc.

Chapter 7. p. 148: Ed Hof/The Picture Cube; *p. 150:* Elliott Erwitt/Magnum; *p. 152:* Bob Bouchal/© Little, Brown and Company; *p. 156:* Peter Simon/Stock, Boston; *p. 163:* © Jill Freedman/Archive Pictures; *p. 166:* Richard Younker 1981/Click/Chicago; *p. 168:* Hemsey/Liaison Photo Agency.

Chapter 8. p. 186: Eddie Adams/Liaison Photo Agency; *p. 189 (left):* Hugh Rogers/Monkmeyer Press Photo Service; *p. 189 (right):* Sybil Schackman/Monkmeyer Press Photo Service; *p. 193:* United Press International; *p. 195:* Mary Ellen Mark/Archive Pictures; *p. 200:* United Press International; *p. 202:* © Twentieth Century Fox Film Corporation/Museum of Modern Art, Film

Stills Archive; *p. 204:* © Diane Grahm-Henry 1981/Click/Chicago.

Chapter 9. p. 210: Abigail Heyman/Archive Pictures; *p. 215:* © George W. Gardner 1972; *p. 216:* © Chris Brown/The Picture Group; *p. 219:* National Archives; *p. 222:* Charles Harbutt/Archive Pictures; *p. 224:* © Universal Pictures/Museum of Modern Art, Film Stills Library; *p. 229:* Peter Jordan/Liaison Photo Agency; *p. 230: Trail of Tears* by Robert Lindneux, courtesy of Woolaroc Museum, Bartlesville, Oklahoma; *p. 234:* Charles Harbutt/Archive Pictures.

Chapter 10. p. 240: Wendy Maeda/*The Boston Globe*; *p. 243:* © Deborah Gewertz, Department of Anthropology-Sociology, Amherst College; *p. 247:* International Museum of Photography at George Eastman House; *p. 251 (left):* Mimi Forsyth/Monkmeyer Press Photo Service; *p. 251 (right, top):* Mimi Forsyth/Monkmeyer Press Photo Service; *p. 251 (right, bottom):* Rhoda Sidney/Monkmeyer Press Photo Service; *p. 257:* Pam Hasegawa/Taurus Photos; *p. 259:* SYLVIA by Nicole Hollander © 1982 Field Enterprises, Inc. Courtesy of Field Newspaper Syndicate.

Chapter 11. p. 278: Michael Rizza/The Picture Cube; *p. 284 (left):* David Strickler/Monkmeyer Press Photo Service; *p. 284 (right):* © Abigail Heyman/Archive Pictures; *p. 287:* Bob Bouchal/© 1982 Little, Brown and Company; *p. 288 (top):* © Abigail Heyman/Archive Pictures; *p. 288 (bottom):* Donald L. Miller/Monkmeyer Press Photo Service; *p. 293:* Joseph Dennehy/*The Boston Globe*; *p. 297:* Reprinted by permission of Tribune Company Syndicate, Inc.

Chapter 12. p. 304: Alain Keler/Sygma; *p. 308:* © Anthony Howarth/Daily Telegraph Magazine/Woodfin Camp & Associates; *p. 310:* Malcolm S. Kirk/© Peter Arnold, Inc.; *p. 312:* © George W. Gardner; *p. 314:* © Charles Harbutt/Archive Pictures; *p. 318:* © Joel Gordon 1980; *p. 323:* © Joel Gordon 1982; *p. 327:* © Teri Leigh Stratford 1980.

Chapter 13. p. 336: J.P. Laffont/Sygma; *p. 339:* © Kal Muller 1982/Woodfin Camp & Associates; *p. 342 (left):* © Ellis Herwig 1980/Stock, Boston; *p. 342 (right):* Diego Goldberg/Sygma: *p. 348:* United Press International; *p. 353:* Philippe LeDru/Sygma; *p. 355:* © R. Darolle/Sygma; *p. 361:* Jim Pozarik/Gamma-Liason.

Chapter 14. p. 366: © Charles Harbutt/Archive Pictures; *p. 369:* Paul Conklin/Monkmeyer Press Photo Service; *p. 371:* David S. Strickler/Monkmeyer Press Photo Service; *p. 374:* Culver Pictures, Inc.; *p. 379:* Bryce Flynn/Picture Group; *p. 380:* Brian Seed/Click/Chicago; *p. 384:* © Frank Siteman 1979/The Picture Cube; *p. 385:* United Press International.

Chapter 15: p. 392: Ken Kobre/The Picture Group; *p. 395:* United Press International; *p. 397:* Culver Pictures, Inc.; *p. 399:* Don Wright/The Miami News; *p. 400:* Alain Nogues/Sygma; *p. 404 (top):* United Press International; *p. 404 (bottom):* Black Star; *p. 408:* Elaine Isaacson/The Picture Group.

Chapter 16. p. 416: © Joel Gordon 1981; *p. 421: Pat Lyon at the Forge* by John Neagle/Courtesy, Museum of Fine Arts, Boston. Herman and Zoe Oliver Sherman Fund; *p. 423:* Mark Godfrey/Archive Pictures; *p. 427:* Jean-Pierre Laffont/Sygma; *p. 431:* Bruno Barbey/Magnum; *p. 435 (top):* Central Office of Information, London; *p. 435 (bottom):* Alice Grossman/The Picture Cube.

Chapter 17. p. 452: Mattison/Gamma-Liaison; *p. 455:* United Press International; *p. 458 (left):* © Joel Gordon 1978; *p. 458 (right):* © Bill Burke/Archive Pictures; *p. 465 (left):* J. R. Eyerman, © 1973 Time Inc.; *p. 465 (right, top):* Photos Kleinberg/Sygma; *p. 465 (right, bottom):* Christian Vioújard/Gamma-Liaison; *p. 468:* By John Fischetti © 1972 Chicago Daily News/Dist. by Field Newspaper Syndicate; *p. 470:* Abbas/Gamma-Liaison.

Chapter 18. p. 478: Judith D. Sedwick/The Picture Cube; *p. 483:* Private Collection, photo courtesy James Moroney Inc.; *p. 484:* Paul Conklin/Monkmeyer Press Photo Service; *p. 487:* Mark Brett/Liaison Photo Agency; *p. 491 (left, top): p. 491 (right, bottom):* © George W. Gardner; *p. 495:* Michael Putnam/© Peter Arnold, Inc.

Chapter 19. p. 500: Dick Pietrzyk/© 1981 Click/Chicago; *p. 503:* Culver Pictures, Inc.; *p. 506:* Michael Kagan/Monkmeyer Press Photo Service; *p. 513 (left):* Michael Kagan/Monkmeyer Press Photo Service; *p. 513 (right):* © Jack Spratt/The Picture Group; *p. 516:* Bill Owens/Archive Pictures; *p. 522:* Mark Godfrey/Archive Pictures; *p. 524:* UFA/Museum of Modern Art, Film Stills Archive.

Chapter 20. p. 530: Cary Wolinsky/Stock, Boston; *p. 533:* Culver Pictures, Inc.; *p. 535 (top):* G. Rancinan/Sygma; *p. 535 (bottom):* Pénélope Chauvelot/Sygma; *p. 537 (top): Tremont Street, Boston* by Philip Harry/ Courtesy, Museum of Fine Arts, Boston. Karolik Collection; *p. 537 (bottom):* © Cheryl Shugars 1982; *p. 539:* From *The Wall Street Journal*, by permission of Cartoon Features Syndicate; *p. 543:* © 1974, United Artists Corporation, by permission of Woody Allen and United Artists.

Name Index

Subject Index